TIPPETT
THE COMPOSER AND HIS MUSIC

TIPPETT

the composer and his music

IAN KEMP

Oxford   New York

OXFORD UNIVERSITY PRESS

1987

Oxford University Press, Walton Street, Oxford OX2 6DP

Oxford New York Toronto
Delhi Bombay Calcutta Madras Karachi
Petaling Jaya Singapore Hong Kong Tokyo
Nairobi Dar es Salaam Cape Town
Melbourne Auckland

and associated companies in
Beirut Berlin Ibadan Nicosia

Oxford is a trademark of Oxford University Press

First published 1984 by Ernst Eulenburg Ltd.
First issued as an Oxford University Press paperback 1987

British Library Cataloguing in Publication Data
Kemp, Ian, 1931–
Tippett: the composer and his music.
1. Tippett, Michael—Criticism and
interpretation
I. Title
780'.92'4   ML410.T467
ISBN 0-19-282017-6

Library of Congress Cataloging in Publication Data
Kemp, Ian.
Tippett, the composer and his music.
Reprint. Originally published: London: Eulenburg
Books; New York: Da Capo Press, 1984.
Bibliography: p.   Includes index.
1. Tippett, Michael, 1905– . 2. Tippett,
Michael, 1905– —Criticism and interpretation.
I. Title.
ML410.T467K43 1987   780'.92'4 [B]   86-21806
ISBN 0-19-282017-6 (pbk.)

Printed in Great Britain by
Richard Clay Ltd.
Bungay, Suffolk

CONTENTS

CONTENTS

for Sue

PREFACE AND ACKNOWLEDGEMENTS

It would have been impossible to write a book of this kind without the collaboration of Sir Michael Tippett. I would like to record my profound gratitude to him for providing me with so much information that could have come from no one but himself, for his patient explanation of innumerable points of biographical and musical detail and for his encouragement.

Writing about a living composer who is also a personal friend (I am not related to Tippett, although we have one name in common) confers great advantages. I hope I have made good use of them. But it has disadvantages as well. I discovered that his willingness to recall earlier events in his life or to explain something about one of his works could disturb his compositional process and the peace of mind necessary for it. In November 1973 he wrote: 'The more I write (letters) – tiddlypom – the more I write. And the more I regret writing. And it distracts *me* from where I am *now* and what I'm having to do *now*.' By limiting myself to questions in conversation I realised that I could still make him uneasy, even physically so. So I began to assemble information indirectly. This was a tactic he understood perfectly well for it was all of a piece with what he had already reminded me of. At an early stage in the preparation of this book, I had asked him why Jack, in *The Midsummer Marriage*, is led in as a false Sosostris; he replied airily that he wanted to get the whole cast on stage for Sosostris's aria. This was obviously an evasive reply and his way of saying that I would have to find out the answers myself and evaluate them myself: however accurate the book might be factually, it would have little real interest unless it were also an independent response to its subject.

Like most people, Tippett is far more concerned with what music sounds like than with the way it is composed; he wants his own music to communicate directly in its own terms. But the terms of music cannot be circumscribed. If Tippett is suspicious of analysis ('fatally easy ... only make-believe'), the way his music is composed remains of great importance. If he is content that his music should arouse intuitive sympathy, the extent of this sympathy still stretches well beyond the 'purely musical'. Whereas much of this book provides factual information it is also therefore a personal interpretation – of Tippett's creative process, his techniques, his beliefs, his achievement, his music.

Tippett has a keen memory; but naturally it is selective and on occasion it has proved unreliable or has deserted him. What he has told me has, wherever possible, been checked and if necessary corrected. It has been filled out with help from many individuals who have given me of their time, knowledge and advice. Of these I would particularly like to thank Tippett's brother, Lieut.-Commander Peter Kemp, his cousin, Cecily Evans and his lifelong friends, David and Larema Ayerst. I owe special thanks to Sir William Glock, who has edited the book with unusual care and to Meirion Bowen, who has read the typescript and made valuable suggestions.

I would also like to thank the following: Cyril Allinson, John Amis, Leslie Arnold, Barbara Banner, Ken Bartlett, Walter Bergmann, Albert Bilson, Alan Bush, William Byers Brown, David Cairns, John Cruft, Eugene Cruft, Oliver Davis, Peggy Deller, Valerie Eliot, Sir Dingle Foot, Wilfred Franks, James Fraser, Christopher Fry, Lord Gardiner, Marabel Gardiner, Alexander Goehr, Reg Groves, Sally Groves, George Guest, David Harrison, Karl Hawker, Geoffrey Hill, Imogen Holst, A. Christopher Lake, Tom Leonard, Stella Maude, Fred B. May, William May, Joyce McGroarty, Philip Moore, Sybil Morrison, David Moule Evans, Leslie Orrey, Henry Pelling, Ruth Pennyman, Robert Pollard, Raymond Potter, Priaulx Rainier, Betty Reid, Luke Rittner, James Robertson, Erika Seelig, Phyllis Sellick, Peter Stern, John Strange, Rosamund Strode, P.D. Trevor-Roper, Charles Thomas, Raleigh Trevelyan, Alison Watson, Peggy Whittle, Carrington Wood, Robert Woodridge and Alan Woolgar.

Grateful thanks are also due to the following for permission to reproduce copyright material:

Sir Michael Tippett for unpublished music and writings; Schott and Co. Ltd for all examples from Tippett's music and for extracts from his libretti; George Allen and Unwin for an extract from 'Song' in Alun Lewis, *Ha Ha Among The Trumpets*; the Author's Literary Estate and The Hogarth Press (for the world, except the territories below) and Harcourt Brace Jovanovich, Inc. (for the USA, its dependencies and the Philippine Islands) for an extract from Virginia Woolf, *Between the Acts*; Eric Bentley for an extract from his *The Life of the Drama* published in the USA by Atheneum Publications, New York; Collins and the Harvill Press, London, for an extract from Boris Pasternak, *Doctor Zhivago* (trans. Max Hayward and Manya Harari); Faber and Faber Ltd (for the world except the USA) and Harcourt Brace Jovanovich, Inc. (for the USA) for extracts from T.S. Eliot, *Four Quartets* (Copyright 1943 by T.S. Eliot; renewed 1971 by Esme Valerie Eliot) and *Murder in the Cathedral* (Copyright 1935 by Harcourt Brace Jovanovich, Inc.; renewed 1963 by T.S. Eliot); Faber and Faber Ltd (for the world, except the USA) and Farrar, Strauss and Giroux, Inc. (for the USA) for an extract from T.S. Eliot, *On Poetry and Poets*; Hamish Hamilton Ltd (for the United Kingdom and British Commonwealth) and Harper and Row, Publishers, Inc. (for USA and Canada) for an extract from Dmitri Shostakovich, *Testimony* (ed. Solomon Volkov); Oxford University Press for an extract from Alan Bush, *Prelude and Fugue for piano* and for extracts from Maud Karpeles (ed.), *Cecil Sharp's Collection of English Folk Songs*, and from R. Vaughan Williams, *National Music*; Routledge and Kegan

Paul Ltd for extracts from Michael Tippett, *Moving into Aquarius* and for an extract from Sidney Keyes, 'Song: The Heart's Assurance' from *The Cruel Solstice*; Routledge and Kegan Paul Ltd (for the United Kingdom and British Commonwealth) and Princeton University Press (for USA, Canada and Open Market) for extracts from *Collected Works of C. G. Jung* (trans. R.F.C. Hull), Bollingen Series XX, Vol. 9, I: *The Archetypes and the Collective Unconscious* (Copyright © 1959, 1969 by Princeton University Press); Vol. 9, II: *Aion: Researches into the Phenomenology of the Self* (Copyright © 1959 by Princeton University Press); Vol. 11: *Psychology and Religion: West and East* (Copyright © 1958, 1969 by Princeton University Press). Excerpts reprinted by permission of Princeton University Press; M.B. Yeats and Anne Yeats (for the world, except the USA) and Macmillan Publishing Co., Inc. (for the USA) for extracts from 'Lapis Lazuli', 'The Circus Animals' Desertion' and 'High Talk' from *The Collected Poems of W. B. Yeats* (Copyright 1940 by Georgie Yeats, renewed 1968 by Bertha Georgie Yeats, Michael Butler Yeats and Anne Yeats) and for extracts from 'Her Dream' and 'Parting' (Copyright 1933 by Macmillan Publishing Company, renewed 1961 by Bertha Georgie Yeats).

Finally, I gratefully acknowledge financial assistance from the Universities of Aberdeen, Cambridge, Leeds and Manchester and from St John's College, Cambridge.

And – to conclude – loving thanks and apologies to Gill, Alexander, Francesca, Kirstin, Robyn and Susanna for having to endure my preoccupation for what must seem like most of their lives.

Ian Kemp
Manchester 1984

For this paperback edition, misprints have been corrected, a few additions and alterations made and the List of Works and Bibliography brought up to date. I would like to take this opportunity to record my thanks to Jessie Dodson, whose name I much regret omitting from the first edition, and to David Fallows, whose help in proof-reading was invaluable.

I.K.
1986

A Short Biography

Family Background

Cornwall contains dolmens, megaliths, stone circles, stone crosses – visible reminders of its one-time status as the last outpost of Celtic culture in England. Tippett is proud of his Cornish origins and has referred to them in print, as, for example, when writing that his affection for Germany 'began perhaps when my Celtic ancestors had their homeland in bronze-age Bavaria'.[1] His tall, rugged and rather wild physical appearance underlines the point. It is tempting to develop the matter further and find correspondences between his origins and his interest in Yeats, or between the Celtic belief in the transmigration of souls and his interest in Jung, or between the combination of severe formal design and delicate decorative tracery in Celtic metalwork and a similar combination of factors in (some of) his music. Such correspondences are of course too vague to contribute much towards an understanding of his work; and they overlook the fact that Tippett is Anglo-Saxon as well as Celtic and that in any case he did not set foot in Cornwall until his late teens. Yet to him his Cornish origins are important. They have assured him that the more visionary or fanciful aspects of his creative imagination are inborn, and not affectation. If such details as have been discovered of his forbears contrast rather prosaically with these intuitions, it should be remarked that they represent only tiny fragments of his background and only the beginnings of an answer to the question of where his creative gifts sprang from.

There is little evidence of creative or imaginative talent in recent generations of the Tippett family. By the mid-nineteenth century that branch of it to which Michael Tippett is related owned estates around Camborne, and from there spread out to other parts of south-west Cornwall, taking on respectable positions as solicitors, bankers, clergymen and naval officers.[2] But Tippett's immediate forbears, in particular his father and paternal grandfather, were inventive and even daring in their various ways – qualities which Tippett himself inherited in good measure. And the Tippett coat of arms (to which the family does not seem to have established a legal right) bore the motto 'Non robore sed spe' (Not by strength but by hope) whose sentiments accord tolerably well with the composer's own philosophy of life.

The later career of Tippett's grandfather, George Frederick John Tippett (born in 1829 or 1830), caused the family such embarrassment that they preferred not to mention his existence. His place in the family tree is obscure and as a consequence the line of Tippett's own descent cannot be

traced precisely. This is a mystery which delights him. In any event George
Tippett was Cornish. It seems that he was educated in Truro (where he
was a cathedral choirboy) and he met his future wife, Mary Stripp May, in
Penzance. There was some opposition to the marriage and this may be the
reason why George Tippett broke with tradition, left Cornwall and was
married in London, in 1854. He quickly asserted his enterprising character.
According to family history he was at one stage a silversmith, but by the
time he had settled in London he was a 'builder', what would now be
termed a property developer. In this capacity he prospered and at the
height of his success became extremely rich. Anecdotes circulated to the
effect that he was offered a baronetcy by the Prince of Wales in exchange
for clearing debts (a proposition he did not accept), that he spent £60,000
laying down a cellar (at which point his doctors forbade him to drink) and
that he gave a substantial part of his fortune to the Countess of
Huntingdon's Connexion (a sect of evangelical persuasion akin to the
Calvinistic Methodists), presumably at the instigation of his wife who had
become intensely religious. He was obviously a resourceful man, prepared
to take risks, and a practical one, being an accomplished carpenter. All this
may be said to have been inherited in some degree by his grandson. It is
less easy to say whether his specifically musical gifts were strong or creative
enough to have survived a dormant generation (Tippett's father was not
really musical at all) and emerge fully developed in Tippett himself.
George Tippett had a tenor voice of such arresting quality that his singing
could silence the congregation at a Moody and Sankey evangelical meeting
and oblige it to listen to him alone, and he became a friend of the celebrated
nineteenth-century tenor, Sims Reeves, for whom he apparently deputized
on occasion. He also knew the music historian and journalist, Sutherland
Edwards, who gave him tickets for London concerts. Some musical talent
did therefore run in the family, and there is poetry in the fact that he was
baptized with the same Christian names as Handel.

George Tippett had eleven legitimate children and kept two mistresses,
by whom he had several more. His wife died in 1885. In the latter part of
his life his fortunes began to decline to such an extent that by 1895 he was
an unregistered bankrupt. He attempted to retrieve his position by leasing
a mine in Wales and setting up a company to operate it, with share capital
provided by his son, Henry Tippett. In order to acquire working capital he
obtained cash from banks on the assurance of invoices purporting to
represent payments due to the company for the supply of ore. Several
thousands of pounds were obtained in this way and though most of it was
spent on machinery and accommodation and wages for the miners, the
company did not in fact supply an ounce of ore. If the mine had quickly
become profitable the stratagem would have remained undiscovered and
the whole venture set on a proper footing. But within a year he found
himself unable to settle his accounts with the banks and the company was
wound up, the largest creditor being his son, Henry Tippett. In January
1899 George Tippett was indicted at the Old Bailey for obtaining money
from banks by false pretences and a month later was sentenced to nine

months imprisonment.[3] He was released from prison before serving the full term and died shortly afterwards, on 21 July 1899.

This was a tragic end to the career of a man who had lived with style and who had operated highly successfully within the framework of Victorian capitalism, whatever the present estimate of its ethics. Had he been a prophet he might have been amused at the thought that each of the next two generations of his family would also see one of its members in prison (though for markedly different reasons). And he doubtless would have approved of the unconventional attitudes of the composer grandson he never saw. As it was, Michael Tippett's introduction to the independent strain in the family was effected through the more circumspect behaviour of his father.

Henry William Tippett was born in London in 1858 and educated at Brighton College (his father had a second, weekend home at Brighton) and Oriel College, Oxford, where he graduated in law in 1879. He was the second son of the family. But since his elder brother had emigrated to South Africa at an early age, he soon found himself obliged to accept the role of the eldest son. This limited his freedom of action. As was customary in those days, he was expected to help his father support the rest of the family and not to marry himself until his sisters had found husbands or been given ample time to do so. He gracefully fulfilled both requirements. He worked in collaboration with his father, did not take a holiday for twenty years nor marry until his father had died and he was forty-four. After leaving Oxford he began work in London, qualifying as a solicitor's clerk. Though not articled he quickly earned a reputation as a free-lance lawyer and entrepreneur. He made investments of his own, notably in the Lyceum Theatre, and also founded the City and West End Property Company (which was eventually bought up in the 1960s). His adventurous streak asserted itself in a striking way when he bought eight million acres of land in Paraguay, intending to look for state wealth reputedly buried somewhere in the country by the defeated Paraguayan dictator, Francisco Solano Lopez. He travelled to Paraguay, but had to return to England shortly afterwards, because of his father's court case. A more sober investment followed in 1902. One of his earlier dealings had been to lend money to a client for a mortgage on a hotel in France, with the usual condition that should the repayments not be made the ownership of the hotel would fall to him. The client failed to meet the condition and Henry Tippett decided to retire from his various enterprises and, though retaining some shares in the property company, to invest most of his resources in Hôtel Beau-Site, Boulevard Beausite, Cannes. By the time he had married he was a hotel proprietor, taking residence during the winter seasons and leaving the day to day running of the hotel to a manager. Henry Tippett showed remarkable flair as a hotelier. Beau-Site was a hotel on a grand scale. He enhanced its reputation for providing the best cuisine on the Riviera, enlarged its facilities, notably by the addition of a winter garden and some hard tennis courts, and he counted the King of Sweden among his guests. In order to make room for the winter garden he had cut into the rock at the back of the hotel and the resulting supply of red gravel gave him the idea of turning the existing grass tennis courts into hard ones. Wanting to capitalize on the tennis tradition at Beau-Site he commissioned William Renshaw to design them (Renshaw was one of the twin brothers who dominated the Wimbledon championships in the late 1880s) and Beau-Site became the venue for international championships where such players as Suzanne Lenglen and Jean Borotra would on occasion find that their ball boys were the sons of the proprietor. (Tippett greatly enjoyed tennis and in early heats of championships he also acted as an umpire.) The hotel has now been converted into flats but a plaque set into the wall of Boulevard Beausite commemorates its place in the annals of French tennis:

Ici en 1881 dans le parc du Palais Beau Site sur les premiers courts édifies dans notre pays naquit le tennis français. En souvenir de tous les champions français et étrangers qui sur ces courts s'affrontèrent en des tournois mémorables.

Henry Tippett met his future wife in the home of one of his brothers-in-law, a general practitioner who had taken into his family a mental patient and had asked Isabel Kemp, a young nurse from the hospital where he acted as anaesthetist, to be companion for her. Henry and Isabel Tippett were married at St Thomas's, Westminster, on 22 April 1903. Isabel Tippett was twenty-two. Their first home was a small country house in The Sigers, Eastcote, Middlesex. In late 1905, by now parents of two sons, Peter and Michael, they left Eastcote for Suffolk, because the 'damp climate' of Middlesex did not suit Isabel Tippett's health. The home where Tippett was brought up was an early sixteenth-century farmhouse on the outskirts of the village of Wetherden, in remote and beautiful countryside about half-way between Bury St Edmunds and Stowmarket. It had an acre of garden and farm buildings attached. Henry Tippett changed the original name of the house, St Briavels, to Rosemary Cottage, presumably because he did not want to be associated with hagiolatry. (In 1553 Mary Tudor stayed there, and left her nightdress behind, while *en route* for Framlingham Castle during the attempt to put Lady Jane Grey on the throne.)

Tippett's father was a gentle, kindly man with a quick sense of humour and much practical commonsense. He was the stabilizing influence in the family. Tippett always sided with him in family disagreements. He was widely read, anxious to teach and explain matters of all kinds to his children to whom he gave free run of his large library when they were old enough (before this he would read weighty biographies to them and, as relaxation, the novels of Stanley Weyman and Edgar Wallace). He was a free thinker (and as such the source of Tippett's sceptical views on religion) and a liberal humanist temperamentally committed to the tenets of *laissez-faire* and the Manchester Liberals, as his working career testified. He was never active in politics, though he was a member of the National Liberal Club. In early manhood he inherited his father's musical friendships and took some interest in artistic life in London and Paris, becoming an *habitué* of Covent Garden and the Paris Opéra. But although he would hum passages from his favourite opera, *Samson et Dalila*, and occasionally talk about music, he had no real feeling for it.

Isabel Clementina Binny Kemp, born in 1880, was the thirteenth of fourteen children. Her father, Alexander Davidson Kemp, was a civil servant on the staff of the Exchequer and Audit Department and her mother, Annie Webster, the daughter of a rich officer in the Bengal Army. Like the Tippetts, the Kemps were an unusual family.[4] Although stemming from Anglo-Saxon Kent, they developed interests which more strongly suggest Celtic links, or at least links with Celtic eschatology, than did those of the Cornish Tippetts. They were attracted to theosophy and spiritualism and were likely to switch from high Anglo-Catholicism at one moment to female freemasonry the next – this despite the outward conservatism of their males, who included clergymen, doctors and solicitors, as well as an admiral and a general. They were less remarkable however for their male progeny than for their domineering and often startlingly nonconformist females. This was evident in Isabel Tippett's mother, who had challenged the canons of good taste at an early age by becoming an art student and exhibiting at the Royal Academy, and by holding unconventional political views, especially about the role of women. It was more pronounced in her mother's cousin, Charlotte Despard. Mrs Despard was an extraordinary woman who exerted a strong influence on Isabel Tippett and on Tippett himself. She was the sister of Sir John French, later the Earl of Ypres. After the death of her Irish husband she moved to Nine Elms, Battersea, promoting charitable schemes in the slums of south London and joining various left-wing political parties. She also joined Mrs Pankhurst's Women's Social and Political Union, but finding that too violent in its tactics, she formed, in opposition to Mrs Pankhurst, the Women's Freedom League, the non-violent, explicitly pacifist yet still 'activist' wing of the suffragette movement. Isabel Tippett greatly admired Charlotte Despard, even adopting her practice of wearing a black lace mantilla instead of a hat. She too became a suffragette, was arrested from time to time for chaining herself to railings and in 1913 was imprisoned in Holloway for a fortnight for taking part in an illegal protest meeting in Trafalgar Square. Her contribution had been to organize the means by which an audience was attracted. (She purchased a quantity of dinner bells from a shop in the Haymarket where her husband had an account and distributed them among the suffragettes in the square; when a bell rang and a policeman was about to apprehend the ringer, another bell sounded from elsewhere in the square, the process continuing until the police got the measure of the situation and arrested those responsible.)

Tippett's mother was in several respects the opposite of his father. She was a red-haired extravert of immense drive, inclined to moralize and always convinced of the rightness of her views. She was a generation younger than her husband, a Tolstoyan and a Shavian, and a sympathizer of the Labour Party (although she eventually became apolitical). She inherited some of the artistic ambitions of her mother. She did not take up painting until her old age, but in Wetherden she had lessons in voice-training, singing drawing-room ballads in a gravelly voice, and began a short career as a novelist. Eight novels were published, at her husband's expense, between 1909 and 1923, under such titles as *The Power of the Petticoat*, *The Waster* (about the no-work ethic of an artist), *Living Dust* (about a widower who keeps his wife's ashes in an urn on the mantlepiece) and *Passing the Love of Women* (lightly touching on homosexuality). She also wrote plays, one of which, based on an episode from Norman Douglas's *South Wind* (about a bishop who pushes his wife into the sea), was produced at a London theatre club. Her creative pretensions helped to establish an environment in which Tippett's own pretensions could be viewed with at least some understanding; and her commanding personality certainly shaped his attitudes and taught him to stand by his own beliefs. Inevitably however, friction developed between her and Tippett and her persistently critical and overweening manner[5] even led, in his early forties, to a complete, if temporary break in relations. Eventually she came to respect his beliefs, whether or not she shared them. Her 'proudest' moment was when Tippett was sent to prison.

In some ways the Tippetts were conventionally middle-class. They lived comfortably and could afford a cook, a nursery governess, two parlour maids, a gardener and a chauffeur (they possessed the only cars in Wetherden). Yet within this protected exterior they were unusually lively and enterprising, well ahead of their time and remarkable in encouraging independent thinking and behaviour in their children. Tippett was perhaps unlucky that a slow decline in family finances coincided with his period of formal education. But he was certainly lucky to have been brought up in so stimulating an environment.

With the outbreak of the First World War Henry Tippett came to an agreement by which he rented Beau-Site to his manager. There followed however a French government moratorium on rents and in any case the hotel was subsequently commandeered for war-wounded. So no income was forthcoming. Economies were necessary at Rosemary Cottage, especially since the children had just started at preparatory school. The servants left; when at home for holidays the children performed domestic duties and kept hens (Tippett's was called Henrietta), selling the eggs to their parents. Henry Tippett took out a mortgage on his house and turned his garden into a smallholding, sending vegetables to London each week. When this tactic failed, Isabel Tippett took on a job as a speaker for the National Savings movement. But by the end of the war debts had accumulated and with the sharp fall in value of the franc to the pound Henry Tippett was in serious financial difficulties. He sold Rosemary Cottage, cleared the mortgage, and he and his wife left England for France, where he could avoid paying tax on dividends from his property company and where revenue from Beau-Site bore a closer relation to the cost of living. The children remained in their English boarding schools. Since the manager of the hotel was now the lessee, the Tippetts were unable to stay there unless they paid hotel charges and although they and the children

were invited as the manager's personal guests from time to time they could
not afford to settle permanently at Beau-Site, living instead in small hotels
and boarding houses. The family fortunes then suffered another setback for
in 1921, when the franc was depreciating even more rapidly than before,
the manager exercised an option to buy the hotel. Henry Tippett had now
lost his major asset. But he loved the continent, his wife loved travelling,
and supported by investment from the proceeds of the hotel sale and
dividends from the property company, they decided to continue a nomadic
existence which would see them in small hotels in France, Corsica, Italy,
Yugoslavia and Germany, for a year or so at a time, until their finances had
recovered enough, largely through the success of the property company, to
enable them to return to England in 1932. What this meant as far as the
children were concerned was that although they would see their parents in
the holidays, travelling across Europe to Beau-Site or wherever it was the
Tippetts had temporarily settled, from 1919 (Tippett was then fourteen)
they had no real home.

During their continental exile the Tippetts occasionally visited England
for business or family reasons. It was on one of these visits – a holiday
in Cornwall with their children in the summer of 1924 – that Henry
Tippett decided to change his name. There was a family precedent for
taking this unusual course. In the mid-eighteenth century a Tippett forbear
had married into a Vivian family, one of whose descendants left an estate to
a Tippett cousin on condition that he change his surname to Vivian; so
from that time part of the Tippett family became Vivians. But although
Henry Tippett claimed that his reason for changing the name was that he
had lost patience with being misaddressed as Mr Pippett, Whippett,
Snippett or whatever, his true reason for doing so was obscure. It was
probably connected with the disgrace of his father's imprisonment. In any
event he now by deed poll became Henry Tippett Kemp, and his sons also
changed their names, Peter[6] permanently and Michael for only a few
months before reverting to his real and, as far as he was concerned, better
name.

The Kemps could have settled on the continent for good. What
prompted their decision to return to England and start a new life there
(when Henry Kemp was seventy-four) was less sentiment than the feeling
that they ought to provide some employment during the depression.
Accordingly Henry Kemp bought a house, in Timsbury near Bath, large
enough to require three servants and a gardener. Later they took in some
Jewish refugees from Germany. At the beginning of the Second World
War, by which time the house and garden had become too big for them,
they moved to Exmouth. In 1943 Henry Kemp was badly injured by the
blast from a high explosive bomb. For someone with a less tough
constitution the injuries would have been fatal, but he lived for almost
another year and was eighty-six when he died in July 1944. His wife
survived him for twenty-five years and died, aged eighty-nine, in
November 1969. Longevity is another family characteristic Tippett seems
to have inherited.

Childhood and Schooling

Tippett was born in a London nursing home (51 Belgrave Road, Pimlico) on 2 January 1905. He was a delicate baby whose health gave such cause for alarm that a clergyman uncle was called in for a midnight christening – when he was named Michael Kemp Tippett. A wasting fever was diagnosed, due less to physical frailty than to an inability to digest cow's milk, and a drastic remedy of brandy and meat juice was prescribed. The baby's health promptly improved. But he developed a taste for this diet, so much so that it was some time before he could be weaned from it. This was the first instance of Tippett's capacity to profit from misfortune.

He was a good-tempered, obedient child and he and his brother Peter (born 11 February 1904) spent a happy boyhood in the pleasantly rural and sheltered atmosphere of Wetherden, where there was always plenty to do (riding Suffolk punches at harvest time, setting night lines for pike, playing bicycle polo in the lane, walking down to the village blacksmith to watch the horses being shod) and where there was a busy social life (Rosemary Cottage was often full with visiting relatives and friends). The boys were allotted a barn each for private study and another was set aside for amateur theatricals supervised by their mother. Isabel Tippett was particularly concerned that her children should acquire that robustness of health which was the hallmark of a well-bred family, and when they were still quite young she established a routine of exercises in the garden before breakfast and long walks every afternoon, which was to continue until they went to preparatory school.

In November 1909, when Tippett was nearly five, she engaged a nursery governess, Jessie Brand. His early education was patterned like a conventional schooling, with lessons in the usual subjects (Latin and French being taught by a retired schoolmaster in the neighbouring village of Woolpit), end of term exams and holidays at the normal times. It also included music, and the boys were given piano lessons by a succession of local teachers. From the start Tippett showed an aptitude for music, spending long periods at piano practice and delivering his party pieces with the airs of an accomplished performer. His gifts were above average but they did not appear exceptional. When he was about ten he began to feel the first stirrings of his instinct to compose. This was simply a matter of extemporizing enthusiastically at the piano, making what were obviously inchoate sets of sounds. But for him they represented his first excitement at the prospect of inventing music. His early ambition had been to become a scientist but now he told his parents that he wanted to become a composer. They however had little idea of what the word composer implied. There was no real musical tradition in the family, they lived far from a centre of musical activity and naturally they did not take him seriously.

The Tippetts' attitude to their son's curriculum may have been conventional but it was perfectly reasonable, for even if they had understood they had a composer on their hands it is unlikely they would have allowed music to take precedence over his general education. In one respect however it was distinctly unconventional. Tippett's father was an agnostic. His mother, though at first orthodox in her religious views (she took her children to the local parish church – and Tippett greatly enjoyed joining in the singing) later became an agnostic too,[7] not so much through her husband's influence as through that of a Liberal agnostic friend of his. As he was growing up Tippett found himself therefore in an environment in which 'divinity' was not included in his official curriculum. Religion was a subject for critical discussion. For a short period, Tippett believed himself a convinced Christian and he excitedly communicated his feelings to his parents, informing them that they should realise there really was a God and that accordingly they should adapt to his way of thinking. But soon he became an agnostic too – and a precocious one: while still at preparatory school he wrote and circulated a small tract refuting deism.

In September 1914, when Tippett was nine, the conventional schooling process began. He was sent to Brookfield Preparatory School (now Forres School) in Swanage, Dorset, where his brother was already a pupil. His curriculum eventually included Greek (which fascinated him) as well as Latin, and piano lessons continued, though they were soon suspended with the outbreak of war and the elimination of 'extras'. His determination to be in the centre of things overcame his fear of the boisterous society and his inability to present the conventional passport to acceptance, skill at games. He was moderately content there and left in July 1918, when he was due to go to public school.

At this point his father had considered engaging a private tutor. His mother however preferred him to go to a tough 'manly' school and her view prevailed. On the advice of an uncle who lived near Edinburgh, Tippett was entered for a foundation scholarship at Fettes College. He won a scholarship and went to Fettes in September 1918. Piano lessons resumed, and he started learning the organ and, briefly, the chanter. He sang treble in the choir and discovered Mozart while playing the piano in an arrangement of the G-minor Symphony (K550) with the school orchestra. But his interest in music and scholastic subjects was overshadowed by the spartan and forbidding atmosphere. Fettes at that time was a characteristic if extreme example of the British public school. Bullying and sadism were commonplace and tacitly regarded as necessary stages in the tempering of young gentlemen. The ageing headmaster, a distant and awesome figure, left the running of the school to the prefects and housemasters, who zealously upheld the principle that the younger boys were the property of the older. One of Tippett's letters to his parents must have been unusually if innocently explicit about sexual practices at the school, for in the spring term of 1919 they unexpectedly arrived from the south of France, and, as Tippett subsequently discovered, threatened to expose the school in the press unless the headmaster was removed. A new headmaster was in fact appointed and the old one resigned or retired at the end of the academic year. Tippett himself would gladly have left at this point, but a letter from the new headmaster persuaded his parents that he should return and help create a fine school. No one realised what this really meant until Tippett

was confronted by his housemaster and obliged to give an account of the
sexual morals of every boy in the school, or at any rate every boy he knew.
It was enough to have had to betray the unwritten law of schoolboy
confidences but apart from that he was 'guilty' himself, having already
been seduced by a boy to whom he had become closely attached. He was
placed in an acute moral dilemma. Some expulsions followed. His final
terms at Fettes were exceedingly unpleasant. The only solution was to
leave and the only way to do this was to reveal the full details to his
parents. Towards these his mother was puritanical, his father more
considerate. But the tactic served its purpose and he did leave, in March
1920. By this time he thought he had managed to break the public school
practice by which the second year bullied the first, the third the second,
and a certain moral toughness in his makeup may be said to derive from his
period at Fettes. But his experiences there were so traumatic that they left
an almost total amnesia and for many years afterwards Tippett never
referred to them.

His five terms at Fettes coincided with his parent's growing financial
difficulties. His father now came over from France and found him a school
of entirely different character, for which the fees were about the same as the
'extras' at Fettes. This was Stamford Grammar School in Lincolnshire.
Compared with the grim and monumental Victorian gothic of Fettes, the
school was small (there were about fifty boarders and 150 day-boys) and
unpretentious; and it was close to the centre of Stamford itself, a typically
English market town with attractive buildings made from local limestone.
Tippett entered Stamford School in April 1920. He immediately found life
more congenial, making friends with the sons of farmers and doctors who
would invite him to their homes on half-holidays. He also developed
rapidly in academic work, especially history. By the end of the following
summer he had reached the sixth form, when he gave up classics (which
was perhaps too closely associated in his mind with Fettes) for science and
advanced mathematics. At the same time he was appointed a prefect of the
boarding house.

At Stamford Tippett's musical abilities were made use of – he played the
piano for hymn singing at school assemblies. But apart from that and
Saturday evening 'sing-songs' for the boarders, at which he was the star
performer, there was no official musical activity at the school, no music
master and no chapel choir (the boys went to town churches for services).
For music he depended on Frances Tinkler, his piano teacher, and Henry
Waldo Acomb, the junior English master.

His piano playing progressed under Mrs Tinkler, a warm personality
and an excellent teacher who held an influential position in local musical
society particularly through the reputation of her ex-pupil, Malcolm
Sargent (himself an old boy of the school). Mrs Tinkler guided Tippett
through some of Bach's *Forty-eight Preludes and Fugues*, some Beethoven and
Schubert sonatas and some Chopin pieces and he practised assiduously
early every morning and, when he was a prefect, while the rest of the school
was having PT. Mrs Tinkler also gave him some singing lessons. When his

family, friends and school were opposed to his enthusiasm for music she was the only person to give real encouragement and the only person he could confide in.

At this time Sargent, in his mid-twenties, was musical director of the Stamford amateur operatic society and founder conductor of the Leicestershire Symphony Orchestra. For one term he kept an eye on musical activities at the school by, for example, dispensing fatherly comments on a performance of Bach's C-minor Concerto for two keyboards which Tippett gave with another boy and an orchestra organized by Mrs Tinkler. (After he had left school but was still living in Stamford, Tippett sang under Sargent's baton as a member of the chorus in performances of Planquette's *Les Cloches de Corneville* with the local society and played a non-singing part, the King's Fool, in Edward German's *Merrie England*.)

Acomb had been an undergraduate at Cambridge and he occasionally brought friends from there to give musical weekends. In this way Tippett was introduced to a curious assortment of pieces, including Mozart's Piano Concerto K488, Dowland songs and English folk-songs (he became an expert exponent of 'John Barleycorn', 'Searching for Lambs', 'Waly, waly' and, when he wished to defy authority, 'The Miller of Dee', pointedly emphasizing its refrain of 'I care for nobody'). Acomb sometimes took boys to concerts – a recital by Pouishnov, an orchestral concert under Sargent at Leicester including Ravel's *Mother Goose Suite*, which was the first piece of twentieth-century music Tippett had heard and one which made a deep impression on him, especially the 'petit poucet' movement.

But all these musical activities were isolated events and in general Tippett's musical gifts were left to develop on their own. Other interests began to take shape at this time. He became absorbed in old furniture, architecture, occultism, pogo sticks, mesmerism, drama (playing Portia and Mrs Malaprop to fine effect and producing small plays himself). He extended his reading through the stimulus of Acomb who introduced him in particular to Greek drama and Samuel Butler (whose *The Way of All Flesh* contained an episode, in chapters 42 and 43, strikingly reminiscent of his experiences with the Fettes housemaster).

With his own circle of friends he was already an outstanding personality and an enthralling conversationalist, always one move ahead of everyone else, cheerful and vivacious, refreshingly light-hearted in his attitude to authority and rules. His least favourite book at this time was Ovid's *Tristia*, because of its melancholy atmosphere. He taught his circle to question received ideas, stand on their own feet and challenge the system. The school was run according to a conventional 'play the game' philosophy. For a while Tippett did so. He enjoyed hockey and became quite good at it. Although he detested rugby and cricket (he campaigned for tennis instead) he played nonetheless. He conformed to religious observances. He became notorious for his jocular remarks in divinity classes but he did not attempt to force his views on other boys. He privately learned Italian, entered himself for an examination set by London University and passed it – partly to irritate the headmaster, whose permission was not asked, and partly because he wanted to anyway. Eventually however his non-conformity became more open. A rebellious attitude to the school cadet corps was followed by a refusal to belong to it at all and an undisguised atheism led to difficulties with the headmaster, who could not understand his apparently irrational behaviour. Tippett refused to contribute to the collection at school services (other boys would put a hand in and then take it straight out) but at the same time he would make clandestine visits with his friends to St Mary's, the local Anglo-Catholic church, because he was fascinated by the drama and dramatic possibilities in the mass. His influence on the school was in fact negligible but he gained the reputation of a dangerously subversive character who needed taming. Matters came to a head when he decided that in order to be logical he would boycott house prayers for a fortnight. The headmaster responded by removing his prefectship and informing his parents that he would not be allowed to return to the school after the summer term of 1922.

Tippett was now seventeen-and-a-half and his parents initially planned to send their gifted but wayward son to Oxford or Cambridge, where he could obtain qualifications leading to a well-paid job in law. But by this time Tippett himself was determined to study music and become a composer. Even though he still had no clearer conception than did his parents of what being a composer meant, he firmly rejected all proposals for an alternative. His father wrote for advice from the headmaster, who replied that the idea was absurd, and from Malcolm Sargent, who thought the same. It was then decided that the only thing to do was for Tippett to train as a concert pianist. So he was put in lodgings in Stamford in order to study with Mrs Tinkler. (The headmaster put Tippett's lodgings out of bounds to his schoolfriends but he continued to see them.)

For a while he practised Mozart's K488 and then, during the winter of 1922/3, he explored ways in which he might teach himself composition. From a Stamford bookshop he ordered a copy of Stanford's *Musical Composition*. In the second chapter, headed 'Technique', he found examples of the difference between harmony and counterpoint which settled the matter. He was going to write contrapuntal music. Mrs Tinkler claimed to have no knowledge of the subject but put him in touch with the organist of St Mary's, who gave him lessons in species counterpoint (the traditional teaching method) and allowed him to practise the organ in exchange for singing tenor in the choir. Mrs Tinkler gave him some lessons in harmony with Stainer's *A Theory of Harmony* [1876]. He wrote a few pieces of the simplest kind. Then, quite by chance, his parents met a professional musician in a train who advised them to send Tippett to the Royal College of Music in London. He was called to see the director, Sir Hugh Allen, who asked him a few general questions and what his favourite fugue in the '48' was (Tippett replied the second but on being asked its key could not remember), and on the strength of this interview Tippett was admitted to the RCM on 30 April 1923, a few weeks after the beginning of the summer term.

Tippett's boyhood added up to much more than the fumbling and haphazard prelude to a musical career it might seem. In several respects it was out of the ordinary. His father's connections with France and belief in the importance of foreign languages (he himself spoke fluent French and Spanish) meant that Tippett was an accomplished French speaker at the age of nine and that he had acquired, even then, an awareness of European peoples and manners markedly less insular than that of his contemporaries. He had inherited a sharp intelligence and an instinct to question current shibboleths. His parents had encouraged this independence – whether by design or lack of interest is of little consequence – and later obliged him, for example, to make his own way across the continent during school holidays to wherever it was they had temporarily settled. This was no small matter for a young teenager prone to travel sickness and, despite his private cure for it (marmalade), likely to tempt fate by opening the door of a carriage in a continental express travelling at speed and climb down to the steps below in order to gulp in fresh air. Luckily Tippett was too young to have been caught up in the 1914–18 war; but he was old enough to have seen those reassuring pictures of soldiers marching off to the strains of 'It's a long way to Tipperary' whose subsequent destruction was to prove a major factor in the formulation of his pacifism. Whatever the disadvantages of eight years of British boarding schools they had at least introduced him to the less pleasant features of middle-class ethics and enabled him to undergo the hazards and rewards of testing his own convictions. If the educational methods of the 1920s made little provision for musical talent they were flexible enough to permit entry into the RCM on the judgement of the director rather than the evidence of examinations.

When he arrived at the RCM Tippett had developed the maturity to make the best of his opportunities.

Student Years

For Tippett the world of music opened out by the Royal College of Music was a revelation. Within a few weeks he experienced the exhilaration of a person at last in the presence of something he had been intuitively seeking but which he had hitherto been unable to find. He had been to only three or four concerts in his life but now he could go several times a week. He developed a voracious appetite for music of all kinds and all styles, listening to everything from plainchant to jazz. He regularly attended Promenade Concerts (hearing the 1924 season in its entirety), Beecham seasons at Covent Garden and Mozart performances at the Old Vic, and he rarely missed the opportunity to hear and see such visitors as Stravinsky and Ravel, Furtwängler and Weingartner, Chaliapin and Melba, Pavlova and Karsavina, the Busch and Léner Quartets. Music was only one component in the remarkable upsurge of artistic activity in post-war London. Through a new circle of friends – especially Aubrey Russ, a music and theatre enthusiast, and Roy Langford, for a time manager of the Lyric

Theatre, Hammersmith – he could now also pursue his interest in the
theatre: Shakespeare, Restoration plays, Ibsen, Shaw, O'Neill, Strindberg,
Toller, Cochran reviews.

Against this intoxicating activity academic demands were more sobering
but no less decisive in fixing his resolve to become a composer. In someone
less single-minded his lack of any genuine training in composition might
have been a disadvantage. Comparisons with apparently more sophisticated peers could have sapped his confidence and he could have been
tempted to fabricate one of the several modern styles current in the 1920s in
order to keep pace with the inevitably competitive spirit of the RCM.
Instead, his relative ignorance brought advantages. He was discovering the
major classics for the first time, without the superficial veneer of
understanding that an early musical environment might have brought him.
By contrast, contemporary English music seemed to him to be amateurish
and he soon decided that his first priority would be to leave considerations
of artistic expression aside and secure a technique. Composition exercises
were therefore no drudgery. He had abundant energy, the capacity for
sustained hard work and the patience to realise that acquiring this
technique would take a long time. The main thing was that he knew what
he wanted to do.

Composition studies, with Charles Wood, began with species counterpoint, the harmonization of chorale melodies from Bach's *Orgelbüchlein* and
the provision of accompaniments to themes by Haydn, Mozart and
Beethoven – this, as Tippett later noted, the same method Rossini had used
when teaching himself composition. Tippett was then set more extended
tasks involving the composition of complete pieces. Wood's method here
had been inherited from Stanford, who in turn had been trained in a
German tradition stretching back as far as Weinlig, Wagner's teacher.
Wood gave Tippett a model to imitate (usually from Haydn or Beethoven),
having first discussed a number of aspects: the basic construction, the
relative length and balance of the sections, the principal modulations, the
number and quality of the themes and the general character. Tippett was
fortunate in having such an accomplished and sympathetic teacher for his
first composition studies. If these studies were limited in scope, they were
thorough. They emphasized the nature of musical function as well as the
minutiae of syntax, developing an attitude he was to find of permanent
value. And if he was occasionally asked to work at a subject which had little
or no practical relevance to his compositional ambitions, then at least he
learnt the 'positive value of negatives' – that to persevere with and eventually exhaust the resources of such a subject was to reach a point at which
another subject of genuine relevance was automatically summoned from
within his own psyche. Wood's death in 1926 was for Tippett a sad loss.

After a few months at the RCM Tippett realised that he could not rely on
his teacher to provide him with everything he wanted. From Wood he had
no instruction in counterpoint, other than the species method. So he began
his own systematic survey. He started with Palestrina and the Renaissance
polyphony he was instinctively drawn to, and planned to reach the

twentieth century in slow stages. There could be no hurry in this matter and Tippett was satisfied with his calculation that he would be forty before he could, as it were, belong to his own period. He would discover what was being performed at Westminster Cathedral (where Sir Richard Terry was then Director of Music) and the Anglican churches and before hearing the work in question would copy it out in the Parry Room Library of the RCM. By this laborious but time-honoured method he studied a substantial quantity of liturgical music, both continental and English. When giving him exercises in modern choral music Wood had taken Brahms as a model, that is, he had placed emphasis on a style of harmony filtering into English music via Parry, and a style of word-setting based on German texts. Tippett wanted to set English texts, and to continue his study of counterpoint. He therefore decided to investigate the English madrigal. The best way to do this seemed to be to find a small choir to conduct. He asked the registrar of the RCM if such a choir could be found for him. Quite by chance the representative of a group of musical enthusiasts living in and around Oxted in Surrey had at that time asked the RCM if a student could conduct the small choir they intended forming. So began, in October 1924, Tippett's practical study of the English madrigal. During his four years at the RCM his self-imposed teaching course did not follow the precise sequence of his original plan. But he was to acquire a detailed knowledge of a wide variety of musical styles and a particular love for the music of Handel and Beethoven.

After Wood's death Tippett had to find a new teacher. At this point he could have studied with Vaughan Williams. But he felt that however academically respectable Vaughan Williams's methods might be, he would be unable to escape the influence of a composer whose style to him lacked intellectual fibre and whose affinities with folk-song seemed too narrow. What he wanted was instruction in harmony, having no sympathy with the whole harmonic system he had encountered to date. So he decided to devote all his prescribed composition time to studying harmony with C.H. Kitson, who, Tippett hoped, would provide him with the rigorous grounding he needed. In the event he found work with Kitson arid. He remained with him until the end of his student period, but it was not until the late 1930s that he felt he had gained a genuine understanding of harmony and tonality.

His second study was the piano, with Aubin Raymar. Raymar struggled vainly to get Tippett to practise and it soon became apparent that he would never acquire the technical skill to perform in public. Nevertheless he was introduced to a great deal of music, from Scarlatti and the standard classics to Debussy, Ravel and Bartók (*Allegro barbaro*), and he became tolerably proficient. He did not learn any other instruments at the RCM, though shortly after, when he was living in Oxted, he decided to acquire some knowledge of stringed instruments and practised, in succession, the violin, viola and cello. He did not practise hard enough to develop any real technique in any of them either but at least he gained a working knowledge, which was all he had intended.

His other study at the RCM was conducting. Though he eventually
graduated to the senior class of Adrian Boult, most of his time was spent in
the junior class of Malcolm Sargent. Sargent concentrated on the practical
problems associated with directing amateur choirs and orchestras and with
accompanying singers at the piano. There was only a modicum of actual
conducting, the emphasis being laid on observing and asking questions. He
decided to supplement this activity by attending Boult's rehearsals with the
first orchestra. For four years Tippett stood at Boult's side on Friday
afternoons, further extending his knowledge of conducting technique, of the
repertory and of the sounds of orchestral instruments. In addition to
routine concerts the first orchestra played for student operatic performances. Tippett thereby learnt several standard operas, as well as such
works as *Parsifal* (for which he was a *répétiteur*), *Pelléas et Mélisande* and *Hugh
the Drover*. In his later years at the RCM he conducted, in an energetic if
ungainly fashion, single works or single movements at open concerts of the
second orchestra. Beethoven's Leonora Overture No. 3, Brahms's Tragic
Overture and excerpts from Handel's Concerto Grosso in G minor, op.6
and Rimsky-Korsakov's *Scheherazade* were among the works heard under
his direction.

He gained two minor awards at the RCM – in 1926 a Signor Foli
Scholarship, awarded to composition students, and in 1927 the Dove Prize,
for 'general excellence, assiduity and industry'. But he had little real
success as a composer. His music was not heard at the public rehearsals of
the Patrons' Fund of the RCM (an important series specially endowed for
young composers and performers and for which the London Symphony
Orchestra was engaged) until several years after he had left: in July 1935
the first movement of his Symphony in B flat was performed (under his
own baton and not that of Sargent, who conducted the rest of the
programme). He never won the Arthur Sullivan Prize, the composition
prize to which budding composers most aspired, nor the Cobbett Prize,
another composition prize. In 1929 he entered for the Mendelssohn
Scholarship, but was placed *proxime* to David Moule-Evans, a fellow
student at the RCM. Yet his composition became increasingly assured and
if he showed few signs of real individuality, among his contemporaries at
least he gained a reputation as a fluent melodist who wrote in unusually
extended paragraphs.

The academic record of Tippett's RCM years does not give the
impression of a major talent nicely poised at the start of a promising career.
But neither does it suggest a slow decline into respectable mediocrity. He
knew exactly what he wanted. What he could, he got from the RCM. What
it was unable to offer him he sought out elsewhere. Someone so sure of his
aims and with so little to show for them may be judged a product of the
general feeling at the time that if you were British you could accomplish
anything; but in Tippett's case it seems rather that he was following an
inner compulsion to do what he must. In the summer of 1928 he failed his
B.Mus. examinations (which he sat as an external student of London
University, since the RCM confers no degrees in academic music). But he

passed them the following December and left the RCM on the eighth of that month.

When first entering the RCM he had agreed with his parents that he would eventually study for a doctorate in music. Now that he had acquired his B.Mus., he decided to spend no more time on paper qualifications and to concentrate on his immediate requirements as a composer. These were simply to find the environment in which to compose unmolested. He wanted to detach himself from academicism and to continue working with amateurs, far from what he considered the potentially stifling atmosphere of professional music.

Oxted

While a student Tippett had lived in London University lodging houses or in flats with friends. Now he had to find a more permanent home. He wanted a peaceful spot away from London, where he could walk out in the countryside without a human-being in sight. The obvious answer was somewhere in or near Oxted, a small town on the southern slopes of the North Downs, where his success with his madrigal choir had by now earned him a leading position in its artistic community. He enjoyed the freedom to explore the English madrigal and operatic tradition as he wished. He also valued the friendship of local families, mostly city commuters and their wives, who in turn were fascinated by the vitality of the young student in their midst and anxious to help him. He commanded respect from the men and with his unruly hair and generally impoverished appearance drew out the maternal instincts of the women. In fact many of these families were to remain firm friends, in particular John, later Sir John and Evelyn Maude, Sidney and Mabel Parvin and Eric and Dorothy Shaxson. Evelyn Maude discovered that a flat was to let at the local preparatory school, Hazelwood School. With furniture provided by his parents, Tippett duly settled there in early 1929.

He was to remain in Oxted until 1951. This first home was one half of Chestnut Cottage, a building originally planned as staff accommodation for the school sanatorium. In 1932 he moved into 1 Whitegates Cottages on the farm of Sidney Parvin, again living in one half of a double cottage. Here, although only twenty minutes from the local railway station, Hurst Green Halt, he was deep in the countryside and some distance from the *nouveau riche* housing of Oxted itself. The cottages nestled at the foot of the Downs, fields and wooded hills to one side, a stream and undulating meadows to the other – surroundings so picturesque that they might have seemed the province of a gentleman composer anxious to escape into an arcadian paradise. Tippett stayed there until 1938, by which time he had been able, with financial help from his father, to buy the whole cottage and the half acre of land surrounding it. Then, by means of a loan arranged through John Maude, he built himself an entirely new and singularly inelegant red-brick bungalow (confusingly named Whitegates Cottage) a

few yards away on the same site, renting out the old cottages to Ben and
Miriam Lewis and to their daughter and son-in-law, Bronwen and Jack
Wilson. Ben Lewis was an ex-miner, now a road worker for the local
council. His wife did some housekeeping for Tippett.

Hazelwood School was very small (only about twenty-five boys) and
Tippett naturally came into contact with its activities and teachers. One of
these was Christopher Fry, the English master, who was subsequently to
provide texts for several of Tippett's vocal works. Soon Tippett was
persuaded to play the organ at chapel services and to provide some casual
music teaching. Later in 1929 the headmaster found himself in need of a
French teacher and Tippett accepted the job, carefully ensuring that it
would still leave him time for composition. The salary of £80 per annum,
plus occasional financial assistance from elsewhere, provided him with just
enough to live on. He did not particularly enjoy schoolmastering but he
was a natural teacher and, except when quashing classroom malefactors,
genial and approachable. Many of the boys were introduced to music
through his gramophone listening sessions or in his singing classes, where
he favoured a mixture of arias from *Messiah*, Cecil Sharp arrangements of
English folk-songs and excerpts from Curt Sachs's *Album of Oriental Music*.
At this time he expressed the view that Handel was the greatest of all
composers and made no secret of his (temporary) dislike of Wagner.

The original Oxted choir had wanted to work in a conventional way, by
entering the local East Kent and West Sussex Music Festival and winning
prizes. Tippett found that the repertory demanded by this event was not to
his taste, so he disregarded competitive work and concentrated on the
music he liked. Instead of Stanford's *Songs of the Fleet* or Elgar's *The Spirit of
England* the choir was asked to purchase Byrd's 'Though Amaryllis dance
in green'. Music by other madrigalists was added, and his lively and
serious approach brought an unexpected quality and ambition to the
choir's work. It increased in size, broadened its scope, gave concerts (one of
which did include the *Songs of the Fleet* plus Tippett's own early unpublished
Piano Sonata played by Cyril Smith) and in general made its mark in a
community eager to welcome it.

Oxted already possessed a flourishing dramatic society, the Oxted and
Limpsfield Players, an enterprise deriving its impetus from the Little
Theatre Movement, which stimulated the growth of amateur theatre in
England between the wars. By this time the local Barn Theatre had been
built and Tippett had persuaded the Players to combine with his choir and
extend their activities into opera. He calculated that some of the choir were
good enough to take leading parts and that the rest could sing in the chorus
or play in the orchestra; with a few professional players opera would be
perfectly feasible. His policy was to introduce the subject gradually, but
with a choice of works which proclaimed enterprise and imagination. The
first venture, in March 1927, was Vaughan Williams's one-act *The
Shepherds of the Delectable Mountains*, in a double bill with the play of
Everyman. In April 1928 his realization of the eighteenth-century ballad
opera, *The Village Opera* was performed; in October 1930, Stanford's *The*

Travelling Companion. In February 1930 there were performances of Flecker's *Don Juan* with incidental music by Tippett himself.

For his first major conducting venture the Vaughan Williams was an ambitious choice. This was the work's first amateur performance and the composer came to see it, interested also no doubt by the effect of a double bill carefully unified by the common theme of the Christian soul entering heaven. Tippett's interest in ballad opera was prompted by the successful revival of *The Beggar's Opera* at the Lyric Theatre, Hammersmith, during the early 1920s. Looking through examples of the genre at the RCM he came across an original edition of *The Village Opera* and decided to perform it, attracted particularly by the idea of a 'village' community producing its own opera. (*The Village Opera* of 1729 is a pasticcio by Charles Johnson, and not the later *Love in a Village* with music by Arne, which by coincidence was revived at the same time in the Lyric Theatre.) This was a large-scale undertaking, editorially as well as dramatically. The original edition contained the full text but only the voice lines of the songs. With the scantiest knowledge of eighteenth-century performance practice Tippett made an elaborate realization of the music for chamber ensemble and compressed and adapted the action. He composed some music of his own and rewrote both text and music for the final scene of Act II, in which the two pairs of lovers unsuccessfully attempt to elope by night. This scene was singled out by *The Times* as the most successful. What particularly attracted him to *The Travelling Companion*, the first and only genuine opera he performed at Oxted, was its lively fast-moving choral style. This taught him that English choral writing need not be weighed down by what had seemed an endemic lethargy. Doubtless he was also moved by the story, in which (to use the Jungian terminology which later fascinated him) a mana personality helps the hero to win the princess by dispossessing her of her magic, that is, by depriving the anima of her power.

These performances gave Tippett invaluable first-hand experience of the workings both of dramatic music and of what amounted to almost the whole of the English operatic tradition except Purcell (whose music he was to discover later) – ballad opera, early twentieth-century opera and incidental music, and the most recent example of that tradition. He showed considerable diplomatic acumen in persuading the Players to view this individual and certainly highly subjective repertory as in their best interests as well as his own.

He was able to explore further operatic by-ways when conducting another amateur operatic society during this period – though he did not control its repertory as he would have wished. Towards the end of 1929 he became conductor of the operatic society of the Music School of the Hackney Institute in London. He was invited in the first place because its own conductor was hesitant to take charge of the ambitious project it had embarked on, a production of Holst's *The Perfect Fool*. Tippett was attracted by the Holst work and stayed for productions of *Martha*, *Ruddigore* and *The Emerald Isle* (Sullivan, completed by Edward German) by which time he had lost interest and in any case had other commitments.

Under the auspices of the Players he gave two major concerts in Oxted, one of his own music and the other of *Messiah*. Both were to have important consequences. The first was given on 5 April 1930 by his choir and largely professional soloists and orchestra (paid for by Evelyn Maude); it was conducted by his friend from the RCM, David Moule-Evans. The programme consisted of a Concerto in D for two flutes, oboe, four horns and strings, three songs for tenor and piano to poems by Charlotte Mew ('Afternoon Tea', 'Sea Love' and 'Arracombe Wood'), Variations for piano on 'Jockey to the Fair', a String Quartet in F and finally *Psalm in C*, a work for chorus and orchestra with text by Christopher Fry. The performance of the two works with orchestra suffered from under-rehearsal and the inevitable difficulties associated with performances involving amateurs (during the final rehearsal the missing double-bass player was eventually found on the golf course). Nevertheless the concert drew appreciative comments from the critics of *The Times* and *The Daily Telegraph*.

The *Messiah* performance was the result of an outing with boys from Hazelwood to the Royal Albert Hall in London, when the work was given in a cut version by the large choral and orchestral resources in favour at the time. Tippett was perplexed by the disparity between the cumbersome forces and the lucidity of Handel's music. Having examined the original scoring in the Chrysander edition, he decided to perform the work as Handel seemed to have written it. He had little idea of the tradition of continuo playing, but he could certainly conform to Handel's instrumental specifications and employ choral forces to match. The performance, on 15 November 1931 (repeated on 2 December in Caterham), was, at his request, a free one and the audience was able to buy the Novello libretto at 1d. He prefaced each part of the oratorio with a short talk about the formal plan and content of the work. Tippett here was less concerned with the idea of 'music appreciation' than with making known an illuminating formal discovery of his own, which he was to turn to artistic account eight years later when he conceived the plan of his oratorio *A Child of Our Time*.

The moderate public success of the Oxted concert of his own music was encouraging. Yet as far as he was concerned it revealed that he had not written a single work with a personality of its own. This was a harsh self-criticism, for some works at least were prophetic of certain aspects of his later style. But he was temperamentally incapable of compromising with his own artistic standards and, like many composers before him, he decided that he would at this comparatively late stage need to take lessons again. He diagnosed a failure of technique: until he had won a fluent and versatile technique he would not acquire the necessary individuality of expression. Tippett remembered a single tutorial, on variations of texture in a Mozart quartet, given at the RCM by R.O. Morris when deputizing for Wood; and he knew Morris's pioneering book on sixteenth-century polyphony[8] (which had previously shown him a way of studying counterpoint without recourse to species methods). Morris agreed to accept him as a pupil. Since Tippett could not pay for lessons himself, Morris arranged for him to be enrolled once again as a student of the RCM, to receive a grant and to be exempted from attendance at classes and from other student obligations.

In September 1930 Tippett began a course of study which lasted until July 1932. Morris considered the works performed at the Oxted concert wayward and undisciplined and straightaway advised Tippett to set them aside and turn to matters of style and form. Although he was the only sixteenth-century specialist Tippett had met, Morris's first four terms of study were devoted almost entirely to the analysis and composition of fugue, examples being taken from Bach's '48'. Then in the final terms he turned to free composition, and exercises in orchestration. The result of this was Tippett's String Trio in B flat, a work which shows a considerable advance in technique. Shortly before the lessons concluded Morris encouraged Tippett to take some private tuition in orchestration from Gordon Jacob. An attempted orchestration of the Trio followed, but Tippett did not gain much from Jacob's tuition apart from an introduction to the principles of orchestral balance as expounded by Rimsky-Korsakov. Like many of his contemporaries, Morris was a Sibelius enthusiast. So indeed was Tippett: his pseudonym when submitting work for RCM composition prizes consisted of the first two bars of Sibelius's Symphony No. 5. Traces of Sibelius may be detected not only in the String Trio but also in the first major work Tippett wrote after leaving Morris, his Symphony in B flat. Subsequently both works were withdrawn because of this unassimilated influence. The study with Morris was deeply beneficial however and there is no doubt that Tippett's compositional maturity stems from it.

During these early apprentice years Tippett's energies were naturally concentrated on composing, studying and performing. But being a composer did not limit him to that alone. Another essential part of a composer's equipment was, in his view, simply being receptive to what life had to offer – friendships, ideas, places, books: he organized his routine so that he could respond to the enthusiasms and preoccupations which were developing in him. Another was knowledge of languages. His father had brought him up to take this as a matter of course. He knew French and Italian already. In 1927 he had learnt a little Serbo-Croat on the train to Belgrade, where he had travelled in response to a telegram from his favourite cousin, Phyllis Kemp. (She was lecturing there in Slavonic languages and studying folk culture,[9] and was hoping that Tippett could help patch up an ill-fated love-affair of hers.) The priority however was German. He began to teach himself, with a Hugo primer. Then he inched his way through Goethe's *Wilhelm Meister* and *Faust*. He soon decided he would need to go to Germany to learn the language properly. He had been there once before, when in 1926 he went on a walking holiday through Ludwig II's Bavarian castle country before reaching Munich for a performance of Wagner's *Ring*. What little German he knew then had been culled from a pre-war Baedeker guide-book. Now, three years later, he wanted to find a place where he could settle down for the summer vacation, learn German and compose in peace. Francesca Allinson (whom he had met through Phyllis Kemp) suggested that he go to a Kinderheim at

Markdorf, about five miles from the northern shore of Lake Constance, where her German cousins had built up a home for some ten Berlin children orphaned by the war. Conditions were primitive but his rent would be minimal. As it turned out this was not an ideal way of learning the language either, since a south German dialect was spoken and the mother of the home was anxious to practise her English. But his German did improve and the main objective of the stay was duly fulfilled.

Visiting Germany that summer fitted into a pattern by which Tippett, like many of his contemporaries, would venture every holiday into an as yet undiscovered part of England or the continent and explore the countryside or retrace the steps of some literary or musical hero. This pattern had begun in 1923, when he visited Cornwall for the first time. He was hardly a committed *Wandervogel*. Determined exercise with a rucksack and tent and the popular cult of rambling were uncomfortably associated with the clean living favoured by the middle-class background from which he was trying to escape. But he loved the countryside and travel was relatively cheap. In any case such holidays were not intended merely for relaxation. At the Kinderheim he found that the beauty of the countryside and the friendliness of the people deepened the affection for Germany which he had already gained through music. This was never to leave him and was later to have a marked bearing on his attitude to the Second World War. Through the Kinderheim he was also able to pursue his interest in progressive education. The eldest pupil at the Kinderheim was given a free place at the well-known school of Salem, also situated on the northern shore of Lake Constance. Tippett took advantage of this arrangement to visit the school where Kurt Hahn (who later founded Gordonstoun School) fostered ideals of civic duty through self-discipline. Tippett did not like Salem, since to him it seemed merely a superior version of a British public school. But he was much attracted to the ideals of the Odenwaldschule (another experimental school, near Frankfurt am Main, where Paul Geheeb had created a system by which children ran the school themselves), until the children confided in him that they were 'not allowed to be children'. The school which attracted him most at this time was Dartington Hall. An Oxted neighbour had been headmaster during the first stages of the school's development and his Oxted friends Eric and Dorothy Shaxson sent their children there. In the 1930s Tippett was twice invited to teach at Dartington, and had it not been in remote Devon he might have agreed.

Tippett's interest in progressive education was genuine enough. It revealed alternatives to the education he had himself received at Fettes and Stamford, and progressive schools promoted the role of music more seriously than did traditional ones. But it arose chiefly because he liked children and not so much because of an enthusiasm for educational methods in themselves. Subsequently he considered all such schools too closely associated with affluence and he became a supporter of state education.

What sustained his interest in the subject during the 1920s and '30s was his friendship with David Ayerst. To say that Tippett's friends were carefully chosen would give a false impression; but he certainly benefited from them. Ayerst, who had gained a first in history at Oxford and had become chairman of the Labour Club there, was now a journalist on the *Manchester Guardian*. He introduced Tippett to left-wing politics and acted as Tippett's mentor on historical matters. He was also interested in educational methods, later in life becoming a schoolmaster and then an H.M. Inspector of Schools. Ayerst and his wife have remained two of Tippett's lifelong friends.

In 1932 Ayerst introduced Tippett to Wilfred Franks, a gifted but impecunious painter. Tippett fell in love with Franks. This was to prove the most intense emotional involvement of Tippett's life and it is perhaps no coincidence that his first genuinely individual music, his String Quartet No. 1, should date from the early years of the relationship. Franks had trained at the Bauhaus for a period. On his return to England he became a Trotskyist and a pacifist, regarding painting simply as a political weapon. For a while Tippett's views corresponded with those of Franks. When, in the late 1930s, Tippett's own commitment to left-wing politics began to wane, he felt he could lay the burden of his political responsibilities on Franks's shoulders. 'You be a revolutionary for me.' This was not a wholly frivolous remark, and neither did it seem so to Franks who is still a supporter of the Workers' Revolutionary Party and a contributor to *News Line*.

Ayerst also introduced Tippett to W.H. Auden, through whom he met T.S. Eliot. Tippett did not become a close friend of either poet; but with Eliot he developed a relationship rather like that between apprentice and master which was to prove by far the most fruitful he had with any living artist.[10]

Tippett had read Eliot's poetry from his student days and had been deeply impressed by Eliot's critical writings ever since the first publication, in 1932, of his *Selected Essays*. Eliot's ideas about the need for a poet to recognize the vitality of tradition – to cultivate a historical sense and the capacity to transmute personal emotional experiences in order to belong to it (the essay 'Tradition and the Individual Talent') – had already influenced Tippett's thinking profoundly. He had also been strongly influenced by Eliot's theory of 'dissociation of sensibility' ('The Metaphysical Poets') which had corrupted English poetic tradition from the Puritans onwards, because Tippett found in it not only a convincing explanation of why English composers had failed to live up to Tudor and Jacobean musical traditions but also a compositional attitude (Eliot's 'amalgamation of disparate experience') through which that tradition might be revitalized. When the opportunity arose to meet Eliot, Tippett was able therefore to make the most of his good fortune. Their friendship began in 1937, in unusual circumstances. The six-year-old son of F.V. Morley, one of Eliot's co-directors at the publishing firm of Faber and Faber, suffered from speech difficulties. He also had a remarkable musical gift. Knowing of Tippett's interest in education through music, Auden suggested that Tippett, whose Oxted cottage was within cycling distance of

Morley's Surrey home, might be able to help the boy communicate. Tippett duly visited the Morleys twice a week – and not only because he wanted to help the boy: he also wanted to become part of a family again. Eliot, for roughly the same reasons, was a regular visitor at that time and the two met there, playing endless games of Monopoly with the boy and generally contributing to household activities. Tippett and Eliot subsequently had a number of short conversations together in Eliot's office at Faber and Faber, at first about drama and later about wider and more general subjects. It would be more accurate to describe these conversations as tutorials. Although Eliot's second love was music and although he liked Tippett and respected his intelligence, Tippett himself was not particularly interested in exchanging views about music. He wanted to learn. He went to Eliot for advice. Eliot told him what to read, and having read the book recommended Tippett would return and ask what to read next. In this way Eliot introduced him to the poetry of Yeats (whom Eliot considered the greatest living poet) and to the philosophies of the Neo-Thomist, Jacques Maritain, and of Susanne Langer, both of whom appealed to Tippett's instinct to categorize and distinguish genres by showing him that aesthetics could be examined in this way as profitably as could music. Eliot also introduced Tippett to the work of the English scholar, Basil Willey, whose *Seventeenth Century Background* (London 1934) – which could be described as a large-scale corroboration of Eliot's seventeenth-century 'dissociation of sensibility' – was to have a formative influence on his thinking and provide the basis from which his own views on the split between science and art, 'fact' and 'fiction', were to develop.

At the time of their first meetings, Eliot had recently completed *Murder in the Cathedral*, was now engaged on *The Family Reunion* and was in general preoccupied with the problems of verse drama. With Tippett he discussed his ideas about the nature of poetry, drama and music, and the relative weight of dramatic action, gesture and music in the mixed arts of play, ballet and opera. Tippett found Eliot's analysis of these matters profoundly illuminating. When drafting the plan for *A Child of Our Time* in 1939 he asked Eliot to write the text. By encouraging him to write it himself Eliot was largely responsible for Tippett's subsequent decision to be his own librettist. Tippett later described Eliot as his artistic godfather and said that Eliot taught him all he ever learnt about the nature of drama. This was perhaps an overstatement. But it was a measure of the debt he felt. At a time when the bible of the musical establishment was Constant Lambert's *Music Ho!*, his was the *Selected Essays* of T.S. Eliot.

Of Tippett's other friends at this time the ones who meant most to him were Phyllis Kemp, Evelyn Maude and Francesca Allinson. Together they formed part of a polarity in his life between relatively calm and enduring relationships with women and more intense and volatile ones with men. His cousin Phyllis Kemp was the only member of his family with whom he had preserved a genuine friendship since childhood. Although Tippett's subsequent Trotskyism brought about an almost irreparable break (she became a fervent Stalinist), as the black sheep of their respective families the two were naturally drawn to each other in their earlier years when, in any case, Tippett's relations with his parents were severely strained. She introduced Tippett to the poetry of Hopkins and Owen, and to Marxism,[11] a commitment she had developed in Yugoslavia. A more powerful influence was exerted by Evelyn Maude. She fell in love with Tippett. An unusually sympathetic person, she did not allow her feelings to interfere with her firm but not prudish principles of integrity. For his part Tippett seems to have regarded her as a kind of mother figure. She played a major part in civilizing the rather wild student composer, introducing him to the writings of Jung and Goethe and to those of the English mystic, Evelyn Underhill, and in general acting as a sympathetic sounding board to whatever views he wished to test out. Francesca Allinson[12] was an accomplished musician, a choral conductor and a specialist in folk-song whose knowledge of the subject provided Tippett with much of the folk-song material he was to use in his earlier music. She was a dainty, lively person and Tippett was very attached to her. For over ten years they had what might be described as an *amitié amoureuse*. Her early life was overshadowed by goitre and though an operation in the early 1930s removed the physical burden she remained subject to depression. In the summer of 1945 she committed suicide. Her death affected Tippett profoundly. During the war she had lived out of London and circumstances therefore had kept them apart. Nevertheless, having seen little of her in the final years of her life, he felt partially responsible for her action. Five years elapsed before he could bring himself to write a work in her memory (the song cycle, *The Heart's Assurance*).

Music and Politics in the 1930s

After leaving R.O. Morris Tippett felt rather unsettled. He possessed the compositional technique maybe but still had not written any work with which he was fully satisfied. His self-confidence had not been helped by a visit to Auden in the spring of 1932, who showed him passages from his highly sophisticated work-in-progress, *The Orators*, and thereby inadvertently drew attention to the somewhat prosaic character of Tippett's latest work, his String Trio. Immediately afterwards however Tippett had visited David Ayerst, in whose house he met Wilfred Franks and other students returning from a work-camp in the Cleveland district of North Yorkshire, when a new venture had been proposed which was to prove a turning point in his career. Ayerst suggested that he take charge of the music at the next of these work-camps and arranged that he meet the camp organizer, Rolf Gardiner.

The work-camps were an offshoot of activities centred on Ormesby Hall, near Middlesbrough, a Georgian family seat owned by Major James Pennyman. In the early 1930s the depression severely affected East Cleveland. The ironstone mines which had been supplying enough iron ore to make Middlesbrough the largest steel-making centre in Britain were now standing idle, many of them never to open again, since it was cheaper to import ore from Spain. In order to help the unemployed miners gain some degree of independence and solvency, Major Pennyman founded in 1931 an association of clubs in three pit-villages in the Cleveland Hills – Boosbeck, Lingdale and Margrove Park – and persuaded a local landowner to donate some ground for use as allotments. Within a year or so the Cleveland Unemployed Miners' Association had ten acres of market garden, poultry, goats, pigs, bees, a cobbler's shop, tailoring schemes, and a furniture workshop run by the noted designer Bernard Aylward. The initiative for this had come less from Major Pennyman, a typical army officer and country squire, than from his wife Ruth and from her friendship with Rolf Gardiner. Gardiner had earlier that year discovered the extent of the hardship in Cleveland and had then organized the first of a series of work-camps to supplement and consolidate these activities. This was held in April 1932, the village of Marske, near the coast, supplying the accommodation and the work taking place at Boosbeck.

Gardiner's political and cultural philosophy[13] had been influenced by D.H. Lawrence, and more particularly by Georg Goetsch, a German educationist whose teaching methods had so impressed C.H. Becker, the Prussian education minister, that he was given official support to put his ideas into practice and build a new kind of training college, the Musikheim in Frankfurt an der Oder (designed by Bartning, and opened in 1929). Goetsch was a talented musician and had been a leading spirit behind the Marske work-camp; but he was not available for the second one. So although administrative ability was to hand there was no one to organize the music. Thus came the invitation to Tippett to take part.

Before this happened Gardiner was anxious that Tippett should attend a summer course for foreigners at the Musikheim to learn something of work-camp techniques. In the summer of 1932 Tippett and Francesca Allinson, who had also been persuaded to take part, did so, using the occasion to take a holiday and visit Prague and other parts of Germany as well.

Tippett's reaction to Gardiner's ideas was guarded, as was that of Ayerst, Franks and Allinson. He was disturbed by his political theories and he could take no more seriously than could the miners an atmosphere of nature worship, chivalry and woodcraft. He agreed to go because he was at a loose end and because it gave him the opportunity to move out of the middle-class environment of Oxted and yet continue to work with amateurs. In the circumstances opera was an improbable venture. But he decided to attempt a production of *The Beggar's Opera*, a shortened version of which was given in 1933 at Boosbeck, where the second camp was held, with local people taking some of the leading parts (a miner's daughter was Polly and a milk roundsman Macheath) and a few student singers and instrumentalists. The opera was an unqualified success. A more ambitious project was planned for the following year, an entirely new folk-song opera, *Robin Hood*, with music by Tippett and text by a team of Ruth Pennyman, David Ayerst and Tippett himself, the three working under the radical pseudonym of David Michael Pennyless. The choice of subject was not an arbitrary one, and in several places the authors forsook period flavour and identified directly with their audience, including, for example, the following in the final ensemble:

> And every man and every maid
>   Shall freely live in peace.
> None shall be rich nor any poor,
>   The curse of hunger cease.

The performers this time included village children, who were required to return to school in the afternoons to learn Latin so that they could sing 'Angelus ad virginem' at the wedding celebrations for Marret (the unusual name chosen by Ruth Pennyman for the heroine). Again the occasion was a success. For Tippett his first opera proved not merely a passing stage in the formation of his style, but a significant event, since fourteen years later he included some of its material in his *Suite for the Birthday of Prince Charles*.

A second important consequence of Tippett's connection with the work-camps was an invitation to direct, at Morley College in south London, a weekly 'class' designed to help unemployed professional musicians keep in practice. The promoters of the London Council for Voluntary Occupation for the Unemployed, an organization formed to co-ordinate various centres for the unemployed in south London at that time, were Eva Hubback, principal of Morley College, and Allan Collingridge. Collingridge was an associate of Gardiner and the invitation came through him. The inspiration behind the orchestra though, and its real founder (and secretary), was Wilfred Franks's father, Dan Franks, a string player and teacher who had been told by his son of Tippett's abilities.

It was natural that Morley College should assume responsibility for providing occupational and educational activities during unemployment, since according to its charter of 1888 its primary objective was 'to promote by means of classes, lectures and otherwise the advanced study by men and women belonging to the working classes of subjects of knowledge not directly connected with or applied to any handicraft, trade or business'. This meant however that, technically, Morley's work was non-vocational. Special permission had to be obtained from the London County Council before the rehearsal class could take place. But this was forthcoming and Tippett was appointed tutor for the LCC at sixteen shillings per hour.

Weekly two-hour rehearsals during college terms began in the autumn of 1932 and the first concert of the class, now called the South London Orchestra (subsequently with 'Morley College Professional Orchestra' added in parentheses) took place in Morley College on 5 March 1933, with a programme reflecting the tastes of its players and potential audience, rather than those of its conductor.

MEYERBEER	March (*Le Prophète*)
WEBER	Overture: *Euryanthe*
J. STRAUSS	Waltz: Du und Du

WEBER	Softly sighing (*Der Freischütz*)
MENDELSSOHN	Scherzo, Nocturne and March (*A Midsummer Night's Dream*)
ROSSINI	Overture: *William Tell*
HANDEL	Oh, sleep (*Semele*)
SMETANA	Dance Suite (*The Bartered Bride*)
ELGAR	Pomp and Circumstance March No. 1

The South London Orchestra soon became the major success of the unemployment scheme, so much so that when, in 1936, conditions eased and other classes stopped, the orchestra refused to disband and indeed continued until October 1940.

With the rapid growth of the film industry in the late 1920s and early '30s, theatre owners, especially in London, soon discovered they could do more profitable business by converting to 'talkies' and dispensing with their pit musicians, hundreds of whom from the silent cinema, variety theatres and some West End theatres were left without a livelihood. Young performers just out of college found the profession in disarray. The position was worsened by the general rise in unemployment. This was the situation the South London Orchestra was designed to meet, and if the financial benefits deriving from concert-giving were so small that they could hardly in themselves account for the success of the orchestra they did offer the players some hope of financial improvement. The players created a system by which income from concert receipts would be shared out equally. On a good night they might net £1 10s each, and on a bad one, 6½d. Musicians' Union fees were paid only when Tippett managed to have the orchestra engaged for an outside event, and this took place on two occasions only. On the first, in June 1937, the orchestra played for 'Lights o' Lambeth', a pageant devised as part of the coronation festivities for George VI. The music was not particularly to Tippett's liking and hence the orchestra was conducted for the first and only time by someone else, F.W. Holloway, the musical director of the pageant. Six performances in an open-air theatre in Brockwell Park drew in audiences of about 30,000 people every night. Success led to the promotion two years later of another pageant, a 'Symphony of Youth'. This had a cast of about 1,000 children and was a 'musical spectacle in two acts expounding the progress of youth and dedicated to its spirit'. For Tippett it was a more congenial enterprise. Sixteen performances took place. Heavy rain fell every night however and the pageant, intended to provide funds for the Belgrave Hospital, was a financial disaster.

In general the orchestra's programmes were of standard classics in the well-tried formula of overture, concerto and symphony or, when playing for schoolchildren, of popular lollipops. Tippett naturally was interested in the unfamiliar, but such a work as Stravinsky's Violin Concerto – the most 'advanced' work performed by the orchestra – was a rarity. Tippett's own music was played however and his Symphony in B flat, *A Song of Liberty* and Concerto for Double String Orchestra were all first performed by the South

London Orchestra. For some concerts Tippett persuaded distinguished soloists to give their services free and such names as Harriet Cohen, Myra Hess, Irene Scharrer, Cyril Smith and Solomon appeared on the programmes.

The success of the orchestra was due to the professionalism of its playing, the corporate spirit of a body of men all in the same predicament, and to its sense of social responsibility (concerts were given in schools, hospitals and churches, as well as in Morley College itself). It was also due to Tippett's personality. The players were mostly more than twice his age. But they quickly recognized in him a musician of exceptional ability, without pretension but determined that quality should be paramount (he abolished the playing of the national anthem at concerts, not for political reasons but because it interfered with the music). He was endowed with a remarkable capacity to convey what he wanted. He paid little attention to conventional stick technique but once the players had learnt to follow him, which evidently was like learning a different way of speaking, they found his intentions and his manner of transmitting them clear and inspiring. The leader, Fred B. May (whom Tippett appointed when he was only twenty and who subsequently played under many well-known conductors) reported that Tippett was a genuinely fine conductor whose closest counterpart was Rafael Kubelik.

The most profound effect on Tippett of the North Yorkshire work-camps had nothing to do with music at all. Tippett's political inclinations, even from his schooldays, had been left of centre. For a while his dislike of middle-class values had been too personalized for him to think beyond his immediate environment. In any case such feelings were quickly displaced by the attractions of post-war London and the artistic ferment which broke out over the whole of Europe in the 1920s. Some hopefully believed this to represent the dawning of a new era. Tippett soon regarded such ideas as illusory, not through scepticism but because he could not identify with the artistic nihilism of Dada and the fringes of the surrealistic movement (unlike many of his contemporaries, he acknowledged the seriousness of the Dadaists' position), and, more particularly, because he began to discover the true facts of the 1914–18 war. What first opened his eyes to the realities of war was, surprisingly, *The Four Horsemen of the Apocalypse*. A popular film starring Rudolph Valentino, for Tippett it was a revelation of violence and destruction: of the horror which could turn thousands of cheerfully singing soldiers into corpses on Flanders' battlefields. The film left an indelible impression. It gave him a presentiment of a vocation – that one day he would express his concern in music. Another powerful influence was exerted by the preface to Shaw's *Heartbreak House*. This not only offered an interpretation of the causes and consequences of the war, but also set out clearly the moral choice open to creative artists. Were those young artists, 'essentially gentle and essentially wise', who had forced themselves to 'pervert their divine instinct' in order, as they thought, to defend the very existence of civilized values, right to do so? Tippett could not believe they were. But all such feelings remained unfocused and there was little to alter them until his friends told him about the conditions in North Yorkshire, and, in particular, until he himself, at Boosbeck, was confronted with realities harshly at variance with the sheltered atmosphere of Oxted.

In 1934 J.B. Priestley published *English Journey*, an account of the 'three Englands' he visited the previous year: the Old, the Nineteenth Century and the New. His Nineteenth Century England was the Midlands and the North, where unemployment brought with it poverty, degradation and hopelessness on a scale almost impossible for later generations to imagine. Priestley did not visit Boosbeck. But Stockton and East Durham are not far away and he described them, and their appalling conditions. During his first Boosbeck camp Tippett lived in a tent with other camp workers; during the second he lodged with an unemployed miner and his wife, Mr and Mrs Jack Brough, in a terraced street where only one man was employed. Maybe the conditions at Boosbeck were not quite as severe as at Stockton and East Durham and maybe the Miners' Association had made some difference. In any event Tippett was moved as much by the human qualities of the people there as by their poverty. Despite the demoralizing effects of the depression they retained their warmth and resilience. Doors were never locked, in case a neighbour needed help, and when someone was sick the women would organize a voluntary rota to sit up all night with the patient. Boosbeck kept its band, its male voice choir, flower and vegetable shows, and some of its inhabitants even saved enough to go to the Redcar races. Behind this however were the stark facts of social deprivation. The worst sufferers were children. The incident which affected Tippett most deeply occurred during a hike with Wilfred Franks through mining areas in the Tees Valley. They stopped for a picnic of bread and cheese and apples when some children, covered with sores, appeared from nowhere, picked up the breadcrumbs, grabbed the apple cores and ran off eating them.

After experiences of this kind Tippett was bound to ask himself whether he had any right to continue writing music. It was not enough simply to show compassion or to identify with the deprived or to express anger at their plight. Some more positive action was called for. He had in fact taken an important step before visiting Boosbeck. One way of harnessing his musical instincts to a political conscience was to follow the lead of his London friends, Francesca Allinson and Alan Bush, and conduct choirs associated with the working-class movement. Francesca Allinson conducted the Clarion Glee Club, founded by Rutland Boughton, composer of *The Immortal Hour* and a supporter of left-wing politics. Through Allinson, Tippett met Bush, conductor of the London Labour Choral Union, a federation of choral societies to which Allinson's was affiliated and of which Bush was Boughton's successor. In late 1932, having given up his teaching at Hazelwood School, Tippett got his name included on the staff-list of conductors for the Education Department of the Royal Arsenal Co-operative Society. He was then asked to conduct two choirs in south

London sponsored by the RACS, one at Abbey Wood, the other at New Malden. Although the co-operative movement in general was identified with the Labour Party, the only co-operative society directly affiliated to it was the RACS and with this connection Tippett had already moved to the left of the political spectrum.

The Labour Party had however shown itself to be weak during the General Strike and subsequently when in office. The single political philosophy which seemed to take a stand against poverty at home and fascism abroad was communism. Tippett accordingly began to learn more about it, encouraged by Phyllis Kemp who persuaded him to read Marx. What crystallized his political thinking however was reading not Marx, but Trotsky.

British Trotskyism in the 1930s developed from the Balham Group,[14] a faction within the Balham branch of the British Communist Party, which challenged the official line dictated by the Comintern, was 'liquidated' and in 1933 set up a party of its own, The Communist League; this was for a time the British Section of the exiled Trotsky's mouthpiece, the International Left Opposition. One of its members, campaigning for new recruits at Morley College, persuaded Tippett to buy its paper, *The Red Flag*, and other printed propaganda. The issue for November 1934 advertised the recently published *History of the Russian Revolution* by Trotsky. This Tippett read. It had a decisive effect on him, confirmed by other pamphlets and by John Reed's *Ten days that shook the world*, an American revolutionary's classic eye-witness account of the October Revolution, commended by Trotsky. (This Tippett read in the original edition of 1919 and not the censored version subsequently published by the British Communist Party.) He became a Trotskyist – and, as it seemed at the time, for several good reasons. Stalin's doctrine of socialism in one country was of no relevance in Britain when set against Trotsky's internationalist doctrine of permanent world revolution spearheaded by the proletariat; Trotsky's faith in the elemental force of society and the logic of history was in itself sympathetic; his account of Stalin's revolutionary credentials exposed a ruthless opportunist who had perverted the ideals of the early leaders and who was anxious to deny the revolutionary quality of the proletariat because this would have jeopardized his own position. And Stalin's intellect was obviously no match for Trotsky's own brilliance as a writer, polemicist and leader. Although Stalin's show trials and purges had only just begun and were so incredible that they could hardly be understood, Tippett had nevertheless gained some inkling of the repressive police state of Stalin's Russia and with it confirmation of his approval of Trotsky.

By the beginning of 1935 the Communist League had disbanded. It was no longer recognized by the secretariat of the International Left Opposition, because it had rejected the secretariat's order to infiltrate the Independent Labour Party and make that the centre of British Trotskyism, in preparation for the declaration of the Fourth International (when theoretically Trotskyists all over the world would rise and overthrow the Stalinist Third International, the Comintern). Various other groups had sprung up claiming Left Opposition sympathies. It was a confused situation and Tippett did not know much about it. The British Communist Party on the other hand slavishly enforced every decree from Moscow. The only course of action he saw open to him was to join it and attempt to pursue the Trotsky tactics of changing it from within. So when later in 1935 Phyllis Kemp decided it was time for them to join the party, he agreed. Along with two other friends he first of all submitted to a cross-examination from Emil Burns, the well-known party worker whom Kemp wanted to 'lead them in'. At the cross-examination Burns asked her what she had read and was answered with, 'the whole of Marx and Lenin in the original'. Tippett was about to reply almost as impressively with Trotsky's *History* but prudently offered Marx instead. He duly became a card-carrying member, entering under his own name, unlike the others who gave assumed names.

There was no party branch at Oxted, so, rather oddly, he was attached to one some distance away, in north London at Camden Town. He was assigned a street 'cell' there and intended forming another at Oxted too. But his membership was short-lived. He attended only one or two branch meetings and took almost no part in official activities, having soon discovered that he would not be successful in converting his colleagues as the Balham Group had done, particularly as the branch was involved with local problems he knew little about. Transport difficulties added to the pointlessness of the venture. Within a few months he left. Years later he discovered that he was on the NKVD's list of wanted men, but as far as he knew nobody attempted to assassinate him.

He then found that there were more Trotskyists about and became more open in his allegiance. Several events at that time confirmed that his decision to leave the Communist Party had been opportune. In early 1936 the various Composers' Unions in Russia held their 'creative discussions' following Stalin's attacks on Shostakovich in *Pravda*, from which it was clear that Soviet composers would be intimidated into accepting the precepts of socialist realism. Tippett could not disguise his own view that the artist should have complete freedom of expression. The public trials of Zinoviev and Kamenev in August 1936 and information that pro-Stalin communists in the Spanish Civil War were shooting in the back their 'comrades' of the Spanish Trotskyist movement POUM (Partido Obrero de Unificacion Marxista) all helped to present Trotskyism as a serious and respectable alternative to Stalinism. What disturbed Tippett as much as anything else was the effect Stalinism had on Phyllis Kemp, who shortly after the trials arrived at his Oxted cottage, in the company of a party official, to announce that there was blood between them: 'We shall never see each other again.' Tippett appealed to her to preserve their friendship on a purely human level but she refused. (When the party line changed, she did get in touch with him again; before she died in 1983 their friendship revived.) Tippett continued to read Trotskyist literature sent from abroad, from Belgium, France, Spain and the USA, translating where necessary for fellow sympathizers. Since Trotskyists in England were so few he kept on the lookout for potentially more powerful groups, and he joined the Socialist Anti-War Front, revived in 1938 shortly before the Munich conference, largely by Trotskyists, in order to promote the view that war was inherent in capitalism and would be eliminated only by a co-operative socialist order.

For some while Tippett accepted the pure doctrine of world revolution and despite evidence to the contrary clung to his conception of Trotsky as a non-violent idealist. But whatever its theoretical basis and its apparently rational and healthily pragmatic ethic, his commitment to Trotskyism was in practice ambiguous. He never joined a Trotskyist party and never got involved with sticky political in-fighting. Although he would have answered to being a Trotskyist until late 1938 or so, a slow disenchantment had set in long before that.

Some indication of the restlessness of these years can be gauged from a summary of Tippett's work with choirs during the 1930s. In the spring of 1934, while adjudicating at an annual London Labour Choral Union competition, he expressed disapproval of the test piece, 'April is in my mistress' face' by Morley, explaining to the participants that the English madrigal arose when the bourgeois, now capitalist class, was looking for some amusement in its homes. In October he provided his South London Orchestra for a large-scale historical pageant, part of that year's centenary celebrations of the Tolpuddle Martyrs, which depicted the struggles of a working-class family from the industrial revolution until the present day. Bush composed the music for it. During the week of rehearsals and performances Tippett's persuasive manner impressed many of the large cast of singers and actors. Seven performances of this Pageant of Labour were given at the Crystal Palace, Tippett conducting two of them. In that same autumn he was chairman of a 'concert demonstration' of workers' songs at Morley College, himself teaching the audience phrase by phrase a newly written song, and at the end of the concert making some closing remarks about the class war with such emotion that he was unable to finish. In March 1935 he introduced another demonstration of political songs by Eisler, whose music provided a model of the type he and Bush favoured.[15] In April he was in Strasbourg, with a choir drawn from Bush's LLCU and from his own Abbey Wood choir, participating as a first tenor in the first 'International Workers' Music Olympiad', a utopian venture created as evidence of working-class solidarity in the face of fascism. In an article published later, Tippett wrote that the occasion taught infinitely more about international socialism than book knowledge.[16] Eisler was one of the adjudicators (the English choir came joint first with a choir from Paris). Tippett himself continued to adjudicate for LLCU competitions, using such opportunities to encourage choirs to include political songs in their repertory and himself writing *Miners* for chorus and piano (text by Judy Wogan, a friend of Francesca Allinson), an efficient but characterless piece of propagandist drama based on the techniques of Das Rote Sprachrohr, the pre-Hitler 'Agitprop' troupe in Berlin for which Eisler had been composer and pianist. In 1936 he was present at the non-party conference in the Whitechapel Art Gallery to which representatives from all choirs favouring social change were invited and out of which emerged the Workers' Music Association. Bush was elected chairman, Tippett a member of the first executive committee.

It gradually became apparent to him however that politically orientated music had little appeal to those for whom it was written. For a while Tippett persisted in the belief that his choirs should sing political songs. But they wanted to sing light opera. If the genre itself was not particularly attractive to him, it nevertheless showed that music answered an emotional demand whose sources stretched well beyond political boundaries and that there was nothing he could do to change this. The choirs had to perform well in competitions run by the London Co-operative Society in order to qualify for financial help towards operatic productions. Under Tippett they duly succeeded, and he found himself rehearsing and performing Gilbert and Sullivan again, *Merrie England*, *Martha* and a second production of *Robin Hood*. By 1937 his views had changed markedly. Although he had in no way ceased to identify with working people and indeed continued with his choirs in the hope that he could remain in contact with them (a vain hope as it turned out, since personnel became increasingly middle-class), he no longer believed that musical propaganda could do anything to improve their position. He would even criticize the choice of Eisler songs at LLCU competitions. His own repertory with co-operative choirs speaks for itself: in 1938 and '39 he produced at a co-operative hall in Peckham Rye in London two children's operas of his own with a clearly non-political content, *Robert of Sicily*, adapted by Christopher Fry from a poem by Longfellow, and *Seven at One Stroke*, with a text by Fry based on a Grimm fairy-tale.

The main cause of these changing attitudes was *War Ramp*, a revolutionary play he wrote himself. It was performed, under the auspices of the Labour League of Youth, in various Labour Party premises in and around London during the spring of 1935, with a cast consisting partly of actors who had performed in the Crystal Palace pageant and partly of his own friends. The idea for the play had emerged in discussions with Jeffrey Mark, a fellow student at the RCM of unusual versatility, both composer and economist. In this latter capacity he wrote two books on the banking system,[17] which he saw as the principal reason for the exploitation of the working class. Like Ezra Pound, he had been influenced by C.H. Douglas's theory of 'social credit'.

Tippett was interested not so much in the financial panacea as in the simple fact that the economic system depended on the supply of bank credit. His play was designed to expose the moral degeneracy of this practice, especially as it affected a war economy, and to present his argument with such dramatic and didactic impact that audiences would be roused to action. The props and costumes were of the simplest kind and the play, like *Miners*, thus in the 'Agitprop' tradition. The intensity of Tippett's feelings can be judged from the foreword he wrote for the play:

We have tried in this play to present the irreconcilable clash between payment for war in arms and legs, and payment for war in money. The sinister farce of the money ramp, though satiric, is presented with a fair degree of accuracy. The figures are not far short of the truth, and the whole process is simplified so as to be presentable on the stage, but not thereby misrepresented in principle.

To those who imagine that payment for purchases and trade is all a matter of currency, we need to point out that in every big capitalist country about 98% of the existing purchasing power is really loans from the banks. About 2% only is notes and coin issued by the State, money as we commonly understand it. The bankers hold a dominating position in advanced capitalist countries and their shareholders share out the 'rewards' of this colossal usury. 1–10% is paid in interest to them for these bank loans without which *capitalist* society could not go on. Bankers are no worse than other exploiters under capitalism, but they hold the key positions, and that more and more as they buy out the industrialists.

In a war the money ramp assumes unbelievable proportions. And the usury and the bonus share capital generated in a war (exactly as we show it in this play) is grimly compensated by the slaughter of the men at the fronts, and the starvation of the women and children in the rear. And after the war is over, the men and women do not cash a farthing of the increased rent, profit and interest. On the contrary they must 'pay' for these till kingdom come, as taxes for the national (!) debt; suffer bad conditions and low wages in order that the industrialists can compete in an artificially dwindling world market, by undercutting the workers of a rival country. International 'patriotic' competition means international falling wages. Even within 'our' Empire, Lancashire unemployment and starvation wages had been accentuated by British prohibition of Indian Trades Unions. As capitalism becomes frantic in its efforts to survive, only the armaments industry flourishes.

The question we ask in this play is a serious one for us all. If the murderous weapons of war are to be forced again into our hands, what are we going to do with them; where is the real enemy?

The play involves two principal groups of actors, representing the government and the bank. War is declared. The Prime Minister, a small-minded hypocrite, appeals in the name of king and country for a national effort. The government asks the bank for financial support and at a secret meeting it is arranged that the government call in all gold coinage and give it to the bank (or, in the play, a sinister figure named Pluto who is periodically heard shifting his stock of gold under the floorboards); this money is replaced by paper money guaranteed on government stocks, as much being printed as the bank thinks necessary to bring support for a government war loan at 4 per cent, which will be paid later from taxes. The War Profiteer and International Financier obtain enormous sums from the bank by borrowing at 3 per cent, buying war loan at 4 per cent and providing this as security for further loans at 3 per cent. Though worried by its lack of gold coverage the bank is assured of backing from international sources, including its ostensible enemies at Berlin and Frankfurt. As a bank assistant says: 'Finance and credit must be international in the end. It's only socialists and people like that who fight one another in modern warfare.' The war ends, the bank draws in its credit to support the gold standard and invests abroad, causing unemployment and low wages at home. The soldiers return, wounded, unemployed and ignored. The play ends with a soldier telling his friend: 'But there's a job for me to do yet. I've got to get my gun back somehow.'

These final lines were a logical consequence of the action. But having carefully analysed the causes of social injustice and found that the only possible outcome was revolutionary violence, Tippett recoiled from his own conclusion. He could not believe that violence, either in theory or practice, was inevitable. Over four years were to elapse before he found an alternative.

This conflict between an instinctive pacifism and political idealism was eventually resolved not by reasoning but by the force of events. The Munich crisis of 1938 hastened the eruption, as he saw it, of a war which would feed on bestiality. With the Nazi pogrom of November 1938 his disillusionment with political idealism was complete. The misery of the Jewish refugees, the assassination of the German diplomat in Paris by the seventeen-year-old Jewish boy, Herschel Grynspan, all those events which led up to the pogrom were terrible enough, but what disturbed him also was the inertia of left-wing organizations in Britain and their unwillingness to help the thousands of Jewish refugees left stranded and dying on the Polish-German frontier.

To these unanswerable questions had been added a serious personal problem. In August 1938 Tippett's relationship with Wilfred Franks had just reached a painful conclusion, so painful that he was unable to come to terms with either the wretchedness of separation or the emotional turmoil it let loose. In his distress he found himself turning to Francesca Allinson and even contemplating marriage with her – which meant that he was also struggling with the ethics of whether to acquiesce in the social convention of marriage when the only real justification for it was that they both wanted to have children. It was a crisis in which every value he believed in seemed to be slipping out of reach.

What first gave him some sign of recovery was, surprisingly, a short book-review. Evelyn Underhill's interpretation of the symbolism in Blake's *Illustrations of the Book of Job* revealed that in the illustration marking the turning point in his series Blake had charted a psychological upheaval strikingly similar to his own. Here Job reaches that 'extreme of interior dereliction in which he can no longer distinguish between the action of Satan and the action of God'.[18] Although Tippett is not particularly responsive to the visual arts, this single illustration of Blake may be said to have influenced him as profoundly as any piece of music. It provided the incentive to pursue the promise of understanding he had already gained from reading *The Psychology of the Unconscious* by Jung: that is, it accounted for his decision to undertake a course of Jungian analysis. David Ayerst had introduced him to the Jungian analyst John Layard some time before (the future author of a classic book on dream therapy, *The Lady of the Hare*). For four months Tippett took to Layard accounts of his dreams. Layard provided an interpretative method which Tippett eventually felt he could apply more profitably by himself and from late January until the end of August 1939 he conducted his own self-analysis. This began with evident approval from his psyche for in the first dream he had after leaving Layard he dreamt that his garden was full of 'work-in-progress' – vast excavations and large numbers of workmen. His dream sequence reached an extra-ordinary yet conclusive ending with two dreams, in the first of which he was, as it were, reassured about the therapy to come and in the second (just two nights before war was declared) subjected to a necessary and liberating 'death'.[19]

This experience marked the major turning point in his life. It meant that he now could re-dedicate himself to his fundamental vocation of composer and set aside his involvement in politics, or at least in party politics. From his analysis, he drew not only an understanding of the private and general forces which had prompted it but an emotional and intellectual balance which left him better equipped artistically. The price to be paid for his new confidence was a feeling if not of loneliness – his warm and spirited personality ensured that he could find congenial company as often as he wished – then that of being alone, of knowing that only through himself could he sustain a sense of purpose. This did not mean that he was denied serious friendships with other people; but it did mean that he resisted the temptation to recapture the profound emotional experiences he had recently undergone because he knew that such experiences were both transient and certain to throw his life out of balance.

Tippett would doubtless have become a pacifist in the Second World War without the insights gained from dream analysis. But they certainly confirmed his position and enabled him to draw away from extremes and resolve some of his conflicts of the 1930s. His particular discovery was of the Jungian 'shadow' and 'light' in the single, individual psyche and of the consequent futility of projecting the 'shadow' on to someone else or of a nation projecting it on to another nation – of the need therefore for the individual to accept his own divided nature and attempt to reconcile and profit from its conflicting demands. In an essay written later Tippett expressed it thus: 'The only concept we can place over against the fact of divided man is the idea of the whole man.'[20] In political terms this meant that acts of war so disrupted the attempted balance that any idea of moral integrity in the human animal was fatally compromised. He began writing the music of *A Child of Our Time* – which, as well as deriving from the political events surrounding Grynspan's assassination of the German diplomat, is also a metaphor of his own experience – on 4 September 1939, the day after war was declared.

In retrospect it is easy to dismiss Tippett's political activities during the 1930s as naïve dabblings in territories he did not understand: Tippett was simply following the romantic fashion to align with the dangerous and exciting politics of the left-wing. But it was not so clear-cut. While the evils of fascism were obvious enough, few people in Britain seem to have had any real idea of the enormities that were being perpetrated in the name of communism or socialism. From a safe geographical distance it was possible, for those too young or too bitter to question the credentials of regimes claiming moral authority, to interpret what unsavoury stories they did hear as unfortunate but temporary expedients in the establishment of a benevolent social order. The first book to expose NKVD techniques of torture and labour camps, Iulia de Beausobre's *The Woman who could not die*, was not published until 1938. By that time many of the left-wing intellectuals who were at all serious in their politics had joined the Communist Party: it appeared the only plausible alternative to fascism and it offered a banner under which fascism could be fought in the Spanish Civil War. Tippett had however already shown himself to be more sophisticated than these by rejecting the Communist Party before he had joined it. His reading of Beausobre's book was a confirmation of what he had already imagined, rather than a shock. He did not fight in the Civil War, for his pacifist instincts were too strong. On one occasion he visited the Trotsky headquarters in Paris to offer help of some kind but immediately left when it transpired that the workers there thought he wanted to join the POUM forces. If he stayed on the sidelines this was less because he had misgivings about Trotsky's tactics or even because British Trotskyists were so few and disorganized as to be impotent: it was rather that it was extremely difficult to know what to do at all.

Tippett's predicament could perhaps serve as an illustration of the predicament of the left-wing in general during those years. Yet for all his involvement, his was not a genuinely representative case. However much he may have wanted to commit himself to politics he was always fighting a losing battle with his creative instincts, whose demands were so imperative that when his conscience urged him elsewhere he was continually forced back to his desk to wrestle with problems of composition. This was true before his dream analysis; and long before September 1939 he had been obliged therefore to accept that he was a composer – not a conductor and even less a political activist or social worker. He had been obliged to accept an inherent contradiction between his egalitarian principles in political affairs and what must be called his élitist principles in matters of artistic quality. In this the latter were bound to predominate. The influence of politics on his creative development can be exaggerated. What he did was to make use of his experiences. Politics had, for example, introduced him to a breadth of human feeling he felt able to reach through his music. Marxist terminology for describing the class-war could be a valuable tool when preparing texts of vocal works. If the primitive rhythms and acceptance of Soviet cultural dogma in Eisler's workers' songs seemed to him to have an enervating effect on the music of Alan Bush (who joined the Communist

Party in 1936), then at least this sharpened his own instincts for a simplicity of real individuality. In an essay of about twenty years later, he wrote that

> most of the seemingly non-creative things an artist does – whether to take up teaching; to enter politics; to undertake Jungian analysis – are really phases of the inner creative life; and directed therefore to the ends of the art he practises. These non-creative activities are only secondary.[21]

Not all composers would accept that such social or personal awareness was relevant or desirable. Yet for Tippett it was now a self-evident truth. Even if his naturally gregarious and compassionate disposition had not led him to such a standpoint anyway, he would certainly have argued that a composer's authority is impoverished if he elects to disregard all aspects of his humanity save his appetite for composition.

Exactly how this philosophy was to be expressed in music was a separate matter. Despite the originality of his music of the mid- and late-1930s Tippett seems for the time being to have remained unconvinced that his command of the subtleties of his craft was sound enough to convey his moral concern adequately. He continued to exercise his technical skills in works basically heuristic in purpose. Or, it could be said that he considered his depth and range of historical understanding too limited to escape the dangers of provincialism: he therefore needed more time for reading and study before risking open statements about the human condition. Or again it could be said that, like many other artists, he wanted to compensate for the apparent disintegration of European society by a return to older, tested values. In any event his music of this period asserts the objectivity of a work of art rather than its sociological function or its quality as subjective expression. Significantly, his most 'committed' work, the 1937 setting of Blake's *A Song of Liberty*, is his weakest and he has never published it. A desolate little phrase conceived a year later at the time of the Munich crisis was not used until 1942 (when it became the subject for the fugue in his String Quartet No. 2). Though written in the turbulent year of 1935, his first work to show an unmistakably individual style, his String Quartet No. 1, is notably free from dark forebodings or tendentious rhetoric, and much the same could be said of its successors, his Piano Sonata No. 1 of 1936–8 and his Concerto for Double String Orchestra of 1938–9. However they are interpreted, these three works are unquestionably affirmative in character. It was ironic that when Tippett felt he had acquired the necessary skill to write a work overtly concerned with contemporary events, circumstances should have rendered affirmation a value less easy to believe in. Nevertheless *A Child of Our Time* still concludes on a note of encouragement, and this fundamental optimism, hard-earned in the 1930s, has remained with him ever since.

The War Years and Morley College

With the outbreak of war and the suspension of adult education, Tippett lost the income from his co-operative choirs. He was not particularly sorry about losing jobs which had become increasingly uncongenial, but his situation was precarious and accordingly he began looking for a new post. He was offered a job at Dartington and another, teaching Latin at Hazelwood where he had first become a schoolmaster. He accepted the latter, because it meant he could continue to live near London. He stayed until July 1940, by which time adult education had been restored and he had returned to his choirs. Then, in October, he was offered the job which was to bring him more satisfaction than any other. On 15 October 1940 Morley College was hit by a high explosive bomb and completely destroyed, apart from an extension built three years earlier. At almost the same time its Director of Music, Arnold Foster, had to leave London because Westminster School, where he taught, was evacuated. Tippett had deeply admired Morley's principal, Eva Hubback, from the start of his association with the college, and when she asked him whether he would take over a virtually non-existent choir (only eight voices) and build up musical life again, he did not hesitate. 'Classes' with the choir began in a nearby schoolroom later that October. (At the same time, his fast-diminishing South London Orchestra was obliged by the disappearance of its rehearsal accommodation in Morley College to disband for good.) Tippett's directorship was to last for the next eleven years.

During the war Tippett still managed, as in earlier years, to organize his life so that he had some freedom to compose. Morley College occupied him more than he wanted (it took up on average about two days a week plus the time spent organizing and financing concerts) but this still left three or four days a week for his own work, with the weekends kept clear for relaxation.[22] With the Morley salary of £125 per annum, a £100 retaining fee from Schott (his publisher) and some help from his friends he was able to eke out a frugal but productive existence, writing four major works as well as several minor ones.

In the first year of the war he continued with the composition of *A Child of Our Time*. By October 1940 he was writing Part 2 of the oratorio, whose narrative, almost journalistic, tone was grimly endorsed by German air raids: he began the 'Terror' chorus with the sound of bombers overhead. Several houses around his bungalow were damaged or destroyed, and he was continually expecting that his would be the next to suffer, for which reason he planned to distribute among his friends copies of those scores he thought worth preserving. This direct experience of war hastened his decision to take up an open commitment to pacifism. In November he joined the Peace Pledge Union, and on 16 November, when his age-group was called up under the National Service Act (he was then thirty-five), he applied for provisional registration as a conscientious objector.

The PPU was founded in 1935 by the Revd Dick Sheppard, as a result of a letter sent to the press inviting those who were opposed to war to send him a postcard containing the pledge: 'I renounce war and never again, directly or indirectly will I support or sanction another'. Sheppard received 100,000 postcards, including one from Tippett. For several years after that Tippett's priorities had taken him away from the peace movement but in the early months of the war his interest was reawakened by the quality of its leaders and his decision to join was a natural consequence. Tippett eventually became a prominent member of the PPU. During the war he gave support to many young pacifists frightened by the realities of conscientious objection, visiting farms and other places where they were housed up and where he felt able to offer some encouragement and practical help. He also spoke at PPU meetings.

The official procedure for conscientious objectors was well-organized and, compared with the notorious 'cat and mouse' tactics pursued in the 1914–18 war, remarkably humane. As a first step, an objector was required to apply for provisional registration. This meant that he could not be called up for military service until his case had been heard by a tribunal – consisting of five well-known local citizens of proved standing and impartiality. The objector himself was represented by counsel, a solicitor and one other person, who could be a trade union official, relative or friend. Four courses of action were open to these tribunals. They could award unconditional registration, which meant that the objector was free to do as he wished; conditional registration, the objector being registered on condition that he undertook some approved occupation, such as farm or hospital work; non-combatant service duties; and finally he could be struck off the register and obliged to join the services as ordered. If, after appeal, an objector failed to comply with the decision of the tribunal, he would then be prosecuted by the police on a criminal charge.

Although Tippett had applied for provisional registration in November 1940, his case did not come up before the South East London Tribunal at Lambeth until 3 February 1942, when he was given non-combatant military duties. He appealed against this decision. At the Appellate Tribunal on 30 May that year he was given conditional registration – full time work with Air Raid Precautions, the National Fire Service or on the land. He refused to comply with these conditions and eventually, on 21 June 1943, appeared before the Oxted Police Court and was sentenced to three months' imprisonment (the minimum term). He conformed to the requirements in Wormwood Scrubs, qualified for the one-third remission and was released on 21 August.

These are the bare facts of the case. But they provide little evidence of the crisis Tippett lived through. Even though he had the moral support of several well-known figures in the musical world (Arnold Bax, Adrian Boult, Benjamin Britten and Peter Pears among others), he was not given to heroics and he could have agreed to the urgings of friends to compromise and accept one of the many alternative jobs they arranged for him to be offered after the Appellate Tribunal: music organizer for ENSA in Northern Ireland Command, librarian for the RAF Orchestra, choir-training with the National Fire Service, social work in London. But Tippett

was determined not to betray his convictions, nor to betray the thousands
of young objectors, who might value the example of an older man when
faced with the obloquy levelled at 'conchees', regarded by prison authorities and many others as worse than professional criminals. While he
was prepared to accept that opposing beliefs could be held equally strongly
and passionately (in this respect it is worth noting that he mixed naturally
with and gained the respect of those, such as high-ranking army officers,
whose views differed sharply from his own), he insisted on respect towards
an individual's inner compulsion to reject the war machine and everything
to do with it. He did not believe ends justified means nor that war could
bring a moral gain; he had an almost prophetic knowledge of what would
be perpetrated in its name, the concentration camps, the Dresden fire
raids, Hiroshima, and argued that such means perverted everything
humanity stood for. He believed that his moral duty was to serve the
community as a musician. Faced with so intransigent a position, and
despite the advocacy of Gerald Gardiner KC (later Lord Chancellor) and
his distinguished solicitor Robert Pollard (who acted for several conscientious objectors), and the support of David Ayerst (now a colonel attached to
the War Office), Eva Hubback and Vaughan Williams at the trial,[23] the
tribunals and the trial magistrates had no room for manoeuvre, and
Tippett realised this. His mind was made up and the prison sentence
followed automatically.

Wormwood Scrubs was theoretically for small-time offenders only but in
the war it housed all varieties of criminal and was very crowded. Tippett
found himself next door to a rapist, a murderer was further down the
corridor and there was a black-marketeer, who paid other prisoners by
cheque to do his work for him. Apart from fifty or sixty conscientious
objectors the largest group was of court-martialled soldiers who wanted to
stay in prison and who therefore did their best to disqualify themselves
from remission. During the first few weeks of their sentence prisoners were
forbidden to talk in the prison yard and were kept in solitary confinement
in their cells from 4.30 in the afternoon – where they sewed mailbags
(without thimbles). The objectors refused to undertake work connected
with the war effort, so for their day-time duties they were put in a workshop
separate from the other prisoners and told to continue sewing mailbags.
Afterwards, as senior prisoners, they could talk in the yard and use the
recreation rooms, and since the warders discovered that they really were
non-violent they were allowed to go from one part of the prison to another
unescorted.

At a PPU meeting in October 1943 Tippett said that when in prison he
was struck most of all by 'the gaiety and vitality of the group of young
comrades there. It was as though having made the fact of their moral
integrity clear by submission to imprisonment they were yet able to turn to
the community around them and to live in generous contact with its
members'.[24] He was the oldest of the objectors and felt responsible for
advising and comforting those who were in distress, of whom, however,
there were very few. To these he was a calm and purposeful figure and on

other occasions – as when directing the prison orchestra, an assemblage of instruments playing chaotically, or when turning the pages for a Pears/ Britten recital[25] – a cheerful one. But in general he had little enthusiasm for anything, even reading. Prison obliged him to accept a fundamentally impassive state in which all he could really do was meditate.[26]

On the day of his release he was welcomed by a large group of sympathizers at the prison gates and taken to a performance of his String Quartet No. 2, which by a happy coincidence was being given that afternoon in the Wigmore Hall by the Zorian Quartet. The celebrations continued in the evening, when he travelled to Cornwall with some friends (John Amis, Antony Hopkins and his wife) for a short holiday in Mevagissey, and next day reached a farcical climax with their apprehension by the local coastguard for nude bathing, a circumstance which could have brought another summons had not Tippett asked a friend who lived nearby (A.L. Rowse) to intercede with the magistrates. All the same, he was still in an uncomfortable position, since there was no technical reason why he should not have been charged again for failing to comply with the tribunal's conditions and given a second sentence. This he believed a real possibility the following spring, when *A Child of Our Time* was given its first performance and when its composer might have been in prison. But nothing came of it and the authorities left him alone.

By this time Tippett had been Director of Music at Morley College for over three years. After a decade of comparative seclusion, working largely with amateurs in order to explore the English musical tradition at his own pace, he had returned to central London and was already building up a reputation for the college and for himself. The tradition of music at Morley dated back to the early years of the century when Holst had been director. This Tippett continued with immense skill and energy. As director he was without personal ambition, content that others take the limelight and that the name of the college should depend on its imaginative programmes and its hospitable atmosphere. He was astute enough to delegate extensively and give his full support to those he had appointed – this a quality he had observed in Eva Hubback, who showed the same confidence in him. He undertook no teaching himself and, apart from overall control of musical policy, simply conducted the choir. He enlarged it from the initial eight voices to thirty by the 1941/42 season and to over seventy by the end of the war. His personal charm and willingness to undertake the unglamorous chores of music-making ensured that the choir was a contented and co-operative group, what jealousies there were being restricted to those ladies competing for his favour. He had few problems in attracting female voices. Male voices, though less easy to come by, were drawn from a variety of sources, including medical rejects and emigrés. Morley became strikingly cosmopolitan. Not the least of the reasons for this was his ability to attract to the teaching staff several distinguished musicians who had been trained in Europe: Walter Goehr, since 1933 well-known in English musical life, who agreed to take on the orchestra; Matyas Seiber, equally distinguished as composer and teacher, who took a composition class and whose knowledge extended from serialism to jazz; Walter Bergmann, whose enthusiasm for the recorder led to the introduction of a recorder class and concerts of eighteenth-century music. Tippett came in for some hostile criticism for these 'foreign' appointments – from Vaughan Williams among others (although in general Vaughan Williams was a warm and fatherly figure with whom he got on well enough). Tippett though was anxious that Morley should not only set high standards but also become a haven for those whose lives had been uprooted.

The musical advantages of this policy were inestimable. Quite apart from the fact that the stimulus of his three chief members of staff contributed to the most enterprising concerts given in London during the war, and for several years after, Tippett himself benefited considerably from his contact with musicians trained in a German tradition. Walter Goehr in particular, who had been a Schoenberg pupil, brought to their collaboration a profound knowledge of this tradition and a scrupulous musicianship which Tippett had not encountered before. His naturally catholic tastes fed on such contacts. The advantages were not one-sided. For his part, Goehr was greatly impressed by Tippett's originality and he became the first conductor to champion Tippett's music – within a series of imaginatively planned orchestral concerts at the Wigmore Hall. The Concerto for Double String Orchestra, for example, was given its official first performance there on 17 July 1943, in company with the Prelude to Part 2 of *The Childhood of Christ* by Berlioz, Haydn's Trumpet Concerto, five orchestral songs by Wolf and Fauré's *Dolly* suite.

Holst had begun a Purcell tradition at Morley College, and this Tippett continued with such single-mindedness that a chance visit to any concert given under his supervision would probably have been rewarded with an unknown anthem, ode or chamber work. Tippett had been introduced to Purcell's music by Francesca Allinson in the 1930s, when he became fascinated by its rhythmic vitality and by its expressive harmony. But his real enthusiasm was born with the fortuitous discovery of some Purcell Society volumes in the debris of the college in October 1940, which revealed an entirely new element of coloratura and baroque virtuosity. Having no inhibitions about the ethics of authentic performance, he gave a performance of one of these works the following year – on 22 November, an appropriate date for the *Ode for St Cecilia, 1692*. The choir numbered twenty-eight, contraltos sang the countertenor parts, recorders substituted for trumpets, there were no timpani and the continuo was played on a piano. Even so, the occasion generated considerable interest, for Purcell's odes were practically unknown at the time. Purcell performances at Morley proliferated. The crucial event took place in 1944, when Tippett met Alfred Deller. Deller was a lay-clerk at Canterbury Cathedral (for which Tippett had been invited to write what was to become his motet *Plebs Angelica*) and on hearing his remarkable countertenor Tippett immediately recognized the voice he believed Purcell had been writing for; Deller himself had already discovered Purcell's alto solos and needed little persuasion to sing at Morley. So, on 21 October 1944, the sound of a real countertenor was heard in Purcell's music for the first time in many generations. Since that time a large repertory has been opened up by Deller and his successors.[27]

During the war symphony orchestras and the BBC were playing little more than the hackneyed classics and Tippett attracted a significant audience for his Morley concerts. As well as Purcell, he favoured Gibbons, Dowland, the other Elizabethans, Monteverdi, and twentieth-century composers such as Stravinsky, Hindemith and Britten. Monthly concerts in the Holst Room, which could accommodate no more than 150 people, were usually full and the choir also gave occasional concerts elsewhere – the National Gallery, Friends' House (in Euston Road), the Wigmore Hall. The personal magnetism of Tippett drew many eminent musicians to Morley, some already known, some yet to make their names, some composers, some writers. As well as Deller and the principal staff members already mentioned, such names as Maria Lidka, the Zorian Quartet, the Amadeus Quartet, Noel Mewton-Wood, Benjamin Britten, Peter Pears, William Glock, Antony Hopkins, Anthony Milner, Peter Racine Fricker (who was to succeed Tippett in 1951) became associated with the college at one time or another. Some representative programmes will highlight the character of those years:

7 November 1942
GIBBONS   Pavane and Galliard
                 Three Anthems
                 Keyboard music
                 Three String Fantasies
                 Three Madrigals
                 The Cries of London

5 December 1942
MOZART   Divertimento K334
SEIBER   Pastoral and Burlesque (*first performance*)
TIPPETT   Adagio from Concerto for Double String Orchestra
STRAVINSKY   Dumbarton Oaks (*first performance in England*)

10 April 1943
J.C. BACH   Quintet in E flat
Recorder music by MORLEY, WILBYE, LOCKE, DOWLAND
J.S. BACH   Cantata No. 189
Sixteenth-century Dances
J.C. BACH   Quintet in D

1 May 1943
MONTEVERDI   Madrigals
DOWLAND   Songs

21 June 1944 (Friends' House, Euston Road)
GIBBONS & PURCELL   Anthems
BUXTEHUDE   Two Cantatas
BRITTEN   Hymn to St Cecilia
VAUGHAN WILLIAMS   On Wenlock Edge
J.S. BACH   Cantata No. 4

21 October 1944

TIPPETT	Plebs Angelica
GIBBONS	O sing unto the Lord
BARTÓK	Pieces from *Mikrokosmos*
HANDEL	Spande ancor a mio dispetto
PURCELL	Music for a While
	Elegy on the Death of Queen Mary
	My Beloved Spake
HOPKINS	Piano Sonata

4 March 1945

PURCELL	Trio Sonata
HINDEMITH	Ludus Tonalis (*first performance in England*)
J.S. BACH	Trio Sonata in C

20 October 1945

BRITTEN	Quartet No.1
PALESTRINA	Stabat Mater
VERDI	Quartet

Tippett's formula for these concerts, a mixture of unfamiliar music old and new with little or nothing from the nineteenth century, could have been borrowed from the Sackbut concerts organized by Peter Warlock and Cecil Gray in the 1920s, which juxtaposed Gesualdo, Purcell, Van Dieren, Bartók and Schoenberg. But he was not at the time aware of this precedent. Some hints for possible programme building came from BBC broadcasts, the occasional concert in the Courtauld-Sargent series of the 1930s and from those promoted later by Gerald Cooper at the Wigmore Hall. Morley concerts however were essentially of his own devising, and they reflected his personal tastes and attitudes. In this latter respect it is worth noting that although he eventually agreed to be first speaker and lead the discussion at the first concert on 2 April 1943 of the Society for the Promotion of New Music, he really was not in favour of public concerts devoted entirely to unknown or little-known living composers and would have preferred the continental procedure, recommended by Seiber, of private concerts and meetings between colleagues.

Most of Tippett's extra-compositional energies during the immediate post-war period were also devoted to Morley College. Work there expanded. With a limited guarantee from the Arts Council, the Morley College Concerts Society was formed and declared its governing artistic principle to be 'the performance of works not usually performed which are of cultural, educational or historical interest'. So Tippett continued to pioneer, now on a larger scale, a type of concert which other organizations either could not conceive or would not risk. In May 1946 the first performance in Britain of Monteverdi's *Vespers* was given, under Walter Goehr, and in subsequent years several other unfamiliar works (Monteverdi's *L'Incoronazione di Poppea*, Stravinsky's *Les Noces*, Martin's *Le Vin Herbé* and Seiber's *Ulysses*) were introduced with such style that the Arts Council invited the Society to give three concerts in the newly opened

Royal Festival Hall, as part of the 1951 Festival of Britain. These concerts marked the official culmination of Morley's musical campaign. In some ways they typified the tradition Tippett had created. They included the Monteverdi *Vespers*, Tallis's forty-part motet, *Spem in alium* (which had been recorded under Tippett for HMV in 1949), Beethoven's C-minor Piano Concerto, Britten's *Les Illuminations*, Tippett's *A Child of Our Time*, Stravinsky's *Babel* and *Ode* and the first performance in Britain of Orff's *Carmina Burana*. Yet in other ways they were at odds with the essential spirit of Tippett's directorship, which had been to create an intimate, co-operative atmosphere, buzzing with conversations and activities covering all manner of subjects from politics to invertible counterpoint (and as such a paradigm of the wide-ranging vitality of Morley College itself) and owing allegiance to no one. It was perhaps no accident that Tippett's resignation from Morley in the summer of 1951 followed these concerts – even though the real causes lay elsewhere.

The most important of these was that Tippett's personal commitment to Morley College had began to wane after the death, in 1949, of Eva Hubback. She had not been particularly interested in music but she recognized the importance of what Tippett had been doing and always gave him encouragement and moral and practical support. When, for example, Vaughan Williams wrote complaining that too few English musicians were at work in Morley during the war, she replied that he ought to be pleased that, under Tippett's direction, Purcell's music was being performed. She arranged that Tippett could take summer terms off to get on with his own composition and although she strongly disagreed with his pacifism she spoke for him at his trial and had no hesitation in keeping his job open for him while he was in prison (Imogen Holst took over in the interim). For his part, Tippett was devoted to this remarkable woman whose vigorous, humane and generous personality was so much like his own. Her death spelt the end of his association with Morley, especially as he did not like the subsequent break with the tradition of a woman principal. He had, in fact, already been thinking of a move on grounds of health: in 1948 he had developed severe hepatitis, partly the result of the strain of writing his opera *The Midsummer Marriage* and of breaking off its composition in order to write a song cycle for Pears and Britten (*The Heart's Assurance*, only two songs of which were completed at the time). Having discovered that he could earn some secondary income as a broadcaster he eventually decided that he could afford to give up Morley entirely and devote himself almost exclusively to composition, living on what occasional jobs came his way and on what he received from his music. At this point he was invited to become the chorus master of the newly formed Philharmonia Chorus but he declined.

In the same year of 1951 he sold his bungalow and land in Oxted, and with the proceeds and some financial support from his mother (who now came to live with him) moved to Tidebrook Manor, near Wadhurst in Sussex. The house was nearly dilapidated when he bought it and it had a minimal number of habitable rooms; but it was spacious and unlike the red-brick Oxted bungalow was of real if motley character – Tudor, Georgian, Victorian. It possessed an air of rather decayed gentility. There was a large garden, constantly threatened by undergrowth, and a kitchen garden where Tippett, in polo-neck sweater, shorts and sandals nurtured his home-grown produce. Surrounding the garden was an expanse of tall trees, so that the whole setting looked like a clearing in a forest – or a stage-set for *The Midsummer Marriage*. Tidebrook set the seal on his new freedom to compose. Whereas the first two acts of the opera took five years to complete, the last, written in Tidebrook, took eighteen months.

After the war Tippett's growing reputation as a composer and as an astute observer of the social and political scene brought him closer to the public eye and ear. He began to play a major role in PPU affairs, along with such names as Benjamin Britten and Alex Comfort, acting as a 'sponsor' (a kind of vice-president whose name adds lustre) and speaking at several public meetings. In December 1946 he was a member of a deputation to the Labour Government protesting against their intention of removing unconditional registration in their post-war plans to extend conscription. Partly as a result of this, unconditional registration was retained in the National Service Act of 1947.

His pacifism also briefly revived his political involvements of the 1930s. In 1948 Phyllis Kemp contacted him for the first time since before the war.[28] Shortly afterwards he received an invitation to be a delegate at a Cultural and Scientific Conference for World Peace to be held in New York in March 1949, at which Shostakovich would be present. This was an item of cold war propaganda designed to show that intellectuals under Stalin were living in ideal conditions and that Western intellectuals and pacifists should marshal themselves under the Soviet banner of the 'peace' movement. By now Tippett was well seasoned in the political tactics of luring the gullible into a sense of euphoria and then springing a shock demand. He refused to go. He would have liked to talk to Shostakovich as a human being but not to meet him on a polemical platform, nor to be party to the impossible question which in the event was put to Shostakovich: did he agree with the *Pravda* article which described Hindemith, Schoenberg and Stravinsky as decadent bourgeois formalists and lackeys of imperialism whose music should be banned in the USSR? The unhappy Shostakovich said he fully agreed.[29] The platform applauded. Had Tippett been on it he would have been forced to enter the political arena he had been carefully avoiding for fifteen years. He had already refused to attend a similar conference in Poland, and later he declined to be a guest of the Union of Soviet Composers at a Moscow conference shortly after the Soviet invasion of Czechoslovakia.

None of this meant that Tippett's political sympathies had taken a turn to the right. He was equally emphatic, for example, in refusing to align himself with the views promoted by the literary periodical *Encounter*, at that time the main English mouthpiece of the CIA's reply to the 'peace' movement. It meant rather that he now understood 'politics' in a different light. For him, the priority was not to engage in party or national politics but to assert fundamental human and moral values. His 'political' activities were therefore devoted to the cause which most fully represented such values, pacifism, and to the creation of music which would, hopefully, be an active agent in sustaining them.

Apart from his public responsibilities as a member of the PPU (which led to his nomination as president in 1956, a titular position he still holds), Tippett's commitment to pacifism continued on the less conspicuous and more personal paths it had taken during the war. In the mid-1960s however Tippett's attitude began to change. He considered that PPU policies and ideas should be in the hands of younger people and he had become increasingly reluctant to take an active part in the organization when his own views had grown ambiguous. While pacifism was obviously a continuing moral issue, as events in Vietnam, Africa and Northern Ireland had borne out, Tippett was also inclined to believe that the spread of nuclear weapons and the politics of détente had turned pacifism into an anachronism. These views did not, in truth, reflect a seriously argued position. They showed rather the degree to which his commitment to composition had grown more urgent as he himself had grown older and how pacifism had slowly been ousted from the central position it held for him during the war and the post-war period of conscription. Yet he has not deserted the PPU and as recently as 8 August 1977 he spoke out, while opening a PPU exhibition at St Martin's-in-the-Fields, London, against President Carter's plans for the neutron bomb.

Writings and Performances

Tippett's broadcasting had begun in January 1943, with a 'Portrait of Stravinsky'. Very few talks were commissioned from him during the war, doubtless because the BBC at that time considered him a mildly subversive figure, and because he himself was worried that his pacifism might cause embarrassment. More enlightened attitudes were possible afterwards and with the creation of the Third Programme in 1946 he found himself taking a modest but significant part in the current growth of interest in the arts. In 1947 he gave seven talks, illustrated by his Morley colleagues, on Purcell and his relationship to the English tradition, and by the 1950s he was giving four or five a year. These included a discussion, for the Asian Service, about corporal punishment in public schools, reflections on moving house, for Women's Hour, and, for the Third Programme, a talk on pride for a series on the seven deadly sins and some carefully argued essays on the philosophy of music. In 1958 he published a number of these, together with other writings, as a book: *Moving into Aquarius*. This was an important milestone, absorbing six months' time and effort. The book demonstrated the increasing quality of his conceptual analysis and his confidence to face, albeit subjectively, simple yet fundamental issues that more world-weary minds were too sophisticated or too short-sighted to look at.

His twin themes are the artist as himself and the artist in relation to society. In this latter respect he occasionally overworks his resentment of a society too philistine to accept the creative imagination. But in general his views are balanced enough. He offers no panaceas, but explores his themes from a remarkable breadth of culture and from a variety of viewpoints, delving deep into the past and ranging beyond as well as within Europe, in the process arriving not so much at conclusions as at a number of questions. That these questions are difficult, if not unanswerable, is less important than that they are posed, for they concentrate attention on the points at which music can lift problems out of the province of words and resolve them in its own terms. When, for example, in a discussion about transcendent moments in theatre from Euripides to Yeats and Eliot, the point is reached where discursive argument finally has to bow out, he affirms the reality of such moments with the statement: 'The miracle was the fact.'[30] The substantiation of this will be found in the individual listener's response to such works as *The Midsummer Marriage* or *King Priam*. In his introduction to the essay 'Too Many Choices' he writes: 'Then there is the problem of Time. This seems to me so strange that I do not discuss it properly in this paper at all.' But he certainly discusses it in his oratorio *The Vision of St Augustine*. Another example could be taken from the title essay, in which Tippett examines artistic contributions to the present mutation in the nature of civilization, borrowing from astrology the idea that the 2,000-year world month of Pisces, which began with the birth of Christ, is ending and that a new one, Aquarius, is imminent. His critique of those twentieth-century artists who have helped to deliver this phenomenon is equivocal: their midwifery is 'disconcertingly and ungraciously factual'. He then presents what seems an equally equivocal question and answer: 'Would modern art be warmer if modern man had found his soul? . . . That art will speak again entire is as sure as the Zodiac.' Although he is more explicit in the second edition of the book (1974) and there rather guardedly postulates an Aquarius of compassion, his real answer had already been given in a corpus of works which do 'speak entire', reconciling the opposites of formal rigour and sensuous beauty, of reality and fantasy. Tippett has written that his function is to 'try to transfigure the everyday by a touch of the everlasting' and 'to project into our mean world music which is rich and generous' – in other words, to create musical images which compensate for the failings of the world as it is. And for this the artist can have 'no reward but in the joy of doing it'.[31]

In 1958 he had in truth not much reward other than the joy of doing it. If he had been slow to develop as a composer, the quality of his music had been conceded even more slowly. In some ways this was no major worry to a composer prepared for indifference or hostility and satisfied that this quality would in time find its place. Yet the response of a small group of sympathizers can hardly sustain a composer for ever and Tippett understandably was concerned to seek out a wider public.

In the spring of 1939 Scott Goddard wrote an encouraging article,[32] the first on Tippett's music to be printed. But since none of it had been published, this had little effect. That year Tippett submitted his Piano Sonata and Double Concerto to Oxford University Press, who rejected them, as did Boosey and Hawkes. In the same year his Double Concerto was rejected by the British Section of the ISCM and by the BBC. These setbacks were however being overtaken by a train of events which was eventually to lead to Tippett finding the publisher with whom he has remained ever since. In March 1939, during one of the intervals in the first (concert) performance in England of Hindemith's *Mathis der Maler*, a friend had persuaded Tippett to overcome his shyness and be introduced to the influential Willy Strecker of the publishing firm of B. Schott's Söhne in Mainz.[33] Strecker asked Tippett to send some scores to Germany. Sensing that Tippett thought this request routine courtesy and no more, Strecker then gave him his professional card and said he would like to have Tippett's early scores as well as recent ones so that he could see how he was developing as a composer. Copies of the Sonata, the Concerto, the early Symphony and *A Song of Liberty* reached Mainz a few weeks before the outbreak of war. Shortly after war was declared, Tippett heard from Hugo Strecker, Willy's son, a director of the London firm of Schott and Co. Ltd (who had received a letter from Mainz via a neutral country), that Schott (Mainz) would like to publish the Concerto and possibly the Sonata. 'Being a born internationalist I thoroughly enjoyed this outcome and thought it a good omen.'[34] The scores were put in safe keeping; they were apparently destroyed when the fire services pumped water into the Mainz cellars during the winter of 1943/4. Since the London firm published no contemporary music at that time and claimed that the engraving had to be done in Mainz, Tippett was at first prepared to wait until the war was over. But he soon grew dissatisfied with this state of affairs. Through Rimington, Van Wyck Ltd, a private record company whose discs were made by Decca and which had recently launched an enterprising catalogue with Russian songs sung by Oda Slodobskaya, he negotiated a recording of the Sonata, played by Phyllis Sellick, hoping to promote a marketing venture by which record company and music publisher work together. If this idea was not to be fully realized until the 1970s (when the Philips label and Schott entered into a collaboration of this kind), he did find some moderate success at the time. The recording was released in August 1941 and attracted attention. In *Scrutiny* of January 1942 Wilfrid Mellers predicted that Tippett would 'play an important part in the destiny of English music', and in *The New Statesman and Nation* of 1 November 1941 Edward Sackville-West had written with similar foresight. The most valuable critical comment appeared on 25 April 1943, when William Glock began his regular article in *The Observer* with the statement: 'A new composer has emerged in English music' – rather in the spirit of Schumann's championship of Chopin.

The success of the recording obliged the managing director of Schott in London to publish the Sonata, and a rough-and-ready edition, then called

Fantasy Sonata, was issued in 1942. Thereafter Tippett's music slowly became available. By the time of the Oxted trial, barely a year later, Vaughan Williams was able to declare Tippett's music a 'distinct national asset' – an opinion bravely echoed by the British Council, who obtained parts of his String Quartet No. 2 from Schott for despatch to and broadcast from Sweden, during the composer's term of imprisonment.

With the vindication of Tippett's commercial instincts, Schott was persuaded to finance and issue a subscription recording of the Double Concerto, which was publicly performed and recorded, again while the composer was in prison. Schott's distribution outlets were not sufficiently wide for the new recording to make much impact beyond the limits of a publisher's promotion campaign (an unsolicited but favourable review appeared in *The Gramophone* about eighteen months later, in May 1945), and for the time being this was the last item in the recording/publishing project. But it did induce the London Philharmonic Orchestra to play in the first performance of *A Child of Our Time*, an event of crucial importance.

This took place on 19 March 1944 in the Adelphi Theatre, London. By then the work was already three years old. Although he had arranged a private printing of the text in 1942, Tippett had hesitated to arrange a performance, partly because of practical difficulties but more because the work was hardly in keeping with the war effort. In 1942, Walter Goehr, though extremely enthusiastic, had advised him to wait. In the following year Tippett was persuaded by Britten to reconsider the position. His preference was to mount concerts solely with the resources of Morley College and his friends; but this was clearly impossible. With the help of Goehr, John Amis and others, the necessary forces were engaged and assembled and the performance duly took place, in a typical Tippett/ Goehr programme, which also included Mozart's *Masonic Funeral Music* (K477) and G-minor Symphony K183. Despite reservations, notably about the use of spirituals, reviews were on the whole favourable; *The Times*, for example, reporting the work as 'strikingly original alike in conception and execution'. Tippett, now nearly forty, had become established overnight.

Nevertheless it was widely believed in the 1940s and '50s that the effort needed to come to terms with his music was disproportionate to the satisfaction to be gained from it. Although it was acknowledged to contain fine moments, it was criticized as the work of a dilettante, weakened by a profusion of extra-musical allusion. A critical commonplace was that Tippett was straining to say something he was technically ill-equipped to do. Another objection was voiced by Malcolm Sargent who, on being asked by the BBC to conduct the first performance of the *Fantasia Concertante on a theme of Corelli*, rang up Tippett's publisher to say: 'My one interest is in removing all this intellectualism from English music.'[35] Tippett withdrew the work from Sargent and conducted it himself. (This, however, did not prevent *The Times* from treating him as a gifted but untutored schoolboy. 'The excessive complexity of the contrapuntal writing in the earlier part of the work defeated its own ends; there was so much going on that the perplexed ear knew not where to turn or fasten itself.')[36]

The real reasons for these criticisms were twofold. Firstly, Tippett's rhythmic innovations seemed to flout the practicalities of music-making; in consequence performances were infrequent and, when they did take place, often unconvincing. Secondly, though prepared to discuss freely the aesthetics of music, Tippett would do no more than generalize about his own music, which encouraged the view that while his verbal literacy was formidable, his musical literacy was not.

For some years the only conductor who led a sustained crusade on Tippett's behalf was Walter Goehr. His efforts were occasionally reinforced from unexpected quarters, as when Hans Schmidt-Isserstedt brought the orchestra of the North West German Radio to the Royal Festival Hall in London on 28 November 1951 and imparted a conviction to the Double Concerto which English orchestras with limited rehearsal time were unable to achieve. The work was now considered worthy to rank with Elgar's *Introduction and Allegro* and Vaughan Williams's *Tallis Fantasia*.[37] The other side of this coin could be less gratifying, as when Herbert von Karajan conducted *A Child of Our Time* on Turin Radio in 1953. Karajan informed Tippett that he was going to have an interval in the middle of Part 2 of the work (after the spiritual, 'Go down, Moses') and not as Tippett had written it. And he did.

The next English conductor to champion Tippett's music was John Pritchard, who conducted the first performance of *The Midsummer Marriage* at the Royal Opera House, Covent Garden, on 27 January 1955. The mixture of derision, bewilderment and admiration which greeted this première has become legendary. Coming in the middle of an arduous opera season, which had already seen the premières of three other British operas (Britten's *The Turn of the Screw*, Berkeley's *Nelson* and Walton's *Troilus and Cressida*), it was perhaps not surprising that the judgement of most critics was hasty, for certainly the libretto is exceedingly complex and it was against the libretto that most of the criticism was levelled. By comparison the musical idiom was generally considered tame and reactionary; if it did win approval, approval was supplied rather as an afterthought. The occasion also provided good copy for gossip writers. On the day before the performance a large-scale feature, signed James Thomas, appeared in the *News Chronicle* under the headline, 'This Opera Baffles Us Too, Say Singers'. 'Not since Salvador Dali tried to introduce a flying hippopotamus into the cast of Strauss's *Salome*', it read, 'has the Royal Opera House had such a baffled cast on its hands as the one which will launch Michael Tippett's *The Midsummer Marriage* into the world tomorrow night.' If this was a trivial instance of the English partiality for debunking something not understood, it was a typical reaction to the opera. The most extraordinary episode in Tippett's laborious struggle to win acceptance occurred with the first performance of his Symphony No. 2 on 5 February 1958. The BBC Symphony Orchestra under Sir Adrian Boult broke down in the first movement (shortly before the second-subject group) and had to begin the work again, Boult turning to the audience and saying, 'My fault entirely, ladies and gentlemen.' This was partly true, for he had condoned the insistence of the leader, Paul Beard, that Tippett's rhythmic groupings in the string parts should be altered to give the appearance of regular four-semiquaver groups per crotchet beat, thus distorting the character of the music and not after all making it easier to play. Attention was momentarily diverted from Tippett to the BBC Symphony Orchestra, and then directed back again when on 21 February 1958 a letter from R.J.F. Howgill, Controller of Music at the BBC, appeared in *The Times*.

> May I bespeak the neutrality of your columns to uphold the technical proficiency of the BBC Symphony Orchestra? The music critics of at least three journals have implied that it was unequal to the correct performance of certain passages in Mr. Michael Tippett's new symphony. In spite of Sir Adrian Boult's public admission that he misdirected them the blame has been ascribed to the players. One critic, who at the hearings seems to have a more intimate acquaintance with the work than the players themselves, claims that he detected another 'false entry' at the second performance. This is categorically denied by conductor and players. In music, practicability of text may not be the concern of the critics; to orchestral players in the mass it may mean the difference between confidence and doubt. The comprehensive technique of the BBC Symphony Orchestra is equal to all reasonable demands.

The proposition that Tippett was amateurish summarized the attitude of a generation, who needed to be put out to grass before his music could be presented sympathetically. The turning points came with the first performance of his second opera *King Priam* on 29 May 1962, also conducted by John Pritchard, and above all with a BBC studio broadcast the following year of *The Midsummer Marriage*, conducted by Norman Del Mar. The quality of Tippett's music was now recognized widely enough to dampen the fire even of those critics who had regarded the strikingly new language of *King Priam* as a perverse repudiation of what was best in his earlier music. In 1965 Tippett's sixtieth birthday gave occasion for further reassessment, and by the time *The Midsummer Marriage* had returned to Covent Garden in 1968, conducted by Colin Davis, who became Tippett's most persuasive interpreter, a change in attitude had been confirmed in performers, critics and public alike. His music has of course remained challenging and technically difficult, and the fact that it does not guarantee an easy or popular success for conductors has meant that only a few works have as yet established a firm place in the international repertory. But of Tippett's stature there is no longer any doubt.

Several institutions, notably the state and the universities, sought to identify themselves with his newly won acclaim. In 1959 he was awarded the CBE, in 1966 he was knighted and in 1979 he became a Companion of Honour. Honorary doctorates have been conferred by the Universities of Cambridge (1964), Trinity College, Dublin (1964), Leeds (1965), York (1966), Oxford (1967), Leicester (1968), North Wales (1968), Bristol (1970), Bath (1972), Warwick (1974), London (1975), Sheffield (1976),

administrators two men in their early twenties, Luke Rittner (later to become Secretary General of the Arts Council) and Anthony Tootal, who quickly justified Tippett's confidence in them and who naturally warmed to his way of treating everyone as equals, however inexperienced they might be.

The most dramatic instance of his faith in young ideas occurred shortly after he was appointed director of the festival, when he invited the student leaders of local universities and colleges to a meeting to discuss what they wanted the festival to include. Out of this emerged plans for a pop festival. An audience of 7,000 was anticipated but 23,000 arrived for the 1969 Bath Festival of Blues. The city had seen nothing like it before and was agreeably surprised: there was only one arrest. A bigger event was planned for the following year, a two-day festival of blues and progressive pop. This time the audience numbered a quarter of a million.

Tippett also instituted an annual Director's Choice concert, a chamber recital reflecting his anxiety that contemporary music should find an important place in the festival even if it could not by the nature of things occupy a significant proportion of the main concerts. Another innovation was a series of Young Performer recitals, short concerts of about an hour given by musicians recently out of college and beginning their professional careers. Further innovations included brass band concerts and such curiosities as a hot-air balloon meeting and the publication of a musicians' cookery book.[41]

Some of the festival programmes pointed to Tippett's growing interest in North America, and the USA in particular. His first visit there had been in July 1965, when he was invited to be 'composer-in-residence' at the Aspen Festival (against the wishes of its director, Darius Milhaud). He returned to the USA in April 1968 when he conducted a concert with the St Louis Symphony, deputizing at short notice for the ailing Stravinsky, and again in 1969 when he conducted the Zagreb Philharmonic Orchestra in Philadelphia. By the time he made his next visit, to Boston, Chicago, New York and Northwestern University, Evanston, Illinois (this last for the American première of his opera *The Knot Garden*), in February and March 1974, his stock had risen dramatically (largely through the impact of the recording of *The Midsummer Marriage*) and his music was received with even greater enthusiasm than it had recently won in Britain. Subsequent visits included one to the University of Austin, Texas, where he gave the Doty Lectures on Fine Art, a return to Chicago in October 1977, when his Symphony No. 4 was given its first performance by the Chicago Symphony Orchestra under Sir Georg Solti, a return to Aspen in the summer of 1978, when he was again 'composer-in-residence', and a return to Boston in May 1979, when *The Ice Break* was given its American première by the Opera Company of Boston under Sarah Caldwell.

Tippett has grown profoundly attracted to the USA – its history, art, the polyglot culture of its big cities, the half-forgotten English culture still preserved here and there on the east coast, the spectacular scenery of the West, the ancient worlds of New Mexico. At the same time he has begun to lose faith in the capacity of Europe to sustain the humanist tradition with which he identifies so fiercely and has begun to find its true custodian in the country which has now become almost a second home to him. So far as his music is concerned this has not meant that the expressive source of his inspiration has shifted; rather has his ambit widened. In his earlier music it was already apparent that he belonged to an English tradition, stretching back to Purcell, Byrd, the metaphysical poets, Shakespeare, in which the artist is 'constantly amalgamating disparate experience', as Eliot put it, forming new wholes from 'falling in love and reading Spinoza' and from 'the noise of the typewriter and the smell of cooking'. The Double Concerto, for example, is compounded of Gibbons, Beethoven, folk-song, jazz and much else besides. Tippett might have been obeying Mahler's injunction to 'embrace the world'. At that time the world was largely Europe. As Tippett's music has gone out into the world, the world has become a bigger place and in following his music Tippett's own expressive world has been enlarged. His works written since 1966 – *The Knot Garden*, *Songs for Dov*, the Third and Fourth Symphonies, *The Ice Break* – are influenced not only by specifically American musical styles such as blues, boogie-woogie, the music of Ives, but also by the specifically American characteristics of spontaneity, candour and the instinct to explore.

Following his own music has also taken him to Africa and the Far East. In April 1975 he was in Zambia for a performance in Lusaka Cathedral of *A Child of Our Time*, given partly by native Zambians and partly by expatriate English. In the spring of 1978 he was in Australia, attending performances in Perth and Adelaide, where *The Midsummer Marriage* was given by the State Opera of South Australia and where he conducted his own Symphony No. 4. He used the occasion to visit Java and Bali. The restrained Buddhist drama, the more extrovert Hindu dancing, and the various styles of gamelan orchestra made a profound impression on him. He had attempted to re-create the sounds of gamelan gongs in his Piano Sonata No. 1 some forty years earlier. With the actual sounds in his ears his earlier enthusiasm was revived and it has borne fruit in his recent Triple Concerto for violin, viola, cello and orchestra.

As Tippett has grown older, composing has not become easier for him. But greater financial security has enabled him to pattern his life as he wishes, taking frequent holidays abroad (not only in pursuit of his own music) and, in particular, concentrating his compositional energies on those large-scale works natural to his style. He has also been able to keep more closely to a daily routine: composing in the mornings; walks in the afternoons (when pre-compositional thinking about new works takes place) plus correspondence or copying; relaxation, such as listening to the radio, watching television or reading, in the evenings.

Tippett has always been an avid reader. In his earlier years, he enthusiastically entered into the literary tradition of the 'whole of Europe' (as Eliot demanded of the modern poet), and more, and emerged with a remarkable capacity to enlighten, to clarify and classify. Literature has made him conscious of his vocation as an artist, and not merely as a composer, and of the correspondingly greater pressure to state his beliefs clearly when the basis from which they are formed is so much wider. David Ayerst[42] has drawn attention to his preoccupation with, at various times, Butler, Bergson, Shaw, Goethe, Blake, Whitman, Frazer, Jung, Yeats and Eliot. Two radio broadcasts in the 1970s, 'With Great Pleasure' and 'Personal Anthology', in which Tippett introduced excerpts from his favourite writers, have given an informative supplement to Ayerst's list: Shakespeare, Dickens, Hopkins, Housman, Owen, Auden and Solzhenit-syn.[43] In his introductions to these excerpts Tippett revealed something of their significance to him, which was that they provided verbal metaphors of the same kinds of subject that occupied his musical thinking. In Blake's *The Tyger*, for example, 'unanswerable questions are made poetic fact'. In *Lapis Lazuli* Yeats makes poetry from the 'heroism and gaiety of war, not the pity' (as had Owen). The dominant impression gained from such broadcasts is of Tippett's anxiety to find explicit confirmation or articula-tion of the more elusive ideas and feelings he himself wishes to express through music. It is as if he needs the assurance that his ideas are not personal caprice but part of age-old human endeavour. He reads therefore not merely to learn, or to find enjoyment or diversion (though he is a compulsive reader of thrillers), but to locate a way of expressing something of whose existence he is already aware. Having recognized what he is looking for, he may dismiss the larger part of the book in question as irrelevant. The process can be described as a form of kleptomania – which accounts for the fact that while Tippett is an absorbing lecturer and conversationalist he has never been a composition teacher (at least, he has never set himself up as one).[44] Teaching might have compromised his compositional ambitions in any case, but, equally important, he regarded himself as not sufficiently objective in outlook to have been very good at it.

Tippett's tastes in music are catholic. He listens to a great deal of contemporary music, 'serious' and pop, and is not at all reluctant to ask his younger and better informed musical friends what he should listen to. He is particularly interested in the music of younger British composers, not least because he knows many of them personally. But nothing written by the post-war generation of composers, British or otherwise, however useful or intriguing he might find their compositional or instrumental techniques, has aroused in him the same excitement or enthusiasm that earlier composers have done. For a BBC 'Desert Island Discs' programme in April 1968, he chose the following eight works: Monteverdi's 'Chiome d'oro' (Boulanger recording), 'Dido's lament' from *Dido and Aeneas* by Purcell, Schubert's C-major Quintet, 'Dawn and Siegfried's Journey to the Rhine' from *Götterdämmerung* by Wagner, Stravinsky's *Symphonies of Wind Instru-ments*, 'The Fourth of July' from Ives's *Holidays* Symphony, Bessie Smith's recording of the St Louis Blues and his own Symphony No. 2. In earlier years Dowland, Gibbons, Handel and Gershwin would doubtless have found a place, as would Bruckner and Shostakovich in more recent ones; and Beethoven would have been represented at almost every stage of Tippett's career had it been possible to reduce his importance to a single work. But, allowing for a bias towards encouraging his listeners to explore the less familiar, these works gave a characteristic enough sample of his preferences.

Tippett has continued to live in the country, where he can shut himself 'away from the noise and activity of the town in order to find some kind of inner silence'.[45] In 1960 he left Tidebrook and settled in Parkside, a Georgian house of mellow Cotswold stone in the village high street of Corsham in Wiltshire. A gate at the bottom of his walled garden led out into the extensive woodlands of Corsham Park, designed by Capability Brown, where there was ample opportunity for his long afternoon walks. By 1970 Corsham had become uncomfortably urbanized and in the spring of that year he moved to a large, recently-built house made of natural materials outside and in, set high on the wooded slopes of the Marlborough Downs overlooking the Vale of Malmesbury.

Life in a 'personal sanctuary'[46] brings its dangers, of which Tippett has long been well aware.

> The artist who has to animate his imaginative powers in order to create, endangers partially or altogether at times his sense of reality. In my own experience this is a true possibility. One guards against it as a doctor guards himself against constant exposure to disease, or perhaps more exactly as a psychiatrist guards himself against the neuroses of his patients.[47]

Thus, Tippett has contrived to keep his distance from the archetypal sources of his creativity lest too close an identification with them should disturb his equilibrium. That he should think in these terms at all is of course an extraordinary thing. It suggests that he is continually dicing with insanity – that the reasons for the perfectly normal aspects of his lifestyle, such as keeping weekends free for relaxation (they are usually spent with friends), having regular holidays, or undertaking his various external commitments, are in fact deadly serious. It suggests that his ability to judge his own music, responding to some parts of it with deep feeling while criticizing others with unaffected detachment, is the result not so much of sagacity as of dire necessity. How successful he has been in separating himself from his own creativity can be gauged from small but telling traits of personality: when, for example, referring to one of his own works, he will use the definite article rather than the possessive pronoun (as with most composers); if he transcribes a passage of manuscript incorrectly, he will say 'it got wrong', not 'I made a mistake'. In informal surroundings, he is fond of assuming the role of master of ceremonies whose function it is to stick pins into whichever conversationalist shows signs of drifting into pretentiousness. He is indeed naturally convivial and inquisitive. But his playfulness can also be seen as a mechanism by which he protects himself from serious discussion – or from those alternative viewpoints which might arouse his creative demon. Total separation of, as it were, creativity and humanity would however lead to spiritual suicide. When Tippett does invite serious discussion, it seems therefore that he is deliberately exposing that 'open wound' which is the hallmark of the creative mind, deliberately testing his beliefs in the market place where they cannot be insulated by the walls of his composing studio.

The forbidding and somewhat isolated figure emerging from these observations is not however a Tippett many people would recognize. There seems little real danger that he should lose his 'sense of reality'. In professional matters, he is practical and businesslike. In general, he exhibits a rich mixture of complementary qualities: exuberance, reserve, quicksilver intelligence, straining flights of imagination, tenderness, realism. Those who have come into contact with him would doubtless add a ruthless streak of egocentricity and even a touch of the prima donna; but the characteristics they would most readily draw attention to would be friendliness, spontaneity, generosity, an instinct to brush aside conventional courtesies and come straight to the point, exchanging thoughts and ideas on an equal and purely human footing. He has a remarkable ability to offer constructive encouragement and to stir the feeling that the human animal has within him an infinite and infinitely worthwhile capacity for enrichment. If all this were to be marshalled under one single quality, it would be of what may be called Tippett's mature youthfulness – his knowledge of how to absorb and profit from experience and of how to retain his confidence in youthful vitality, vision and vulnerability.

It has become a commonplace to remark on the physical signs of this quality, Tippett's youthful appearance and restlessly active manner. Yet if this overlooks the toughness of the man, and even if it ignores the fact that he is, after all, well into his seventies, it remains true that a correlation exists between his physical appearance and the vigorous, questing nature of his music. It would be equally true to say that this is the result of his attitude of mind. Since 1970 he has suffered from macular dystrophy, a localized degeneration of the retinas. This has meant that he cannot read without a large magnifying glass and that he has to compose on specially made manuscript paper with widely spaced stave-lines; to conduct he has to commit scores to memory. Since about the same time he has also suffered from a mild heart complaint and persistent attacks of the same kind of 'intestinal neuralgia' that seems to have afflicted Berlioz. But he has not been unduly restricted, and he continues to compose and plan works which will take him well into his eighties.

THE COMPOSER AND HIS MUSIC

CHAPTER ONE

1923·34

Formative Attitudes

When he first arrived at the Royal College of Music in London, Tippett found the world of music exhilarating but confusing – a disordered pattern of styles and techniques lacking any evident hierarchy of values. He could have closed his mind to outside influence and, having gained a basic musical literacy from the RCM, taken Hans Sachs's advice, made his own rules and followed them, as many composers appeared to be doing at the time. But he mistrusted iconoclastic measures and private systems. Instinctively, he would attempt a solution to a problem only when he had isolated and categorized its components. So he decided patiently to disentangle the pattern and then to work out his own compositional objectives, find his own models and gain a technique. Creative individuality, if he had any, would emerge in due course. This strategy was not evolved overnight; it was to be profoundly influenced by his reading of Eliot (see p.23). Eventually it took a form corresponding to the strategy he was to ascribe to Purcell.[1] In showing how Tippett trained himself to become a composer, the present chapter takes as its starting point his interpretation of what may be called the Purcellian syndrome.

Purcell's unique musical language, as Tippett saw it, was the result of developing the already perfected styles and techniques of his Tudor and Jacobean forbears and of integrating this native inheritance with new styles and techniques from abroad. The essence of composition lay therefore in the integration of disparate material. For the young Tippett the position was analagous, if not so clearcut. What exactly was his musical inheritance and what exactly were the new ideas from abroad? As far as he was concerned, his inherited styles and techniques were those of the whole of European music (and more), including but not limited to English ones. His tasks therefore were to develop skills in them all, to try to uncover an English tradition and in particular to decide whether the folk-song movement of the time was significant. New styles and techniques from abroad were less easy to assess because critical ability in these matters matured more slowly and was likely to be based on unrepresentative samples. He eventually settled on two elements, jazz and the new classicism: jazz (used in the widest sense of the word) for its own sake and also as a kind of vernacular, valuable because it could reach a wide audience; neo-classicism largely through Stravinsky, to whose music and ideas he responded with particular sympathy.

Tippett's neo-classical sympathies were responsible for another decision he took at this early stage, which was that the component parts of his proposed stylistic integration – the musical genres, the contrasts of character – should be kept distinct, creating large-scale forms by the tensions and interrelationships between them. This may also be seen as an intuitive recognition of Blakean or Jungian ideas about energy deriving from the tension of opposites. In any event it meant that when he was studying academic techniques – fugue, canon, chorale prelude, sonata, passacaglia and so on – Tippett was not blindly submitting to traditional disciplines but building up a vocabulary of basic expressive methods.

In his initial exploration of the repertory he quickly began to pick out the styles and composers that seemed most significant and which could teach him most. He developed a marked distaste for the romantic and nationalistic music which might have been expected to make the most direct impact on an impressionable young musician. He eventually took the view that however admirable their individual accomplishment nine-teenth-century composers in general had created nothing new or important and had been content merely to add a personal gloss to what already existed, thus confusing the boundaries between musical genres and obscuring the clarity of gesture and content he was seeking in his own music. The nineteenth-century preoccupation with harmony was also unsympathetic. The major nineteenth-century composer for him was Berlioz, for the lucidity of his melodic lines and the transparency of his scoring.

Tippett was far more interested in contrapuntal music, in the rhythmic counterpoint of the sixteenth and early seventeenth centuries, and especially in the English music of this period and the long flowing lines from which its counterpoint was created. In this context harmony, the anguished non-structural harmony found in the darker madrigals of Weelkes and Monteverdi and in the songs of Dowland, became a clear and precise expressive tool. The benefits of Tippett's early study of sixteenth- and seventeenth-century music lay fallow for several years but they nevertheless went deep and eventually surfaced in the late 1930s as the first fruits of his maturity.

As for eighteenth-century composers he liked Domenico Scarlatti, for his crisp and colourful textures. Bach, to him, was an ambiguous figure, greatly to be admired and from whom many technical skills could be abstracted – as was impressively confirmed when Tippett studied with Morris – but curiously characterless as sound (this perhaps a reflection of performing practice in the 1920s). All he remembers responding to in the Brandenburg Concerto No. 5, for example, was the cadenza in the first movement. He found little drama in Bach, an element conspicuously evident in Handel, whom he regarded as by far the greater composer. His love for Handel centred on the op. 6 Concerti Grossi, which he felt had an irresistible drive, a rhythmic vitality, clarity of line and spontaneity of musical invention without peer.

Of the Viennese classics, he was especially attracted to Haydn and his string quartets, for their own sake and because he became increasingly fascinated by the quartet medium as such. His favourite set was op. 76, and out of that, No. 2 in D minor (the Quartet whose first movement contains some strikingly Tippett-like 'anticipatory' rhythms. See p.100). But of all composers the one who meant most to him and who gave him the most lasting musical tutelage was Beethoven. He was almost obsessed with the music of Beethoven during his RCM days and for long periods listened to little else. The Busch and Léner Quartets regularly gave complete Beethoven cycles in London in the 1920s and also made recordings, through which Tippett became so familiar with the quartets that he had to stop listening to them. His particular favourites at the time were opp. 95 and 132. The principal lessons he learnt from Beethoven concerned the vitality of formal process, how the ebb and flow of musical movement is to be created, developed and controlled. Beethoven offered an enormous repository of musical gesture. Beethoven therefore represented organic form, both within and between movements regardless of the genre (Tippett saw little distinction, for example, between *Fidelio* and the symphonies).

Tippett's preoccupation with Beethoven accounted in some ways for his indifference to Brahms, whose lyricism seemed at the time to obstruct motivic development and whose intermezzo-like middle movements avoided large-scale formal problems altogether. Wagner was tarred with the nineteenth-century brush – although Tippett later developed a deep admiration for Wagner and learnt two things in particular from him: that an empty stage can be filled with sound and that operatic proportions must be carefully articulated.

All these judgements on older music reflected the exclusive preferences of a young man, and they were conditioned to some extent by the climate of the times. In the 1920s Handel's operas, for example, enjoyed a revival on the continent and Handel has in any case always been an English favourite. The editorial labours of E.H. Fellowes were revealing the glories of Tudor and Jacobean music, and the pre-eminence of Beethoven has remained inviolate, whatever the generation concerned. Later these judgements mellowed and were enlarged, Tippett admitted new figures to his pantheon of masters, Purcell being a notable example, and he remained open to ideas from any- and everywhere. Yet they were crucial in formulating his early outlook, in which personal and national elements, as manifested in nineteenth-century music, were set aside and inspiration drawn from Beethoven, the eighteenth century and further back, and in which he found that his response to non-English music was just as genuine as that to early English music, however greatly he loved this music and however clearly the elements of a specifically English tradition could be seen in it. And they were also crucial in their practical application, for they gave him a store of models from which he could, when in compositional difficulty, deduce guiding principles.

Tippett's interest in the English tradition was initially a consequence of his discovery of Elizabethan and Jacobean music. Later it was deepened by his understanding of Eliot's theory of 'dissociation of sensibility', which helped him to identify the mixture of 'art' music and the vernacular in that tradition and to account for its decline after the death of Purcell. Purcell did not exert any real influence on his thinking until the early 1940s, when Tippett encountered that brilliance of vocal style and originality of word-setting which then seemed the most vivid manifestations of it. A particular obstacle in the way of his early understanding of Purcell was the figured bass. In the 1920s and '30s, he paid more attention to ballad opera than to Purcell, both as a genre in itself and for its significance as a storehouse of folk melody.

His most urgent contact with the English tradition was a result of the folk-song revival in the early part of the century. The pioneer work of Cecil Sharp as a field collector, his skill as a polemicist and the practical and moral support given him by Vaughan Williams and others combined to lift the subject into the forefront of musical politics. Sharp considered the ballad opera effectively useless as a source of folk-song, because the versions contained therein were corrupt. He believed that the purity of the songs he had unearthed could be the basis for the revival of English music, as English literature had depended on the publication of folk-ballads in the mid-eighteenth century for the emergence of the romantic poets and novelists. These assertions were made from positions of authority and carried great weight and influence, as the numerous followers of Vaughan Williams and Holst testified. They were bound to be taken seriously.

The first shots in the campaign had been fired by Cecil Sharp in his book *English Folk-Song: Some Conclusions*, first published in 1907. Here are some key remarks from the chapter headed 'The Future of English Folk-Song'.

No School of Music has yet arisen and flourished in Europe that has not primarily been concerned with the expression of national aspirations... The natural musical idiom of a nation will, therefore, be found in its purest and most unadulterated form in its folk-music... We may look therefore to the introduction of folk-songs in the elementary schools to effect an improvement in the musical taste of the people, and to refine and strengthen the national character. The study of the folk-song will also stimulate the growth of the feeling of patriotism.

Nearly thirty years later, Vaughan Williams, in his book *National Music* of 1934, and from a position of even greater authority, was still upholding and developing these ideas.

Art, and especially the art of music, uses knowledge as a means to the evocation of personal experience in terms which will be intelligible and command the sympathy of others. These others must clearly be primarily those who by race, tradition, and cultural experience are the nearest to him: in fact those of his own nation, or kind of homogeneous community (p.39)... I do hold that any school of national music must be fashioned on the raw basis of its national song (p.74)... If [the artist] consciously tries to express himself in a way which is contrary to his surroundings, and therefore to his own nature, he is evidently being, though he does not know it, insincere (p.6).

Setting aside the jingoistic sentiments, common enough before the 1914–18 war and even more so thereafter when a wave of nationalism swept across the whole of Europe in one way or another, the important questions prompted by Sharp and Vaughan Williams were, to Tippett, does the English musician feel such a deep bond with his folk-song as proposed, and in what way is his national song so English? For his part, Tippett's first musical excitement had come through Mozart's late G-minor Symphony, which affected him far more deeply than the Cecil Sharp folk-songs he learnt at Stamford School, much as he liked them too. And, to him, a more solid and productive source of inspiration than folk-song was Elizabethan music. To suggest that folk-song should be the exclusive basis from which a musical culture should spring simply flew in the face of experience.

As for the Englishness of the Sharp songs, a more detailed investigation was called for. In the 1930s, Tippett and Francesca Allinson began to ask why it was that these songs, predominantly gentle and ruminative in character, should be so different from the more lively ones in the *Fitzwilliam Virginal Book*, in *The Beggar's Opera*, or in the Chappell collection *Popular Music of the Olden Time* (1859). Principally through observing a correspondence of phrase structure (ABBA) between the Sharp songs and those in *The Petrie Collection of the Ancient Music of Ireland* (Dublin 1855), Allinson came to the conclusion that the Sharp songs were profoundly influenced by Irish folk music, as a result of the influx of Irish labourers during the industrial revolution. Purity could not be granted the Irish product either, since its chief protagonists, blind itinerant harpers, had in turn been influenced by Corelli and Handel. From an examination of Sharp's manuscripts, Allinson also discovered that Sharp's proposition that English folk-song commonly contained quintuple or septuple rhythm (eagerly accepted by Holst and Vaughan Williams whose music contains a significant number of sections entirely in these tempi) was not the case: the 5/4 time signature allotted by Sharp to the famous song 'Searching for Lambs', for instance, is in fact present in only one of several manuscript variants of the song. So Sharp's defence of the racial purity of English folk-song was based on wishful thinking rather than genuine research.[2] A final word may be taken from A.L. Lloyd's classic book on the subject, *Folk Song in England*.

> Persuasive as Sharp's 'Conclusions' seem, we are not a great deal the wiser about what makes English song different from anyone else's because so many of the peculiar characteristics he had hoped to isolate are not really peculiar at all, but are shared by many other peoples.[3]

Tippett's reactions to the music of Holst and Vaughan Williams had brought him to roughly the same conclusions as Allinson long before she put them on an academic footing. He acknowledged the courage and imagination of these composers in breaking away from German hegemony and he admired Holst, in particular,[4] for laying himself open to change and enrichment from non-European stimuli. Holst's experiments with English word-setting avoided the four-square rhythms of the Victorian hymn; his interest in modal parallel harmonies, in bitonality, in quintuple and septuple rhythms (however shaky their theoretical foundation) all contributed to an unmistakably original language. In *The Hymn of Jesus* Tippett recognized a kind of oratorio which, in his estimation, was to prove the mainspring of English choral music for some years to come. Yet Holst had no more been able to escape the pervasive pastoralism of the time than Vaughan Williams. This Tippett found disturbing, because its concentration on the folk idiom excluded too much (even within its own lights it drew only from rural as opposed to urban folk-music). It discouraged sustained musical thinking and encouraged aimless rhapsody. He liked the *Tallis Fantasia* of Vaughan Williams, for example, until the ubiquitous viola solo made its appearance. As with that work, the *Pastoral* Symphony seemed, to him, to begin at least with an expression of the ache in the soul whose authenticity no-one could doubt; but after that he got bored. He found the G-minor Mass a poor copy of the five-part Mass of Byrd. Whereas Vaughan Williams drew on Byrd's harmonic sentiment he, Tippett, would like to draw on his harmonic passion. Fast movements were reduced to the inane heartiness of the scherzos of the *London* and *Pastoral* Symphonies. In general he regarded both Holst and Vaughan Williams as lacking in technical skill and this was one reason why he was determined to acquire it for himself.

If this disposed of the racial sanctity of English folk-song and if the prognosis for a folk-based style was bleak, Tippett nevertheless did not reject folk-song. Its attraction was too powerful to resist and he used it in his own music as a major stylistic ingredient until 1939, and even after that wrote occasional folk-song arrangements. He liked many of Sharp's tunes for their own sake and he examined a wide range of folk melody from other and earlier collectors, especially with the help of Allinson. He did not believe that a folk-based style need necessarily result in melodies exhausted of life after their first phrases were over, nor that it could not, with the injection of Austro-German development techniques, sustain a linear momentum. Much of his music of the 1930s is evidence of these beliefs. In addition, he was attracted to folk-song for its promise of a vernacular. Its place in his thinking was thus parallel with that of jazz – and at this point his twin objectives converged.

Jazz seemed to offer a vernacular on an international scale and was therefore of potentially greater value. Though genuine, his interest in jazz during his student years was in fact rather vague. He was fascinated by the novelty of it, by its rhythms, its instrumental ensembles, the virtuosity and humanity of its chief exponents and by its warnings of the pretentiousness lurking behind the temples of high art. For many years it acted as a form of correcting mechanism: in the 1930s he would listen to Hindemith's String Trio No. 2 (which he admired) and then, as a complement, would play records of Bessie Smith. But he did not gain any understanding of the specific technical novelties of jazz until the late 1930s.

Jazz, however, was not only a new language from abroad. It also appeared to be affecting the direction taken by the English tradition, as represented by the post-Vaughan Williams generation. Walton and Lambert were Tippett's own contemporaries and in the 1920s and '30s the most influential leaders of this new direction. They ignored the Vaughan Williams school entirely and sought an integration of English and continental idioms, notably the jazz idiom. If their total rejection of folk-song was at variance with Tippett's less extreme ideas, their aims still corresponded in many ways with his own. The test however was in their music – and this he found of only marginal interest. Though such works as Walton's *Portsmouth Point* Overture and *Sinfonia Concertante* were permeated by the 'wrong note' technique Tippett scorned, and though they exhibited a typically breezy English wit (an attribute notably absent in Tippett's mature music), they did have a kind of movement about them – up and down, backwards and forwards, like a boat in a pond – and they did escape from the Housmanism of the times. Yet jazz-influenced works, such as Walton's *Façade*, Lambert's Piano Concerto and *The Rio Grande*, suffered from the same failings Tippett had diagnosed in continental counterparts. None of these works, whether by Ravel, Milhaud or even by Stravinsky, seemed to have done any more than reproduce mannerisms. They might have documentary value, but the jazz was unassimilated. This, to Tippett, was the important point and until he had himself learnt how to use it constructively, his interest in the subject would have to remain enthusiastic but unproductive.

Most of the published information or opinion about 'serious' contemporary music available to Tippett was of an ephemeral kind, and for considered judgements he was limited to Adolf Weissmann's *The Problems of Modern Music* (1925) and the provocative *Survey of Contemporary Music* (1924) of Cecil Gray. He was hampered by the paucity of recordings and concerts, but he heard what he could, examined published scores and eventually concluded that contemporary music could offer no new archetypal forms or gestures to compare with those he had already found in Beethoven and earlier composers. In general, contemporary music represented to him a rather frantic and desperate search for roots within some central tradition. Yet the temper of the 1920s and '30s had one positive and indeed decisive feature – the neo-classical music of Stravinsky, which gave proof of the validity of his own compositional ambitions. Tippett was deeply responsive to Stravinsky, whom he regarded as the real master of the twentieth century. He could not gain much from Stravinsky's techniques but he was to be reassured by the fact that the music he himself wanted to write belonged to an aesthetic which received the imprimatur of Stravinsky's *Chroniques de ma vie* (1935). So, if the letter of the Purcellian idea of marrying inherited styles with new ones from abroad could not be adopted, he found himself applying the spirit without prompting.

Tippett summed up the relevance of other contemporary composers for

himself in a series of judgements which may be considered cavalier or
brilliantly perceptive according to taste. Whatever view is taken of them
they cannot be dismissed as casual opinion for they have not materially
changed in the ensuing fifty years and more. In Debussy, for example,
Tippett recognized a new sensibility, finer than Ravel's, because it had
'magic': Debussy knew how to 'lay out a sound'. Schoenberg was to him
not new at all, merely the tail-end of the nineteenth century; and the
twelve-note method addressed itself to only the most primitive elements of
vocabulary, at the expense of language. Webern was a composer crippled
by his rejections, his rejection, for example, of perfect intervals. Berg he
found more sympathetic than either, though if *Wozzeck* had to be
acknowledged the perfect twentieth-century opera, that was a cheerless
outlook. From Bartók he learnt the idea of colouristic dissonance.
Hindemith appealed to him for his clean, classical style and his contrapuntal skills, and also in a more sophisticated way: as a writer of what Tippett
took to be utility music, Hindemith was Tippett's own antithesis. In the
early 1930s Sibelius stood very high in his estimation and provided
constructional models for a new kind of sonata form which were to have
important consequences. Apart from Sibelius the contemporary composer
who taught Tippett as much as anyone else was his own contemporary,
Alan Bush. Tippett particularly admired Bush's *Prelude and Fugue* for piano
and *Dialectic* for string quartet, and Bush's ideas about contrapuntal
writing and thematicism – the derivation of material from one thematic
germ (which, oddly enough, *he* had gained from the twelve-tone waltz in
Schoenberg's op. 23) – were important factors in Tippett's attempt to
transcend the twin influences of Sibelius and a folk-song style.

By the mid-1930s Tippett had absorbed or discarded what other
composers had to offer him and in any case had drawn back from too close
an involvement with new music lest this would prejudice the development
of his own style. He had written his first mature work after a process of
learning and discovery taking over ten years. None of the music he wrote
during his student years is particularly interesting as music or really worth
reviving. But it has genuine relevance as an index of Tippett's temperament – of his conviction that if his music had the beginnings of quality this
would eventually emerge, and of his patience in accepting that the priority
he laid on acquiring a technique would entail such protracted effort. And of
course it has relevance for what it prefigures of Tippett's later music.
Without hindsight this would not be easy to determine, for it is concerned
more with musical process than with the invention of striking or
memorable phrases. Indeed its anonymity of language might encourage the
view that the 'transcendent capacity of taking trouble' will of itself lead to
the creation of works of art. Suffice it to say that Tippett's student works
represent an apprenticeship rather than a search for a style.

Student Works

Tippett has rejected most of the music he wrote when an RCM student, either destroying it or allowing friends to take it away. Of the surviving works, one of the earliest is his adaptation of *The Village Opera*, written between 1927 and 1928. This can be taken as an initial and representative example of how seriously he took his commitment to learning the craft of composition.

His interest in the work derived from his interest in ballad opera. If *The Beggar's Opera* remains the only ballad opera hardy enough to have kept a place in the repertory, *The Village Opera* is a characteristic example for it was first produced and printed only a year after *The Beggar's Opera* had launched the genre – that is, when the genre was still young and vital. The story of *The Village Opera* tells how two pairs of lovers (one pair disguised as gardener and chambermaid) eventually confound the machinations of a preposterous old country squire and two roguish footmen. The music, as in the original 1729 edition Tippett worked from, contains over sixty popular tunes of the day, printed in voice-line only with no indication of how they should be set. Apart from making cuts in the dialogue, he transposed some of these tunes and substituted others or his own in places, in order to increase the sense of tonal connection and to give the individual characters more idiomatic music. He added recitatives and dances, and while in general conforming to the original, he used the occasion primarily as an exercise in harmonization, instrumentation and in the control of musico-dramatic shape. His most radical alteration was in Act II, the second scene of which he entirely rewrote as an uninterrupted piece of music rather like a Mozartian finale. In this elopement scene, the two girls wait at their bedroom windows for their lovers to climb up; the plan is discovered at the last minute through the unchivalrous behaviour of the footmen. Tippett begins with a melodrama, two solos and a duet (all in 5/4). Then follows a quartet, sextet and nonet, the sections linked by accompanied recitatives and the whole remaining just within the bounds of a folk-song style. This is the most effective scene in the opera, and it shows how anxious Tippett was, even at this early stage, to test his ability to create operatic tension. For the rest he concentrated on the more straightforward task of providing appropriately coloured accompaniments to the songs. There was nothing perfunctory about his approach: he devoted as much care to the treatment of minor characters as to the major ones. Example 1, from a song for the hero's manservant, gives the rejected original song (though the text was too good to lose), his own new one and an indication of the instrumentation (the opera is scored for flute, oboe, horn, string quartet, harpsichord and piano; only the harpsichord is not used here).

The relatively elaborate accompaniment in this example is symptomatic of Tippett's predilection for contrapuntal textures, even if at this stage he had not broken away from simple arpeggio figurations. The remaining works of this period (see List of Works, p.498) show him continuing to manipulate traditional genres and forms and continuing to develop

Ex. I

Original Edition 1729
Air III: The Logan Water

My Dol - ly_ was the_ Snow - drop fair, _____

Pno. *f*   Str. *p*   Fl.   Pno.

1. Cur - ling_ En - dive was_ her Hair; The frag - rant Jess - a -
2. Breasts in_ swel - ling Mush - rooms rise; Her Waist, the streight and_

Vlns.   Fl. Ob.   Ob.   Hn. Vla.

mine her Breath; White Kid - ney - Beans her e - ven_ Teeth.
up - right Fir; But all_ her_ Heart was

Two_____ Dai - sies_ were her eyes; Her Cu - cum - ber.

conventional contrapuntal skills. His *Psalm in C* (1930) for chorus and orchestra is of interest for its instrumental specification, which includes a solo string quartet. In itself not a particularly novel feature at the time (even Lambert's *The Rio Grande* contains a solo string quartet), it is nevertheless an intriguing indication of his affection for Handel. A note on the score reads: 'The "Concertino" is a string quartet of the four leaders; the "Concerto Grosso" is the rest of the strings. (The principle employed is that of the Handel Concerti Grossi.)' In fact there is little Handelian about his use of the quartet and the music as a whole is laboured in effect. By far the best of these early works are two real string quartets, one in F minor, the other in F major, written between 1928 and 1930.

From his earliest student years Tippett had been attracted to the quartet medium. The sounds of Haydn, Mozart and Beethoven rang through his ears to such an extent that he would have found it difficult to invent a truly original idea even if he had wanted to. At that time originality of material was however less important to him than development of musical process and the quartet, which seemed to possess a finality and purity more compelling than any other medium, was the ideal context in which to flex his muscles.

The principal compositional objective behind the two quartets is to integrate a Beethovenian and a folk-song style – a curious compound on the face of it, yet Tippett argued that if Beethoven could introduce folk-themes in his Rasumovsky quartets and modal harmonies in op. 132, there was no reason why he could not attempt something comparable himself. This idea is strikingly clear in the opening sonata-allegros, in which dramatic argument between the Beethovenian (or, in the case of the F-major work, the Haydnesque) and the folk-song style is sustained with great deliberation. These movements also reveal his determination to mould the folk-style to classical developmental patterns, that is, to invent lyrical themes of varying structure and function and with varying accompanimental tex-

tures, and thereby to enforce contrapuntal ingenuity. In Ex.2 part of the
first and second subjects of each quartet is shown, to illustrate the degree of
contrast Tippett made for himself and, in the lyrical themes, to illustrate
the growing versatility of his treatment of both phrase-structure (6-bar
phrases in the one, 3 + 5-bar phrases in the other) and accompanimental
texture (inventive use of arpeggio figuration and imitative counterpoint
respectively).

Ex. 2

(i) **String Quartet in F minor**

(ii) **String Quartet in F major**

The middle movements are the most successful, perhaps because though still mainly based on the sonata principle, their more schematic forms do not set so high a premium on intuitive control of mood. Yet both works are carefully, almost self-consciously balanced. It seems that Tippett was determined to test his ability to dispose several forms on a large scale, asking himself such questions as how does one write argumentative music, serene music, graceful music, eloquent music, and how are these elements to be placed in a complete work? The quartets contain two different answers to these questions. In the F-minor there are five movements: allegro, allegretto, chorale prelude, rondo, variation on the sonata-allegro; in the F-major, four: sonata-allegro, largo, allegretto, slow fugue with fast introduction and coda. Of particular interest is his cautious treatment of the 'finale problem', much in the academic wind at that time. In both finales he brings back material from earlier movements, a device he was to use later on occasion, but unexpected here since it recalls the nineteenth-century aesthetic he affected to despise.

The most individual feature of the quartets is Tippett's treatment of tonal relationships. Modulations are determined less by structural con-siderations than by the nature of the thematic material he wishes to introduce. In the case of the two second subjects in Ex. 2 this is the bright, open sound of D major; the resulting mediant relationships are quite fortuitous. When the composer's priorities are of this kind, difficulties arise and although expressive rather than structural use of tonality was to become a characteristic fingerprint, the curious tonal organization of the sonata movements in the quartets reflects a problem Tippett did not really solve until his Concerto for Double String Orchestra.

The final impression left by these works is of a struggle to reproduce Beethovenian gestures on an extended scale, out of which emerges a genuine breadth of phrase, a natural feeling for contrapuntal textures and a disdain for impressionistic effect. If their vocabulary lacks character, Tippett's intentions were soundly based and remained fundamental for the later composer. Though 'student' works, they are serious and accomplished. After the performance of the F-major Quartet (certainly the better of the two) at his Oxted concert of 1930 Tippett decided however that their lack of character was a fatal defect and he decided to remedy matters by studying with Morris.

While with Morris, he wrote his String Trio in B flat, a three-movement work more succinct in its procedures, livelier in rhythm and fresher in texture. It still holds to conventional forms however, to the folk-style (though only in the slow movement) and it still recalls first-movement material at the end of its finale. Tippett's absorption with classical techniques seems to have reached an impasse. In retrospect this work can be interpreted as a kind of *reculer pour mieux sauter*, for his next important work, though nominally in B flat again, also in three movements and containing an elaboration of the Trio's *quasi adagio* for its slow movement, is of markedly different character. This Symphony in B flat was the first work Tippett wrote after leaving Morris. Its purposeful character may be said to derive from Morris's teaching, and perhaps from the fact that it was also the first work he wrote after visiting Boosbeck. He completed it in October 1933 and, after a performance with his South London Orchestra at Morley College, revised it in the spring of the following year. (Apart from the removal of a folk-style theme in the finale, one that in fact bears a striking resemblance to the closing theme in his Double Concerto, the revision consists of some cuts and compressions to tighten the formal structure.)

In every respect the Symphony is a marked advance on previous works, and symptomatic of the advantages to be gained from rejecting past accomplishment and venturing into new territories – here, breaking away from the strict classical forms Tippett was so attached to and testing out formal methods Morris's enthusiasm for Sibelius had encouraged him to investigate. The work is unmistakably Sibelian in character. But it was not a fruitless exercise, because a number of Sibelius's techniques subsequently became absorbed into his mature style, and because it is a fine work anyway, roughly comparable in character with the contemporaneous Symphony No. 1 of Walton.

Its decisive novelties concern formal procedures in the outer movements. In the first, Tippett employs Sibelius's technique of drawing out motivic fragments into long extended paragraphs. Thus, after a short, slow

introduction, there follow five sections, each developing the material heard
in the first, the length of the first three following the proportions
approximately of 3:5:8, the remaining two of 6:2. The whole movement
was conceived as continually developmental. Tippett did not however
entirely discard his Beethovenian inheritance. Thus the first section is a
kind of exposition with first and second subjects, the second a 'development
section one' based on second-subject material, the third a 'development
section two' and the climactic section, the fourth a 'recapitulation' in
reverse, and the fifth a coda. In the last movement, a much simpler rondo
form, Tippett applies this technique on the melodic plane only. The lyrical
second subject (modelled on the horns' theme in the finale of Sibelius's
Symphony No. 5, the model for the whole movement) is built up by
expanding and then contracting the phrase lengths, all of which begin with
the same motif (as had the first three sections of the first movement).

The language Tippett invented for filling out these formal schemes was,
ultimately, derivative – as can be seen in Ex. 3, the beginning of the second
section of the first movement, which includes 'first subject' (*a*) and 'second
subject' (*b*).

Ex. 3   **Symphony in B flat**

The influence of the Symphony on Tippett's later music was far-reaching. Although he reverted to classical forms soon after writing the work and continued to use them until his Symphony No. 2, adaptations of the Sibelian method began to reappear with his Concerto for Orchestra and are quite explicit by the time of his Symphony No. 3. Of more immediate relevance was his enlargement of syntactical resource and his absorption of particular Sibelian characteristics into his own subsequent language. One of Sibelius's typical fingerprints is the unobtrusively introduced chromatic appoggiatura, gradually swelling to a sharply articulated release: an example of this in Tippett is at (c) in Ex. 3. The resulting dissonance gives the Symphony much of its harmonic bite. In later works he was to turn this little idiom into highly individual semitonal clashes. When Sibelius expands it into significant rhetoric, as if the music is being forcibly wrenched away from a position of comfort, an effect comparable with the beginning of the finale of Tippett's Symphony may emerge, or with the beginning of the second movement of his String Quartet No. 1 (see Ex. 26). In later works, this becomes a characteristic gesture, as in Ex. 112 (bars 4ff) from his *Fantasia Concertante on a theme of Corelli*. So although Tippett eventually decided not to publish the Symphony, because of its unassimilated Sibelian influence and of what he considered unsatisfactory transition sections, it is easy to understand why he delayed ten years before reaching the decision. From this crucial, preliminary integration of the old and the new emerged his String Quartet No. 1, the work in which he finally discovered his individual style.

In the concert works mentioned thus far Tippett set store on inventing and developing material in its own terms, without regard to other than purely musical considerations. With operatic works however a different approach was called for. His adaptation of *The Village Opera*, that is, his use of pre-existent material, was already evidence of the distinction he drew between musical material as such and musical material as a means for creating dramatic effect. In his four early 'operas', *The Village Opera*, *Robin Hood* (1934) and the two children's operas, *Robert of Sicily* (1938) and *Seven at One Stroke* (1939) – it should be mentioned that the two children's operas are included in the present context because they are obviously 'student' works, even though written some years after Tippett had found a mature style – most of the material is borrowed or 'given', in the sense of being a formula. Before embarking on a genuine opera of his own he could, by this method, take a detached and critical view of the distinction and gauge his capacity for placing particular types of material in relevant dramatic situations. None of the operas is pretentious enough to qualify as a study or sketch for what ultimately became his first opera, *The Midsummer Marriage*, yet three at least were necessary and important exercises in that direction.

Robin Hood's subtitle is 'A Folk-Song Opera', an exact description of its genre, a ballad opera with folk-songs instead of 'ballads'. There are altogether about twenty songs in it, most of them traditional. The work is nicely tailored to the amateur accomplishments of the forces available (see p.26) and includes six solo parts (soprano, contralto, two tenors, baritone and bass) and plenty of work for the chorus (including a group of choirboys). The 'orchestra' comprises oboe, horn, violin, cello and piano. The text is calculated to be entertaining (it amusingly recalls 1930s slang) and, more to the point, to speak directly to the audience for whom it was written. There are many allusions to landlords and poverty. Here is the text of a song sung by Robin Hood's men after they have tied up Lord Lamkin, the warden of Sherwood Forest:

> Oh God who made the cottager,
>   He made him strong and free;
> But the devil made the landlord
>   To steal from you and me.
>
> So God he made us outlaws
>   To beat the devil's man;
> To rob the rich, to feed the poor
>   By Robin's ten year plan.

This song comes in the middle of Act I, by the end of which it has transpired that Lamkin wants to marry Marret (a farmer's daughter, whose parents, as representatives of an older generation, are pointedly unprincipled), that Marret is in love with Alan-a-Dale, and that Robin Hood will unite the lovers and obtain £10,000 ransom for Lamkin. In Act II this duly happens. Disguised as a blind harper Robin Hood forestalls the wedding of Lamkin and Marret and distributes the ransom to the poor while Friar Tuck marries Marret and Alan-a-Dale.

The text of the opera is skilfully engineered dramatically and Tippett's hand in it can be deduced from the deft placing of the principal musical moments. The musical settings are distinct improvements on the Sharp style, more than that being inappropriate if the songs were not to be travestied or the performers overstretched. From the point of view of operatic workmanship the most successful moments are the following three: a very simple four-part unaccompanied round of Tippett's own, 'By oak, ash and thorn' (the still centre of the Act I finale), the medieval 'Angelus ad virginem' sung by choirboys while Marret waits to be married to Lamkin (a subtle use of dramatic irony, an innocently beautiful tune sung while the innocent beauty herself is in tears) and Robin Hood's 'This is thy true love' (the emotional climax of the opera, when Robin Hood blesses the lovers to a folk-like theme of Tippett's own and of much greater intensity than the other traditional tunes). In these numbers Tippett must have demonstrated conclusively to himself how music can lift the drama out of the everyday and impart a quality of experience all its own – as was confirmed fourteen years later by his use of the last two of them in his *Suite for the Birthday of Prince Charles*.

The number which stands out above all others however is the overture (also used in the *Birthday Suite*) – a rather jaunty music, alive with rhythmic tension and generating a momentum which sails over obstacles (barlines)

like a trained athlete. After ten years of compositional apprenticeship
Tippett was entitled to expect some reward for his labours, but this augury
of his mature style appeared apparently unbidden and he seems not to have
recognized it, for it is quickly overtaken by the efficient but predominantly
staid vocal music of the rest of the opera.

The crucial, rhythmic novelty of Ex. 4 may be interpreted as the result of
an integration of folk-dance and jazz. The fast tempo and melodic contours
are folk-dance elements (the material a transformation of the tag phrase in
the Helston Furry Dance) and the 'anticipatory' rhythms (as between bars
2 and 3, see also p.100) jazz elements – even if the jazz (strictly, from piano
rags) has as yet only the superficial appeal of a new plaything. Tippett's
interest in folk-music had hitherto concentrated on song rather than dance
and it seems hardly an accident that his music should gain in novelty and
freshness precisely when it was injected with the dance element. In this
respect the results vindicated his disapproval of the rigid division between
dance and song favoured by contemporary theorists and his more general
idea that the new would emerge from an integration of styles.

Ex. 4   **Robin Hood**

The *Robin Hood* overture cannot however obscure the fact that the opera as a whole remains a student work of only marginal importance. It is too dated and the music generally too conventional to arouse any more than academic interest. Much the same could be said of *Robert of Sicily*, and even more of *Seven at One Stroke*. Like *Robin Hood* they also were the outcome of strictly practical considerations and their significance again lies in the way Tippett used the occasions to experiment with operatic techniques.

In 1937 he had agreed to the request of the Royal Arsenal Co-operative Society to take on a choir of about twenty-five primary schoolchildren at New Malden in London. Their voices were capable only of unison singing (they were, as Tippett noted, barely strong enough to match a trumpet and so could not divide into separate parts for full harmony). In order to lend some tonal variety to their ambitions and to get away from Victorian harmony to a cleaner sound, Tippett proposed that all five children's choirs sponsored by the RACS (including ones from Earlsfield, Peckham, Tooting and Woolwich) should combine in a joint venture, each rehearsing alone and coming together for the performance. Apart from the choirs, his performers consisted of clarinet, trumpet, cello, piano and bell.

His main idea for *Robert of Sicily* was to use the theatrical device of processions, which had greatly impressed him in a Max Reinhardt production of a miracle play he had seen in Cologne while on holiday there with Christopher Fry. Fry produced a text which skilfully accommodated unison singing in processions and the theme of a religious miracle. It is based on Longfellow's poem 'The Sicilian's Tale' from *Tales of a Wayside Inn*, a moral tale of how the ignorant and arrogant King Robert of Sicily is brought to book. He is summoned by his brother the Pope to Rome for Holy Week, at which point an Angel appears, to take his place as King and to downgrade him to court fool. In this capacity he goes to Rome, and refuses to kneel with the rest of the people listening to the Easter service from St Peter's. But when he hears from inside the church the voice of the Angel singing a plainchant hymn, a miracle occurs, he does kneel, and on his return to Sicily the repentant King is restored to his throne.

The work again follows the pattern of a ballad opera, with extensive dialogue divided by musical numbers (almost entirely of traditional material). In the first part the alternation of rousing community songs and plainsong alleluia and Magnificat nicely reinforces the mixture of comic and serious in the text. At the climax, the Easter service and the return to Sicily, the music is continuous. It leads from plainchant in all voices with instrumental support to the unaccompanied solo voice of the Angel, an example of how the very simplest of musical means can create a moving effect. This effect is not squandered because the succeeding numbers gently reduce the tension until they conclude with a setting of the haunting Scottish folk-song 'Ca' the yowes' – this is a demonstration of the fact that music can perform a dramatic function regardless of its ostensible verbal meaning (the rather abstruse reference to home-coming in the song would certainly have been lost on the audience, even if it could understand the Scottish dialect).

No doubt *Robert of Sicily* was another useful exercise to Tippett. Its present interest however lies more in the identity of some of the individual numbers. The 'Boating Song', accompanying the voyage to and from Sicily, is a French cradle-song which he used later in his *Suite for the Birthday of Prince Charles*. 'Ca' the yowes' had already been used in his Piano Sonata No. 1, where however it is not stated explicitly. 'Non nobis Domine', the canon ascribed to Byrd, which is used in the final scene of the opera, appears again in *The Shires Suite*.

The success of *Robert of Sicily* accounted for the composition of *Seven at One Stroke*, Tippett's second children's opera, or 'play for children' as the title pages read. It was also written in collaboration with Christopher Fry, and was scored for the same forces plus flute and violin but minus the bell. Fry's text here is an updating of the Grimm fairy-tale 'The Valiant Little Tailor', which tells how a tailor killed seven flies with one flick of his towel and made use of this feat (though without reference to his victims) plus a lot of native wit, to advance his position in the world. This work is in a pantomime tradition. However successful in that respect, the music, a perfunctory sequence of numbers deriving from musical comedy and the weaker moments in *Hansel and Gretel* and Gilbert and Sullivan, suggests that Tippett did not take it very seriously. In 1939 he had more pressing musical commitments. By this time he had learnt as much as was practically possible from his other three operas and *Seven at One Stroke* was simply a job to be fulfilled dutifully and with tolerable efficiency.

CHAPTER TWO

1934-52

The Composer in Context

When he was fourteen Tippett's philosophy of life (according to a cousin) was to take the 'evolutionary jump' – to make a daring, supreme effort and thereby find himself transported into an unknown and exciting area of experience. Something of this kind seems to have occurred with his String Quartet No.1 of 1934–5. Having written music laudable and painstaking but in the last resort characterless, he now, without warning, produced a work with an instantly recognizable signature of its own, quite different from anything he had written before. A hint of this new style may be perceived in his *Robin Hood* overture, and perhaps the deliberate fusion of old and new techniques in his early works had ushered in a period of incubation rather than one of mere apprenticeship. But neither this, nor the occasional stylistic precedent, nor even the changes in his private life at the time, can fully explain a metamorphosis as remarkable as that between a caterpillar and a butterfly. All that can be said is that it took place. Tippett had discovered his individual voice. Of this he was well aware. The manuscript of the Quartet's finale bears the inscription 'Damn braces. Bless relaxes.' (from the 'Proverbs of Hell' in Blake's *The Marriage of Heaven and Hell*), as if to say that creative constraint has finally been thrown to the winds and that far from losing everything he has instead found a new identity. This is most obvious in the finale but is not limited to that movement alone.

The present chapter attempts to show what the constituents of Tippett's individual voice might be and how he tested and developed them in various contexts during that prolonged span of about eighteen years which may be called the first period of his maturity. The period is divided into four stages, reflected in the final four sections of the chapter. In the first of these sections, those seminal works announcing the formation of his new language are examined in detail. They show how from somewhat raw beginnings in his String Quartet No. 1, Tippett gradually refined his new language until it was fully realized in his Concerto for Double String Orchestra. These works embody his first mature exploration of the sonata principle. The second section shows how his development reached an intermediate climax when he turned to the more dramatic form of oratorio. *A Child of Our Time* is notable also for containing the first presentation of those psychological ideas to have a crucial bearing on his opera *The Midsummer Marriage*. In the third section he is shown continuing and, for the time being, completing his exploration of traditional genres and of the sonata principle. The final section of this chapter is devoted to *The Midsummer Marriage*, the fruit of Tippett's long-term strategy and ample vindication of it. *The Midsummer Marriage* belies its status as a first opera. It is composed with such mastery that it emerges as the crux of Tippett's entire output, the fulfilment of an artistic programme which remains the touchstone against which all his works can be measured. Tippett's 'first period' may accordingly be understood as an enormous upbeat preparation for the composition of *The Midsummer Marriage* and the works in it exercises – albeit exercises on a grand scale. As such they may appropriately be examined not only for their musical quality and significance but also for what they reveal of Tippett's creative methods, of his unusually clear-sighted assessment of his compositional objectives and of the growing precision with which he pursued his course of action.

As a background to the subsequent discussion of individual works, the next section of this chapter concentrates on Tippett's interpretation of general technical matters, structural, tonal and harmonic, and finishes with an extended study of his rhythmic language, undoubtedly the most original feature of his style.

A chapter emphasizing technique cannot describe what Tippett's early works are really like or what responses they arouse. Some attempt to do so may be helpful however, in order to sketch out the expressive and historical world to which they belong and to which later remarks may be related. Their rhythmic and contrapuntal energy is decisive. This is what makes them bracing and challenging, the qualities which ensure that they are heard as argument and not as cushioning against it. Together with an unaffected melodiousness and a harmonic style so elusive that it rarely suggests 'harmony', these characteristics form a musical language remarkable for two apparently contradictory qualities. On the one hand it seems perennially youthful. It is spirited without being frivolous, tightly reasoned without being pretentious. On the other hand it evokes strain and tension. It asserts that what it uncovers is not a personal discovery, with finely etched contours, but a less tangible and more dense phenomenon which can be expressed only in terms of idea or large abstraction. Such dualities are of the essence of Tippett's music. If it were possible to divide music into two categories, one of self-sufficient works indifferent to acceptance or rejection, the other of works which urge the listener to contribute by coming forward and meeting them half-way, then Tippett's would belong to the second category.

In 1941 he wrote that his aim was 'to steer clear of a heavy, Germanized and too serious work'.[1] Although written of his Piano Sonata No. 1 and allowing for a momentary rush of xenophobia in wartime Britain, this was a helpful introduction to his music in general, as well as an index of native musical climate at the time. New music was new British music. Tippett contrasted with both the increasingly nostalgic style of such composers as Walton and Bliss and the earnest pastoralism of the Vaughan Williams school. The composer with whom he showed greatest affinity was Britten. Britten and Tippett were for many years bracketed together as composers who both strove after clean and clear statements in their music and who led English music away from provincialism into a more continentally orientated style based on a wide knowledge of musical tradition. In retrospect the differences between the two composers appear more obvious than the similarities; but in the 1940s the important thing was that two distinctive personalities had established roughly the same priorities.

When set in a wider context, Tippett's music of the 1930s and '40s fits squarely into the prevailing neo-classicism of the period, one in which the baroque orientated neo-classicism of the 1920s had given way, though not surrendered, to a neo-classicism more lyrical, euphonious and humanistic. The rise of fascism now drew out a powerful reassertion of classical and romantic tradition, as is testified by such works as the violin concertos of Bartók, Berg and Schoenberg, Stravinsky's *Perséphone*, Hindemith's *Mathis der Maler*. When writing his own works of the 1930s Tippett was therefore adding his distinctive voice to a European sensibility, even if his language drew from a wider background, bar the romantics, than the composers mentioned above.

During the war years *A Child of Our Time* made his status as a European composer more explicit. Yet by the 1950s, when *The Midsummer Marriage* was given its first performances, it seemed to many observers that Tippett had withdrawn from his earlier position. To the traditionalists the opera's relationship with the English pastoral inheritance was too ambivalent. To the avant-gardists his language was irrelevant. The central line of development in European music at that time appeared to be leading to a kind of hermetic abstraction, markedly different from the abstraction of the neo-classical music of the 1920s. Then the use of traditional models reflected a desire to give stability and meaning to a culture which had nearly destroyed itself in a world war; now, in the generation of composers emerging after the Second World War, there developed a neo-classical attitude apparently so anaesthetized by the inhumanity of war that it could no longer make contact with the human at all. It wanted to 'reconstitute a way of writing that begins with something which eliminates personal invention', as Boulez wrote of his *Structures* of 1951.[2] Boulez was voicing an extreme view but it was representative of a powerful aesthetic, suggesting that tonality was an anachronism and that the splintered, abrupt gestures of such a work as *Structures* embodied an historical imperative. Even those more senior composers who held fast to traditional expressive values or to the discoveries of their pioneering days wrote music quite at variance with the affirmations of Tippett's opera. The period was also characterized by such bleak, sombre and menacing works as Varèse's *Déserts*, Shostakovich's Symphony No. 10 and Britten's *The Turn of the Screw*. Either way the only other important composers who seemed to stand back from the immediate pressures of the time were Messiaen and Carter. Despite their widely differing outlooks, Tippett, Messiaen and Carter have much in common. Like *The Midsummer Marriage*, Messiaen's *Turangalîla-Symphonie* of 1946–8 concentrates on the theme of love, draws from oriental culture, finds means for expressing the timeless and makes use of diatonic harmony. Carter's

String Quartet No. 1 of 1950–1 explores, as does Tippett's opera, the relationship between 'external time' and 'dream time'.[3] If three works of this calibre challenge the prevailing aesthetic then that aesthetic needs to be defined less rigidly. These works show that within the ascetic neo-classicism of the post-war years were contained the seeds of a new romanticism, strongly disciplined but no less anxious than its nineteenth-century counterpart to restore the potential of music as an overtly expressive and inspiriting art. By the 1960s this inheritance had begun to dominate Western music. Far from a lonely exercise in private myth-making *The Midsummer Marriage* stands out in this context as a seminal representative of its age.

Compositional Techniques

Form and Tonality

If the style of first-period Tippett is neo-classical it follows that his approach to classical structure is of crucial significance. How and why he used what forms he did use and how he used tonality to serve structural ends are important questions. After hearing the second movement of his Quartet No. 1 Tippett decided that he would discard the Sibelian approach to the sonata-allegro in that movement and return to the Beethovenian model. Beethoven's sonata-allegros embodied a formal procedure so fundamental as to demand recognition as an archetype, one which could be avoided only at the cost of mutilating a composer's expressive resource. The basic property of a Beethovenian allegro, as Tippett saw it, can be reduced to that of an argument between passionate and lyrical sound. Music gives form to human feelings. If such feelings can be described as active (in the sense of movement between opposites) or passive (in the sense of remaining essentially the same) then there is no escaping the power of the Beethovenian model to articulate the former, dynamic pattern of human experience and to provide examples of how the movement between such opposites (here expressed as the passionate and the lyrical) can be organized, so that the ear is taken naturally from one place to another without a break in sound. By the tightness of its argument the Beethoven-ian model demands the counter-balance of movements expressing single-ness of emotion. Apart from simple song forms and, to a certain extent, variation forms, the most important form of this type was for Tippett the fugue. It also acquired the status of an archetype, not least because it is flexible enough to accommodate a multitude of different expressive moods while remaining essentially unitary in character.

Tippett's concern for the precise definition of expressive mood is central to these considerations. Music can convey the richness and immediacy of human emotions and at the same time lend them distance and, paradoxi-cally, urgency by the strictness of the forms within which they are contained. His music shows that he has been reluctant to allow the intensity of the particular moment to lift into its own flight of fancy and challenge the strength of the basic design. Yet he has obviously not wanted to deny intensity, which is why the choice of forms is so important. The form must in itself be a metaphor of the expression.

Tippett's classicizing temperament and his concern to learn a craft meant that he had no desire to alter the four-movement shape of the classical sonata. His interest in Beethoven, and in Jung, had underlined the strength of this shape. Four is the symbol of wholeness and Beethoven had dramatized the imaginative willpower needed to attain wholeness by focusing attention on his finales, the agents of wholeness. In Tippett's view the formal problems encountered in planning a work could be reduced to three questions. Where in the four movements should the fundamental ingredient, the dramatic sonata-allegro, be placed? How should the relative weight of the other movements be disposed in relation to it? What should the character of the finale be? In his String Quartet No. 1 he approached these problems from the most awkward angle possible, perhaps accentuating them in order to clarify them. Sonata-allegros (or sonata-allegro equivalents) coming second hardly exist in the classical repertory. His disposition of the remaining movements in that work is skilfully conceived, especially the idea of a fast fugal finale whose intricacy of workmanship would provide some balancing weight while its monothematicism would not undermine the dualities of the sonata movement. In his Piano Sonata No. 1 he continued his quite conscious experimentation with these problems. The sonata-allegro now comes third. In subsequent works it comes first (Concerto for Double String Orchestra and Symphony No. 1), last (String Quartet No. 2) and not at all (String Quartet No. 3).

Having settled his approach to large-scale formal design there followed the question of how this design was to be tonally articulated. From his earliest days as a music student Tippett was disturbed by his inability to understand classical harmony and tonality. He became a pupil of C.H. Kitson at the RCM in order to do so. When this tactic failed he tried to teach himself. He took the subject very seriously, read standard academic textbooks, and, after they had proved as dry as Kitson, sought out major works from abroad. In this way he read Schoenberg's *Harmonielehre* and, some years later, Hindemith's *Unterweisung im Tonsatz*. The Schoenberg he found pedantically Germanic: chord tables appearing to expound the theses that chords are separate entities and that music is a series of chords. The Hindemith was, to him, equally far from the truth. Eventually, as late as 1938, he encountered Vincent d'Indy's *Cours de Composition Musicale*. This book, and especially the chapter 'La Sonate de Beethoven', while not contributing much to his understanding of harmony, offered an approach to and a rationale of tonal process which he found profoundly sympathetic.

In considering methods of development,[4] d'Indy made a number of observations of particular value to Tippett, notably the simple but crucial one that a development section can be in a state either of 'immobilité' or 'translation' (expressed also as 'en repos' or 'en marche'). The principal lesson learnt from d'Indy however concerned the control of modulation, or the structural use of tonality. This is seen in relation to an ascending or a descending cycle of fifths, the former creating 'clarté', the latter 'obscurité'. D'Indy provided a scale of effects: modulation to the first 'fifth' (C–G ascending, C–F descending) was 'assez faible'; to the second (C–D, C–B flat), 'accidentale' or 'passagère', because there are no notes in common between the key pairs; to the third (C–A, C–E flat), much more decisive. Modulation to the fourth 'fifth' (C–E, C–A flat) was the most powerful and energetic of all, the maximum limit of 'clarté' or 'obscurité'. After that modulations became ambiguous or disorientating in effect, since the fifth 'fifth' ascending (C–B) is the same as the seventh 'fifth' descending, and the sixth 'fifth' (C–F sharp) is the same from both directions.

In May 1938 Tippett was asked to write a report on a congress held in London in preparation for the festival of the International Society for Contemporary Music which took place there the following month. What he in fact wrote was an apologia for tonality and d'Indy, provoked by an observation in the congress that what made music 'contemporary' was absence of tonality.

> Would someone explain the tenacious emotional satisfaction of the tonal system? Here is the answer. The artistic use of the tonal system is based on the fact that music whose tonal centres are rising in the scale of fifths produces an effect of ascent (struggle, illumination), while tonal centres descending the scale of fifths produce an effect of descent (resignation, despair). Beethoven was the great master of these effects. The first movement of the 'Hammerklavier' sonata is a skilfully continuous use of ascent, while the first movement of the 'Appassionata' is an equally continuous descent. The listener is not directly conscious of these effects. His response, I think, is centred in a complementary movement of the stomach muscles. Contemporary life has not given us iron stomachs, very much the contrary.[5]

The significance of d'Indy's teaching therefore was not only that it enabled Tippett to construct logical tonal schemes. It also provided him with the basis for controlling fluctuating emotional moods.

Harmony

In recent years Tippett has been fond of observing of his first-period works that there is not a single chord in any of them – a legitimate hyperbole if the essentially contrapuntal nature of these works is to be contrasted with the more harmonically orientated language of his later music. As a general guide the observation is however closer to the truth than might be expected. Although he occasionally employs the block sonorities of 'four-part harmony', normally he avoids them: chordal harmony of this type is indeed not typical of early Tippett. Why this should be so is no doubt due to the fact that he associated 'harmony' with that nineteenth-century retreat into self-expression he found so distasteful. His music could not be a confessional. It was designed to stimulate, to refine autobiography into self-sufficient images of, rather than instances of, emotional experience – and this was effected largely through counterpoint. His harmony is intuitive, subtle and elusive, and because it lacks the theoretical foundation upon which his treatment of tonal organization depended, its behaviour is difficult to rationalize. It suggests rather than states and encompasses wide harmonic areas without staking immediate claims on ownership.

Ex. 5   String Quartet No. 2

This is apparent even in passages which do stem from the conventions of four-part harmony. Every chord in Ex. 5 (the first episode of the fugue in String Quartet No. 2) can be found in Franck or Wagner. But the passage neither modulates (an eventual modulation is carried out with three chords only) nor confirms the tonality, nor does it stabilize points of harmonic tension. It articulates the structure, compensating for the rigidity of the fugal exposition by releasing a paragraph of continuously flowing movement. The principal reason why the passage does not sound anachronistic is that Tippett disregards the siren calls of the cadential 6/4 and floats into his very personal realms of harmony as expressive colour. In this characteristic technique he draws from a wide range of historical reference. The pivotal chord of C major at bar 5 of Ex. 5, for example, creates its moment of serenity through a fleeting reference to the widely spaced chords of C major in the slow movement of Beethoven's String Quartet in A minor, op. 132. The final chords in *The Midsummer Marriage* gain added resonance for summoning up the splendours of the climactic chord of A major in Tallis's *Spem in alium*. Tippett's gesture does not depend on the allusion but it undoubtedly benefits from it. In the same way the time-honoured device of a switch from major to minor in Ex. 6 guarantees the desired expressive effect; but this is heightened through the reference to Beethoven's Symphony No. 7 where the switch heralds not gloom but renewal of energy. In *The Midsummer Marriage* Tippett developed such

Ex. 6

(i) **The Midsummer Marriage**

(ii) **Beethoven: Symphony No. 7 (Scherzo)**

confidence in the technique that he was even able to introduce a tiny reference to Gershwin's *The man I love* without disturbing the atmosphere (see the bracketed phrase in Ex. 83). Allusions of this kind need not be so specific. The opening of String Quartet No. 3 (Ex. 7) is coloured with the vital desperation of the blues and the more anguished moments in Purcell, but no particular pieces are suggested and the listener is left to decide for himself what the precise expressive intentions might be.

Ex. 7   **String Quartet No. 3**

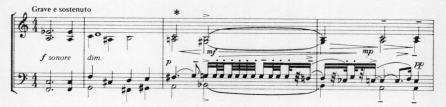

Few of these allusions could have been assimilated into the texture of Tippett's music unless the harmonic environment had been sufficiently fluid to admit the actual pitches of their originals. In this lies the essence of Tippett's harmonic practice. It may be compared with that in a renaissance motet, where a network of possibilities and relationships grows around a central tonal axis. Tippett's harmonies, within the limits of a germinal tonality, move freely and are conditioned more by melodic shapes or expressive demands than by the authority of functional harmonic progressions, functional bass lines or melodic shapes deriving from the triad. In this context he can settle on any chord or chordal implication he wishes to and nourish its qualities as sound rather than function, pursuing a harmony, as it were, vertically as well as horizontally. In brief, Tippett's harmonic methods are modal.

At this stage in his career his harmonic vocabulary is also to some extent modal, in that it derives partly from the church modes. But this should not obscure the fact that his methods, regardless of vocabulary, are modal in the wider sense of the term: modality, the free movement of parts within the broad but circumscribed limits of a mode, set of pitches, intervals or chords. Tippett is thus a characteristically twentieth-century composer, joining company with many others, some of the most striking being Scriabin, Stravinsky and Messiaen, for whom harmony has also been a means of creating a sense of suspended animation, of relishing the qualities of the present rather than conquering an uncertain future. His methods have not been so radical as those of the composers mentioned for he has not regarded the resources of functional harmony as a group of dangerous clichés – to be avoided, lampooned or refurbished. He has simply made them correspond with his own expressive instincts. In Ex. 8, the beginning of the first aria in *Boyhood's End* and a typically contrapuntal texture in which harmonies are implied rather than stated, the music certainly

Ex. 8 **Boyhood's End**

(Ex. 8 cont.)

grass - y dew - wet Earth,   from day
to day,   from year   to
year.

f quasi cadenza, brillante

progresses from the tonic to the dominant. But the final 'chord' of F major
is also a clear sound of release, a symbol of burgeoning springtime, and as
such the product of a modal 'wandering' within a set of mildly dissonant
chords hinging on B flat: it is not approached through the 'strong'
progressions of functional tonality. The order of the implied harmonies is
less important than their kinship within a basic complex and the speed
with which delicately, almost timidly placed points of emphasis follow one
another.

By the time of *The Midsummer Marriage* Tippett had become so skilled in
handling modality of this sort that he could if necessary abandon
dissonance altogether and without forfeiting his individuality limit himself
to an almost exclusively triadic vocabulary. The excerpt from Mark's 'Lark
Song' in Ex. 79 is full of the most banal components of triadic harmony –
root positions and first inversions. Yet the sound is as fresh as the dew. It

celebrates a characteristic discovery – that if harmonic progressions rise to the sharp side of a tonic and then apparently contradict the process by sinking towards the flat side (or do the same in reverse), the result is not tautology, or anticlimax, but a flowering, a revelation of hidden perspectives.

The essentials of Tippett's harmonic vocabulary appeared as early as the first bars of his String Quartet No. 1. They are compounded from pre-existent models (thus putting into immediate effect his planned integration of styles) and they acquire their distinctive character from persistent contrapuntal collisions in semitonal dissonances. Such dissonances are always approached by logical, melodic routes, but at the same time they are deliberately sought after, in order to drive the music forward. Three principal types can be distinguished – resulting from an anticipation of the subsequent harmony, from collisions between notes individually behaving traditionally, and from the simultaneous use of a modal substitute note and a natural note. Collectively they make up a typical Tippett idiom.

The first type (see Ex. 25, *a*) derives from Tippett's early affection for Sibelius and has already been described in connection with the Symphony in B flat. A later instance may be found in Ex. 97 (asterisk).

The second type is at once more conventional and more individual. It is closely related to traditional teaching on suspensions, appoggiaturas, auxiliary notes and harmony notes. Yet the actual dissonances (as at Ex. 25, *b*, bar 9, which is caused by the octave displacement of the viola's auxiliary note) are strictly of the twentieth century and typical of the ambiguities of Tippett's idiom. On the one hand they belong to the principles of modality (the chord at *b* above, or the last bar of Ex. 47 No. 1 (i), which combines two chords to make one sound) and on the other to traditional principles of dissonance and resolution, through the behaviour of their individual parts.

The third type (Ex. 25, *c*) is sixteenth-century English in origin. It recalls those melodic curves in music of that period which rise to a flattened seventh and fall to a leading note, and those harmonies resulting from a superposition of such sevenths found in composers from Tallis and Byrd to Purcell. It is a highly characteristic Tippett fingerprint. It has some affinity with 'blue-note' clashes but is quite different from the major/minor dissonance of Bartók, Stravinsky and their imitators. Instances of its melodic use can be seen in Exx. 51 and 58, of its harmonic use in Exx. 7 (bar 3) and 40 (bar 7).

Melodies and harmonies of this latter type ultimately derive from the church modes, from Tippett's affinity with an idiom whose instability actively encourages wide-ranging, undogmatic expressive gestures. As well as unstable sevenths, the modal system includes unstable thirds, sixths and to a lesser extent seconds and fourths, and Tippett gradually absorbed such variables into what may be seen as a single mode, containing the full chromatic range of pitches but remaining essentially diatonic in character. This process can be followed by comparing, for example, the first theme of his Concerto for Double String Orchestra (Ex. 17), which contains ten pitches, with that in his Symphony No. 1 (Ex. 66), which contains all twelve.

The influence of church modes on Tippett's harmonic progressions accounts for his favourite supertonic, subtonic and subdominant relationships (relationships untypical of the central harmonic tradition of the eighteenth and nineteenth centuries). Their influence on his harmonic vocabulary accounts in particular for the components of one chord, a 'tonic' with minor third and major sixth, which may be considered the Tippett chord *par excellence*. It crystallizes in one sound the sense of both repose and movement. An example occurs in Ex. 7 (asterisk).

A similar effect is made in an additional type of dissonance entering Tippett's vocabulary at the time of his Symphony No. 1 – fourths chords. Bar 3 of Ex. 9 below draws some of its dramatic point from the impassive, rather dry qualities of a chord constructed synthetically. But its harmonic context also suggests a more traditional interpretation in which there is an implied resolution of an appoggiatura (the D).

Ex. 9   **The Midsummer Marriage**

Tippett's sensitivity to the ambiguities of fourths harmony and his resource in handling it is of special interest. Many twentieth-century composers have used fourths, both as 'new' harmonies in their own right, as in Bartók, and as members of a harmonic hierarchy, as in Hindemith. Tippett is unique in extracting such variety of expression from them. At one extreme he can emphasize their angular abstractions in order, as it might seem, to make the philosophical point that an apparently intractable language can yield to more human contours (see Ex. 67). At the other he can surround them with an aura of tenderness that is Debussy-like in its shimmering tactile presence (see Ex. 90). He was able to use fourths with such ease because they grew quite naturally out of his melodic language, out of, that is, his fondness for the modal intervals of seconds, fourths and sevenths. The 'motto' from the slow movement of the Double Concerto, a pair of melodic fourths, is audibly derived from the folk-like main theme. In

Boyhood's End melodic chains of three fourths are quite prominent and chains of up to four fourths dominate his Symphony No. 1, where Tippett first used fourths chords as such. It is possible that he was prompted to do so by hearing Hindemith's music at that time, but the idea was already latent in his own music. Having tested his ability to dispose the idiom both melodically and harmonically Tippett absorbed fourths into the much more diverse harmonic language of *The Midsummer Marriage* where they so closely approach a harmonic norm that they are frequently used in parallel motion. It was not until his Piano Concerto of 1953–5 however that fourths chords entirely lost their quality of dissonance requiring resolution and became consonances analogous in function to triads. Colin Mason[6] pointed out that the number of notes present in chords of this type is five (or that they consist of four superimposed fourths) and deduced their stabilizing function from the presence of an inverted triad within the five notes. It should also be mentioned that such chords contain no semitonal dissonance (a property arising only when five or more fourths are superimposed) and can therefore be used to release harmonic tension in passages where semitonal dissonance preponderates.

Rhythm

In music of the later nineteenth century, rhythmic innovations took an increasingly subordinate position to innovations in other parameters. Apart from Berlioz, Brahms and some Nationalists, composers of the period were content to accept the regular 3/4 or 4/4 bar as the basis of rhythmic articulation and did little to develop the expressive and structural potential of rhythm, thus nicely illustrating the point that rhythmic enervation is in direct proportion to a society's decadence. If the twentieth century is to take heart from its creative artists it is then a matter of importance that rhythmic energy should be reasserted – as it has been through Stravinsky, Bartók, Ives, and more recently through such composers as Tippett, Messiaen and Carter. Rhythmic energy is the hallmark of Tippett's style: his creative identity springs directly from it. His significance however lies less in the fact that he has made a major contribution to a vital trend in twentieth-century music than in the particular complexion of his contribution. By associating rhythmic energy so closely with the idea of regeneration, he has given rhythm the decisive role in the formulation of a philosophy; and by articulating this philosophy broadly in terms of a received musical language he has shown that regeneration can grow from within and need not be imposed from without.

If Tippett's rhythms emanate from the roots of his artistic personality it is natural that, like his harmonies, they should lack theoretical support. Admittedly, their fusion of the components of a received rhythmic vocabulary (rather than the invention of new gestures) suggests the conscious application of the principles of stylistic integration he had drawn up as a student. But in fact they materialized as a result of entirely unconscious forces in his creative imagination: the birth of Tippett's rhythmic language, in the finale of his String Quartet No. 1, was quite spontaneous. He may have experimented with methods of notating this language (the published score of the Quartet finale represents the best of three attempts) but its identity had already been shaped by intuitive judgements. A preliminary assessment of its essential features must equally rely on subjective responses.

Tippett's rhythms are lilting and buoyant; their energy is unforced; they are characterized by understatement. They do not, as with Stravinsky for example, lead to new concepts of musical form: they revitalize the old ones, an ambition more modest but in some ways more testing. What in particular makes them so individual is the absence of a regular 'beat' but the presence nonetheless of widely spaced 'beats' at a higher level of rhythmic organization than that implied by the co-ordinating metre (usually of quavers). The predominant impression given is of an irregular but gently insistent sequence of downbeats – not particularly decisive downbeats, because they are lightly stressed and so widely spaced, but downbeats all the same, resisting formation into the natural out-and-in or right-and-left downbeat and upbeat rhythms of breathing or walking. This is an extraordinary impression. It sets up a delicate balance between, on the one hand, the broad, flowing and almost leisurely movement of the extended downbeats and, on the other, the unpredictable and confined movement of the interior rhythms which separate them. The poise deriving from widely spaced points of articulation is contradicted by the restlessness caused by the irregularity of such articulation. The music evokes both abandon and reticence, the relaxed and the precipitate, the compliant rhythms of the singer and the darting rhythms of the dancer, the measured rhythms of poetry and the fluid rhythms of prose. It is an extremely subtle mixture, richly ambiguous and very characteristic of Tippett.

It might be thought that intractable problems would confront the composer attempting to preserve the balance in the equations suggested above. Unless his phrase structures were crudely simple, the sharply focused interior rhythms would threaten to obliterate the sense of poised length. Tippett's retention of traditional phrase structure is however both clear and elegant enough to provide one reason why this is not the case. Another is the sheer quantity of events in his thematic material. This is so challenging to the ordering instincts that the listener is forced to impose some kind of overall coherence on the music by seeking out the longest comprehensible units. In doing this his attention naturally falls on the component phrases; and these divide into the familiar groupings of sentence or period structure.

Four typical themes are given in the examples below: the fugue subject from String Quartet No. 1 and, from String Quartet No. 2, the 'first and second subjects' from the first movement and the main theme from the scherzo. The phrases are shown by square brackets. As in subsequent examples in this section, the music is re-notated to show the true rhythms[7] and re-barred to show the 'beats' referred to above, each bar being one such beat. Other annotations are explained later.

In Ex. 10 the four phrases form a sentence structure. The second

Ex. 10 **String Quartet No. 1**

phrase is a varied repeat of the first, with lyrical expansion; the third arrests the lyricism with a complementary dynamic compression and the characteristic use of sequence; the last phrase both concludes the subject by limiting itself to the one motif (marked *a* in Ex. 10) whose relative anonymity does not demand further elaboration and leaves it open-ended, because the music then proceeds to the fugal answer. The two phrases of Exx. 11 and 12 form the antecedents of period structures. Here the first phrase is followed not so much by a varied repeat, as in sentence structure, but by a contrast. The consequents of period structures usually form balancing repeats, or near repeats, of their antecedents and since this is what happens in Exx. 11 and 12 the consequents are not illustrated. The full period structure of Ex. 13 is given however, in order to show the melodic variation of a rhythmic repeat.

Ex. 11 **String Quartet No. 2**

Ex. 12 **String Quartet No. 2**

Ex. 13   **String Quartet No. 2**

In all these themes traditional forms of melodic exposition, as described above, supported by the orientating function of the beats enables the broad spans of the phrase structure to be easily recognized as such and a fundamental shape to be imposed by both the psychological need to find one and the character of the music itself. This shape is then set in motion by the springing interior rhythms.

The above considerations provide some 'psychological' explanation of the expressive effect of Tippett's rhythms and of why the listener tends to hear them in large structural groups. Before an analytical explanation can be uncovered it is necessary first to distinguish their principal technical features.

With one exception, the rhythmic components of Tippett's language are drawn from the common currency of the present and previous centuries. The disposition of these components may be unexpected, but their identity remains familiar and is rarely distorted by melodic angularity or rhythmic displacement. When Tippett uses syncopation it is readily heard as such (as in bar 2 of Ex. 10 or the second half of bar 6 of Ex. 11) and thus can easily be distinguished from the exception, anticipatory rhythm, with which it bears a superficial resemblance.

The term anticipatory rhythm is used to describe a particular rhythmic nuance, as in the tied note of bar 1 in Ex. 10. It is highly ambiguous in effect for it comprises both a weak and a strong accent. The articulation occurs before a pulse and is not generated by one as in conventional syncopation; it is sustained and thrown on to the pulse, which though not articulated is still sensed. The idiom's first appearance in the *Robin Hood* overture smacks of rather self-conscious mannerism. In the quartet movement of Ex. 10 however it appears quite naturally, as one component in a phrase and not the dominating one. In fact it was so unsolicited that Tippett initially did not know how to notate it. This difficulty was perhaps not surprising for the idiom derives from a confusing variety of sources.

Jazz is the most obvious and the one Tippett himself is most ready to acknowledge since it marks the successful outcome of his attempt to absorb a style he not only liked for its own sake but which for him offered the promise of a vernacular. With the publication in 1938, shortly before he began work on his Concerto for Double String Orchestra, of Winthrop Sargeant's pioneer work on the subject, *Jazz: Hot and Hybrid*,[8] Tippett was able to place his enthusiasm for jazz on a sound theoretical footing and identify the parentage of his anticipatory rhythms to his satisfaction. (In the Double Concerto they are notated in definitive form – as, for example, in the tied note of bar 1 of Ex. 17.) That they were already a characteristic if unobtrusive part of his rhythmic vocabulary suggests however that they were the result not only of his instinct to borrow from jazz what he found novel and vital in it nor even of his instinct to pin down this novelty to one technical feature, but that they were also the product of a much older musical inheritance. A typical gesture in late Beethoven is the placing of dynamic weight not on the strong beat but on the anacrusis, producing an effect of search and discovery or of inward strain without romantic pathos. A well-known instance is given in Ex. 14 (i). Tippett had demonstrated his sympathy with such gestures in the very first bars of his String Quartet No. 1 (see Ex. 25). Converted into a fast tempo Beethoven's idiom would yield such a phenomenon as that in Ex. 14 (ii). Tippett's anticipatory rhythm is only marginally less close to Beethoven than to jazz. Another possible source is the unusual method of word-setting found in sixteenth- and seventeenth-century English vocal music, such as that in Ex. 14 (iii). Whatever its sources this component is the most novel in Tippett's rhythmic vocabulary and it contributes significantly to that characteristic lilt mentioned earlier.

Ex. 14

(i) **Beethoven: String Quartet op. 127**

(ii) **Beethoven: Grosse Fuge op. 133**

(iii) **Byrd: Magnificat** (*The Great Service*)

It remains however only one of many components; and the individuality of Tippett's rhythmic language derives not so much from the identity of its components as from their fusion into discrete units and the juxtapositioning of such units to form larger groupings. Additive principles therefore lie at the centre of his language. Additive rhythm is a convenient but imprecise term. Its inventor, Curt Sachs,[9] used it indiscriminately to refer to two quite distinct types: that in which the beat is constant, although its interior construction is asymmetric, and that in which the beat is continually changing, whether the interior construction is asymmetric or not. The former type differs from the familiar divisive rhythm only in so far as its interior construction is asymmetric. Otherwise its premises are the same. The latter type differs radically, because it forfeits the stabilizing influence of a regular beat. Additive rhythm has become too valuable a term to be rejected. The most convenient solution is to call the two types fixed- and free-additive rhythms respectively.

Within the category of free-additive rhythms there are again two types: those which can be organized according to arithmetical procedures and those which cannot. Examples of the former are Blacher's 'variable metres', Messiaen's 'chromatic rhythm' and Carter's 'tempo modulation'. To these Sachs's term numerical rhythm might reasonably be applied – even though he evidently thought of it in a different way. The latter type is not susceptible to codifiable analytical methods. It is not organized independently of other parameters and is therefore subject to the influence of an infinite number of factors, thematic, gestural, colouristic etc. It is common in Stravinsky, and in Tippett – doubtless one of the reasons why Tippett holds Stravinsky in such high regard. The term free-additive can now apply to it without confusion, but with the rider that so loosely defined a technique will obviously be applied in numerous ways.

Fixed-additive rhythms are rare in Tippett. He used them only twice in his first period and even on those occasions he sought means of easing or obscuring the rigidity of the technique, presumably because the continual repetition of a single rhythmic unit obstructed organic growth and cramped his naturally lyrical style. A short description of the two movements in question will show how carefully Tippett explored the technique before rejecting it in favour of free-additive rhythm.

The first strain of the theme in the variations movement of his Piano Sonata No. 1 is given in Ex. 15. Fixed-additive rhythm is obviously appropriate in a theme for variations, which by definition needs the quality of somewhat dogmatic statement. (Its anticipatory rhythms are by now typical features of his style, as is the construction of each bar, with unarticulated downbeat.) Tippett clearly was determined to preserve the idea of construction by units of five and indeed to apply this to the movement as a whole. The quintuple rhythm is echoed in the phrase construction (in the first strain, five-bar groups disguised by overlap, and in the second, nine-bar groups divided 4+5) and in the overall design (theme followed by five variations, plus restatement). Yet, significantly, he abandons the quintuple rhythm at one point in the concluding strain of the

Ex. 15

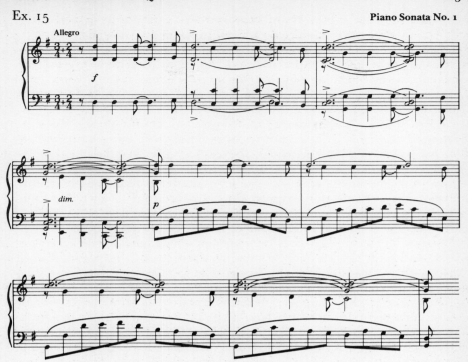

theme, and in the variations themselves he subjects the 3+2 unit to
progressive modification. The table below shows how the two durations of
this unit are affected.

Notated time signature	Tempo indication	Effective duration
Theme $3/4 + 2/4$	Allegro ♩ = 138	𝅗𝅥. + 𝅗𝅥
Var.1 $3/4 + 5/8$	Allegro ♩ = 138	𝅗𝅥. + 𝅗𝅥♪
Var.2 $4/4 + 2/4$	Allegro vigoroso ♩ = 152	𝅝 + 𝅗𝅥
Var.3 $4/4$	Meno mosso ♩ = 44 [♩ = c. 𝅗𝅥.]	𝅗𝅥. + 𝅗𝅥.
Var.4 $3/2 + 3/4$	Molto allegro ♩ = 192 [♩ = c. ♪]	𝅗𝅥. + 𝅗𝅥♪
Var.5 $13/16 + 2/4$	Allegro moderato ♩ = 104	𝅗𝅥.♪ + 𝅗𝅥

In variation 1, the second duration is augmented; in variation 2, the first.
The durations reach equilibrium in the central third variation. In
variations 4 and 5 the reverse procedure takes effect. By its diminution of
the second duration, variation 4 complements variation 1. Variation 5

should conclude the process and contain a diminution of its first duration. But this would have produced a unit of two minims and thus overshot a return to the theme. As may be expected in Tippett, a preconceived plan yields to demands of expression and function. Variation 5 comprises therefore a rhythm close enough to the original to lead naturally into it yet particular enough to preserve the essential nature of the rhythmic treatment throughout the movement.

In the short aria 'What have I done to you, my son?' from *A Child of Our Time* the basic unit is again a 5/4 bar divided 3+2. But here it remains unchanged throughout. Although this aptly symbolizes the plight of the mother, powerless to help her son (see p.161), Tippett clearly sensed a threat to his natural rhythmic buoyancy and attempted to counteract it by introducing canonic imitation on the third crotchet of each bar, thus obscuring the basic rhythm. It was perhaps the only tactic he could have adopted, given the decision to write in fixed-additive rhythm. But the rhythm is in fact so insistent that no genuine modification is effected.

Free-additive rhythms are far more characteristic of his style and their distinguishing features may now be deduced from the four themes of Exx. 10 to 13. The rapid quaver metre in Exx. 10 and 13 bears some resemblance to rhythmic procedures in Bartók and Stravinsky, the only two contemporary composers whose rhythmic language could have exerted any real influence on Tippett at this time; and indeed, in his String Quartet No. 1, he had not fully absorbed their influence for the persistent and mildly abrasive quaver attack occasionally recalls the stamping or chanting rhythms of Eastern European folk-music. The presence however of lyrical elements (legato phrasing and relatively long note values) as well as dance elements (staccato phrasing and relatively short note values) means that what preponderate are light, scampering rhythms, quite different from the fixed-additive rhythms and the very simply proportioned note values of Bartók and even more foreign to the free-additive rhythms of Stravinsky, where traditional phrasing has no place and where forms are commonly constructed from an opposition between static and shifting durations. Stravinsky can be heard in such abstract terms because his rhythmic material is often reduced to almost algebraic simplicity, for example, nothing but crotchets and quavers. In Tippett the durational patterns are influenced by classical procedures of thematic development and by melodic/rhythmic shapes drawn from a richer stock of inherited gesture. His themes are less 'pure' than Stravinsky's and as a result his free-additive rhythms resist classification as compounds (additions) of twos and threes, as in Sachs's schema, and instead group themselves into larger units. In the first bar of Ex. 10, for example, the quaver units are given as 9 and not 4+5 (or 2+2+2+3). In the first bar of Ex. 11 they are 7 and not 4+3. Additive groupings of 4+5 and 4+3 would, admittedly, have indicated the slight *ictus* at the dividing points but they would have ignored the aural fact that the music 'floats' between its main beats and that comprehension by groups of quavers is held in abeyance until a new beat occurs. The chronometric length of a beat may be determined by the number of quavers but its effective length is determined by its relationship with its neighbours. In this way the music assembles into a number of beats of varying duration, that is, it creates the downbeat impression mentioned earlier.

This impression is consolidated by two other factors: Tippett's indifference to functional harmonic progression, which deprives his music of clear harmonic upbeats and directs attention to its accentual qualities, and the irregular length of the beats, which directs attention more specifically to their beginnings, their downbeats. (In music with regular beats the importance of the downbeat retreats into the background.) If however this music really did consist of nothing but undifferentiated downbeats it would lose that sense of poise mentioned earlier. The downbeat impression is in fact merely the first stage in an interpretative process. On a higher level of rhythmic organization the beats form into a hierarchy of values by which some are stronger than others. In this lies a rhythmic principle: of two successive beats the longer generates greater anticipation and tension and therefore throws greater emphasis on the following beat. Expressed in another way, a beat will be weaker, an upbeat, if longer than its successor, stronger, a downbeat, if shorter. By this phenomenon an almost subliminal pulsing of contrasting strengths of downbeat stress is created, providing the chief technical reason for the sense of poise and the characteristic spring and elasticity in Tippett's rhythms.

This principle may yield to the immediate influence of dynamic, tonic or agogic accent but in general it holds good. It produces quite complex results. By adapting the method of Cone[10] these can be expressed graphically through six symbols: – ⁄ ＼ for first, second and third stress downbeats, arranged in increasing order of weight; ⌣ for upbeats; and ⌣̄ or ⌣̣ for 'reflexive' beats, in which downbeats are transformed into upbeats and vice versa. The scansion pattern of the four phrases of Ex. 10 would read: –⌣|⁄⌣⌣̄|＼⌣⌣̄|–⌣. This can be explained as follows. In the first phrase the longer second beat is an upbeat, leaving the first as a first stress downbeat. In the second phrase the first beat is preceded by the first clear upbeat in the music and is therefore a downbeat of greater strength. It is given as a second stress downbeat. Since the following upbeat is shorter than the comparable beat in the first phrase (11 as opposed to 12 quavers), the downbeat following that is not so strong. Yet this downbeat becomes longer than the preceding upbeat. It therefore acquires the property of an upbeat and is given the symbol of a reflexive beat. As an upbeat it is 14 quavers long, the longest beat in the fugue subject, and it therefore heralds the strongest of the downbeats, that at the beginning of the third phrase. The construction of the third phrase is similar to that of the second: a sequence of beats of increasing duration. The two phrases are respectively of 9, 11, 14 and 6, 8, 11 quavers. The scansion pattern is therefore the same. The fourth phrase likewise repeats the proportions of the first and its scansion pattern is also the same. The scansion pattern for the fugue subject as a whole is thus a nicely symmetrical scheme, the inner and outer phrases rhyming with each other and defining the closed nature of the musical idea.

A more accurate picture of the relative strengths of the downbeat stresses could be devised with a system giving – to a first stress downbeat, = to a second and so on. The pattern thus emerging would confirm the richness of rhythmic content and the functional quality of the articulation: – ◡|≡ ◡ ◡̆|≡ ◡ ◡̆|= ◡. (The third phrase, for example, begins with the strongest stress, as is appropriate for the climactic phrase about three-quarters of the way through.) But for present purposes a scansion system of the first type distinguishes the varied stresses clearly enough. The scansion patterns of Exx. 11 and 12 would read ◡ˊ|◡–◡◡̆ and ◡–|◡ˊ respectively. In the first, the pattern is of a controlled decrescendo of downbeat stress, in the second, an increase. These may be reduced to a single downbeat and a single upbeat, appropriate articulations for 'first and second subjects'. In Ex. 13 the pattern is ◡◡̆ˊ◡|–◡ repeated. This produces an arched dynamic, appropriate for a theme developmental in character. Scansion patterns cannot of course reveal all the rhythmic subtleties of such themes. Tippett's skill in, for example, binding the first phrase with the abruptly contrasting second phrase of Ex. 13 (by the modulating rhythm of bar 4, whose compound time provides a neutral setting out of which a new rhythm can emerge) can only be seen in musical notation. They illustrate rhythmic diversity and, in particular, the degree to which varied stress contributes towards rhythmic function.

In order to emphasize this important point, the examples given above have been somewhat oversimplified, in as far as they omit supporting textures. Yet rhythmic function is not seriously questioned by Tippett's contrapuntal textures, which reinforce rather than obscure rhythmic character. The counterpoint to Ex. 11, for example, is effectively in rhythmic unison with the theme; that to Ex. 12 is more accompanimental than polyphonic. In fact contrapuntal activity serves not only to support the themes but also to urge them forward – with little thrusting accents, like anticipatory rhythms or, more particularly, like incipient canons. When Tippett writes real canons the textural complexity is more dense – it occupies a mid-point between monophonic and polyphonic presentation – but it is not different in kind. The accentuation is now continuous. What distinguishes Tippett's canons is the point of entry of the second voice, which commonly occurs at a point rhythmically 'dissonant' with that of the first. The accentual effect is most pronounced in fast movements where some highly idiosyncratic music emerges. One of the most remarkable of Tippett's canonic treatments is in the introduction to the aria 'The soul of man' in *A Child of Our Time*. As an introduction, the music here plays a subordinate role in order not to pre-empt the effectiveness of the voice entry. At the same time it introduces a sense of animation, in keeping with the character of the aria. This double effect is achieved through the canonic writing, which creates both animation and, by the rhythmic behaviour of its phrases, what may be termed a rhythmic diminuendo.

In the first phrase of Ex. 16 the canon is by melodic inversion, a procedure which immediately diverts attention from the linear to the rhythmic and prepares for the ostensibly more conventional canonic writing in the remaining phrases. Here however the groupings of the eleven-quaver pattern in the upper part are not followed exactly in the lower part. By their regularity these repeated trochaic scansion patterns nonetheless relax the tension and lay out an accompanimental texture ready for the voice entry. For Tippett canonic techniques are not only a means of increasing animation; as with monophonic presentation of themes they can also be used to articulate function.

Ex. 16 A Child of Our Time

The rhythms of the examples above are geared to a quaver metre; yet in practice this metre is obliterated by the larger and seemingly indivisible units of crotchets, dotted crotchets, minims, etc. In fact if metre is suggested at all Tippett's widely spaced downbeats propose an affinity with the minim or, more accurately, with the concept of the tactus – this another indication of how he parts company with other contemporary innovators in rhythm for whom metre is associated with short note values rather than the minim or semibreve proposed by the tactus. Yet while he has never rejected the expressive resource of a clear metrical background, his most characteristic rhythms rarely operate against a genuine recurring metre of this kind. Surprisingly, in view of its apparently free articulation, the first movement of his Concerto for Double String Orchestra is one such exception. (Although most of it is notated in 8/8, the whole of it could have been notated in 2/2 had Tippett been less concerned with practical problems of performance.) Why this should be so is no doubt due to the fact that the Double Concerto introduces that most striking and individual of all aspects of his rhythmic style, a rhythmic polyphony arising from the combination of such lines as have been examined above. The technique is so novel that Howard Smither could find no place for it in his pioneer and ostensibly comprehensive classification of twentieth-century rhythm.[11] To correlate two or more independent lines of such complexity obviously presents a major challenge to the creative imagination and it was perhaps not so surprising therefore that with his discovery of the technique Tippett should have used metre as a means of orientation. Nevertheless it is unobtrusive (it even allows a hint of inner rubato) and in subsequent works using rhythmic polyphony he discarded it.

The essentials of Tippett's rhythmic polyphony are contained in the Double Concerto's opening theme (Ex. 17). The rhythmic independence of the two lines of this theme is so marked that there is a danger of incoherence, increased with the jettisoning of functional harmonic support. Tippett avoids incoherence in several ways: by the 2/2 metrical background in orchestra 1 (an 'eight-bar theme'), by the mixolydian modality common to both lines, by their complementary expressive character and, particularly, by the clarity of phrasing. The phrases of each line build up into period structure, ABAB, whose balanced shapes are strong enough to create a general if not very firmly established sense of completion on their own, without the addition of harmony. The textural layout, AB over AB^1, then AB^1 over AB, recalls another traditional formal technique, voice-exchange, dating back to English music of the thirteenth century.

Ex. 17   **Concerto for Double String Orchestra**

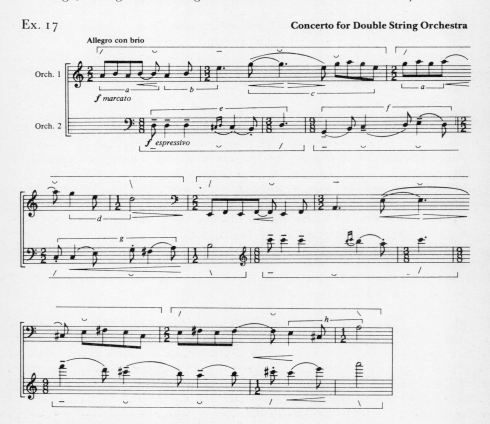

(both orchestras doubled at the octave above and octave below)

Such considerations are important. But the clinching formal determinant is rhythmic. The superposition of rhythms creates a new rhythm, a consequence of the fact that between the two lines there can be either no coincidence of stress, in which case comprehensibility is suspended, or a variety of types of coincidence, in which case a new pattern of beats at a higher level of rhythmic organization is created, their significance depending on weight and position in a phrase. In the diagram below the new scansion pattern of Ex. 17 is shown by the second of the two scansion systems described earlier. (Dotted lines indicate points of coincidence.)

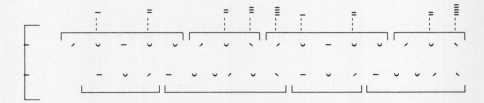

The new pattern defines and characterizes the period structure of the theme. The antecedent is both concluded and projected into the consequent by, respectively, the strongest stress up to that point and an even stronger one. The consequent follows the course of the antecedent until the decisive final stress, when for the first time the rhythms of the two lines coincide in identical strong stresses and thus satisfyingly complete the structure.

When writing in more than two parts, when, that is, stretching comprehensibility to its limits, Tippett either reduces rhythmic complexity in the single lines or teams up lines in pairs so that they are rhythmically consonant with each other. In this way a texture that might be thought impenetrable will yield to a scansion pattern no less controlled and functional than that in the Double Concerto theme. Example 18 is taken from the most complex texture Tippett wrote in his first period, the double fugue of his String Quartet No. 3. Although contrasted, the two subjects (S1 and S2) have the same scansion pattern and form a pair, until they break apart in order to allow the fugal answer to cut through. At this point

Ex. 18   **String Quartet No. 3**

(Ex. 18 cont.)

counter-subject 1 (CS1) is joined in rhythmic canon by counter-subject 2 (CS2), a procedure which restores the idea of paired units. Here, with all four subjects heard simultaneously, the peak of rhythmic complexity is reached. But the new scansion pattern in the diagram below shows that the passage is a simple dynamic ascent. The statement of the twin subject increases and subsides in rhythmic weighting; the answer echoes but intensifies the process.

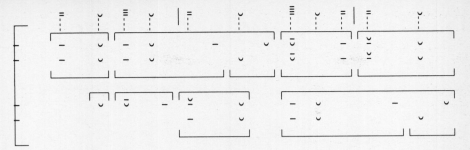

The examples given so far in this section have been taken from thematic material. While the essentials of Tippett's rhythmic language can legitimately be found in his themes, in so far as they represent intuitively conceived hypotheses of musical argument, they would have been almost unusable had Tippett not learnt how to exploit his discoveries and extend his control of rhythmic function in themes to that in transition and development sections. A study of his rhythmic language must therefore account for his ability to effect rhythmic modulations as well as rhythmic statements. There is nothing new in the idea of rhythmic modulation. The point here is simply that the complexity of Tippett's basic material demanded an exceptionally skilful use of it.

Tippett first mastered rhythmic modulation in the opening movement of his Double Concerto. The exposition of that movement can provide a representative example of how he applies the technique. The main theme (Ex. 17) is followed by a transition and a 'second subject', given in Ex. 19 (notated, as before, in the true rather than published rhythms). The transition is in two sections, the first absorbing some of the energy of the theme and gradually simplifying its rhythmic polyphony until a point of rhythmic unison and rhythmic neutrality is reached, out of which the second section emerges, a re-grouping of forces in preparation for the 'second subject'. Like the opening theme this is a period structure. Unlike that theme however it is in rhythmic unison, a simplification in one respect which permits a complexity in another: its phrasing is markedly less

Ex. 19   **Concerto for Double String Orchestra**

(Ex. 19 cont.)

symmetric. These procedures can be observed in the plan (Ex. 20) of the basic rhythmic motifs and durational values.

At the beginning of the transition, tension is reduced by sequence, by canon as opposed to polyphony and by the 'inexact' augmentation (x^1) of the three-minim rhythmic motif (x) in the theme. This motif is shortened and reversed, a procedure which throws the upbeat on to its second value, in preparation for the 'new' motif x^2 (a diminution of x^1), which by its novelty has the authority to break the asymmetry and initiate a calmer rhythmic flow – the canons now enter on a 'consonant' value and the minim values are grouped in pairs. The cadential three-minim motif acts as an upbeat to the second section.

Ex. 20   **Concerto for Double String Orchestra**

(Ex. 20 cont.)

Here the four-semibreve motif creates a relaxed, neutral background (grouping by fours is the most natural rhythmic pulse in Western music). The pulse is quickened by the three-semibreve motif and its conversion into the even quicker pulse of six minims. The final phrase combines the minim pulse with x^2. This phrase serves to introduce the principal rhythmic procedures in the formation of the 'second subject' and, by its braking non-retrogradable rhythm, to conclude the transition.

The 'second subject' (its period structure indicated by capital letters, as in the main theme) integrates the principal durational values in the main theme, minims and dotted crotchets, not, as there, by superposition but by juxtaposition. The A phrase of the antecedent is a non-retrogradable rhythm, as befits this point of structural articulation, but it is 'inexact', appropriately creating an effect both of stasis and movement. The B phrase is a diminution of A, repeated. In the consequent, B^1 leads by steadily increasing values to the climactic C phrase, which integrates the minim pulse with the 'new' motif x^2. The (varied) repeat of B^1 and C^1 is an acknowledgement of the psychological fact that this particularly arresting passage needs to be repeated if it is not to sound inconclusive.

An attempt has been made in the previous pages to uncover a rationale behind Tippett's rhythmic language, partly to show that his rhythms are organic, to reveal, that is, his remarkable inventive, developmental and integrative skills, and in particular to define his originality. Some of the preceding paragraphs may have suggested parallels with Messiaen. Whatever philosophical attitudes Tippett may have in common with Messiaen, his rhythmic techniques are sharply contrasted. Tippett's are organic rather than synthetic; they support rather than determine musical behaviour. In this respect he appears to have closer links with Bartók and Stravinsky but again, as has been shown earlier, his additive rhythms have little to do with those of the earlier composers. If Tippett's connections with the great twentieth-century innovators are remote, his connections with his English contemporaries, Lambert and Walton, are even more so. All this is perhaps obvious enough and Tippett's originality self-evident. Yet if he is conspicuous among twentieth-century innovators in drawing so little from his immediate predecessors and contemporaries, he cannot have drawn so much entirely from within himself. No composer works in total isolation. Interest in the nature of Tippett's rhythmic language centres precisely on this fact – that its most clear parentage lies in music written over 350 years before. This may be accounted an extreme instance of the neo-classical attitude among twentieth-century composers, or an exemplification in musical terms of Eliot's thesis that the true nature of the English tradition went underground with the advent of the Puritans, not to surface again until the twentieth century. Whatever the reasons there is no doubt that Tippett's monophonic rhythms bear a closer resemblance to those in Elizabethan and Jacobean music – especially the fast-moving balletts of the madrigalists, the quicker-tempo songs of the lutenists and the instrumental fantasias of such composers as Byrd and Gibbons – than to any other. Indeed so marked are the correspondences that from the evidence of such music as the Weelkes and Dowland excerpts in Ex. 21, it would seem the ultimate source, at least of his monophonic rhythms.[12]

Ex. 21

(i) **Weelkes: On the plains Fairy trains** (*Balletts and Madrigals*, 1598)

(ii) **Dowland: Clear or Cloudy** (*Second Booke of Ayres*, 1600)

As for his polyphonic rhythms, their source is not to be found in twentieth-century music either. In Tippett's only possible model, Stravinsky, polyrhythmic techniques derive from the superposition of ostinati and this is entirely uncharacteristic of Tippett in his first period. An isolated passage (Ex. 22), from the finale of Haydn's String Quartet op. 71, No. 3,

Ex. 22   **Haydn: String Quartet op. 71 No. 3**

offers an eighteenth-century counterpart. As with monophonic rhythms the prime source remains Elizabethan and Jacobean – especially those instrumental fantasias where the points of entry continually subvert a sense of regular metre (see Ex. 23). Tippett's fondness for a particular Gibbons fantasia[13] (which he uses in his Divertimento *Sellinger's Round* and in his Symphony No. 4 without any stylistic incongruity) underlines his affinity with the vitality and lyricism of this music.

Ex. 23   **Gibbons: from No. 2 of Nine Fantasies of Three Parts** [c. 1620]

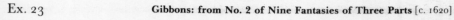

Such correspondences should be regarded however as illuminating rather than conclusive. They overlook the curious fact that Tippett's study of such composers as Weelkes, Dowland and Gibbons finished long before it bore fruit in his mature music and that he did not encounter Gibbons's fantasias until after he had written his Double Concerto. In any case counterpoint in English fantasias is imitative whereas Tippett's is 'free'.

What distinguishes the rhythms of the Elizabethans from those of their European contemporaries is what distinguishes Tippett's from those of his: the varied downbeat stresses. English is a stressed language. The Elizabethans may have awakened Tippett's sensitivity to the rhythms of English, but once awakened it led him to develop well beyond a mere renewal of their idioms. The composer who stimulated him most in this respect was Purcell. In a broadcast of 1947[14] Tippett contrasted Purcell's and Handel's setting of the word 'shepherd' in 'Nymphs and Shepherds' and 'He shall feed his flock' respectively, much to Handel's detriment because *he* had missed the opportunity Purcell seized with relish to create a characteristic rhythm of the word. Like Purcell, Tippett responds to all that is typical of the English language – sounds and inflexions as well as stresses. The determining rhythmic factor in such a passage as that in Ex. 24 is as much the delicacy with which vowels are set as fidelity to stress rhythms. This is especially noticeable in his treatment of diphthongs: 'feed' and the 'chil-' of 'children' are given three and two notes respectively.

Ex. 24   **A Child of Our Time**

If such a clear connection exists between Tippett's rhythms and the English language it is natural to assume that his music is influenced by English prosody. Apparent confirmation of this is found in the score of his String Quartet No. 2, which contains the direction that the finale should be played with a 'decisively sprung rhythm'. This movement does indeed suggest the influence of the 'sprung rhythm' of Gerard Manley Hopkins, in that its varied stresses within a regular 4/4 time signature reflect the principal characteristic of sprung rhythm – freely chosen but isochronous patterns of metrical feet. But regular metre is not typical of Tippett and, ironically, this movement is the weakest in the quartet. In his only setting of Hopkins, the madrigal *The Windhover*, he entirely disregards Hopkins's fixed metrical foot. It may be that some kind of creative misunderstanding has occurred by which Hopkins's prosody has stimulated Tippett's feeling for stress rhythms; but if so this appears to have been unconscious. By the same token it is possible to find correspondences between Tippett's rhythms and, for example, the twentieth-century revival of the 'strong-stress' prosody of Anglo-Saxon poetry or the wide variety of foot and of line length in English poetry in general. It could be said that the elusive relationship between quantity and quality of syllables in English poetry is reflected in the equally elusive relationship between metre and rhythm in Tippett's music. It could even be said that the introduction of the typically English trochaic rhythm of crotchet plus quaver in his Double Concerto gave the finishing touch to the creation of a wholly individual style. But in the absence of a definitive theory of prosody such ideas cannot be tested.

What can be said is that Tippett's rhythms are profoundly English. They are rooted in Elizabethan music and in the sounds of the language; and they are enriched by cheerful and profitable acts of plunder on musics and languages of all kinds. This is of course true not only of his rhythms but of his music in general – which shows how successfully he fulfilled his early philosophy that the new would emerge from an integration of native tradition with influences from abroad. If native tradition is predominant, this is simply because a composer needs a secure and fertile base to work from. In the 1930s and '40s it was inevitable that if he were honest he would find this in his own culture. It is equally true that exclusive involvement in one culture leads to decay and with his assimilation of foreign influences Tippett both kept faith with his philosophy and in the process reanimated a tradition that had lain dormant for centuries.

The Sonata Principle: Four Early Works

String Quartet No. 1

The manuscript of the unpublished original version of this work is headed 'Quartet No. 1 in A, op. 2'[15] and dated 23 September 1935. There are four movements: an introductory slow movement, an allegro (not a sonata-allegro, though the function is the same), a second slow movement and a fugal finale. Tippett grew dissatisfied with the first two movements and in 1943 replaced them with a single new one. This three-movement work was eventually published in 1946, two years after the publication of his String Quartet No. 2.

The original first movement is of an intense elegiac beauty, acting as a foil to the resolute urgency of the second. It is the first genuinely characteristic piece Tippett wrote and it is a pity that his dissatisfaction with the following allegro obliged him to discard it. In several respects it is typical of the mature composer, not least in its textures, whose lines are frequently packed tight, like the strands of a plaited band, and then allowed to weave in and out of each other as the textures themselves move through a shifting sequence of layers. Emphasis on movement accounts for Tippett's interest in line and in contrapuntal interplay between lines. The 'first subject' (most of the exposition of the movement's shortened sonata form is given in Ex. 25) is thus a process, rather than a theme, designed to carry the music to the 'second subject' (cello, bar 9, prefigured in viola, bars 5–6), which though of conventionally lyrical character is again more of a gesture than a melody. Material of this plastic, almost athematic character is common in much of Tippett's subsequent output. Attention is focused less on the material as such than on its contribution to an organic flow.

Ex. 25   **String Quartet No. 1**
                                                                            (original version)

In general the movement's tonal relationships are classical: the exposition concludes in the dominant and the recapitulation in the tonic. The means by which these structural points are reached however are modal. The exposition is articulated in a sequence of tonalities running down the Aeolian mode, A–G–F–E, a procedure entirely foreign to the classical method of reaching the dominant and one whose novelty is emphasized by the pointed use of second-subject material for both G (bar 9) and F (bar 12). Of particular interest is Tippett's use of B flat at bar 5/6, not as a neapolitan progression, but for its colouristic properties. When the melodic/harmonic tension of bar 4 is released, the B flat conjures up a warm, soothing sound, whose function is expressive, not structural. This is the first mature example of a characteristic technique.

In the second movement, Tippett's formal ambitions seem to have taken precedence over everything else and as a consequence the music is rather pedestrian in content. Its anonymity of language contrasts uncomfortably with the individuality of the other movements and Tippett's instinct to judge music by what it sounds like and not by its technical pretensions inevitably led him to reject it. Nevertheless, the movement's proportions are skilfully handled and its function as dramatic allegro never lost sight of.

As in his Symphony in B flat, Tippett wanted here to write a fast movement not tied to classical sonata schemes yet having the structural weight of a sonata-allegro. In this case it is preceded by a slow movement, as opposed to a simple introduction. This meant that the material needed to be more diverse, in order not to be swamped by the slow movement, and more compressed, because it was for a quartet and not a symphony. The movement is in five sections, tabulated below, the italic letters indicating thematic material and the numerals the number of bars. Example 26 provides most of the opening statement, with italic letters corresponding to those in the table.

statement	$a \atop 3$	$b \atop 2$	$a \atop 3$	$b \atop 3$	$c \atop 5$	$d \atop 3$	$b \atop 4$	
exposition	$a^1 \atop 10$	$c^1 \atop 9$	$b \atop 2$					
development	$a \atop 3$	$b \atop 6$	$a \atop 3$	$b \atop 9$	$c \atop 25$	$d \atop 62$	$x \atop 9$	$b \atop 8$
recapitulation	$a^1 \atop 12$	$c^1 \atop 10$	$b \atop 2$					
coda	$a \atop 3$	$b \atop 6$	$a \atop 15$	$b \atop 3$	x			

Ex. 26   **String Quartet No. 1**
                                                                   (original version)

As in the Symphony the movement combines a classical structural scheme with Sibelian developmental methods. The opening statement provides a pool of motifs, each with a specific function. Thus *a* wrenches the music upwards and away from the mood of the slow movement and at the same time becomes the 'first subject', a^1; *b* and *c* are both transitional in character, *b* a means of dissolving the tension and *c* of increasing it before turning into a cantabile 'second subject', c^1; *d* has a codetta function. The main interest lies in the extreme deliberation and self-discipline with which Tippett extended motifs *c* and *d* in the development section, so that their potential is fulfilled to a point of exhaustion. Even if his unyielding 3/4 eventually proves to exert a deadening influence, Tippett's escape from motif *d*, an upward-moving cello cadenza marked *x* in the table, eases the rigidity and is an imaginative invention, comparable in gesture to a jazz 'break' (though not consciously used as such). The coda begins like a second development and leads into a second (unbarred) cello cadenza, which this time curves downwards into a richer tone colour in preparation for the second slow movement.

These cello cadenzas were retained in the revised first movement (the first considerably altered, and now appearing after the exposition as opposed to the development, and the second almost literally) – symptomatic both of Tippett's desire to recover something of the flavour of the original and of the inherent value of his original ideas. There are other retentions. Although the first subject of the revised movement embodies a new thematic idea, and must do since it now begins the whole work, it still retains the typical wrench followed by a release (Ex. 27), and the 'modal' harmony of the original first movement is retained in the first two bars. The

Ex. 27   **String Quartet No. 1**

original figure of Ex. 26c is also retained, as a transition to the second subject (Ex. 28), which is itself a reshaping of the original codetta motif.

Ex. 28   String Quartet No. 1

Despite these correspondences the revised movement sounds different. It is vivid and assured, where the original was dogged, and having dispensed with the sagging motif of Ex. 26b Tippett now sustains a vigorous onward sweep. Not the least of the reasons for this is that he had in the meanwhile learned the art of rhythmic modulation. The time signature of 3/4 remains unchanged but his adjustments of pulse between the principal subject groups cunningly conceal the basic metre and enable him to curb the natural inclination of his tempo to lapse into a formless sequence of downbeats. This means of shaping a movement was a Beethovenian inheritance. The Sibelius influence had been set aside and, as has been noted, Tippett had meanwhile come to the conclusion that the Beethovenian sonata-allegro was something he could not do without.

Whether approached from the original or the revised movement, the slow movement of the Quartet needed the contrast of uniformity of mood; it is in fact an extended arch of lyric melody. Its form is that of a pavan. Classic examples of the pavan, as in the English virginalists, are in three equal sections each repeated (often with variation), the whole designed so that the principal line is carried across the sections to form one extended thematic unit. Tippett's expressive metaphor here is that of a song, a song in which all the parts sing and yet still produce a unified sound of the same dynamic level at any given point. The length of his melodic lines, whether in the principal or subordinate parts, may owe something to his experiments with melodic prolongation when writing under the influence of Sibelius; but their shaping is wholly individual and symptomatic of his willingness to take the 'evolutionary jump', to go beyond the forbidden corner and find himself in some unexpected paradise. In Ex. 29, the first section of the movement, the upper E flat in the 1st violin part of bar 1 could be expected to lead to the note below, as could the A flat which does in fact follow it. By riding over the melodic tension in this way, Tippett creates another tension which threatens to break the texture apart. In the second phrase (bar 3) the challenge is accepted, whereupon the threat dissolves and the music discovers an exquisite calm, no less so for containing what appears to be an echo of Strauss's *Tod und Verklärung* (bar

5). If a composer can use a nineteenth-century commonplace and still retain his identity, then he has surely reached maturity.

Ex. 29   String Quartet No. 1

This movement embodies the first example of that long soaring melodic line characteristic of so much of Tippett's output. It here subdivides into two wide curves for each main section, the first rising to a magical height (as in the passage just discussed), the second to a passionate climax; in the final section these elements are integrated and both are included in both subsections. Melodies of this type are not wholly dependent on a feeling for line. Much of their shaping is determined by the need to resolve dissonance. Every bar contains examples. Such dissonances lead to a curiously ambiguous use of tonality, partly influenced by nineteenth-century progressions (in that there are, for example, several mediant relationships, as between bars 5 and 6) but more strongly by Tippett's idiosyncratic use of tonality as expressive colour. The tonal structure of the whole movement is as follows:

A_1: D flat–D–E flat– B_1: B minor/G flat–E– C_1: G flat–E flat–
A_2: G–A flat– B_2: B minor–G– C_2: E flat–D flat

A broadly traditional tonal scheme is present, the most remote tonalities occurring in the central sections and the final sections returning to closer relatives of the opening D flat. But the D flat acts as a point of departure rather than a structural tonic. The A flat at the end of the second section is not heard as a dominant, nor is the G flat in the penultimate section as a subdominant, even though such traditional interpretations would be likely. These tonalities are heard instead as sonorities, evoking associations from an inherited language of feeling. The G in the second section, for example, creates a fresh, open sound (albeit unpleasantly suggestive of Elgar) needed at this juncture to lead the music away from the more closed sound of the beginning. The E flat in the penultimate section recalls an E flat of the final part of Debussy's *Prélude à l'après-midi d'un faune*, a sweet nostalgic remembrance, appropriate to the closing pages of a movement.

The control of such tonal methods requires exceptional finesse and it cannot be said that Tippett had mastered them at this stage. The return to D flat at the end of the movement is perfunctory; a more conclusive effect would have been obtained by remaining in E flat. He was still searching for a genuine understanding of the structural use of tonality and had in the meantime to be content with intuitive methods.

The finale of the Quartet breaks open the closely woven textures of the adagio and is from every point of view a major contrast. In fact the contrast between the neo-romanticism of the adagio and the neo-classicism of the finale is so marked that the Quartet as a whole barely escapes the charge of being a patchwork. But it would be missing the point to regard this as the consequence of eclecticism or of failure to conceive a work in its entirety. It was rather the practical application of Tippett's compositional premise that each movement should keep to its own specific genre and that a comprehensive musical statement would emerge from the interaction between polarities.

The finale appears to be a kind of eighteenth-century rondo, three statements of a main theme separated by two episodes. The emotional temperature is relaxed and the audience, spared the need to concentrate too hard, can afterwards depart happily humming the themes, or at least fragments of them. All this holds good until it is discovered that the finale is not a rondo at all but a fugue, the appearance of the 'theme' being exposition, middle entries and final statement respectively. Why the composer juggles with the listener's expectations in this way can be answered firstly by saying that playfulness is part of the character of the movement, and that had the opening sounded like a fugue subject an intelligent audience would have responded to such apparent academicism with a sigh of dismay. A more significant answer concerns Tippett's attitude to Beethoven. If Beethoven could revitalize an apparently out-dated form like the fugue and, in particular, produce so radical a transformation of the genre as that in the finale of his Piano Sonata in A, op. 101, there was no reason why he, Tippett, should not also make the attempt to give it validity in a contemporary idiom. The fundamental answer, however, concerns Tippett's compositional need to find musical forms symbolizing singleness of emotion or of mood, as a complement to the dramatic allegro.

Tippett achieves his opening illusion in several ways. He takes advantage of the quartet medium by allotting the subject to two instruments (cello and viola) in octaves and by reinforcing this sound by the addition of the other two instruments long before the subject is complete. Thus the whole quartet is playing while only one contrapuntal 'voice' is expounded. He further subverts the expectation of a single part to a single 'voice' by introducing at strategic points semitonal dissonances in a kind of heterophony to colour the line (this a Bartók influence), giving the subject a hard edge which draws attention to its intrinsic quality rather than its function as a fugue subject. Fugue subjects are normally of one or two phrases only, the incompleteness of melodic structure appropriately generating expansion and development. Tippett's however is of four phrases, and although it is tonally open-ended, completeness of melodic structure is what initially gives it the character of a rondo theme rather than fugue subject (see Ex. 10).

The fugal exposition is relatively long, because the subject is so long. It proceeds in a traditional way, but with marked individualities. The subject itself has covered a wide tessitura and thus has already occupied the textural area that would normally have been available for the remaining 'voices'. The succeeding entries are characterized therefore by an elaboration rather than an expansion of texture. This spreads upwards from the cello part, which keeps the subject to itself in all three succeeding entries. Countersubjects preserve heterophony and the allied feature of jumping from one instrument to another, until at the final entry all the instruments are playing in a complex four-part counterpoint. Harmonically this is a large-scale presentation of the home tonality of A major, elements of its tonic, dominant and subdominant echoing that sequence of tonalities in the preceding entries. This is shown in Ex. 30 (counter-subjects are indicated by CS): the notation here is as published.

Ex. 30   String Quartet No. 1

(Ex. 30 cont.)

The two episodes, rather inconsequentially, use bitonality. In the first, for the violins, this is not disturbing, since one of the tonalities preponderates and the harmonic piquancy has a genuine structural function after the saturation of A major in the exposition. (Bitonality was suggested to Tippett by the opening scherzo in Holst's Concerto for Two Violins.) In the second, with three contrapuntal parts (though all four instruments are involved) and the consequent extension, to its limit, of the relationship between tonalities a major third apart, the sound is more confusing. On both occasions Tippett restores equilibrium by a passage based on pedal points in A major and thus does not attempt to integrate the bitonality with the prevailing harmonic language. Bitonality is used simply as a means of creating contrast. This he obviously regarded as a rather crude experiment, for bitonality does not reappear in his work until his Symphony No. 2 of twenty-two years later.

The first episode is also of interest for containing an extended addition, written after Tippett had heard Samuel Dushkin playing Stravinsky's Violin Concerto. There are no quotations from the Stravinsky, but the open-string fiddling on solo violin has an unmistakably Stravinskian ring about it, however skilfully Tippett has stitched in his interpolation. Despite these curiosities the proportions are nicely balanced, not least because of the eventual elimination of the counterpoint from two-part canon to a single part (in rhythmic augmentation with accompanying phrases) and then to a final rhythmic unison of all instruments.

Tippett's liking for fugue is naturally an indication of his liking for contrapuntal textures. It also implies a dissatisfaction with forms associated with the idea of tune and accompaniment, such as baroque dance forms or nineteenth-century music in general. Two of the most obvious features of this movement are the resistance of its themes to the role of either tune or accompaniment and their refusal to be confined by the conventional accompanimental device of a repeated rhythmic pattern. In this respect the character of the movement is conditioned by the fugal form, that is, by its basic formal metaphor. This character is however too vital to be determined by any one formal or expressive mould. What gives the movement its crucial position in Tippett's output is, as has been shown in the previous section of this chapter, its rhythmic language. This deserved some critical acknowledgement; but in the mid-1930s, when the radicalism of music was reckoned in terms of harmony more than anything else, the relatively diatonic harmony of the Quartet concealed its originality and Tippett was left unnoticed. Had he been in any doubt of the authenticity of his new language he could have changed direction and attempted some new style. But during the next four years he slowly, deliberately and in almost complete obscurity set out to consolidate his compositional gains. At the end of this period he had written only three new works (discounting the children's operas), a miserable output when measured against the popular yardstick of the prolific, untutored artist. But it was enough: one moderate work, one very good work and one work of genius. The vixen, in the fable, has lots of cubs, while the lioness has just one, a lion.

A Song of Liberty

The unpublished *A Song of Liberty* is a setting for chorus and orchestra of the final section of Blake's 'The Marriage of Heaven and Hell'. It was written in 1937 and completed on May Day – a date which points directly to the political motivation behind the work. Blake's text, an encomium upon the French Revolution (written in the heady days before the Terror), is used by Tippett as an intimation of the socialist revolution he then hoped to be near at hand. This however is less important than his decision to turn to the allegorical and symbolic vision of Blake, rather than a contemporary writer specializing in topical content, and to compose in a style of his own, rather than adapt and simplify in response to political demands, as was the practice of contemporary composers such as Eisler and Bush. By 1937 Tippett had realised that, in his own case at any rate, an appeal to a wide audience would need to be based on texts releasing deeper and more powerful sentiments than those tapped by propagandist tracts, and that an attempt to short-circuit contact with such an audience by diluting his own style would have at best only temporary advantages. These were crucial

decisions and if *A Song of Liberty* must be counted a failure, the failure, like
that of the second movement of his String Quartet No. 1, was a failure of
apparatus rather than intention.

Blake's text is in three parts: a description of the psychic process by
which revolution was born, a salute to its success ('Empire is no more!')
and a final 'Chorus' concluding with the words 'For everything that lives is
holy'. This gave Tippett a musical scheme of declamatory recitative
culminating in a fortissimo climax, and choral fugue – a kind of fantasia
and fugue in which compressed musical energy is released in soaring
intertwining contrapuntal lines. The fugue is the best section of the work,
partly because its very short text allowed the music to take wing, and partly
because Tippett invented here a combination of vocal line and decorative
instrumental support which enabled him to capitalize on his natural
lyricism and his new-found rhythmic suppleness. Example 31 illustrates a
language that was ultimately to blossom into the choruses of *The Midsummer
Marriage*.

Ex. 31   **A Song of Liberty**

The opening section is however too anonymous in character for its intended compression of musical energy to have any more than an attenuating effect, and its climax therefore sounds like a gratuitous rhetorical cliché. As a whole the section is uncomfortably reminiscent of that English style of choral writing, stemming from Parry's *Blest Pair of Sirens*, in which 'naturalness' of enunciation is a cloak to hide a lack of musical substance. However respectable its source in madrigal technique, a form composed of numerous short sections each illustrating a line of text will possess no musical necessity unless the musical ideas themselves are characteristic. Yet while such a passage as that in Ex. 32 could be accounted turgid and weighed down by the density of its verbal imagery, it can also be seen as the beginning of a choral style which will crystallize into, for example, the Scena of Part 3 of *A Child of Our Time*. What Tippett did was to isolate the functions of chorus and orchestra, and then integrate them, by giving the chorus the task of presenting the text and the orchestra that of providing a complementary gloss, in the process creating independent lines of some breadth.

Ex. 32

A Song of Liberty

A Song of Liberty can be interpreted as an autobiographical parable of how Tippett attempted to reconcile his politics with his instinctive pacifism, and of how the latter, celebrating the sanctity of life and bypassing political sentiments altogether, eventually 'defeated' the former. In musical terms, the diatonic defeated the chromatic. Although the diatonic was rapidly becoming Tippett's natural language, its victory was however an uneasy one, for the anonymity of his chromaticism left it ill-equipped to do battle on equal terms. The diatonic emerges therefore as contrast rather than consequence. The lesson of *A Song of Liberty* was not however to discard chromaticism; it was to refine it. Once Tippett had, in his next works, developed motivic techniques, chromaticism became a powerful and valuable expressive resource.

Piano Sonata No. 1

In 1936 Tippett wrote a set of variations for piano on a theme of his own. While writing *A Song of Liberty* he put them aside; subsequently he used them as the first movement of his Piano Sonata No. 1, completed in July 1938. The Sonata, as published in 1942, was originally called Fantasy Sonata, because at the time of composition Tippett accepted the view that a sonata should have a strictly classical sequence of sonata-allegro, slow movement, scherzo and finale and that his unconventional sequence of variations, slow movement, sonata-allegro and rondo-finale disqualified it from the title. By the time the 1954 edition had been published it was clear to him that the Sonata belonged to a group of works (those discussed in this chapter) which were concerned with classical structure and not at all with the idea of free fantasy. At that point he re-titled the work.[16]

Tippett's Piano Sonata No. 1 is, to quote the composer, 'the first work where the various personal stylistic ingredients are almost completely integrated'.[17] If not fully mature therefore, it is nevertheless highly individual and marks a crucial transitional stage in his development. Its transitional nature is shown, as a positive factor, by its foretaste of the bright, fresh language of his Double Concerto and, as a negative one, by Tippett's rather uncertain handling of broad design and various other structural and stylistic details. Placing the sonata-allegro third was not in truth a clear structural decision for it was forced on him by the nature of the opening movement. A dramatic allegro could not have followed the variations without creating too high a concentration of musical argument at the beginning, and it could not have been put last without demanding perhaps too much of his creative imagination at that stage. In this respect he evaded the 'finale problem'. All the same this did not affect his determination to work within classical structures.

This can be felt at the outset. The variations contain the typical ingredients of a Beethoven set, with slow variation, *minore* variation and a variation in a contrasting key. In general they suggest a miniature sonata on its own (this a reflection of the independent origin of the movement). The theme and first two variations, in which the tempo quickens and the energy is spent, are followed by a slow variation, a scherzo variation and, after a cadenza variation (having some parallels with the G-minor episode before the final variation in Beethoven's *Eroica* Symphony finale), the final variation, a restatement of the theme. In character they take the listener on a kind of world tour, both geographically and chronologically. They lead back in time from the central-European romantic tradition (variation 1) and a severely contrapuntal style recalling the baroque (variation 2) to the rapid scalic figuration of Elizabethan virginal music (variation 3). Then they return via the folk-music of Scotland (the 'scotch snaps' of variation 4) and Indonesia (variation 5) to the restatement of Tippett's theme, whose contemporary idiom and amalgam of folk (modal) and 'art' (tonal) music is now set in relief.

The theme itself is in two parts, each repeated with variation. Obvious models for Tippett's varied repeat in a traditionally bipartite structure can be found in Beethoven's Quartets opp. 127 and 131. But the real model, at least as far as the opening thematic statement is concerned, seems to have been those Elizabethan variation sets in moderately fast tempo, such as Byrd's 'Walsingham' or 'The Carman's Whistle', in which the theme is presented unaccompanied and then repeated with keyboard texture around it. Tippett's first strain is presented in octaves, like a peal of bells or a trumpet call to attention, and is then repeated in a flowing lyrical harmonization (see Ex. 15). In its first presentation the second strain begins to integrate the three elements of octaves, lyricism and harmonization by including the octaves and the lyricism; in its harmonized repeat the process is completed. It is an exquisitely balanced theme, self-contained yet inviting elaboration through its interior variation.

The most striking single feature of the movement is its rhythm (discussed on pp.102–4). The individual variation containing most promise of Tippett's subsequent rhythmic development is the second, whose two-part invertible counterpoint is so engineered that the anticipatory and 'normal' rhythms bounce off each other in a sequence of rapid impulses (Ex. 33).

Ex. 33   **Piano Sonata No. 1**

The most ambitious variation is the fifth. This attempts to re-create the sonorities of gongs in a gamelan orchestra (prompted by 78 rpm recordings of Indonesian music Tippett heard at that time) and also, through its pedalling indications, those of unusually tuned semitones. Apart from the central variation, whose stabilizing function is reflected in a ternary form without repeats, it is the only variation to disturb the basic proportions of the theme. Here the first part is not repeated and the repeat of the second is condensed. This heightens the improvisatory character of the variation and breaks the pattern in preparation for the final clinching statement – an effect not fully achieved in the original version, where the first part was repeated (though, as usual, with variation) and the second greatly extended on its first appearance. This original extension is given in Ex. 34, which was replaced by bars 11 and 12 of the printed edition.

Ex. 34   **Piano Sonata No. 1**
                                                            (original version)

(Ex. 34 cont.)

In the slow movement Tippett pursued his interest in combining folk-song with a classical style, in this case the Scottish folk-song 'Ca' the yowes' (known by the first line of the text Burns wrote for it) with the two-part keyboard invention. Conjunction of two such sharply differentiated idioms ultimately proves impossible, because they are too extreme to submit much one to another. As a result the movement is uncomfortably sectional in character. Yet Tippett's approach typifies both his compositional ambition and his preoccupation with musical symbols of reconciliation. He disguises the incongruity of style by suggesting rather than stating the folk-theme and by using its opening motif as the main motif of the invention. Doubtless one of the reasons why he chose 'Ca' the yowes' for the melodic basis of the movement was because *its* opening phrase is an inversion of that of his variations' theme. In Ex. 35 (i) the notes of the folk-theme are added in small type in order to show the degree of melodic transformation. (Tippett's method here obviously recalls Elgar's in the *Enigma Variations*, though there is no secret about Tippett's theme.) In Ex. 35 (ii) the beginning of the invention is given, and in Ex. 35 (iii) an analysis of the motivic derivations, whose severely disciplined working illustrates the extent to which Tippett concentrated on thematicism at this time. As has been remarked, his interest in thematicism was stimulated by Alan Bush, whose influence here stretched beyond the purely technical to the actual substance of the music. Example 35 (iv) demonstrates Tippett's debt to Bush.

The movement is a very simply constructed ternary form, three appearances of the folk-theme, separated by two appearances of the invention (which functions as episodic material). The semiquaver figuration of the invention flows into the accompaniment of the central statement of the folk-theme, and its imitative counterpoint is taken over in the final, quasi-canonic, statement. If these procedures cannot conceal the move-

Ex. 35

(i)

(ii)

(iii)

(iv) **Alan Bush: Prelude and Fugue op. 9** (1928)

ment's incongruity of style and the inherent difficulty in combining diatonic and chromatic idioms, they nevertheless give it a convincing expressive shape.

The third movement is a scherzo, a dynamic Beethovenian or even Chopinesque scherzo, bursting on the scene with all the exuberance of a young man celebrating his new-found strength. As the dramatic sonata-allegro it is also destined to carry the main weight of the whole work. In this respect it lacks variation of rhythmical pace and is too short to achieve its purpose wholly satisfactorily: a movement serving two almost contradictory functions was perhaps an excessively demanding prescription and Tippett never attempted it again. These remarks however are set against an ideal standard. What strikes the listener is not that the ideal is unfulfilled, but that the music is so alert. It opens, characteristically, with a gesture as opposed to a theme. This recalls the opening of Vaughan Williams's Symphony No. 4 (Vaughan Williams had by this time started to write some of his best music and Tippett's earlier judgements were moderating somewhat) and it can be heard as a product of the stark and menacing spirit of the times. Tippett does not remain in this mood for long however. It is quickly transformed into one of exhilaration and then, through a pattering transition, into one of rapt lyricism (a folk-style theme). The exhilaration erupts again. There are altogether six themes or thematic ideas.

The tonal organization contains two particular departures from the classical norm: the subtonic relationship, or modulation to the second 'fifth' in a downward cycle, at the opening, and the tritone relationships B to F and E flat to A (see Ex. 36). To move in a downward cycle at the beginning of an outgoing sonata movement is an illogical step by d'Indy's tenets. The tritone relationships, although a clear part of the composer's design, are never approached logically, and unless the E flat were chosen as the fourth 'fifth', the point of maximum 'clarté', the choice of keys seems arbitrary. However the relationships in the table below (Ex. 36) are interpreted, they do not suggest that Tippett had fully absorbed d'Indy's theories (white notes for major keys, black for minor ones).

Ex. 36   Piano Sonata No. 1

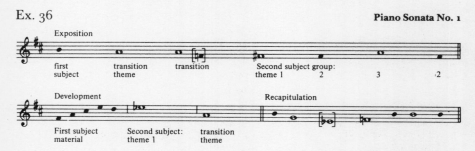

The tonal organization of the finale is also somewhat speculative. The exposition (the movement is a kind of sonata-rondo with a concerto-like 'development' section) is traditional, but the recapitulation begins in the

remote key of E flat (the fourth 'fifth' in a downward cycle) and moves to B
flat before the final statement of the theme in the tonic G. There is some
logic in moving out in an ascending cycle of fifths and returning through a
descending one. But the effect is oddly, if engagingly, precarious.

Despite these curiosities the movement's function is admirably fulfilled.
It is a classically light-weight, almost jaunty rondo, emphasizing pianistic
bravura. Its most obvious feature is its nod in the direction of jazz. The
rondo theme recalls the rhythm of the cakewalk (Ex. 37, bracket *a*), the
polyrhythms of 'secondary rag' and, notably on its appearance at the very
end of the work, blues harmonies (not to mention the cheeky pay-off line).
Though less overtly jazzy, the second theme still belongs to the same idiom
and includes more sophisticated polyrhythmic treatment in a combination
of 3/4 and 2/2. Elsewhere the musical language is decidedly European
however and if Tippett had wanted to absorb jazz within his idiom he was
as yet content merely to lay out the ingredients of such an integration.

Ex. 37   **Piano Sonata No. 1**

Tippett's piano style reflects his fondness for the toccata-like brilliance of
Domenico Scarlatti and for the clarity of line achieved by limiting
sonorities emerging from the use of the sustaining pedal to a discreet
minimum (Tippett learnt Scarlatti through the piano). The Sonata
abounds in transparent two-part textures and bare octaves. Scarlatti's
ability to spread sounds over the whole of the keyboard is also recaptured.
Tippett himself was not a good enough pianist to invent new ways of
treating the instrument and in the last analysis the keyboard layout of
every bar is derived from a particular style or composer, Scarlatti being one
of many: there are also echoes of the English virginalists, Bach, Beethoven,
Brahms, Ravel and Stravinsky. This means that there is little response to
the incidental detail of sonority characteristic of the great composer
pianists. Tippett's rather doggedly maintained textures and his evident

belief that additional resonance can be obtained by hitting the keys harder also obstructs an original piano style. The work's originality is not to be found therefore in an arresting or ingratiating pianism, nor even in Tippett's ability to keep in play the relative claims of the piano as harmonic and contrapuntal instrument (with the scales tipped in favour of the latter). It is to be found in its rhythmic language, its multiplicity of styles, and in a characteristic difficult to define but ultimately the most significant of all. Some of the Quartet and much of this Sonata conveys a spirit of confidence in the vitality of things, an almost missionary belief in the power of music to carry the listener through to an awareness of discovery and illumination. This is what gives these works their rare quality, whatever their faults; and this is the process which reaches a climax with his next work, the Concerto for Double String Orchestra.

Concerto for Double String Orchestra
Tippett started writing his Double Concerto soon after completing the Sonata, finishing it on 6 June 1939. The 'concerto' of the title refers to his interest in Handel's Concerti Grossi and in the dramatic effect of contrast, in these works, between fast and slow music and between a full sonorous body of strings and a concertino group. Apart from the fact that it is for strings, the Double Concerto seems however a far cry from Handel, until it is recognized that the work's more obvious parentage, the tradition established in Elgar's *Introduction and Allegro* (1905) and Vaughan Williams's *Fantasia on a theme of Thomas Tallis* (1910) is itself derived from Handel – Handel's eighteenth-century trio sonata concertino having been replaced by a nineteenth-century string quartet. The Elgar/Vaughan Williams tradition became a strong one, and not only for its quartet concertino; several works testify to its resilience, such as Warlock's *Capriol Suite* (1926), Bliss's *Music for Strings* (1935) and Britten's *Variations on a theme of Frank Bridge* (1937). In 1932 the tradition had been given a new impetus by the formation of the Boyd Neel Orchestra, intended initially to revive the eighteenth-century string repertory, primarily Italian. It was hardly surprising therefore that Tippett should have been drawn into the tradition, especially since with the revival of eighteenth-century music it appeared to have come full circle.

Yet his ensemble of two orchestras was an unusual one. The Vaughan Williams does contain two orchestras, but for antiphonal effects or for added weight. Tippett's orchestras do not create antiphony, in the sense of echo effects: they carry and clarify the argument. Nor are they much used for added weight since the texture is primarily contrapuntal; if one orchestra borrows a part from another or one line transfers to another this is more for practical than dramatic reasons. The relationship established between the orchestras is in fact quite different from that of the most obvious models. It is a concertante relationship, finding a close contemporary counterpart in a work well outside the English tradition, the *Music for strings* [double string orchestra], *percussion and celesta* (1936) of Bartók. It springs from the character of the opening theme. Here (see Ex. 17) two powerful three-octave lines, markedly independent of each other in rhythm, though equally distinctive in character, are presented simultaneously. They are then reversed, a process which demonstrates that neither carries a subordinate role. This immediately creates a dialectic which of its nature asks to be unfolded by two equal groups of instruments, and which in any case needs such forces if aural confusion is to be avoided. In working out this dialectic, the triple-octave texture naturally contracts from time to time and conversely the two-part counterpoint expands into three or four parts. Ten parts were available to Tippett, but in keeping with the original idea the music is usually confined to two or three. In short, the work's scoring derives largely from its musical substance and only incidentally from Tippett's response to an artistic climate.

In general design the Double Concerto, like its predecessors, is traditional – or so it seems. A concerto grosso in three movements acknowledges a debt to the Vivaldi/Bach tradition; one whose movements are, respectively, in sonata form, modified ternary form and sonata-rondo form belongs to a Beethovenian tradition. Baroque and classical traditions are not however easily fused and in this respect Tippett presents another instance of his characteristic instinct to draw new life from an amalgam of apparently incompatible elements. Formal traditions of the baroque and classical periods are not the only such oppositions. There is also an opposition of style, the continuous uniform movement of the baroque being allied with the discrete movement of the classical, to which are added folk-song elements, not to mention Tippett's own original vocabulary. The Double Concerto is an extremely lyrical work: the taut lyricism of its first movement derives from the dance, the flowing lyricism of the second from song and in the third movement there is a combination of both. Yet from this omnipresent lyricism Tippett manages to derive a motivic technique whose workings belong to the dramatic style of Beethoven.

The structural divisions of the opening sonata-allegro are not immediately obvious. The energy of the movement, the absence of the lightening effect of melodic decoration and of the conventional punctuations of rubatos and ritardandos, a motivic argument so sustained as to smooth down the edges of thematic individuality and leave instead a kind of rolling thematic cohesion – all these features combine to create the impression of a seamless whole, a single act of exultation, an alleluia. But when the focus is narrowed down a little, the standard divisions of exposition, development, recapitulation and coda (the first such in Tippett's output) fit into place clearly enough. Each of them begins with the same material, with, that is, the opening theme, which therefore acts not only as a classical 'first subject' but also as a ritornello theme in the manner of a baroque concerto.

The influence of this theme on the work as a whole is far-reaching. Its influence on the scoring has been mentioned; that on the rhythmic character has been examined in earlier pages. Here it is important to note its influence on the behaviour of the sonata-allegro. If a sonata-allegro consists of an argument between the passionate and the lyrical, the question arises as to how these two elements are to be presented. In the

Beethovenian model they appear successively. In the opening theme of the Double Concerto they appear simultaneously. By his immediate telescoping of the dramatic, *marcato* 'first subject' of orchestra 1 with the lyrical, *espressivo* 'second subject' of orchestra 2 Tippett forfeits conventional means of structural articulation. He has, as it were, played his ace in the first round and placed a high premium on his ability to alter the rules of the game as he goes along. It is not easy to describe this theme unequivocally. Certainly, it can be heard as a self-contained statement, a *fait accompli*, its tensions melting into a unified, reconciled whole. On this level Tippett's sonata-allegro conforms to the Beethovenian model only in so far as the divisions of statement (exposition), elaboration (development) and restatement (recapitulation) are archetypal and inescapable components of formal design. But the theme can be heard in another way. It is of course two themes. The jostling gravid friction between them demands that the music release, explain and grow in a way quite different from the formalized patterning suggested by the first interpretation. This in fact is what happens. The music does proceed in a dramatic way deriving from the Beethovenian model, though without the formal resource offered by conventional disposition of thematic material.

The first consequence of the initial thematic jostling is that neither theme can expand towards a fulfilment of its character because of the retracting power of the other. Both are therefore less clearly etched than they might have been and cannot be relied upon to articulate the form because they are not stable enough. Their compensating, protean virtues are however turned to advantage. Tippett uses them not so much as themes, but as a pool of eight motifs from which the material of the complete movement, and indeed the whole work, can be derived. The fundamental shapes (taken from the corresponding motifs in Ex. 17) are given in Ex. 38. Tippett treats these motifs in a variety of ways – as uncharacterized melodic motifs, as rhythmic motifs, in simple sequential repetition and in elaborate transformation. In every sense they are germinal. The first six are continually present in Exx. 17 and 19, the two examples making up the exposition of the movement. The remaining two are introduced as characteristic ingredients in the first and second sections respectively of the development. By the coda Tippett has exhausted the possibilities of linear extension of his motifs and now develops two new ones, the first a transformation of *a*, the second of *e* and f^1. The questions posed by these motifs, appearing so late and so briefly in the movement, are resolved in the next, where they become fugue subject and counter-subject.

Ex. 38   **Concerto for Double String Orchestra**

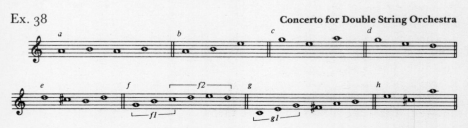

All the motifs are too short to be formally assertive on their own; but their intervallic coherence (they are variations of one another) endows them with the collective authority to carry the ear naturally into new textures, new thematic dispositions and, in particular, new gestures. Tonality obviously assumes a decisive responsibility in articulating the form, but to this must be added Tippett's use of gesture. If the motivic substance of such gesture is essentially the same, the expressive character can be wholly different. The exposition moves from concentrated vigorous polyphony to flowing, expansive monody (compare Ex. 17 with the final bars of Ex. 19): the passionate has been superseded by the lyrical. Having laid out the expressive premises of the movement, Tippett then proceeds to explore their implications. Almost immediately, at the beginning of the development, he unites the two; but the intensity thus generated proves to be so highly charged that the music rapidly breaks up into exhausted fragments. Out of this emptiness appear distant, ethereal siren calls. This is a new gesture, the psychological demands of a musical argument leading to those unexpected dimensions whose integration within abstract design creates the tensions of musical vitality. These high sounds call into being correspondingly low sounds, and out of the murky, rather Sibelian underworld slowly emerges the confident gesture of the opening theme, and the recapitulation is under way.

Apart from its function as an area in which tonal equilibrium can be established, the coda serves to accommodate the logic of a final clinching polyphonic statement. After each previous appearance of the opening theme, the complex polyphony had slowly loosened. Obviously a work based on such a theme could not be allowed to deny its pedigree and finish on a note of laxity. As a foil to the imminent dense polyphony, Tippett now creates two moments of lyrical release, the second a particularly eloquent phrase on the cellos, which seems to call attention to the import of what follows. The final section is a *tour de force* of contrapuntal ingenuity. In the table below (Ex. 39) it can be seen how the orchestras unite to form a single complex, out of which emerge two textural units, the first a network of

Ex. 39   **Concerto for Double String Orchestra**

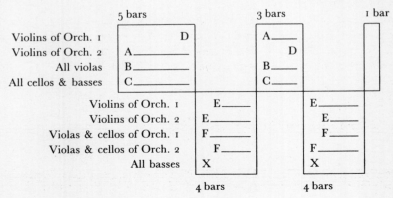

superimposed motifs, the second a kind of double canon or round whose parts exchange roles. The unbending strength of the second 'swallows up' the first, which is reduced from five bars to three and then, in the last bar, to one.

Musical gestures such as those described above and the consequent mutation of expressive meaning are the essence of the concerto. This raises intriguing questions of identity. If the 'feminine' motif e (Ex. 17) can both yield to pressure (Ex. 19, bar 11) and penetrate the texture to touch that vital nerve through which the moment of revelation is released (Ex. 19, bars 50–1) and if this vibrant yet passive moment is associated with an inversion of the 'masculine' motif a, do the terms masculine and feminine have meaning any more? Sexual analogues of this kind are frequently suggested by Tippett's music. By their questioning of received opinion they disclose not only an enlightened contemporary view of roles and behaviour but also, through persuasive reality of the music, proof of its validity.

The slow movement constitutes Tippett's last sustained attempt to integrate folk-song with classical form. As in his Piano Sonata No. 1 the folk-song model is 'Ca' the yowes', though here the tune is used as a basis for the phrase structure and only in broad terms can Tippett's theme be heard as a melodic paraphrase of the original. Melodically the theme is derived from the pool of motifs in the first movement, as Ex. 40 illustrates. Yet whatever its motivic connections and however wide its range (two octaves, and hence outside the compass of the normal human voice), its paramount feature is vocal lyricism and as such it is a calculated foil to the dance lyricism of the first movement.

Ex. 40   **Concerto for Double String Orchestra**

The 'Englishness' of this gravely beautiful theme derives in part from its harmony, especially the clash at bar 7 (which belongs to a family of dissonances stemming from Ex. 25 c), and in part, of course, from its folk-song origin. In some ways the movement sings the swan-song of twentieth-century English pastoralism (significantly, with a Scottish tune). Yet it is more than that. The intensity of the theme rapidly obliterates associations prompted by the standard folk-song setting, and lifts the music into an entirely new emotional world, having some kinship with Elgar maybe, or, more closely, with Weelkes or Dowland, but essentially one of Tippett's own. The treatment of the climax is especially characteristic. It is an impassioned, almost desperate climax, which rather than sustain the harmonic tension instead spills over on to the unexpectedly serene plateau of the triad of E major. E major is not so much part of a harmonic progression as a sound evoked for its associations with some kind of heavenly comfort (as in many other works using E major in this way – 'Comfort ye' from *Messiah*, for example, or the slow movement from Schubert's String Quintet).

Tippett's compositional problem was to find a structural scheme into which such intensity of expression could be channelled. In this context the ensuing fugato, with its contained, distanced formality, acts as a complement and not a disruption, as had tended to be the case in the slow movement of the Sonata. Nevertheless the difference between a folk-song and a neo-classic fugue is considerable and Tippett's problem remained extremely complex. Not surprisingly he used a model to help him solve it; this was the slow movement of Beethoven's String Quartet in F minor, op. 95.

Beethoven's movement begins with a simple motto theme, and then proceeds to its main idea – the juxtapositioning of a homophonic paragraph of intense, lyrical beauty with a contrapuntal paragraph (a fugato) of slighter emotional weight recalling the manners of the baroque. The rest of the movement is concerned with the integration of these apparently contradictory gestures. Tippett follows Beethoven's procedure fairly closely. Both movements are in D. Beethoven's fugato leads, after an exposition and an extended stretto episode, to the remote key of A flat, at which point the motto returns and directs the music back to the tonic for a counter-exposition, when the subject now appears with a new counter-subject. Tippett's fugato consists of an exposition only, leading to a brief return of his motto idea and then a counter-exposition. At this point Tippett echoes Beethoven's tonal scheme: his counter-exposition begins in A flat (minor). It likewise has a new counter-subject, bearing in fact a close resemblance to Beethoven's original counter-subject, while at the same time being a variation of Tippett's own first one. Example 41(i) gives Tippett's subject with both counter-subjects. Example 41(ii) gives Beethoven's subject and original counter-subject. (The example also illustrates Tippett's motivic working: motif *j* is a transformation of the first new theme in the coda of the first movement, motif *k* a transformation of the second, and motif *l* is from the motto theme of this movement.)

Ex. 41

(i) **Concerto for Double String Orchestra**

(ii) **Beethoven: String Quartet op. 95**

[Allegretto]

Beethoven's counter-exposition is the start of an extended process by which his fugue subject is gradually eliminated. Firstly, its identity is obscured by successively closer points of entry. A disorientating pattern of inversion and *recte* further questions its identity, and then its limbs are systematically dismantled so that eventually only one interval and finally only one rhythm is left. The rather anonymous motto theme ushers in a return of the lyric theme, greatly expanded because it now does not need to accommodate itself to a non-existent fugue subject. Beethoven's process therefore is not of integration at all: it is of liquidation. Tippett's temperament is not so extreme. At the risk of leaving his tensions not fully resolved he does attempt to integrate his material. His counter-exposition proceeds by *recte* and inversion, as in Beethoven, but without the obscuring effect of accumulated stretto nor the systematic dismantling of the subject. In fact the climax of the movement is marked by the appearance of the complete fugue subject plus an extended treatment of the lyrical motto theme, as if, by preservation of the lyric, he intends to demonstrate the common intensity of feeling in all three thematic ideas.

In Beethoven's final paragraph his fugato subject does make a fleeting reappearance, but only as a submerged echo, as if to demonstrate that it no longer has any influence. The second half of his theme now flowers into such pure lyricism that at the end it needs the release of a miniature cadenza. In Tippett the fugato subject reappears at exactly the same place, but as a self-contained event ushering in what initially sounds like a new development. It is only when this section alights on the central cadence of the main theme and then continues, as in Beethoven, to an expansion of its second half, complete with miniature cadenza, that it can be heard retrospectively as part of one final paragraph.

If Tippett's eventual thematic alliance is an uneasy one, this is chiefly because the structure of a folk-theme is self-sufficient and resists that moulding of contour demanded by a dialectical formal scheme. As an instance of abstract musical logic, the movement is not wholly convincing. Yet as an expressive metaphor of the need to integrate, however imperfectly, it is powerful and moving precisely because of its limitations.

To have dismissed the slow movement as if it had never happened would have required a Beethovenian ruthlessness foreign to Tippett. At the opening of the finale, he avoids the self-confident gesture concerned only with itself. Instead he ushers in a group of motifs, all bright and alert as befits a finale, but fragmentary and not assuming the stability of a decisive statement until twenty bars have elapsed. At this point a bold theme is announced *fortissimo*. The rondo theme of the movement is, therefore, two themes, and the relatively loose construction of the movement as a whole is foreshadowed by the subdominant, relaxed relationship of the second theme (see Ex. 42).

Ex. 42   **Concerto for Double String Orchestra**

Ex. 43   **Concerto for Double String Orchestra**

The second subject (Ex. 43(i)) is one of Tippett's most entrancing melodies, at once so simple as to appear a natural and unquestioned part of the language of music and at the same time fleeting and elusive – despite its exquisitely arched shape slipping out of reach once an attempt is made to capture and define it. It appears only twice in the movement, here and in the recapitulation, but its influence is crucial, for without it Tippett could not have justified the work's most individual formal feature, a lyrical coda embodying an entirely new theme (Ex. 43(ii)). The new theme derives motivically and in spirit from the folk-theme of the second movement, in which respect it serves to clinch the integration of 'folk' and 'art' music in the Concerto as a whole (and, with its Scotch snaps, to clinch Tippett's internationalism in the matter of folk-music). If its novelty is somewhat diluted by these considerations, it remains a new theme nonetheless and what clinches that is its C-major tonality, a sound barely touched on before and one whose remarkable expressive effect in this context provides the most conclusive evidence of how Tippett, with his Double Concerto, finally acquired a secure and imaginative command of tonal organization – or, in other words, of how he adapted d'Indy's theories to his own purposes.

His methods are at their clearest in the first movement. The modality of the A to G relationship in the exposition shows that he was not to be a blind follower of d'Indy, for the effect of this second 'fifth' in a downward cycle, theoretically one of, let us say, 'incidental darkening' of the emotional climate, is in fact of sunny release. If the nature of the musical idea (the A/ G relationship in the opening theme) challenges the theories then the theories will be ignored. Over the extended span of the rest of the movement, however, Tippett strongly endorses them. The table (Ex. 44) sets out the principal tonalities.

Ex. 44   **Concerto for Double String Orchestra**

Despite the G, the music is wrenched to E, the classical dominant, for the beginning of the development. The first part of this is a rapid course to C sharp, the fourth 'fifth' ascending and the relationship of maximum brilliance. The music at this point is indeed brilliant. Tippett then dramatically switches to the opposite pole, to F minor, the fourth 'fifth' descending, and the point of maximum darkness. He continues the descending cycle until he reaches the sixth 'fifth', E flat minor (fig. 6, miniature score). This is the point of greatest ambiguity, and Tippett signals the fact by paying an irrelevant, almost Haydnesque call to the threshold of the tonic, before returning to the tonal progress of the movement as a whole. The next step in a descending cycle is A flat; the next step in an ascending cycle (after C sharp, the last one reached) is also A flat. The logic of Tippett's position is unassailable. This fifth 'fifth' ascending and seventh 'fifth' descending is, in d'Indy's terms and

Tippett's, again ambiguous and the music now underlines the point with a long passage in whole-tone harmonies which effectively obscures any sense of key and leaves the way open for the recapitulation. The coda uses up the remaining important relationships – the third 'fifth' ascending, F sharp, and the third 'fifth' descending, C – and the movement is complete. It offers a textbook illustration of the structural and dramatic use of functional tonality.

Having put d'Indy's ideas to the test Tippett never lost sight of them. They proved to offer scope for an infinite variety of expressive content. As well as the seriously argued, the playful, for example, could find a place – as is shown in the finale. The movement begins in D, and its double theme is in D–G. At its second appearance, the beginning of the development, it is in E–A, the next pair of keys in an ascending cycle. In its final appearance, at the recapitulation, it is at the furthest point in the cycle (short of being ambiguous), C sharp–F sharp. The second subject appears first at the furthest distance from D, in A flat. When it returns in the recapitulation, it is in B flat, two steps towards 'home' in a descending cycle. At the next structural point of lyricism, in the coda, the music has gone two further steps, into C, in which tonality the movement ends. Thus while the rondo theme starts at a point of neutrality and reaches out towards a position of maximum brilliance, the second subject starts at the point of maximum warmth (d'Indy's 'darkness' does not describe the effect of the music) and returns to the security of 'home'. The two themes move in diametrically opposite directions. What prevents this tonal organism from spinning out of sight is the stabilizing influence of, paradoxically, the development section, which is in the same key for most of its duration. The key in question, A, serves a double function, for it also creates a long-range sense of balance by recalling the tonality of the first movement.

However effective these tonal manipulations, the most individual feature of the movement remains the use of C major at the end, the tonality appearing not simply because it fits in the scheme outlined above but because Tippett wanted to conclude the work with a broad, out-going sonority having something of the quality of an apotheosis. This he achieved by using the harmonic colouring of a tonality inseparably associated with such ideas. To use tonalities for their expressive properties has remained one of Tippett's most characteristic techniques. The coda of the Double Concerto was, at the time, the boldest and most emphatic vindication of it.

Apart from this use of harmonic colouring, the techniques described above are perhaps of greater interest for what Tippett does with them than for what they are. With rhythm however the situation is different. In the Double Concerto his characteristic rhythmic polyphony appears in mature form for the first time, as does his assimilation of the jazz-influenced anticipatory rhythm (see pp. 100–101). The crucial influence of jazz on this work is not however to be limited to one component of rhythmic vocabulary. The real parallel is found in an interplay between an underlying metre and rhythms continually leaping away from it. Because this is so pervasive, Tippett here discloses a more profound sympathy with the spirit of jazz than any other 'serious' composer – apart perhaps from Carter, and from the special case of Gershwin. This may seem an extreme remark. In justification, it should be noted that those who have been influenced by jazz – Ravel, Stravinsky, Milhaud, Krenek, Martinů, Copland – were content to add a few colourful items of vocabulary to a language which otherwise remained untouched. The only other composer who made serious use of jazz was Weill, not so much in his instrumentation or his foxtrot rhythms, as in his elevation of the monotonous steady metre to the status of a compositional principle, against which all manner of harmonic, melodic and formal masterstrokes could be set. In real jazz, however, there is an attempt, never quite fulfilled, to break away from the gravitational pull of the steady metre. This renders Weill's use of it one-sided, if not negative. Tippett creates an inclusive synthesis, by preserving a counterpoint between the metre and the attempt to transcend it.

Tippett's metrical basis is of course not overt: he alters the equal relationship, in jazz, between metre and rhythm to one in favour of rhythm. Nor are the techniques by which metre is transcended primarily derived from jazz. Yet if these are important differences, on another level they establish an identity. Jazz itself is a synthesis of African and European music: Tippett's music is compounded of similarly diverse elements used creatively to make something new. When, in the first movement of the Double Concerto, with only the most delicate reminders of the basic 2/2 and with an extremely allusive use of functional harmonic progression, Tippett creates a sense of being carried along without 'visible' support, of being airborne, of being part of a continual dance, he is using jazz to contribute to a philosophy. The drabness of life, symbolized by the steady metre, can be overcome, if it is used as one part of an opposition engendering vitality, energy, even exhilaration.

The Double Concerto's extraordinarily sustained expression of the energy and constructive potential in the human soul singles it out as exceptional by any standard, and especially so when considered against the time of its composition. Tippett was acutely aware of the political situation in Europe in the late 1930s. Yet his Concerto seems to profess a wilful indifference to it. To his first small audience it perhaps did not matter much whether his music made a contemporary statement or not; but for Tippett this music represented what in retrospect can be seen as an article of faith. Art should not mirror its times. It should offer a compensation, a symbol of what might be aspired to rather than what is. In this respect Tippett belongs to a Beethovenian tradition far removed from much contemporary music of the 1930s, which although also indisputably cheerful in aspect wore its cheerfulness as a bright article of clothing to be put on or put aside at will. Stravinsky's Concerto in E flat, *Dumbarton Oaks*, (1938) is a case in point of a work set forth ready-made, with little interior indication of what human forces prompted its making. The difference between such a work and Tippett's Double Concerto is that Tippett's assurance is audibly earned. It has been reached both on an objective level, through a process of taut and lucid argument, and on a subjective level, through his willingness to face those dark areas of experience which could have turned the Concerto's character into one of resignation. 'And that', as Helen in Forster's *Howards End* reasoned of Beethoven's Fifth Symphony, 'is why one can trust Beethoven when he says other things.'

A Child of Our Time

Historical Background

Tippett's first ideas for what eventually became *A Child of Our Time* were unconnected with the specific historical events upon which the work is actually based. They gathered around a general desire to give artistic shape to a complex of ill-defined but essentially compassionate emotions deriving from his reactions to the 1914–18 war, and from his feelings towards the socially deprived or exploited. The central concept emerging from these emotions was of rejection, and of the figure of the outcast or scapegoat upon whom such rejection is projected and through whom it ostensibly is justified. His own schooldays had made him peculiarly sensitive to such issues. After he had seen the effects of unemployment in North Yorkshire and London in the early 1930s they became more sharply focused. At this time his feelings were as much of anger as of compassion. Still believing that political action could bring about social reform he looked for a dramatic subject which could stimulate such reform through the immediacy of its presentation. His first plan therefore was for an opera. A possible subject was mooted in conversations with Charlotte Despard, his elderly cousin who was now, in her nineties, a supporter of Sinn Fein, the left-wing republican party in Ireland. The subject was of the Easter Rising, the rebellion in Dublin in April 1916 after which fifteen Sinn Fein leaders were shot by the British for their part in the attempt to bring home rule to Ireland. Tippett thought it could exemplify the merciless fight of capitalism to retain authority and, in the Sinn Fein martyrs, present resonant and contemporary scapegoat figures. Easter symbolism could also be used to postulate hope for a new springtime. He studied a great deal of Irish history before considering a scenario. Difficulties arose as soon as he had envisaged his opening scene, a committee meeting of republicans. What would they be doing? He put the problem to Jeffrey Mark, a close friend at that time. Mark thought that they would be drinking from a large whisky bottle. Tippett thereupon accepted that the whole project was artless and unworkable; the plan for an opera collapsed.

The plan for a dramatic work remained however and through the stimulus of Mark came to fruition in the play *War Ramp* of 1935. As has been noted, this play posed more questions than it answered and obliged Tippett to recognize that potentially pacifist beliefs would have to be reconciled with his social and political conscience. But it did have a negative value, by making him realise that what he wanted to express was too complex for dramatic treatment in an opera and that his ideas would need the framework of oratorio for presentation and discussion. This in turn suggested a work in the tradition of the passions, where his concept of the scapegoat would find an appropriate place and where a narrative is related not as a stimulus for dramatic action but simply in order that the moral implications arising from it can be considered. This new project lay dormant for three years, partly because he was then engaged in fashioning his musical style in other works, and partly because he could not conceive a meaningful subject in times overshadowed by the rise of Nazism.

But in late 1938 a rapid sequence of events gave shape to his original ideas. The outcome of the Munich conference in September would inevitably, as he saw it, be war; with the November pogrom in Germany and Austria a virtual state of war already existed, history having overtaken what hopes there might have been for reconciliation. The shock of the pogrom and the personal tragedy of Herschel Grynspan, the seventeen-year-old Jewish boy whose assassination of a Nazi diplomat in Paris precipitated the brutality, was so powerful that Tippett immediately found his emotions had crystallized into a clear picture of an oratorio based on these particular events.

The title of the work emerged as an indirect result of his listening to a BBC broadcast of Berlioz's *L'Enfance du Christ* (which he loved) on Christmas day that year. Tippett found himself musing on why it was that the once universally accepted image of the Christ-child seemed to have lost its emotional power,[18] and following this train of thought, he bought a copy of the 1938 English translation of *Ein Kind unserer Zeit*,[19] the last novel of the German-Hungarian writer Ödon von Horvath. Apart from giving him the title of the oratorio, Horvath's brilliant and frightening book[20] provided a remarkable parallel with the fate of Grynspan.

It is the story of a young Nazi soldier whose illusions gradually disintegrate, after he discovers that the captain he had tried to rescue was not dying a heroic death but committing suicide ('we are no longer soldiers, but wretched robbers, cowardly murderers') and after he has been invalided out of the army on a pitifully inadequate pension. He tries to find the girl he has fallen in love with but never spoken to. But she has lost her job, for becoming pregnant by another soldier now dead, has been put in desperate financial straits, and has obtained an abortion for which she has been imprisoned. His bitterness suddenly overrules him and he murders a representative of her employers, an aged small-time accountant. Two days later the nameless, deranged soldier lies in the snow, frozen to death.

Horvath's story confirmed that Tippett's central concept of the scapegoat was part of an age-old recurring pattern in human existence. Although prompted by contemporary events, the oratorio would have therefore more than documentary relevance. It would be a kind of modern passion, in which the scapegoat does not die voluntarily but instead acts violently and pointlessly, vainly trying to match himself against the 'man of destiny', the Hitler, Caesar, or other faceless adversary. It would ask what happens when acts of apparently righteous indignation end in catastrophe.

When Tippett first read about Grynspan and the ensuing Nazi pogrom (in newspapers and, particularly, in the magazine *Picture Post* of 26

November 1938), the essential if not the complete picture was clear. The principal historical facts are given below.[21] It is doubtful if a complete account of Grynspan's life will ever be made.[22]

On 31 October 1938 a Polish government law was due to take effect, by which Polish passport holders living abroad for more than five years would not be re-admitted into the country without a special visa. The law was designed to relieve Poland of the problem of repatriating the thousands of Jews of Polish origin living in Germany and Austria, a problem which Nazi anti-semitism gave her every reason to expect and which she was not prepared to deal with. The Nazis retaliated by informing the Polish Government that Polish Jews would be expelled from Germany unless they were allowed to return to Poland at any time without the special visa. This the Poles refused to do on the grounds that they could not absorb large numbers of people in a short space of time. In order to pre-empt the Polish law, the Gestapo was ordered on 27 October to arrest 15,000 Jews and take them to the Polish frontier. This was done with savage precision. A number did manage to escape into Poland, but by 6 November there were still nearly 6,000 at the frontier station of Zbonszyn (near Poznan), stranded without possessions, with little hope of any livelihood in Poland even if they were able to get there, some living without shelter, some in tents, barns or stables. Many died, committed suicide, were driven insane or afflicted with disease. The Polish government refused to admit these 'stateless' citizens, who could speak only German. Eventually, at the end of January 1939, the Nazis agreed to allow them to return to Germany to sort out their affairs, where it was said their money could be banked and transferred to Poland. A small number of these refugees were admitted to Britain and the USA.

Herschel Grynspan was the son of a Polish Jew who had settled in Germany before the First World War. Grynspan left his native Hanover in 1936, intending to emigrate to Palestine. But in fact he went to Paris, living there with an uncle and aunt. In August 1938 he was served with an expulsion order by the French authorities because he did not possess a residence permit, and from that date his uncle sheltered him illegally. On 3 November he received a postcard from his sister telling him of his family's arrest and deportation, and of their suffering on the Polish frontier. Four days later, on 7 November, Grynspan bought a revolver and walked in to the German Embassy in Paris, asking to see the first secretary. He was shown in to the third secretary, Ernst vom Rath. He protested about the treatment of Jews at the Polish frontier and then fired five shots, two of which hit vom Rath. Grynspan made no attempt to escape.

On the following day Jewish newspapers in Germany were ordered to stop publication and anti-Semitic demonstrations began. Vom Rath died the day after that. The Nazis used the assassination as the pretext to unleash a pogrom of unparalleled brutality: those who survived it experienced a trauma so deep that they could remember its details only with the greatest difficulty. On that night – the infamous Crystal Night of 9 November, so-called by the Nazis because of the acres of broken glass lying in German cities the following morning – there were thousands of arrests and beatings all over Germany and Austria, synagogues were burned, some people were stoned to death, shops were attacked and plundered. Goebbels, on announcing the 'justified and understandable indignation of the German people', then ordered the violence to stop. But the arrests continued. The Jewish community was told to pay £83m, insurance claims and passports were confiscated, students expelled from universities and children from schools, and Jews were ordered to repair and pay for property damage.

The composer who attempts to transmute such blind collective sadism into a work of art can be charged with a kind of blasphemy; and indeed the English are peculiarly vulnerable to it, having little first-hand experience against which to measure delicacy of feeling. Yet to do nothing can equally invoke censure. No creative artist worthy of the name will avoid a subject because treating it might appear hubristic, tasteless or naïve. In writing his oratorio Tippett was following the conviction that a composer has a moral responsibility to address himself to the problems of his time. The question therefore was not whether the work should be written, but how it should be written, from what standpoint and in what style. In this Tippett had already taken the fundamental decision, which was to avoid specific reference to the historical events and to make it general and universal. The Grynspan story would be considered as both representative of the contemporary situation and of an archetypal pattern in human existence. And of course music's capacity to illuminate the deeper levels of common humanity would be used hopefully to induce the instinct to heal and close divisions. In this way *A Child of Our Time*, though of quite different emotional temperature, would adhere to the philosophy exemplified in the Double Concerto – that art should offer an aspiration, a compensation, and not rest content with an impassive reflection of its subject.

The Text in General
After having planned the broad shape and character of his work Tippett asked T.S. Eliot to write the text.[23] Eliot was a natural choice for Tippett, since he both greatly admired the poet's work and also had reason to expect that Eliot would find the writing of an oratorio text congenial. The two had recently spent some time together discussing music, which was Eliot's second interest, and verse drama. More pertinently, discussions had centred on Eliot's ideas about stage works which mixed several arts – play, opera, ballet – and on his perception that the three ingredients of dramatic action, music and gesture would be in a particular order of priority according to the genre. Thus, in the play the order would be dramatic action, gesture, music; in opera, music, dramatic action, gesture; in ballet, gesture, music, dramatic action. These simple but decisive distinctions profoundly influenced Tippett's own thinking, especially on the making of opera. As far as oratorio was concerned, Eliot's principle could presumably have been applied to produce a hierarchy of music, text and, a distant

third, drama. In any event, when agreeing to Tippett's request, Eliot obviously understood that the text writer would be in a subordinate position, for he asked that his part be spelt out for him. He wanted a precise scheme of musical numbers and the quantity and quality of the words to go with them. Tippett then prepared a careful typescript of what at the time was headed 'Sketch for a Modern Oratorio'[24] (although within it was already contained the phrase 'the child of our time' and an indication that this might be the title).

Apart from the musical scheme, this included his own suggestions for a text, invented or borrowed, along with accompanying explanations of his intentions. Eliot considered the 'Sketch' for some weeks, and then gave the unexpected advice that Tippett should complete it himself, for it was already a text in embryo. Also, 'Anything I add to it will stand out a mile as so much better poetry.'[25] Since, however, the music would for the most part dominate the words, whatever 'poetry' Eliot might contribute would be obliterated and irrelevant, or at best obtrusive. Eliot also advised Tippett not to 'let the poets loose on your librettos; because they are going to do with the words what your music should do.' He should use extremely simple, familiar words, like those in the Bible. Unless Eliot, the famous poet, was glad to be relieved of the responsibility of working with a virtually unknown composer or was uneasy about associating himself with the deeply Jungian influences in the 'Sketch', his advice must have been based on the judgement that Tippett had both sufficient literary skill to construct his own texts and such certainty of verbal intention, or in other words, such certainty of musical intention, that no one else would be able to fulfil his wishes as effectively as the composer himself. If mildly flattering, the advice was practical and realistic; from that time, Tippett has always written his own texts for major choral and operatic works.

In the 'Sketch' he had exemplified many of Eliot's precepts without prompting, by instinctively using a language of simple, pithy statement and by adapting what he already knew rather than writing something professedly original. For the first chorus, for example, he had, as he explained to Eliot, been thinking of these lines from Wilfred Owen's early poem, *The Seed*:

> War broke. And now the winter of the world
> With perishing great darkness closes in.

His own idea for a text used Owen's seasonal symbolism and the very short sentence, and added a new element, deriving both from Jung's conception of the 'shadow' or the dark side in the human psyche and from a haunting visual picture of the earth turning in space, from the film *The Green Pastures*.

> The world turns on its dark side.
> It is winter.

The language is very simple, even oversimple as Tippett himself has described it; but it resonates and allows for an expanding as opposed to a circumscribed image. The definitive text begins exactly as given above.

By adapting Owen in this way Tippett was acknowledging an aesthetic attitude very close to that of Eliot, by which the urgency, vividness or passion in a creative artist's expression is given power and coherence through its connection with a continuing artistic tradition and its adherence to a firm structural basis. This acknowledgement is made explicit in the motto of the oratorio, a half-line from the final chorus of Eliot's *Murder in the Cathedral*, 'the darkness declares the glory of light'. Here Eliot twists and re-fashions 'The heavens declare the glory of God' from Psalm 19 in such a way as to postulate both the unchanging nature of human experience in an apparently chaotic world and his own contemporary theology that the existence of God can be proved by the existence of evil. Tippett, as can be seen with hindsight, takes Eliot several stages further by ignoring the theology altogether and using the half-line to express the psychological premise that darkness and light are not corollaries but one and indivisible.

Elsewhere, direct allusions to Eliot are few, but those that can be identified are striking. 'The garden lies beyond the desert', from the Scena in Part 2 of the oratorio, recalls a similar image in the fifth section of *Ash Wednesday*. In the penultimate section of the work Tippett stands an Eliot line on its head. The central chorus of Part 1 of *Murder in the Cathedral* begins with a reference to Hebrews 13:14:

Here is no continuing city, here is no abiding stay.

The Tippett line reads:

Here is no final grieving, but an abiding hope.

And one of the least felicitous of Tippett's lines, 'I am caught between my desires and their frustrations as between the hammer and the anvil', from the tenor solo in Part 1 of the oratorio, is, ironically, an echo from a sentence by the Third Priest in Part 1 of the same Eliot play:

What peace can be found
To grow between the hammer and the anvil?

Allusions to or borrowings from other contemporary poets are, as far as can be ascertained, limited to such remote correspondences as 'A terrible beauty is born' from Yeats's *Easter 1916* with 'A curse is born . . . They took a terrible vengeance' from the beginning and end of the Scena in Part 2 of the oratorio. For the most part Tippett's language takes its cue from the rich variety of image in the spirituals – biblical, poetic and homely. Some criticism has been levelled, and by the composer himself, at the rather pretentious confusion of abstract and concrete in such lines as the 'hammer and anvil' cited above. But these are rare and in general the text is direct and evocative. If difficulties arise they are not with the words as such but with the highly compressed philosophical and psychological ideas they frequently embody. Most of such ideas stem from Tippett's interest in the writings of Jung.

Jung believed that the unconscious part of the human mind can be divided into two components: the personal and the collective. The personal unconscious is that whose contents were at one time conscious and are now forgotten or repressed. The contents of the collective unconscious lie much deeper. They were at no time conscious and the individual has no part in their acquisition. He inherits them. They are a repository of the accumulated experience of mankind over thousands of years. They represent powerful forces which when activated in some way can cause both noble and humane behaviour and violent and irrational behaviour in individuals or societies. In as far as they are unconscious they cannot be fully known; their form appears to be literally incomprehensible to the human mind. Yet something of their nature can be revealed through symbols – as in dreams in particular and also in religious experience, myths, works of art. Here the contents of the collective unconscious assume perceptible symbolic forms, whether sensual, visual or verbal. We may also add musical, though Jung himself was curiously reticent about music.[26] By identifying and interpreting such forms, especially those which could not possibly have been created exclusively from personal experience, Jung was able to offer a basis for an understanding of human behaviour.

The concept of the collective unconscious has met with considerable scepticism: anything can apparently be demonstrated by anything and amateur psychologists can frolic in waters far distant from the prickly ground of real psychology. Jung's thesis makes the uncomfortable proposition that facts and intuitions are interdependent. To the creative artist however it at once gives authority to the idea that if he wishes to address a wide audience he will be better equipped to do so by acknowledging the collective unconscious. When asserting that 'the composition of oratorio or opera is a collective as well as a personal experience',[27] Tippett was expressing precisely this view. Most successful composers of large-scale 'public' works, such as oratorios, have presumably fashioned their styles instinctively to such views without giving a thought to the collective unconscious, even if they had heard of it or, in the case of earlier composers, of more poetic formulations of the same concept. Tippett on the other hand had already made a study of Jung, for private non-musical reasons, and had found that Jung illuminated not only personal emotional problems, but a wide range of philosophical, social and artistic matters in addition. To a self-conscious artist such as Tippett, one moreover inescapably bound to the prevailing neo-classic aesthetic that the intellect and not only the feelings should be *heard* to contribute to the making of music, there was no reason why such insights should not nourish his creative work as well as his private life.

Jung called the sources of the symbolic forms mentioned above archetypes. For the most part he regarded these as personifications, in that the majority reveal themselves to consciousness as recognizable if not necessarily known human or near human beings. He called them 'self-portraits of the instincts'.[28] One such archetype is the 'shadow'. Jung's views on whether the shadow is a personal or a collective figure varied somewhat but eventually settled in favour of both, with the collective taking the decisive part. The shadow therefore represents the unconscious as a whole. It is 'that hidden, repressed, for the most part inferior and guilt-laden personality whose ultimate ramifications reach back into the realm of our animal ancestors and so comprise the whole historical aspect of the unconscious'.[29] Since it embodies those aspects of personality most individuals refuse to accept, it is frequently projected on to someone else. Familiar shadow figures in literature are Caliban and Mephistopheles. The simple message of Jung's work was that a balanced, mature and integrated personality could be achieved only if such archetypes of the collective unconscious are recognized and accommodated to the complementary needs of the conscious mind. This could be taken further. In 1937 he wrote, apropos the ugly political tensions in Europe:

> Such problems are never solved by legislation or by tricks. They are solved only by a general change of attitude. And the change does not begin with propaganda and mass meetings, or with violence. It begins with a change in individuals. It will continue as a transformation of their personal likes and dislikes, of their outlook on life and of their values, and only the accumulation of these individual changes will produce a collective solution.[30]

Jung believed therefore that the only hope for a peaceful Europe was that the problems should be tackled at source, and individuals become more tolerant and compassionate through an understanding of their unconscious minds – from every standpoint an illusory and impossible ideal but in the face of impending catastrophe one with the force of emotional necessity. Tippett believed essentially the same thing. In 1944, when the catastrophe ('possible because everyone is able in entire unconsciousness to project his inferior side on to the enemy')[31] had been a reality for several years, he echoed Jung's sentiments in the following terms: 'The only concept we can place over against the fact of divided man is the idea of the whole man.'[32] But his crucial formulation of this idea (crucial, in that it was the result of personal experience) had already been made in the text of *A Child of Our Time*. Here, in the penultimate section of the work, headed General Ensemble, the formulation is more poetic and at the same time more Jungian.

> I would know my shadow and my light,
> so shall I at last be whole.
> Then courage, brother, dare the grave passage.

'Shadow', as explained, refers to the unconscious; 'light', though not used by Jung as a technical term meaning the rational conscious mind, nevertheless 'always refers to consciousness'.[33] With 'the grave passage' Tippett used his own imagery to describe a journey into the unconscious.

These lines are of great significance to Tippett. Not only do they express metaphysical beliefs; they also postulate a music deriving its character from the tension of opposites – precisely the music he had already been writing and was to continue to write. Twenty-five years later he was still underlining their significance. They are the 'ground bass, the credo; all my more elaborate dramatic works are an exploration of [their] meaning. It is the only truth I shall ever say.'[34] A decade after that he was more circumspect: 'I hold it to be just possible for individuals, but impossible for collectives in our present climate of self-righteousness; of groups, societies, nations.'[35] If his later works seem to dissociate themselves from the conviction with which the belief had previously been sustained, they nevertheless continue to endorse its essentials, as can be heard in, for example, the endings of his Third and Fourth Symphonies.

As a postscript to the above it may be noted that while the burden of these lines is philosophical Tippett at the same time continues, Eliot-like, to weave additional strands into them. In the oratorio they are followed by the final spiritual, 'Deep River'. The title and substance of this derive from the closing pages of the first part of Bunyan's *Pilgrim's Progress*, in which Christian and Hopeful have to cross a deep river before entering the celestial city. In this ordeal Christian is encouraged by Hopeful's exhortation: 'Be of good cheer. Jesus Christ maketh thee whole.' With Tippett the inference is that Jesus Christ can accomplish nothing of the kind. But the metaphor is retained, that wholeness may be achieved after a new baptism, a 'grave passage'. 'Brother', incidentally, is the mode of address between Hopeful and Christian as well as between members of left-wing political organizations, a reference Tippett at the time of the oratorio presumably still endorsed. It also indicates that the soloists have left their metaphysical or dramatic roles and reached a position of equality among themselves.

The Text in Detail
When preparing for his performances of *Messiah* in 1931, Tippett made a close study of Handel's oratorio and discovered that its tripartite shape embodied three basic formal and dramatic functions: the first part is prophetic and preparatory, the second narrative and epic (from the birth of Christ to the world's end), the third meditative and metaphysical. Tippett particularly admired this scheme and adopted it for *A Child of Our Time*. Here the first part is concerned with the general state of oppression, the second with the actual historical events, the third with meditation and interpretation. This scheme creates a kind of mirror form, moving from the general to the particular and then back to the general again. The individual parts reflect this on a smaller scale, by beginning with the cosmological, gradually narrowing the focus down to the human (in Part 1, representa-

tive man and woman, in Part 2, the individual, in Part 3, humanity in general) and then opening out to the universal.

In its detailed patterning the work embodies another tradition, that of the Bach Passions. The distinguishing feature of the Lutheran passion is of course the congregational chorale. Tippett wanted to include this as well, because it was precisely through the chorale, or something like it, that he could make contact with deep-seated collective responses. He needed a style with the quality of a vernacular. Though in some ways well suited to such a purpose the chorale was however an anachronism in a period suspicious of the protestant ethic and caught up in political tensions far removed from those of Bach's time. Furthermore Tippett wanted to speak to the atheist, agnostic or Jew, as well as the Christian. After rejecting such alternatives as folk-songs and Jewish hymns, because they like the chorale were also exclusive, he finally decided to use negro spirituals. He lit on this imaginative solution in an unexpected way, hearing a black singer on the radio singing the spiritual 'Steal away' and being suddenly aware, at the phrase 'the trumpet sounds within-a my soul', of being moved by something far deeper than the spiritual appeared to deserve as tune or text. The spiritual epitomized a fundamental emotional experience, not limited to oppressed blacks in nineteenth-century America but understood everywhere. Having settled on the contemporary equivalent of the chorale, Tippett obtained a collection of spirituals from New York[36] and found that there were spirituals for every situation he needed.

This was the stage he had reached when he asked Eliot to collaborate. He had conceived a complete musical scheme along with some preliminary ideas for the text. When writing his own therefore, he knew precisely which musical forms his words would need to match.

The oratorio begins with a three-part opening section, which Tippett has compared with the Prologue in Heaven near the beginning of Goethe's *Faust*, Part 1.[37] The first chorus paints a broad picture of the world in darkness. As in the *Faust* scene, where Mephistopheles's mission is explained and with it the nature of the play to be enacted, there follows an aria in which the alto solo, as 'personification of the soul',[38] puts forward Tippett's diagnosis of the situation and the nature of the discussion to follow. (An attempted explanation of the 'soul', another important Jungian term, is deferred until the corresponding alto aria in Part 3 of the oratorio, in which, unlike the present aria, the term is crucial to the sense of the words.) Tippett calls this aria 'The Argument', borrowing the heading from Blake.

> Man has measured the heavens with a telescope, driven the gods from
>   their thrones.
> But the soul, watching the chaotic mirror, knows that the gods return.
> Truly, the living god consumes within and turns the flesh to cancer!

Man has acquired great technological skill through the exercise of rational scientific values. But he has overemphasized their importance and ignored or suppressed awareness of the unconscious (Greek gods are personifications of Jung's archetypes). The unconscious will inevitably reassert itself with far more destructive or corrosive power than would have been so had it been accepted and accommodated.

But as well as destroy and debase, the awesome qualities of the unconscious can illuminate and compensate. This is a frequent theme in Tippett's writings. Much of *Moving into Aquarius* is concerned with an extension of it – that music, as carrier of archetypal images, should be accorded a social status consistent with its function as a corrective to the dehumanizing advance of technology. It is a beguiling and ultimately irrefutable thesis. Yet at the same time it is simplistic and arrogant, for what interest, other than academic, can it have for those trapped by the realities of political oppression? In a way Tippett concedes this, as the following Scena illustrates, with its disorientating alternation of desperate questions from the chorus and elliptical answers from the alto solo. 'Is evil then good? Is reason untrue?' If we must accept the gods and embrace what appears to be evil and if we must deny rational enquiry and rational behaviour, what then are the precepts by which we can live? The answer is an apparent *non sequitur*, and less an answer than a proposition. 'Reason is true to itself; but pity breaks open the heart.' Rational enquiry is inviolate and unquestioned but it is irrelevant in matters of the heart and it is through the heart that the gods are apprehended. However touching, this is a mockery to those not in a position to indulge in philosophical speculation and experiencing the opposite of pity and compassion. 'We are lost. We are as seed before the wind. We are carried to a great slaughter.' Tippett acknowledges the terrible fact that nothing can prevent the onset of indiscriminate savagery, least of all an argument in explanation of it.

These then are the questions posed in the oratorio. Why does such savagery occur? What happens when it does occur? Are there any means by which it can be avoided? Although prompted by the events of 1938–9 and in vital respects a protest against precisely those events, the questions stretch well beyond historical limits and eventually reduce themselves to the single question of why men should mete out such inhumanity to one another: an enormous, intractable question, to which every age seeks an answer. In no other way does Tippett reveal his identity as a composer more clearly than in his determination to confront such a question head-on. It is also characteristic of him that the final lines of his opening section should not strike a note of absolute despair. 'If we are seed, we are at least seed; and if to a great slaughter, this may be a collective sacrifice out of which new attitudes and reconciliation may spring.'[39]

The remainder of Part 1 of the oratorio gives shape and human meaning to this metaphysical exposition. The bass solo, in his capacity as narrator-cum-evangelist ('considered as a father-God figure'[40]), tells of persecuted minorities 'in each nation'. Tippett now confirms that his opening chorus did indeed refer to the world and not to Europe alone, for the soloist points, albeit somewhat obliquely, to Russia, whose purges and prison camps had recently been exposed in Iulia de Beausobre's *The Woman who could not die* (1938), to lynchings in black ghettos in the USA, as well as to the November pogrom and to starvation among the English unemployed. The text of the following Chorus of the Oppressed, 'When shall the usurer's city cease?', takes its cue from the central thesis of *War Ramp* and its manner from Isaiah 14:4, 'How hath the oppressor ceased! the golden city ceased!' After this expression of the anguish of a human group the focus sharpens on to the more poignant anguish of the individual – in Tippett's words, the ordinary man and ordinary woman.[41] The two arias ask how is it possible for the natural impulse to express love and give love to grow in a world of denial and rejection, and reach heart-rending intensity with the final words of the soprano: 'How can I comfort them [my children] when I am dead?' Out of this emerges some kind of release in the first spiritual, 'Steal away to Jesus'.

This spiritual echoes the final chorus in Part 1 of *Messiah*, 'His yoke is easy, his burthen light'. In the same way, Part 2 of *A Child of Our Time* begins with a chorus echoing the opening chorus of Part 2 of *Messiah*, 'Behold the Lamb of God'.

> A star rises in mid-winter,
> Behold the man! The scapegoat!
> The child of our time.

Here however there is no simple analogue. Whereas the unaffected theology of the spiritual is employed without qualification as an authentic expressive metaphor reaching beyond its purely Christian significance, in this chorus Christian symbolism is employed that it may be shown as hollow. The chorus is exemplary and almost bitter in function. The sacrificial lamb who died in order to atone for the iniquities of man no longer exists and the sacrifice of the contemporary scapegoat serves only to redouble such iniquities. To accept Christian symbolism with one hand and reject it with the other exposes an unresolved contradiction in the text which cannot be obscured by its carefully assimilated verbal style. Tippett's musical solution to the problem of fusing the naïve and the sophisticated is, as will be shown, far more persuasive.

Having set the scene, he now turns to his narrative reconstruction. As explained, he avoids specific, named mention of the historical events or of the places or persons involved. But his references are unmistakable. In three concise recitatives the bass tells of the anti-Semitic campaign in Germany, of how Grynspan, referred to simply as 'the boy', was one of those who managed to escape to a 'great city', and of the postcard from Grynspan's sister at the frontier (using what were incorrect press reports, Tippett makes this a letter from his mother). Each stage of this narrative is dramatized with a brief set-number – a Double Chorus of Persecutors and Persecuted, a Chorus of the Self-righteous and a Scena for the quartet of soloists. The second chorus depicts the attitude of those countries who will not receive homeless Jews and particularly the British refusal to receive

more than a token few, and to the sufferings of the thousands stranded on
the Polish frontier.

> We cannot have them in our Empire.
> They shall not work, nor beg a dole.
> Let them starve in No-Man's-Land!

In the Scena the boy ignores the sane advice of his uncle and aunt and
desperately searches his mind for a means of saving his mother. The
heightened emotional intensity of this part of the oratorio demands more
frequent collective involvement if it is not to veer dangerously close to the
condition of opera, and the second spiritual, 'Nobody knows the trouble I
see, Lord', appears already at this point.

The next section describes Grynspan's assassination of vom Rath. It is
characteristic that Tippett should here avoid anything remotely suggestive
of dramatic realism. This second Scena is markedly different from the first.
In cool, factual tones the bass (who had assumed the role of the uncle in the
previous Scena) resumes his narrative function, while the alto (who had
been the aunt) becomes 'personification of the soul' again. She interprets
each step in the narrative. The final sentences are as follows: 'He shoots the
official – '; 'But he shoots only his dark brother – And see – he is dead.'
Tippett's restraint at this point goes so far as to obscure the crucial word
'shoots' with the only moment of overlap in the Scena, when in his anxiety
the bass interrupts the alto. The alto's interpretation is that Grynspan has
been overcome by 'demonic and destructive' forces from within himself and
has shot, or attempted to shoot, only his 'dark brother', his shadow.

The narrative part then culminates in the 'Terror' chorus, the November
pogrom. ('Burn down their houses! Beat in their heads! Break them in
pieces on the wheel!') A corresponding reaction of bitterness is channelled
through the spiritual 'Go down, Moses'. Tippett heads this 'A Spiritual of
Anger' – perhaps not only a reflection on the vengeful Jehovah of the Old
Testament but also a reminder that the same chorus which has just sung
the 'Terror' is now singing in a spirit of righteous indignation.

After this the tension slackens and the narrative gives way to an
imagined picture of the boy in prison and of the mother grieving over the
tragedy which has overtaken them both. Tippett here found difficulty in
effecting a transition to the concluding spiritual of comfort, 'O, by and by',
for the intervening alto solo contains the only perfunctory passage in the
whole text.

> The dark forces rise like a flood.
> Men's hearts are heavy: they cry for peace.

The opening chorus of Part 3 picks up the winter symbolism of the
corresponding earlier choruses. There is no suggestion in any of them that
winter is abating. But in the second one, the phrase 'a star rises in mid-
winter' is a presentiment that a small spark of illumination has been struck,

as well as a reference to the star of the three wise men and to the old idea that the birth of an outstanding human being is associated with a rising star. And in this last chorus, there is a further shift of emphasis.

> The cold deepens.
> The world descends into the icy waters where lies the jewel of great
>   price.

Even if this is adjudged a recondite statement requiring a high degree of poetic sympathy before it can mean anything, Tippett's ability to give emotional expression to the idea of promise, of eventual liberation must be conceded. In fact the text embodies another Jungian expression of great significance. The world descends into its unconscious state (water is a common symbol of the unconscious) where unconscious powers overtake it. Yet this descent also marks a conscious search for what lies at the core of the psyche – the numinous archetype of the 'self', Jung's term for a new centre of personality created from an integration of conscious and unconscious elements, of what a person thinks he is and what he also is. The self contains a continuous flow of psychic energy through which a new beginning, a new purpose can be achieved. It takes various symbolic forms: a child, a saviour-figure, a mandala and what Jung called 'the treasure hard to attain' – a flower, the philosopher's stone (which alchemists attempted to re-create in visible form), a jewel. The jewel in the text above represents therefore the idea of renewal, of rebirth. It also means that experience of the dark forces of the unconscious is a necessary prerequisite before the self can be found; or, in the harsh terms of the oratorio's political background, that war is inevitable if peace is to be created.

These are disturbing and challenging propositions, which can be fully grasped only by an effort of imagination. But they can be elaborated and refined, and as if by way of appeasing the discursive intellect, Tippett's alto solo now explains how this rebirth may be brought about.

> The soul of man is impassioned like a woman.
> She is old as the earth, beyond good and evil, the sensual garments.
> Her face will be illumined like the sun.
> Then is the time of his deliverance.

It is reached, that is, when the 'soul' is revealed. When casting his alto solo as 'personification of the soul' Tippett was not being at all vague. In Jungian terminology the soul is a vitally important concept, referring to the 'inner attitude, the characteristic face, that is turned towards the unconscious'.[42] It compensates for conscious attitudes and behaviour, and acts as a bridge between the two parts of the psyche. It manifests itself as an archetype, the anima for a man, the animus for a woman, which embodies man's timeless experience of woman and vice versa. Everybody has an inborn image of the opposite sex. What this might actually be and in what form it is symbolized varies enormously. In general, the anima can be said to possess both erotic allure and secret, irresistible, age-old wisdom. The most celebrated pictorial representation of this manifestation of the anima is the *Mona Lisa*. In his text Tippett is obviously referring to that aspect of the anima which is warm and passionate, gentle and compassionate. When this archetype is uncovered an electric charge will flow within the psyche, and, hopefully, shift its centre to that realignment of the self alluded to in the chorus.[43]

The opening chorus and this alto solo comprise the scenario for Part 3 of the oratorio. They parallel the Prologue in Heaven in Part 1. The following Scena between the bass solo and the chorus returns to earth with a dialogue on the detailed realities of the situation. To anguished questions from the chorus the bass provides the unavoidable answer that time must take its course and that, given patience, healing will come with it. The 'man of destiny' (Hitler's self-appointed role) is dismissed as having consigned himself to his own hell of loneliness. 'What of the boy, then?' To this the bass gives the terrible and absolute reply: 'God overpowered him.' For him there was no redemption: the black power of his unconscious overwhelmed him and destroyed him. In 1939, this was a startling and even blasphemous statement, and no doubt Tippett meant it to be, for if not he could with little difficulty have rephrased it to suggest gods, or something of the sort, rather than God. But its real significance lies in what Tippett himself has to say about Grynspan's action and fate. Tippett is not at all consoling or sentimental; while his answer may be that of a pacifist, it is none the less uncompromising for that: Grynspan is dismissed as summarily as was the 'man of destiny'. His action may have been comprehensible, but by allowing himself to be overtaken by God-like, archetypal forces and 'make a judgement in God's name',[44] he denied his humanity and, inevitably, was broken. There is no point in seeking an answer in the fate of Grynspan. The answer lies in ourselves. With this decisive change of direction Tippett sets in relief the central message contained in the first lines of the following General Ensemble, already quoted. After this the remaining lines can, in the seasonal symbolism of the work, affirm the birth of spring.

> Here is no final grieving, but an abiding hope.
> The moving waters renew the earth.
> It is spring.

When writing *A Child of Our Time* Tippett seems to have been unaware that it might have prophetic qualities. Even though the crucial word 'pity' from the Scena in Part 1 obviously recalls Owen ('My subject is War, and the pity of War. The poetry is in the pity ... All a poet can do to-day is warn'), his attention, in objectifying his text, was fixed on the particular fate of Grynspan and its implications, and not on sounding warnings about inexorable patterns of unavailing protest or of war and peace. Yet if his argument were correct, the work would have such a quality – as has turned out to be the case. A recent child of our time is Jan Palach. Certain aspects have been inverted (shots have been fired at Gandhi, Martin Luther King and Pope John Paul II as well as at tyrants); but its basic premise has never ceased to have relevance, as wars, repressions and tensions since 1945 have continually demonstrated. This is simply that 'we suffer, as individuals and communities, from a kind of moral pride that will not let us acknowledge that the roots of all fears and shames and hatreds are in ourselves'.[45] When the pride breaks, then will come some hope of recovery.

None of this of course could carry much weight unless the music itself had the strength to do so. It might be objected that something is missing from a work which seems to require such extended exegesis before it can be understood, and the music, admittedly, is in one sense merely a gloss on these Jungian ideas. But it is a gloss in its own terms. There would have been no point in writing the work at all if Tippett had doubted the capacity of his music to tap the unconscious and convey a part of its contents to conscious hearing.

The Music

Tippett's central compositional problem in *A Child of Our Time* was to refine the musical language of the spirituals so that, firstly, they contained concepts and feelings of a more sophisticated order than in the originals and, secondly, so that their language was integrated with his own. He did not want to juxtapose the two idioms in a kind of surrealistic collage, nor to discard his own style in favour of a secondhand re-creation of a popular one. The only existing work he could have used as a model for the setting of spirituals was *Porgy and Bess*. But Gershwin's idiom was too idiosyncratic and too much shaped by dramatic demands to be of help for the more formalized presentation he had in mind. Accordingly, he obtained from the USA recordings of what he hoped would be reasonably authentic performances of spirituals by American singing groups, including some by the Hall Johnson Choir (which he remembered from the sound track of the film *The Green Pastures*). Although of little value in terms of musical idiom, in terms of presentation the Johnson recordings were decisive, for they provided him with a model he could use.

Naturally, the spirituals veer towards a jazz style. (The score directs that they should be sung with a strong underlying pulse and slightly 'swung'.) Tippett was anxious to capture this flavour, as it was a vital part of his attempt to create a collective vernacular. There was no intrinsic difficulty in assimilating jazz into his compositional style since he had already done so. Such a spiritual as 'O, by and by' (Ex. 45) sounds as if it could almost have been composed by Tippett, so close are its rhythms to those of, for example, Ex. 17. What 'jazziness' there is in the rest of the music (in the soprano aria of Part 2 and the alto aria of Part 3) is therefore even less obtrusive.

A much more difficult problem was posed by the need to integrate the spirituals' harmonic and melodic style. In one respect the problem was an asset. Once he had relieved it of cliché, the static harmonic language of the spirituals would, by comparison with the shifting harmonies of his own

Ex. 45

A Child of Our Time

music, provide of its own accord the necessary points of rest. But the degree of harmonic contrast would remain disturbing unless he prepared some common ground between the two. Tippett's chosen common ground is intervallic – partly because his style at that time was more melodic and contrapuntal than harmonic, and partly because his 'harmonization' of the spirituals was to be so pure in its diatonicism that it could almost be said to 'exclude all harmonies whatsoever'.[46] He abstracted a characteristic interval from the spirituals, the minor third, and used this as the basic interval for the whole work. In the spirituals the interval is generally found between the fifth and flattened seventh of a given tonic. With the tonic note it therefore gives rise to two other intervals, the fifth and the flattened seventh. The simplest instance of their presence in a spiritual is in 'Nobody knows'.[47] (See Ex. 46. The bracketed groups in this example, marked *a*, *b*

Ex. 46

A Child of Our Time

and *c*, refer respectively to the minor third, the fifth and the flattened
seventh.) Example 47, from Part 1 of the oratorio (numerals indicate
musical numbers), illustrates Tippett's resource in deriving a variety of
motivic beginnings from these three intervals. His method ranges from the
relatively straightforward use of the minor third in, for example, No. 1(i),
to more subtle usages in which the interval is regarded as a musical space
to be filled out (No. 2(ii)) or expanded and developed as a chromatic motif
(No. 3). The same method is applied throughout the rest of the oratorio.

Ex. 47   **A Child of Our Time**

Such motivic techniques represented a significant advance in Tippett's compositional development. They showed that he was now able to write concisely in a chromatic idiom, without sacrificing his individuality and without preventing his lyric gifts from developing freely. (In this connection it may be noted that the nearest he came to using a leitmotif technique is with the two appearances of the 'child of our time' phrase (Nos. 9 and 28) and of the 'It is winter' phrase (Nos. 1 and 9), inverted at the words 'It is spring' (No. 29).)

As far as larger considerations of formal structure and gesture were concerned, Tippett had already planned to adopt a characteristic formal principle of the Bach Passions: a sequence of narrative recitative, followed by a brief, highly-charged descriptive chorus, whose energies are then released in a contemplative aria. Though this sequence does not appear in literal form in the oratorio its influence can be plainly felt, especially in the pattern of short, fast section followed by longer slow one. The Bachian model remained however somewhat restricting. In order to provide greater flexibility Tippett introduced two other formal types, the operatic scena and the orchestral interlude. The former allowed for more dramatic presentation where necessary, as in the first Scena of Part 2, and also permitted a dialogue between the metaphysical protagonists and the real actors in the drama. The orchestral interludes, according to such models as the Pastoral Symphony in *Messiah* or the Praeludium to the Benedictus in Beethoven's *Missa Solemnis*, allowed time for important events to be absorbed or introduced. For the recitatives he obviously could not use the eighteenth-century model of organ/harpsichord and cello continuo. But he retained the idea of spread chords at the opening of a phrase and of the single bass line. This bass line (given initially to the cellos and subsequently including the double-basses as well) is the sole instrumental support in recitatives and is an ingenious solution to the continuo problem, even if its spare texture creates a somewhat cloying effect, not wholly relieved by the spring of natural speech-rhythms.

As a final means of imposing unity on the work Tippett designed a tonal structure of considerable subtlety. An abbreviated plan of the tonal centres in the work is given in Ex. 48 (numerals indicate musical numbers). It will be seen that the opening choruses create a kind of progressive tonality. Each moves to its own dominant which in turn becomes the tonic of the succeeding one. The tonalities therefore follow a rising sequence of fifths, which nicely corresponds to the growth of promise across the work. Part 1 ends in its relative major, Part 2 in the relative major of its dominant (these, tonal metaphors of gradual release from the associations of the respective tonics) and Part 3 ends in its own dominant, the most emphatic tonal progression of the three. This has multiple meanings: an indication that the 'jewel' may be found; that the final C sharp is related to the intitial E of the work as an extended progression to the third 'fifth', and the whole work therefore exhibits a progression from 'dark' towards 'light'; and that the frequent leaning towards its own relative, E major, indicates another extended progression from E minor to E major, with its allied associations. That none of these meanings can be said to predominate and in particular that the final bar of the work edges away from an apparently conclusive E major to a restrained C sharp minor indicates, perhaps, Tippett's reluctance to dogmatize, or his anxiety not to be misinterpreted as in favour of the triumph of good over evil, or some such cliché.

In general, the tonalities of the outer parts are structural in function, of the inner, dramatic. The function of the opening Prologue in Heaven is confirmed by its closed tonal design; the corresponding section in Part 3 is

Ex. 48   **A Child of Our Time**

a transposed repeat of this design, though its third sub-section moves away
from its tonic in a descending cycle of fifths, reflecting the course of the
argument to the terrible final statement. At the climax of No. 1 there is a
modulation to E flat minor. This tonality becomes the tonic of No. 2 and
establishes a relationship seven steps away in a descending cycle of fifths.
According to d'Indy's theories it is an ambiguous, uncomfortable relationship, and so it sounds. Nos. 5, 6 and 7 pick up this relationship and very
gradually carry it forward – with tonalities of F minor, C minor and G
minor, the fifth, fourth and third 'fifth'. There can be no coincidence in the
appearance of the darkest relationship of all, the fourth 'fifth', precisely
when the focus is set on the individual human being (the tenor solo). The
numbers of Part 3 follow a more intricate pattern. The Preludium before
No. 29 provides a striking tonal contrast, the A flat major being used
largely for its capacity to evoke a mood of tranquillity. No. 29 itself acts as a
kind of tonal recapitulation, returning to the opening dominant; its
modulation to A major is again an evocative use of the tonality.

In Part 2, the tonalities reflect the shifts in the drama either by their
place in the particular tonal symbolism of the work or by their evocative
properties. Thus in Nos. 16 and 22 the tenor returns to his C minor from
Part 1, and in No. 15 the soprano to her G minor (her D minor in No. 23 is
an extension of this). The tonality of C sharp minor is associated with
death or terror (Nos. 11, 17, 19). The C major of No. 13, the Chorus of the
Self-righteous, illustrates the composer's verdict on a tonality whose self-
assurance (deriving from its use by classical composers) is in this context
an affront. What is interesting about the spirituals is not so much that their

tonalities evoke Beethovenian determination (C minor, No. 16) or vehemence (F minor, No. 21), or the spring-like qualities of A major (No. 25),
but that, apart from the 'new' tune for No. 16, they all appear in the
tonalities given in Tippett's source-book. Here is impressive evidence of the
universality of such tonal symbolism.

The orchestral prelude to *A Child of Our Time* (see Ex. 47, No. 1(i)) at once
announces the scale and character of the work. The mood is set by a
snarling trumpet triad, the slow tread of whose succeeding harmonies
sounds like a descent into Hades. There is already a marked contrast in the
answering phrase on the strings, a compensation, so when the trumpets
return *piano* the menace is softened and the second answering phrase need
no longer assert its quality as compensation: it can take on a more firmly
shaped identity of resignation, lament. In a single classical four-phrase
statement of considerable breadth (it stretches over as many as twenty-five
bars) Tippett therefore has laid out both the underlying tensions and the
specific forms of his idea. In addition, he has done so in an idiom rich in the
multiple resonances a wide audience can respond to. The gestural
correspondence of the opening with the openings of such works as Vaughan
Williams's *A Sea Symphony* or Walton's *Belshazzar's Feast* places the work in
an English choral tradition. Within the music are also embedded covert yet
powerful reminders of a European tradition. Example 47, No. 1(i) recalls
the motif of Amfortas's suffering from Wagner's *Parsifal* (cf. Ex. 49(i)) and
Ex. 47, No. 1(ii) that of Sachs's stoicism from *Die Meistersinger* (cf.
Ex. 49(ii)). Whether or not such allusions are deliberate the risk attached
to an idiom of this kind is that it flattens the distinctive contours of a
composer's personal handwriting and, with it, the music's communicative
edge. It is a risk Tippett has always been prepared to take. In this case it
pays dividends largely because the rhythms in the string phrases remain so
characteristic.

Ex. 49

(i) **Wagner: Parsifal (Act II)**   (ii) **Wagner: Die Meistersinger (Act III)**

The following alto aria introduces another feature of the work – the use
of obbligato instruments in an eighteenth-century manner for the vocal
solos, in keeping with the Bachian prototype (and also in keeping with the
economic instrumentation of Berlioz's *L'Enfance du Christ*, the work which
had contributed so strongly to the inception of Tippett's oratorio). All these

solos have characteristic orchestral timbres. The pungent yet plaintive sounds of the cor anglais and bassoon in this aria form the first in a series of sound platforms which stretch across the whole work in finely judged gradations. In general these lie within a narrow sound spectrum, though Tippett does not follow his procedure slavishly and from time to time enlarges his resources to include, as in the case of this aria, a much larger wind section plus the full brass for the climax.

This is not the only way in which the aria sets a precedent. Given the eighteenth-century prototype Tippett might have been expected to use the da capo form. But this would have been the wrong expressive metaphor, as well as an anachronism. A da capo aria, with its associations of an 'exit' aria, is a completed closed form. To preserve a dynamic impulse and to reflect the density of his conceptual thought, Tippett needed a form with the quality of a proposition, one so charged with meaning that it demanded a consequence – some continuing elaboration or rejoinder, or simply some time in which it could be absorbed. All the arias in the oratorio consist of one single melodic unit, with no development sections or rounding recapitulations (although plenty of incidental verbal repeats). And they all have their consequence. Here Tippett has written an exceptionally extended one in the form of a canonic Interludium for two flutes (the only wind instruments not used in the aria) over a pedal note in the cellos, to which is added a lonely viola (perhaps an image of the soul's, the alto's, presence in the heart of things, rising and then falling, unacknowledged).

At this point Tippett's adaptation of the Bachian pattern of short chorus followed by longer solo makes its first appearance. The trumpet triad returns and contorted questions by the chorus are answered by compensating alto phrases and a repeat of the Interludium. This interchange introduces more than the conceptual premise of the oratorio: it also renews two musical procedures already established, the pairing of menace and conciliation in the four phrases of the orchestral prelude and the pattern of aria plus consequence. Since however this Scena as a whole develops and expands these procedures rather than simply restates them, the reappearance of the Interludium *in toto* fits uneasily into the context, a formal weakness underlined by the developmental character of the ensuing final two 'phrases'. The trumpet triad leads this time not to a conciliating phrase but to a disorientating choral fugato ('We are as seed'). A further formal weakness can be observed here, for by the time the fugato has been worked out the musical energy generated needs room for expansion rather than the abrupt full stop (the end of the 'Prologue in Heaven' section) in fact provided. However compelling in immediate terms, this Scena requires very sympathetic handling if it is to fulfil its expository role in the structural scheme.

In keeping with their more simple objectives the remaining numbers in Part 1 are not so ambitious as the opening section. They form a triptych. Each panel is a direct and unambiguous portrayal of human suffering. The choral fugue (Chorus of the Oppressed) is laid out in two parts like a strophic aria. With its shifting chromaticisms and close stretti it fittingly symbolizes a weary and uncomprehending people vainly and with growing anxiety searching for an escape from themselves and from the Kafkaesque prison they are immured in. The orchestral ritornello which frames the tenor aria ('I have no money for my bread') gives freer rein to this anxiety, which now has a touch of venom in it. But the tensions arising from its syncopations can find no outlet either and the music falls back into the more resigned rhythms of the aria proper. Here Tippett has deliberately used a tango rhythm (or at least that tango variant suggested by Weill in the 'Zuhälterballade' of *Die Dreigroschenoper*), in order to evoke the familiar if in this case dispiriting sounds of popular music and thus set his tenor (the 'ordinary man') in an immediately recognizable environment. The aria has none of the pungency of the Weill. But neither is there any hint of pastiche, because the rhythm is a natural outcome of the rhythm of the ritornello and is in any case simply a framework upon which characteristic melodic and harmonic shapes and other rhythms having little to do with the tango can be built. The soprano aria likewise evokes popular dance rhythm, though less plainly. It has something of the flavour of a lullaby or a waltz or even of a dimly perceived foxtrot. The compositional subtlety here is that the merest suggestion of a dance rhythm is enough to associate the aria with the anguish of the tenor and give the composer opportunity to concentrate on the more sharply human plight of the 'ordinary woman' ('How can I cherish my man in such days?'). This soprano aria ends with one of the supreme moments in Tippett's music, a transitional vocalise so poignant as to set off that instant shock of recognition which floods the eyes with emotion. But human kind 'cannot bear very much reality', and although the soprano continues to grieve in a floating melisma the spiritual 'Steal away' with its familiar cadences comes as a relief as well as a release.

The setting of 'Steal away' is not so simple as it sounds. It is a persuasive example of art concealing art, as is shown when Tippett's harmonization is compared with any typical instance from a popular song-book. Tippett always intended to harmonize the spirituals in the purest way possible. What did present compositional problems to him was the manner of presentation. He eventually found a model for this in the recordings by the Hall Johnson Choir mentioned above. They introduced him to the practice of using soloists as 'leaders' in the choral sections, as well as to the solo plus response form of the central sections, the spirituals as a whole therefore being cast in the ternary shape of chorus, solo, chorus. This means that when the tenor solo, as in 'Steal away', is the 'leader' and singing with the tenors of the chorus, he is not merely being provided with a chance to warm up in preparation for his genuine solos in the central sections; he is given the responsibility of articulating the tune and carrying the chorus with him. It is a remarkable effect, suggesting a desire to sway and encourage rather than control, and as such entirely in keeping with the emotional climate of the spirituals as a whole.

Part 2 moves swiftly to the crux of the drama. Whereas the opening chorus of Part 1 is tightly formalized, consisting of two strophes with introduction and coda, the opening chorus here is more dramatic and open-ended. It gives birth to three quite distinct musical gestures – an icy stillness on 'A star rises', a full-voiced choral rhetoric on 'Behold the man' and then the culminating phrase introducing the child of our time. This latter is not in fact particularly arresting in itself, approaching dangerously close to that earnest brand of sentiment worn by the face of established piety. But its minor thirds link it with the intervallic matrix of the work, and it is just characteristic enough to serve as a pointed reminiscence at the end of the Scena in Part 3 (see Ex. 50).

Ex. 50   **A Child of Our Time**

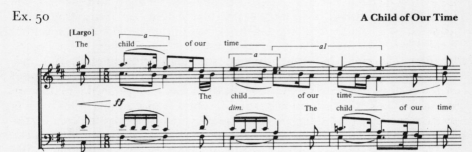

The two fast-tempo choruses that follow are also open-ended in shape. In the first a sequence of distorted echoes rebound between the 'persecutors and the persecuted'. In the second, imitative inverted entries quickly converge on the unanimous assertions ('Let them starve in no-man's land!') of those whose bigotry is so unreasoned that there is no answer to it. Tippett ironically associates this chorus with 'English' musical idioms: with the clashes between flattened sevenths and natural leading notes and with the typical rhythms of his own arising from English speech-rhythms. There is also an allusion to the chorus 'Sei gegrüsset' from Bach's *St John Passion* (see Ex. 51).

Ex. 51   **A Child of Our Time**

If the Englishness of this chorus is Tudor in origin, the opening soprano arioso of the Scena for solo quartet recalls another era. But it is difficult to see precisely what Tippett intended here by conjuring up the spirit of the *Enigma Variations*, unless it was simply that Elgar's theme crystallizes a universal mood of valedictory sorrow. In the event the mood is rapidly superseded by the imperative utterances of the other three singers. These rise to a knot of chromatic tensions as the boy tries to free himself from those urging caution. The spiritual 'Nobody knows' is especially apposite here and at the same time it is so skilfully treated that its quasi-canonic textures both represent the impossibility of shaking off restraining forces and fuse the language of the spiritual with Tippett's own contrapuntal style.

The next Scena, describing the assassination of the 'official', continues the fragmentation which had begun in the previous one. It is a series of little recitative and arioso sections, the recitatives adopting the manner of the narratives, the ariosos that of the alto's exhortations. Out of this fragmentation emerge two extreme emotional states, one of revenge, the other of threat.

The 'Terror' chorus fulfils its dramatic function by harnessing luridly expressive musical motifs (all deriving from the variant a^1 in Ex. 47, 3(i)) to a strictly disciplined formal scheme. It is an austere fugue, with three regular counter-subjects (and passages therefore of four-part invertible counterpoint) and a rigid ternary structure of exposition, episode, middle entry, episode, recapitulation, defined tonally by the disorientating sixth 'fifth' relationship in the middle entry. Example 52 is part of the recapitulation.

The spiritual 'Go down, Moses' is set as a chorale prelude, the tune a cantus firmus while canonic counterpoints deriving from it weave above. Apart from its dramatic function it also acts as the dynamic climax to the narrative section of the oratorio.

The necessary period of reflection is provided by an orchestral interlude, a close canon between the violins and flutes sounding like a silent screeching of anguish. This interlude serves two purposes, for it acts also as a ritornello to the ensuing aria for the boy in prison. Whatever criticism may be levelled against the aria – that it prolongs the introspective element at a time when the demands of musical proportion call for some relief from sombre colourings· and a heavy pulse – there is no doubt that it is an affecting portrayal of the lassitude and the sheer waste imposed by state retribution. And its dense contrapuntal fabric shows how much Tippett had advanced since the diffuse chromaticisms of *A Song of Liberty*.

Wholesale retreat into lethargy is warded off in the next aria, where the anxiety of the mother prompts a much faster tempo and some almost jazzy cross-rhythms in the accompanying parts. At this point it might perhaps have been expected that Tippett would continue generating the emotional tension needed to precipitate the consoling, unbidden dream of escape presented in the final spiritual 'O, by and by'. But the transitional alto solo reverts to a slow tempo again and as a result the effect of the exquisitely

Ex. 52   A Child of Our Time

beautiful setting of the spiritual is somewhat vitiated.

At the opening of Part 3 the return to metaphysical subject matter is marked by a return to the abstract formal design of the opening of Part 1. The chorus here is again in two strophes, with introduction and coda. But at this stage in the work it was not to be expected that the strophes would be so simple as before. They now contain two gestures (thus nicely absorbing the dramatic style of Part 2), the first a bold symbol of the world descending into 'the icy waters', the second an image of the 'jewel of great price'. Here Tippett has hinted at the motionless luminosity of the Jungian self by writing what initially seems to be a perpetual canon by inversion, that is, something which remains the same whatever angle it is viewed from. But this image can as yet be only a likeness and its revolving pattern is in fact squeezed into a cadence (see Ex. 53).

Ex. 53   A Child of Our Time

Apart from the 'Terror' chorus, the succeeding alto aria, 'The soul of man', is the only number in a sustained fast tempo and the only one not geared to its bass line. It is at once the finest and the most characteristic. This of course is wholly appropriate since it holds the key to Tippett's 'solution' of his oratorio's metaphysics. Nonetheless it draws attention to the imbalance of tempi in the work as a whole and to the fact that the oratorio would have benefited from more music in this style. The aria highlights the dilemma facing the composer dealing with such momentous subject matter, which is that musical demands assert themselves regardless of the subject matter.

The aria's rhythmic style has been examined above (see p.106). The vocal writing in the oratorio as a whole has already shown what limitless capital Tippett could draw from his Purcellian inheritance, simply by taking the rhythms and nuances of the English language at face value. (These lessons could be applied to instrumental music too; the dotted crotchet plus quaver rhythm in the following Scena obviously derives from Purcell's setting of the word 'music' in 'Music for a While'.) His use of vocal melisma in this aria draws from another aspect of the Purcellian inheritance. Earlier numbers include brief melismatic shapes as a means both of colouring a word and of opening out a melodic phrase so that it can flower. But here the melismas do not really need their attendant word in order to convey their expressive meaning. They take on an independent existence as expressive metaphors in their own right (see Ex. 54).

Ex. 54   **A Child of Our Time**

In other respects the aria marks the culmination of the methods common to all the arias in the oratorio: it contains the most extended treatment of the model of a single thematic sentence and the most thorough treatment of the idea of obbligato instrumentation. The four sentences of the text are reflected in the four phrases of the theme, the obbligato instrumentation in a correspondingly fourfold sequence of strings, wind, brass and tutti.

The series of apocryphal pronouncements and anxious, almost frantic questions which comprise the Scena between the bass solo and the chorus restores the prevailing mood. The conceptual substance here is more refractory and is presented even more aphoristically than elsewhere in the work; accordingly the musical sense of exertion, of wrestling with forces which yield only unwillingly is more marked. The bass's pronouncements are expressed in a chromatic idiom which eloquently conveys the struggle that has gone into their making (see Ex. 55). After this climax of imaginative concentration the canonic Preludium for two flutes and cor anglais provides a period of repose, of poise before the final clinching statement.

Ex. 55   A Child of Our Time

The quality of statement in the 'General Ensemble' explains the presence in the cellos and basses of insistent immovable crotchets, which might otherwise have seemed a stylistic intrusion. Here they assume the function of a ground bass. Above them Tippett adds various counterpoints and draws out a wide aspiring arch as a trope to the principal element, a long melody of over twenty bars, apportioned phrase by phrase to the solo quartet. The whole work has been leading to this moment. It says much for Tippett's technical assurance that he can summon up reserves of lyricism precisely when he needs them. The interesting point is that none of the individual strands of this melodic complex are particularly original in themselves, and were it not for their rhythmic style they might almost be termed pedestrian. But collectively they bloom into a kind of cosmic embrace, whose meaning can no more be circumscribed than can that of the text (see Ex. 56). The chorus takes this music to itself and the Ensemble finally flows into a rapturous, wordless benediction from the soloists. A premonitory modulation then leads down to the more familiar strains of 'Deep River', which can now symbolize the universality of the philosophical 'solution' by involving, for the first and only time in a spiritual, the full performing resources. In the central section echoes of the soloists' vocalise are united with the more reassuring accents of the chorus, a moving symbol of integration between psychological illumination and the need to live with the world as it is, and one deriving its authenticity from the fact that it is a consequence and not a dogmatic assertion.

Ex. 56

A Child of Our Time

A Child of Our Time showed that Tippett had acquired a highly developed control of dramatic gesture and pacing, a distinctive vocal and choral style and an ability to dispose unifying techniques over a wide canvas. Such technical advances cannot of course create genuine artistic unity by themselves. But the work does have unity, nowhere more evident than in those passages where it is most threatened, the transitions from Tippett's 'own' music to that of the spirituals. Unity is at once the work's strength and its weakness. Given Tippett's well-founded interpretation of oratorio as a genre requiring predominantly meditative content, there remained the purely musical danger that fast tempo sections might be too short to warrant the emphasis on those in slow tempo. This danger is not always averted, as has been suggested. The listener sometimes yearns for a light touch to offset the occasional heavy uniformity of tempo. Yet such passages are redeemed by an eloquence so persuasive that it can meet and defeat on its own ground the hypothesis that the conceptual content of a work of art must ultimately capitulate to the purely aesthetic.[48] *A Child of Our Time* is not in any narrow sense a political work. But what it has to say about the human condition seizes the imagination as surely as the music through which it is expressed.

Completion of a Strategy

Minor Works

During the next six years Tippett wrote some dozen works. Half of them were relatively small-scale, composed for particular performers or special occasions. They testified to growing public recognition, a situation promoted by his activities at Morley College and later, by the successful first performance of *A Child of Our Time*. Yet for him their real value was otherwise. They taught him two things: how to organize his working life so that important works could be kept in cold storage while less important ones were being attended to, and how to turn their demands to good account. None of them is insignificant. They represent the genres of madrigal, motet, brass canzona, chorale prelude and, for a second time, the the 'English' string piece. The core of Tippett's music of this period however is contained in five substantial works not written to order: a concertante work for piano and orchestra, a solo cantata, two more string quartets and a symphony. In these he finally completed his strategy for testing his compositional mettle and was ready to embark on the long-delayed task of writing an opera. They are discussed below, after a brief examination of the 'occasional' works.

The Source and *The Windhover*, the madrigals written in 1942 for his choir at Morley College, form a contrasting pair, one slow the other fast, unified by both ending with characteristic melismas and on the same tonic. Although they both pay scrupulous attention to word-painting, *The Source* is more like a part-song than a madrigal, consisting basically of a harmonized melodic line varied on its repeat. *The Windhover* on the other hand is a true madrigal, in the sense that it is through-composed. Here Tippett was so bewitched by the idea of capturing the flight of a falcon that attention to word-setting and word-painting is carried to almost obsessive lengths. Since few of the twenty or more bright little images are given room for expansion the work suffers from an excess of undeveloped motifs and unvarying textures, and it sounds congested. Despite its rhythmic inventiveness it lacks genuine impetus. The madrigals showed that Tippett was not really at ease in small-scale forms of this type. By the time he wrote his only other madrigal, *Dance, clarion air*, ten years later, he had profited from their example and now composed in extended paragraphs.

In his two motets Tippett undertook tasks more congenial to his musical imagination, and they are correspondingly better works. The motet, or at least that renaissance model dear to him, needs fewer words than the madrigal and it provides the environment in which lyricism can flourish. The first of them, *Plebs Angelica* for double choir, was written in late 1943 at the request of the precentor of Canterbury Cathedral, the Revd Joseph Poole.[49] Tippett, the agnostic, naturally had reservations about writing for the Anglican church. But he could recognize the power of some of its fundamental beliefs, even if the terms in which they were expressed might be different from the ones he would have chosen himself. The motet is a setting of a Latin poem which exhorts the angelic host (*plebs angelica*) to carry the faithful into paradise: an age-old symbol therefore of the destiny of the messenger figure – the angel, prophet, creative artist – to reveal the jewel-like depths of the soul, and as such highly sympathetic to both Tippett and his sometime patrons.

The resonant acoustic of a cathedral accounts for the motet's pure intervals and predominantly triadic harmony, as does the traditional division into decani and cantoris. From another point of view these features can be seen as Tippett's act of homage to the English tradition of church music from which he had drawn so much. If there is affectionate pastiche in Tippett's music, this is the nearest he got to it. The false relations and idiosyncratic chromatic turns (Ex. 57, bar 7) stem from English music from Tallis to Purcell, and the treatment of the two choirs owes a debt to Tallis in particular. Tippett's design, alternating responses in imitative and homophonic style until the central climax when the choirs share thematic material and eventually unite in eight-part harmony, is reminiscent of Tallis's methods in the forty-part motet *Spem in alium*.

Ex. 57   **Plebs Angelica**

If *Plebs Angelica* may be termed a motet 'da chiesa', *The Weeping Babe* is one 'da camera'. It belongs to the tradition of Byrd's polyphonic songs and is designed for a twentieth-century equivalent of an Elizabethan chamber, the private sitting-room with radio for musicians. It was commissioned by the BBC for a programme called 'Poet's Christmas' and has a specially written text by Edith Sitwell. Her contemporary interpretation of the nativity carol (her poem, beginning 'The snow is near gone', ends with the lines below)

> Why must those winter flowers know the cold
> Of the world's heart, and those bitter years,
> The nails of thy Cross, my sweet flower's thorn?

is given a personal gloss by Tippett. The work is really a memorial for Bronwen Wilson, who was killed when a flying bomb demolished the pair of Oxted cottages Tippett rented out. Her two children were unhurt; her husband recovered in hospital. *The Weeping Babe* is an intimate, hauntingly beautiful work, with some especially tender harmony.

The commission to write an opening fanfare for the celebrations marking the fiftieth anniversary of the consecration of St Matthew's Church, Northampton in September 1943 was arranged by Britten (whose own *Rejoice in the Lamb* was first performed at the same time). Britten wanted to help Tippett gain some recognition. In his turn, Tippett doubtless wanted to be able to serve a useful social role and produce a competently and responsibly made artefact – as proved the case. The thematic material of this *Fanfare for Brass*[50] is certainly drawn from the familiar stock of brass flourishes, and it is recognizably the work of its composer. Yet it leaves an oddly inconsequential impression, as if Tippett had somehow contrived to spike his own guns. The modesty of the work cannot be attributed wholly to a desire not to pre-empt the effect of what was to follow it. It seems rather that something in Tippett, perhaps dramatized by the priorities of wartime or by the fact that the Fanfare was the first work he wrote after his release from prison, rebelled against the idea of becoming an 'official' artist. Subsequent commissions were accepted only if they were inherently sympathetic or if they simply endorsed what he was writing anyway.

Modesty of a different kind lies behind his only organ work, the *Preludio* written to precede a 1946 performance of Monteverdi's *Vespers*. Here his chief concern was the eminently practical one of preparing an audience for the first performances in Britain of a work he held in high regard. The *Preludio* is thus a short chorale prelude on two sections from the *Vespers*: an introductory ricercar on the invocation 'Sancta Maria, ora pro nobis' from the *Sonata sopra Sancta Maria*, followed by a simple harmonization, in Monteverdi's rhythm, of the hymn *Ave maris stella*. Tippett reveals his identity only in the closing bars, and then gracefully retires, leaving his work poised on Monteverdi's dominant.

By this time his Symphony and String Quartet No. 3 were already behind him and he had no need to prove himself. The last of his 'occasional' pieces comes therefore as a kind of relaxation before the enormous effort required for *The Midsummer Marriage*. His *Little Music for String Orchestra*, written for a medium which gratefully accommodates the serenity of language he was now able to summon up, is the slightest of his three string works (its first performers numbered 6, 4, 4, 3, 2), but it is boxed and labelled with the almost theatrical flourish of an artist who can now display a trick or two. A lordly survey of the company, with a twinkle in the direction of Bartók, and out comes a gem in the colours of the Ritual Dances (see Ex. 58). And the work is concluded with another little *trouvaille*, as the artist tiptoes away while the company is still savouring his ability to take them to a land galloping with wild horses. It was a nice way to bring down the curtain on a compositional period.

Ex. 58   **Little Music for String Orchestra**

Fantasia on a theme of Handel

Scene 1, as it were, of Tippett's career could not have ended like that unless its protagonist had been tempered by a series of trials. All his major works of this period reflect the process in miniature, emerging after concentrated struggle into a mood of repose or jubilation. And all therefore exemplify the philosophy that the best things in life are free only to those who have experienced enough to know that that is true.

The composition of the *Fantasia on a theme of Handel* for piano and orchestra derived from several stimuli: Tippett's attraction to a concertante style, frequently cultivated at the time, in which the participants could converse at a modest level of argument and not be committed to the extended symphonic rhetoric of a full-scale concerto; his admiration for the brilliant piano cadenzas in Lambert's *The Rio Grande*; and from a more specifically technical interest in varying the inner construction of asymmetric phrase-lengths. The work is a set of variations, and demonstrates a more radical type of thematic transformation than in his Piano Sonata No. 1.

Handel's theme had been a favourite since Tippett's schooldays at Stamford, when he developed an enthusiasm for the novels of Samuel Butler. In Chapter 5 of *Erewhon* the theme is quoted by Butler in order to give some idea of what the giant statues guarding Erewhon sounded like.

Their heads were carved in the shape of 'a sort of organ-pipe, so that their mouths should catch the wind and sound with its blowing'. Tippett was less concerned with the theme's function in the novel however, than with its quality as music. It haunted him for nearly twenty years before he finally gave way to its promptings and wrote the Fantasia.[51]

The work was begun before *A Child of Our Time*, that is, immediately after the Double Concerto was completed in June 1939. When he completed the text of the oratorio in September, Tippett set the Fantasia aside in order to write the oratorio's music. A gap of about eighteen months interrupted the composition of the Fantasia. Colin Mason[52] perceived a change of style in it which he ascribed to the influence of the oratorio and in particular, with the supposed quotation of the *Dies irae* motif, to the influence of the Second World War. In fact the motif in question is not the *Dies irae* and neither is there any change of style, unless the whiff of Franck or Rachmaninov in variation 4 is considered to be that. In its own terms the Fantasia is homogeneous enough. Nonetheless it is a curious work and this is due largely to a failure of integration of a more fundamental kind. The Handel theme is so powerful and assertive in character that it is not really suitable for variations at all. It does not yield readily, and fixes itself in the memory so strongly that its reappearance at the end evokes a self-confidence disturbingly remote from an age which has had to search hard for its assurances, and thus robs the variations of some of their vitality. It might almost have been better to have begun the work with the first variation and left Handel to the end.

Tippett however seems to have relished this problem, for after its initial presentation the theme is brushed aside with an almost arrogant gesture (somewhat reminiscent of the solo entry in Stravinsky's Concerto for piano and winds), as if to say that Handel's challenge will be accepted and met on its own ground. As has been suggested, Tippett conducts a losing battle. Yet the work is a densely wrought example of his style, consistently lively and coloured with that invigorating pianism associated with the Piano Sonata.

The variations are grouped to form a kind of sonata – a first movement (variations 1, 2 and 3), slow movement (variation 4) and scherzo (variation 5), followed by development, cadenza and fugal finale. Their tonalities form a chain of descending thirds, starting in A (the fifth 'fifth', very distant from the home tonic of B flat) and continuing with its relative F sharp minor and proceeding in this way in a descending cycle of fifths from D to G. The development eventually turns this G into G minor, the relative of the tonic. Its material consists of ideas from the variations in reverse order (the '*Dies irae*' being an inverted variant of the theme of variation 4), a process that likewise leads to a return of the Handel theme, now transformed into a fugue subject.

The main compositional interest lies in Tippett's highly sophisticated variation technique and in his treatment of phrase-lengths. One of the attractions of the theme to him was its asymmetric construction, of 7 + 13 bars. He loosened its tight rhythms by adding a *meno mosso* at the beginning

of its second part, thus allowing himself the freedom to launch into cadenzas at these places in the later variations. But he adhered to the dimensions of the theme, seeking variation in the interior rhythmic groupings.
This was a device he had noticed in classical works, where, for example,
an eight-bar phrase could be divided 3 + 5 and not 4 + 4. Example
59 illustrates this feature in relation to the first seven bars of the theme.

Ex. 59   **Fantasia on a theme of Handel**

Boyhood's End

The cantata *Boyhood's End* for tenor and piano was written in early 1943 for
Peter Pears and Benjamin Britten. Tippett wanted to write a solo cantata,
as opposed to a set of songs or a song cycle, because being a form in which

one person sings directly of a single situation it was appropriate for
conveying what he described as a 'personal response to nature felt as a
mirror for a state of soul'.[53] He found a suitable text in the chapter headed
'Boyhood's End' in the autobiography *Far Away and Long Ago* of the writer
and naturalist W.H. Hudson, in which Hudson as an old man remembers
his emotions on his fifteenth birthday when he first feared he would lose the
sensitivity and immediacy of his contact with nature.

The cardinal point about Hudson's text is that it evokes memories. It is
drained of the sap, the root-forms of immediate experience and is conceived
in such terms as 'to feel the same old surprise and delight at the appearance
of each familiar flower' or 'the wide hot whity-blue sky'. Tippett's
sympathy with the rather dusty pastoralism of Hudson may be said to link
him with the early twentieth-century English school of song writers. But
the manner in which he expresses this sympathy also links him with the less
circumscribed aesthetic attitudes of a later generation. Artists of Tippett's
generation, knowing of the carnage of the First World War and now
working in a second, could see no point in flaunting the red lifeblood: that
was being spilt anyway. Art needed to act as a shield, behind which
distanced reminders of the existence of that lifeblood could be harboured.
In order to serve that purpose its material had to be durable and almost
inanimate, yet resilient enough to present cogent images of renewal.
Boyhood's End is a rather dryly textured work, highly circumspect in its
control of musical material and perhaps lacking a kernel of raw experience.
But it certainly is a cogent image of renewal. It is one of the most striking
instances of the neo-classical attitude in Tippett – especially evident in the
tensions created between a subtly allusive evocation of mood and the use of
severe formal design and of lucid textures originating in the baroque.

Boyhood's End is like a baroque cantata in that it comprises a sequence of
recitatives and arias with corresponding passages in syllabic and lyrical
style; the piano fulfils the role of the continuo. It may be compared with the
solo cantatas of Bach, Handel or Alessandro Scarlatti, with the characteristic twist that it again echoes the sonata archetype – recitative (introduction), aria (first movement), recitative (slow movement), aria (scherzo),
aria (finale). Tippett's real model, however, was Purcell, and especially
that earlier form of cantata, such as *The Blessed Virgin's Expostulation*, in
which declamatory recitatives are followed not by *da capo* arias but by the
simpler melodic paragraphs of songs. In his lyrical sections, Tippett writes
neither *da capo* arias nor songs but he is closer in spirit to the latter, and if
the recitative sections lack the vividness of Purcell this is due to the
character of Tippett's text rather than a failure to benefit from Purcell's
example. What gives the work a special place in Tippett's output is its re-
creation of Purcellian vocal coloratura. Without this he would have lacked
the necessary resource for the composition of *The Midsummer Marriage*.
Coloratura in Purcell emphasizes virtuosity for its own sake, a distancing
effect highly sympathetic to a neo-classical temperament; paradoxically, it
also charges virtuosity with a sudden expressive eloquence whose impact
has nothing to do with executive skill at all. For this reason coloratura

cannot be the whole *Affekt*. It is used as an expressive device. So with *Boyhood's End*: it appears only once in the work – in the first aria. Whereas the actual notes of the passage in question are not likely to stick in the memory, the coloratura, a means of energizing the climactic phrase so that, like its text, it dances, is indeed memorable. It crystallizes the feeling of enchantment aroused in the earlier part of the aria (as well as showing how Tippett has adapted the Purcellian spirit to his own purposes by drawing from other sources in addition, notably the Monteverdian *trillo* and the polyrhythms of jazz: see Ex. 60).

Ex. 60   **Boyhood's End**

Because it is used so sparingly, coloratura of this type and ornamentation in general must however be counted as incidental features. The essence of the work lies in its supple vocal lines and in the generous arcs of melody flowing from them. A sense of natural movement is one the work has to evoke if it is to be true to its subject matter and its prose rhythms. But it is thereby in danger of drifting into enervating rhapsody, and Tippett duly applies a check on this by contrapuntal interplay between voice and piano and by the discreet use of the strophic principle in all sections, apart from the first. The most subtle check however is made through harmony. For long stretches the harmony is characteristically modal, but it is always ready to be directed towards cadential articulation, as in the closing bars of Ex. 8 (p.93), and thus to mark out the tonal design of the whole work. Continuing experiments with sonata weightings, notably in the unusual, voluptuously floating finale, impose their own tonal restraints. Yet the carefully plotted network of relationships, in which the germinal tonality of A eventually comes to rest on its subdominant, itself paints the emotional course of the work. Tippett's sedulous approach to compositional technique during this period can be inferred from a comparison between the tonal design of *Boyhood's End* and that of his String Quartet No. 2 (Exx. 61 and 62). In the Quartet he applies 'abstract' as opposed to 'programmatic' logic and rigorously works out the implications of the progression at the beginning across all four movements.

Ex. 61   Boyhood's End

Ex. 62   String Quartet No. 2

String Quartet No. 2

Experiments with tonal construction in Tippett's String Quartet No. 2 are symptomatic of the much wider considerations prompted by this fascinating and exquisite work. As the first to be conceived after *A Child of Our Time* it set a pattern in Tippett's output by which dramatic works were followed by complementary instances of 'pure' music. In this case the chosen medium showed how much importance he attached to the classic vehicle of pure music, the string quartet. It is possible to detect a certain reserve in

Tippett's approach to other media. But with the string quartet it was different. It was the medium in which he worked most naturally and flexibly, the one most suited to the lyrical and contrapuntal gifts of a composer still in some ways committed to a private and almost introspective exploration of his musical personality. He wrote three quartets during this period, in the process producing examples in three, four and five movements (respectively, String Quartets Nos. 1, 2 and 3).

In his String Quartet No. 2 Tippett decided to put the main structural weight on the finale, which is therefore a dramatic Beethovenian sonata-allegro. From this decision sprang the character of the rest of the work, and in particular that of the first movement. Here again he attempted something very rare, a fast movement containing the substance of a Beethoven allegro but in a lyrical style without dramatic tensions and contrasts. The only obvious precedent for this was to be found in Beethoven himself, in the opening movement of his Piano Sonata in A, op. 101. Although Tippett may have drawn support from Beethoven's example, his formal design is however entirely his own.

He creates his expressive effect through his natural lyricism, his lithe rhythms and especially through sonata form: Tippett uses sonata form only to undermine its basic principles. In the classical prototype there is a sharp contrast between the 'passionate' and the 'lyrical', the first- and second-subject material, which means that the transition section has the precise function of getting from one to the other. The tensions between them are gradually resolved in the development so that the recapitulation marks a dramatic act of reconciliation, effected traditionally by the acceptance of the tonic key by both groups of material. In Tippett's movement contrast between the two groups is minimal. They are both lyrical; the main theme of the second subject is clearly derived from the first subject's accompanying part; and both subjects begin with the same rhythm (see Exx. 11 and 12, p.99). The transition, which is also lyrical, turns out to be as well suited to connecting the second subject with the first as the other way round, for in the recapitulation, which begins with the second subject, it appears in identical form, apart from being transposed. Since the recapitulation states the material in reverse order and moreover with the second-subject material in the subdominant and not in the tonic, the movement as a whole assumes an ABCBA arch form, that is, a closed symmetrical form with none of the dramatic divisions of traditional sonata form.

This may seem an unduly ponderous way of describing what sounds an effortless flow of music, weaving and gliding like birds in free flight. Certainly some aspects of the movement, notably its rhythms and textures, are now so recognizably Tippettian that in the last analysis they must stem from purely instinctive modes of expression. Yet if Tippett's developing technical resource is to be charted, his skill in marshalling his language is worth underlining. Reference has already been made to rhythmic aspects of the movement's thematic material (see pp.104–106). Its tightly woven textural bands are of particular significance, since having forfeited dramatic tension and contrast, Tippett depended largely on variations of texture to articulate his structure. The first subject is in a compact middle register. The transition is signalled by little crystalline flourishes in the first violin (the only unconvincing feature of the movement, for the flourishes are not developed and hence sound somewhat incongruous); it then opens out the texture by means of a passage in bare octaves (a frequent device in Tippett for lifting the music from one section to the next) and another passage in sequential imitation. This gradually rises until it reaches a relatively high tessitura for the main second subject. Further bare octaves, starting low and releasing the tension generated by so much high music, usher in the subsidiary themes. They start in unanimous homophony and therefore have the authority to set the music on a downward course. It then fans out for a codetta absorbing everything that has gone before into one all-embracing texture from high to low, the first appearance of four-part counterpoint in the movement. A contraction into the middle register, and the development can ensue with the same texture as at the opening.

The spare lines of the slow movement, a fugue, now form a genuine contrast. There is also a contrast in mood, for even without knowing that the fugue subject was conceived about three years earlier as a direct response to the Munich conference, there is no mistaking its poignancy. If the first movement encapsulates the idea of wonder at the living movement in things, this encapsulates the idea of sorrow, of the worm in the bud, the weight of centuries of suffering. The fugue is the most intensely expressive Tippett has written, and one of a very small number of works to re-create nineteenth-century chromaticism in a twentieth-century idiom.

Its effect derives largely from tensions between rigidity and flexibility. The subject (Ex. 63, violin 1) is treated as if it were five bars in length, in that the entries follow each other mechanically in multiples of five bars. Yet it is really a seven-bar theme, whose last three bars melt into a codetta/counter-subject (Ex. 63, viola: its first two bars are the final two bars of the codetta/counter-subject) which then continues as a regular counter-subject. Thus there is already a characteristic rhythmic polyphony even though the pulse appears to be a straightforward three-in-a-bar. The middle entries are always ten bars long; the episodes begin identically and then become progressively shorter, until at the end of the movement they

Ex. 63   String Quartet No. 2

break the ten-bar patterning of the subject entries. Example 63 is the last entry in the exposition.

The scherzo (see Ex. 13, p.100) is a beautifully judged complement – light and capricious, like a ball dancing on a jet of water. In this way it provides the necessary contrast of speed and texture. Its other structural function is transitional: it acts as a link between the unitary forms of the first two movements and the dualities of the last. The emphatic subdivisions of a conventional scherzo and trio would have created too abrupt a change at this point and Tippett here conceived a novel adaptation of the prototype in which the distinction between scherzo and trio is smoothed over and the form made open-ended: continuous variations on the scherzo/trio unit, rather than the closed form of scherzo/trio/scherzo. So that the variations principle should not itself become too assertive, it is applied very sparingly. The variations are more like a sequence of adjustments, made to accommodate the tonal scheme and Tippett's natural inclination towards the sonata dialectic (the trio sections are by way of being exposition, development and recapitulation). The movement is a particularly informative example of Tippett's rhythmic style. Some aspects of this are discussed above (see p.106).

Having now reached his finale Tippett could hardly compose as if he were starting at the beginning. As well as bearing the main structural weight of the work, his Beethovenian sonata-allegro had to act as a kind of summation, after the manner of the finale of Beethoven's op. 131. Principal material from the earlier movements is therefore woven into the fabric by means of ingenious transformations: the first subject derives from the first movement, the second from the fugue and the 'new' theme at the beginning of the development from the trio of the scherzo. These transformations are so extreme however that they provide only the most tenuous of aural reminders of their origins and the movement ultimately depends on the musical substance as it is. Of all the sonata-allegro movements in the first period of Tippett's maturity this one conforms most closely to the Beethovenian prototype. The distinction between the 'passionate' and the 'lyrical' is drawn fearlessly, almost defiantly. But Tippett was not so successful here as elsewhere in getting from one to the other. The rather frantic lunge at the second subject is plausible in the exposition for it might be expected that its compressed energy would be given freer rein in the recapitulation. But in fact it returns exactly as before (apart from the necessary transposition), as does the second subject, and as a result the awaited climactic apotheosis does not materialize. What is left, a beautiful coda recalling the mood of the opening of the work, does not quite compensate for this failure of nerve.

If not a faultless work, Tippett's String Quartet No. 2 is nevertheless profoundly original in language, the most endearing and the most classical of his quartets. In it his exploration of the Beethovenian allegro was effectively concluded. Although he continued to experiment with formal weightings in his Symphony No. 1, the opening allegro of that work is far distant from the dramatic prototype.

String Quartet No. 3

In his String Quartet No. 3 of 1946, written about three years after No. 2, Tippett discarded sonata movements altogether. The reason for this was not that he had tired of them or thought them in some way disposed of. It was that having in the meanwhile heard all the quartets of Bartók, he changed his attitude to the quartet medium. In a broadcast talk,[54] he explained how Bartók's music had questioned his ideas of what a quartet should sound like. In Tippett's view, Bartók began to break open the traditional quartet sonority deriving from the Viennese classics and eventually to such an extent that it seemed as if he were not writing a quartet at all. Tippett himself was temperamentally incapable of drawing so close to the barrier between quartet and some other medium, and neither could he follow Bartók in seeking out new string techniques. His quartet contains none of the arresting sonorities of Bartók, nor do any of its motifs have that tactile quality of a sound-object. It is true that superficial resemblances may be detected betweeen, say, the repeated-note patterns at the climax of the introduction in Tippett's String Quartet No. 3 and the first movement of Bartók's String Quartet No. 5, or between the quasi-impressionism of its fourth movement and Bartók's 'night music' pieces. But this is unimportant. Bartók's influence was far more subtle, and an illuminating example of how one composer's influence on another is at its most profound when transmitted in terms of idea rather than stylistic mannerism. Bartók forced Tippett to consider the elementary but fundamental question of sound. And Tippett responded entirely in his own way.

He has not explained exactly how he reasoned out his response, but his String Quartet No. 3 offers several indications of what this might have been. It was not a question of inventing the brilliantly incisive gesture which would clamour for notice. On the contrary, Tippett used thematic material of traditional origins, with the properties almost of formulae, so that by merging his material with what might be considered the background – the root identity and colour of the musical processes, as opposed to the counters with which they are conducted – he brought that background into the foreground and thereby directed attention to its essence. Emphasis is therefore laid on sound as an expressive metaphor in its own terms. Significantly, the String Quartet No. 3 was preceded by the invigorating but rather dry orchestration of Symphony No. 1, and this would in any case have been a natural impulse.

It was reinforced by the more particular demands of formal design. Having decided to use the five-movement form of Bartók's String Quartets Nos. 4 and 5, Tippett was obliged to consider a new type of formal weighting in which the movements balance each other rather than evolve from each other as in the four-movement model. His solution was to simplify the components and cast each movement in a unitary form, in order that the balances could be clearly set. Thus the three fast movements are all fugues and the intervening slow movements strophic forms. This inevitably postulated homogeneous sound characteristics for each movement and thus neatly confirmed the basic premise.

The sounds of each movement are accordingly all-pervasive and at one with themselves, and fully perceptible only when a movement has run its course (or most of it). They are flowing sounds, gaining definition through addition and accumulation. The listener senses that what is there has always been there and simply needs time to be formed anew. In this context novelty is irrelevant: the objective is to make sounds and textures characteristic. The five movements could be loosely described as translucent, singing, vigorous, rhetorical and liquid.

In some ways these were dangerous tactics. By sacrificing the musical idea's instant individuality Tippett ran the risk of being dismissed as trite, as well as setting a high premium on the authenticity of his music's essential content. But they were lineaments of his compositional personality already. The difference in his String Quartet No. 3 was of degree.

If then the thematic material of the Quartet was to be more reticent than that of, for example, the String Quartet No. 2, how was it to be prevented from sinking into anonymity? The fugue subject from the first movement will serve to illustrate how Tippett answered this question, by laying out a sound whose provenance is so immediately and disarmingly recognizable that its surface elements can be taken for granted, and whose substance is at the same time charged with those idiosyncrasies which give it individuality. Example 64 is composed of such expressions as are the stock-in-trade of the high baroque – a rhythmic patter, little appoggiatura figures. But its length already gives pause for enquiry (is it really a fugue?) and its strangely elusive tonality proclaims a later age. The most subtle clue to its identity comes at the beginning, where an innocent upbeat figure conceals a highly individual anticipatory rhythm (as in the explanatory addition to Ex. 64).

Ex. 64   String Quartet No. 3

All the themes in the Quartet could be examined from this point of view. As for their general purpose, they serve to introduce the typical sounds of their respective movements. Example 64 draws out a finely spun thread, with exactly the requisite strength to bear its own weight and stretch across a wide hollow, until it fastens on to another thread on the other side and instigates the busy preparation of a fabric worthy of Queen Mab. As a whole, the movement is correspondingly delicate, teeming with activity.

If it is accepted that each movement is to be identified by a single characteristic sound, Tippett's use of two sounds in his slow introduction to the first movement seems contradictory. Here there is both a sonorous harmony and a wriggling tailpiece, implying the oppositions of a sonata dialectic quite foreign to the proposed expressive world of the work. Maybe it was likely that Tippett should court such expectations and then casually direct his music elsewhere, just because the prodigious contrapuntal achievements in the fugal finale of his Symphony No. 1 had given him the confidence to flourish any compositional sleight of hand he chose to. Indeed the presence of three fugues in the one work is evidence of the relish with which he exercised this mastery. But these are tangential reasons. Deeper ones can be found in the work itself, notably in its proportions. It is a relatively long work and some indication of its dimensions was needed at once if the opening fugue were not to sound attenuated. The dualities of the introduction serve therefore to introduce the idea of expansiveness. Tippett skilfully elaborates this idea by allowing the tailpiece to grow into a mood of cheerful exuberance, rather than the gritty resolution proper to a sonata-allegro; and when this exuberance withdraws, leaving only a tiny sound in its place, it is clear that sonata oppositions are far distant. At this point the fugue begins. So the tailpiece is the precursor of the fugue subject, its kinship confirmed by a rhythmic connection (Ex. 64, bracket *a*) and made complete when it marks the first climax of the movement. The sonorous opening harmony behaves differently however (see Ex. 7, p.92). Admittedly it is woven into the texture at a later stage and uncovered as the climactic revelation of the movement; but this is a dramatic stroke on Tippett's part and no indication that its identity can be altered or clarified, as with the tailpiece. It *is*. Its sounds are immutable and ever-present. It is glowing, deep red, a source of vitality. If its sounds are heard in this way its function becomes clear. It is the *ur*-sound from which life springs and without which nothing can happen. The duality therefore is inevitable and necessary. It is tempting to follow this line of thought and see the Quartet as a parable: the first movement depicting birth and childhood, the second early experiences of love, the third the vigorous prime of life, the fourth questionings on the meaning of life, the fifth an apparent anti-climax or compromise, which eventually is shown to be rich and rewarding. If this interpretation seems credible, Tippett's String Quartet No. 3 would not be the first quartet to which its composer had attached a secret programme.

Certainly the second movement corresponds with such a scenario. In form it is very simple: two strophes, one major one minor, in each of which the theme is heard in the tonic and then in an abbreviated form in the dominant. The violins have the major version, the viola and cello the minor, the theme slowly winding its way across the whole quartet from the highest register to the lowest. An introductory passage precedes each strophe and then concludes the movement. This is an apt symbol of the unchangeable yet changing voice of love, beginning in a serene and rapturous stratosphere where no obstacles can impede its course and slowly descending to sadder and wiser territories. The most poignant contribution to this discourse is made in the introductory passages, where the viola, accompanied by pizzicato cello, takes the role of a loving, patient counsellor preparing for the vision to ensue. Of all the movements Tippett had written by this time this one most fully justifies the assessment of him as a visionary artist. Yet its vibrant lines and melting harmonies are made by transmuting nineteenth-century 'horn fifths' and the most familiar of idioms from the English pastoral school (Ex. 65).

Ex. 65   String Quartet No. 3

As the scherzo-like core of the work the central fugue is the most densely wrought movement and, characteristically, the most vital. It is a *tour de force* of contrapuntal and rhythmic ingenuity. Some aspects of its rhythmic language are discussed on pp. 109–11. At its central climax it generates such contrapuntal density that it almost expires from exhaustion. The recovery provides one of the most attractive moments in Tippett's music.

The fourth movement is the most difficult to bring off. It can sound like an undigested exercise in Bartókian impressionism, or as a venture into a type of rhetoric uncongenial to Tippett's temperament, or as a curious miscalculation – the third of its three burgeoning strophes emerging into a furious preparation for what turns out to be a disappointment. Tippett himself has not been wholly satisfied with the movement, since after the Quartet's first performance he altered the opening of the finale from an unaccompanied statement of its chorale theme to its present richer texture, presumably to give body to the sound and thus offer the fourth movement something worth reaching for. As recently as 1975 he altered it again by directing that the finale should dovetail with the last bar of the fourth movement. Certainly some special pleading is necessary if the expectancy generated by the fourth movement is not to be squandered. But if the earlier interpretation of its place in the scheme of the work is accepted, then at least it has dramatic point as an introduction to a finale whose want of incisive gesture is not an evasion of the 'finale problem' but a natural consequence of the work's conceptual premise.

Tippett would not have cast his finale as a chorale prelude simply in order to shuffle the pack and bring out another of the available fugal options. A chorale is a hymn and a hymn usually conveys thanks about something. In this context the thanks must be for nothing less than the richness of life. This music flows in warm, liquid textures and eventually leads to a final statement of the chorale with a clinching last phrase added to it. The work ends on a note of profound assurance.

Tippett's String Quartet No. 3 was his last major work before *The Midsummer Marriage*. A string quartet is not an obvious preparation for an opera, but it is precisely because this Quartet contains three examples of the most 'abstract' of musical forms that it exemplifies his natural instinct to think dramatically. Each of the fugues is a dramatic metaphor. This can be shown by reference to the tables below.

FUGUE 1

Introduction	
Exposition 1	beginning with unaccompanied subject and introducing three regular counter-subjects subordinate in character
Development 1	leading to climax based on motif from Introduction
Exposition 2	beginning in two parts; shorter
Development 2	leading to climax based on harmony of Introduction

Exposition 3   beginning in three parts; shorter still (introduces
                 stretto) based on Development 1
Codetta

FUGUE 2
Ritornello

A
  Exposition   double fugue, with two regular counter-subjects
                 subordinate in character
  Episode 1   a) canonic
                 b) 'Trio' motif in violins

B
  Middle Entry 1 subject 1 in canon by inversion at the fifth; short
                 link to
  Middle Entry 2 subject 2 in canon by inversion at the octave
  Episode 2   a) pedal
                 b) 'Trio' motif, inverted, in viola and cello
                 c) codetta

Ritornello

A
  Recapitulation in four parts
  Episode 3   a) as Episode 1a
                 b) as Episode 1b, in four parts

Ritornello

FUGUE 3
Introduction   pre-figuring fugue subjects and introducing
                chorale theme
Exposition   three subjects, all subordinate to chorale
Episode 1   based on all subjects, leading to entry of first half
                of chorale theme and entry of fugue subject 1
Episode 2   based on subjects 2 and 3, and concluding with
                entry of subject 1
Episode 3   based on subjects 2 and 3, and leading to entry
                of complete chorale theme and subject 1
Episode 4   as Episode 2, inverted
Episode 5   as Episode 1
Recapitulation of all subjects, with chorale theme
Coda   chorale theme with concluding phrase and tonic
                pedal

The first fugue is expository in function and therefore, unlike a
conventional fugue, consists of three expositions. While the expositions get
progressively shorter, the developments grow progressively longer, thus
indicating that despite its expository nature the movement is not a closed,
symmetric statement. The second fugue is designed to reassert vitality after
the meditative conclusion of the first slow movement. It therefore begins
with a decisive gesture of its own, called Ritornello in the table, and then
proceeds to the fugue proper. As the centrepiece of the Quartet it is the
most rigorous in contrapuntal technique and is appropriately more

symmetric than the first. Necessary points of relaxation are provided by three sections marked 'Trio' in the table, which return at regular intervals to create a basic form of scherzo with three trios. The third fugue shows some family resemblance to the others in that, typically for Tippett, it is compounded of two elements: chorale theme and a subordinate fugue subject, which with its two counter-subjects makes up a trio of equally weighted parts. (In the other movements the two elements are, respectively, fugue plus material from the introduction, and double fugue.) Its function as finale is symbolized by its closed mirror form.

Symphony No. 1

Tippett had planned to write his Symphony No. 1 several years before it took material form. He pondered its broad design while in prison in the summer of 1943 and started work early in 1944, completing it on 25 August 1945. Most of it therefore was written in wartime. But it does not project direct responses to war and is not a typical 'war' symphony, as are such instances as Shostakovich's Seventh and Eighth, or Stravinsky's Symphony in Three Movements or even Vaughan Williams's Sixth. It is the most forceful manifestation in this creative period of Tippett's instinct to weigh his personal response to a situation and conceive his answer to it long before putting pen to paper. Far from indicating imperviousness to war, the almost obsessively optimistic abstraction of his symphony makes a deliberate and pertinent statement about it. In crude terms this may be expressed as insistence on the resilience of the human animal. It is a large statement, and appropriately so in a form which traditionally serves to embody the highest aspirations of a composer. The work is not comfortable to listen to: it invites action rather than provides reassurance. It carries conviction because it is argued with such intellectual passion, such single-minded attention to the development of material that its character is not only validated but transformed as well. By the end of it Tippett has disclosed that extraordinary artistic phenomenon by which intensity of workmanship eventually generates a new being, in whose presence the listener can only stand in awe.

In style the Symphony is severely contrapuntal. Its instrumentation is designed to clarify, to analyse the contrapuntal lines: sensuous sonorities for their own sake are non-existent. In the two passages which superficially approach this quality – the codetta theme in the first movement and the trio of the scherzo – richly absorbent spreads of string tone function as structural articulations and are not concessions to euphony. Tippett uses each instrument and each family of instruments as components with fixed colouristic and dynamic properties to be deployed, according to the needs of the form, in varying molecular proportions. Since most of the counter-point is in three parts only, instrumental combinations are determined largely by questions of balance. Tippett has explained how he was guided in this matter by the principles of Rimsky-Korsakov,[55] in which one line of the string body is equal, in the *forte*, to one trumpet or one trombone, to two horns, or to four woodwind instruments. The result is a crisp and often

stark network of lines modulating in and out between mixed tone colours
and lighter, more brilliant primary ones, in the process isolating those
motifs which take on independent existences. In his first mature work for
full orchestra it was perhaps to be expected that Tippett would deliberately
test out techniques of this kind. That the results of his near didactic
methods should be so individual was however less predictable. Many of the
sounds in the Symphony reappear in later works. The only other composer
who adopted a comparable approach to the orchestra at this time was,
surprisingly, Webern.

In a lecture given before the Symphony's first performance[56] Tippett
suggested that his audience would be in the right frame of mind for hearing
the work if they imagined the first movement as an arrow, the second a
circle, the third a star. He was evidently defeated by the fourth – which
simply shows that these hieroglyphs were not part of his original
conception. But they are nice evidence of how practically he applied
himself to the task of introducing a new work and they are indeed helpful
clues to the work's character. The first movement is a dynamic sonata-
allegro, pursuing an unswerving course to its pre-ordained conclusion; the
second a set of mirror variations on a ground bass; the third a scherzo and
trio, glittering with points of articulation and held together by a lambent
centre. The finale is a double fugue. It is difficult to see what hieroglyph
could have represented that, unless it were the yin-yang symbol, and this is
unlikely to have been particularly instructive. Doubtless Tippett was
anxious that his finale in particular should make its effect without
assistance.

In design the opening allegro may be compared with the Beethovenian
prototype. But in character it is uniquely personal. Tippett avoids the self-
conscious opposition between the 'passionate' and the 'lyrical' of the finale
of his String Quartet No. 2 and returns to a style of rhythmic polyphony
deriving from his Double Concerto. The passionate is scaled down to the
vigorous and the lyrical is not stated abruptly but reached as a necessary
point of rest: there is no longer any genuine 'second subject'. The
exposition comprises two principal themes, plus a transition section
containing three themes and a final codetta section, making six thematic
groups in all. The work is thus laid out on a very broad scale, and this in
the first instance is what distinguishes it from the Double Concerto. The
thematic groups, though interconnected and motivically interrelated, are
distinct in sound and function. The major difficulty presented by the
opening of a long movement in Tippett's rhythmic polyphony is that the
style is intrinsically powerless to make the quick, decisive introductory
gesture. Its dynamic impulse leaves it no time to do so. Instead the gesture
has to be expressed as a full thematic statement and this will sound too
lightweight unless its rhythmic character is firm rather than supple.
Tippett's solution to this problem was to put the main thematic weight at
the bottom of the texture and to restrict its rhythmic articulation, initially
at least, to crotchets and quavers. In truth this opening theme is not wholly
satisfying, for its repeated crotchets can sound pedestrian, or even rather

jolly, unless they are handled with a delicacy which would in fact conflict with their character. Nevertheless it is rich in content. It contains all the essential diatonic intervals and its counterpoint is skilfully designed to end in unison so that the approving stamp on trumpets and violins can emerge naturally out of it.

Ex. 66   Symphony No. 1

Example 66 is half the opening theme, which is completed by a developing repeat. The second theme follows immediately, a more relaxed and eloquent neighbour, strangely prophetic of a theme in the first movement of Tippett's Concerto for Orchestra. Its second half is a free inversion of its first. The three transitional passages serve to regain the rhythmic impetus and prepare a textural calm, itself a preparation for a grinding canonic crescendo to the rhetorical climax, out of which emerges the codetta theme. This is a highly characteristic moment – a beautifully timed expression of release and reward for having withstood the logic of percussive accentuation for so long. The music flows in generous phrases, as if surveying the heights it has just scaled (Ex. 67).

The whole exposition is thus presented as a single paragraph. After a classically shaped development it returns *in toto* to form, with a short coda, a serenely poised whole. It is a sonata-allegro in keeping with Tippett's natural style, accommodating dense contrapuntal thought and the ebb and

Ex. 67

flow of dramatic movement without compromising itself to the letter of the
Beethovenian model.

The slow movement was originally conceived as an answer to the
criticism that Tippett's music had no bass to it. Such at any rate is the
reason he has been inclined to offer for the presence here of a ground bass.
Actually the movement has no firmer anchorage to a bass as harmonic
foundation than any other of his slow movements, since the ground is a
driving line functioning as the lowest in a characteristic three-part

counterpoint of lines; only at cadences does it become harmonic orientation. The real reason for the ground bass stems from Tippett's love for the
ground basses of Purcell and from his desire to use the form in a context
where its essentially static nature can act as a foil to the developmental
sonata-allegro.

Tippett emphasizes this static quality by reversing the sequence of the
movement's sections to form a set of mirror variations (not a palindrome, a
device he did not use until his *Songs for Achilles*, written fifteen years later).
For the most part the variations are grouped in pairs, a natural
consequence of the diminuendo from *ff* to *pp* in the ground itself.
Variations 1–2 and 3–4 are shaped as crescendo and diminuendo. Along
with variation 5 they begin with a lonely solo instrument (clarinet, oboe
joined by bassoon, and horn with solo viola in canon) and then build up to
a climax, the first of almost Mahlerian intensity, with jagged triadic
figures, the second of more submissive contours yet splintered by fragmentary phrases on a trumpet. In variation 5 these form into distant menacing
fanfares. The still centre of the movement, a trio for flutes, sounds in this
context like a lullaby. After such poignancy the rest of the movement
cannot be a routine return to the opening. In variation 7 (= 5) warmer
colourings of strings replace the forlorn horn and viola, and before this
variation is over the submissive contours of variation 3–4 flow into the
single variation 8, which is now all that is needed of the original double
variation. Variation 9–10 is the original 1–2. The crescendo of variation 10
leads into a coda.

The movement is an imposing example of its form and in particular of
Tippett's ability to sweep across the regular four-bar phrases of the ground
and create more free-ranging shapes. But it is a good deal more than that.
In mood it is sombre and harrowing, to be compared with the brooding
slow movements in some of Shostakovich's later symphonies. The ground
becomes a symbol of ineluctable forces against which the rest of the music
offers Sisyphean resistance; certain passages, notably the fragmentary
figures in variation 3–4 and the succeeding distant fanfares, inevitably
suggest a programmatic basis. It is impossible to avoid the conclusion that,
despite what has been suggested above, the movement is a direct comment
on war. If this is so then the vitality of the last two movements is even more
persuasive evidence of the work's central character.

The scherzo is the maverick among Tippett's fast movements, because
the vast majority of its 3/8 bars have regular accents and are thus curiously
uncharacteristic. Tippett did not write in this rather stiff manner again.
But to say this is to be wise after the event. In the context of the symphony
the rapid accentuation contrasts effectively with the steady pulse of the
slow movement and it revives the work's spirit with genuinely Beethovenian panache. It erupts with energy. And the irregular groupings of 3/8
bars show a fine ear for rhythm as a form-building agent.

Tippett was stimulated to write in this rhythmic style by some music of
Pérotin in the (old) *Oxford History of Music*.[57] He has explained how he used
this medieval material.

I had observed how Pérotin wrote vocal trios all in triple time in which, after a few bars of plainsong in crotchets, the voices took off in a flying hoquet on a chosen vowel in bumpy quavers. Yet the effect of these hoquets was always to have a very strong accent on each bar. This allied itself in my mind with the presto crotchets of some Beethoven scherzos, which equally have an accent to each bar. Thus I saw what seemed to me a new material for a symphonic movement of a scherzo kind.[58]

What he found in Pérotin therefore was a new way of re-creating the one-in-the-bar Beethoven scherzo of, in particular, the Seventh and Ninth Symphonies. But he also found a new style and a new formal method.

Example 68(i) below quotes the first section of Pérotin's conductus *Salvatoris Hodie* in the *OHM* transcription.[59] Its first seven bars constitute the 'plainsong', the remainder the 'flying hoquets'. Ex. 68(ii) is the opening of Tippett's scherzo, in which a brief ritornello-like passage is followed by an extended episode. Though by no means a 'crib' of the Pérotin, Tippett's music obviously derives from it.

Ex. 68

(i) **Pérotin: Conductus 'Salvatoris Hodie'**

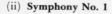

(ii) **Symphony No. 1**

In the complete *OHM* excerpt, comprising the first four-line strophe of Pérotin's text, the technique of treating each line as conductus plus *cauda* creates a form in which the conductus sections remain approximately the same in length while the *caudae* show a tendency to expand. Tippett took this idea as well, subjecting an initial strophe to two varied repeats in which expansion continues. In the table below the relative proportions of Pérotin's strophe and Tippett's three strophes are compared (numerals indicate numbers of bars).

PÉROTIN	*Strophe 1*	TIPPETT	*Strophe 1*	2	3
Conductus 1	7	Ritornello 1	7	8	9
Cauda 1	13	Episode 1	14	31	62
Conductus 2	6	Ritornello 2	7	8	9
Cauda 2	15	extension	9	9	9
Conductus 3	7	Episode 2	11	16	17
Cauda 3	12	Codetta	8	9	16
Conductus 4	6				
Cauda 4	41				

No mysterious numerology can be ascribed to these figures. They simply emphasize the deliberation with which Tippett applied his structural idea. The interesting thing is that the idea harks back not only to Pérotin, but also to the developmental methods he had learnt from Sibelius. His eclecticism is nowhere more strikingly shown than in this movement, which draws from Pérotin, Beethoven, Sibelius and, in the trio, the English virginalists.

The trio is a pavan, the form Tippett had previously used for the slow movement of his String Quartet No. 1. The Elizabethan prototype is less clear here than in the Quartet, not so much because the music is at a fast tempo, but because its ocean of string sound, spreading across the scene like a huge smile, is so friendly a contrast with the often strident and always volatile disposition of the scherzo that the contrast is already enough by itself. How the composer prolongs one richly accompanied melodic line to form a total of 118 bars is perhaps, in this context, of small importance. All the same, the melody is worth examining if only to show that Tippett never does the same thing twice. In the earlier pavan there are the traditional three sections, each followed by a varied repeat. Here the three sections comprise a theme and two varied repeats, the second a free inversion, the third a free transposition. The shape of the whole soars, dips and then soars even higher. The success of this scheme depended on the breadth of the theme, and Tippett conceived here one of his finest and most characteristic melodies, continually renewing itself from within. Its three phrases foreshadow the tripartite form of the trio as a whole (Ex. 69).

Ex. 69   **Symphony No. 1**

Fugues *within* a symphonic finale are relatively common occurrences – but *as* a finale? Apart from Tippett's Symphony No. 1 it is hard to think of one. Although the fugue declined in status anyway between the period of Beethoven and that of twentieth-century neo-classicism, the major composers of the twentieth century had good reasons for discarding the idea. The intimate proportions of a fugue subject and the linear nature of fugal texture are naturally suited to a small ensemble or even a solo instrument;

when transferred to a symphony orchestra they run the risk of sounding grossly inflated. It would perhaps have been part of Tippett's temperament to venture into such dangerous territories. But in choosing to do exactly this, he knew what he was about. He had proved that he could use fugue dramatically, both within a movement and as a component of a large-scale work. He had already written a fugue as finale to a string quartet and was shortly to complete his tally of fourteen or so fugues in this period with five more, two of them finales (by the last of which, in his *Little Music*, he almost flaunted his mastery of the form by nonchalantly throwing it to the winds half-way through the movement). In any case his compositional regimen insisted that he confront the 'finale problem' in the most uncompromising way possible. Each of the other movements in the Symphony is clearcut in form and there was no reason why he should jeopardize the integrity of his neo-classical symphony at the last moment. On the contrary, the fugue is the culmination of the work, the most strictly composed and the most decisive assertion of its character.

The finale is a double fugue in the true sense of the term. There are two subjects, one dynamic, the other lyrical. Neither dominates the other and neither, curiously, dominates the music. Tippett solved the problem of symphonic fugue by the opposite of what might have been expected – conceiving subjects not strikingly original in themselves yet powerfully expressive all the same. They are agents of expression rather than expressive agents, and allow the ear to concentrate on the behaviour of the music *qua* music. It is the method of his String Quartet No. 3.

The distinction between cliché and genuine creative invention can be illustrated by a comparison. The first subject, for example, might have begun like Ex. 70 (granting its composer the licence of a subdominant answer). What Tippett actually wrote (Ex. 71) transforms this convention-al gesture. Trills and colouring harmony immediately give life to it, so that an age-old formula becomes a vibrant, relevant presence to which the second motif can respond: that is, by being in diminution, it acknowledges the relevance of the first, breaks the tension and releases, like a filly from the starting gate, a line of rapid semiquavers themselves impelled by enough energy to sustain their momentum across two more appearances of the subject. It is dramatic music, and still only a fugal exposition. What registers is the nature and course of the action, not the list of runners.

Ex. 70

Ex. 71

Seen from a distance the action is simple and inevitable: there are two opening sections (one for each subject), a central development and a final section in which the subjects are combined. In detail it is more complex. The movement is a fascinating example of how Tippett used d'Indy's principles to regulate progressive tonality. Its goal is the tonality of E, and all the major points of tonal emphasis are designed to lead to this. Example 72 contains a plan of the movement, indicating these points as relationships within d'Indy's scheme. In the first section the subject entries in exposition and counter-exposition take the tonalities on an ascending cycle to the fourth and fifth 'fifths', the maximum point of brilliance in relation to E. The second section begins from the complementary point of maximum warmth on a descending cycle. In the development the entry of subject 1 'uses up' the remaining fifth, while subject 2 begins a movement back to E. In the final section the tonalities of subject 1 perform a dual function: from the point of view of their ascending cycle they approach the E from its flat side, as any other way would be tautologous; at the same time they invade the descending cycle of subject 2. The second group of subject entries reinforces the homing process with a *reculer pour mieux sauter*, which also absorbs a tonal complex involving all the relationships in a descending cycle. The final E could not be more emphatically reached, especially since it has been hinted at throughout the course of the movement.

Ex. 72   Symphony No. 1

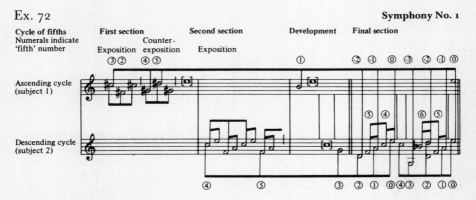

Tippett's control of expressive behaviour is equally sure-footed. He organizes his first two sections so that they have both sufficient structure in common to match each other and thus to form one large-scale expository statement, and sufficient individual freedom to remain true to their subjects. The first section comprises a three-part exposition of subject 1 with two counter-subjects (see Ex. 71), a short episode, a counter-exposition and another episode which drives to an abrupt halt – a schematic process in keeping with the tight and rather peremptory character of the music. Subject 2 emerges, a retrograde inversion of the first. There is another three-part exposition with, this time, a 'redundant' entry, already symptomatic of the subject's tendency to expand. The episode which follows is considerably longer and freer than that in the first section. It culminates in a counterpart to the first section's counter-exposition, a set of middle entries in stretto. In the development section Tippett begins to adjust the character of the subjects. Against a background of either semiquavers (from the first subject's counter-subject 1) or quavers (from the counter-subjects of subject 2) they are fragmented and then built up afresh. By stretching their inherent characteristics to extremes Tippett makes them not caricatures of themselves but, literally, each other. The two are indivisible. He can now demonstrate the logic of his position. Three statements of subject 1 are combined with two of subject 2; and after a short lull the process is repeated with the positions reversed. This is a remarkable example of integration, prompting the same sexual cum metaphysical questions touched upon earlier in connection with the Double Concerto (Ex. 73).

Ex. 73   **Symphony No. 1**

Tippett's counterpoint here does not promote a conventionally homo-geneous euphony. The themes generate such intensity that they are eventually consumed by the heat. In the coda the three-note fourths-motif (Ex. 71, *a*), derived from a counter-subject (although it is more a motto than a counter-subject),[60] finally falls on the tonic E, and is there reinforced by the bass drum. It expands by augmentation, double augmentation and then disintegrates. Across this the two subjects slowly disintegrate also until all that is left of the trills of subject 1 and the song of subject 2 are ever-expanding strokes on the bass drum, throbbing like an enormous heartbeat, an image of pure energy. It is an extraordinary and astonishing conclusion – and an appropriate climax to a body of work representing ten years of concentrated compositional effort in search of the vitality of things.

The Midsummer Marriage

Compositional Background

Tippett took about seven years, from 1946 until 1952, to compose *The Midsummer Marriage*. Ideas for the opera had taken shape in his mind long before 1946 however. Its genesis dates from as early as 1941, a year which itself marked the end of an extended period of thought and experiment in the 1930s, originally to have concluded with a neo-classical *opera buffa*.

The turning-point in this remarkable sequence of events occurred late in 1940. At that time, when he was composing *A Child of Our Time*, Tippett's plan for a comic opera coincided with an entirely different one which, though still for a comic opera, was prompted not by the technical demands of a kind of graduation exercise but by the need to relax and restore the balance after his exertions on the sombre oratorio. He even went so far as to draft out a scenario for such a piece, to be called *The Man with the Seven Daughters*.[61] Putting pen to paper in this way however seems to have made him realise that salted though it might be with the macabre, with social realism and with psychological *trouvailles* ('of course you realise at once that having seven daughters he is the most unconscious man in creation'), a witty entertainment was incompatible with his true instincts. Within a short time the foil to *A Child of Our Time* had been overtaken by a much

larger and more serious project deriving from the insights set out in the
final section of the oratorio.

As such it was also a dramatization of the psychological discoveries of his
own emotional upheavals of 1938/39. It is easy to understand how Tippett
would have wanted to recapture and profit from these experiences, to show
how positive feelings could be disentangled from the raw nerve-ends of
emotion and formed into a new equation, a new concentration of purpose,
in effect, a new birth. If Jung's concept of the unconscious were valid, and
Tippett had good reason to suppose that it was, it also followed that such a
project would by definition have far wider application, one moreover which
had particular urgency in the political climate of the early 1940s. And it
received the imprimatur of Eliot's thesis that the artist is one who struggles
to transmute his 'private and personal agonies into something rich and
strange, universal and impersonal'.[62] Tippett himself did not perhaps
foresee that his project would prove to have so insistent a life of its own.
The precise moment of operatic conception was unbidden and involuntary,
a 'first illumination', as he described it in his essay 'The Birth of an
Opera'.[63] The images thrown up here (they are given in full below) so
reinforced his conscious thinking that he now had no choice but to pursue
their implications.

Between 1941 and 1946 Tippett was therefore not only completing the
various works discussed in the previous section of this chapter but
gradually moulding his project into a workable shape. By the time he
started the composition of *The Midsummer Marriage* he had conceived an
operatic ground-plan ready to be given musical and dramatic substance.
So the opera really took over ten years to write.

None of the obvious reasons for this – natural caution over a first full-
length opera, Tippett being a slow worker and his score being unusually
complex – fully explains why the composition was so protracted. The
crucial reason is to be sought in the nature of the work itself, for it is not an
opera in the conventional sense, with plot and strongly contrasted characters. It is more a dramatic allegory. Its drama is precipitated not by human
interaction or the obvious laws of cause and effect but by the inner impulses
of individuals who curve around and past each other in a way recalling
the language of dreams. This kind of material necessarily drew him into
a debate with forces in his own psyche. It consequently introduced tensions
between intellectual and instinctive priorities which required extreme
patience to resolve. In his essay Tippett expressed the matter as follows:

> I know also that somewhere or other, in books, in pictures, in dreams, in
> real situations, everything is sooner or later to be found which *belongs* for
> all the details of the work, which is, as it were, ordained. And everything
> is accepted or rejected eventually according to whether it *fits* this pre-
> ordained *thing*, which itself will not be fully known until it is finished.

This 'thing'[64] can be variously described as the hold exercised on his
imagination by the images mentioned above or, more prosaically, as an

exploration of the meaning of the line 'dare the grave passage' from *A Child of Our Time* or, more poetically, as the idea that love can be presented dramatically as the supreme symbol of illumination and self-knowledge. That the 'thing' should be 'ordained' is a consequence of the fact that some aspects of these perceptions are unconscious: while they can be recognized they cannot truly be created. It may be accepted that opera in some guise or other is the medium most suited to the projection of analogues of the inner life, and countless composers from the Florentines onwards have treated it as such; but no other composer has used it to explore the psyche in so deliberate a fashion as Tippett in *The Midsummer Marriage*.

It would be wrong however to give the impression that the opera is a psychological treatise. Tippett offers an experience. If this experience can be described in terms of an idea and its development then the idea is, let us say, the stalk out of which grows a fully formed leaf, with its living forms, textures and substances. By concentrating on the intricate network of lines which makes up the dry skeleton of that leaf, as much of this section will do, one is nonetheless acknowledging the eloquence of the music. The music sweeps the listener into its own expanding universe with such persuasiveness that it immediately wins confidence in Tippett's affirmations. The music is easy to submit to. But it is *dramatic* music and without some understanding of the opera's libretto, appreciation must be incomplete. This is what prompts the extended enquiry, in the second part of this section, into the meaning and structure of a libretto which on its own may invite summary dismissal as pretentious or obscure.

An initial approach to *The Midsummer Marriage* can hardly rest content with the information, correct though it may be, that the opera attempts to illuminate the unconscious and to encourage the capacity for renewal such illumination brings with it; or that its 'message' is that problems in personal and social contact can be alleviated, if not wholly resolved, when the ignorance human beings have about their unconscious minds is removed; or that it tells of how lovers elope, quarrel, undergo various mysterious experiences and then are reunited. The difficulties lie in the mysterious experiences, for here Tippett has taken his characters into realms far removed from the reasonably plausible worlds of myth or fairy-tale. To those who have not studied *A Child of Our Time*, his premises will seem as unfamiliar or as controversial as his remark that the 'real revolution of our time' is the 'discovery and invention of the Unconscious'.[65] Yet these difficulties are less formidable once it is accepted that many of them result from Tippett's free use of whatever parallels he can find in cultural or anthropomorphic tradition to give shape to his artistic vision. His test of relevance is his own instinct. Whether the authorities he consults are reliable or not is beside the point. His allusions, references and borrowings do not constitute bits to be pieced together into some kind of mosaic, still less are they a display of cultural sophistication. They simply amount to those ideas which 'fitted' his 'pre-ordained thing'.

An opera of this kind invites new dramatic procedures or, if not that, a thorough reappraisal of existing ones. Tippett could draw on few ready-made solutions, and he could not afford the luxury of inventing non-traditional ones – the reward a novel conception might seem to offer its composer – because his material is so deeply embedded in human experience that some acceptance of traditional procedure was vital if the work were to be comprehensible. It was not surprising therefore that before starting composition he should have decided to draw up a kind of operatic balance sheet. He had already written four ballad and children's operas. Now he was as anxious to define the nature of opera as he had been to define that of the sonata before embarking on his instrumental works of the 1930s. Accordingly he singled out what, for him, were its essential features and reduced them to a set of four 'rules' which could be used to monitor the progress of composition. These rules are described in 'The Birth of an Opera' and they are worth examining here for their elucidation of the rationale behind the opera and of Tippett's working methods.

The first rule runs as follows. *The verse dramatist carries out on the words themselves operations which the composer effects by music.* Tippett derived this rule from Wagner's idea that to have serious pretentions as drama, opera should take its cue from contemporary theatre, where the heart of dramatic development would inevitably lie. Tippett subsequently explained that he thought Wagner had 'got it right when he said in *Oper und Drama* that you could no longer have the Shakespearian theatre with a great many scenes in each play'.[66] In order to make the transcendent manageable, Wagner had instead condensed such an enormous story as that of Tristan and Isolda into just three continuous acts, and in the process had been obliged to invent a contemporary theatre of his own since the necessary apparatus did not exist before. For Tippett, the situation was not so extreme. A workable theatrical apparatus did exist – that of the English verse-dramatists of the 1930s and '40s, Eliot in particular. The plots of their plays interested him only marginally. What interested him profoundly was their poetic technique, and the light this threw on the distinction between words for stage play and words for opera: in the former the crucial moments of heightened emotion are created by the words, in the latter by the music. In this apparently elementary observation lay the real significance of Tippett's first rule, for it clarified and indeed justified his function as librettist. No amount of literary skill could redeem an opera unless its dramatic and emotional substance were expressed by its music. The music must dominate in an opera, or, to borrow an expression of Susanne Langer Tippett has often cited, in an art mixing several arts, one (here music) 'swallows' the other (the text).[67] In an article about the nature of song Tippett put the matter more bluntly.

> The music of a song destroys the verbal music of a poem utterly. I am inclined to think that a composer responds less to a poem's verbal sound, when he chooses that poem as a vehicle for his musical art, than to the poem's situation, lyrical or dramatic.[68]

When writing an opera the composer therefore chooses situations. At a conversational or explanatory level of interest, situations will need words carrying greater conviction as words than elsewhere, but as situations approach higher levels of emotional tension then the words become progressively less important. They reach a stage at which they retreat into the background. They become metaphors, not sets of ideas for 'illustration' in a kind of musical onomatopoeia. In as far as Tippett is not a poet or a playwright himself he took such metaphors from all manner of sources. 'We composers have to be general magpies, and collect where we can!'[69]

Tippett's practice of writing his own librettos has drawn adverse criticism, and a critic bent on exposing a maze of undigested references could make short work of the libretto of *The Midsummer Marriage*. But if he did he would merely be announcing his inability to distinguish between a libretto and a play. A much more reasonable comment, frequently made, is that Tippett could at least have invited the collaboration of a librettist, in order to give coherence to his ideas and eliminate the occasional naïvities of verbal expression. In fact he did try to work with one,[70] but he gave up when it transpired that his material was so personal that the result could only have been a damaging compromise. For him the writing of an opera was not a question of looking around for a suitable subject. It was one of giving definition to existing impulses in themselves operatic. This being so, then the only person who could faithfully translate these impulses into words, assess their function as narrative or elaboration, stand back and judge whether they 'fitted' or not, was the composer himself, who would already have conceived an outline of his situations, their musical proportions and character, their sequence and so forth. Improvements could be made and advice taken, but having set out the verbal infrastructure the essential task in that respect was already complete. The functions of composer and librettist are in Tippett inseparable and speculations about a possible isolation of the two fruitless.

The second of his rules concerns the opera's subject matter. *The more collective an artistic experience is going to be, the more the discovery of suitable material is involuntary.* This rule seems to have been designed as a reassurance that the mythological background to the opera was genuine, and that Tippett's prolonged search for appropriate material would eventually be rewarded with approval from his own psyche. This background is examined in detail on subsequent pages.

The third rule, in effect, is a reaffirmation of Tippett's artistic credo. *While the collective, mythological material is always traditional, the specific twentieth-century quality is the power to transmute such material into an immediate experience of our day.* A succinct if rather crude summary of this credo would be of writing music relevant and valuable to a society which has witnessed the deeds committed in and the changes wrought by two world wars. An artist who turns his back on these things is, to use some words Tippett once quoted with diffidence but evident approval, 'free to crawl into the shelter of the safe old methods and rot'.[71] As applied to opera, and particularly to a work whose subject matter is mythological, this rule was easier to state than to put into effect. It was no longer possible, as it had been for Wagner

and the Romantics, to insulate such subject matter against its application
to real life by spinning a web of fantasy round it (however 'real' that might
be in psychological terms) and by peopling it with figures none of them
recognizably of any period: such an approach carried a moral stigma. Yet
the mythological material could not be gainsaid. Wagner's method had
been to enter into a sort of pact with his audiences by which disbelief was
suspended for a guarantee that the fantasy world would not be broken. By
adopting a different standpoint Tippett forfeited a crucial advantage.
Drama depends on the probable. If his opera was to interpret mythology
by juxtaposing fantasy and reality, if, that is, he was blatantly to advertise
the improbable by contrasting it with the probable, then he courted
disbelief continuously and compromised his work's plausibility as drama
from the start. To summon up the improbable, 'magic' moments through
the sternly logical procedures of music would seem no solution. Yet of
course it was – or at any rate would be, provided music's capacity to
overthrow conventional logic, to make probable the improbable, was fully
exploited. By placing the emphasis squarely on his music Tippett took the
decisive step of staking the success of his opera on this alone. He could not
really depend on help from stage setting and action, for they could turn
against him by visibly exposing any discrepancy between intention and
fact. His music therefore had to achieve two objectives: it had to create its
own persuasive logic, and in those passages where such logic was irrelevant
– the transitions between reality and fantasy – its qualities as pure sound
had to be compelling enough to carry the listener into an entirely different
range of experience. It is possible to detect a certain caution in Tippett's
attitude to all this, as if he were deliberately balancing his undoubted
commitment to the profound issues he raises (and his genuine fear that
archetypal forces could get out of control) with the thought that perhaps
the whole thing was absurdly high-minded. On the one hand he writes
such a scene as that between his hero and heroine in the Act I finale:
Jenifer, with moral rectitude, asks Mark if he is aware of the price to be
paid for experience of Dionysian ecstasy and Mark answers that moral
values are of no consequence in the face of such consuming passion. On the
other hand Tippett throws cold water on his whole apparatus by, for
example, having his Ancients, the stewards of that apparatus who normally
speak in grave philosophical aphorisms, utter such remarks as 'What's the
matter now?' or 'Lifted to such lofty heights, I do' (when accepting a
challenge from the 'villain' King Fisher). The voice of self-deprecating
irony is unobtrusive in *The Midsummer Marriage* but it is there nonetheless.

The above considerations already take for granted some of the implications of Tippett's fourth rule, which is a translation into more technical
terms of the simple premises of the first one. *In opera the musical schemes are
always dictated by the situations.* This rule might be paraphrased as meaning
that the music itself should create, should *be* the situations – in which case
the distinction between music as music and music as drama is a fine one.
The 'situations' can be regarded both as stages in a musical dialectic and as
dramatic situations in the normal sense of the term. Either way Tippett

seems to have regarded the sequence of musical forms and procedures by which the situations could be articulated as belonging to an archetype of dramatic expression as fundamental as that he had earlier perceived in the sonata. At its clearest this archetype can be found in the set number tradition of early nineteenth-century Italian opera, and this underlies the construction of Act I of his opera particularly. More pertinent to the technique of an opera concerned with 'continuous illumination' is the reworking of this tradition in the middle and later operas of Verdi. Tippett learnt many lessons of dramaturgy from Verdi, practical ones of, for example, allowing time for characters to get on and off the stage, as well as more musical ones concerning the use of 'recurring' motifs and the use of timbre to create mood. The most important lesson however concerned the weaving of set numbers into a continuous fabric. In this latter respect Tippett obviously learnt from Wagner as well. What he learnt most of all from Wagner was the use of the orchestra to establish an atmosphere or a sense of place. The sunrise at the end of the opera, the stage empty of people but filled with almost visible music, could hardly have been conceived without the example of such a scene as the awakening of Brünnhilde in the last act of *Siegfried*.

This rule leads to the conclusion that Tippett conflates the techniques of Verdi and Wagner in a way recalling the method of Berg in *Wozzeck*. And in as far as Tippett regarded *Wozzeck* highly as opera, if not as attitude, his own opera can be seen as a creative criticism of it. However, apart from references to Mozart's *The Magic Flute*, that is about the extent of the musical information conveyed in the rules. They concentrate on the dramatic and the conceptual. Even so they merely introduce the subject and a much more detailed examination of the mythological and conceptual background to the opera is needed before its meaning can begin to be understood.

The Libretto

The opera bears a Greek motto, with its translation: 'You shall say: I am a child of earth and of starry heaven.' This comes from the Petelia Tablet (now in the British Museum), one of the so-called Orphic Tablets or Gold Leaves of the late fourth century BC found in graves in southern Italy and Crete.[72] It is part of a text engraved on gold-leaf, rolled up and enclosed in a tiny cylinder connected to a fine chain, which was evidently designed to be worn as an amulet by a dead man on his journey through the underworld. The texts contain ritual formulae, and instructions about the topography of Hades and about how to produce favourable answers from its denizens.

By using this motto as a sort of gateway to his opera Tippett makes several points. The opera itself will act as an amulet, a ritual protection during the journey the listener will make into the underworld, the unconscious. It will enact the dangers and delights of this journey, objectifying them and presenting them in a formalized dramatic framework. The journey is dangerous because man is divine ('I am ... of starry heaven') and his godlike attributes, the archetypal forces in his psyche, will be encountered. But he cannot escape the responsibilities of his humanity either and the opera will take place on 'earth' as well. Tippett also makes the crucial point that whereas the author of his motto may have held to a literal belief in Orphic eschatology or in pure magic or in both, he himself believes that such texts and practices represented attempts to find metaphors for profound psychological truths and as such they are as valid now as ever they were. Perhaps even fourth-century Greeks did not really believe that their dead could drink in Hades from the well of living water, but the idea that death is a journey to be concluded by a rebirth or that in order to live one must undergo a 'death' is fundamental to mankind, appearing in countless ritual guises throughout the ages. His opera is therefore an initiation ceremony, a baptism, a *rite de passage*.

This is obviously a strange subject for an opera, and in order to establish a frame of reference in which intangible or supernatural presences could be accepted Tippett decided from an early stage that his work would include dancing: dance, to quote Susanne Langer, creates an 'image of a world of vital forces, embodied or disembodied'.[73] For this reason he originally referred to the opera as 'the masque'. But by 1946, when he began writing the libretto, he had decided that the work was more like an opera than anything else and it had become an 'Opera in Two Acts' (Act I ending where the present Act II ends).

It was provisionally titled *Aurora Consurgens* or *The Laughing Children*. The Latin title is that of a thirteenth-century alchemical treatise, discovered by Jung,[74] referring to the wisdom (*sapientia*) conferred by the 'Queen of the South' who, wearing a crown of stars, appears like a rising dawn (*aurora consurgens*). The stars symbolize a wheel or the sun, which itself symbolizes psychological wholeness. According to alchemical writings the wheel is turned by the four seasons. *The Laughing Children* is an allusion to a couplet from 'Burnt Norton' in Eliot's *Four Quartets*:

> Go, said the bird, for the leaves were full of children,
> Hidden excitedly, containing laughter.

The bird is saying that children can rejoice in the transcendent beauties of moments when the eternal and the temporal meet, but not adults:

> ... human kind
> Cannot bear very much reality.

It may also be mentioned that a few lines before the couplet in question, Eliot's image for the transcendent moment is the lotus, whose significance to Tippett is explained later.

Both titles are in their ways reasonable indications of the opera's subject. But the beguiling alliteration of the eventual title confers obvious advantages. It is attractive on its own account and tells that the opera is a 'comedy'; and of course it summons up the enchanted world of *A*

Midsummer Night's Dream. Tippett's opera has much in common with the Shakespeare. It also has two pairs of lovers in a magic wood, it interweaves fantasy and reality, and it capitalizes on the idea that 'midsummer madness' signifies a willingness to accept the workings of the imagination. It also is a dream.

Most operas, in effect if not by design, explore the world behind the external trappings of human behaviour. That is indeed one of the prime justifications for the genre, its very nature announcing a covenant with the strange and marvellous. In so far as art in general seems, in contemporary estimation, to have superseded religion as the favoured representative of the unconscious, opera in particular can lay claim to being an especially well-endowed sub-representative. Music mirrors the fluidity of unconscious activity more directly than any other art and opera uses real human beings as counters. What is surprising is that so few composers have sought to combine opera with another eternally valid projection of the unconscious, the dream, and form an alliance potentially, at least, more persuasive than any other. Strauss in *Die Frau ohne Schatten*, Schoenberg in *Erwartung* and *Die glückliche Hand*, Shostakovich in *The Nose* and Weill in *Lady in the Dark* are among those who have approached such an idea. Only in *The Midsummer Marriage* however does it become explicit. It would be overstating the case to say that the opera is planned wholly as a dream; for one thing it continually shifts from dream to (qualified) reality, and besides, it can be understood in various other ways. But it persistently uses dream images, and this explains many idiosyncrasies of character and content.

A dream can be described as a vision of the unknown, taking place during intervals out of time. The opera creates the illusion of a short stretch of time expanded by an enormous parenthesis. A few minutes after the beginning the lovers meet; a few minutes before the end they meet again to the same music and it seems as if the intervening two and a half hours or so have taken place in some other dimension. Sequences of events in a dream provide their own justification; only when awake does the dreamer try to discover a comprehensible pattern of cause and effect. So with the opera. In dreams, people are sensed as presences rather than physical beings and in the opera the characterization is similarly muted, with none of the magnified contrasts or the concrete individuality usually associated with the genre. Perspective in dreams is either missing or very deep, in which case there is no blurring of focus whether the foreground or the background holds the attention. The opera exhibits a similar phenomenon, as if the spectator is witnessing one of those strange miracles of nature when the light, the clouds, the atmosphere and the sun suddenly combine to create the effect of a visitation: the horizon is as clear as the foreground and everything vibrantly coloured and shaped.

Why the opera can be experienced in these terms relates to Tippett's interest in Jung: to the belief that dreams offer metaphors of unconscious activity and can be regarded as pointers towards self-understanding; and to the insights gained during Tippett's analysis of his own dreams, when he himself encountered that range of image which sanctioned a comparable diversity in his opera. The language of dreams could therefore provide the environment in which a dramatization of 'the experiences of knowing the shadow and the light' could plausibly be acted out. Although not occurring in an actual dream, the images presenting themselves as the 'first illumination', and Tippett's interpretation of them, reinforce these correspondences. In 'The Birth of an Opera' Tippett described them thus:

> I *saw* a stage picture (as opposed to hearing a musical sound) of a wooded hilltop with a temple, where a warm and soft young man was being rebuffed by a cold and hard young woman (to my mind a very common present situation) to such a degree that the collective, magical archetypes take charge – Jung's *anima* and *animus* – the girl, inflated by the latter, rises through the stage flies to heaven, and the man, overwhelmed by the former, descends through the stage floor to hell. But it was clear they would soon return. For I saw the girl later descending in a costume reminiscent of the goddess Athena (who was born without father from Zeus's head) and the man ascending in one reminiscent of the god Dionysus (who, son of earth-born Semele, had a second birth from Zeus's thigh).

Supposing that Jung himself had agreed to collaborate on the libretto, an improbable but convenient hypothesis, it may be imagined that he would have accepted the above as a basis for a scenario; and then perhaps, on the grounds that integration of personality may be achieved vicariously through witnessing a collective rite or ceremony, in this case an opera, or that a rite is a dam to 'keep back the dangers of the unconscious',[75] gone on to expand it into a full-scale individuation process, an exemplary exploration of the unconscious. The opera has many points in common with this model and a comparison between the two is instructive.

The Jungian individuation process (as relevant to perfectly 'normal' people as to those with real psychological difficulties) may be described as an undertaking in dream analysis which aims to remove the barriers to self-understanding by revealing the archetypes one by one, until a synthesis and re-orientation between the conscious and the unconscious is created. Although archetypal dream images may in practice occur in a variety of orders and groupings, progress in individuation depends on their conscious identification and assimilation in a specific order: shadow, anima/animus, 'mana personality'[76] and self (this was Jung's earlier view at least: later he recognized that there could be individual variation in the order of assimilation). An attempted definition of the first two archetypes has been given already, in the section on *A Child of Our Time* (see pp. 156, 162). These can be manifested only through a relationship with someone of the same and the opposite sex respectively. The mana personality is, for a man, the wise old man, and for a woman, the great mother. These archetypes will be manifested only when the anima/animus has been accepted and understood as the mediator between conscious and unconscious – when, that is, it has forfeited some of its immanent power, its mana. The mana now released is taken over by both conscious and unconscious and appears in the above projections. These embody the dominant sexual characteristics within the individual, the primordial masculine logos and the primordial feminine eros. The danger is that identification with such awesome forces, possible because the conscious mind has contributed to their revelation, will inflate the ego and invite retaliation from the unconscious. So a delicate balance has to be preserved and it is on this level ground that the existing ego can be 'sacrificed' and a re-orientation can occur, through an image of the self (p.162).

The action of the opera may be summarized as follows:

Midsummer day. The scene is a clearing in a wooded hilltop, in the middle of which is a temple surrounded by a group of buildings.

ACT I (morning). The chorus assembles for the run-away marriage of their friends, Mark and Jenifer. They are frightened away by a group of dancers from the temple, led by Strephon and followed by the two Ancients. A sword dance. Mark arrives and stops the dance, demanding a new one for his wedding day. He quarrels with the Ancients who then usher the dancers away. When Jenifer arrives, she says she has no intention of getting married: 'It isn't love I want, but truth.' She climbs a stone staircase near the temple and disappears from sight. Mark in turn disappears into a cave. King Fisher, Jenifer's father, accompanied by Bella, his secretary, arrives in search of his absconding daughter. Convinced that Jenifer is in the cave, he first tries to persuade the Ancients to open its gates and when that fails agrees to Bella's suggestion that Jack, her boy-friend who is a mechanic, should be asked to help. Jack tries to force open the gates but a mysterious voice from within warns King Fisher not to meddle. At the climax of his frustration Mark and Jenifer return, strangely transfigured. They both sing of their experiences and finding themselves in even sharper disagreement, go off again in opposite directions, Jenifer into the cave, Mark ascending the staircase.

ACT II (afternoon). Strephon begins a dance, but is interrupted by the chorus and then by Bella and Jack. It being midsummer day, Bella proposes to Jack. Three ritual dances follow, in each of which Strephon, in various animal transformations, is hunted by a female dancer, similarly transformed. At the climax of the third he is nearly caught and killed but at that moment the dance is stopped by the terrified cries of Bella, who has been watching with Jack. The dancers vanish. Jack comforts Bella and restores her composure.

ACT III (evening and night). The chorus celebrates after a meal. King Fisher sends them away to escort Sosostris, his private clairvoyante, who will outwit the Ancients and return Jenifer to him. The chorus reappears, not however with Sosostris but with an impostor who turns out to be Jack. He is exposed and in the ensuing confusion the veiled figure of the real Sosostris appears. She describes from the pictures in her bowl a vision of Mark and Jenifer making love. King Fisher loses patience. Jack is given a belt, holster and pistol and commanded to unveil Sosostris. But he refuses to do so. Instead he chooses his own destiny and goes off with Bella. King Fisher unveils Sosostris himself, thereby revealing an incandescent bud, which slowly opens into a glowing lotus flower. Within are seen Mark and Jenifer transfigured as the Indian gods, Shiva and Shakti, in mutual embrace. King Fisher aims his pistol at Mark, at whose glance King Fisher falls dead. While the She-Ancient comes forward and addresses the audience, his body is carried into the temple. Strephon and his dancers then perform the fourth ritual dance, a fire dance, in front of the transfigured couple. Strephon sinks exhausted at their feet and is absorbed into the flower, which gathers together and bursts into flames. The scene becomes a chilly morning. Dawn breaks. Mark and Jenifer enter, in normal clothes though 'dressed for a wedding'. She now accepts the wedding ring, and they disappear into the distance. The sun rises.

Many of these mysterious events can be explained by reference to the Jungian model. Tippett firstly, through his dancers, creates the mental space in which such events can arise naturally, and then he introduces images or situations for all four archetypes, in the 'correct' order. Some initial difficulty is presented by the fact that Jung used the word for the first of them, the shadow, to mean three things: the personal shadow (the manifestation in dream images or in a concrete figure of the repressed or unrealized characteristics of an individual pertaining to his or her sex), the collective shadow (a genuine archetype, 'the lowest levels of which are indistinguishable from the instinctuality of an animal'[77]) and the unconscious as a whole (the 'shadow' side of the personality). Tippett seems to have used all three meanings. The personal shadow is not necessarily a negative figure, since it can represent unfulfilled potential as well as repressed embarrassments, as is evidenced in literature, for example, by the twin figures of Dante and Virgil or Christian and Hopeful. It is a 'living part of the personality and therefore wants to live with it in some form'.[78] In the opera Mark's personal shadow is Strephon. In a sense he *is* Strephon. While implying he has to some extent come to terms with his personal shadow, for Mark shows at the beginning of the opera that he knows Strephon already, the presence of Strephon more specifically indicates an intuition of the world behind Mark's youthful illusions and therefore his readiness for what ensues. This character pairing is an extremely ingenious dramatic device for it enables Tippett, in Act II of the opera, to focus directly on imaginative understanding by limiting the character to Strephon only. At the end of the opera the absorption of Strephon in the fire symbolizes the total integration of the shadow. It may also be mentioned here that the emphasis laid by Tippett on Strephon suggests that the opera is not really about Mark and Jenifer but about Mark alone.

Unless King Fisher is regarded as representative of the collective shadow (and while feasible, this is not wholly convincing since he has another role to play), Tippett has included no obvious manifestation of this concept. It may be argued however that the appearance of Jack as the false Sosostris amounts to a very particular type of the collective shadow. If this is the case Jack's appearance would be of the 'trickster-figure',[79] a product of the collective shadow designed, by its irresponsible and buffoonish character, to divert attention from the presence of imminent forces almost too frightening to contemplate. In effect, it is a sign of an awesome happening – as is the case, for Sosostris herself then appears. So, although this archetype appears 'out of turn', it could be said that Tippett introduces a variant of it nonetheless.

There is no doubt however that he uses the word shadow to mean the unconscious as a whole. Just before Jenifer begins her ascent in Act I she addresses Mark: 'For me the light! For you, the shadow!' In context, this is the only possible interpretation of the term, since Mark then goes into the cave, as age-old a symbol of the entrance to the underworld as a stairway or ladder is of the entrance to heaven. All the same it is somewhat misleading. Mark would be deceiving himself if he thought that it was simply the shadow he was entering. The quarrel has precipitated (in Jungian fashion, i.e., through interaction between the sexes) the emergence of a much deeper and more particular aspect of the shadow, the anima. In the same way, Jenifer is not seeking light simply in the sense of conscious awareness: she is overtaken by the archetypal power of that idea in her psyche, the animus.

She returns, partially transfigured as the war-like goddess of wisdom and the hunt, Athene, possessed by her animus, he as the effeminate god of the ecstasies of the vine and the flesh, Dionysus, possessed by his anima. As Tippett points out in the passage quoted above and in his libretto, the fact that the mothers of these divinities were respectively divine and human and that they were born out of the head and thighs respectively of Zeus, reinforces the symbolism. (That they were born of Zeus and not their real mothers is an indication of the process of rebirth now set in motion. What their common father signifies is not clear.) These are classic archetypal symbols, highly compact illustrations of the concept in its essential form. To say that however begs the question of what the essential form might be. Such an elusive concept will inevitably be expressed in subjective, imaginative terms, however 'collective' its essence. While this first manifestation of the anima/animus is relatively easy to grasp, what Tippett does next is less so. Mark and Jenifer then go off in complementary directions, he this time to the 'light', she to the 'shadow'. They seek the other side of their respective archetypal experiences. The anima is not only 'feminine' instinct and sensuality; it is also withdrawn inertia. The animus is not only 'masculine' spirit, intellect, logic, it is also fierce concentration. When the two reappear in Act II, he as Strephon, she as 'girl dancer', it is already clear for this reason that the Ritual Dances are acting out archetypal behaviour at a very deep level of perception. In order to escape the pursuing girl dancer, Strephon constantly transforms himself – into hare, fish, bird. In order to catch him, the girl dancer likewise transforms herself – into hound, otter and hawk. These dances say that the female animus is a ruthlessly predatory creature, and the male anima her pitiful victim. But who knows a hawk from a handsaw? Since Mark and Jenifer are also experiencing what is within themselves, the dances also mean the opposite – that the hunter is within the male, the quarry within the female. It is a neat geometric equation.

Tippett's treatment of the 'mana personality' is equally individual. Mark does not encounter the figure of the wise old man at all and, according to theory, the great mother archetype would appear for the woman only. But Sosostris's vision is vouchsafed to both Jenifer and Mark, not to mention all the other characters on stage. Tippett is clearly saying that while creative wisdom is 'feminine' in essence, it is accessible to both sexes. From Mark's point of view Sosostris is a further manifestation of the anima, that is, a compensating archetype of the great mother as wisdom (*sapienta*, see p.216), now that his acceptance of the other anima projections has confirmed his detachment from primitive understanding of the anima as physical mother. It should be mentioned here that the two Ancients might be regarded as mana personalities. In so far as they act pompously and are apparently indifferent to human predicaments they behave according to Jung's conception of mana personalities in their initial projections; and although they do not, as in the Jungian model, become progressively more reasonable and integrated, their music does (see p.252). What they lack however is the numinous quality of a Sosostris.

The mandala symbol Tippett uses for the archetype of the self has been made familiar from Jung's writings. Mandalas are semi-abstract, circular patterns (mandala is Sanskrit for circle), created either spontaneously or as an aid to contemplation. The most beautiful examples are from Tibetan Buddhism and have the basic form of a lotus flower, at the centre of which is often depicted the Hindu god Shiva, the timeless essence of being, locked in eternal embrace with his female counterpart, Shakti, from which conjunction springs the creation of the world. Mandalas are not necessarily Eastern, nor are they relics of defunct religious belief. Jung discerned mandala patterns in cultures ranging across the whole world, both in distant ritual and in the creative imagination of his contemporaries. He regarded them as one of the oldest and most widespread images of the self.[80]

Tippett has been criticized for choosing so esoteric a solution to his dramatic problem, and justly, for there was no pressing need for his visual symbol to be so specific. The lotus flower and Hindu deities strike little or no resonance in a Western audience, however accurately or authentically they are presented on stage. At least that was so in the 1950s. Three decades later, the situation is not quite the same – already some vindication of Tippett's evident conviction that such universal symbols would have a subliminal effect and, with the gradual erosion of cultural boundaries, a more direct one. The reason for his choice can however be seen from a different angle. If the 'sacred marriage' of the light masculine and the dark feminine were to carry emotional weight the only metaphor he could have used was a sexual one. And if an important theme of the opera was that illumination flows from love, the answer was the same. That theme is not particularly original, but it remains the only absolute truth common human experience will corroborate. For 2000 years Christian civilization has been so frightened of sex that no generally understood and accepted metaphor of this truth has evolved, despite ingenious devices for getting round the problem. Even though the Christian myth is in essential respects the same as a primitive *rite de passage*, Tippett could not, for example, have used such a metaphor as Christ and his church bride, since that is too circumscribed and in any case promises rebirth only after real death. At the same time actual love-making on stage, even supposing it to have been permissible, would have introduced a realistic dimension entirely foreign to the opera. The idea had to remain allegorical, ritualized, and fixed in some cultural tradition. The only tradition to have embraced the idea was Indian.

And another factor must be taken into account. The twentieth century has seen an enormous expansion of historical knowledge. With this has developed as real a sense of identity with human aspiration in the untold past as with human aspiration in the immediate present. A corresponding alteration of historical awareness has occurred. For Tippett this seems to mean that the Christian conception of history or time as a unique event from genesis to world's end has given way to one in which time continually revolves and repeats. 'I ally this sense of the past with those Indian religious myths of creation which ... are designed to enforce the idea that creations and aeons have already been, and will be yet, innumerable.'[81] His symbol therefore offers a paradigm of perpetual renewal.

Whatever may be said about Tippett's solution, comparison between the operatic events and the Jungian model establishes a clear connection between the two. Tippett's debt to Jung is self-evident; as it is, the opera could hardly have been conceived without Jung's insights.[82] There is no need to labour the point, but two further correspondences are worth mentioning for their exemplification of how Tippett interpreted and developed the model, of how the correspondences are at once close and tenuous.

The individuation process should involve two people, the 'patient' and the analyst as well, who averts possible self-deception or self-inflation by ensuring a realistic contact with the world as it is and as it must be lived in. This is reflected in the opera by the characteristic switching between the transcendental world of Mark and Jenifer and the mundane world of King Fisher and, to a lesser extent, of Jack and Bella. Jung considered that the process could take place without external prompting, especially in the first half of life when most people have a naturally perceptive and workable understanding of their emotional needs. This idea is accommodated by

Jack and Bella, who encounter transcendental experience *en passant*, so to speak, and thereby acquire enough subliminal enlightenment to go off and get married without elaborate self-questioning.

At this point the correspondences begin to fade. Jung was not doctrinaire by inclination, but he was unusually firm in his belief that an individuation process deliberately undertaken was appropriate only at or after middle age. He reasoned that only then would the ego be mature enough to accept the idea of integration. Although Tippett was himself middle-aged when he wrote the opera, he implicitly rejects this view, since Mark and Jenifer, who 'endure for us the perils of the royal way', are young people. And they needed to be if another central theme of the opera was to be preserved – the idea that youth and vitality, represented by Mark and Jenifer, will always prevail over the old order, represented by King Fisher. Tippett also knew that the outcome of a real-life individuation process was uncertain, and had he acted as dispassionate commentator on the human condition the opera would doubtless not have driven so powerfully towards its affirmative conclusion. Far from reflecting uncritical acceptance, his attitude to Jung therefore emphasizes the degree to which he was held in sway by his own, overriding idea. And, given his personal and theoretical experience, it also illustrates the degree of will-power needed to sustain the force of this idea and actively suppress those Kafkaesque presences, such as the retributive Eumenides of Eliot's *The Family Reunion*, which stalk the avenues of the mind as insistently as the more exalting archetypes. His working out of archetypal concepts is in fact highly individual. The dominant impression left by the Act II Ritual Dances, for example, is of a richly ambiguous mixture of the elemental destructiveness of the female and, through the thrilling sounds of the music, the sado-masochistic pleasure of the male. Whatever credence may be apportioned to this view of the sexes, it remains an exceedingly challenging one and so independent an interpretation of Jung's concepts that Jung is left far behind.

Jung's role in the creation of *The Midsummer Marriage* may be said therefore to have been vital but partial. It should be measured more in terms of relevance than influence. Tippett took what he wanted from Jung, and then went on to give shape to his idea by drawing on a wide range of other writers, composers, traditions and intuitions. What he wanted was some kind of structure within which to dramatize the idea of renewal.

Jung himself drew attention to the number of folk and religious rituals which centre on the idea of rebirth, and an important body of writings on this and allied subjects had appeared in England in the early part of this century. Tippett's wide interests and his voracious appetite for reading had already led him to some of this literature, in particular to the twelve volumes of Frazer's *The Golden Bough*, an enormous corpus of material on myth and folk-ritual whose underlying theme concerned fertility. When he first read it (in the late 1920s) Tippett was interested only in a general way; but when he began to consider the details of his opera he found that particular rituals described by Frazer had taken root in his imagination. In trying to discover more about them, Tippett explored other writers. For

Frazer, ritual was simply a means for obtaining material advantage. He explained it in terms of primitive magic (deriving, as he thought, from the fallacy that an analogy is a likeness). His successors thought differently and interpreted such myths and rituals as a means for obtaining spiritual advantage. Of these, one of the most important to Tippett was Jane Harrison. Her *Themis*[83] exerted a strong if rather shadowy influence on the opera.

In trying to trace the origins of Greek religion, and indeed of religion as such, she came to the conclusion that the familiar Olympian divinities were a kind of intellectual artifice designed to charm away the influence of real religious attraction, which lay in the cults of Dionysus and Orpheus. Behind these lay a pristine initiation ritual, reliving and reaffirming nothing less than Life itself (she referred to Bergson's concept of *l'élan vital* in an attempt to clarify what she meant). This instinct was channelled through the death and resurrection of a communal representative of the most obvious manifestation of Life, the annual cycle of nature. She called this year-spirit the 'Eniautos-Daimon'. So, while the Olympian gods could not be written off, neither could the Eniautos-Daimon. 'It might almost be said that the Olympians stand for articulate consciousness, the Eniautos-Daimon for the sub-conscious.'[84]

The relevance of *Themis* and of initiation to *The Midsummer Marriage* is already clear. What gives the book its special significance however is its hypothesis that in the ritual of the year-spirit lay the origins of drama. The ritual itself was of the killing, dismemberment, eating and rebirth of a divine victim, with Dionysus as the most frequently encountered protagonist. The protagonist gradually became personified as a king or a hero who battles with an enemy, and the ritual acquired a set format. This, according to Jane Harrison, consisted of the following Aristotelian events: an *agon* or contest between the king and his enemy; a *pathos*, the sacrificial death (which death is announced by a messenger and followed by a *threnos*, a lamentation); and finally a *theophany* (in which the slain king is discovered, the *anagnorisis*, and then, through an abrupt change of mood, the *peripeteia*, revived in some form of resurrection or *apotheosis*). In a sub-chapter to her book Gilbert Murray[85] demonstrated that parallels between the above sequence and the formal structure of Greek tragedy were so close that they could not have been fortuitous. He found the closest parallels in Euripides's *The Bacchae*. His only modification was to add a *prologue*, in which there was an expository scene followed by a choral dance.

F.M. Cornford[86] applied Murray's theory to comedy and found that in the earliest extant examples of the genre, the plays of Aristophanes, there also was an underlying formal structure, which not only showed an almost exact correspondence with tragedy at certain points but an even closer resemblance with what was known of Dionysian, i.e. phallic, ritual. 'Tragedy' was therefore in essence 'comedy', with the happy ending omitted because of its obscenity. In Cornford's scheme the Aristophanaic structure begins with a *prologue* and a *parados* (the entry of the chorus, divided into two, one half for each contestant in the *agon*), and an *agon* and

a *parabasis* (in which the chorus address the audience directly). Then
follows a *sacrifice* and a *feast*, interrupted by the appearance of an *impostor*,
and the play concludes with a *gamos* (marriage) and a *komos* (a festive
procession). The first two items correspond with the prologue in a tragedy.
The next two correspond with the *agon*. (The *parabasis*, according to
Cornford, was a residue of an earlier ritual in which the divided chorus
pleads its respective causes and was therefore part of the *agon*.) The next
two correspond with the *pathos* and *theophany* (the sacrifice, as when the old
man in Aristophanes's *The Knights*, for example, is cooked by the sausage-
seller, is the sacrifical death, the feast the ritual eating of the victim's flesh,
the two representing the *apotheosis* through which he is brought to life
again). The remaining elements are peculiar to comedy. The impostor, the
false hero who claims a share in the victory, seems to have the function of
confirming the status of the real one. The final two items are of particular
interest, in so far as they seem to embody the true *theophany* of the original
rituals. The *gamos* is a descendant of the ritual of the 'sacred marriage', in
which the regeneration of life is ensured by the most powerful symbol
possible – a sexual union between the risen god-figure and a representative
of the mother goddess. The *komos* is a descendant of the ensuing procession
of worshippers, following in the wake of the phallic god-figure. Cornford
therefore suggested that tragedy and comedy sprung from the same roots,
tragedy taking a form emphasizing death and resurrection, comedy one
emphasizing fertility and the sacred marriage.

If the central theme of *The Midsummer Marriage* was to be of renewal, if
this concept was so fundamental as to be at the root of all religious belief
and dramatic expression as well as of modern psychology, and if the basic
outlines of that dramatic expression, as manifested in the Greek play-
wrights, could help articulate what he, Tippett, wished to represent – if all
this was so, then the relevance of the preceding paragraphs to the opera is
clear. The table on p.227 shows how close the parallels are.

Every one of the Greek components is present at some point in the opera.
Its detailed structure and character is of course no more a literal repeat of
the model than was Aristophanes's structure a repeat of *his* inherited model
(his plays are not so simple and uniform as the table suggests).
Aristophanes refashioned and parodied. Tippett likewise adds his own
gloss, reflecting the fact that over 2000 years' worth of artistic enterprise
has intervened, that his scenario manipulates three dramatic threads
(Mark and Jenifer, the lovers and King Fisher, Bella and Jack) and that he
approaches a great social issue, regeneration after war, with the weapons of
the imagination while Aristophanes approached his contemporary issues
with the weapons of satire and ribaldry. Because Tippett's opera is more
'serious' it embraces the components of tragedy as well. It is in any case not
a 'comedy' in the conventional sense of the term, with a pair of romantic
lovers encountering the 'unexpected hindrances to an eventual marriage',
as Tippett himself described the 'one' comic plot.[87] Whatever romantic
accretions the word marriage may have acquired in the intervening years,
for Aristophanes the *gamos* was only a symbolic way of saying something.

GREEK TRAGEDY	GREEK COMEDY	JUNG	TIPPETT

Prologue
    Exposition
    Choral Dance
	Prologue
	    Exposition
	    Parados
		Shadow	ACT I
			Prologue
			    Parados (entry of chorus)
			    Dance
			    Exposition

Agon	*Agon* *Parabasis*	Anima/animus	*Agon 1* (Mark v. Jenifer)
			ACT II *Agon 1 contd.* (Ritual Dances)
Messenger *Pathos* *Threnos*	*Sacrifice*	Trickster Great Mother	ACT III *Feast* *Komos* (entry of Jack – *Impostor* – as false Sosostris) *Messenger* (Sosostris), or *Agon 2* (King Fisher v. Ancients)

Theophany
    Anagnorisis
    Apotheosis
	Feast and
	Impostor
			Parabasis 1 (Ancients to audience)
			Agon 2 contd. (King Fisher v. lovers)
			Anagnorisis (revelation of Mark and Jenifer)
			Pathos (death of King Fisher)
			Parabasis 2 (She-Ancient to audience)
			Threnos (lament for King Fisher)

	Gamos *Komos*	Self	*Apotheosis, Gamos, Sacrifice* (transfiguration, sacred marriage, fourth ritual dance) Epilogue

His brides turn up at the last minute and solely in order that sexual union may be implied. Jenifer's role in *The Midsummer Marriage* is not quite so functional, but certainly the absence of a named female counterpart to Strephon, not to mention the absence of a 'negative' animus figure in the Ritual Dances, suggests that the spirit of Aristophanes is at work on this level as well.

The principal divergence from the Greek model concerns King Fisher. Setting aside the manner of his death (Tippett could hardly have had him boiled alive, as with Demos in *The Knights*), the important fact is that he does die: he is not revived. In Aristophanes the part of the Old Man was the one through which the author spoke for himself and he always emerged victorious in the end as the bridegroom. The Young Man is a minor part and never the hero. The reason for Tippett's change of emphasis is obvious.

In the first *agon* of the opera the outcome is inconclusive, because that is the way with the battle between the sexes. But in the second, Mark defeats King Fisher. Youth conquers age.

To make this theme come alive, the character of King Fisher had to be drawn boldly and plausibly enough for the scales not to be tipped too heavily against him. Tippett therefore gives him a name which conjures up a figure with vital mythological associations. The Fisher King of the Grail legends[88] is identified with life and fertility, the fish being a sex symbol. He has become impotent through wounding, sickness or old age and as a consequence his lands lay waste. He and his lands are restored to health only through the intervention of a hero who succeeds after a prolonged quest in finding the castle of the Grail and asking the meanings of the various objects, which are sex symbols, displayed there. Tippett has a double purpose in evoking this legend. Like Wagner's *Parsifal*, which is a variant of it, the legend ultimately derives from the old ritual of the death and rebirth of the Eniautos-Daimon, and it therefore fits neatly into the mythological structure of the opera. As with the Aristophanaic model, it has one feature however to which Tippett adds his own gloss. In the legend, the hero does not usurp the king's position: he simply brings about its restoration. Tippett alters this – as does Wagner (though restored to health by Parsifal, the old king Amfortas loses his kingship). Mark does not merely succeed King Fisher; he removes him from the scene altogether. The significance of his action stands out because it confounds legendary expectations.

Tippett elaborates the function of King Fisher in other ways. By the transposition from Fisher King he not only lowers the tone somewhat but also emphasizes the contemporaneity of the opera (on the analogy of King Oliver, Duke Ellington or Count Basie). And by casting him as 'a business man' he is able to associate the world of business, commerce and mechanization with imaginative sterility, and underline the point by giving King Fisher the manner and speech of such a Shavian *bête noire* as Boss Mangan in *Heartbreak House* or Undershaft in *Major Barbara*: vulgar, overweening, sentimental, philistine – yet with the occasional touch of truth which lifts him out of caricature.

The most important contemporary allusion however is to the Fisher King of Eliot's *The Waste Land*. The diversity of allusion in the opera mentioned thus far already shows how much Tippett owed to Eliot's creative attitude – his insistence on the interconnection and interdependence of human feeling and aspiration and his practical exemplification of it by the use of motifs, references and quotations from cultures remote in time as well as in distance. Tippett learned a very great deal from Eliot. But this did not mean he had to agree with him. Eliot's protagonist watches over a decaying Europe, from which all values have been drained away. After the death of the Fisher King the final section of the poem offers no resurrection, no imminent hero, only the faint glimmer of a hope Eliot had to go to India to find. Eliot's use of Sanskrit in his concluding lines may have sanctioned Tippett's evocation of Hindu deities at the climax of the opera. But the spirit of the two endings is quite different. Eliot's is valedictory, vulnerable, acquiescent, while Tippett's glows with the ecstasy of absolute conviction. It is as if the opera were designed as some sort of consolation for Eliot, that the death of his fisher king was not in vain and that the waste land would be redeemed – or that the visions of supreme transcendental experience which haunt the pages of the *Four Quartets* (another Eliot work profoundly influencing *The Midsummer Marriage*) like a series of wasted opportunities, could be made into realities.

The character of Sosostris, also borrowed from *The Waste Land*, can be similarly understood. Madame Sosostris has reduced *her* calling to the level of a fortune-teller, and her remarks come true in a way she did not intend. King Fisher evidently sees the character in that light too, for he addresses her as Madame and eventually does not believe what she says. Tippett's Sosostris is however the genuine mouthpiece of the god, the Pythia at Delphi, the oracle. Her vision is true because it must be.

But this does not fully explain her function. Clearly she is no more a conflation of elements, squashed into some synthetic shape, than is any other of the characters. She is not just a counter in a game, punctually though she appears as messenger figure in both the Greek and Jungian schemes. Yet, if she really is a messenger from the unconscious, she must also be the voice of the creative gifts which make that possible. Whatever her place in the drama, she is also therefore the voice of the composer himself, describing the nature of the divinatory process.

Tippett has explained how he found a way of articulating this process in Valéry's *La Pythie*,[89] a poem about the sufferings of the oracle – fated to lose her womanhood yet give painful birth to the inspiration of Apollo, who eventually takes over her personality entirely and allows a 'new and white' voice to escape from her tormented body. Sosostris's aria charts the struggles and rewards of the creative artist, and follows Valéry's sequence in doing so. Valéry, however, is not responsible for the climactic sentiment in the aria:

> I am what has been, is and shall be.
> No mortal ever lifted my garment.

These words are those Beethoven kept on his writing desk, always in front of him, copied in his own hand and framed under glass.[90] He obviously saw them as applying to himself, the bearer of timeless, unknowable truth whose destiny it is to transmit, whether he wants to or not, some part of that truth whose significance is beyond even his understanding. Tippett did not know of Beethoven's interest in these words when he chose them for his libretto. All the same, there is perhaps something a little disquieting about a composer who sets words Beethoven never dared set. Equally there is no doubt of the authenticity of the music at this point in the opera – some of the grandest and most awe-inspiring Tippett has conceived.

Throughout the ages writers have said that the true poet has no choice but to seek transcendent knowledge of truth and wisdom through love for a woman. Robert Graves is one of the most recent to do so. His *The White Goddess* contains a rich quantity of ideas on this and allied subjects which Tippett found of signal relevance to his opera. In *The Midsummer Marriage* Tippett gives Graves's *Ewigweibliche* a more contemporary slant however. Sosostris certainly fulfils the essential poetic requirements, but from a different angle: she is not an outward projection of the goddess, but the figure within, the anima in her guise as earth mother whose consort the poet is destined to be. For Graves the price of this gift is a death, a torment of callousness, treachery and mockery.[91] The death that Tippett acknowledges is of a different order: the lucidity which results from the confrontation with the goddess is more precious than the agonies and ecstasies of the struggle itself. Oddly enough, this in fact is what Graves himself seemed to be saying when he based his whole book on a story with such an ending. *The White Goddess* is a detailed interpretation of a Welsh romance, exemplifying what Graves called the 'single poetic Theme': the birth, life, death and resurrection of the God of the Waxing Year, the central episode being an account of the god's (and the poet's) losing battle with the God of the Waning Year (the poet's other self, his shadow) for the love of the goddess. As such it had an important part to play not only in confirming the validity of the structure of Tippett's opera but also in formulating its dramatic action – as may be seen from a brief account of 'The Romance of Taliesin'. It is the story of how young Gwion obtained inspiration and knowledge from the cauldron of the goddess figure Cerridwen, by licking some drops which bubbled out onto his hand. The cauldron had been prepared for the benefit of her own son and thereupon she pursued Gwion relentlessly. He tried to escape by turning himself into a hare, but she turned into a greyhound; he dived into the water as a fish, she became an otter; he flew into the air as a bird, she became a hawk. Finally he turned into a grain of wheat, so she became a chicken and swallowed him. Then however she found herself pregnant, and Gwion was born a second time. Cerridwen threw him into the sea. But he was rescued by a prince, for which service the newly-named Taliesin repaid his master by confounding his enemy through superior powers as a wise and inscrutable poet.

The idea of evading capture by a series of animal transformations is a familiar component in the mythology of the sex-chase or in the reign of a sacred king, or, in Jungian terms, a familiar strategy for countering the anima, who often appears as an unknown young girl or as a dancer, as well as in animal transformations. Its inevitable end is often indicated by a seasonal order of events. Dionysus and Proteus are typical male figures, Thetis and Leda female ones. The idea has survived in recent folk-song, as, for example, in the following:

> Young women, they'll run like hares on the mountains:
> If I was but a young man, I'd soon go a-hunting.
> Young women, they sing like birds in the bushes:
> If I was but a young man, I'd go and bang the bushes.

> Young women, they'll swim like ducks in the water:
> If I was but a young man, I'd go and swim all after.[92]

Tippett had ample evidence to support the idea of using Gwion's escapades as the scheme of the Ritual Dances in the opera. Furthermore, the transformations themselves have appropriate symbolic meanings. The hare used to be regarded as a royal animal (it was also associated with sacrifice, because it has a habit in scrub fires of waiting until it is on fire itself and then dying a lingering death), as were fish and many species of bird. One of the most intriguing aspects of Taliesin's success is that his poetic powers were expressed in extended riddles. This, in Graves's view, was a means of disguising the heresy they contained (the identification of the Christian sacrament with the details of the ritual eating of the Eniautos-Daimon). It would be stretching a point to say that a similar riddling operates in Tippett's opera. Nevertheless, the correspondence is present, and perhaps further testimony to the hold Graves's book exercised on Tippett's imagination.

Along with Jung, Aristophanes and Eliot, Graves makes up a quartet of literary figures who can be regarded as the presiding geniuses of the opera's mythological structure: an extraordinary group, but clearly a beneficent one. If one of Tippett's voices had reproached him for this apparent retreat into antiquarianism or pedagogy, the other might have replied, in the words of his favourite Blake, 'Men are in a less distinguished Situation with regard to mind than they were in the time of Homer'.

Tippett has long been attracted to the proposition that a subject is complete only when it has reached a quaternity and it would be fitting if the present survey of the opera's origins could stop at this point. But many other figures contributed to the cauldron of ideas from which the opera sprang. To track them all down would be unnecessarily pedantic, but two of them, Mozart and Shaw, are of special significance.

The work which exerted a more direct influence on *The Midsummer Marriage* as opera than any other was Mozart's *The Magic Flute*. Strictly musical correspondences are few. But *The Magic Flute* offered Tippett practical solutions to problems of dramaturgy and in particular convinced him that his opera would not be a private exercise in myth-making but part of a living operatic tradition, as continued in such works as Weber's *Oberon* and most of Wagner. This tradition, as Tippett put it, is of the Quest, 'the incidents of which are traditionally extraordinary and supernatural, depicting as they do some continuous illumination of the hero.' Both the Mozart and the Tippett belong, therefore, to the tradition of the Grail legends. But they also belong to a deeper mythological substratum, for Mozart's plot derives from passages in *The Golden Ass* by Apuleius and from those writings of the first century BC historian, Diodoros, which describe initiations into the cult of the ancient Egyptian gods, Isis and Osiris. Like the Eniautos-Daimon, Osiris was slain and brought to life again.

More tangible correspondences between the operas can be briefly summarized. There are similarities of place and of character: an Egyptian temple near the Pyramids, a Greek temple within an environment suggesting Stonehenge; two pairs of lovers, one 'spiritual', one 'earthly'; the Orator, the Ancients; priests, dancers. There are less obvious similarities, such as that between the final invocation to the sun-god Osiris by his priest, Sarastro, and Tippett's final invocation to the sun itself. And certainly there are other, more subtle transformations.

It would be wrong to suggest by this that Tippett's opera is an artificial edifice pillaged from tried and tested formulae. He took over some of Mozart's operatic apparatus because it fitted his 'pre-ordained thing', and his borrowings, if they may be called that, simply indicate his recognition of what was appropriate. Where Mozartian premises clashed with his own, they were rejected. At the beginning of their trials in *The Magic Flute*, Pamina has no choice but to accept the strange behaviour of Tamino and follow his example. With the lovers in *The Midsummer Marriage* it is the other way round. And at this point the final literary godfather enters the arena. Bernard Shaw's influence is perhaps not so fundamental as that of the others, but it is pervasive, in the sense of acting as a touchstone against which Tippett's ideas, both dramatic and conceptual, could be measured.

In the preface to *Man and Superman* Shaw notes with approval the fact that in Shakespeare's plays 'the woman always takes the initiative'. She is the pursuer and contriver, he the pursued and disposed of. In his own plays, women are the practical ones, they run rings round their victims, they have the surest understanding of their sexual appetites, they have the vision. *Getting Married* is a case in point. Not only is there a visionary character (the coal-merchant's wife, who speaks in a trance of the transcendent gifts of love: she is a distant prototype for Sosostris) but also a feminist heroine. An hour or two before her wedding Edith suddenly announces that she is not going to get married after all – because, as it turns out, of the discriminatory marriage laws. Jenifer has other reasons for postponing her marriage. All the same, as Tippett revealed in his essay, this was the scene which prompted his first visual picture of the rising action of the opera. Shavian precedents of this sort perhaps confer some kind of literary and social respectability on Jenifer's action, as does the fact that after about seventy years Shaw's conception of the New Woman acquired legal sanction. Nevertheless, however discredited the Romantic conception of woman as passive, ever-indulgent redeemer may be, Tippett's experience is still a remarkable instance of how a relatively insignificant dramatic episode can germinate ideas fertile enough to grow into a whole opera. Tippett's own anima must be powerful indeed. Or perhaps creative impetus really is feminine. Perhaps Shaw did not exaggerate.

Such speculations are not entirely out of context. Many of Shaw's more mystical ideas were sympathetic to Tippett, especially as they in turn had been taken from Bergson. (It was through Shaw that Tippett read Bergson, whose ideas about creative evolution and about the experience of time held great interest to him.) If it had not sounded so ingenuous, the expression Life Force (Shaw's translation of Bergson's *élan vital*) might have found a favoured place in Tippett's own writings. Life Force is a way of referring to the life-affirming impulse which flows from an active profession of all human drives and instincts, and as such is closely related to the premises of the opera. In Part V of *Back to Methuselah*, Shaw took the idea into the realm of metaphysics. When the holy war between mind and body has been left behind by old age, there can emerge an ecstatic state of pure thought which so relishes living that Life itself can expand indefinitely (the play takes place in 31,920 AD) and gather an intensity such as to annihilate the barriers to understanding, make it possible not only to understand creation but to become the actual source of creation. (At least, this is the conclusion the bisexual earth mother Lileth, the personification of the Life Force, seems to be leading to at the end of the play.) This concept is embodied in the characters of the He-Ancient and the She-Ancient. They have not yet reached the ultimate state but from their omniscient positions they serenely and rather patronizingly expound their vision of creative evolution to their neophytes, whom they address as 'children'. Tippett lifted these figures bodily into his opera; and while he left most of their philosophies behind, he brought their *mise-en-scène* with them. Shaw's play is also set in a hillside clearing, with a Greek temple and a path of stone steps rising away from it. There is no cave, but there is a grove opposite. And the play begins with a dance accompanied by flutes, concluded by a handclap; the next dance is stopped, when the He-Ancient bumps into one of the dancers, Strephon. The correspondences are so exact that it seems as if Tippett is using Shaw's setting as a point of departure in order to show what *Back to Methuselah* really ought to mean.

Tippett's Ancients are more a dramatic convenience than philosophical spokesmen. With their dancers as votaries, their role is something like that of a Greek chorus; they are guardians of inherited knowledge, and they put this knowledge to wholly didactic purpose only once in the opera, in the *parabasis*. Tippett was more interested in the character of Strephon, in Shaw a tenderly drawn figure in whom the pain of heartbreak is never really assuaged, but now vastly expanded into the Mark/Strephon pairing. With this Tippett draws away from Shaw and sets his drama on what is in fact a much more practical and realistic footing. Heartbreak *can* be overcome by the deliberate sacrifice of illusions and be turned into a source of rejuvenation. It should be added here that Strephon also derives from Gilbert and Sullivan. Strephon, the hero of *Iolanthe*, is billed as an 'Arcadian shepherd' (the name is borrowed from Sidney's *The Arcadia*); really he is a 'fairy down to the waist – but his legs are mortal'. He enters singing and dancing and playing the flageolet, for it is his wedding-day. The divided personality gives occasion for some salacious *doubles entendres* in Gilbert and Sullivan. If Tippett wishes to say something about sex, he is more direct about it. The allusion serves principally to emphasize the division between spiritual and physical, but it also prevents the character from becoming too solemn.

The previous pages have uncovered the etymology of most of Tippett's cast of characters. The remainder can be examined briefly. He originally called his hero and heroine George and Margaret, presumably after the saintly dragon slayers. But these names were perhaps too ordinary. In any event both still have royal names, as befits their ritual status, and Tippett's personal interest in them is shown by their having Cornish names as well, Mark recalling the Cornish King Mark of Arthurian romance (who doubtless had *his* origins in the Fisher King legend) and Jenifer Queen Guinevere, wife of the Cornish King Arthur (Jenifer is a Cornish variant of the name). Tippett's unusual care in these matters echoes his approval of a sentence of Confucius that he quoted in his early essay, 'Contracting into Abundance'.[93] 'If an object is correctly named, something essential is contained in the name regarding the nature of this object.' Tippett went on to add his own corollary that if an object is incorrectly named it will be incorrectly valued. The naming of the characters is not therefore to be taken lightly. Even the seemingly conventional names of Jack and Bella are precisely judged. His brisk and self-assured secretary is pretty: hence Bella. Jack is a mechanic. A dictionary definition of Jack is 'man of the common people'; it is also a word applying to mechanical contrivances replacing manpower. It is also a familiar name for a Cornishman.

Similarly with the opera's title. As has been seen the word 'marriage' embraces both the familiar meaning and the idea of marriage between the dark and light sides of an individual's psyche – or of the sacred, royal, incestuous marriage, the *hieros gamos* of ancient religious tradition. 'Midsummer' makes play with the old belief that since midsummer is the turning point of the year anything might happen on that day. It also suggests fire-festivals. Until the comparatively recent past midsummer fire-festivals used to blaze out all over Europe at the summer solstice, huge bonfires being kindled (usually by 'need-fire', friction by rubbing two pieces of wood together) and made the centre of general merrymaking – dancing and singing, and the custom of jumping over the flames and/or driving animals through them. Sometimes a human effigy or a decorated tree was burnt and the ceremonies often concluded with a procession of lighted torches. A large number of these ceremonies are described in *The Golden Bough*. Tippett was particularly fascinated by some South German ones in which lovers would leap over the flames hand in hand, the higher they leaped and the higher the flames, the better for them.[94] Frazer linked fire-festivals with the myth of the Norse god Baldur, who was killed by a sprig of mistletoe and then burnt at sea. By this argument (which drove straight through the Christianizing of the ceremony and its connection with St John the Baptist) he reached the conclusion that fire-festivals were ultimately related to a primitive initiation ceremony – what, in Jane Harrison's terminology, would have been the ritual of the Eniautos-Daimon. Fire-festivals represented the killing of a failing god in order that his spirit might be resurrected in a more worthy successor.[95] Fire has always been regarded as a means of purification and release from bodily constrictions, a fit preparation therefore for communion with the gods.[96]

Modern psychology equates fire with passion and particularly sexual passion. Jung took this view a step further, regarding Eros as an archetypal bearer of light, in all senses of the word, and thus of energy, whose power to overwhelm the psyche was fully understood by those who kept it at a distance through myth or ritual.[97] Of all the meanings of the symbolism of the fire dance at the climax of Tippett's opera, perhaps the most significant is that it is a ritual.

Tippett's stage setting was obviously conceived with as much care as his title. A clearing in a wood suggests an ancient magic circle within which the sacred ritual could be enacted safe from outside interference. Tippett does not however seem to have been so sure how to describe what his setting should look like. It is one thing to release the imagination into a world where art, religion and communities have not been driven apart by opposing dogmas, another to confuse it by teasing allusions to a Greek temple suggesting Apollo's temple on Parnassus at Delphi and a megalithic monument suggesting Stonehenge. The music is not at all surrealistic in this way. Stonehenge seems to predominate, for the 'semicircular group of buildings' around the temple is an unmistakable reference to the extended semicircle of stones embracing the central altar-stone there, the so-called 'horned gate' (whose shape derives from the belief that spiritual energy flows from a bull's horns and from its visual suggestion of receptivity, readiness to link the human with the divine). The stage directions at the end of the opera confirm the connection: the buildings then should be seen only as 'ruins and stones silhouetted against the sky'. Tippett obviously wanted his directions to lead to the mythology behind them, but it is difficult to see how allusions to Stonehenge can be avoided if they are to be observed reasonably faithfully.

As if the fabric of ideas discussed in the previous pages was not rich enough already, one further strand must be added. Tippett's sketchbooks reveal that the *I Ching*, the 'Book of Changes', was also occupying his attention at the time of composition. A considered assessment of this surprising fact will no doubt be made in due course. In the meanwhile a brief examination shows that there is some general correspondence between the opera and the book, in that the course of the action relates in some degree to a particular sequence of trigrams, the so-called Inner-World Arrangement.[98] This is a circular, self-repeating sequence, representing the life-cycle of the phenomenal world of the seasons – day and night, life and death in all its aspects. Given Tippett's interest in Eastern and Oriental culture, it is easy to understand how he might have wanted to bestow a kind of ecumenical benediction on the opera by relating his own dramatic sequence and his own interpretation of historical and psychic movement (the opera's action is rotational and is perpetually in a state of change) to a philosophy which likewise unites the idea of immovable rigour with that of continual transformation. The first trigram, *Chen*, the Arousing, is associated with the decisive movement of awakening, of thunder, of running feet, of spring, and of everything which that word implies. The opera begins with incisive chords, which perhaps might suggest thunder, and scurrying scalic passages which might suggest running feet. Certainly the chorus come in running, and the busy semiquavers in the orchestra might also suggest the winds which, as in the next trigram, flow in as a result of the reanimation of nature through the thunder. But this already shows that a literal and uninformed interpretation along these lines becomes fanciful, for the speed of change is here too quick and elsewhere too slow to posit a close connection. The Chinese book of wisdom may have contributed to the opera but it obviously was not a determining factor.

Many other factors did contribute, and some of them are mentioned in the pages that follow. Now however it is appropriate to gather together the principal ones discussed thus far and consider what relevance they have towards an appreciation of the opera.

Tippett has frequently been criticized for his supposed habit of pursuing the simple with such doggedness that it expires under the weight of the complexity heaped upon it. He certainly belongs to that type of artist who brushes aside the sophistications of his day and asks exceedingly simple questions, in the case of *The Midsummer Marriage*, 'How do you give purpose to life?'. Questions of this sort naturally provoke charges of naïvety. They accumulate so many other questions as to seem unanswerable, or at best to belong to the province only of fools and philosophers. They are not at all simple. But they are still worth asking, and if Tippett may be accounted quixotic in doing so, answers couched in terms of music are likely to carry more conviction than most. In any case the seriousness of Tippett's own answer is as undeniable as its complexity is inevitable. At the centre of this complexity is a modern re-creation of the myth of the Eniautos-Daimon – the idea of a renewal through sacrifice. The theme of the opera is the 'single poetic Theme' of Robert Graves. Clues to its meaning can be found in Jung, to its structure in Aristophanes and Graves, its technique in Eliot, its apparatus in Mozart and Shaw. Once these clues begin to form into a coherent picture then admittedly they seem to take fright and scatter in all directions again. And this is the point at which the commentator needs to turn to the music, the mechanism which keeps them in focus and justifies the whole undertaking.

The Music

An opera relying so heavily on music must obviously present its credentials from the start. And *The Midsummer Marriage* duly does so. By the time its first three scenes are over Tippett has established his music's primacy as agent of dramatic expression, shown what it can do in this respect and shown how the work's structure is to be articulated. In his earlier output a certain inhibition can be detected, the product of a tension between his naturally expansive lyrical style and the strictness of the forms within which it has been disciplined. In the opera, despite the fact that he has experimented with hardly any of its forms, there is a sudden loosening of the reins and the music surges forward with a momentum as elemental as the diurnal cycle within which the work is contained. Its language ranges from a triadic tonality so simple that Tippett had never risked it before to a chromatic and textural complexity equally uninhibited. It displays an ability to weigh the emotional temperature of dramatic situations and set them in place with uniquely appropriate material, in short an instinct to squander ideas rather than hoard them, recalling the munificence of a Verdi. While an earlier work, such as his Symphony No. 1, might eventually reach a comparable freedom of expression in its closing pages, it seems as if the opera is itself the closing pages of a work embracing the whole of his previous output.

In his earlier music Tippett had already demonstrated what limitless capital could be drawn from the expressive and structural resources of tonality. It is fitting therefore that *The Midsummer Marriage* should end with not so much the evocation of a sunrise as the chord of A major, the assertion of a tonality. How Tippett manipulates tonality in the opera is less clearcut. Logical and imaginative tonal schemes can be perceived quite easily in his earlier music. But the more the tonal organism of *The Midsummer Marriage* yields its secrets the more mysterious it becomes. If A major is understood as symbolizing the 'light', E flat, its opposite, the 'shadow', tonality can be seen to reflect the course of the action faithfully enough. From this line of argument, the effect of a tonality depends on the direction from which it is approached – from an ascending or descending cycle of fifths. Example 74 illustrates the theoretical basis for this

Ex. 74   **The Midsummer Marriage**

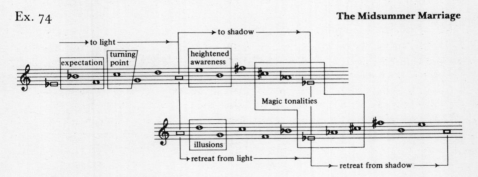

interpretation, with generalized verbal indications of the character of particularly important tonalities. Example 75 provides an abbreviated tonal plan of the opera, with indications of the main dramatic events. From these diagrams it can be seen that, for example, Act I begins in B flat and modulates to A, ending with the same tonalities in reverse order. The effect at the beginning is of exploration, at the end of reassurance: one progression is on an ascending cycle of fifths, the other on a descending one. The Ritual Dances descend from A minor to E flat minor, and from that extreme point of darkness rise to the last tonality, D major, before reaching the 'light' of A major. They are a tonal paradigm of the opera's conceptual premise. The 'shadow' tonality of E flat is represented by the impersonal figures of the Ancients, its more numinous manifestations appearing in the close relatives of A flat and C sharp. In general these tonalities show how a dramatic tonal structure, conditioned largely by Tippett's sensitivity to tonal colour, could still be founded on abstract logic.

Ex. 75   **The Midsummer Marriage**

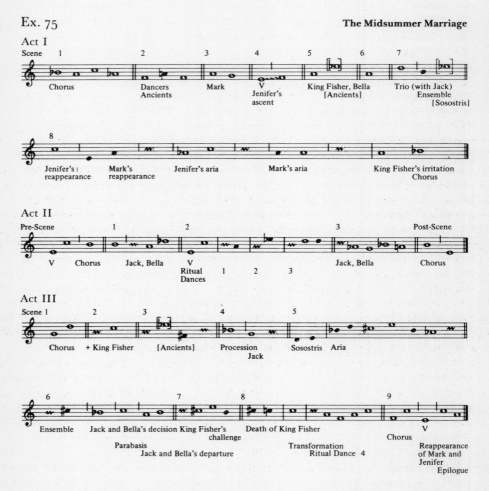

Yet an interpretation of this kind cannot provide a complete explanation of Tippett's procedures. It would have been logical for him to have reserved A major, the tonality of illumination, for the final pages alone. But it is the ever-present central tonality. Its appearance in the first scene, where it also marks the sunrise, and in the fourth ritual dance is undoubtedly consistent. There seems little justification for its use elsewhere however. If A major symbolizes the ecstasy of Mark (Act I aria), the irritation of King Fisher (Act I finale) and the domestic ambitions of Jack and Bella as well as the idea of psychological fulfilment, then Tippett has been either extremely careless or extremely subtle. It seems that a rationale of his tonal symbolism would have to extend beyond simple tonal analogues of the type described above and admit sonorities and textures as significant co-ordinates. As yet no coherent theory of such factors has been developed. An interim assessment of Tippett's procedures must therefore rest content with the observation that A major symbolizes immediacy of experience, whether uplifting or humdrum, sought after or merely stumbled upon, and that its particular complexion is determined by sonority.

Incomplete answers of this kind may be unsatisfactory in some respects. But at least they set in relief the simple facts that Tippett's use of tonality is profoundly original and that he can persuade his listeners of the abundant life still to be drawn from tonality, in particular, major key tonality. If this is equated with the fortunes of his characters then the message of *The Midsummer Marriage* is unmistakable.

The style of this message is immediately apparent in the brief orchestral prelude. It creates an expectant, exuberant atmosphere and it also announces an important feature of the work as a whole: the music will celebrate the immanence of the present and give short shrift to nostalgic hopes or memories, or to comforting havens of self-absorption. In this prelude Tippett writes no real themes: there is simply an accumulation of energy. Its broad paragraphs nicely add substance to motifs themselves shaped to be neither strikingly original nor neutral and thus unable to steal a march on what follows. The varied repeat of the first paragraph introduces a particular feature of the opera, and indeed of much of Tippett's music – development by sequence, whether overt or disguised. The method is applied both to the construction of discrete melodic units and to open-ended transitional sections. In his later music it occasionally becomes a mannerism, but here its cumulative musical thought is obviously well suited to an opera concerned with continuous illumination.

The motifs assemble into a constellation of gently turning movement. Out of this flow long, canonic lines in the chorus which weave into a single ribbon of sound marking the climax of the first scene: an invocation to the sun. The sun rises, the mists clear and the music settles on a long cadence. As well as introducing the chorus and the time of day, the music uses its own resources therefore to introduce a 'situation' of controlled excitement. Three principal gestures modulate from one to another and form a coherent dynamic and expressive shape: spirited activity in the orchestra softening into choral arioso which, after a central punctuation (an 'echo' effect for the double chorus), flowers into full-bodied lyricism with both forces, choral and orchestral, combined. The logic of this process is not, however, wholly rounded, for there are no recapitulations and the tonality progresses from B flat to C (having in the process touched on the central tonality of A). It is thus left ready for its continuation.

On an earlier page it was shown that the music for *The Midsummer Marriage* needed to fulfil two objectives: it had to be dramatically convincing on its own account and not rely on help from stage action, and it had to create convincing shifts of sensibility from the everyday to the 'magical'. The first of these objectives has now been achieved – or at least, with most of the opera yet to come, Tippett has cultivated a readiness to accept this as probable. Now he addresses himself to the second objective.

The transition into the world of the imagination is indicated on stage by the appearance of the temple buildings and the subsequent appearance of the Ancients and the dancers. Musically, it is evoked by a 'magical' sound. Everything at this point depends on whether this sound is authentic. Reactions to it will depend on the individual. All the commentator can say is that it does indeed transmit the spectator into a sharper, more delicate and responsive sensitivity (see Ex. 76). It is very simple, and it verges dangerously close to the simplistic – but that was a necessary risk to take if it were to fulfil its function instantly. And it is actually not so simple. On paper it looks like three bars of 2/4, but it is one bar of 5/4, with a characteristically elusive scansion pattern. The most interesting thing about it is the scoring, the sound. Tippett's 'magic' instruments are almost exactly the same as Mozart's in *The Magic Flute*: flutes and bells (celesta) as opposed to flute and bells (keyed glockenspiel). If Tippett borrowed from Mozart in this way it may be taken that he did so not because he unthinkingly accepted the example of a master composer but because Mozart's sounds were the contact which lit up recognition of something deeper. Precisely why flutes and bells should have the property of evoking the numinous is impossible to say. But there can be no accident in the fact that, for example, the legendary Orpheus charmed his victims by playing the flute, or that maenads in Greek vase paintings are frequently depicted playing flutes and crotales, or that the flute is associated with operatic 'mad' scenes. In any event Tippett's magical sounds here are not a local solution to a particular problem. As it turns out, they are the only solution. With the addition of muted horns (which hark back to Huon's magic horn in *Oberon*: they are introduced at an appropriate moment in a later scene), flutes and bells, in numerous and varied permutations, are always used when Tippett wishes to evoke the world of the imagination. The realistic orchestral shiver of excitement which follows these sounds is so natural a reaction to them that it is hardly necessary for the chorus to employ words to endorse their effect. When they return, the chorus retreats, as from something strange and disturbing.

Ex. 76   **The Midsummer Marriage**

So, within his first scene Tippett has shown that he has the equipment to fulfil both objectives. By the time the next two scenes are over he has also revealed the structural basis of the opera.

In keeping with its characteristic shifting between a real and a fantasy world, the opera is modelled on the distanced structure of a 'number opera' while at the same time disguising the boundaries between numbers in order to admit a free flow of imagination. In the traditional pattern of a number opera the sequence would run as follows: chorus, framing a solo for the tenor, and a solo for the soprano; then, following the entry of the baritone, a development of the relationships in progressively more complex ensembles – duet, trio and finale with stretta conclusion. As will be seen, Tippett's act bears a close resemblance to this pattern. His immediate problem concerns his 'chorus', for it is a double chorus, one part of singers, the other of dancers. Their function as background representatives of the natural and the supernatural had to be established swiftly otherwise the speed and lightness of the opera would have been jeopardized; by the same token the appearance of the tenor could not be withheld until the whole 'chorus' was over otherwise the proportions of the opera would have been attenuated. Tippett's solution to this was to distinguish the two components of his chorus by musical style and structure, to weld them into a unit simply by juxtaposing them and then to overlap the appearance of the tenor with the second component. The tenor was thus left poised for his solo.

The singing chorus has been introduced by a freely dramatic musical form. As if to compensate for their other-worldly nature the dancers are by contrast set in a more stylized musical context. The little march accompanying their entrance at the beginning of the second scene does not sustain the mystery of the magical sounds (even though there is a prominent flute part, for Strephon). It is the prelude to a ritual within a ritual, and as such it is deliberately formalized and curiously ambivalent in tone, at once familiar and remote. It summons up the enchantment of an antique fairyland. On a signal from the Ancients, the dancers perform a sword dance. In origin a sword dance is a miniature re-enactment of the old ritual of the Eniautos-Daimon, the actual killing being represented by a symbolic decapitation of the victim through the interlocking of swords in the so-called lock, nut or knot. The dance therefore is an unspoken prologue to the opera, rehearsing the essential course of the action. Even if none of this is known the music is eloquent enough. Its impassive, rather quaint renaissance flavour is tinged with sadness and this adds poignancy to what otherwise would have sounded an irritating constraint on the exuberance of the opera thus far. It acts as an unwelcome but not unexpected reminder that innocent enjoyment of things is short-lived and maturity hard won (see Ex. 77).

Although the score does not indicate as much, it seems obvious that Mark's imperious call to stop the dance should coincide with the point at which the knot is made. The dance resumes, but Mark breaks it up again, demanding a new one for his wedding day. His attempt to 'change the unchanging ritual' precipitates an argument with the Ancients. The

Ex. 77   **The Midsummer Marriage**

Ancients are not particularly sympathetic characters. They converse in the maddeningly self-assured tones of unanswerable authority and seem more concerned with sustaining that authority than using it to exercise a little human understanding. There is indeed an uncomfortable friction between the instinct to cast such elderly people in the role of grandparent figures, a dependable source of affection, and the facts of their sententious pronouncements. This is a pity, for the depth of experience they represent could have been linked to a corresponding depth of human relationship and thereby eased rather than obstructed contact with the magical world they come from. But Tippett stood firmly to his conception of them as functional guardians of the impersonal, unconscious laws of life and left it at that. At any rate they provide the necessary dramatic conflict. Mark rebels against their apparent obduracy. Equally inevitably, they reprove him, by ordering a repeat of the old dance instead of the new one he asks for, and when the He-Ancient trips Strephon, Mark sees this exemplification of the laws of life as sheer perversity and not to be taken seriously. After the Ancients and the dancers have gone he quickly regains his composure and dismisses the whole episode.

The musical justification for Mark's reaction lies in the fact that Tippett concludes the scene with the little march which opened it, and thus the whole scene, unlike the first, is neatly squared off and isolated. It can be regarded as a thing apart. This is a courteous and shrewd tactic for it also gives the audience time to ponder their own reaction to the supernatural world. Another advantage is that it enables Tippett to introduce his hero without inventing an artificial context for the purpose.

Mark's first phrases are arresting and decisive, yet at the same time almost casual. None of them is recapitulated and each seems drawn from a limitless supply of similar material – a splendidly apt portrayal of a character overflowing with generous impulses but unable to discriminate between them (see Ex. 78).

Tippett's third scene, a scena and aria, is structurally and psychologically a necessary point of rest after the ceaseless activity preceding it. The astonishment of the (singing) chorus at the episode with the Ancients and dancers is expressed in a buzzing orchestral background made up, surprisingly, of canons. One of the most intriguing features of the opera is the use of contrapuntal textures of this sort – textures normally associated with weighty sentiments – to effect delicate transitions to the light-hearted

Ex. 78

'real' world of the opera. Mark explains that he has known the Ancients since boyhood and then reminds the chorus of why they are in this 'magic wood'. If there is to be no new dance then at least a 'new song to greet her'. Thus the verbal apologia for the aria. Musically Tippett lets the buzzing background run to a halt while the voice gradually branches out from a monotone to the lyrical writing which is to be a feature of the opera.

The aria certainly does mark a point of rest. Its ruminative and improvisatory melismas eventually become so rhapsodic that they almost fall asleep. They are prevented from doing so only by the arrival of Jenifer. Put in another way, Tippett stretches out the pastoral mood close to the point of inertia so that Jenifer's arrival can be as unsettling as being woken from a pleasant dream. In consequence her entry is as effective a *coup de théâtre* as was Mark's.

There are further reasons for conceiving Mark's aria in this way. He is waiting for his beloved. He is tender and vulnerable, filled with thoughts of unassuaged giving yet unable to channel these thoughts into a fixed purpose because she is not there. In short, he is held by illusions. Tippett's music conjures up this mood with harmonies and melodic phrases of the purest diatonicism and as natural and unforced as the lark-song to which the text refers. They circle around in a spirit of idyllic aimlessness. The phrases are appropriately lyrical but equally appropriately they lack that incisive shaping which would change mood into action (see Ex. 79).

Ex. 79   **The Midsummer Marriage**

Tippett reinforces the aria's function as structural articulation by casting it in a stable but unobtrusive ternary form – only the 'lark' melisma of the first section returns in the third. This recalls Mozart's technique of ensuring melodic coherence by using the same tag phrase at the end of both sections; Tippett's method is in fact similar to that in the 'Portrait Aria' of *The Magic Flute*, an aria he has cited as a precedent for his own.

With this aria Tippett concludes his exposition of his work's basic premises and the ensuing dramatic development can now take place in a language and environment the listener has learned to accept.

Jenifer's arrival is signalled by an abrupt change of tempo and a hint of the tonality which will be associated with the magical transcendence of a kiss (a hovering between B major and E major). But 'Today there'll be no wedding'; her behaviour rapidly directs the tonality to darker areas, the thematicism to more incisive shapes, and the form to episodic procedures. Mark tries to appease her with a line of his lark-song, but she will not respond and she thus hastens the quarrel which ends with her sweeping him aside and climbing away out of sight.

The one serious dramatic flaw in the opera is contained in this scene. It must be assumed that Jenifer arrived prepared to have a reasonable discussion about her attitude; but to have decided that the moment to come to grips with her intellectual substance should be the day of her wedding betrays a calculated indifference to the feelings of a lover who could legitimately regard such egocentricity as treacherous. A genuine dramatic tension has therefore been set up. But Tippett forfeits this advantage with a confrontation not nearly bitter or violent enough to provoke an upsurge of archetypal behaviour; and the tonality of Jenifer's crucial phrase 'Now I know where I shall go' is too close to the tonalities already established to suggest that anything out of the ordinary has happened. After what is no more than a tiff the idea that Jenifer should ascend an unexpectedly material stone staircase seems gratuitous. This is the first piece of operational as opposed to expository magic in the opera and the work's credibility here receives a jolt. The section needs special pleading in terms of stage business if it is to carry conviction.

In the succeeding passage Tippett firstly evokes an aura of mystery with the sound of muted horns, the sound which completes his 'magical' apparatus. Then he gives it substance by condensing it into a motif of very particular significance (Ex. 80), memorable on its own account and neatly punctuating the division between scena and aria as well as underlining the importance of what Jenifer is saying. This motif has other properties however. It has a heroic ring to it, suggesting intense concentration of energy and demanding release in a balancing concluding phrase. Tippett trades on this expectation in an extremely skilful way, using it as the

Ex. 80 **The Midsummer Marriage**

tension which will sustain interest in Jenifer's aria, even though the presence of her aria here means a postponement of this psychologically necessary consequence. In fact it seems as if Tippett actively courts disaster. However apt a symbol of Jenifer's flight from reality, her rising line of serene cantilena is so simple in contour and harmony that the slightest lapse into banality or short-windedness could break the tension and bring the whole aria toppling to the ground. But, like his heroine, Tippett treads a tightrope with masterly aplomb and when Jenifer has finally disappeared there is a sense of relief as heartfelt as that on witnessing the successful outcome of some dangerous feat of exploration.

After this celestial moment – Jenifer at the top of her voice and there dissolving into vocalise as the girls of the chorus are left, as it were, hanging in mid-air – Tippett releases the tension in a carefully controlled transition. It bears some resemblance to a comparable passage in Verdi's *Falstaff*. When Alice's reading of Falstaff's letter becomes genuinely moving Verdi deflates the situation with a comic cadential trill and choral laughter. Tippett begins to deflate his situation with a similar peal of mocking choral laughter from the girls, just enough to register as laughter but not such as to bring it to earth with a bump. Mark is left humiliated and in despair, and the intensity of his music temporarily gains the upper hand over the laughter and the off-stage callings of King Fisher (which in the best traditions of *opera buffa* now add to the confusion). The men of the chorus urge him to his feet and he is suddenly possessed by the opposite of despair, resolution. To exactly the same motif as in Ex. 80 Mark makes his decision to enter the 'shadow'. Tippett brings back the motif whose non-completion had determined the character of the intervening music and now, while it still clamours for fulfilment, provides just that: a decisive cadential answer. The return of the first motif is an unobtrusive but firm way of rounding off the whole scene and a fascinating example of how Tippett puts a 'recurring' motif technique to structural as well as expressive use. The cadential answer not only provides the necessary fulfilment; it also opens out the drama again, a process effected by its musical novelty and by the fact that Tippett depicts Mark's plunge into the cave with another new motif – an orchestral cadenza of canons on a striding, chromatic figure (see Ex. 81).

Ex. 81   **The Midsummer Marriage**

After this the laughter of the men of the chorus has a challenging edge to it. King Fisher's first move is to accept the challenge and silence everybody. 'What are you laughing at? It's no laughing matter if my daughter's left me for a bastard.' (Mark indeed is a bastard.)

Back in control, King Fisher calls Bella; and the mood instantly lightens into the opera's first piece of *recitativo secco*, as Bella is told to ask the inhabitants of the temple where Jenifer might have gone. Bella is quick and sensible, a soubrette with something of the charm of Susanna in *The Marriage of Figaro*. The orchestra recalls the 'din, din' tinklings of Susanna's mistress to confirm the point. Thus prompted she rings a bell conveniently hanging by the temple doors. Out come the Ancients, to a grave 'classical' variant of the little march heard earlier. There follows an amusing three-way conversation in which Bella darts up and down stage retailing questions and answers from King Fisher and the Ancients. But since King Fisher clearly has no hope of understanding the answers the Ancients depart without notice. Bella is ready for such an emergency. She suggests getting Jack to force open the gates. This makes good sense to King Fisher and Bella goes off to fetch Jack while King Fisher turns to address the chorus – or, in musical terms, Tippett takes a grip on a rather wayward situation and prepares for the aria of the baritone, the last of the main characters and one whose aria needs to contrast markedly with the other two if its effect is not to be squandered.

The way Tippett does this is of particular interest. There is nothing unusual about some of his procedures. The aria is the longest of the three. Mark's and Jenifer's were one-tempo cantabiles like early nineteenth-century cavatinas, their more complex arias proper being reserved until later. King Fisher's is already a full-scale aria, in fast tempo and relatively elaborate in construction – two stanzas, the second part of each in faster parlando style after the tradition of the old dupe's patter song. Other procedures are less traditional. Certainly Tippett could hardly have sat in judgement over his evil genius and equated quality of character with quality of music. But he does not paint King Fisher with bold distinguishing marks either. In fact the musical language of this aria is so consistent with that of the opera as a whole, and it has such an exhilarating swing to it, that only by the natural colour of the baritone voice does it suggest the presence of a dark impediment. It takes its place in the dream-like flux as effortlessly as the rest of the music. And this is the point. Tippett has underplayed the element of contrast in order to preserve the essential character of the opera.

King Fisher likes to give the impression of generosity: in the first stanza he offers money to the men for finding Jenifer (in the second the girls refuse). But underneath he is an opportunist, and this is shown by the music, whose numerous little motifs give nothing away. They are short motivic statements rather than motivic developments and sound as if forced from lips too tight to accommodate them. Such attention to detail is really a Mozartian inheritance: nothing is unimportant, least of all the portrayal of unsavoury characters whose humanity is merely mixed in different proportions from that of the others. In this aria Tippett also goes to the Mozartian length of painting one word with more care than it merits. In the disdainful line 'You fancy people may despise me' what he fastens on to is the word 'fancy'; the line is set in the highest part of the voice and with a glowing orchestral texture which lifts the music well above the mundane level of the situation and does not sound at all like disdain (Ex. 82). But since words in arias tend to retreat into the background, the passage serves a purely musical purpose, establishing one extreme of texture which will be followed by its opposite and then locked into position in the middle register with a cadence.

King Fisher's aria has served to clear the stage of the chorus. At this point in the traditional formal scheme, when the development of the action is under way, there would be a duet followed by a trio. Tippett writes both at the same time. With the arrival of Jack and the return of Bella, three characters are on stage, but the music is a duet.

Ex. 82   **The Midsummer Marriage**

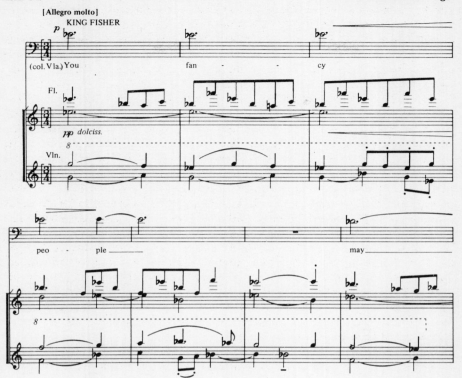

Jack and Bella are subsidiary characters and neither is given the theatrical entrance of a principal. Jack sets to work without preliminaries, to a businesslike sequential phrase in the orchestra. This sounds as if it knows where it is going, but in fact it always runs into complications. For the time being these are ignored by King Fisher and the two sing the first section of a dancing little duet which reveals Jack as an obliging individual who will cheerfully undertake whatever he is asked. In the middle section the complications momentarily steal the limelight, as Bella slips in with one of the most haunting phrases of the opera and then assumes control in the final section of the duet (see Ex. 83).

Amorous asides are holding up proceedings and King Fisher impatiently demands that Jack returns to work. This is the beginning of a large ensemble, carefully designed to grow in complexity until its accumulated tensions of anxiety and frustration are released in the magical return of Jenifer and Mark, and the opening of the act's finale. Its principal musico/dramatic function therefore is of extended anacrusis. It can also be seen as a trio with chorus and as Tippett's continuing use of the traditional set-number pattern, the preceding 'duet' now being followed by a 'trio'. To put these numbers in quotation marks is in part to show how subtly Tippett has recreated the traditional model but more to qualify the 'trio' in

Ex. 83   **The Midsummer Marriage**

particular. Here he adds another element, the warning voice of Sosostris
from behind the gates of the cave, and thus makes it more like a quartet.
The off-stage voice is the dramatic agent in Tippett's scheme. He has
carefully prepared for this unexpected event, firstly through the 'complications' in the duet, two groups of sounds which contrast markedly with the
rather workaday language of the duet itself, and secondly through the
magical sounds heard earlier. The warning voice is encased in a halo of
flutes and muted horn and immediately evokes the mysterious promptings
of the imagination (see Ex. 84).

Ex. 84   **The Midsummer Marriage**

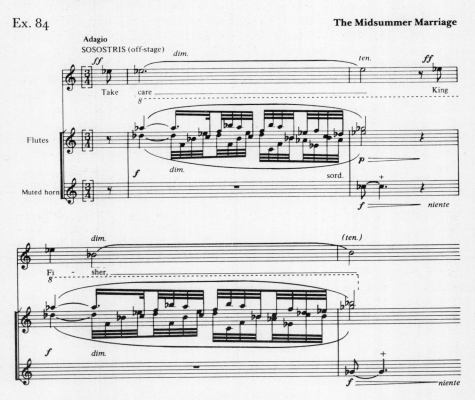

A dialectic of timbre is set up between Ex. 84 and the ensemble proper,
and the form and character of the ensemble is largely a consequence of it. It
is designed in three sections, like a choral ode with strophe, antistrophe and
epode, or like the AAB 'Bar' form found in Wagner operas. The strophe
and antistrophe are themselves in three sub-sections, consisting of music
for King Fisher's frustration, for the warning voice, and for Jack and Bella
with the chorus. The chorus now returns, the girls in the strophe, the men
in the antistrophe. The sub-sections become progressively longer and at the
beginning of the epode King Fisher's frustration is prolonged still further as
he frantically demands that Jack gets on with the task of forcing open the
gates. The characters on stage are all in opposing states of mind at this

point and this provides the dramatic justification for the final part of the epode. But in effect the music takes over the drama entirely, building up from a *stretto fugato* to a powerful and disturbing climax as the various conflicts are subsumed by what sound like the birth-pangs of some tremendous event. Jenifer is revealed, standing at the top of the stone staircase in her partial transfiguration as Athena. It is an astonishing moment, conceived with unerring theatrical instinct and made credible purely by the music.

The magical sounds now take over. As she climbs down, her slow steps are marked out by the celesta (whose notes are sustained by violins) and little rustlings on the flutes. When she reaches the ground she is received by string phrases of the utmost stillness as if hardly daring to move in the presence of such transcendence. She sings in a trance of a 'very gracious heavenly wonder'. In this context the boorish remarks of King Fisher are bound to provoke a change and Jenifer is stirred to leave her self-communings and announce the return of Mark, to precisely the same motif Mark himself used when he plunged into the cave. This musical reprise has a striking effect. It jumps backwards in time and links the 'magical' passages in a continuous thread, so that the intervening scenes seem to be relegated to a position of lesser importance. Tippett applies the same technique on a wider canvas later in the opera.

Mark duly returns, luridly transfigured as Dionysus, and sings in similarly rapt phrases of the triviality of mundane existence and the intoxicating wonders of the flesh. Jenifer, as possessed by her animus as he by his anima, sees this as a challenge and the motto of the opera suddenly rises to the surface, complete but divided among the protagonists. She brandishes her new discovery, 'I am a child of the starry heaven', and he his, 'I am a child of the fruitful earth'. This premonition of the inconclusive result of their coming *agon* is expressed in a circular stalemate of harmonies (see Ex. 85).

Tippett breaks it open with the appearance of the Ancients and dancers to ceremonial fanfares sounding like an announcement of a jousting match. He now has his whole cast on stage for the main body of the finale. (As before, the entry music of the Ancients has a period flavour to it; with each entry the style grows more up to date and after suggestions of the renaissance and the classical it now recalls the nineteenth century, or at least that nineteenth-century style associated with Franck. By the time the Ancients have made their last appearance their music has been absorbed within the style of the opera as a whole.)

The Ancients first demand that Mark and Jenifer stop their wrangling and argue their respective causes in a civilized way. Operatic precedents for a singing contest can of course be found in Wagner's *Tannhäuser* or *Die Meistersinger*. But Tippett's contest is not between rival songsters or rival musical persuasions. It is between the light and dark sides of the personality and its real model is not Wagner but, as has been noted, Aristophanes.

In the Aristophanaic model each contestant is supported by his half of

Ex. 85

the chorus which in turn is represented by a leader. The dramatic content is simple: the half-chorus encourages its contestant, the leader invites the contestant to begin his argument, the contestant does so. His main argument is followed by a short peroration delivered at a faster speed in order to drown the expected audience invective and enable the contestant to leave the arena with a Parthian shot. Correspondences between this scheme and Tippett's finale are close. His singing chorus has already shown its respective allegiances in earlier scenes of rather stereotyped male and female behaviour. The dancing chorus have thus far performed as a unit but now they divide up as supporters of Mark and of Jenifer, and provide the leaders, in the form of the Ancients. Tippett's leaders retain their impartiality, however, for they act as master and mistress of ceremonies and the cause they champion is their own philosophy. The He-Ancient orders the contest to begin and the She-Ancient enjoins the contestants to shun spiritual pride. 'Pride has subtle and peculiar power to swell the stomach but not heal the heart.'

In broad design Jenifer's aria is conventional – bipartite in form, preceded by a scena, with the slow and fast sections of so many operatic arias (concluding with a fast section was obviously determined by considerations of musical and psychological balance, rather than by the Aristophanaic model). And there is nothing original in associating the sounds of a high lyric soprano with the purest and most translucent states of being. What makes this aria exceptional in Tippett's output is the power of its musical symbolism, especially in the transition from the scena to the slow section and in the slow section itself. If evidence were needed of music's capacity to disclose hidden reaches in the human psyche then this aria would provide it. After Jenifer has explained that it was for the sake of her 'poor straightened soul' that she left Mark and climbed away into the heights, her experiences begin to reform, the music seems to jettison material support and the layers of her mind are parted to reveal extraordinary singing sounds, gently weaving a spell among themselves. They arouse oddly contradictory sensations. They both approach and recede, they are a yielding carpet of colour and icy blue points of light, they welcome and are dangerous. Jenifer herself does not appear wholly confident of belonging there for her vocal line floats across this territory as if not daring to set foot in it. The sounds themselves are another permutation of Tippett's magic apparatus, two flutes and celesta, the celesta line doubled by solo violin, and Jenifer's line given to a solo viola and an oboe when she is not singing herself. To this complex Tippett adds another instrument, a solo trumpet, which contributes unearthly ceremonials between the phrases of the melodic line (see Ex. 86). The trumpet is also a visual symbol, for one of the 'girl dancers' is instructed to play on a 'silver trumpet', presumably to associate Jenifer's state of mind with the silvery moon goddess.

The fast section takes Jenifer into rapturous coloratura, as, in a dancing duet with the trumpet, she describes how the 'congregation of the stars began to dance'. Her voice flowers into exquisitely poised melismas, so irresistible that the girls of the chorus are drawn in as well and not only sing but also move to the rhythms with the dancers.

This tableau is cut short by King Fisher. He in turn is cut short by the He-Ancient. 'All comment is clearly out of place while judgement is suspended for the half.'

Mark's aria is not laid out with the same clarity of form as Jenifer's. Hers reflects absolute conviction. His is more wayward. It is in three parts, in progressively faster tempi. The first is rather stiff, as he leads 'his' chorus and himself through the previous events. 'How did the lover look when she had gone?' At that time he was a stereotype, a point confirmed by the orchestra, whose guitar-like strummings recall a conventional lovesick serenade. But to accept this shows that he has already changed. Once past the 'gate of horn' he entered a world in which conventions were left far behind. The second part moves more freely as he remembers his journey through the 'labyrinthine maze of fear', and then, with a clash on a cymbal (as in Jenifer's aria, there is now a visual symbol, a 'man dancer' with a cymbal representing the metallic resonance of the earth), Mark suddenly recovers his feelings of intoxicating sensual freedom. This at any rate is what the words convey, with their references to the frenzies of Euripides's

Ex. 86   **The Midsummer Marriage**

bacchantes. It cannot be said though that the music of this final part of his aria re-creates Mark's experiences as compellingly as Jenifer's. Its proud lines and strophic form with variable ending are certainly an appropriate symbol of the perpetual renewal of physical ecstasy, but these lines do not generate the necessary melodic abandon (see Ex. 87). Even so, the music reaches a fine climax, capped by the interruption of Jenifer on a top C. Gloatingly she holds up a mirror to Mark's face, to show him the beast he has become and how impregnable her own moral position is. Her coloratura now has a touch of Handelian ostentation. Mark raises a 'golden branch' (golden bough, or bacchic thyrsus, see note 95) and Jenifer's mirror falls to the ground. The Dionysian defeats the Apollonian. Feminine instinct has defeated masculine logic. But both Jenifer and Mark know that a Nietzschian interpretation of this order is superficial. Jenifer again takes the initiative. To the same music which depicted Mark's descent into the underworld she now seeks that side to her personality which has given Mark such power, while he in turn seeks what had given her such conviction. As she plunges into the cave, a reprise of Ex. 81 puts a concluding stamp on these extraordinary events.

Ex. 87   **The Midsummer Marriage**

By this time quite enough of the 'magical' has occurred to be absorbed at one stretch and Tippett quickly brings proceedings back to earth, firstly with the by now characteristic texture of a fugue (a tiny double fugue), as King Fisher conducts exasperated exchanges with the chorus, and then with a reprise of the opening orchestral prelude, overlaid with the rejoicings of the 'laughing children' (see p.216). These ensure that the act does not betray its content and end in an emotional void, but that on the contrary it ends with fervour. For all its excitement this structural recapitulation is not however wholly convincing. It imposes a formality at odds with the progressive development of the action and obviously would not have been needed had Tippett kept to his original plan of proceeding now to the second *agon* between Mark and Jenifer. If he had done that though the act would have been disproportionately long and the sub-plot of Jack and Bella unduly condensed. His only solution would have been to compose some entirely new music for the end of Act I – which perhaps he should have done.

Act II explores deeper realms of experience than before and accordingly its structure is even more symmetric than the little opening scene with the Ancients and dancers in Act I with which Tippett instituted a correlation between psychological depth and stylized musical organization. The act is laid out in strict arch form: prelude, chorus, duet, dances, duet, chorus, epilogue. It functions as an interlude between the main structural arguments on either side. In character it may be compared with the reading of a fairy story, the music at the beginning and end sounding like the opening and closing of the story book, and the intermediate sections introducing a romance which melts into a central chapter where the animals come to life. A good fairy story should properly enchant its listeners, and the Jack and Bella duets indeed contain the most exquisitely tender music Tippett has written, placed with the utmost finesse just on the right side of sentimentality. But it should have its quota of terror as well. The animals of the Ritual Dances have nothing of the urbanity of those in, for example, *The Magic Flute*. Here they are red in tooth and claw. Tippett's observation of the laws of the countryside is so coldly precise that the dances could have become almost too frightening to contemplate had he not set them at a distance with musical procedures as abstract as anywhere in the opera, and had they not that quality of psychological truth which willy-nilly draws the listener into their aura.

To make his listeners believe in that truth Tippett needed to re-establish the opera's supernatural world immediately. He does this with a most remarkable musical gesture. It is as if with one stroke of his wand a magician had summoned a timeless expanse of sunlight, trees, haze, sparkling rivulets, a host of unseen presences basking in the warmth of summer afternoon. To trespass in such a territory would seem an act of unpardonable vulgarity – unless, that is, one belongs to it anyway. The listener's passport is contained in the first four bars, a musical evocation of the most universal introduction to the transcendent, a kiss (see Ex. 88). It is remarkable enough that Tippett should have formed his musical metaphor from so scientific an observation of its physical properties. Remarkable also that his 'magical' sound apparatus should prove so versatile. (To the two flutes is added a discreet clarinet, and the cascade of tingling sensations is

given point by the substitution of plucked harp notes for celesta; muted
horns and bell (gong) complete the picture. On this, so to speak, abstract
magic is imposed the more tactile presence of Jenifer's silver trumpet,
softened by attendant trombone.) What proclaims the hand of a master is
Tippett's ability to present in a single imaginative act this unmistakably
authentic world of sound, and then to allow the consequences of that sound
to permeate every corner of an empty stage with music seemingly tuned to
the pulse of creation. This music can claim to be the English equivalent of
Debussy's *Prélude à l'après-midi d'un faune*.

Ex. 88   **The Midsummer Marriage**

The climax of Tippett's prelude is marked by the appearance of
Strephon: he therefore is the central figure. Having introduced the idea of
the supernatural Tippett then proceeds to show how it can be understood
by anyone who cares to, by unobtrusively linking it with the 'everyday'
world of the chorus and of Jack and Bella. The first of their duets
eventually becomes so absorbed in its reverie that it slips quite naturally, as
the lovers kiss, into the introductory music again, and the stage is set for
the Ritual Dances.

Before the first duet the chorus is heard off-stage singing what sounds like a four-part madrigal. Actually it is a round, or at any rate a tune which could go on repeating itself indefinitely. As such it cheerfully mirrors the renewal of the midsummer season and the everlasting battle of the sexes. It may be described as a twentieth-century 'Sumer is icumen in'. Tippett does make it into a round at one point (asterisk in Ex. 89) by putting it in canon (but it does not really fit). This is when the semi-chorus accompanying Jack and Bella enter.

Ex. 89   **The Midsummer Marriage**

With the introduction of (off-stage) human voices the individual situation of Jack and Bella can move into the foreground. Jack simply wants to enjoy a pleasant afternoon. Bella has something more particular in mind. Like Jenifer in Act I, she immediately takes charge and like the cuckoos of which the chorus has just sung, cunningly uses the occasion as a pretext with which to flaunt her engaging charm, dangle unspoken promises and capture her mate. Naturally she is wholly successful, and expeditiously so for she acquires a compliant fiancé and the prospect of a neat little house and home all in the recitative preceding the duet. It might be objected that Tippett has not provided much of a love story if its most endearing component, the first responses and awakenings, is so briskly despatched in favour of the domestic aspirations of the heroine. But he is less concerned with the love story as such than with creating a receptive atmosphere where the thoughts of the lovers, and the audience, can flow unhindered into the world of the Ritual Dances. In any case Bella's behaviour represents only one stage of her emotional life. By the time she has witnessed the dances and come face to face with the consequences of not at that point going off with Jack (at least that is presumably what is meant by her Act III lines: 'O Jack, why did I trust myself and not trust you, there in the shadow of the wood?'), she has realised that she has unloosed feelings and responsibilities she is unable to manage by herself. In the meanwhile Jack too has changed, from a lap-dog to an individual with a will of his own. For the moment, however, all is simple, idyllic and bewitching.

After Jack has agreed to marry Bella, they settle down for the duet proper – music of disarmingly innocent diatonicism. It constantly seems likely to drift into triviality but always slips past such hazards at the last moment, as if, like Bella, it were playfully teasing something actually less playful than it appears. In the first section Bella looks forward to being a housewife, Jack a provider. The rhythm is of a country dance, the form a simple binary form, with a caesura in the middle lightly touching on the real depth of their feelings by recalling the magical harmony of Ex. 88, bar 4. The second section is a lullaby, as Bella retreats into her imagination and pictures herself cradling her baby to sleep. There is no suggestion of caricature. If reminder were needed of 'the force that through the green fuse drives the flower' (the Dylan Thomas line Tippett quotes in *King Priam*) this music would provide it. Bella's croonings are entirely unaffected yet driven by a force greater even than her own fantasies – in musical terms, strong enough to lift the tonality far from its apparent roots into regions where solid support is no longer relevant (see Ex. 90).

Ex. 90   **The Midsummer Marriage**

[to Ex. 88]

In this dreamlike state the two slowly move away under the trees, there to experience the vision of Mark and Jenifer's psychological conflict, and their own, to be acted out in the Ritual Dances. Bella wakes up, in a 'dazzle of sunlight', when the vision reaches an unbearably savage climax. This apparently existentialist denouement is such an affront to any respectable view of life that Bella cannot accept it. She forcibly thrusts it out of her mind by occupying herself with her own reassuringly familiar, protective ritual. She does her hair and touches up her face. Her aria is shaped in the appropriately conventional form of a swing-era standard: 'verse' and 'chorus'. Its sound, however, recalls the invention of Mozart, who can be imagined responding with similar relish to the little pictures of stray wisps of hair, awkward tangles, caressing strokes of the hairbrush, the ever-so-deft artistry with the hairpin. 'Many a man's been caught for good in a girl's hair' sings Bella in the 'chorus' (the only real 'tune' in the whole opera), and she knows precisely what she is up to (see Ex. 91).

Ex. 91   **The Midsummer Marriage**

All the same she could not have behaved quite like that without the experiences of the dances. She could not have admitted Jack into her boudoir at all unless she had been excited by the prospect of letting him see some of her secrets fall away from her. Tippett explores the paradox of her situation by preceding the aria with a duet scene itself full of contrasts. Jack utters comforting clichés and Bella abruptly shifts from sobbing and trembling to a sudden rush of blood as she decides what she will do. Jack's clichés are only verbal: musically he is wholly individual and in the process he introduces a short motif (Ex. 6(i), bracket *a*) which may be considered the counterpart to Mark and Jenifer's 'light' and 'shadow' motif.

In the duet scene which follows Bella's aria the music is a condensed repeat of the earlier one. The situation is the same but the roles reversed: Jack is worried about working for King Fisher again and now *he* needs to be reassured. Bella quickly does so and the two run off to find their friends. The off-stage chorus are heard singing their round (from the point at which they had earlier left off) and the act ends with a final recapitulation of Ex. 88.

This recapitulation completes the structural scheme. But it serves two other purposes, allaying anxiety that the magic might be irrecoverable and, because it returns to the beginning, suspending the whole act in a place out of time. In my beginning is my end. If we are at the beginning again was the act an illusion? – a question reinforced by the presence of the magical music in the middle also. In this context the effect of the Ritual Dances is subliminal and the structure of the act can be seen as a means by which their realism is, by its insubstantiality, converted into metaphor. Tippett applies the same technique to the structure of the opera as a whole.

What the Ritual Dances might mean dramatically and psychologically has been discussed on earlier pages. Here it is worth mentioning only that they are in no way a *divertissement* or a concession to some operatic convention. They are inextricably connected with the nature and rationale of the work, a point confirmed by the fact that the ritual they enact is not completed until Act III, when the fourth dance takes place. In Act II they reach that stage at which the seasonal transformations of the sacred king can no longer avert his inevitable death or, in other words, at which an individual's most cherished estimate of himself is to be broken for ever.

The ritualistic aspect of the dances is emphasized by their stylized presentation. In the prelude Tippett restates his musical *mise-en-scène* and reintroduces Strephon (to some strangely wayward music sounding as if a timid nocturnal creature were venturing from his hideout). In the 'transformation' the magical sounds of Ex. 76 invest the trees with life. In the 'preparation for the first dance' the tree-dancers, to appropriately industrious music, arrange themselves in the shape of a field and then seem to stand to attention. Strephon, costumed as a hare, takes his place, as does the girl-dancer, costumed as a hound. Formalities over, the dances can begin. The earth in autumn. The hound chases the hare.

It is immediately clear that Tippett writes with an eye for realistic detail almost French in its pictorialism and far from the English tradition of pastoralism from which his music nevertheless also derives. In that tradition a hound chasing a hare might have provided occasion for a rollicking folk-dance. Tippett however is keenly observant of the facts of the case. His music is descriptive and narrative. His hound must be a harrier rather than a greyhound: greyhounds hunt by sight and this animal hunts by scent. She bounds along over rough, rocky terrain, pricking her tail, swinging her ears and sniffing rapidly. When she warms to the scent she runs faster and having picked it up lets out ugly yelps. The hare (the male hare, appropriately in this context, is called a jack), who has been squatting in his form, senses danger and flies off. Hares are tricky customers. Their movement is highly unpredictable. They jink and zigzag, dart sideways with a spring, spin round and run backwards along their tracks. They will abruptly sit stock still, ears pricked, listening intently. They like running in circles and then leaping out. All this is vividly shown in the music. Example 92 is the beginning of the second of four divisions on a ground bass – a suitable form for a dance introducing the idea of inexorable pursuit. The upper stave shows the hare (or Strephon, still with the magic instruments of flute, bell, here triangle, and muted horn), the lower the hound. In the last two divisions the hound threatens to catch the hare and the ground bass accordingly gains ground on itself by being compressed into shorter note values. If he had been caught the hare would have cried like a child, but he manages to escape, and his jubilation, and that of the audience, is expressed in a rhythm returning to the strictly human world of the polonaise, originally a triumphal march of warriors, more recently associated with the spirit of heroic chivalry.

Ex. 92   The Midsummer Marriage

(Ex. 92 cont.)

After a repeat of the 'transformation' and 'preparation' music (a process which sounds rather laboured in the concert suite Tippett made from the dances but which in the opera house serves to reaffirm the ritualistic aspect, as well as giving the solo dancers time to go off-stage and change costumes), the dancers now arrange themselves to form trees on the banks of a river. The waters in winter. The otter chases the fish.

This dance, like the next, also has an open-ended repeating form whose component strophes shrink in a kind of musical fear as the hunter closes in on her quarry. Each strophe consists of four elements. In the first, the watery scene is set; bassoons and horns impart a forbidding depth to the river and violas add cold eddies. Then the fish, a trout perhaps, appears (Strephon's flute now changed into the liquid tones of a pair of clarinets). He rises from his lie and snaps at some flies, plunges down and then up again, snaps at some other ones and gobbles them down (this, if it is what Tippett intended, is depicted realistically enough, although it might be thought that Tippett's uncertainty about fish behaviour – they do not surface to breathe as the libretto has it – resulted in the music sounding as much like an otter as a fish: the otter, a rather clownish performer, twitching his whiskers and seeming to play on a toy trumpet). All this has attracted the attention of the otter, who slips into the river and heaves with powerful muscular movements against the current while the fish darts back to safety. The fourth element depicts the foaming eddies of the water churned up by the otter. In the third strophe the fish, in his anxiety to escape, gets stuck in a tree-root and is hurt while wrenching himself away. The polonaise has a catch in it. In his transformation as a bird Strephon therefore is wounded. He has a broken wing.

The 'preparation' for the third dance reflects this new state of affairs. The confident air of the previous two is lost; even though the dancers keep busily to their task of sowing a field of spring corn, they sound pensive, as if they were reluctant to prepare for a drama whose outcome they would prefer not to see. But knowing also that this will not be the real end of the drama their music gains a kind of desperate exhilaration. It is swept aloft and lands on a perfectly pitched cadential triad for four solo violins. The air in spring. The hawk chases the bird.

The violins and high woodwind embroider a tapestry of little leaves quivering in the breeze. The bird hops out into the field (Strephon's tessitura sinks as the dances progress: he is now a bassoon) and starts pecking at the grain to a motif which amusingly indicates his awkward thrusts into the furrows and his satisfaction with the produce (see Ex. 93). (It also suggests another picture, of the bird perched on a stalk and slipping off.) He hears the song of his mate in the tree tops (a melody for oboe) and tries to fly up to her. But since his wing is broken his flutterings (trills) are useless and he falls to the ground – to precisely the same motif which marked Strephon's fall to the ground when he was tripped by the He-Ancient in Act I. The hawk swoops down, but the bird has hopped away just in time. As the drama approaches its climax the sub-sections become shorter and more agitated, the song of the mate more plaintive and halting (it changes from 6/8 to 7/8 and 8/8) and the music for the hawk more menacing. At the end it is obvious that the bird will be killed.

Ex. 93   **The Midsummer Marriage**

The vivid pictorialism described above remains the most immediately attractive feature of the Ritual Dances, and of the concert suite, much of whose success is due to it. But such success cannot depend solely on pictorialism: for one thing the fourth dance contains none at all and its liberating conclusion is as vital to the formal scheme of the suite (opening allegro, slow movement, scherzo and finale) as it is to the meaning of the opera. This meaning would be destroyed if the dances addressed themselves purely to the visual instincts. Felicitous though Tippett's translations from the natural image to the musical motif may be, the motifs are the stuff of his drama and its meaning remains intact because through them he creates and sustains mood, from the tiniest fluctuations within a single dance to the crucial general sense of danger, threat and raw terror which spreads across the first three and is transformed into one of ecstatic release in the last.

Act III is planned in two extended paragraphs, the first slowly gathering intensity as it leads to Sosostris's aria, the second moving rapidly from there to the culminating ritual dance. After King Fisher has challenged the Ancients to a contest for his daughter Jenifer, the act leads therefore to its first *agon*, in which King Fisher, in the worst traditions of businessmen, employs someone else to do his work for him. Sosostris is his surrogate. When this tactic misfires and he sees that his adversary is not the Ancients but the power of sexuality, he tries first to employ Jack to destroy that power and when that tactic misfires too, he is obliged to conduct the contest alone. In this exposed condition he falls back on the only weapon he can think of, a pistol. In the second *agon* he is defeated by the sheer force of personality of the lovers; or it might be said that his virility has to capitulate before Mark's. The scene is then set for the revelation of the transfigured lovers in the ritual dance.

The sustained dramatic development of this act is in marked contrast to the stylized patterning of Act II; it demands greater concentration of its listeners. As if to soften the edges of the contrast the beginning is earthy rather than magical, leisurely, almost casual in mood, its characters occupying themselves with the eminently human habit of trying to bypass their responsibilities by carousing. There is no real dramatic substance. The chorus have just finished their evening meal. Wedding or no wedding they are continuing the party into the night. Tippett constructs the scene like a drunken eighteenth-century concerto, the ritornello theme being assigned to the soloist (an on-stage fiddler who plays for dancing) and the episodes to the full chorus. This procedure enables him to place greater emphasis on the episodes and thus have the fiddler effect an unobtrusive transition (via an altercation with a tipsy reveller) to the choral invocation to wine (Ex. 94) which caps the scene. The tonality of the previous sections staggers between an appropriately rustic Dorian mode on A and a clear G major, so that the whole section acts as an extended upbeat to the invocation.

Ex. 94   **The Midsummer Marriage**

The text of Ex. 94 provides one explanation of why this music darkens towards the end. The real reason for it is that having re-established the scale of his opera Tippett now needs to move the action forward to the point at which the drama can resume. To the same signal which introduced the sword dance in Act I the chorus are quickly sobered up by the realities of the situation: King Fisher has summoned them – for they know not what. They split into their opposing factions of men and women; the mood becomes anxious, the texture thins out and then condenses into the three-part counterpoint accompanying King Fisher's blustering arrival, complete with belt and holster. What he asks them to do is not however so unpleasant. They cheerfully echo his command to go out and welcome Sosostris (see Ex. 95).

Ex. 95   **The Midsummer Marriage**

These first two scenes sound so natural that the technical skill with which Tippett has given them coherent musical shape is, in the opera house, taken entirely for granted. The distinction between Exx. 94 and 95 illustrates how Tippett invested them with that harmonic and gestural stability without which the whole would have drifted inconsequentially and which at the same time serves different functions. The first is intermediate, the second conclusive. Accordingly the first is modelled on 'sentence' construction – each phrase flowing sequentially into the next. It has an implied content of six six-bar phrases (Ex. 94 is the second), a strategy Tippett uses to inculcate a sense of breadth. But he writes only five phrases and turns the last three into a transition to the next section of the scene. Thus emerges a structural punctuation without too firm a brake on the forward-moving character of the music. The second theme is modelled on the more formal design of 'period' construction – two balancing (though asymmetric) pairs of phrases, each pair (Ex. 95, brackets) providing a question and answer. Tippett allots the first pair to King Fisher, the second to the chorus and separates the pairs with episodic material. This procedure absorbs both solo and chorus in one concise, clinching statement. Tippett was obviously well aware of what he was doing, for the music here and especially in the short succeeding codetta contains a wicked allusion to the final scene of *Die Meistersinger* by Wagner, a composer not noted for economical statement.

With the chorus out of the way, King Fisher can turn to the Ancients. To a condensed recapitulation of the music used for the same purpose in Act I, Bella rings for them and they emerge from the temple likewise to the same sounds as in Act I. King Fisher comes to the point. To rather theatrical flourishes (little battle cries in the trumpets) he delivers his challenge. As the Ancients say later, he 'shows a certain courage of his own'. At this juncture Tippett inserts a four-part ensemble on a pedal point and a duet embodying a vain attempt by the He-Ancient to persuade King Fisher to withdraw. Both sections are usually cut in performance, for the good reason that although King Fisher's challenge marks a crucial turning-point in the action, its musical urgency is not sufficiently powerful to justify the contemplative outcome. Furthermore King Fisher's weapon for the contest, Sosostris, has not yet been introduced, so it is difficult for an audience to accept the seriousness of the situation. It is better therefore to continue straight to the Berliozian gesture with which King Fisher repeats his challenge. The Ancients accept. The chorus returns, with whom is thought to be Sosostris.

An operatic procession is often an excuse for gratuitous spectacle. As has been suggested, Tippett's is founded on other premises. It nevertheless does provide occasion for an impressive scenic display, Jack at the head of the procession, wearing the conical hat of a professional jester and a green cloak presumably intended to cast him in the role of Jack-in-the-Green, the old midsummer custom by which the representative of the ailing god roams the streets in a wickerwork pyramid of green leaves and branches before, in the original ritual, being set on fire. Here the chorus provides the branches (or substitutes in the shape of flags and banners). What Tippett's appropriately demotic music suggests at this point is simply the exhilaration of good-humoured buffoonery. But when Jack is unmasked the music suddenly lights up, as if flames were licking its structure: it glows with an intensity curiously at variance with the almost farcical events on stage. There is no need to quarrel with Tippett's dramaturgy here for this short passage contains some of the most thrilling music in the opera. Nevertheless the question remains of why Tippett should have conceived the scene in this way, and the only plausible answer is that he deliberately sought to activate some archetypal memory of the excitement, terror and catharsis of ritual death embodied in the original Jack-in-the-Green custom. He wanted to prepare his audience for the imminent supernatural happenings. It is in this light that his procession's obvious indebtedness to the 'Turkish' variation in the finale of Beethoven's Ninth Symphony can be understood. In Beethoven, that variation is not merely an expression of its composer's republican sympathies: it also forms part of a sequence of musical gestures by which a popular style, converted in the succeeding fugal variation into an elevated style of intense argument, serves to highlight the sophisticated material to come. So with Tippett. The correspondence is underlined by a thematic connection between his processional music and the music of Jack's unmasking (see Ex. 96).

Sosostris is announced to a new variant of the 'magical' sound apparatus – muted horns and bells, the latter now consisting of real (tubular) bells as

well as celesta, and a gong in addition. An unearthly incantation on the brass (to a motif reminiscent of the 'treaty' motif in Wagner's *Ring*, perhaps implying that a price has to be paid for the ensuing vision, or perhaps simply echoing the signal for the appearance of Erda in *Siegfried*) – and the strange veiled 'contraption' is there for all to see. Tippett has prepared for Sosostris's aria with such care that its effect could easily be forfeited. And indeed he almost invites anticlimax by suggesting that, earlier hints notwithstanding, the audience will now be spared the interminable Wagnerian narration of events thus far: 'I needn't tell Madame Sosostris all the story.' (Ironically enough, some of Tippett's own music here is usually cut.) But another and a particularly beautiful variant of the 'magical' apparatus restores the atmosphere, and the aria begins.

It is an extraordinary conception, Tippett staking everything on the power of twelve minutes of slow music (there is no stage action) to hold an audience on the metaphysics of artistic creation. That he does hold his audience is a measure of the quality of his music. It is a classic account of the creative process, laid out in four sections, each describing a particular stage. From inchoate beginnings illuminated by sudden flashes of insight a struggle develops to give shape to ideas intractable yet clamouring for fulfilment, whose very fulfilment denies the humanity of their creator. The second section culminates in a magnificent but terrible acceptance of this destiny (see Ex. 97). Once such struggles are over something is both given and taken away. The composer is given the lucidity through which his visions of the soul can be formed and at the same time he is deprived of his own identity. As himself he dies: he becomes an instrument. Tippett's music of lucidity is as serene as any he has written. It moves in a state of rapt spirituality, impervious to fashionable conceptions of 'contemporary' music, yet unmistakably original in voice, quietly asserting that the sources from which Handel and Mozart drew their inspiration are as fresh as the air we breathe. A stab of pain breaks the spell – a phrase marking the 'death' of Sosostris (as well as that of King Fisher later in Act III) – and in

Ex. 97   **The Midsummer Marriage**

the final section of the aria she looks into the sombre depths of her crystal
bowl, her music rises and clears, and she perceives her vision. What she
perceives – a meadow where Jenifer among the flowers welcomes the
'glorious lion [St Mark] of love with symbol erect' – is vital to the course of
the action; but how Tippett himself conceives visionary music is more
immediately relevant here. With his 'magic' instruments he constructs a
fabric of short ostinati, interrelated but of varying lengths, which combine
into sound patterns at once the same and always different – a marvellously
apt symbol of the infinite, timeless nature of Sosostris's vision (Ex. 98). The
composite pattern never repeats itself *en bloc* (it would not do so until the
flutes' music in Ex. 98 had been repeated 108 times), although Tippett
subsequently does adjust it in order to reflect the narrative course of the
vision. In some respects this technique derives from Stravinsky, but its real
origin stretches back to medieval isorhythm, where fixed rhythms and
pitches (Roman numerals and brackets respectively in Ex. 98) lead
independent existences in the same melodic line. This technique has
proved a valuable addition to Tippett's expressive resource and he has
used it in various later works, notably in the 'vision' section of *The Vision of
St Augustine*.

King Fisher calls the vision a 'disgusting trick' and breaks Sosostris's
bowl; but the influence of her music cannot be gainsaid. No more than his
character can Tippett himself deny its effect. He skilfully engineers his
drama to accommodate this emotional imperative by ignoring King
Fisher's activities and allowing the chorus to remain held by memories of

Ex. 98   **The Midsummer Marriage**

* Fl. & Cl. doubled by solo Vln. & Picc.

the aria. What they identify with in particular is the tremendous statement of Ex. 97, here simply its tonality and later, immediately before the revelation of Mark and Jenifer, its actual notes. In the meantime the atmosphere is dispelled only when King Fisher commands Jack to put on the belt and holster. This 'brutal dress' (Tippett's pacifism momentarily comes into the open) and King Fisher's next command that Jack unveil Sosostris provoke Bella into action. Bella, who earlier was no more able to accept her vision of the Ritual Dances than King Fisher can now accept Sosostris, has matured and she knows that tampering with such authentic experience invites catastrophe. She cries out, in order to prevent Jack committing sacrilege. The focus switches to him. Will he become a mercenary or will he respond to deeper promptings and retain his integrity? The chorus, representative of humanity at large, ask Jack and Bella to make the choice on their behalf as well and while a large ensemble builds up, the chorus initially following Jack and Bella in canon and then branching out independently, the Ancients move towards the footlights and deliver, to a cantus firmus chorale, that hard but challenging aphorism which could well have stood as motto for the opera had Tippett not been more concerned with the living of life than the contemplation of its meaning.

> Fate and freedom propound a paradox.
> Choose your fate but still the god
> Speaks through whatever acts ensue.

This is the opera's main first *parabasis*. Though extremely dense the texture is not impenetrable and it is a pity that this relatively short section – barely two minutes long – has always been cut in performance. In some ways it is the most characteristic moment in the opera. Undoubtedly it is the most audacious, Tippett appealing to his live audience precisely when Sosostris's aria, and his own credo, has begun to take effect.

In any event it is now Bella who inspires Jack to defy King Fisher. Whether Jack chooses fate or freedom is not clear, but he certainly chooses

Bella and his own pride while that still generates enough momentum to carry them into their future. They disappear, borne aloft on the exultant phrases of the Act II round.

King Fisher is left to unveil Sosostris himself. He does so to music which depicts both the brutality of his actions and the travail of some supreme event in the making. As he tears away the last veil and the chorus sing Sosostris's credo as a litany of appeasement ('No mortal ever lifted my garment'), what emerges is not Sosostris nor cosmic disaster but a lotus flower, whose petals slowly unfold to reveal Mark and Jenifer transfigured as Shiva-Shakti. The psychological significance of this *anagnorisis* stretches understanding to its limits and Tippett does not pretend otherwise. Its unusual musical complexity is the result not so much of its wealth of detail as of Tippett's conflation of two apparently irreconcilable elements – the 'magic kiss' music of Act II and the present brutal music of King Fisher, itself severed by choral canons. Although this technique obviously requires considerable compositional finesse if it is not to sound chaotic the fact that Tippett superposes rather than integrates material betrays his own almost passive attitude to his denouement: it can be accepted but not fully comprehended. The listener is, as it were, stunned by its impact. The 'dead' music of King Fisher's collapse[99] is therefore peculiarly appropriate and his funeral march even more so since it allows time for active concentration to develop again – a process encouraged by the addition of a second *parabasis* from the She-Ancient: 'Blessed be the dead. For which of you do minister with love to the dying under the broken house?' If somewhat elliptical her words here are clear in general meaning. They remind the audience that the capacity to identify with an imagined stage death should not be mistaken for the capacity to fulfil the human duty of attending to the dying and respecting the sanctity of death. Once again Tippett steps out of his opera and pits it against real life.[100]

The funeral march consists of five repetitions of a ground bass, each, except the last, with the same neo-Purcellian harmony and the same choral laments, whose cadences nicely reinforce the ambiguity of its tonality: it recalls the C sharp minor of Sosostris's credo and introduces C minor in preparation for the C major of the 'transformation' music.

If the seemingly unending repetitions of the ground bass symbolize death, the re-emergence of the 'transformation' and 'preparation' music symbolizes the opposite. The 'preparation' music has been heard twice before, on each occasion associated with a stage action, though not corresponding particularly closely to it. By all conventional yardsticks a further recapitulation here would be a disappointingly tame substitute for that revelation of something new expected at the climax of a drama. But events on stage, the kindling of need-fire, now create a sudden identity of music and action and in consequence the music lights up with new meaning. Strephon turns a stick in a wooden block and makes sparks (Ex. 99, brackets *a* and *b* respectively); while other dancers fan the glowing tinders (bracket *c*) the stick bursts into flames. Tippett's symbolism is abundantly clear. Life, in this context, means fire, the generation of sexual passion and the illumination flowing from it. This is the power to have annihilated King Fisher and to be exemplified in the final ritual dance.

Ex. 99   **The Midsummer Marriage**

The final dance is subtitled 'The voluntary human sacrifice' – the willing, knowing submission of individuality in the transcendence of love. Strephon dances the rite of midsummer. Like Stravinsky's sacrificial virgin he eventually dies, having relinquished the emblem of his individuality, the lighted stick, to his true self, the transfigured Mark and Jenifer. But unlike Stravinsky, Tippett does not stop here. The dance continues. And in Tippett's scheme of things it is vital that it should continue, for unless transcendence springs from sacrifice or, in other words, unless Mark and Jenifer experience an absolute from which they can draw limitless strength for their future lives together, then the whole opera is prejudiced. A respectable pedigree lies behind Tippett's dramaturgy here. Many composers have sought to re-create the experience of transcendence. Almost without exception they have done so not explicitly but in terms of metaphor. This is partly, no doubt, because the presumption in attempting otherwise is little short of blasphemous; but the more compelling reason is that direct confrontation with such overwhelming forces invites personal tragedy. Had Scriabin completed his *Mysterium* there is good reason to suppose that he would have entirely lost his wits in the process. The question therefore is not whether such forces should be kept at bay through metaphor but which metaphor to adopt. Surprisingly few composers have used that of making love. Of those who have, the most successful have set their metaphors in contexts which pre-empt too circumscribed an interpretation of their meanings. In the 'Royal Hunt and Storm' from his opera *Les Troyens* Berlioz wrote perhaps the most literal and subtle example, but it remains after all a description of a hunt and a storm. Even the duet in Act II of Wagner's *Tristan und Isolde* is couched in terms of the metaphysics of night. These composers cannot be accused of prudish diversionary tactics. They simply wanted the sexual metaphor to tap the deeper transcendental power of the idea. If not as graphic as Berlioz nor as symbolic as Wagner, Tippett is more direct than either. He presents his metaphor for what it is – a sacred marriage, ritual love-making, and he casts it in a language as realistic in its evocation of human experience as were the Act II dances in their depiction of animal behaviour.

The principal compositional technique used is canonic. This is already an apt musical equivalent of the identity of two in one. When, as in the exclusively canonic first section, it is applied to Tippett's dancing rhythms and exploratory lines, it creates an intricate backcloth, alive with movement, but still a backcloth and as such also a symbol of the retreat of the individual into a generality. In the second section this generality fuses into two components – a torrent of unison semiquavers in the orchestra which support and generate a unison song in the chorus. Initially the chorus is limited to thrusting percussive accents, so that its presence as added sound quality is hardly noticed. But while Mark and Jenifer, now with the addition of the Ancients, continue to provide their canonic gloss, its lines grow more fluid, develop into exquisite melodic shapes and eventually embrace the whole texture, solo voices included, spilling over into an unforgettable phrase heard three times in succession. Mark and

Jenifer respond with ecstatic melismas. It is an extraordinary climax. It creates a burning yet curiously calm and effortless intensity, epitomized in its culminating phrase which concentrates anguish and release in one gesture (see Ex. 100, chorus).

Ex. 100   **The Midsummer Marriage**

The opera is really over, though only after the melismas have been steadied, the choral caption set in place and the familiar sounds of the Act II prologue have brought the whole scene to rest, can the listener draw breath and assess his reactions to it in, as it were, the cold light of morning. As if to demonstrate that he has his feet on the ground, Tippett now provides just that – shivers on the flutes, harsh cock-crows on the trumpets and a shudder in the double-basses. 'Was it a dream?', the chorus enquire. Does the eloquence of Tippett's music really convince us that new beginnings are always possible? The chorus offer a beautiful invocation to the sun: at least the sun always rises (although it may be noted that this second invocation is more circumspect than that in Act I). By way of agreement the birds begin to sing and soon the dawn chorus is in full voice while a wordless hymn of thanksgiving forms in the background.

The dawn chorus is a canonic variation of the main theme from Mark's lark-song and as such also a sign that the opera is about to retrace its steps. Mark and Jenifer meet to exactly the same music as in Act I – but with a different continuation. He gives her the wedding ring 'in this magic wood on midsummer day', and a repeat of this earlier music alters course too, leading not to the phrase associated with the cavalier sentiments of 'If no new dance ...' but to a transformation of it, set to a text (from Yeats's *Lapis Lazuli*) compressing into two lines the experience of a lifetime:

> All things fall and are built again,
> And those that build them again are gay.[101]

As Mark and Jenifer disappear with their friends, their voices echoing in the distance, and as two final stanzas of the hymn ring out to welcome the dawn, Tippett's reminiscence technique reaches its apotheosis. These last two recapitulations are plainly audible: the whole opera, like its second act, has returned to its beginnings. In a sense, it does not seem to have got anywhere. But the opera has taken place nonetheless and while Tippett's musical technique at this point underlines its subliminal, dream-like effect, his musical argument over 700 pages of full score has won him the right to convert formal courtesies into conclusive statement. His characters all gone under the hill, his music now can occupy the stage by itself. Halting as if unable to suppress delight at its newly gained freedom *The Midsummer Marriage* ends with as certain, splendid and uninhibited a celebration of its art as can be heard in twentieth-century opera.

CHAPTER THREE

1952-58

Operatic Aftermath

With *The Midsummer Marriage* Tippett had achieved what he had set out to achieve: the opera marks both a culmination and a fulfilment. He took a rest from composition after completing it (writing his essay 'The Birth of an Opera'); but its sounds continued to echo in his imagination and he soon responded to them, producing an important group of works for the concert hall. The language of these works in turn began to crystallize into the radically new style of his second opera, *King Priam*. So while *The Midsummer Marriage* concluded a major period in Tippett's stylistic evolution, it also released what turned out to be the inspiration for *King Priam*, a work fertile enough to sustain his invention across a further major period of creative activity as prolonged as the first. The subject of the present chapter is the intervening transitional period.

The most obvious feature of this period is its variety. By writing *The Midsummer Marriage*, Tippett seems to have found himself in the position of a Dante encountering his Beatrice for the first time, of experiencing that 'flame of charity' in which everything is transformed in an inspiring light. Hitherto his rather purist attitudes could not countenance the idea of entertainment music, for example, or *Gebrauchsmusik* for amateurs, but now he wrote in both genres. Most significantly, he wrote a piano concerto. The solo concerto was the only important genre he had not attempted in his first period, presumably because he could not then separate the idea of a solo concerto from nineteenth-century rhetoric and because limp examples by senior English composers of the time offered no solutions to the difficulty. But *The Midsummer Marriage* (and a performance, by Walter Gieseking, on his return to England after the war, of Beethoven's Piano Concerto No. 4) convinced Tippett that he could now contain the rhetoric of a concerto within the flowing, lyrical idiom he had newly developed.

Despite this special significance to Tippett, there is of course nothing unusual in writing a piano concerto. By so doing, and in composing his other major works of the period (a song cycle, another string piece, a sonata and a symphony), he was in fact continuing to promote what he had believed from the beginning – that renewal should grow from within a tradition and not be imposed from without. This is not to say that by persisting with a long-held belief Tippett had run out of creative invention. On the contrary, the period upheld the force of his belief by generating precisely that renewal upon which it depended.

The period lasted for about six years, from autumn 1952, when Tippett

completed *The Midsummer Marriage*, to autumn 1958, when he started work
on *King Priam* – though for the purposes of this chapter it is taken to include
works written during the composition of the earlier opera as well. As a
period of transition it is unusual. It is characterized by two interlocking but
somewhat contradictory processes, neither of which leads directly to the
new style: some of the implications of *The Midsummer Marriage* are extended
to a point almost of extinction, while others are condensed into the
materials from which the new style was to develop. Most of the works
follow the first process. Only in his crucial Symphony No. 2, completed in
November 1957, is the second process clearly evident, and even this work
marks a stage halfway along the line between the two operas, rather than
one at the end of it. The period traces therefore not a gradual change from
one style to another but a slow withdrawal, then a judder, to be followed
abruptly by the fully-fledged language of *King Priam*. This metamorphosis
was perhaps less radical than that which, some twenty-five years earlier,
had resulted in Tippett's String Quartet No. 1. But it was remarkable
enough. At the time it provoked the criticism that Tippett was an
opportunist, desperately trying to reanimate a moribund language, or that
he had traded his true gifts for a gauche imitation of contemporary fashion.
In fact the period offers another example of Tippett's capacity to conduct a
long-term strategy by working simultaneously on two levels. In his
compositions, he was exploring the style of *The Midsummer Marriage*. But its
ethos, the imaginative world with which he had been engrossed for so many
years, was draining dry. He rejected it, and half consciously and half sub-
consciously was pondering the character and genre of the dramatic work to
succeed it. 'Bit by bit the new style for the new opera became clear. By the
time I had hammered out a satisfactory libretto for *King Priam* I had
understood the musical style essential to it.'[1] The same kind of process had
occurred while Tippett was pondering the musical style of *The Midsummer
Marriage*, and although this opera bears a much closer resemblance to the
works preceding it than does *King Priam* to the works discussed in the
present chapter, it still contains many features which at the time were new
to Tippett's music. These are the features he developed in this transitional
period.

   The stylistic novelties of the period derive from the simple fact that *The
Midsummer Marriage* is a work for the stage and not for the concert hall. In
order to characterize human actions and feelings Tippett needed to invent
musical gestures that were explicitly dramatic, and which had therefore
been irrelevant in the abstract and severely logical arguments of his earlier
music. The function of such gestures is to depict a particular stage event –
the rushing demisemiquavers of Mark's entry, the graceful clarinet and
violins as the high-heeled Bella minces from King Fisher to the Ancients,
the fusillade of brass as King Fisher commands Jack to unveil Sosostris. In
so far as they represent something actual and immediate, these gestures
create contrasts that interrupt the lyricism of the opera, for which reason
there are relatively few of them (what instances that do exist being
succeeded by lyrical counterbalances). There are enough however to

comprise a significant addition to Tippett's stylistic resource. Such
contrasts as those in the first movement of his Piano Concerto or in the slow
movement of his Sonata for Four Horns (see Ex. 101(i) and (ii)) are a direct
inheritance of the opera. When condensed into the more sharply textured
blocks of, for example, the slow movement of his Symphony No. 2
(Ex. 101(iii)), they form clear links in the chain which leads to the
structural methods of *King Priam*.

Ex. 101

(i) **Piano Concerto**

(ii) **Sonata for Four Horns**

[Lento cantabile tranquillo in stilo notturno]

(iii) **Symphony No. 2**

[Molto tranquillo]

These gestural characteristics are a product also of Tippett's heightened sensitivity to sound. In his earlier music he makes little use of 'instrumental colour', presumably because the concept then smacked of self-indulgence. But in *The Midsummer Marriage* he welcomes sonority as a dramatic agent analagous to gesture. In the events from the opera referred to above the sounds contribute to the effect as powerfully as the notes. The most obvious example of this feature is the 'magical' motif for flutes and celesta (Ex. 76), which clearly illustrates his growing interest in the sonorous properties of a musical idea, for it reappears, in various transformations, not only throughout the opera but in the transitional works of this chapter, and in subsequent works as well.[2] The fortunes of this little motif are vividly representative of general and, from the point of view of Tippett's creative development, progressive tendencies for his music to become more compressed and self-sufficient.

At the same time a development in the opposite direction was taking place, this deriving from the fact that *The Midsummer Marriage* is not just a stage work but a particular stage work, with its own subject matter. Conveying 'continuous illumination' demands expansion rather than compression, and the overriding effect of the opera is indeed of burgeoning paragraphs, melodious, richly textured and borne on a powerful ground-swell. Not surprisingly this was the dominant feature of the works written in its wake. Even if the impulse generating the opera had receded into the distance its musical style was bound to be carried along by its own momentum. Eventually this momentum flagged, but in the meantime some extremely beautiful music materialized. By the first movement of his Piano Concerto Tippett had however reached a crisis point, for its sweet lyricism has left the muscle and tension of *The Midsummer Marriage* so far behind that, at the climax, it is no longer capable of renewing itself. The slow movement of the Concerto marks the real turning point. The feature that had contributed as much as anything else to the crisis, melodic decoration, is now challenged on its own ground, and is obliged to capitulate. The immensely complex decorative patterns in the solo part do not really decorate anything: they attempt to enrich a rigid sequence of canons in the orchestra and succeed only in reaching a stalemate whose solution is handed over to the orchestra. The outcome of this little drama was that Tippett turned to more crisp thematicism and more taut structure in the finale of the Concerto and in the works that followed. Once robbed of a firm melodic backbone, decoration had been revealed as debilitating in effect.

It would be wrong to suggest that Tippett's pursuit of decoration was unproductive. In his earlier music there was little of it: melodic lines are tightly thematic and motivic. But in the spontaneously exuberant atmos-phere of *The Midsummer Marriage* decoration was obviously appropriate and it generated some of his most marvellous music – the controlled abandon at the heart of his *Fantasia Concertante on a theme of Corelli* and that re-creation of the Celtic spirit of ecstatic profusion (such as can be seen, for example, in the Book of Kells) which pervades the first movement of his Piano Concerto. In the opera two types of decoration preponderate: an embellishment of a line and a trope to a line. The first is a way of making a line more eloquent: the decoration makes it throb, pulsate with life. The trumpet part in Ex. 86 gives an example. This type remained an important expressive resource in Tippett's music. The second type both explains and enhances a line. It might be described as ornamental counterpoint. In Ex. 88 the line is in the brass; the decorations in the wind give meaning to it. When however this second type is deprived of its linear foundation its condition becomes precarious, in that it can easily degenerate into quasi-impressionistic effect or pure capriciousness. At the climax of the *Fantasia Concertante* Tippett makes dramatic capital out of these dangers. When the decorative trope in the high parts seems likely to become entirely self-absorbed, function is restored at the last moment by the entry of the lower parts; now that the steersman has taken full control a profound sense of relief as well as excitement ensues (see Ex. 102).

Ex. 102   **Fantasia Concertante on a theme of Corelli**

(Ex. 102 cont.)

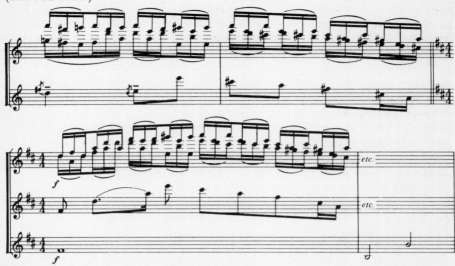

In the first movement of the Piano Concerto the decorative profusion is in even greater danger, for it does float away into uncharted waters (see Ex. 101(i), bracket *x*), as if its steersman had fallen asleep. It is part of Tippett's genius that such voyages lead to unexpected treasure (bracket *y*); but he is also aware that any more than a sight of the treasure will lead to disorientation and this jolts him to his senses and an abrupt change of course (bracket *z*).

The language of the Concerto suggests that Tippett had deliberately carried decoration to an extreme in order to find out precisely how far it would go. The results of this exercise were not negative for apart from the music it produced it revealed that the instinct to decorate was also an instinct to sharpen his feeling for sonority. The sonorities of Exx. 101 and 102 are almost as striking as their shapes. Decoration of this second type is at one with the progressive as well as the more indulgent tendencies of the period.

Decoration can even be seen to contribute to the sharper harmonic sense Tippett developed as a consequence of the distinction between tune (voices) and accompaniment (orchestra) in *The Midsummer Marriage*. An interest in harmony often implies a corresponding slackening of interest in rhythm. Decoration of the second type is usually associated with a single rhythmic value, and in neutral rhythmic environments of this kind features of a new harmonic language start to take shape. Beginnings of this rather oblique approach to harmony are present in the first song of *The Heart's Assurance*, where amid the apparently decorative demisemiquavers of the piano part, an ingenious method of pedalling indicates their essential content, which is harmonic. Example 103(i) illustrates that the actual harmonies are the result not of contrapuntal movement, as was predominantly the case in Tippett's earlier music, but of a directly harmonic imagination – in particular, of the conflation of discrete harmonic units: a fourths chord and a so-called 'chord on the leading note', to which is then added a triad. The unobtrusively dissonant harmony of this example, all the notes belonging to a single tonality, was followed by more pungent sounds, involving both the addition of an overtly harmonic imagination to his existing modalism (Ex. 103(ii)), and the combination of two or more tonalities (Ex. 103(iii)) – though the latter was initially more for colouristic effect than tonal function. The Symphony No. 2 is characterized by explicitly bitonal or polytonal harmonies used functionally: their component tonalities interact and generate structural tension (Ex. 103(iv)). By the end of the Symphony such harmonies have become strong enough to stand alone, and this was one of the most important resources Tippett had acquired by the time he came to write *King Priam*.

Ex. 103

(i) **The Heart's Assurance**

(ii) **Symphony No. 2 (First movement)**

(Ex. 103 cont.)

(iii) **Piano Concerto**

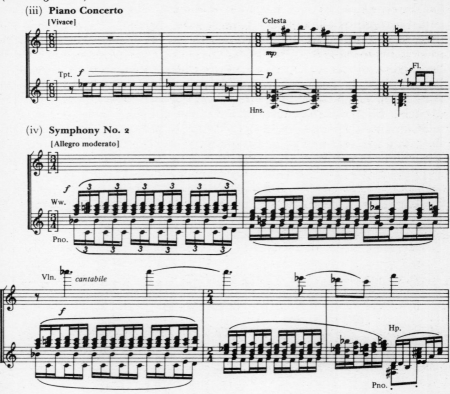

(iv) **Symphony No. 2**

As was suggested above, Tippett's rhythmic language did not develop much beyond the point it had reached in his earlier music. Indeed it is difficult to see how it could have done, without abandoning pulse and articulation completely. Tippett held fast to his earlier rhythmic gains. But as a consequence of his sharper harmonic sense, he also began to lay greater stress on the more traditional articulations of fixed-additive rhythm (see p.102) and, via this route, his rhythmic language began to embrace the rhythmic discoveries of other composers, Stravinsky in particular. In technical terms this meant that his rhythmic patterns now showed a greater tendency to repeat. Extended passages in fixed-additive rhythm, as, for example, the 3+3+2 of the principal theme of the scherzo of his Symphony No. 2, occur for the first time in his music since *A Child of Our Time*. Even when the technique is applied to transitional (as opposed to expository) material its stabilizing influence can be plainly felt. The transition to the second subject in the first movement of the Symphony illustrates how Tippett's characteristic rhythmic polyphony was affected by it (see Ex. 104). This remarkable passage sounds less like a progression to a predetermined goal than a static block so intense that its only resolution is to break open into a new sound altogether. Rhythmic polyphony can therefore no longer be reduced to a pattern of functional beats. It has become more like an extended harmony: the separate strands are triadic rather than modal, and this triadic character is reinforced by the repeats and varied repeats consequent on the additive groupings. The resulting 'harmony', as in, for example, the conflation of triads (of G, A and D) in the last two bars of the passage, is a dense polytonal aggregate, whose energies are compacted in one vertical moment. Repeating rhythmic patterns serve the same expressive ends. They are symptomatic of an aesthetic that would free the musical moment from functional obligation and set it in isolation, to be savoured for its sonorous properties alone.

Ex. 104   **Symphony No. 2**

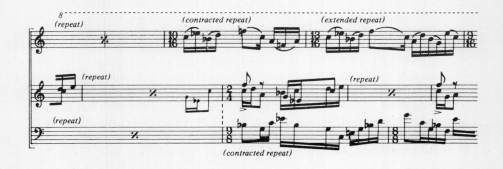

(Ex. 104 cont.)

In Ex. 104 the emphasis therefore is on the static. Yet this emphasis is relative. When examined in detail the passage shows that Tippett had not really forsaken his long-held understanding of music as a dynamic flux; on the contrary, he had begun to develop a new way of asserting it. The passage contains the seeds of a new type of free-additive rhythm, new to his music and particularly associated with Stravinsky, in which momentum is generated by an interaction between varying durations, some static and repeating, some dynamic and changing. That Tippett should have used this technique was a consequence not of a study of Stravinsky but of changes in the nature of his own musical language. Motivic cells are no longer components of fully-realized melodies but single entities in their own right, confined to very simply proportioned note-values. The emergence of this technique can be traced in the top line of Ex. 104, where two groups of fixed-additive rhythms lead into two of the new free-additive type. Reading in semiquaver units, the passage consists of $8+12$ repeated and $(4+3)+$ $(4+3)$ repeated, followed by more complex patterns containing the static and dynamic elements referred to above: $(4+3)+3+(4+3)+6+(4+3)+2$ and $(3+4)+6+(3+4)+8$.

Tippett did not develop the implications of this technique to their fullest extent until the scherzo of the Symphony. This movement contains at once the first and the most concentrated example of it in his output, a section in which every element is fixed and immobile save the rhythmic and in which rhythmic procedures therefore are at their most explicit (see Ex. 105).

In isolation, this section, more than any other in Tippett's music, sounds like Stravinsky (though it would be difficult to refer to a particular Stravinskian original). But in context it has a dramatic function. It is a stabilizing element, necessary after a precarious violin solo had seemed about to topple over; at the same time it is a source of concentrated energy, ready to break out into lyricism. As such it is entirely in accord with Tippett's own way of symphonic thinking and naturally it is subsumed within the progress of the movement as a whole. Likewise, Tippett's rhythmic procedures here conform in general to the Stravinskian model; but in detail they are wholly individual. Significantly Tippett's free-additive rhythms involve a device quite uncharacteristic of Stravinsky, the splitting of a component cell into two parts. Cells *a* and *b* in Ex. 105, both seemingly indivisible, in fact divide into tiny segments. Bars 1 to 5 of

Ex. 105 establish a behavioural pattern in which rhythms are determined by the disruptive addition of cell *c* to the (apparently) indivisible cells *a* and *b*. The reaction of *b* is to compensate by augmentation, of *a* by diminution. Cell *c* retreats from the new power of *b*, and then stands its ground, while *a* and *b* divide and eventually reform into a new composite cell in which the components are reconciled with one another. This is effected by simple superposition (box *ab*). Once *a* and *b* have established common cause, *c* is free to escape.

Such a 'psychological' explanation of the rhythmic processes here is really the only one possible, for Tippett's rhythms do not form into strictly schematic patterns, numerical or otherwise. They simply obey innate and ultimately mysterious laws of musical judgement.

Occasional Works

Up to *The Midsummer Marriage* even the least pretentious of Tippett's works made some contribution to his systematic charting of the traditional genres. In the present transitional period, major works consolidated the process while minor works, in the main, abandoned it. They form a heterogeneous group, suggesting that having completed a programme of exploration to his satisfaction Tippett was now occasionally content to adopt the role of journeyman composer, writing more or less what was asked of him. Thereafter production fell sharply, because as he grew older he became increasingly anxious to concentrate on what he really wanted to compose.

As has been suggested, these works do not represent Tippett at his best. They tend to reinforce the fact that he was not at ease when writing on a small scale. Nevertheless he did not undertake their composition casually. The hymn tune *Wadhurst*, written in 1958 at the request of the Salvation Army, is a case in point. Tippett had always been moved by the classic beauty of traditional hymn tunes, and having in consultation with a Salvation Army bandmaster discovered that what was wanted of him was a straightforward four-part congregational hymn, to be supported by band, he first planned his hymn as a descant to the familiar tune 'French' (from the *Scottish Psalter* of 1615), known to him as a metrical psalm (No. 121), 'I to the hills will lift mine eyes'.[3] He discarded this idea, because he found the rhythms of the psalm text too evenly grouped. He then discovered another version, by John Campbell, containing freer groupings ('Unto the hills around do I lift up my longing eyes') and wrote a new tune of his own, though retaining the Scottish melodic style. His personal imprint can be seen in a pattern of expanded and irregular phrase lengths and in a harmonic progression from a modal E flat to a tonal A flat, so that the repeated verses flow round in a harmonic circle and do not mechanically stop and start as with most hymn tunes. Such scrupulous professionalism did not guarantee an important contribution to British hymnody; nor did it, in *Music* of 1960, revive the dying tradition of unison singing at the end of competitive music festivals (lusty unison singing to Shelley's 'I pant for the mu-u-sic which is divine' is indeed faintly ridiculous); nor, in the *Four Inventions* of 1954, did it indicate that the sound of recorders could happily be transferred from an eighteenth- to a twentieth-century idiom. But because they are well-made, such works are useful additions to their respective repertories. This in fact is all they aspire to. In his younger days Tippett had regarded the artistic premises underlying Hindemith's *Gebrauchsmusik* as the reverse of his own: useful music, functional music, amateur music then seemed a betrayal of the oracular calling of a composer. Now his attitudes had mellowed. If the works just cited show that the change produced indifferent results, the remaining *Gebrauchsmusik* pieces of the period show that it could yield genuine bonuses. The folk-song settings are charming and original examples of their kind, *Dance, clarion air* one of the few successful twentieth-century madrigals and the cantata *Crown of the Year*, though perhaps too sectional to be easily moulded into a coherent shape by the schoolchildren for whom it was designed, one of the most substantial and attractive of Tippett's works in a lighter vein.

Tippett's naturally expansive style might not easily adapt itself to the concise and the small-scale. But when such qualities were already given, as in folk-songs (or at least the folk-songs he chose to set), then he could concentrate more on presentation than invention. He could make good use of his contrapuntal gifts and in the process offer practical examples of what he considered the proper way to set folk-songs – which was that they should not really be 'harmonized' at all but left alone to speak for themselves, enfolded in an affectionate melodic embrace. In *Bonny at Morn* (1956) the haunting Northumbrian folk-song acts as its own bass, supporting a trio of recorders which wheel above like birds in the morning air (and show that recorders can after all be used imaginatively in a modern idiom). In *Four Songs from the British Isles* (1956) for SATB the settings are considerably more sophisticated, but in approach essentially the same. The tunes are placed in contexts where they can stand out unadorned and free of conventional harmonization. The only exception to this is *Poortith cauld* (Cold Poverty), a Scots song with words by Burns, whose sentiments Tippett perhaps considered too poignant to be delivered without comment, for on the last two of its three appearances he embellishes the lonely tune as if to smooth down its edges and offer some consolation to its doomed lover. Its more conventional harmonization can be seen as an expressive device, the frequent harmonic rootedness symbolizing the heavy weight of poverty. But even in this song Tippett's individual harmonic vocabulary ensures that the integrity of the original is not compromised.

Example 106 is the refrain of *Poortith cauld*. In Burns the refrain appears after each of the five stanzas. In Tippett's setting however its text appears after only the first and last, while its music is fitted to the middle stanzas as well, a procedure which enables him to reduce the song to three musical stanzas with concluding refrain, that is, to adapt it to the suite-like proportions of the set as a whole. *Poortith cauld* is the slow movement, preceded by *Early one morning* and *Lilliburlero* (the English and Irish songs, first movement and scherzo respectively) and followed by *Gwenllian*, a Welsh cradle song which provides a gentle, lilting finale.

Ex. 106   **Poortith cauld**

The set was commissioned by the radio station of Bremen in northern Germany for a festival of European folk-song. Tippett selected a song from each of the countries of Britain in order to 'emphasize the fact, not always appreciated on the continent, that English, Irish, Scottish, Welsh are still to this day different peoples'.[4] The participants at the festival presumably remained unaware of this fact however, for the songs were not performed, being found too difficult. Although they lie within the competence of a good amateur choir they undoubtedly require considerable technical skill for performance. This is a question not so much of mastering Tippett's idiosyncratic rhythms as of reducing vibrato and developing the tonal and dynamic resource to clarify texture and distinguish the tunes from their surroundings. Such technical problems are worth persevering with – providing of course that the music itself is thought to have quality. This indeed is Tippett's own attitude to his amateur music. It is not a body of music for easy enjoyment, or for the development of technical skills or the encouragement of sympathetic responses to contemporary music. It is music pure and simple. As such, though composed with relatively modest resources and accomplishments in mind, it inevitably contains its share of technical difficulties, which, if the effort to do so is considered worthwhile, will surely be overcome.

The difficulties of *Dance, clarion air* (1952) are less technical than interpretative. Perhaps because Tippett was closer in spirit and style to the Elizabethan period than any of the other composers represented in 'A Garland for the Queen' (the abortive attempt to mark the Queen's coronation with a rival to 'The Triumphs of Oriana'), his madrigal has proved the most enduring in the collection. Yet beautiful though it sounds, its sectional changes can appear awkward and the sections themselves lacking in coherent succession unless its performers respond with unusual sensitivity to Tippett's expressive intentions. The opening fanfares introduce not a tune but a texture, as if to announce that characteristic melodic invention and even the madrigalian tradition of word-painting (the next section paints a picture of the tide heaving stones onto the shore) will take second place to the creation of mood and movement. It is not easy to underplay the melodic appeal of the fanfares and concentrate on their mood; but if this is achieved the second section conveys not anticlimax but a sense of expectation. The most individual passage hinges on the carefully prepared main climax in the third section. At this point a joyful hullabaloo might have ensued ('Sound with love and honour for a Queen'); but what emerges is music hushed and still. It is even less easy here to convey a sense of turning the key onto a visionary landscape than it is to establish the basic premise of the madrigal at the start. But to do so is to uncover one of Tippett's loveliest inspirations.

The text of *Dance, clarion air*, as of *Crown of the Year*, was written, at Tippett's request, by Christopher Fry (who produced two 'coronation' texts for Tippett to choose from). Tippett's obvious sympathy with Fry's language suggests that Fry is the only living writer with whom he could have developed a fruitful working relationship and it is a pity that the two have never collaborated on a major work. Their treatment of monarchy in the madrigal and cantata suggests that the institution of Master of the Queen's Music might, surprisingly, in Tippett's hands have been rescued from its association with empty ceremonial and become the expression of genuine collective needs. The concluding lines of *Crown of the Year* – the 'young Elizabeth' telling of a 'morning innocent and clear' – are not conventionally respectful nor are they simply a poetical conceit by which the hopes of a country recently released from war are allegorized. Nor did Tippett set them in this way. His music here speaks of a hesitant, yet increasingly confident and at the same time, to the erstwhile republican, a slightly uncomfortable recognition of the fact that the young Queen does indeed bear the nation's aspirations in her person and that there is a psychological rightness that this should be so.

It is possible that Tippett could have gone on to develop the theme of monarchy on a larger and more public scale. But *Crown of the Year* remains his only essay in this direction – and in any case royalist sentiments are not at the core of it. This is Fry's felicitous interpretation of the New-Elizabethan-Age theory, widely current at the time: the prosperous stages in England's fortunes having occurred while a queen was on the throne, stages that can be likened to the seasons (Elizabeth I – spring, Anne – summer, Victoria – autumn), it follows that the reign of Elizabeth II will be both prosperous and spring-like, and, in addition, by its completion of the circle, the crown of the whole process. From a strictly Viconian standpoint Fry's scenario would of course leave Elizabeth II with winter. But winter, in the shape of two world wars, took place before she reached the throne and that necessary ordeal is what postulates the new spring of her reign. Lest this appear too facile a thesis, a refrain continually warns of the 'dark dying to bear' before spring can return.

As well as containing a feminist slant congenial to a girls' school (the

Ex. 107

work was commissioned for Badminton School, Bristol[5]), Fry's text provided Tippett with an opportunity to write a work of great variety and in many short numbers, which was what he had planned. It also presented him with a neat musical form, and he pursued the implications of this not only by casting the work in a variant of his favourite four-movement form (introduction, scherzo, slow movement and fantasia finale) but also by strengthening its seasonal and historical aspects. The main vocal numbers are preceded by instrumental preludes; unrestricted by words these set the seasons in focus with more vivid colourings than would otherwise have been appropriate, and they establish the historical periods and the general tone of the work by featuring tunes both evocative and refreshingly (even startlingly) familiar.[6] What Tippett did not do was conclude the work with a literal repeat of its beginning – as the title invites. Nor did he follow a cyclic tonal scheme, though he did set a kind of tonal pendulum in motion by which spring swings from D to A, summer from G to E, and autumn (the richest season) from B flat (with central passages in F and E flat) to A flat (including allusions to C sharp, F sharp and B): that is, the tonalities swing in widening arcs from the flat to the sharp side. Winter returns to the D which had heralded spring and the work eventually settles on C, the only tonality not used before. Such subtleties indicate that the work holds deeper meanings than its brightly polished surface would suggest. What, for example, is the reason for the harsh and almost brutal comment on the piano, after the first entry of the voices in 'Hush, nightingale' has been so tenderly prepared (see Ex. 107)? Do the changes for handbells in the 'Prelude: Autumn' signify more than the 'knell of passing day'? Do they conform to the traditional rules of change-ringing? Why does the rather jazzy tune 'Frankie and Johnny' represent winter? Answers to these questions may be offered as follows:

1. The piano, in the wintry key of D minor, represents the night, which is being overtaken by a morning song so entrancing that even the nightingale is obliged to stop singing.
2. Possibly.
3. No.
4. Johnny 'done her wrong, so wrong'. Frankie therefore disposed of him and instituted the women's liberation movement (the tune was a favourite of the suffragettes), from which winter of discontent a new spring is about to emerge.

The important thing of course is not whether these answers are correct but that the questions are posed. A work for schoolchildren will have little value unless it is found serious and stimulating – and *Crown of the Year* certainly has the material for that. It is eventful, moderately challenging in idiom (it derives from Tippett's Symphony No. 2), and if it does not quite exceed the sum of its parts this is due less to the absence of a full-blooded climax than to the inherently delicate sentiments of its final movement. *Crown of the Year* is one of the best of Tippett's occasional works.

As their titles indicate, the *Suite for the Birthday of Prince Charles* (Suite in D) and the *Divertimento 'Sellinger's Round'* were designed to have the immediate and uncomplicated appeal of entertainment music. It was characteristic of Tippett not to have spent too much time on their composition, both being made from pre-existent material and put together with the skill of a craftsman rather than the eloquence of an artist. If ultimately they seem to erect a barrier round Tippett's true musical character and leave a rather dry impression, they still bear his unmistakable imprint and, in the case of the Suite at least, stand in a class apart when compared with other English examples of their kind. Reservations about the Divertimento stem from its confusion of aims. In some respects it is appropriately diverting and lightweight, its musical ideas nicely geared to the soloistic instrumentation of a chamber orchestra and its bevy of quotations and reworkings of period styles almost imparting the flavour of a pot-pourri. Yet at the same time these virtues are compromised by a strange kind of private scholasticism. The work originated as Tippett's contribution to a composite piece commissioned from various composers for the 1953 Aldeburgh Festival, each movement to include reference to the traditional tune of 'Sellinger's Round'.[7] Tippett accepted the commission partly to please Britten and partly because he was fond of the tune anyway, which he had known through Byrd's version in the *Fitzwilliam Virginal Book*. At the time he was preparing for a performance of Purcell's *Dido and Aeneas*, so as well as working in the one quotation he incorporated another, and made that, an arrangement of Dido's first aria, 'Ah, Belinda', the substance of the whole movement. As an example of how Tippett then interpreted Purcell and realized a figured bass it is informative;[8] but inevitably the movement sounds dated and over-romanticized, and indeed rather cranky, for the lachrymose commentary on a solo violin is a decorated version of 'Sellinger's Round'. Having thus made his original brief more complicated than it needed to be, Tippett had no choice, once he had decided to build a complete work from the Aldeburgh movement, but to persist with his scheme of two quotations per movement. The first movement is based on one of the Gibbons fantasias he had discovered after writing his first mature music,[9] and which had then moved him profoundly since he found in Gibbons both proof of the tradition to which he himself belonged and the acme of it. The quotation is a tribute to his own ancestor. The second movement is the Purcell arrangement, and the remaining movements are also based on pieces by British composers with a personal significance to him (arranged in chronological order),[10] and 'Sellinger's Round' is squeezed into the texture of each. The distortion necessitated by this process was curious enough in the original movement. But in the other movements it becomes so bizarre that it is difficult to see why Tippett committed himself to this regimen, unless he felt some psychological need to exercise his technique in complex contrapuntal problems. Tippett has sometimes been accused of working a simple idea to death. This is his only composition to offer substance to the criticism.

With the Suite he had set himself more practicable objectives, fixed his attention on them and produced a correspondingly better work. Tuneful and cheerful, it leaves the listener with the feeling that there is perhaps more to it than immediately strikes the ear. It was commissioned in 1948 by the BBC to celebrate the birth of Prince Charles, and it marked Tippett's first acceptance of the fact that unless he were to be churlish he would occasionally have to accommodate himself to the needs of the

musical establishment, to which he did or would owe quite a lot. Much of
Purcell's music had been written in similar circumstances, and maybe with
this example in mind (Tippett's use of Purcell's ceremonial key of D major
here seems no accident), Tippett approached his task seriously and
tactfully – rather in the spirit of a godfather bestowing good fortune at a
christening. The opening movement recalls the trumpets, the bell chimes
('St Paul's Steeple') and the hymn tune 'Crimond' which were heard at the
Queen's wedding. Thus the stage is set, and by the second movement the
baby has duly arrived, for it is a cradle-song – marked 'Berceuse' in the
score, since the tune is French. (It is taken from Tippett's children's opera
Robert of Sicily, where it is a 'Boating Song' accompanying the court's
voyage from Sicily to Rome.) The third movement is cast as a bedtime fairy
story, the little march which signals the appearance of the supernatural
dancers in *The Midsummer Marriage* framing an exciting version of the
dance-tune 'All round my hat'. 'All round my hat' is a fertility dance. The
protagonist's initiation properly accomplished, the proposed *curriculum vitae*
now proceeds to marriage, represented by the medieval English carol,
'Angelus ad virginem', which Tippett had used as a wedding processional
in his early ballad opera, *Robin Hood*. The main theme of the rondo finale
comes from the overture to *Robin Hood* and so, at the climax of the work, the
young prince is promised a life of happiness and adventure. Naturally,
there is a cautionary episode (the rondo theme also includes the phrase 'O
don't deceive me' from the folk-song 'Early one morning'), but nothing
really can question the assurance of flowers all the way (the Helston Furry
Dance, which had also appeared in the *Robin Hood* overture) and of
everlasting delight (a beautiful 'folk-song' of Tippett's own, 'This is thy
true love and thy only dear', again from *Robin Hood*).

From Tippett's point of view the chief advantage gained from writing the
Suite was that it enabled him to salvage some of the best ideas in his
unpublished early music and present them in the effective and original
manner he was now capable of. His treatment of 'All round my hat', for
example, is a model of what in his early music he had barely envisaged.
The tune is lit up by a sizzling 'counterpoint' rising across the whole
orchestra; and its necessary repetitions are turned to dynamic account – by
an invented codetta (bracket in Ex. 108), which alters the pulse and thus
allows the tune to breathe, despite the almost breathless pace.

Ex. 108   **Suite for the Birthday of Prince Charles**

(Ex. 108 cont.)

Five Major Works

The Heart's Assurance

The first of Tippett's major works of this transitional period, *The Heart's Assurance*, was the product of his decision to write a 'true song cycle', now that in *Boyhood's End* he had already written a cantata (the distinction lying in 'the poet's voice describing rather than an "I" talking'[11]). As a matter of fact *The Heart's Assurance* is not a true song cycle in the classic narrative tradition of, for example, *Die Winterreise* or *Dichterliebe*. It belongs rather to that category, whose prototype may be found in Berlioz's *Les nuits d'été* or Schumann's *Liederkreis*, op. 24, and which was much favoured by Britten, in which an emotional experience too intense for expression in a single song is given room for expansion in a group of songs. Tippett's cycle has no story, only a theme – which he has described as 'Love under the shadow of death'. The work grew out of his affection for Francesca Allinson[12] who died just as the war was ending, a time when sensibilities were already heightened by so many deaths. Tippett's grief, remorse, and his bitterness that the war could have been partially responsible for her suicide were so acute that it was not until five years later, when 'the personal wound began to heal, and, more importantly, as the very real wounds of the war healed', that his feelings had become sufficiently distanced for expression in music. What eased this process was the recently published work of young poets of the Second World War. They, it seemed to Tippett, had been unable to make poetry out of the brutalities of war, as had such men as Wilfred Owen; their best poetry was made out of love. But this was love poetry of a unique kind, since the vibrant affirmation somehow forced from these poets rang out the more poignantly for the pressure under which it was conceived. In the work of two poets, both killed in the war, Alun Lewis (1915–44) and Sidney Keyes (1922–43), Tippett found the words which transmuted personal emotions and stood out as a profession of belief. In the first song of *The Heart's Assurance*, a setting of Alun Lewis's *Song*, the final lines of the poem are intoned on a single note[13] as a kind of motto for the whole cycle:

> [Remember this, Remember this]
> That Life has trembled in a kiss
> From Genesis to Genesis,
> And what's transfigured will live on
> Long after Death has come and gone.

The act of love, like the work of art, has the transcendent power to live eternally. Thus the cycle sprang from the deepest of human instincts: to express love and to make a memorial. It is among the most passionate of all Tippett's works.

The Heart's Assurance is laid out rather like Berg's *Lyric Suite*, a composition written from a comparable emotional standpoint: the odd-numbered songs become slower, the even-numbered faster. The fifth and last song however restores the equilibrium (unlike the Berg) and prevents the cycle from developing an automatic momentum of its own. Tippett thus declares sole responsibility for the behaviour of his organism, and establishes a context in which the supreme triumph of will in its culminating phrase carries the logic of unanswerable experience (see Ex. 109).

The vividness of that music, if not its intensity, can be heard in every moment of the cycle, even in the one song, the (second) title song, in which Tippett twists the evident meaning.

> O never trust the heart's assurance –
> Trust only the heart's fear:

runs the bitter text of Sidney Keyes; but Tippett does trust the heart's assurance and his dancing coloratura says so very clearly (though with the tact of one who has not himself had to wear battledress). Why the cycle

Ex. 109

should have so unusually close an identity of words and music may be ascribed to the influence of *The Midsummer Marriage* and, especially, to Tippett's need in the opera to cultivate a sharper visual imagination. In this connection he has often drawn attention to Schubert's *Gretchen am Spinnrade*, observing that what fired Schubert to write the song was not simply Goethe's poem but the picture it evoked, of the pitiful Gretchen singing at her spinning-wheel.[14] In the poem there is no mention of the spinning-wheel; but in the song it is there all the time. Just how fruitful these observations were can be seen from the fact that secondary images of this kind run through each of the songs of *The Heart's Assurance* – from the scurrying demisemiquavers of the 'endless belt' in *Song* (see Ex. 103(i)), to the rumbling figurations of the 'hurling night' in the third song *Compassion* (Lewis) and to the haunting evocation of the Last Post in *Remember your Lovers* (Keyes), in which Tippett imagined a 'young woman singing out over the Elysian fields to the young men in the fields beyond'.[15] Perhaps the most realistic of these images is of the eponymous dancer of the fourth song (Lewis). She floats in, rises on her points and performs a pirouette (see Ex. 110).

Ex. 110   **The Heart's Assurance**

In these ways background images are formed of such eloquence that they cry out for the precise details which will make them speak. Tippett's response to the individual word in the cycle is indeed as direct and unequivocal as anywhere in his output. In, for example, the following passage from *Compassion*, the emphasis on 'he' contrasts with that on 'she' in the first stanza and prepares for what follows, the man's reactions rather than the woman's actions; 'death', 'shivered' and 'still' are each vividly pointed; and the 'meadows of her breath' are evoked with those singing colourings of A flat which always seem to appear when Tippett touches on the pastoral (see Ex. 111).

Such minute attention to verbal meaning is prevented from lapsing into the purely illustrative by unobtrusive strophic forms,[16] which also serve a more positive role, by setting the inevitability of their own processes against the unpredictable immediacy of the word-setting and thus generating a tension which issues in the vividness mentioned above.

Ex. 111   **The Heart's Assurance**

(Ex. 111 cont.)

Fantasia Concertante on a theme of Corelli

Compared with *Boyhood's End*, *The Heart's Assurance* marks a shift from the abstract to the concrete musical metaphor and this is one of the respects in which it is forward-looking. Its romanticism is hard-edged. The romanticism of the *Fantasia Concertante* on the other hand is more nostalgic. It is as if Tippett recognized that the dream-world of *The Midsummer Marriage* could not last much longer but was nonetheless reluctant to leave it: while such sounds as the dawn chorus in Act III of the opera were still ringing in his ears he would recapture their flavour before they vanished for ever. The work was written with some urgency (a mere six weeks).

It began life as a commission from the 1953 Edinburgh Festival for a work to celebrate the 300th anniversary of the birth of Corelli. Tippett did not know much about Corelli, so he obtained a copy of the only Corelli music that seemed to offer a feasible starting point, the Concerti Grossi, op. 6. Having examined this to him not very stimulating material he eventually decided to use an excerpt from the middle of the first movement of No. 2 in F – a short adagio followed by a tiny vivace. (The principal material of the movement, an allegro, Tippett considered irredeemably conventional and he ignored it.) A friend helpfully informed him that Bach had written an organ fugue on a theme of Corelli (BWV 579);[17] Tippett was pleased with the prospect of stiffening the Corelli with some Bach and gratefully accepted the information. From these unpromising beginnings he wrote what may be regarded as his perfect work.

In choosing such seemingly insignificant material Tippett had in fact responded to his natural creative instincts. Little of his own musical material is particularly original as such. It makes its effect more by what it symbolizes and becomes than by what it is. In his programme note for the first performance of the *Fantasia Concertante* Tippett described the Corelli adagio as of a 'dark passionate kind' and the vivace as one in which Corelli 'explores the brilliance of the violin', going on to say that his own work passes to and fro between 'the dark and the light'. The Corelli excerpt therefore embodied metaphors which he could develop in his own way without restraint. Furthermore, Corelli's language is not so different from that of his beloved Purcell; and, in addition, the excerpt is part of a fantasia movement (rather than a concerto ritornello or a dance movement) and as such belongs to a tradition to which Purcell's viol fantasias belong. Tippett had long been fascinated by these works, especially by their formal construction: a sequence of discrete sections of widely contrasted moods, each emerging from the other and *in toto* building up to a convincing dramatic shape, but without the repeats and recapitulations of later music. Lacking formal orientation of this kind they set a high premium on a composer's intuitive command of dramatic argument. Tippett's *Fantasia Concertante* is a fantasia of this Purcellian type, and the first he had written. (It does contain a brief recapitulation, but this is more a dramatic gesture after the manner of, say, the ending of Beethoven's Pastoral Symphony, than a true recapitulation.) The 'concertante' of the title refers to his retention of Corelli's concertino (two violins and cello) and, by implication, of the contrast between concertino and concerto grosso. The instrumental feature particularly characteristic of Tippett is his replacement of the keyboard continuo with a third group of string players, a 'concerto terzo' – that is, his simultaneous acceptance and refashioning of a tradition according to the emotional needs, as he sees them, of the period to which he belongs. The unusual warmth and richness of sound provided by his thirteen-part string body indicates how important he thought these qualities were, at a time when post-war austerity was still being felt.

The Fantasia opens with a statement of Corelli's 'theme', correct, trim and on a tight rein – like a pony dressed up for a show, its mane plaited, its tail brushed, its flanks gleaming. Tippett then proceeds to shake out the plaits, loosen the reins and ride it out into the open country where it really belongs. He effects this transformation in a sequence of two variations. The adagio element of the theme begins to struggle free, first in a decorative, then in a repeated-note variation (sounding with the eloquent urgency of a Monteverdi *trillo*). During this process the 'concerto terzo' gains the confidence to forsake Corelli's harmony and rhythm, and the adagio pulse quickens to exactly half that of the vivace. The vivace has been waiting for the adagio to arrive, contributing little more than the occasional flourish and a tell-tale touch of consecutive fourths, instead of Corellian thirds. When the two elements have found their rhythmic identity, the time is ready for Tippett, in a very characteristic gesture, to wrench the organism free of its moorings and lift it into a different world entirely – where it is able to ponder the beauty of its surroundings and do what it likes.

Example 112 concludes the first section of the work and at the same time
introduces the second, an index of the mastery with which Tippett converts
the inherently scrappy fantasia form into an instrument serving the
interests of dramatic necessity. Of the remaining sections, each could be
described in terms of its interior construction. But the true character of the
work lies in their function. Thus the second is an exploration of 'the dark
and the light', a silent examination, 'seriously aware', of the contours of the
new world into which it has been admitted and a delighted frolicking
therein; it can also be described as a third variation on the theme or as an
introduction and allegro, the allegro a set of five divisions on a ground. The
third section is a full-throated hymn of thanksgiving; or another, and
particularly Italianate variant of the adagio. The fourth gathers the threads
together and builds up into an ecstatic celebration of everything that has
already happened, and with such all-consuming intensity that the final
section exceeds its proper length by about six times in order to accommodate an emotional need to absorb and reflect on an experience which by the
nature of things can never be repeated. The fourth section is in fact a fugue,

Ex. 112   **Fantasia Concertante on a theme of Corelli**

based on the Corelli/Bach subject, and the last a pastorale – this a salute to the similarly named movement tacked on to the end of Corelli's op. 6, No. 8, the 'Christmas Concerto'. Tippett concludes his work not within the world he has created but outside it – with a little recapitulation of the Corelli. This procedure politely returns his listeners to their seats and permits them to decide for themselves what they think of his work.

The principal material of the Fantasia is all derived from Corelli, even to the extent of admitting the Corelli/Bach subject because, by what may be termed a meaningful coincidence, it is formed from the same motivic unit as the theme. The fugue is constructed with especial skill. It begins, as in the original (Ex. 113(i)), with a single part, thus nicely preserving the melodic line of the previous section, and with an additional, second counter-subject of Tippett's own, which preserves three other features: the repeated notes of the accompaniment to the previous section, the motivic unit of the work, and Tippett's own language (and rhythm) at a point where it might have had to defer to that of Bach (Ex. 113(iv)a). After an exposition of this material there follows what sounds like a relaxing episode; but in fact it is a second exposition, Tippett's counter-subject assuming the role of subject and a new counter-subject being added (Ex. 113(iv)b). In the restatement of this double exposition Tippett's own material is inverted, so what had originally wound its way downwards now slowly rises, until it reaches that extraordinary decorative fervour signalling the final statement, in augmentation, of the basic material (see Ex. 102).

A final point of interest concerns the work's tonal structure. The five sections are in F minor and major, D, A flat, F minor to B minor, and F major: that is, they move to the lower and upper minor third and then to the remaining minor-third relationship, before returning to the home tonic. A singular feature of the work is precisely this, its homogeneity, the feeling it gives of being shown the same thing from several angles. If Lendvai's theory of 'axis' structure in the music of Bartók,[18] tonalities on the same

Ex. 113   **Fantasia Concertante on a theme of Corelli**

(i) Corelli theme

(ii) second section: ground

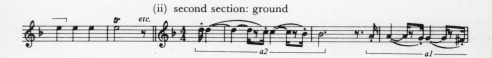

(iii) third section   (iv) fourth section

(v) fifth section

minor-third axis offering different perspectives of each other, is still in need of wider corroboration, here is evidence for its validity.

To describe Tippett's *Fantasia Concertante* as his 'perfect' work is not to claim that it is his greatest – its aims are too modest for that – but to say that it is made with consummate artistry. Of no other work of Tippett can it be said that not a note is out of place, not a moment misconceived or miscalculated. Everything contributes to a certainty of intention so absolute that were it not for the tone of the music the result would be almost frightening. As it is, the music is welcoming, restorative and peaceful. It could perhaps be termed pastoral. But this is a pastoralism active rather than reflective, which satiates the imagination rather than appeases it. What Tippett calls the 'pastoral metaphor' does return in his later music but never again with such luxurance.

Concerto for Piano and Orchestra

Tippett's Piano Concerto is not a work of this calibre, partly because it attempts much more and partly because it is hampered by a pianism not sophisticated enough to measure up to the expressive demands he places on it. The work is big, rich and leisurely in pace: this, at least, is the character of the orchestral sound. The piano tries to match it, but with gestures which often recall the stock-in-trade of precisely those nineteenth-century virtuosi Tippett was trying to avoid. Some passages in the Concerto suggest that he had the example of Brahms's Piano Concerto No. 1 in mind when writing the work, or more particularly of Bartók's Piano Concerto No. 3 – which would have been an excellent model of the type of concerto he favoured. But, unlike Bartók's, many of Tippett's gestures imitate rather than re-create and thus introduce an occasional vulgarity which rubs uncomfortably against the more intimate sections of the work (see Ex. 114).

Ex. 114   **Piano Concerto**

The limitations of Tippett's own piano technique are less evident in the quieter sections. His avowed intention of making the piano 'sing' again (in contrast to the more percussive approach in such works as Bartók's first two piano concertos or those of Prokofiev and Stravinsky) does indeed bear fruit, and especially in the decorative accompanimental passages so typical of the work and in the cantabile moments which are the essence of it. Yet even here it is difficult to escape the feeling that Tippett is not so much resisting the temptation to convert the non-sustaining piano into a lyrically sensuous instrument (as, say, Debussy had done) as unconsciously acknowledging the fact that he is not really capable of doing so (see Ex. 115).

Ex. 115   **Piano Concerto**

The surprising thing is that the Concerto is still compelling enough to emerge intact from such strictures, to assert its personality in spite of them and stay imprinted on the imagination long after they have been forced into insignificance. If flawed, its authority is incontestable, its matter more powerful than its manner. The Concerto, and especially its first movement, is an extreme instance of this phenomenon in Tippett's output, perhaps because it is itself somewhat experimental, its pursuit of the soaring and shimmering lines of *The Midsummer Marriage* or, to be more accurate, the states of mind symbolized by the lines, nowhere more sustained. Outside the context of an opera an artistic intention such as this might seem likely to degenerate into a sophisticated exercise in wool-gathering. But the work proceeds with the inevitability of a sunrise, and the territory revealed is not a featureless expanse – as the discovery of, for example, its secret places indicates (see Ex. 101(i), bracket *y*). Its boundaries however are limited and limiting. Having surveyed his territory, occupied it quietly and unhurriedly, Tippett then withdrew, leaving an enduring record of his visit. Why he should have wanted a piano as companion or why the ostensibly extrovert concerto form should have been chosen for so inward a purpose was due in part to the stimulus of that most inward of concertos, Beethoven's Piano Concerto No. 4. But the deeper reason was presumably that Tippett saw the piano as a member of the 'magical' ensemble of flutes, celesta and muted horns of *The Midsummer Marriage*. It is a celesta substitute, or even the celesta's twin brother. The beginning of the Concerto is already 'magic' music (see Ex. 116).

This music plainly illustrates Tippett's instinct to use thematic material so familiar that it is almost a cliché and to capitalize on that very fact by straightaway leading the listener through its outer surface into its potential as metaphor. It is obviously hazardous to attempt a verbal description of the unfolding meaning of this metaphor. But since the essence of it is so clearly reached in the tiny passage for solo viola, muted horns and celesta already mentioned (see Ex. 101), there seems little doubt that Tippett is here restating one of the central axioms of *The Midsummer Marriage*: once the magic has been unlocked a process is set in motion which leads to the 'jewel of great price'. As a whole the movement is laid out in a strict, if loose-limbed sonata form, but this passage always appears at a different place in the structure, as if to say that its mystery can be approached from many paths and can inspire many outcomes: wonder, peace, resolution. It first appears at the end of the transition, after the opening theme has broadened out into an orchestral paragraph and eventually flowered into a decorative stasis (Ex. 101(i), bracket *y*); it then appears within the grating climax of the development section; finally it appears within the cadenza which, having (unusually) forestalled the recapitulation of the second subject, now leads into it and invests it with a more heroic ring as a consequence.

The paradox of this beautiful movement is that despite the persuasiveness of its metaphor it is defeated by it. As indicated earlier, the climax is unclimactic: it reveals nothing new. In a movement so much concerned with revelation, this is a serious failing. Tippett's extraordinary slow movement is a kind of answer to this charge. Its sound is no longer alluring, its argument is concentrated, almost to the point of pedantry; but at its climax it does reveal something.

An eerie summons from a quartet of horns announces a strange contest which sounds as if staged in some mythical realm whose laws would have each contestant fight his own shadow. The piano launches into a frenetic exhibition of decorative bravura, while the orchestra contemplates an extremely long and an extremely staid theme, in canon with itself: that is, the principal elements of the first movement, decoration and melodic line, separate and follow independent courses. Initially, the result is the most densely textured music Tippett has written. Eventually the tension relaxes, not because either element has capitulated to the other, but because each has retreated from its own extreme position. The decoration becomes genuinely decorative and the line genuinely melodic (simply by going faster). The 'victor' in the process is the line, as with Tippett at any rate it must be, and the contestant with which it is associated, the orchestra, now voices its delight at the outcome in a climactic release of high-pitched string parts, while the piano gracefully reminds it, with a modestly decorated echo of the original orchestral theme (see Ex. 115), that the piano too has found its true identity. The pattern of orchestra answered by piano continues until the piano is received into the warm embrace of the cellos and basses.

This final section is strongly reminiscent of the 'taming of the orchestra' in the slow movement of Beethoven's Piano Concerto No. 4. No doubt the allusion is deliberate (Tippett could have covered it up had he been uneasy about it); and as such it can be read as his tribute to Beethoven. But it can also be read as another example of how he reinterprets his forbears in order to say something. In Beethoven the 'taming' comes at the beginning of the movement. But in Tippett it is at the end, and the piano is tamed, not the orchestra: the individual is reconciled with the collective. By way of confirming the point, the orchestra inaugurates the finale with an unusually extended ritornello, the principal rondo theme; and the piano is quite happy to accept a subsidiary role as provider of the four episodes. So the outcome of the Concerto is an alliance, represented by gaiety in the orchestra, attractive tunes from the piano, a democratic formal scheme (ABC, 1, A, 2, B, 3, C, 4, ABC) and a characteristic twist at the end by which the tonality veers from an E flat tonic to the broad confidence of C major.

The question lingers however of whether or not the first movement has been rejected by these high spirits, whether its beauties were, after all, an illusion. Tippett's own answer to this is equivocal. Undoubtedly the most haunting section of the finale is the fourth episode, a 'magical' duet for piano and celesta: the magic does remain therefore. But too much has happened for it to be the controlling influence again. This section perhaps marks the origin of the overt irony that was to colour much of Tippett's later music.

Sonata for Four Horns

Though short, Tippett's next work, his Sonata for Four Horns, is of considerable significance to his development. Its significance derives indeed from its very brevity. It is concentrated, neat and purposeful, and although it contains a very beautiful slow movement, Tippett makes no attempt to chase the magic of the Piano Concerto, confining his symbolism to the familiar, down-to-earth associations of the instruments for which he is writing. The Sonata's *chasse* is of the purely musical implications of thematic material deriving from hunting calls, its quarry a type of harmony and gesture from which much of Tippett's subsequent output was in fact to develop. In brief, the work is a reaction to the Concerto.

It can of course be regarded as the natural outcome of a commission for four virtuoso horn players. Such a work would by definition be relatively short (the sonority of four horns is too rich for prolonged hearing), be harmonic rather than linear in style (since the sonority is homogeneous) and would present a formidable technical challenge.[19] Yet the important innovations of the Sonata are hardly the trappings of a simple *pièce d'occasion*. It seems that under cover of its modest exterior Tippett was using the occasion to make a crucial preliminary survey of the new ground he was shortly to occupy.

The significance of the work's harmony lies in the fact that the gentle sonorities of fourths chords, as in the Piano Concerto, are superseded by a harmonic norm more pungent and more tangible – stemming from a chord which telescopes tonic and dominant. The interior construction of this 'bitonal' chord is so elementary that it postulates boyish experiments at the piano with 'modern' harmonies. But Tippett's choice not of two superimposed triads but of the more alert sound of a fifth and a triad points rather to his long-standing instinct to reinvest the common currency of harmonic usage and in particular to his newer instinct to fasten on to a chord for its individual properties as sound. The rootedness of the chord isolates it. The opening of the Sonata presents the chord in contrapuntal guise (Ex. 117(i)). Tippett no longer views harmony just as a means to an expressive end; perhaps through having to write in four parts, he begins to relish the sound of four-part harmony *per se*. Through harmony he discovers a way of fixing and holding a musical moment (Ex. 117(ii) and (iii)).

As yet such harmonies remain essentially diatonic, but a decisive step has been taken towards a music which discards the evolving, exploratory lines of the Piano Concerto and concentrates on immediate objectives and clearcut articulation of the progress towards them. As a result of this harmonic emphasis the rhythmic character of Tippett's music begins to change too. While not forfeiting the rhythmic characteristics of his earlier music he now admits fixed-additive rhythms (as in the $(2+2+3) \times 3$ semiquavers of the slow movement) and that Stravinskian variety of rhythmic counterpoint which consists of a rhythmic ostinato with free part added (as in the $5/4$ ostinato accompanying the recall of first-movement material in the final episode of the fugal finale). Such changes affect

Ex. 117

Tippett's treatment of structure as well. Despite the work's title not one of its four movements is a true sonata-allegro, as if Tippett were saying to himself that classical sonata form can lead to diffuseness and must be replaced by tauter structures. His solution is to cast each of the movements in a strophic form[20] (if the fugue can also be considered such) – a simple, but highly significant tactic, for by their nature strophic forms make no presumption to the successfully concluded arguments of sonata form and limit themselves to uncomplicated statements, the alternative aesthetic which in *King Priam* was to be raised to the level of a principle.

In the Sonata, unhampered by considerations of scale or metaphysics, Tippett was able to sit back and enjoy the fundamental pleasures to be derived from exercising his gift for composing music. He treated himself to a kind of holiday task – and in the process produced one of his liveliest and freshest pieces. This is the most important fact about the work, and it would be wrong to gloss over these intrinsic qualities by laying too much emphasis on its place in his stylistic development. Nonetheless, it remains relatively lightweight, and although it did open the way to several decisive changes in his next work, his Symphony No. 2, the splendour of that work inevitably overshadows the pretensions of the little Sonata.

Symphony No. 2
It would be equally misleading to suggest that the Symphony's status as the vital stylistic link with the new language of *King Priam* is more

important than its status as symphony. It has been placed in a transitional period. But the work is in no way tentative. It drives from start to finish with a single-mindedness so intense that on occasion it borders on the hectoring. And while its neo-classicism is less exemplary than that of the Symphony No. 1 it remains firmly wedded to that historical symphonic archetype Tippett had found in Beethoven. It marks the culmination of over twenty years' practical speculation on the meaning of classical structure and is voiced with something of the urgency of a manifesto.

In this Symphony then, Tippett acknowledged the ineluctable necessity of the four-movement Beethovenian archetype and an almost moral obligation to uphold it: the dramatic sonata-allegro, the deeply expressive slow movement, the vigorous scherzo and the triumph of will represented by the finale. The work's fascination derives from precisely these factors, for if Tippett needed to make so vehement a statement about symphonic form he surely did so in response to the challenge of an alternative aesthetic, unconscious though his awareness of such a challenge may have been. (It may have been just because he could not formulate its premises that it constituted a challenge to him.) The Symphony seems to wage a campaign against an unknown adversary, stretching Tippett's defences against assaults from all directions to such a degree that they begin to break under the strain and split off into, ironically, precisely those elements that were to comprise the new symphonic aesthetic he was to develop a few years later. The almost obsessive commitment of the Symphony betrays a sense of insecurity – in which respect the work can be seen as genuinely transitional.

Its opening movement illustrates these features very clearly. It seizes the attention from the outset, with a driving, pounding momentum[21] that sounds as if Hephaestus himself were forging impregnable armour for the protection of some latter-day hero. His materials are refractory but they yield to his elemental resolution. This mood is sustained right through until the end of the movement, when a flourish of hammer blows on the timpani sets the seal on an undertaking successfully accomplished. The textures are somewhat rough, there is no rubato, ritardando or accelerando, and even the lyrical moments are not allowed to forget that they are held in sway by a force greater than themselves. Further linguistic evidence of the character of the movement is provided by strict motivic control and the presence of a second development section, unprecedented in Tippett's output, which absorbs the energy and corrects the imbalances left over at the end of the recapitulation. Yet the counters in this argument are not the germinal or plastic motifs and gestures traditionally associated with symphonic thinking: they are not so much open-ended propositions, as self-contained statements. On a large scale this is reflected in the sharp contrasts of timbre between the main structural groups and the sub-sections within them; on a small scale, by the motifs themselves. Despite the fact that they do yield under pressure, they are arresting and almost peremptory in tone, and when set in close proximity as, for example, at the opening of the movement, their independence is underlined. Thus, while the three motifs (*a*, *b*, *c* in Ex. 118) are motivic variants of one another, the second by augmentation, the third by the conversion of the first two into a (transposed) harmonic aggregate (Ex. 118(ii)) and by a linear elaboration of the resulting harmony, their sonorous characters disclaim the connections. With material of such self-sufficiency Tippett finds himself in a position analagous to that of Stravinsky manipulating brief, irreducible melodic cells. The only developmental techniques appropriate to such material are permutation and repetition. Since permutation implies an anti-teleological,[22] circular or directionless art foreign to Tippett's own thinking, he is left with the resources of repetition. Naturally, Tippett does not limit himself to literal repetition of material. This indeed is the principal point to be made, for the energy of the movement derives in large measure from the way in which he wrenches his material out of its natural inertia and thrusts it forward by force of will. His repetitions include varied repetitions, and they generate new patterns by processes of addition and accumulation. The first repeat of the two-bar motif *a* in Ex. 118 is stretched to three bars. The process in the complete example may be expressed as follows: $(2+3)+(2+5)$; it continues with $(2+3)+(2+6)$. Likewise motif *c* (see brackets in example) may be expressed, in semiquaver units, as $(4+4)+(4+6)$ and $(4+4)+(5+3+5)$. By its nature, material of this kind leads Tippett to that method of free-additive rhythmic development mentioned earlier (see p.288), which results from an opposition between static and dynamic motivic cells. Although the oppositions of the first movement derive largely from non-rhythmic considerations (Tippett's determination to extract some lyrical substance from his dramatic material and his development of the harmony of the Sonata for Four Horns), the effect of them, and especially of the harmonic, is often dependent on the rhythmic.

Ex. 118   **Symphony No. 2**

(ii)

The Symphony marks the point at which Tippett first used overtly bitonal or polytonal harmony. It was characteristic of him to use such harmony not only for its colouristic properties but also as a source of structural tension. By conflating the 'bitonal' (telescoping tonic and dominant) chord of the Sonata with another such chord rooted a tone apart Tippett created a germinal chord (see Ex. 118(ii)) whose inner dynamic of opposing tonalities assuredly does generate structural tension. Yet by combining two or more tonalities in one sound Tippett also reached a stasis, a kind of saturation point – for if the potential of one tonality (say C) for modulation and development is pre-empted by the fact that other tonalities (say G and D) are already present, where can that one tonality go? Of course, several options remain open (and Tippett's 'second subject' similarly conflates three tonalities based on A flat, the warm fourth 'fifth' relationship). But polytonality of this type weakens the force of traditional tonal relationships considerably and explains why Tippett's tonal structures are from this Symphony onwards more than ever dependent on his feeling for tonality as dramatic colour and why his 'modulations' are not gradual changes of tonal perspective but abrupt shifts from one pan-tonal area to another. It is in this context that rhythmic procedures come to the fore. The outcome of the 'first subject' of the first movement is not a release of energy but an implosion, in which tonal conflict breaks apart and accedes to rhythmic polyphony (see Ex. 104).

The slow movement is notable for a new mutation of Tippett's 'magical' sonority – harp and piano, a more prickly sound than before and symptomatic of his growing feeling that the magic can be uncovered only when a tougher surface has been penetrated. A carefully prepared timbral modulation in the first movement has made the significance of this new sound easier to grasp. There the 'magic' appears, briefly but unforgettably, in the characteristic sonority of celesta and muted trumpet (as echoes of the phrases of the second subject – see motif *b* in Ex. 104) and then (in the recapitulation) in the equally characteristic sonority of celesta and flute, to which is added a harp, a conspicuously delicate sound. In the slow movement the harp remains, while the celesta, after the model of the Piano Concerto, is replaced by the piano. The harp/piano duet does not have the authority of Tippett's earlier 'magical' apparatus because it never acts alone, nor does it precipitate a new musical event. Its role is subordinate, but crucial, for it serves as an assurance that the subject matter is indeed the illumination of something deep and mysterious. Without its explanatory gloss, the strange beckoning of the long, opening trumpet solo ('Jenifer's' trumpet, coloured by tremblings on a flute) could not have succeeded in drawing its listeners into the imaginative world of the movement as a whole: it would have sounded too much like a real trumpeter struggling with an awkward part.

This movement, therefore, marks Tippett's return to his preoccupation with musical magic. In his Piano Concerto his approach may ultimately have proved unsatisfactory, but the preoccupation itself is so fundamental to his understanding of what music is that he was bound to return to it and develop new ways of expressing it. Here, he sets the 'magic' and the 'real' in bold juxtaposition, as though to call his own bluff: if the magic fails to hold up, it will sound false. The result of this challenge is a sound with none of the luminous warmth of the Piano Concerto but with a strangely fascinating quality all the same, as if Odysseus were hearing sad and chilling tales from the souls of the underworld (see Ex. 119).

Ex. 119   **Symphony No. 2**

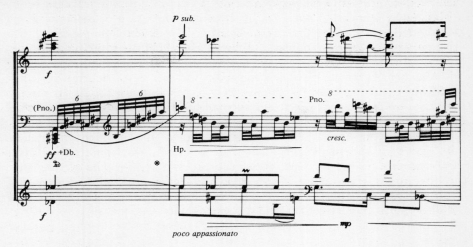

poco appassionato

Tippett's more critical approach to musical magic was to have important structural consequences. As a whole the movement can be described as a song form in two stanzas – and lyricism certainly preponderates: the lyrical duet for cellos from which Ex. 119 is taken is followed by a second lyrical section for the full string body. Yet each stanza is also characterized by the abrupt, fantasia-like juxtapositions referred to above. Those in the first stanza are most marked when the second lyrical section calms a 'realistic' interpolation, by reducing it to a fragment; those in the second, when, at the same juncture, the fragmentation process is carried to an extreme unprecedented in Tippett's output (see Ex. 101 (iii)). Here, the calming factor is not the sound of strings, but a new one, of four horns – obviously deriving from the Sonata for Four Horns (and in later works to become a characteristic Tippett fingerprint) but in this context deriving more from Tippett's need to find a metaphor for the transformation occurring when the magical and the real interact. In this movement Tippett not only foreshadows the structural methods of *King Priam* – the juxtapositioning of discrete sound blocks – but also shows that what determines the instrumentation of such blocks is less the play of instrumental colour than the conduct of a metaphysical argument.

The scherzo courteously acknowledges the plausibility of that visionary movement and then informs its listeners that the time has come to return to earth and get on with things. What it gets on with is a rediscovery of energy and exuberance in preparation for the finale. The slow movement's magic is not forgotten altogether, for the harp/piano duet reappears at the end to cast a spell over the exuberance; but it functions more as structural device than expressive metaphor, and in general the movement is direct and to the point. It is planned as a single dynamic arch, crescendo and diminuendo. The peak of the crescendo is not simply the loudest part of the movement, nor is it the centre of a symmetrically ordered mechanism, as is implied by the movement's palindromic basis. It behaves organically, leading, in three sections, from a concentration of energy (see Ex. 105) to a lyrical release of energy, which in turn is cut short by a scattering of energy: an emotionally satisfying sequence, comprising the climax of the development section, the recapitulation of the 'second subject', and a recall of the principal motif of the development. The movement is structured therefore far more subtly than either Tippett's own description of 'mirror form scherzo' or the following scheme would suggest: A B C (=development) B C A. In broad design it conforms to a preconceived plan but in detail it responds to the intricacy and potential of its material. The first subject, for example (Ex. 120), is one long theme, a complex canon at the seventh, divided among several solo instruments, each 'voice' a duet. The second subject, by way of necessary complement, is two short themes for tutti strings, the first in the simplest texture possible (unison), the second a straightforward tune and accompaniment. Rhythmically, the first subject merely states the additive principle, while the second develops it at some length, introducing techniques which reach their own height of complexity at the climax of the movement (referred to earlier, on p.288).

Ex. 120   Symphony No. 2

The finale begins with a section coming dangerously close to what Stravinsky called 'the monotony of the run' – an introduction so transparently introductory that what actually happens in it tends to lose out to the ordinariness of its function. This is a pity, for the fault lies not in its musical substance but in the fact that the scherzo has already acted as an extended anacrusis and has therefore made further introductions superfluous. Tippett's miscalculation here is symptomatic of his continuing struggle with the 'finale problem'. After his relatively light-weight scherzo he needed a movement resolute enough to balance his opening sonata movement and, in particular, flexible enough to symbolize his belief that lyricism (the 'magic'), if it is to mean anything, cannot simply be stated, an effect without a cause, but must be fought for. His solution is a fantasia movement, whose core is a ground bass on a theme sufficiently rich and

concentrated to provide a challenge to those powers of musical argument
that would justify the eventual lyricism. It is an ingenious solution. And it
is obvious why he should have wanted to emphasize the seriousness of his
Symphony's culminating movement by prefacing it with an introduction.
Presumably, his ideal solution would have been to write an opening section
somehow combining the effect of introduction and exposition all in one – an
almost unrealizable prescription but not in fact so far removed from what
he did write. His introduction fuses the seemingly contradictory states of
blind energy and a kind of trapped desperation: its gestures promise to
escape and take on a purposeful existence, only to subside into chilling
inertia. Musically, a transformation process takes place in which material
from the first movement – the pounding C's, the dancing violin figurations
of the first subject and the 'echo' of the second subject – is moulded into
what soon emerges as the ground bass theme. So, as is axiomatic with
Tippett, an apparent hopelessness contains the seeds of its own recovery;
and because a belief of this order can never cease to have meaning, the
erstwhile irrelevance of his introduction begins to sound vitally relevant.
That this was no trick solution to Tippett's compositional problem can be
seen in the ground bass theme itself. It is terse almost to the point of
unintelligibility, a phenomenon due in part to the toughness his music had
acquired since his earlier uses of the ground bass form but principally to
the fact that if the lyricism is to be properly won it must be won according
to the stated terms of Tippett's conceptual premise. The theme is the
introduction forged and refined into an epigram. It starts with resolution,
begins to dance and then floats into lyricism – significantly, into Tippett's
favourite tonality of A flat, though as yet only cautiously (see Ex. 121). The
eleven variations proceed to elaborate and elucidate this epigram with a
series of dancing counterpoints whose tendency to lyricism is firmly
directed along the path of discursive reasoning. When that has reached its
point of greatest concentration (a group of canons for the strings) the
texture is penetrated by two trumpets, announcing in triumphant, almost
strident fanfares that the stage is set and illumination imminent (see
Ex. 121).

Ex. 121   **Symphony No. 2**

(Ex. 121 cont.)

As is shown in the above example, Tippett pits the course of his
argument against a strict, almost scholastic treatment of the ground bass
principle. Only in the final two variations does he forsake the proportions
and contours of his theme and he does so not simply to effect a transition to
the lyrical section of his fantasia but also in response to the dramatic
impact of the trumpet fanfares. The extraordinary shiver of excitement
which comprises these two variations corresponds with the *anagnorisis* in
The Midsummer Marriage, a moment of shock and recognition. A rapturous
line for unison violins (later repeated on the lower strings) now slowly
winds its way across the fabric of the whole orchestra, supported on a
glittering carpet of sound from the wind instruments and welcomed by
seals of approval from the magical duet of harp and piano. The movement,
and the Symphony, has reached its apotheosis. Tippett's exquisitely
beautiful melody here speaks of his absolute certainty of intention. It is
conceived in dangerously simple terms, tune and accompaniment, and in a
tonality, A flat, whose associations with musical 'magic' in his earlier
output might have made him nervous of using it in this way once again. In
performance its ecstasy, serenity, immediacy, is not easy to capture. But it
is there all the same, and this, its sheer length and its spicy tonal flavour
(resulting from its bitonal colourings, see Ex. 103(iv)) shows that he was
abundantly equipped to beget fresh images and to turn his metaphysical
beliefs into musical fact.

The coda returns the Symphony to its starting point, as if to assure doubters that what has happened was indeed the consequence of those raw, uncouth beginnings. The opening C's lead straight into a vibrant chord, a gesture repeated until it alights on the germinal chord of the whole work, when a solo trumpet voices the strangely exalted and strangely terrifying wisdom of genius. Had Tippett written no more music after his Symphony No. 2 he would still have been a twentieth-century master.

CHAPTER FOUR

1958-76

Tippett's Change of Style

Between *The Midsummer Marriage* and Symphony No. 2 Tippett's style changed, but not so rapidly as to conceal the evidence of organic development. Between the Symphony and *King Priam* however a change occurred of such rapidity that to many commentators of the time it seemed to lack necessity: it seemed the product of change for change's sake, sad witness of a misguided attempt on Tippett's part to restore failing creativity by tearing his natural composing style from its roots and filling the void with all that was uncharacteristic of him – hard, intractable sonorities, an aggressively dissonant harmonic idiom and construction by means of stringing together gestures both crude and short-winded. Superficial, and on this level of observation, gauche echoes of the music of Britten, of Stravinsky (especially of *Agon*) and even of Webern gave substance to such criticisms.

That *King Priam* does mark a radical change in Tippett's development can be illustrated by a comparison.

The Midsummer Marriage	*King Priam*
comedy, with invented story	tragedy, with traditional story
symbolic	realistic
insights	statements
few scenes, flowing into each other	many scenes, abruptly juxtaposed
long paragraphs	short sections
lyrical arias	declamatory monologues
full orchestra	small ensembles

The antitheses above, which look as schematic as those Brecht set up when distinguishing 'dramatic' from 'epic' theatre,[1] show that Tippett's change of style was deliberate, as well as radical. This does not mean however that it can be attributed to some kind of creative aberration. *King Priam* is a problematic work; but far from inhibiting or emasculating Tippett's development, the opera encouraged it, to the extent of uncovering a source of inspiration rich enough to sustain his invention over a 'second period' of maturity as prolonged as the first. Unless that is to be written off *en bloc*, it is obvious that the change was extremely fruitful. The first question prompted by the music of his second period is not therefore whether it was harmful but why it should have happened in the first place. The opening section of the present chapter is concerned with this question and its implications.

King Priam is a ruthlessly analytic account of what happens when the psychological balance symbolized by marriage is knocked awry by responsibilities, war and fate. In *The Midsummer Marriage* Tippett had launched his characters on the assurance of an idyllically happy life together; now he declares that the rewards of marriage will be poisoned by violence and bigotry, the inevitable result being tragedy. Doubtless the principal reason for this apparent repudiation of everything his earlier music had stood for lies hidden in the mysteries of his psyche. Three more prosaic reasons can however be advanced as follows. The first is that having, in *The Midsummer Marriage,* fulfilled the objectives of nearly twenty years of compositional endeavour and proved to himself that he had the technical and intellectual equipment to accomplish whatever he liked, Tippett, temperamentally incapable of resting on his laurels, now felt able to accept any challenge his imagination offered him, immediately and without elaborate preparatory exercises, even to the extent of writing the opposite of *The Midsummer Marriage.* (*King Priam* can certainly be seen in this light, not simply because it is a tragedy but because it is the most didactic and theoretical of his works.) Once he had successfully fulfilled this new objective, he knew he could follow his creative instincts wherever they led him, and in his post-*King Priam* music, up to his Symphony No. 4 (1976–7), Tippett became progressively more direct and idiosyncratic in what he wished to say about the human condition.

The second reason is that *King Priam* is the natural outcome of an accelerating stylistic development. Hitherto Tippett's music had developed gradually, but by the time he had completed the opera the stylistic gap between it and its predecessors had widened so much that the connections seemed barely perceptible. In retrospect *King Priam* can be seen as already the climax of this process, for the novelties of his subsequent works do not reveal unexpected aspects of his musical personality to quite the same degree. But the process continued nonetheless and Tippett's post-*King Priam* music is distinguished by comparably surprising changes of style and emphasis.

The third reason is to do with the 'feel of our time',[2] Tippett's neat evasion of the rebarbative *Zeitgeist*. The music of his first period was written in an age dominated by war: the threat of it, the fact of it and the aftermath of it. The stylistic homogeneity of this music, its overriding concern for sounds emphasizing vitality and renewal, can be interpreted as the consequence of what Tippett saw as a moral obligation to provide a corrective to the age, to 'raise his lyre amid shadows',[3] as Rilke's ninth *Sonnet to Orpheus*, a poem he is fond of quoting, expresses the matter. The stylistic homogeneity of the music to be considered in the present chapter is of a different order. It could be described as heterogeneously homogeneous. It is the product of a creative mind no longer limited by one pre-eminent commitment but set free to occupy itself with the less fundamental but more particular and diverse preoccupations of an age in which the pursuit of individual aspiration became morally respectable once more. From the mid-1950s the world was a different place, war a less obsessive fact of living. Certainly, the threat of nuclear destruction may have promoted the cheerful fatalism of the 1960s, the feeling that since the future was in doubt life had to be enjoyed before it was too late; but the period also saw the abolition of conscription, the politics of co-existence, so-called permissiveness, financial recovery, spectacular advances in technology, considerations which released that genuine exuberance and idealism whose energies were not arrested until the oil crisis of the early 1970s. In the mid-1950s, the signs of such changes were surely unmistakable to a creative artist of Tippett's sensibilities, even if their later manifestations could only be guessed at. The 'feel of the time' had altered. Tippett no longer needed to feed the imagination with images of vitality and renewal, since that was happening already. He needed to invent fresh images and fresh compositional resources, strong enough to adapt themselves to this new situation and strong enough to uphold his unchanging belief that music should offer a corrective. It seems no accident therefore that precisely when the scars of war were being healed and the promise of a more open and compassionate society was being vigorously pursued Tippett should have forged the new language of *King Priam*, an opera about the inevitability of war, the destructiveness of personal relationships and the futility of illusions. No accident perhaps that its epic realism should date from a period when the Hungarian revolution and the Suez invasion would have underlined such apprehensions – or when, with the crisp sensuousness of *Le marteau sans maître* and the dramatic rhetoric of *Gruppen*, the leaders of the ascetic neo-classical movement (see p.87) of the immediate post-war years, Boulez and Stockhausen, were rediscovering their native traditions and ushering in the characteristic neo-romanticism of the next decades. It was perhaps no accident that *King Priam*'s first performance, in 1962, should have taken place just one day before the first performance of Britten's *War Requiem*, a work which epitomized for a generation the new spirit of reconciliation.

None of these reasons for Tippett's volte-face in *King Priam* takes account of its most obvious aspect – the almost reckless self-assurance of a composer prepared to turn his back on past accomplishment, form a new style virtually from scratch and then, not content with that, subject the results to the merciless scrutiny of the most public of arenas, an opera-house. This is so obvious that it would hardly have been worth mentioning, had it not drawn attention to a belief lying at the heart of Tippett's artistic personality. Music is not abstract construction. Whatever the risk to the composer, it must communicate something. That something must in turn reveal, assert, celebrate the *absolute* value of man and of man's living even if, in order to do so, it has to be a full-length opera about someone whose house falls in ruins and who dies amid ghastly brutality. Tippett has no interest in any final 'salvation' of King Priam. He is concerned with his mortality. Whether Priam's life was in fact worth living can be answered only by the individual listener, but there can be no doubt that to Tippett it was and furthermore that it was only through music that such a message could be conveyed. Recklessness or hubris does not come into it therefore. Life has value, and the composer is driven to say so by the force of a moral imperative. Tippett's exemplars in this respect are such figures as Shakespeare, Goethe, Beethoven – not merely because they are 'great' but because they drew inspiration from everywhere and thus speak to everybody: they lend authority to his own artistic ambition to stretch beyond cultural boundaries and reach a universal humanity. They also however led him into a creative predicament, for it would seem pitifully naïve to imagine that a fundamental humanism of this order could have any genuine, practical relevance to a world split into separate ideologies, each preoccupied with defending its own superiority against the apostasy of the others. Yet if the divisions between communism, capitalism, national-ism, religions, technologies and the pursuit of simple self-interest cannot be healed by rational argument, it is at least possible that an 'irrational' medium such as music can touch deeper layers of common humanity and make some contribution towards a collective balance. This is the faith by which a composer such as Tippett justifies his existence.

Of course, few people can afford the luxury of thinking in these terms. And even should it be agreed that creative artists enjoy some special dispensation, it could still be argued that the only creative artists really entitled to do so are those who have had direct experience of regimes promoting the opposite of humanism. This is what Tippett seems to be hinting at in his essay 'Too Many Choices' (written shortly before he began composing *King Priam*), when referring to the predicament of creative artists in the Soviet Union.[4] By this line of argument he could perhaps have concluded that the one legitimate contribution to the humanist tradition produced at the time of *King Priam* was Shostakovich's Symphony No. 13 (1962), a work which paints a harrowing picture of fear and desperation and which still manages to end on a note of consolation. Tippett was by nature haunted by the contradictions presented by these moral problems; but he had in fact grappled with them as far back as the mid-1930s and had long ceased to believe that his position as armchair observer of the political and social scene invalidated his licence to compose. What his sympathy for Soviet artists did was, it seems, to make him more conscious of the privileged position of those free to work within the humanist tradition, thus more conscious of the vulnerability of that tradition and more than ever anxious to uphold it against the challenges of scepticism and rival theologies.

From the former viewpoint, *King Priam* can be interpreted as a profession of faith: the opera presents humanist philosophy at its weakest point, and in a setting remote from everyday experience, so that this weakness cannot be painted over by the plausibility of a contemporary setting. King Priam's life was, ultimately, meaningless. What sort of philosophy is that? Tippett re-plies firstly that Priam had no choice but to live his life anyway; but, more importantly, he shows how music can be used to give concrete form to those stark and unanswerable eternals of experience which for millennia have pro-vided a yardstick against which human sensibility can be measured.

From the latter viewpoint, *King Priam* is, as Tippett has revealed,[5] a conscious attempt to question Marxist ideology. Hitherto he had regarded music ill-equipped to express his antagonism towards totalitarian regimes (Marxist, Marxist-Leninist or whatever); but in 1957 he read a book by the Marxist philosopher-critic Lucien Goldmann which threw down a challenge he felt bound to take up. Goldmann's book, *Le dieu caché*,[6] is a study of 'tragic vision' in Pascal and Racine. Tippett certainly gained some valuable insights from it. What provoked him was, as he saw it, Goldmann's central thesis that tragedy is theatrically impossible in the modern world because the only serious philosophical alternatives, Marxism and Christianity, both postulate an optimistic view of life, the one leading to happiness on earth, the other in heaven. *King Priam* is that impossible artefact, a modern tragedy, and an invitation to the Marxist to pronounce it untragic. (The opera's tilt at Christianity – the presence of a god, Hermes, and the emphatic *finis* on Priam's death – is more muted, presumably because Tippett considered Christianity not so potent a threat as Marxism.) It would be absurd to suggest that the opera is no more than this, or that it is a unique example of a twentieth-century operatic tragedy (though it might, all the same, be argued that its main 'rivals', such works as *Lulu* or *Lady Macbeth*, are not genuinely tragic because their plots could have lead elsewhere had the social circumstances of their heroines been different). But the fact remains that a crucial reason why Tippett wrote *King Priam* was that he wanted to refute Marxist ideology – to show that the 'inevitability' of the communist utopia will always be subverted by (non-economic) factors beyond the control of man's best instincts.

That he should do so in the mid-1950s seems hardly coincidental: the apparent thaw in Soviet politics at this time would, to him, have appeared no more lasting than the 'false spring' of the early 1920s. However plausible in these terms, Tippett's approach may still seem disconcertingly idiosyncratic, if in order to say something about Marxism he should have chosen to do so on the rarefied level of literary criticism and with no reference to the issues in dispute. An answer to this puzzle may never be wholly convincing. If seen from the composer's point of view however, Tippett's course of action becomes quite logical. Thus, intense though his antagonism towards communism may have been, it would have had to be expressed through the only channel he knew, music, in his own terms and on his own ground. If his opera were to be a tragedy, it was characteristic that he should have turned to the ur-tragedy, Homer's *Iliad*, as he had turned to the ur-ritual and the ur-comedies of Aristophanes for *The Midsummer Marriage*. If he had decided to articulate Homer in terms of 'the mysterious nature of human choice'[7] rather than an exposé of communist repression, then this theme served to underline the tragic fact that whatever someone chooses to do and for whatever reasons, honourable or otherwise, the consequences can always be catastrophic. The theme questions the value of human compassion and the validity of the laws of cause and effect, and it thus serves to set in relief those supreme experiences which give rise to such questionings – parenthood, passion, anguish, exhilaration, combat, grief, shame, death. In the process it joins forces with Tippett's humanistic message as well.

It is only with hindsight that Tippett's intentions can be interpreted in this way. To many of its first listeners what *King Priam* 'meant' was simply that Tippett had reacted to criticism that *The Midsummer Marriage* was weak in plot and had accordingly given his new opera a strong story line; this decision necessarily entailed a different sort of music. Tippett *had* taken this criticism seriously, and his constructive response to it offers a salutary reminder that the plain facts of his music can easily be hidden behind a thicket of extra-musical comment. This danger is especially acute with the music he wrote from *King Priam* onwards, which, unlike his earlier music and not therefore representing the working out of a carefully planned compositional programme, does not automatically claim to be examined from a strictly musical point of view. Assuredly, it 'develops' – and Tippett's transformation from a composer of tightly controlled self-discipline to one, apparently, of uninhibited and even reckless spontaneity is a particularly remarkable aspect of his career, not least because the process took shape when he was already well into his fifties (only Janáček presents a similar phenomenon in the present century). This development and the stylistic changes it brought about are determined however by expressive demands, and not by the desire to enlarge a musical vocabulary *per se*. It is precisely for these reasons that the commentator cannot avoid the question of what shaped these demands, what factors accounted for the predominantly extra-musical stimulus behind the works concerned. If in the process the commentator appears to be hunting woozles, that is in the nature of the assignment. He would be naïve to imagine that every contributory factor were equally significant or that the question could be settled with a single answer. Some factors shed more light than others. Tippett's criticism of contemporary composers, which helped define his own intentions; his increasing willingness to accept the status of man of the establishment, which aroused his youthful instinct to scandalize; his withdrawal from active involvement in the Peace Pledge Union, which perhaps showed that while his opposition to violence was channelled into an official outlet his music displayed no signs of violence but that when this was no longer the case it did – all these considerations have various shades of relevance. But none of them bears a consistent relationship with his output. What does is the 'feel of the time'. The commentator is brought round to the inescapable conclusion that this is indeed the decisive compositional determinant. Even if Tippett's pre-*King Priam* music had not communicated 'images of vigour for a decadent period, images of reconciliation for worlds torn by division',[8] his later output would still have spoken by itself of his deeply characteristic instinct to make music serve as some sort of indemnity for the excesses of its period. *King Priam* was written at a time when the value of life was in danger of being cheapened by sentimental illusions.

At first hearing, the remaining works of Tippett's second period may seem less obviously geared to this way of thinking. Abandoning the broad, generalized response and becoming more closely attuned to the specific moods of their time, they appear to endorse rather than compensate – an impression which in some respects is accurate, for the more enlightened attitudes of the 1960s (which in several instances were given legal sanction) and, in particular, the encouragement of the ambitions of young people represented to Tippett precisely what he had been campaigning for in his earlier music. He therefore had good reason to identify with them. Yet once they are examined more closely these later works show that Tippett had not really changed.

It is perhaps too early to summarize the 'feel' of the 1960s and early 1970s; but some attempt in this direction is necessary if Tippett's contribution is to be set in perspective. The extraordinary multiplicity of styles practised during the period can already be reduced to the common denominator of an all-pervading neo-romanticism. To a future historian this may seem an index of the period's failure to measure up to the challenge of the new scientific revolution, its loss of faith in a collective identity and its consequent retreat into subjectivity. In this case, music written from the positivist standpoint that only pre-determined, 'contextual' relationships matter and music written from the Zen Buddhist standpoint that nothing much matters would appear to be the only relevant contributions to the period. But its major composers evidently thought otherwise. None of them was insensitive to the new scientific challenge: their intensely searching investigations into technique, sound production or into musical sociology show how seriously they reacted to its implications. But their music nevertheless comes down heavily in favour of the humanistic. It represents a kind of ecological crusade against the technological, a celebration of man's rediscovered faith in himself or, more particularly, of man's discovery that this faith need not be expressed in terms of striving for achievement nor in terms of the compromises of elders and betters, but that it can be immediately experienced for its own sake. The beginnings of this process were signposted by Stockhausen's *Kontakte* of 1960, a *rapprochement* between the technological and the 'human', after which confidence in the purely human and instinctive grew rapidly, to the extent of admitting appeals to chance (aleatory music) and to the senses (for example, Ligeti's *Atmosphères* of 1961) and of identifying the human with the feelings of the individual once more – Stockhausen's *Momente* 1961–72 and Boulez's *Pli selon pli* 1957–61 are, to a greater or lesser extent, self-portraits. Growing confidence in the positive qualities of human feeling perhaps accounted for the fascination with collage and quotation, techniques which rather than confront, embrace and integrate. Interest in such techniques reached a climax in Berio's *Sinfonia* of 1968, a year which also saw the earlier explorations of the senses and the psyche develop into a neo-expressionism, strikingly overt in Maxwell Davies's *Eight Songs for a Mad King* and Henze's *Essay on Pigs*, deeply contemplative in Stockhausen's *Stimmung*, with its search for an oriental 'inner consciousness'. It was inevitable that these movements should skim dangerously close to the realms of nostalgia or fantasy, and that they should appeal to the devotees

of the neo-religiosity and the 'New Narcissism' of the late 1960s who
believed in imminent spiritual or physical panaceas. They bore a
superficial resemblance to that enthusiastic amateurishness which characterized the ephemera of the period. But such works as have been mentioned
avoid self-deception by the intensity of their feeling and workmanship, that
is, by the instinctive creativity of their composers.

Tippett's relationship with this movement of sensibility is not so
unequivocal as that of the composers referred to above. He was acutely
conscious of the challenge of the new scientific revolution. His writings
continually return to the idea that the destiny of the creative artist is to
compensate for the dehumanizing advance of technology. 'Too Many
Choices' is almost wholly concerned with this idea – and not surprisingly,
since it had recently been dramatized by the launching of the first sputnik,
'the herald of ever more limitless weapons of warfare, youngest brain-child
of our unappeasable death-wish'.[9] Tippett did not necessarily associate
technology with warfare or bloodshed, though he certainly did associate it
with the death of the human spirit. In this essay he expressed his
opposition to abstraction in art, or (to paraphrase what he meant by
abstraction) his opposition to those for whom the work of art 'was no longer
to be thought of as an expression of feelings or ideas, or as a representation
of reality, but rather as the solution of a problem that was unique and
intra-artistic',[10] in terms of choice and sacrifice: by choosing purity and
form, we sacrifice richness and allure. The matter was expressed tactfully,
but there was no doubt where Tippett's priorities lay:

> only by enriching the sensibility in as many directions as possible
> ('Ripeness is all') can the starved soul of the technologist be given fresh
> nourishment to come alive again.[11]

His own music, therefore, could never become an artistic counterpart or
capitulation to scientific methodology. As man remains the sole measure of
art, so does man remain, in spite of evidence to the contrary, the sole
measure of the universe. Scientific advance simply sharpened Tippett's
determination to 'renew our sense of the comely and beautiful'.[12] *King
Priam* can be seen, at least on one level, as an index of how drastic his
interpretation of the comely and the beautiful could become when he was
faced with one agent of that advance, sputnik.

Lying beneath these questions however lay the spectre of another
scientific 'achievement', which affected Tippett much more deeply. He has
been reluctant to voice any firm opinions about the sociological and
psychological impact of nuclear armament, but his music speaks of an
attitude to the subject which contrasts significantly with the evident
opinions of those who responded as to a call to gather rosebuds, or to value
what one has rather than what one covets, or to explode the doctrine that
'goals' and 'solutions' are a *sine qua non* of creative endeavour. Tippett was
not unsympathetic to such ideas, but he could not have believed they were
there simply for the asking. If the pursuit of 'solutions' had been

discredited in sociological and political spheres, this did not mean that 'non-solutions' should be uncritically accepted in the artistic sphere, which was close to suggesting that composers should be lotus-eaters. A 'non-ending' (to transfer to musical jargon) had to be earned and sought after. It represented something akin to a miracle, a level of sensibility in which release from tension could be apprehended only if it were the product of that same tension. Tippett's works of the 1960s featuring 'non-endings' (comprising his Piano Sonata No. 2, Concerto for Orchestra and *The Vision of Saint Augustine*), certainly belong to their period, but with the characteristically exemplary twist that the composer's licence to explore his own feelings in no way exonerated him from his responsibility to present argument, circular though that argument might be.

Tippett's 'non-endings' imply more than this however. They also imply a different sense of time. Herein may be found the crux of his response to nuclear threat.

> That we go on creating and procreating implies that we have our sense of the future as yet intact. But the possibility of nuclear suicide is so recent we cannot yet esteem its challenge.[13]

The challenge is that should the world be destroyed in a nuclear war and there be no future, then there would have been no point in writing music. Tippett's reaction is a sort of compromise. For himself, he must go on writing music anyway; but he is also a (qualified) realist, and if he is not able to stretch confidently into the future, then he can celebrate the present and even look inwards to a mystical world of the imagination where there is no past, present or future. What is the meaning of Time in such a world?

> There is a sense of Time as unique, from Genesis to World's End. And there is a sense of Time as repetitive, or circular – the myth of the Eternal Return. I am uncertain how objective is my feeling that the movement of these two ideas, one against the other, is another aspect of the new world picture.[14]

Feelings about the metaphysics of Time are by definition deeply subjective, but Tippett's examination of them was nonetheless objective enough to give concrete expression, pre-eminently in *The Vision of Saint Augustine*, to the idea both of progression and of stasis – not, furthermore, as abstractions but as elements within the larger and more characteristic idea of revelation. This answer to the challenge of the nuclear age was certainly very personal; but it was not eccentric, nor was it 'romantic' in the conventional sense. It made the point that while the period as a whole seemed to be hiding its head in the sands, its art, at least, could attempt to redeem it, by converting the pursuit of self-gratification into an exploration of the limits of intellectual concentration. And by making the point in terms of a new conception of musical time, Tippett found himself in the company of several other composers – sharply though his approach differed from, for example, the onomatopoeic symbolism of Messiaen's *Et exspecto resurrec-tionem mortuorum* or the confounding of time through ritual in Britten's *Curlew River*, works contemporary with *The Vision of Saint Augustine*.

By the mid-1960s Tippett, like most of his contemporaries, seems to have become used to the idea of nuclear stalemate and from then onwards the nuclear issue provoked no obvious reaction. In any case it was to be expected that after *The Vision of Saint Augustine*, his most extreme response to scientific rationalism, he would return to the more immediate and down-to-earth questions prompted by the 'feel' of the later 1960s and early 1970s. How he would respond to these questions was less predictable. It might have been supposed that he would rest content with the contemplative and detached statements befitting a composer now, after all, well into his sixties. But instead, Tippett launched into a sequence of works of astonishing vividness which address explicitly contemporary subject matter with the passion of a composer in his twenties. Nothing provides a clearer illustration of Tippett's creative temperament than his continual readiness to lay himself open to the immediacy of new experience and to contend with it as in a struggle between life and death. 'Why should not old men be mad?' It was an attitude sanctioned by Yeats, and by Eliot, Goethe and many other of Tippett's artistic godfathers. The price to be paid was an occasional awkwardness (which could verge on the embarrassingly naïve) and a certain incomprehensibility, less to do with Tippett's inevitably personal and even autobiographical choice of subject matter than with the simple fact that he could dare to proffer such comprehensive statements about the human predicament. The cast-lists of *The Knot Garden* and *The Ice Break*, for example, suggest that in these operas he had deliberately included a representative of each and every sort and condition of man; and he appears to have approached his subject matter from every possible angle – the individual in *Songs for Dov*, the group in *The Knot Garden*, representative humanity (more or less) at one with itself in Symphony No. 3, at odds with itself in *The Ice Break*. The reward was that Tippett had kept faith with his humanism. By concentrating on such large subjects he had not evaded its challenge and by admitting its contradictions he had ensured the integrity of his 'conclusions'. The word needs quotation marks, because while all his later music ends with a qualified Yes, the confident affirmations of his earlier music were never to be recaptured. It is as if he were always asking himself whether he might have chosen the wrong line of approach, or whether his beliefs did not represent some monstrous form of self-deception, or at best the vain pursuit of an ideal which was rapidly slipping out of reach. He called this ideal a dream. 'What though the dream crack!'[15] His determination to continue forging new images of reconciliation and of transcendent love remained firm, but at the same time he doubted whether such images really had any power or relevance. The irony of his position is coloured by a touch of desperation. Infinitely vital and inventive though it is, the language of these works develops an almost strident tone, and with it a remarkable candour, which could have been regarded as a typical product of the 1960s and early 1970s had it emanated from the beguiling camaraderie of the period but which in fact emanated from the anxiety and urgency with which Tippett felt he must voice his counterpoint between certainty and doubt. Tippett's candour also derives from his American experience. This is to be assessed not merely in such linguistic details as the use of the blues or of a neo-Ivesian type of harmony and gesture, nor in the Americanisms of his texts. An equation may be perceived between the directness of his mode of address and his feeling that it was in the USA that he would find the most sympathetic and productive response to his fundamental humanism. If the USA was to be the seedbed in which his beliefs were to take root it was not surprising therefore that he should have expressed himself in, to the European at least, the specifically American terms of forthrightness and candour.

Why Tippett's attitudes should have changed so markedly in the fifteen years or so separating *King Priam* from *The Ice Break* can be ascribed in part to accumulated realism, in part to difficulties in his private life, but principally to the 'feel of the time'. To many people the time in question was one of outstanding promise. To Tippett it obviously represented one of disillusion. What could the future hold if man's inability to distinguish between aspiration and fact had reached the stage when the pursuit of Utopia through 'flower power', 'personal growth', the occult and so forth existed alongside the invasion of Czechoslovakia and the killings at Kent State University? His call for some recognition of the common humanity to be experienced through music is, in these later works, more vehement and hard-fought than anywhere else in his output.

Only in his Symphony No. 4, completed in 1977 when he was seventy-two, did Tippett withdraw from so direct an involvement with his times and inaugurate what can already be interpreted as a 'late' period of consolidation and summation. It would be rash to assume that the more serene language of this recent music is simply the lineament of advancing years. It seems equally likely that Tippett has been influenced by a genuine shift in attitude on the part of his old adversary, technology. According to Jacob Bronowski, for whose writing Tippett has the greatest respect,[16] scientists now accept that their apparently factual and conclusive discoveries are no less of metaphors than are those of creative artists. A concordat of this order would certainly, in Tippett's terms, set the seal on a lifetime's endeavour.

Technical Features

In the section above an attempt has been made to discover what was responsible for Tippett's change of style in *King Priam* and for its subsequent mutations. It remains to ask what the specifically musical features of this new style actually were and how they influenced his output.

It would be wrong to suggest that the 'old' Tippett was entirely swept away by *King Priam*. Many passages in the opera, notably the lyrical ones, bear his recognizable imprint. His method of word-setting – the colouring of particular words and the derivation of musical rhythms from the spoken rhythms of English – remained essentially what it had been in his earlier music; and his habit of building melodic paragraphs by varied sequence persisted, as did his 'expressive' use of tonality. Most significantly, the underlying rhythmic vitality of his music was unaffected. His new style may not have promoted any significant additions to his rhythmic vocabulary, but he continued to capitalize on his earlier discoveries and in the process showed that the source of his creative invention had in no way been dammed up by *King Priam*. Rhythmic polyphony, for example, remained an unmistakable feature of Tippett's language, even though his new style, with its very sharp differentiation of line and its tendency towards metric regularity, lent itself less readily to the technique (see Ex. 122). The period introduced one minor addition to his rhythmic

Ex. 122   **King Priam**

vocabulary, a form of rhythmic modulation arising from Tippett's need to relate sections in different tempi. The technique (which in essential respects is the same as Carter's 'tempo modulation') is made possible by the greater incidence of regular metre and of rhythmic ostinati. This provides the basis upon which the technique can operate. Example 123(i) illustrates the junction between the two tempi of the first movement of his Concerto for Orchestra. The immediate effect is of a sudden and dramatic switch into a new tempo. Example 123(ii) shows that the complementary, almost subliminal effect of coherence is achieved through rhythmic modulation – the placing of an irregular rhythmic value over a regular one (the triplet crotchets in bar 2 of Ex. 123(i) over the regular crotchet beat), with the irregular value then becoming the controlling value of the next section.

However intriguing in its workings, this technique was, for Tippett, simply a functional device, and as such it is symptomatic of the fact that his new style instituted no fundamental changes in his rhythmic vocabulary. What did change, however, was the character of his musical invention in general and if this change was of degree rather than kind, it was extreme nonetheless, in some respects representing a major shift of attitude.

Ex. 123

Tippett's musical ideas could previously have been described in terms of becoming, unfolding, growth, development. While these qualities were never lost sight of, the accent now lies elsewhere. The meanings behind his ideas are compacted into single statements. They present; they encapsulate. They characterize in a single gesture. Because they have acquired fixed, aphoristic qualities, they oblige Tippett to construct by accumulation rather than development. This feature is underlined by a method of instrumentation in which unchanging and highly characteristic timbres (a characteristic timbre may be defined as that arising when an instrument sounds least like any other) are presented either in stark isolation or in unusual, spare and even somewhat coarse-grained combinations. This, in turn, is underlined by a pungent harmonic language. If contrapuntal textures create a sense of flow and harmonic ones a sense of arrest, it was inevitable that *King Priam* should demand of Tippett a much more overtly 'harmonic' style than before.

These four features (gestural, structural, instrumental and harmonic) are the most important of the new style. They were all shaped by *King Priam*.

The importance of gesture is a consequence of Tippett's decision to present the natures, thoughts and behaviour of the characters in his opera as a series of unequivocal facts – of statements so categorical that they would naturally arouse the critical comment and 'examination' of the opera's interludes. Characters therefore had to be sharply differentiated. What a character was, thought and did had to be conveyed instantly, with music which both left no doubt about its own meaning and could not be confused with that of another character. Tippett had to compel attention with music which hit the nail on the head first time, or which came 'right with a click like a closing box', as Yeats said of poetic creation. It was from prescriptions of this kind that Tippett developed the essentials of his new style, which then permeated his subsequent concert as well as operatic music.

By setting so high a premium on intelligibility Tippett demanded of himself that he invent a very large number of gestures, so that in his operas the density of dramatic substance could be reflected faithfully and in his concert music he could assemble enough musical material to compensate for the brevity of these gestures and build large-scale forms. The first scene of *King Priam*, for example, contains about twenty gestures, the first movement of his Concerto for Orchestra, nine. Some of them are brief and self-sufficient, others more malleable and suited to expansion. In *King Priam* they are unusually direct, even uncouth, as befits the rough, intractable nature of the subject; in later works they can be more ingratiating. In order to articulate structure and, in his operas, drama, Tippett discriminated very carefully between his gestures' relative quality and weighting. The examples from *King Priam* given below (Ex. 124) illustrate both the general character of Tippett's new style and his ability to invent gestures ranging from the arresting and memorable, to those which, because they serve the subordinate function of covering the stage action, for example (Ex. 124(v)), or of elaborating the tone of a scene (Ex. 124(vi)), are less characteristic.

Gestures of this latter type could, of course, draw dangerously close to the trite or second-hand. Though Tippett did not overstep the mark, his

Ex. 124   **King Priam**

(i) Priam

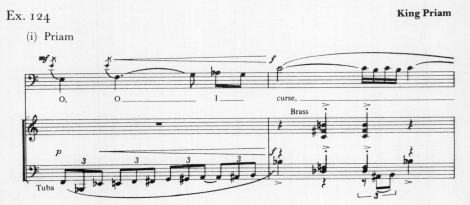

(Ex. 124 cont.)

I curse

(ii) Nurse as anima

There are things left out _____ of your sci - ence.

Harp

(iii) Fretful Paris in the cradle

Fl.

Cl.

(iv) Death

ff

(v) Ceremonial Exit of Priam and Hecuba

(vi) Menelaus as unseen presence

Brass

willingness to evoke stereotypes meant that he came close to it on occasion (Ex. 124 (iv), (v) and (vi)?) and it was this which prompted earlier criticism that *King Priam* was gauche, since it suggested a disparity between gesture and language far more acute than had typified his former re-creation of the eternal in terms of the actual. If, however, Tippett's gestures sometimes seem to lay themselves open to charges of ingenuousness, this is the consequence not of gaucherie but of how successfully he had communicated the uncomfortable truths of his expressive scenarios. However reassuring, for example, his equation between the monstrous contours of Ex. 125(i) and bloodlust, the music all the same is exciting and even exalting. Tippett trades on the ambivalence of such gestures in later works (see Ex. 125(ii)), where comparable material arouses similar reactions of repulsion and attraction – or where he makes the point that the dividing line between will-power and ruthlessness is thin indeed.

Ex. 125

The organization of Tippett's gestural language postulates juxtapositions and superpositions, as opposed to the developments and gradual transformations appropriate to material that invites rather than resists change. So although his gestural units create intricate patternings of repeats and correspondences that might seem to recall a quasi-Wagnerian leitmotif technique, the parallel is misleading, for Tippett's 'discontinuous' music is far removed from Wagner's 'art of transition'. Tippett proceeds by sudden contrasts and by the rearrangement of the components of such contrasts. His music is 'non-developmental', in the sense that it contains no transitions, or at least seems to have none. Nevertheless it still contains the stuff of dynamic movement for its components generate their own interior tensions which then find release in switches to other components. Later in his output Tippett began to allow such tensions some immediate release, in, for example, the rather expressionistic gesture of a decelerating and accelerating rhythm: see Ex. 169, brackets *c* and *d*. But at this stage his components remain tightly compressed and it is this which underlines the fact that their organization, despite its radical surface, is still conditioned by fundamental laws of emotional and even structural logic. Example 126 provides a characteristic example from *King Priam*, which shows that while the degree of contrast is high (the example contains four quite distinct gestures) the effect of the music is nevertheless not of abrupt lurches in arbitrary directions but of highly-charged emotional states following their own natural sequence. What Tippett dismisses as unnecessary are the intervening, 'explanatory' steps. Underlying the expressive logic of Ex. 126 is the purely musical logic of a thematic statement bound to the principles of sentence construction (here, the usual four phrases, with a linking phrase between the second and third).

Ex. 126   **King Priam**

Tippett's differentiation of character and emotion may be sharp and it may give a general impression of vivid units assembling into almost visual, mosaic-like patterns; but such patterns are still held in place by the influence of more traditional structural models. The first scene of *King Priam* contains about twenty gestural units. These units appear and reappear, in literal or altered form, according to the turns of the drama; the drama, however, is also conditioned by Tippett's musical structuring. The sounds representing the birth of Paris are recapitulated at the end, in order not only to emphasize the nature of the decision taken (infanticide, emphasized by a superimposed motif of killing) but also to round off the scene, set it apart and give it the closed, completed shape appropriate to its function as expository prologue. The interior of the scene is also given an appropriate dramatic shape. It is punctuated by three sections of increasing weight – an arietta and a short aria for Hecuba, and a monologue for Priam. Hecuba's aria is the dynamic climax of the scene, Priam's monologue the emotional climax. All three sections are ternary in shape, the most rich in content and unusual in character being the last, a procedure which thus sets Priam in the forefront of the drama.

Tippett's ability to organize and correlate brief, discrete units in this way harks back to his manipulation of larger units in his earlier fantasia forms. The fantasia may justly be considered the true progenitor of the 'mosaic' construction of *King Priam* and its successors. It is less easy to locate the origins of the other structural novelty of the opera – Tippett's superpositioning of material. The technique of building up climactic density by

combining themes stretches back at least as far as the sixteenth century;
but Tippett's approach differs from earlier precedents, even from Stravinsky's technique of piling up ostinati around a principal theme, because his
material steadfastly retains its identity and refuses to submit to a central,
collective unity. Its components expand the texture outwards, rather than
condense it inwards; they form a unity of pluralities. Integration may be
the principal conceptual idea behind such superpositioning but the balance
achieved is a delicate one, depending on the character of the material
involved. At the climax of Act I of *King Priam*, the first example of the
technique, the balance is tense and grating (see Ex. 127). In the women's
trio in Act III, the balance is complete, but it creates a mood of acceptance
rather than achievement.

Ex. 127   **King Priam**

In *King Priam*, the justification for this multi-layered 'collage' technique is dramatic. But in subsequent concert works Tippett developed its potential as a compositional technique on its own, using it to articulate climaxes and as a means of collecting his 'pieces' together and imposing some kind of integrative unity on them. By occasionally referring to its products as 'jam sessions', Tippett acknowledged its expressive ambivalence. It can 'sound' like a mobile, or an animated conversation piece (as in the first movement of his Concerto for Orchestra), an awe-inspiring presence (*The Vision of Saint Augustine*, see Ex. 151) or like a real jam-session, albeit one of anguish rather than exuberance (the Act I blues of *The Knot Garden*). At the mid-point of Part 1 of his Symphony No. 3 Tippett employed the technique in such a way that it caused the opposite of integration: here the textural complexity is so intense that the music breaks apart.

King Priam includes one other important structural technique, related to that of collage but used for much more precise expressive purposes. It consists of the superposition of ostinati. Tippett uses it in order to create a sense of timelessness. He had used the technique once before, in the 'vision' section of Sosostris's aria (see p.271). Now, it does not appear very often but such appearances as there are have great significance because they represent focal points in works particularly concerned with the idea of timelessness. The discontinuity of musical process in *King Priam* already challenges the concept of time as a continuous, 'goal-orientated' flow; the inconclusive ending of the opera, and of its immediate successors, does the same thing – in which respects all these works engage in some form of exploration of the meaning of time. They create the impression of a continual animation of something at rest, of a search for a state of mind that will not be subject to the pressures of striving. Few of them contain explicit attempts to pinpoint an actual 'moment' of timelessness. The most important of those that do is *The Vision of Saint Augustine*. Its 'timeless' moment is however foreshadowed in the vision experienced by Priam just before his death. In Ex. 128, the somewhat earthbound quality resulting

Ex. 128 **King Priam**

from a rhythmic pulse common to all ostinati may have persuaded Tippett to avoid a perceptible pulse in his later use of the technique. In the 'magic island' music from *The Knot Garden*, for example (see Ex. 129), he superposes ostinati of varying lengths and of much greater number, and the effect is correspondingly more ethereal. Behind both examples however lies the same technical idea of a music whose individual components repeat (theoretically) until infinity, and whose composite patterns are therefore always changing while always remaining part of the same tonality – a strikingly apt metaphor of timelessness.

Ex. 129   **The Knot Garden**

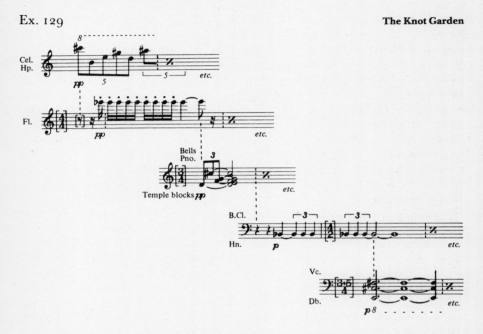

Of course, the technique does not of itself guarantee the effect, which depends equally, if not more, on instrumentation. Harnessed to a clamorous instrumentation, such as that of the 'dissolve' sections in *The Knot Garden*, the technique deadens rather than awakens receptivity, and while this may be admirably suited to the novel scene-changing role Tippett assigns it in that opera, a 'non-music' (the term he applies to these 'dissolve' sections) is clearly the reverse of what his 'timeless' music is meant to convey. Instrumentation is therefore of the greatest importance. Significantly, both Exx. 128 and 129 employ further mutations of the 'magical' apparatus of *The Midsummer Marriage*: the original flutes and celesta combination becomes, for *King Priam*, xylophone and celesta, and for *The Knot Garden*, harp, celesta, flute, piano, bells, temple blocks and more. The less alluring sound quality of the former may be ascribed in part to the fact that Tippett had not yet discovered how to mix the primary orchestral colours of his new style into the more subtle and almost Debussy-like textures of *The Knot Garden*. But it is also a characteristic product of *King Priam* itself. Nothing illustrates the opera's sound quality more clearly than the music associated with its explicitly 'magical' figure, the god Hermes. Tippett's sonority of xylophone and piano differs radically from *The Midsummer Marriage* prototype, from its immediate predecessor, the harp/piano duet of his Symphony No. 2, and even from the xylophone/celesta music of Priam's vision. It is sharp, glittering and somewhat defiant in tone, seeming to make the point that the magic can no longer steal in bewitchingly but must be set apart and protected by a curtain of fire.

This was an extreme, almost theoretical position for Tippett to take. It shows how uncompromising his change of style was and perhaps how necessary it was for him to submit totally to its implications before he could distance himself, assess what it could offer and make refinements. Nevertheless, if Ex. 130 sounds somewhat recherché, a minimum of instruments compounded for maximum effect, it left its mark on the remainder of Tippett's output, which abounds in passages for xylophone and piano and in elaborations of the same ensemble.

Ex. 130   **King Priam**

The xylophone/piano duet also epitomizes Tippett's new attitude to orchestral balance. Previously he had accepted the principles of Rimsky-Korsakov (see p.197) and had treated the orchestra as a kind of absolute, whose interior relationships could be disturbed only at the cost of unintelligibility. The dramatic demands of *King Priam* forced him to abandon the idea of orchestra as unit and replace it with that of orchestra as a set of smaller 'orchestras', whose sharp differentiation of sound matched the sharp differentiation of character, and whose autonomy permitted their casting in the role of protagonists in that continual dialectic with the voices which was integral to his conception of the opera. To reconsider the orchestra in this way was a critical step for Tippett. It meant that he had to give up the foundation of his orchestral thinking to date, the strings, for which he had written some of his best music and which in themselves were an expansion of the string quartet, the medium he had loved most in his earlier career. The strings were no longer a homogeneous body, but at least three, quite distinct sound qualities – violins, violas, cellos and basses. Tippett's almost evangelical commitment to this idea is strikingly illustrated by his distribution of these sound qualities among the three women of his opera – Hecuba, Helen and Andromache respectively (although he did not apply the method rigidly, Helen's violas, for example, always being heard in combination with other instruments).

What gave him the confidence to fragment the orchestra in this way was the example of Stravinsky, who had 'shattered the Rimsky-Korsakov balances', as Tippett expressed the matter.[17] This was a reference to *Agon* (first performed in England in May 1958 a few months before Tippett began *King Priam*), the ballet in which Stravinsky uses a large orchestra as a source from which numerous unusual instrumental combinations can be drawn. In fact, Stravinsky did not so much invalidate Rimsky-Korsakov's balances as render them obsolete. The traditional string body does not exist as such in his orchestra and the new combinations which attracted Tippett never entered into Rimsky-Korsakov's reckoning – timpani and harp; two flutes and double-basses in harmonics; solo violin with xylophone and two trombones; horns and piano. It was from such ensembles that Tippett realised that 'any instrument can equal any instrument in the *forte*, if played in the necessary way',[18] and it was perhaps from Stravinsky's use of such ensembles to differentiate between dance groupings that Tippett derived his own use of the ensemble, and even the solo instrument, to differentiate between operatic characters.

'Orchestra' means 'set of ensembles', small or large, corresponding closely or not at all with received ideas. Once Tippett had reinterpreted 'orchestra' in this way, his imagination responded as if it had unlocked an Aladdin's cave. He immediately started to make good use of his discovery. What previously had been inconceivable now became fact, and what had seemed sterile flowed with life once again. Thus the combination of

Ex. 131

(i) **King Priam**

(ii) **Symphony No. 3**

xylophone and piano, an instrument hitherto reserved just for garnishing and an instrument not really belonging to the orchestra at all (at least as far as Tippett had been concerned); thus the apparently outworn association of trumpets and drums enlivened by piano and additional percussion (see Ex. 131(i)); and thus many other new ensembles – two flutes, harp and horn, for example (see Ex. 137(i)*a*), or three horns, tuba and piano (see Ex. 122).

Tippett's ensembles have none of the elegance of Stravinsky's. If they point to any other composer, it is to Janáček, whose craggy surfaces 'feel' like running the hands over the bark of a tree. The ensembles of *King Priam* are likewise bare and somewhat rough, their components undiluted and refusing to surrender their individual indentities. In subsequent works Tippett mixed his timbres more fastidiously; but his acquisitive ear was still eager to find a new eloquence in sounds of such rawness as double-bass harmonics or trombone glissandos and to assimilate the ill-bred electric guitar, flugelhorn and electric organ. Some of his more raucous ensembles, especially those featuring his expanded percussion section, may at first suggest an inexperienced composer enthusiastically experimenting with instruments he has not yet fully understood (see Ex. 131(ii)). But such ensembles soon take their place in an idiom which, as with nearly all Tippett's music, is bracing and challenging rather than sensuously pleasurable and which, moreover, would stretch out to welcome a great variety of other dialects, rather than ruminate on the qualities of its own. His gestures, that is, are large, even when expressed with small ensembles. This, presumably, is why Tippett has not regarded his ensembles as the basis of chamber music and why he has not contributed to that twentieth-century tradition, inaugurated by Schoenberg's *Pierrot Lunaire* and Stravinsky's *The Soldier's Tale*, of music for small chamber ensemble.

Tippett's new harmonic language may be divided into various chord categories, ranging from the least to the most 'dissonant' – from chords with modal inflections, to bitonal or polytonal chords and to those very remotely related or quite unrelated to modal or triadic origins. This is not to say that his harmony developed from one to the other. The essential features of all categories are present in *King Priam*, either overtly or by implication, and subsequently they reappeared or were elaborated according to the demands of the work in question. The particular quality of Tippett's harmony was determined therefore by the nature of what he wanted to communicate and not by any desire to extend his vocabulary for its own sake. No technical 'method' can be perceived in his work. His new attitude to harmony, an expressive device in its own right, resulted from his new attitude to music in general.

His most euphonious harmonies stem directly from his earlier liking for diatonic discord and, especially, for clashes between modal and diatonic sevenths, of 'blue' notes. The difference between the chord in Ex. 132(i) and, for example, that at the beginning of Ex. 27 is not of musical substance but of contextual meaning: chords are now placed so that there is more time to hear them and thus to appreciate 'harmony' in its traditional nineteenth-century sense as expression of feeling. In this respect they are symptomatic of a very characteristic development in Tippett's harmonic language, brought about by what may be called the compensating mechanism in his creative temperament. If, as was increasingly the case, his music tended towards astringency and discontinuity of feeling, then he would not permit himself to lose sight in the process of the opposite end of the spectrum and would instinctively cultivate a sonorous neo-tonality, precisely for its qualities of warmth and fluidity. The instances of this neo-tonality in Tippett's later output are not numerous, but they are memorable enough to form an integral part of his new language and, in addition, to form the source from which the overt lyricism of his most recent music (notably the slow movement of his Triple Concerto) was to grow. Significantly, the purest example of it occurs in *The Knot Garden*, his most astringent work. The Act II duet between the characters Denise and Mel opens with an orchestral passage (predominantly on 'romantic' strings and horns) which for all its indebtedness to the tradition of chorale harmonization, with firm harmonic bass and fixed number of parts, to 'blue' notes, and, later in the duet, to the polytonal textures of Ives, retains the unmistakable imprint of Tippett (Ex. 132(ii)). It was from music of this character that he went on to write such rich harmonies as those in the coda of *Songs for Dov* (see Ex. 170) and in the slow section of his Piano Sonata No. 3 (see Ex. 184(i)).

Ex. 132

   (i) **King Priam** | (ii) **The Knot Garden**

The frequent Lydian inflections in Tippett's new style also stem from his earlier modality, when the dissonant note (the sharpened fourth) was less a chromatic appoggiatura or a pungent dissonance after the manner of, say, Bartók, Messiaen or Britten, than one member of that group of notes arising when scales on the 'tonic' and 'dominant' are conceived as aspects of a single, wider tonality. What is new about Tippett's treatment of Lydian fourths is that their earlier tendency to provide melodic resolution of semitonal dissonance is held in check, and used to create a kind of ache in the pure sound of the triad (see Ex. 133(i)). In *King Priam* he also elaborated this harmony by setting it within a richer modality. In Ex. 133(ii) the Lydian note (D in bar 2) is surrounded by both 'tonic', 'dominant' and 'subdominant' regions and then released in a form of modality which in fact is more like polytonality. Here (bars 3–4) the general flavour of tonic, dominant and subdominant is spiced by clear references to the actual triads of the three regions.

Ex. 133   **King Priam**

(Ex. 133 cont.)

Bitonality or polytonality was a conspicuous feature of Tippett's harmony before *King Priam*. Thereafter it became more pervasive and relationships between constituent tonalities more remote. Ex. 134(i) illustrates a linear bitonality, A, B flat and E flat, the middle line being a modal scale of B flat with Lydian fourth and flattened seventh. Ex. 134(ii) combines B flat minor with A or D, in a characteristic pattern of fourths. Ex. 134(iii) shows how Tippett continued to include 'fourths' harmony within an idiom that nevertheless remained essentially triadic.

Ex. 134

If the (unillustrated) contexts of the above examples resist explanation in terms of tonal progression, the chords themselves still exemplify Tippett's use of tonality as expressive colour. The first conflates A and E flat, tonalities associated with youth and warmth, or, in *King Priam*, Paris and Helen; the second evokes the dominant of the 'fateful' D minor (Priam having, with his acceptance of Paris, accepted his own death); the third generates

a spark by fusing the bright tonalities of C, G, D and A, and fills the resulting vistas with the honeyed colours of A flat. All these harmonies could therefore be described as enrichments rather than distortions or 'dissonances'.

Tippett did however use explicitly dissonant harmonies, when the
demands of particular works obliged him to cover a wider range of human
emotions than he had done before. These abrasive, expressionistic
harmonies nevertheless also stem from existing procedures. They can be
subdivided into two categories, the first of clusters. Tippett's Piano Sonata
No. 2 contains five-note clusters, their notes running up a diatonic or
Lydian scale from tonic to fifth. They can be interpreted as a characteristic
modal device, the components of a set of notes being compacted vertically
rather than strung out horizontally. They serve here to make a colouristic
punctuation rather than a genuinely expressive point and it was for this
latter purpose that Tippett used clusters most often. The same Sonata
contains a more acid cluster, deriving from his three-note 'bitonal' chord of
tonic note plus dominant third and fifth. In Ex. 135, the fifth has been
flattened (the F natural). Further examples of these clusters, which create
great expressive tension, can be found in Ex. 154.

Ex. 135   Piano Sonata No. 2

The last three notes of Ex. 135 introduce the second category of
'expressionistic' harmonies. The notes form a short, non-tonal motif, and it
was from such thematic motifs that much of *King Priam* was built. There
are two principal motifs of this kind, both associated with conflict (they
represent the birth of Paris, and the disastrous love of Paris and Helen),
which is why they lack the assurance of tonal clarity and emphasize intervallic content, particularly semitones. The first of them (see Ex. 136 (i)) is
used largely as a source of motivic or thematic material. (Ex. 135 also derives
from it.) It created the context in which Tippett found himself approaching chromatic saturation, writing, for example, a theme for Paris which contains eleven notes (Ex. 136 (ii)). Intervallic writing of this kind was extensive-

Ex. 136

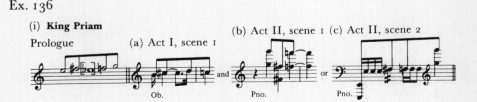

Ex. 136

(ii) **King Priam** Act I, scene 3

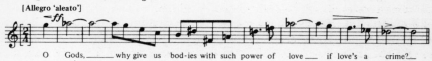

O Gods,_____ why give us bod-ies with such power of love___ if love's a crime?___

(iii) **The Vision of Saint Augustine**

Tam-quam au - di - rem___ vo - cem tu - am de ex - cel - so: Cibus
CHORUS (in octaves)

(iv) **The Knot Garden**

ly developed in *The Vision of Saint Augustine* (Ex. 136 (iii)), and was to culminate in an overtly twelve-note theme in *The Knot Garden* (Ex. 136 (iv)).

It is from the second of the *King Priam* motifs (Ex. 137(i)) however that
Tippett's expressionist harmonies, as opposed to themes, were to develop.
He turns this motif into very astringent chordal variants whose semitonal
(or major seventh) clashes severely weaken tonal reference. He draws on
the pungency of such clashes when, in later works, writing chords whose
density seems to obliterate tonal references entirely (Ex. 137(ii)) – at least,
this would seem the only obvious explanation of chords which now lose
motivic coherence and are held together purely by the force of Tippett's
imagination. Such chords as those in Ex. 137(ii) represent the extremes of
Tippett's expressionistic manner.

Ex. 137

(i) **King Priam**

(a) Helen motif

Act I, scene 3   (b) Act II, scene 1: Paris motif

(ii) **The Knot Garden**

Act I, scene 4

THEA
What_____ is it you do to Flora?

The Knot Garden
Act I, scene 5

Tippett's views on musical form could be expressed through Susanne Langer's maxim that music is 'the morphology of feeling',[19] with, however, the caveat that the forms which give comprehensible shape to the behaviour of feelings are surprisingly limited. Up to *King Priam*, this was, for him, an entirely satisfactory state of affairs. He understood these few forms as archetypes of expression, and he experimented with their treatment, both individually and in combination, in a seemingly infinite variety of ways – having, at the beginning, always decided which of the formal archetypes was most suited to the expression he wished to convey. (It may be noted here that, somewhat against the current of accepted opinion, form, for Tippett, is more a 'mould' to be 'filled in' than the consequence of an initial musical *trouvaille*: he invents notes after he has conceived the form.) Once he had written *King Priam*, however, Tippett began to feel that his existing vocabulary of formal metaphor was becoming inadequate, or, to be more precise, that his reliance on the Beethovenian sonata-allegro to articulate large-scale concert works was in conflict with the new style he wanted to develop. It might be thought that his answer was to discard the Beethovenian model entirely, relying instead on some non-narrative but still essentially dramatic scenario to control the manipulation of *King Priam*-like 'blocks' of material. But Tippett's faith in the Beethovenian model was so strong that to deny it would have amounted to a betrayal not only of his master but also of his most deeply held convictions. In an essay written in 1967[20] he showed how he found a way out of this difficulty by distinguishing between 'historical' and 'notional' archetypes. The 'historical' idea of a symphony is conditioned by middle-period Beethoven; the 'notional' idea embraces many composers (Tippett mentions only Mahler), who may have changed the four-movement 'historical' archetype but who still wrote what are symphonies in spirit and what can justifiably be called symphonies. In this apparently very simple distinction Tippett found a means of keeping faith both with the direction his creative thinking was taking and with his response to an archetype. He could discard the letter but not the spirit of the Beethovenian symphony and sonata-allegro. Nevertheless it took him a long time to put these ideas to the test. Fifteen years separate his Second and Third Symphonies, a period in which his rethinking of the sonata-allegro took the form of assigning the weight of the whole work to it (Piano Sonata No. 2), of reducing its element of conflict to almost nothing while still retaining its intellectual weight (Concerto for Orchestra), of conceiving it in purely dramatic terms (*The Vision of Saint Augustine*), until finally in his Symphony No. 3 he wrote a sonata-allegro that is Beethovenian in its dualities but *King Priam*-like in its juxtapositionings of contrasted material. The interesting thing is that in escaping from the letter of the Beethovenian model Tippett found himself returning full circle to the Sibelian model of progressive expansion he had used in his unpublished Symphony in B flat. And while the idea of a 'notional' archetype enabled him to discard the four-movement symphony in its literal form, both his Third and Fourth Symphonies still hold fast to the four-movement groundplan. Traditionalism in this wider sense is to Tippett not merely an attitude but an unavoidable fact of existence to which music must bear witness.

Tippett's operas exemplify his approach even more strikingly than his symphonies. He has not invented a single new operatic form but in his recreation of the orchestral prelude, the aria, the monologue, the song, the ensemble, the 'character' of the orchestra, and in his disposition and weighting of these and many other formal types, he has shown that tradition can supply a stock of formal metaphor both complete and inexhaustible.

The deepest evidence of his beliefs can be seen in his choice of subject matter, which is of the eternals rather than the particulars of human experience. His approach can be illustrated in a dialogue he might have had with himself. *Question*: what is opera? *Answer*: music drama. If music is the revelation of a person's inner feelings, thoughts and inclinations, then music drama is the revelation of what happens when that person comes into contact with another person or persons, or with a fresh situation or situations. The essence, therefore, lies in *what* happens to people's emotions, not in how or why it happens. Tippett's position is the same as that of the character Isa in Virginia Woolf's novel *Between the Acts*, as she muses on the village pageant:

> Did the plot matter? The plot was only there to beget emotion. There were only two emotions: love and hate. There was no need to puzzle out the plot!

When planning *The Knot Garden* Tippett was considerably influenced by Virginia Woolf's novel. But the idea that the plot was only there 'to beget emotion' had been part of his thinking for several years. *The Midsummer*

Marriage still remains the strongest evidence of it. The very familiarity of the plot of *King Priam* reduces the significance of plot and focuses attention on the emotional responses of the characters. The characters are, however, far more substantial in this opera than in *The Midsummer Marriage* and in some ways *King Priam* marks a concession to the demands of the discursive intellect. This pattern was to be repeated in Tippett's next two operas, though on a less extreme scale. Plausible reasons can be adduced for the situations and events of *The Knot Garden*; but they are not stated explicitly and emotions, the 'loves and hates', are very much in the ascendant. With *The Ice Break*, as with *King Priam*, symbolism retreats into the background: its realism is horribly familiar yet at the time so incidental to the opera's intimate dramatic thread that the listener is still forced back to the common ground of emotion. By placing so high a premium on his music's emotional logic, Tippett of course runs the risk of making his listeners so uncomfortable or of so exasperating the discursive intellect that his operas are dismissed altogether. And by situating his characters in that allegorical hinterland where they seem to tread air rather than the ground, he does the same thing. None of his characters loses a pin, gets bitten by a parrot or has his motor car break down. It could perhaps be said that Tippett is too much of a moralist to stoop down to everyday irritations of life and let them disturb the larger issues he wishes to give voice to. Yet it is precisely in his willingness to prevent his listeners from identifying with familiar human particulars, to deny knowledge of what has caused his characters' predicaments, that the relevance of his operas lies. They insist on attention to the matter in hand and do not allow sentimental sympathy to interfere with it. The matter in hand is the emotions and the characters needed to project emotions. Which emotions are to be projected is determined by Tippett's estimate of what in the universal is most relevant to the contemporary. (In this Tippett's standpoint is certainly that of a moralist.)

Changes in Tippett's musical vocabulary should not therefore obscure the fact that he has continued to declare that renewal still depends on the attempts of the present to forge links with the archetypal past. He has not been indifferent to new trends and genres, as witness the 'indeterminacy' in *The Vision of Saint Augustine* (Ex. 151) or elements of 'music theatre' in much of *The Knot Garden*. And in his increasing anxiety to be clear and direct, the technique of allusion that had been so characteristic of his earlier works can take the form of literal quotation – in which respect his methods correspond with those of many contemporary composers. He does not, however, evoke a general sense of identity with the past, nor rebel against it; quotations are used to achieve specific expressive effects. Schubert's 'Die liebe Farbe' in *The Knot Garden* evokes an artificial nostalgia, artificial because it is by Schubert and not Tippett; the quotation of the rending dissonance from the finale of Beethoven's Symphony No. 9 announces that Tippett is approaching the finale of his own Symphony No. 3 in precisely the same spirit as Beethoven, even though he will draw quite different conclusions. The most striking 'quotation' in Tippett's later music is of the blues – though this is not really quotation at all but Tippett's addition of another archetype to his stock of formal metaphor. When, in the Act 1 finale of *The Knot Garden* and the finale of his Symphony No. 3, Tippett recreates the blues, he neither quotes direct nor does he merely assimilate the vernacular into his language, as he had done with the spirituals of *A Child of Our Time*. For the articulation of certain types of expression the blues became a structural and harmonic imperative to him, strictly comparable with, for example, fugue or sonata form. It is in this sense that the traditional is most clear in Tippett's music – always interpreting tradition as Eliot had done: '... a sense of the timeless and of the temporal together is what makes a writer traditional' ('Tradition and the Individual Talent'). For Tippett, opera, symphony, etc, are the timeless, as are fugue, sonata form – and the blues. Of course, these forms and procedures are not timeless: they are the product of the last 400 years at most, which only shows how intense has been his commitment to the ideals of renaissance humanism.

'King Priam' and Its Vocal and Instrumental Successors

Compositional Background

Tippett's original idea for *King Priam* – that it should be a tragedy with a certain didactic content (see p.325 above) – took shape after he had read Lucien Goldmann's book, *Le dieu caché*. 'Goldmann, through his acute analysis of tragedy in Racine's work, determined the tragic nature of my new opera *King Priam*.'[21] Tippett did not, however, simply read Goldmann and there and then decide to compose *King Priam*. Goldmann acted more as catalyst than tutor. He helped fuse various existing strands in Tippett's thinking, most of which had developed as a result of writing *The Midsummer Marriage*.

Of these, one of the most deep-rooted was contained in the *parabasis* of that opera:

> Fate and freedom propound a paradox.
> Choose your fate but still the god
> Speaks through whatever acts ensue.

King Priam can be understood as an elaborate gloss on these words – as *The Midsummer Marriage* was itself a gloss on the line 'dare the grave passage' from *A Child of Our Time*. In *The Midsummer Marriage* the fate chosen by the lovers leads to happiness. But if Tippett really believed in the truth of his aphorism there was no reason why this should necessarily have been so: the lovers could equally well have met with catastrophe. Of course, once he had, in *King Priam*, switched the emphasis from the younger to the older generation it was to be expected that the workings of fate would be more complex: choice would no longer be a question of acting boldly and idealistically, but of choosing between conflicting imperatives in the knowledge that the consequences would affect others as well as the chooser. But it was hardly to be expected that Tippett's aphorism held such importance to him that he would be prepared to submit it to the ultimate test. In *King Priam* the characters do meet with catastrophe. While *The Midsummer Marriage* says that risks are worth taking, *King Priam* says that 'risk' has nothing to do with it: by their nature and by circumstance the characters are forced to make impossible decisions and live with the inevitably disastrous consequences. The only lasting moral value upheld in the opera is that of exercising choice responsibly. This exemplary, existentialist stance does not in truth represent a complete picture of Tippett's temperament, and this is one of the respects in which the opera can be considered didactic. But what it teaches is as much Tippett's readiness to face the full implications of his beliefs as the simple anti-Goldmannism of the thesis that tragedy has a place in the modern theatre. Goldmann may have 'determined the tragic nature' of *King Priam*, but he was not responsible for the philosophy behind it.

Likewise, Goldmann's 'acute analysis' of tragedy in Racine may have stimulated Tippett to define his own conception of tragedy more closely; but it cannot account for the essence of that conception. In 1953, some three years before reading Goldmann and while the ideas prompted by writing *The Midsummer Marriage* were still fresh in his mind, Tippett, in two BBC talks,[22] had speculated on the subject of music in the theatre, particularly that 'music' which accompanied or created moments of transcendence – as when a character on the verge of death finds himself in a realm of experience which is 'out of time and beyond death'.[23] In Euripides's *Hippolytus*, Tippett had noted, a sense of the numinous is realized through the presence of a goddess, Artemis, and through the verbal music of the dying Hippolytus's awareness of that presence: 'O divine, perfumed breath'. In the interlude preceding the final scene of *King Priam*, the god Hermes sings an aria, 'O divine music', and a split second before his death Priam lives that moment 'out of time', a vision of glassy stillness, conceived musically as a motif which could repeat endlessly (see Ex. 128). That Tippett introduced a god into his opera and that he was even at this stage attempting a musical metaphor of the 'timelessness' which was to be the concern of several of his subsequent works is less important here than that he was, in 1953, already thinking along the lines which would lead to *King Priam*.

The BBC talks also included discussion of the transcendent element in Racine, so Tippett's statement that Goldmann 'brought me to Racine'[24] is not strictly true: it provides another instance of his instinct to read books not so much for information as for illumination of something pre-existent. Thus, Goldmann's insights confirmed Tippett's own perception that a tragic figure, gripped by and accepting the consequences of some supreme passion or commitment and entirely withdrawn from the normal standards of life, would eventually enter a state of mind which was god-like, absolute.[25] Because absolute, it would be incomprehensible to the world at large. When, in Act III, scene 2 of *King Priam*, Priam sings, 'I do not want these deaths. I want my own', he begins to accept his tragic destiny. An orchestral interlude carries his soul from the depths to the heights;

he is able to break every convention of social behaviour and beg for compassion from the killer of his own son. In the final scene he awaits death, unable to communicate with anyone except Helen, whose semi-divinity provides the only contact with which he can identify. Goldmann also confirmed Tippett's perception that the condition of a tragic figure would be 'out of time', by showing that in Racine's *Phèdre*, for example, time is circular or repetitive, not progressive.[26] Phèdre's last words correspond with her first. *King Priam* ends with the same music with which it began, the death of Priam corresponding with the birth of Paris – or of Priam: 'So was I once a baby.'

This latter feature of the opera raises another important point – that the idea of a complete life-cycle was as fundamental to Tippett's conception as the idea of tragedy. Indeed, since he had committed himself to writing a modern tragedy (Homer's *Iliad* is, of course, modern: 'One does not go to a past work of art for the past, but for the present.'[27]), it was logical that he should ruthlessly follow his commitment through from beginning to end: tragedy and the life-cycle depended on one another. In his final libretto, the point is underlined (if somewhat gratuitously: 'For life is a story from birth to death').

In the summer of 1957 Tippett received the incentive to mould his conception into a clear musical shape – a commission from the Koussevitz-ky Foundation for a choral and orchestral work (subsequently changed to an opera). At first, he imagined his work as a dramatic cantata or a choral ballet, to be laid out as a sequence of 'eight, somewhat unrelated scenes'[28] from birth to death. He was persuaded by David Webster (the then General Administrator of the Royal Opera House) that this scheme was really operatic and that he should discuss his plans with the producer, Peter Brook. Brook suggested that if Tippett's new opera were, like *The Midsummer Marriage*, to be based on myth, he should choose a familiar one, otherwise his audiences would not follow him. Brook also pointed out that the use of traditional epic material was a long-standing theatrical practice. Tippett pondered this very straightforward advice and it was at this point that he re-read the *Iliad*. Then, rather surprisingly, since his sympathies had previously been with everything Greek,[29] he decided that it was the story of Priam, King of Troy, that would give life to his conception. What Tippett found in the Trojan (but not the Greek) camp was the family, or rather the opportunity to explore human relationships within the context of the family, as he had done in *The Midsummer Marriage* and was to continue to do in his other operas. The family is the 'true seed-bed for all drama'.[30] What he also found was that sequence of fateful decisions, imposed by uncontrollable forces, which could set in relief the tragic disrelation between honourable human behaviour and the consequences of that behaviour, between the arbitrariness of life and the inexorable rhythm of the life-cycle. At this stage Tippett thought that his 'eight ages of man' would give *King Priam* a symmetrical design of two acts, with four scenes in each. He gave provisional titles to these scenes: birth, boyhood, young love, warriors, women, judgement, mercy, death.[31] His expanded 'warriors' scene subsequently obliged him to recast the opera into three acts (rather as the expanded *agon* of the Ritual Dances had obliged him to recast *The Midsummer Marriage* also into three acts).

The Midsummer Marriage had been criticized for the obscurity of its libretto and its severe demands on production techniques. During the genesis of *King Priam* Tippett ignored a message that Auden wanted to write a libretto for him, because he had already decided, in conversations with Eliot and Christopher Fry, that 'during the period of gestation the composer is advised to eschew the advice of dramatists and seek the advice of stage-producers':[32] that is, he feared he might be tempted by the professional sleight-of-hand of a dramatist (or librettist) to accept ideas which had no connection with his own intentions. Constructive criticism of *The Midsummer Marriage* would therefore be focused on how an opera should be approached and planned rather than on its basic idea. It was for this reason that he discussed his intentions for *King Priam* with Peter Brook and, later, with the German producer Günther Rennert,[33] who told him that he should take from the *Iliad* only those scenes he wanted and not get distracted by anything else. It was for this reason also that he became especially interested in the stage theories and techniques of Brecht. Judging from his own precept that opera should take its cue from contemporary theatre, it was to be expected that *King Priam* would be influenced by Brecht, whose work and ideas had, in the 1950s, begun to arouse wide interest. Tippett saw the 1956 London productions of the Berliner Ensemble and, in the same year, another example of 'epic' theatre, a production of Claudel's *Christophe Colomb* (with music by Milhaud) by the company of Jean-Louis Barrault. Tippett found the productions of both companies extremely exciting, not (*pace* Goldmann) because of their 'political' content – he was as unmoved by the Marxist message of the one as by the Christian message of the other – but because of their theatricality. Evidence that the theories of 'epic' theatre worked in practice accounts in large measure for the 'Brechtian' methods of *King Priam*. But Tippett did not accept Brecht's or Barrault's ideas wholesale.

> The disadvantage of this new-fashioned theatre is precisely in its virtues. We are fascinated by the technique, but at the end of the 'examination' we are little or not at all interested in Columbus.[34]

Thus the virtuosity of the technique could easily smother what for Tippett remained the essential theatrical ingredient, emotional involvement with the characters on stage. He accepted that Brecht had upturned his neo-Wagnerian conviction that a great number of scenes in any one operatic act was unmanageable; he subjected the *Iliad* to the 'epic' technique of extracting from it only those scenes which directly related to his theme (resisting the temptation of including Cassandra, for example, or a love scene for Paris and Helen or the funeral games for Patroclus); and he interlaced his eight scenes with choral interludes employing the 'alienation' techniques of commenting on the action and of explaining what was to happen next (in *Christophe Colomb* the chorus are 'by turn, us ordinary people and the characters of the epic'). All this served to underline his central theme, by presenting the scenes as a sequence of isolated accidents whose arbitrariness could be emphasized in the choral interludes. At this point however Tippett parted company with Brecht, for his scenes ask for precisely the kind of involvement that Brecht's 'non-Aristotelian' theatre dismissed as blind stupefaction, and his interludes examine not sociological but emotional implications. In his final interlude Tippett almost flaunts his rejection of Brechtian ethics by inviting his audience to experience an Aristotelian catharsis: 'O but feel the pity and terror as Priam dies.' Typically, as with Goldmann, Tippett took from Brecht what he wanted and discarded the rest.

The Opera and Its Music

The principal Trojan characters in *King Priam* are Priam, his wife Hecuba, their two eldest sons Hector and Paris, and their sons' wives Andromache and Helen. Tippett included two Greeks, Achilles and Patroclus, not for the sake of a 'comprehensive' picture of the Trojan War but to keep to his central theme of choice: Achilles's decision to avenge Hector's killing of Patroclus by himself killing Hector is the turning point of the drama. Tippett also introduced a group of subsidiary characters – the Nurse, the Young Guard and the Old Man – and an all-purpose Chorus. In the scenes these members of his cast help form the dramatic background against which the principal characters can be set in relief. They are relatively anonymous, which is what permitted Tippett to transfer them from the scenes to the interludes and there allot them the commentating or narrative functions of 'us ordinary people'. The principal characters, on the other hand, are drawn boldly and vividly. Some of them, notably Priam himself and the women, are rather sketchy characters in the *Iliad*. Tippett exercised remarkable psychological insight in his re-creation of Priam – who, after all, had never been made the centre of a drama before. As for the women, he rounded out Homer's descriptions by using material from other early writers (Euripides's *The Women of Troy*, in particular). It was typical of Tippett that he should see the majority of his characters as representative types[35] rather than individuals. This involved some sacrifice in dramatic immediacy, but it nevertheless created an imaginative environment in which the archetypal and even the godlike could be accepted. In *King Priam* there are two semi-divine characters, Achilles (whose mother was the sea-goddess Thetis) and Helen (whose father was Zeus). The behaviour of Achilles suggests his divine parentage only in so far as his instrumental characterization is related to that of the one real god in the opera, Hermes. Helen behaves as if she is truly possessed of superhuman qualities. She says very little, and except in her one aria, makes herself felt by physical presence rather than by her exiguous utterances. Tippett's interpretation of her character owes much to an essay by Freud on the psychological meaning behind the mythological theme of a man's choice between three women.[36] Like the mysteriously silent Helen, the chosen woman is usually dumb. This, to Freud, indicated that she represented death. A man cannot of course but choose death; yet he rebels against his destiny and by a process of wish-fulfilment converts death to love, persuading himself in the process that he is exercising free choice by choosing from a group of three women. By 'choosing' Helen, Paris is not exalting love above the more practical and sociable virtues in a woman; he is choosing death. This, at least, would be Freud's interpretation. For Tippett the situation was obviously less simple. Although Paris's love of Helen does eventually cause his death, the real point is that he chooses love, passion, desire, the body, because he is compelled to respond to an absolute. Tippett dramatizes Paris's dilemma and its inevitable outcome in his most brilliantly imaginative theatrical *coup* of the whole opera – a visionary Judgement of Paris in which the three goddesses, Athene, Hera and Aphrodite, are represented as the three women in his life, Hecuba, Andromache and Helen. The familiar blandishments of the first two – success in affairs and in battle, and the cosiness of a conventional marriage – naturally evaporate when compared with the irresistible allure of Helen.

The technical instrument by which Tippett switches into his visionary scene is Hermes. Hermes is the most surprising member of his cast, for it might have been expected that in an opera so committed to human predicaments Tippett would have removed every single divinity from the Homeric pantheon. But Hermes was an integral part of his scheme of things. He serves as a dramatic expedient to engineer some scene-changes – and he acts as spokesman for Tippett himself. To cast himself as Hermes, the messenger of the gods, may seem excessively immodest and this doubtless is why Tippett offers a disclaimer, by making Hermes behave as an ironic, 'throwaway' character.[37] But when forced to declare his hand Tippett acknowledges that he does see himself as a kind of Hermes. At the still point of Act III, after announcing that 'timeless music' will convey the transcendent experience of Priam's death, Hermes delivers Tippett's credo on the therapeutic power of music to communicate the incommunicable.

> O divine music,
> O stream of sound,
> In which the states of soul
> Flow, surfacing and drowning,
> While we sit watching from the bank
> The mirrored world within, for
> 'Mirror upon mirror mirrored is all the show,'[38]
> O divine music,
> Melt our hearts,
> Renew our love.

As with *The Midsummer Marriage*, therefore, *King Priam* stands or falls by its music, and it was entirely characteristic of Tippett that he should restate this maxim at that stage in his opera when his music's capacity to fulfil its declared aim was most severely tested. In truth, the cathartic moment of

Priam's death does not quite convey the experience of infinite, lucid movement that Tippett presumably intended, and neither does it convey the message of the very greatest of tragedies that the human spirit is somehow ennobled by the sufferings and acceptances of the tragic figure. The music is too familiar – having been heard twice before, when it served as a premonition of Priam's death. It also is too short. But its pretensions emphasize what extraordinary and confident demands Tippett placed on his creativity.

What they also emphasize is the relatively low status accorded the words in Tippett's scale of values. A libretto's structure is certainly of the greatest importance to him. But, as was explained earlier (see p.212), its words matter less than their general quality of meaning. If Tippett's 'An die Musik', quoted above, reads heavy-handedly and rather naïvely, in performance it sounds tender, soothing and uplifting, a necessary foil to the harsh realism of the final scene. This attitude towards libretto-writing is of course a risky one, for if the words are ill-judged where they are particularly conspicuous the effect can be embarrassing – and *King Priam* is not without its share of celebrated Tippettisms.[39] (Many of them are literal or almost literal translations from Homer: cases in point are Hector's taunting of Paris – 'you pretty boy', 'woman-struck seducer' – and Achilles's reproaching of Patroclus – 'Why are you weeping, Patroclus, like a little girl needing her nurse?') But for the most part the opera's text is direct and succinct and if Tippett the writer should falter, he is usually redeemed by Tippett the composer. If, however, Tippett the composer should falter, the opera's structure suffers, not its text. It would be wrong to suggest that *King Priam* is badly weakened by structural miscalculation. The opera is so rich in musical event and so immediately compelling as sound that the listener is quite happy, during a performance, to allow these qualities to take precedence over the impact of the work as a whole. But, as was mentioned before, it remains a problematic as well as a compelling work, and the main reason why the listener is left with a feeling of slight discomfort is that by rejecting his original, symmetrical two-act form, while at the same time retaining its dramatic ingredients, Tippett imposed a structural imbalance on his opera which no amount of producer's special pleading can really gloss over.

Synopsis

ACT I
[BIRTH]

Scene 1	The birth of Paris. The Old Man interprets Hecuba's dream: Paris will cause his father's death. *Priam decides to have Paris killed.*
Interlude	The Nurse, Young Guard and Old Man comment on Priam's decision. Explanation of course of opera.
[BOYHOOD]	
Scene 2	Paris was not killed but given to a shepherd. Priam

encounters the boy while on a bull hunt. *Priam decides to take Paris to Troy.*

Interlude   Comment on this course of events. Wedding Guests announce Hector's marriage with Andromache and report on friction between Hector and Paris. Paris leaves for Greece.

[YOUNG LOVE]
Scene 3   Paris and Helen. After a visionary scene (The Judgement of Paris)
Paris decides to abduct Helen.

ACT II
[WARRIORS]
Scene 1   Priam unites Hector and Paris, who go off to fight the Greeks.

Interlude   The Old Man, through the agency of Hermes, is taken to the Greek camp to gloat over the inaction of Achilles.

Scene 2   Achilles sings nostalgically.
Achilles decides to allow Patroclus to fight Hector in his, Achilles's, armour.

Interlude   The Old Man asks Hermes to tell Priam of the danger.

Scene 3   Hector has killed Patroclus. Priam, Hector and Paris sing a hymn of thanksgiving, interrupted by the war cries of Achilles, who has now been roused to action.

ACT III
[WOMEN]
Scene 1   Hecuba, Andromache and Helen react to the war in various ways. They pray to their tutelary goddesses. Andromache senses the death of Hector.

Interlude   Serving Women comment ironically on the impending collapse of Troy, and on the condition of Priam, who has been shielded from news of the war.

[JUDGEMENT]
Scene 2   Paris tells Priam of Hector's death. In torment, he relives the decision of the first scene. He begins to accept his own death.

Interlude   Instrumental
[MERCY]
Scene 3   Achilles gives Priam the body of Hector. They drink to their deaths, Priam at the hands of Achilles's son Neoptolemus, Achilles at the hands of Priam's son Paris.

Interlude   Hermes announces the imminent death of Priam. He sings of the power of music to express Priam's experience of the transcendent.

[DEATH]
Scene 4   Paris tells Priam that he has killed Achilles. Priam is unmoved. He dismisses Paris and speaks only to Helen. He is killed by Neoptolemus.

As can be seen from the brief synopsis above,[40] the crucial dramatic events in the rising action are four decisions. Once these have culminated in Achilles's return to the battlefield, *King Priam* falls to its tragic end. It therefore divides naturally into two parts, the first a crescendo of increasingly desperate hope, the second a diminuendo of abandoned hope. The formal strength of design in the first act as originally planned can be perceived in the present first and second acts. Each of them ends with a splendidly theatrical ensemble. Together these climaxes belong to a carefully graded dynamic ascent in which the mysteriously exalted climax of the Judgement of Paris is capped by the blood-curdling and eminently realistic climax of the warriors' trio. Heard in isolation, however, they create an abstract structural pattern (ensemble climax at the end of each act) which, in the present third act, is left unfulfilled. This is at the root of what makes *King Priam* vaguely dissatisfying, for it conflicts with the evidence of Tippett's brilliantly faceted new style that clarity of language was to be matched by clarity of structure. Further consequences of his redistribution of acts – the short Act II postulating a ternary design which is then upset by the very long Act III, and the less pointed impact of the complementary all-male and all-female trios at the pivot of the opera – add to the difficulty. It is easy to understand why Tippett felt obliged to expand his warriors' scene, and then separate it from its predecessors for fear of making the first act too long: he needed to allow room for an adequate exposition of the important character of Achilles. He had wanted, in effect, to have two different scenes in the same scene – an impossible prescription.

The most novel structural feature of the opera is the sung interlude. As has been shown, Tippett's main reason for using it was ideological. If his scenes were to be set apart and 'examined' after the manner (though not the political standpoint) of Brecht, it was nevertheless typical of him that his interludes should contain impassioned as well as dispassionate comment and that his characters should frequently slip out of their narrative 'Chorus' roles and react as thinking and feeling individuals.[41] They become progressively more concerned, perplexed and disillusioned at the incomprehensible workings of fate as the action unfolds. Eventually, verbal comment is stifled entirely and all that remains is the eloquent anguish of an instrumental interlude – after which, commenting function is taken over by a god.

In the earlier interludes, touches of drama and of self-questioning introduce a tone not unlike that of Priam's monologues in the scenes proper, a feature which certainly intensifies the impact of the interludes but which also threatens to pre-empt that of the monologues. Tippett avoids this danger in several ways, all of them designed to throw the weight onto the scenes. While the interludes diminish in substance, the three monologues become longer and more complex; the interludes are framed by 'Chorus' sections and thus set apart from the scenes, even though the music is continuous; and the interludes are also differentiated instrumentally, by the less insistent sounds of stringed instruments and of a solo piano. (The only exceptions to this last feature are the interludes in Act II. Unlike the others, these are straightforward narrative transitions – which confirms the fact that Tippett's separation of his 'warriors' scene was a compromise.) The interludes therefore remain strictly interludial in function. They are pauses for breath, repositories of comment. While they do serve as transitions, at least of mood, Tippett makes no attempt to conceal the scene-changing which takes place at the same time. (In this respect he had imagined that cutting techniques derived from film and television might be applied.[42]) For these reasons his scene/interlude patterning does not really follow in the tradition of such operas as *Pélléas et Mélisande* or *Wozzeck*, despite the fact that Tippett's instrumental interlude obviously recalls the famous final interlude of *Wozzeck*. The closest contemporary counterpart is Britten's *The Rape of Lucretia*, though even here there is a marked difference between the predominantly expository function of the Male and Female Chorus in Britten's interludes (not to mention the Christianity of their comments) and the much more varied function of the characters in Tippett's interludes.

The other structural novelty of the opera is the monologue. Priam's monologues, following such models as Boris's monologue in Act II of *Boris Godunov* or Iago's creed in *Otello*, may at first seem a sensible but not particularly original solution to the problem of finding aria-substitutes, the disjunct and declamatory style appropriate to Priam's self-questionings replacing the more flowing cantabile style of arias proper. But as the opera progresses, it becomes apparent that the monologues are creating a very special effect – due, in particular, to the contrast with the opera's real arias (those for the women at the beginning of Act III). While the arias generate structure, the monologues arrest it. The arias articulate and reinforce the external dimension of the action, while the monologues insert parentheses and elaborate the internal. Tippett wanted to explore the inner thoughts of Priam, in which respect the monologues compensate for the fast and ruthlessly factual surface of the opera as a whole. But what these abrupt switches from outer to inner reality also do is suspend the passage of time. This remarkable feature is of course not new in Tippett's work. The 'loop in time' (an image, from Eliot's *The Family Reunion* I.i, which has long intrigued him) at the end of the opera when the music of birth is recapitulated as the music of death, is itself a reworking of the technique Tippett had applied across the whole of *The Midsummer Marriage*. The deliberation with which he applies the technique in the *King Priam* monologues is of great significance, for in *The Vision of Saint Augustine*, Tippett's most extended examination of the idea of timelessness, he raised the technique to the status of a principle.

For the rest, the special quality of *King Priam* stems from Tippett's differentiation of character by sharply defined timbres and motifs. His methods are severe, but versatile enough to distinguish between depth of character as well as between the characters themselves. Thus while some are always associated with a single instrument, others are allotted instrumental ensembles which vary or are enriched according to the individual case. Only in the cases of Hermes, Achilles and Helen does the instrumentation share common ground, because they are all divine in one way or other. Otherwise the characters keep to their own preserves and give the impression of proud, lonely figures able to yield to others or to circumstance only in proportion to the rigidity or flexibility of their associated instrumentation. Priam's music changes most radically. Of the remainder, Helen's is the most elaborate, although its expansion from and subsequent contraction to its opening sound-quality suggests richness of character rather than the capacity to adapt. Hermes's capacity to do precisely this reflects the god's inherently protean attributes. Paris's development from boyhood to manhood is reflected in the change from solo oboe to three oboes (or what sounds like three oboes: in fact the instruments are oboe, cor anglais and clarinet). The complete instrumental characterization is given below. Only the Young Guard is not associated with a particular timbre or motif.

Priam:	2 horns and piano → additional wind and brass → low strings → low wind → xylophone and celesta
Helen:	flutes, harp, muted horn (also clarinet) → violas, harp and piano
Hermes:	xylophone and piano → piccolo and E flat clarinet → wind quartet → string harmonics → flute, harp and piano
Achilles:	guitar → xylophone
Paris:	oboe → 3 oboes
Hecuba:	violins
Andromache:	cellos (and double-basses)
Hector:	trombones
Patroclus:	cor anglais
Nurse:	harp
Old man:	bass clarinet, bassoon and double bassoon

Tippett also uses timbres or motifs to represent characters not in the opera and inanimate things or concepts. War, for example, means trumpets, piano and percussion; Achilles's armour, horns, tuba and piano (see Ex. 122); the unseen presence of Zeus and Menelaus, suitably dark and forbidding sounds. Even the idea of a life-cycle has its own theme (see two bars before Fig. 70 in the score). Add to this a number of timbres and motifs conceived solely as accompaniments to stage business, and Tippett has shown how the 'standard' orchestra could be 'used up' without in any way exhausting its potential. Rather, he had just discovered what could be done with it.

If *King Priam* has a characteristic sound-quality, that is of the harsh, often brutal sounds of trumpets, piano and percussion. But the opera does not establish a real norm against which other sounds can be set in relief. It accentuates a sequence of disparate sound-qualities. These are usually made by small ensembles and some disproportion between private and public scenes results. What also results however is that effect of aural mosaic which is so individual a feature of the opera and which was to influence so much of his later output.

The ceremonial yet curiously frantic fanfares with which *King Priam* opens signal a new directness of expression in Tippett's output. Whereas the orchestral prelude of *The Midsummer Marriage* introduced a general sense of excited anticipation, the prologue of *King Priam* introduces an explicit, if stylized, representation of birth. The fanfares are overlaid with choral cries suggestive of labour pains while in low brass instruments short contractions eventually release a tiny sound, the solo oboe of the baby Paris. The dividing line between simile and metaphor can be very thin. Tippett's intense suspicion of realistic effect had previously kept him at some distance from it but in his increasing anxiety to make the meaning of his music plain he drew ever more close to it. *King Priam* marks the beginning of this process. The whistles (piccolos) as Hector calls the hounds to heel in the scene 2 bull hunt, Achilles's lyre (guitar) and spine-chilling war-cries which bring down the curtain on Act II, the beating wings (high violas) of the transfigured Zeus as Helen recalls her divine parentage in her Act III aria, the slow tear drops as the opera ends – all these are examples of how deliberately he drew from external stimuli while at the same time absorbing them into the fabric of his purely musical thinking. The prologue remains, after all, an exposition, the 'whistles' episodes in a rondo scheme, the war-cries a dramatic means of breaking up the complacent canons of the warriors' trio, the 'beating wings' a central component in the articulation of Helen's tripartite aria, the 'tears' a minute coda.

The first scene of Act II provides a more detailed example of how Tippett converted gestures of this type into an extended coherent form. Its short motifs are not so graphic as the ones referred to above, but they are all directly expressive, mostly of war. From the table on p. 366 it can be seen that the first part of the scene is a rondo and the second, in which Priam arrives to unite his quarrelling sons before they go off to fight, a contrasting middle section (Priam's music is in a calmer tempo) combined with recapitulation. The tight, closed form of the rondo symbolizes the obduracy of the quarrelling sons, while its open-ended recapitulation symbolizes both their departure to the war and their reconciliation. The whole scene is thus cast in a ternary form, with a subtle interlock between the middle section and the varied repeat of the first. Exact equations of this kind between drama and musical structure can be found throughout the opera.

This 'warriors' scene is loud and abrasive in tone, the interlude that follows it even more so (see Ex. 131(i)). What follows next vividly illustrates Tippett's new confidence in handling the age-old theatrical device of contrast. The contrast here is representative of many in the opera, but it is by far the most effective because it is the most extreme, a fearful din followed by the intimate sound of a solo guitar. Tippett's placing of Achilles's song is more than a piece of theatrical expertise however. It introduces a vitally necessary element of lyricism into an opera that had

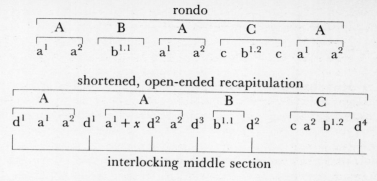

Explanation of symbols: a^1 – timpani/piano (war motif); a^2 – trombones (Hector); $b^{1.1}$ – piano/bass drum (war motif: Hector as 'living hammer', see Ex. 136(i)*b*); $b^{1.2}$ – (Paris's identification with same); c – oboes (Paris, see Ex. 137(i)*b*); d^1 – arrival of Priam; d^2 – horn/piano (new Priam motif); d^3 – low wind (Priam as father); d^4 – brass (Priam's prayer to Apollo); x – xylophone (Priam's killing motif from second monologue).

threatened to become too tough to digest, and it thus gains a significance out of all proportion to its weight. Tippett was not to squander this gain in dramatic density. He greatly developed the lyrical element in arias for Andromache and Helen at the beginning of the next act. The style of Achilles's song both looks forward to the flowing curves of Hermes's aria and back to *The Heart's Assurance*, where the piano provided an accompaniment which is a counterpoint and a harmony at the same time. Here, intricate fingerwork on the guitar also forms harmonies, though they are now based on Tippett's new 'consonance', the bitonal chords marked *y* in Ex. 138 below, and on his use of fourths chords (*x* in the example) to modulate between tonal areas.

Ex. 138   **King Priam**
(i)

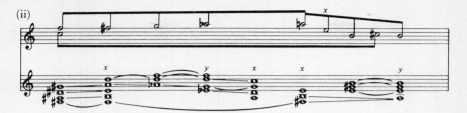

The beauty of Achilles's song is passive and withdrawn, as befits its nostalgia. Andromache and Helen suffer actively, however, and the beauty of their arias compels active involvement. Who was this Andromache who experienced such torment at the death of her husband? Who was this Helen who provoked such vituperation for her sensuality? The answers to these questions have the dramatic function of setting the opera on its downward course, for both arias are overshadowed by a sense of dread. But their beauty leads a life of its own. It is not surprising that Tippett should have returned to the heart-rending eloquence of Andromache's cellos in his Concerto for Orchestra and to the heart-warming richness of Helen's piano in his Piano Sonata No. 2. In the opera the influence of the arias, and of the succeeding women's trio, reduces the importance of Priam himself, who from this point ceases to dominate as he had done.

Andromache's aria is a single line of intense cantabile supported by a complementary line of cellos. Considering it is mere two-part polyphony, it is unusually rich harmonically. Andromache already senses that Hector has been killed, for ghostly transformations of his trombones appear in double-bass harmonics and within her line are premonitions of that extraordinarily simple but profoundly moving chromatic descent with which, at the end of the scene, she accepts that Hector is dead. Some indication of the tone of her aria is given in Ex. 133(i).

Helen's aria is her credo. She asks the metaphysical question, 'What can it be that throbs in every nerve, beats in the blood and bone, down through the feet into the earth, then echoed by the stars?', and her music, varied, impassioned, supremely fulfilled, gives an audible answer: it doesn't matter what it is, it *is*. Tippett writes in an ABB form, a form which, appropriately, has never been given a name in textbooks. The aria begins with Helen's motto harmony (see Ex. 139); its climax is illustrated in Ex. 133(ii).

At the beginning of *King Priam*, Priam himself is presented as confident and authoritative, sharing with his equally confident wife the tonality traditionally associated with royal assurance, D major. Eventually, when he is reduced to resigned despair, all he can do (until the appearance of Helen and his subsequent vision) is dismiss his wife, daughter-in-law and last remaining son to lugubrious, inward-turning phrases in A flat, the 'opposite' of D. In the meanwhile, Tippett charts Priam's gradual disintegration in three monologues of increasing length and complexity. The first of them (scene 1) introduces the only instance of lyricism in

Ex. 139

Priam's music, a haunting phrase expressing his fatal compassion (see Ex. 140). The passage begins in the relative minor of D and then returns to the royal tonic. On its second appearance, however, it veers into F minor, the 'darkest' relationship. Paris shall be killed. When it returns in the third monologue (Act III, scene 2) it is at first wrenched forcibly to the dominant of D, that is, to the 'reality' of Priam's interrogation of the dream figures in the monologue; then, as Priam accepts the full implications of his compassion, it subsides into A flat, the tonality associated with death or at least with preparedness for death. (This is an unusual association for Tippett, who usually connects A flat with a gentle pastoralism.)

Ex. 140   King Priam

These recurrences illustrate the tonal subtlety with which Tippett paints Priam's advancing despair and how the opera continues to exemplify Tippett's use of tonality as expressive colour. In general, however, he achieves his effect by more direct methods – by following the increasingly erratic twists of Priam's self-questionings with music which likewise switches abruptly from one mood or gesture to another. In the first monologue Priam was relatively untroubled: although difficult to reach, his decision was clearcut. The music was calm and was set in a simple ternary form. By the time the second monologue has been reached Priam is much older and he is acutely aware of what his acceptance of Paris will mean. Though he is mature and forceful, his decision cannot be reached so easily. Neither does Tippett attempt to capture his feelings so neatly. The monologue is open-ended, as if to indicate that Priam knows his destiny cannot now be foreseen. It is also more complicated, a bipartite form, each of whose parts contain varied and, as it were, corrective repeats. The second part is based on the passage quoted in Ex. 126. In this monologue Tippett introduces a very characteristic feature, an inner dialogue, or dream interlude, in which Priam interrogates the three figures from the crucial first scene (the Nurse, Young Guard and Old Man) who apparently condoned his original decision. These recapitulations enable Tippett to continue weaving that intricate network of relationships which stretches across the whole opera. Apart from that, they dramatize how Priam's mind is losing its inner cohesion and, in addition, they intensify the quality of mental probing that gives the monologues their special sense of timelessness. The third monologue is almost entirely taken up with inner dialogue. Its musical structure, a tripartite shape reflecting Priam's lurches into despair, fury and ultimately into futile cursing (see Ex. 124(i)), is the least balanced of the three and its material the least sustained. It gives the impression of frenzied impotence mercifully concluded by the benediction of the Nurse (an anima figure, and the most telling of the smaller roles). On the other hand it is certainly the most arresting. It shows Tippett's declamatory style at its most extreme, its furthest from that broad cantabile through which an operatic character most easily arouses sympathy. Tippett's dramatic integrity is strikingly apparent at this stage, for his main protagonist can now arouse sympathy only through his pathos. Tippett does not quite rise to this challenge, for in the next scene, the famous meeting of Priam and Achilles, Priam is upstaged by Achilles, who has some of the most fascinating and affecting music in the whole opera (notably when, to the sounds of a single trumpet and its distant echo, he asks Patroclus in the 'dead lands' to forgive him for returning the body of Hector to Priam). In the last scene Priam is almost entirely submerged in the blind momentum which cuts through him as if he had not been there and not even Hermes's plea that the audience feel pity and terror carries much weight since there is so little to project it on. Priam has ceased to be a human figure at all. What, therefore, is Tippett's purpose in these final scenes? What he does, by accident or design, is trade on the audience's impending sense of absolute and uncontrollable tragedy by quietly shifting the focus from the character, about whom nothing can be done, to the music. It becomes the means by which the tragedy can, in some sense, be uplifting. This process begins with the instrumental interlude, music of immense power and eloquence, is continued in the Priam/Achilles scene, music of extraordinary fantasy, is further continued in Hermes's aria, a moment of enchanted calm before the hectic, fragmentary survey of the principal characters in the drama is finally thrust outwards by the 'birth' music of the prologue, a richly ambiguous moment of despair and jubilation. This, it could be said, is the pity and terror to which Hermes had referred. The opera ends – apart from the tiny coda. As well as representing inward tears, Tippett's coda can also be interpreted as a kind of disclaimer, like the spoken coda that was to give *The Vision of Saint Augustine* a comparable ending.

King Priam is not a perfect work. It does not take wing often enough, its sound quality is too persistently raw and aggressive and it has faults in construction. It nevertheless contains some of Tippett's greatest music.

Minor Works

Between 1960 and 1963, during and immediately after the composition of *King Priam*, Tippett wrote a total of nine other works, all of them closely related to the style or ethos of the opera. Some include direct quotations from it. This might suggest that *King Priam* had acted as a kind of labour-saving device, providing Tippett with the breathing space in which he could fulfil minor commissions without diverting the main course of his creative development, which was now directed towards *The Vision of Saint Augustine*. Most of these works are modest in scope and they increase Tippett's stature by relatively little. Their collective tendency to plunder from *King Priam* reflects not so much the pragmatism of the composer as the potency of the opera. The situation may be compared with that surrounding *The Midsummer Marriage*, with the important difference that since *King Priam* marks the beginning rather than the culmination of a period, its progeny are fresher, more robust and more diverse. Furthermore, they include two major works, his Piano Sonata No. 2 and Concerto for Orchestra, which present Tippett at his most exploratory.

Of the small-scale works, the most intriguing is *Words for Music Perhaps*. It is based on the idea of a 'poem cycle', in which music is not the dominant element as in a song cycle, nor even a means of supporting or illustrating the spoken word, but a deliberately subordinate element, used solely to provide connecting links and a coherent atmosphere in which the poems can be heard to best advantage. For Tippett this was an experiment of great interest. It challenged him to solve some of the problems of weighting between words and music that had always concerned him and it allowed him to make amends, as it were, for the fact that his previous vocal works had 'destroyed' the poetry (see p.212). Here the poetry would remain intact. In addition, the poetry suggested for the purpose (by Anthony Thwaite, at the time a producer on the BBC Third Programme for which the 'work' was originally conceived) was by Yeats, the twentieth-century poet who, apart perhaps from Eliot, meant more to him than any other; and the title of the collection from which most of the poems were taken, 'Words for Music Perhaps', seemed to bestow Yeats's posthumous blessing on the project. *Words for Music Perhaps* has remained a unique example of its kind – which is a pity, since Tippett's (qualified) success might have encouraged other composers to develop the genre. It comprises thirteen profound and passionate love poems,[43] arranged in a sequence that does not always sustain the emotional ebb and flow obviously intended (if Tippett had chosen the poems, it might have done – but it was his fault that he didn't) but which nevertheless creates an extraordinarily powerful impression of the vibrant, oracular voice of the poet himself. It was originally performed with three speakers.[44] It can be done with two. Tippett himself prefers one, male, speaker. His music is for a small ensemble and consists of tiny gestures, vivid enough to make an instant effect but not such as to challenge the poetry. He begins with exactly the same chord that had announced the appearance of Hermes in *King Priam*, here announcing the imminent utterances of another messenger of the gods. As the work continues there are reminders of the music for the Old Man and Andromache, in particular. Tippett's gestures often incorporate transitions of mood between poems. Example 141 illustrates his finesse in this respect.

Ex. 141   **Words for Music Perhaps**

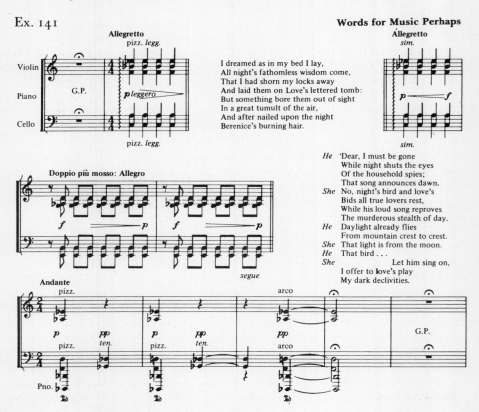

I dreamed as in my bed I lay,
All night's fathomless wisdom come,
That I had shorn my locks away
And laid them on Love's lettered tomb:
But something bore them out of sight
In a great tumult of the air,
And after nailed upon the night
Berenice's burning hair.

He 'Dear, I must be gone
While night shuts the eyes
Of the household spies;
That song announces dawn.
She No, night's bird and love's
Bids all true lovers rest,
While his loud song reproves
The murderous stealth of day.
He Daylight already flies
From mountain crest to crest.
She That light is from the moon.
He That bird . . .
She   Let him sing on,
I offer to love's play
My dark declivities.

As if to redress the balance, Tippett surrounded the 'poem cycle' with no fewer than three song cycles – or, to be exact, two short song cycles and an extended song. These works reaffirm the importance of solo song to him, not least because one of them, the single song, is a setting of the poet, Yeats, whom Tippett was soon to be at pains not to set. *Lullaby* (1959) might have been given the sub-title of 'Song for Helen', so closely does its style correspond to that of Helen's aria in *King Priam*. It does not have the passion of that aria but it echoes the tender, stabbing beauty and adds a quality of its own, derived partly from the artistry of Alfred Deller, for whom it was written, and partly from the fact that the accompaniment is not for piano but for a group of five solo voices. These contribute a comforting gloss to the poem, as if the singer's other self were filling out what he alone had been unable to articulate (see Ex. 142). This compositional idea, appearing also in the *Magnificat and Nunc Dimittis* of a year later, foreshadows the technique Tippett was to develop in *The Vision of Saint Augustine*.

Ex. 142   **Lullaby**

The two song cycles also foreshadow later works. The last of the three *Songs for Achilles* includes the first example of a palindrome in Tippett's music, a device he was to use on a far larger scale in the slow movement of his Symphony No. 3. The justification for it here is dramatic, Achilles's mother, the sea-goddess Thetis, emerging from the oceans for a last meeting with her son, and then slowly sinking back again. The palindrome is not applied with absolute strictness, Tippett's keen ear sometimes adjusting the notes in the retrograde so that the expressiveness of his music is not prejudiced by the technical idea behind it. What he expresses at this point is a desperate sense of finality, of loss and heartbreak made the more poignant because the two previous songs have shown that for all its mad mixture of nostalgia and blood-lust Achilles's life cannot have been futile. The first song is lifted bodily from *King Priam*, which accounts for Tippett's scoring for voice and guitar for the cycle as a whole; the second depicts the warrior Achilles, sustaining Patroclus on the battlefield with that barbarous war-cry which turned all hearts to water. Despite this second song the predominant impression left by the cycle remains one of intimacy. It seems that Tippett's fondness for Achilles insisted that he resolve the question mark hanging over his hero in the opera.

The little *Songs for Ariel* vividly illustrate how the discipline of writing *King Priam* drew out of Tippett the ability to capture extremely complex ideas with extremely, and unexpectedly, simple music. They are the neatest and most attractive of all his songs. They are also his most Shakespearian, not in the obvious sense of being his only Shakespeare settings but in condensing into the smallest space the most profound of truths and of giving the impression that such truths have been hanging in the trees like berries ready to be plucked. Tippett himself obviously thought they were more important than their size suggested, for he used passages from the first two of them – 'Come unto these yellow sands' and 'Full fathom five' – at the denouement of *The Knot Garden* to express ideas which could not have been expressed better with newly composed music. In this context the songs confirm their quality, not only by their persuasive appeals for, respectively, affection and rebirth but also by their ability to withstand the rather coarse orchestration they are occasionally subjected to. In their original form they were part of the incidental music Tippett wrote for a production of *The Tempest* at the Old Vic Theatre in 1962. For this he used a small ensemble of flute/piccolo, clarinet, horn, harp, harpsichord and percussion. Subsequently, the songs were published in an arrangement for piano. The remainder of the incidental music contains many short references to and extensions of Ariel's songs, two additional songs (with words by Ben Jonson), which formed part of an extended interpolation in the Act IV masque, and a number of evocative gestures analagous to those Tippett had used in *Words for Music Perhaps*. Example 143 is the music accompanying Ariel's ushering of Alonso and his followers into Prospero's magic circle. This could be interpreted as a pre-echo of the music Tippett was to write for the close of his Symphony No. 4. But, apart from the Ariel songs, the significance of the *Tempest* music lies not in the music itself but in the close contact it brought him with Shakespeare's play. *The Tempest* was to become the main stimulus behind *The Knot Garden*.

Ex. 143   **Incidental Music to The Tempest**

The other two 'occasional' works of the period are not of the calibre of the Ariel songs, but they show how Tippett's acute musical intelligence could still produce forceful and original music when his full energies were directed elsewhere. His *Magnificat and Nunc Dimittis* was written in response to a commission from St John's College, Cambridge for a liturgical work, to be performed by its Chapel Choir, in celebration of the 450th anniversary of the foundation of the college. Tippett himself chose to write a setting of the evening canticles, doubtless because the Magnificat, at any rate, provided an appropriate element of celebration, and because both texts embodied deeply poetic human situations to which he, an agnostic, could respond without equivocation. He approached the commission, that is, in much the same spirit as when writing *Plebs Angelica* for Canterbury Cathedral – with, however, the difference that in the present case he did not allow his knowledge of the English cathedral tradition to interfere with his own style, as he felt it had done with the earlier work. What particularly attracted him to St John's College was the recently installed trumpet stop in the college organ. The Magnificat begins with a trumpet flourish, a full-blooded, rather brash sound which immediately announces that Tippett will not allow his congregation to lapse into that devotional reverie sanctioned by so much nineteenth- and twentieth-century Anglican church music but that, on the contrary, he will make them sit up. If the opening sounds like a firework display, this is not inappropriate, for it celebrates an event calling for celebration whatever the faith involved – the annuncia-tion, or the universal delight of a young woman knowing that she is to give birth, knowing too that her son will change the face of the world. The choral writing cannot escape that dutiful enunciation of the verses, one by one, typical of the genre; but it contains many felicitous touches, not least in the doxology, which is conceived as a mass of apparently confused sounds sung by the general congregation. Tippett's most imaginative treatment of the text is reserved for the *Nunc Dimittis*. Here a semitonal cluster in a low organ register represents the thumping in Simeon's heart as he is about to meet his Creator. Simeon is too old to voice his own thoughts. All he can do is say 'Lord'. An angel plucks the words out of his thoughts and sings them for him (Ex. 144).

Ex. 144   **Magnificat and Nunc Dimittis**

Tippett's *Praeludium* for brass, bells and percussion includes six horns and two tubas in its instrumentation, a luxury reflecting the fact that Stravinsky's *The Rite of Spring* was performed in the BBC fortieth anniversary concert for which it was commissioned. Tippett does not employ his forces to create a spectacular opening fanfare. Instead, he creates a resonance, long reverberations on the bells leading to a muffled, remote area of the imagination where even the obligatory trumpet fanfares sound *en dehors* (an effect somewhat exaggerated at the first performance, whose conductor, Antal Dorati, took the view that English music should sound like nightingales and who accordingly reduced Tippett's *forte* markings to *piano*). It seems that Tippett wished the celebrations to be kept at a distance. The work is economically constructed (two strophes plus coda) and its material is economical too, most of it sounding like half-remembered, and haunting, fragments from *King Priam* (compare Ex. 145 with Ex. 122) – more like an epilogue, therefore, than a prologue. Why Tippett should have responded to the occasion in this way imparts a mystery to the *Praeludium*, curiously out of proportion to its exiguous substance.

Ex. 145   **Praeludium**

Piano Sonata No. 2 and Concerto for Orchestra

Of the many possibilities for development opened out by *King Priam*, the one Tippett concentrated on most assiduously during the immediate post-*Priam* period concerned problems of structural organization. In the opera the justification for 'non-developmental' procedures had been dramatic. Now, in his Piano Sonata No. 2 and Concerto for Orchestra, he explored ways in which the justification could be abstract and purely musical. The aural effect of these works is of playful bravura. Tippett gives the impression of having renounced the stern control he had exercised over his previous output and of having set his imagination free to frolic as it chose, while he stood back and took snapshots of the attractive patterns it made. In this lies part of the appeal of the Sonata and the Concerto: they dramatize Tippett's readiness to let go of something and take up a new position. They are his most experimental works. But their novelty reflects a deeper undercurrent in his thinking than the merely experimental. They reflect a mounting impatience with traditional forms, and an attempt to find alternatives which would not, however, lose touch with those essential and unavoidable qualities he still perceived in tradition. What is particularly significant about the present two works is that they are rooted in those archetypal forms Tippett had uncovered some thirty years earlier, even though they take him further away from tradition than he had ever been before or was to go afterwards: they abandon archetypal forms as whole-heartedly as he was capable of and extend the 'mosaic' technique of *King*

Priam to its limits, yet both works ultimately acknowledge that these forms are more powerful than the most persuasive of alternatives his intellect can muster. They symbolize a debate between emotion and intellect, whose result was known in advance but whose staging was essential if Tippett were to discover where his ideas led and make use of such conclusions as he reached. It could be said that his conclusions were non-conclusions. All he could do with his self-sufficient units of musical material was fit them together in a collective collage. All he could do after that was repeat the whole process. The results therefore were non-developmental, circular patterns. It was of course precisely in this phenomenon that Tippett found a metaphor of deep interest to him. Circular movement created a different sense of musical time, replacing the idea of progress towards a goal with that of activation of an ever-recurring continuum.

The Piano Sonata No. 2 is short in duration (eleven minutes), but dramatic in impact and dense in substance. It comprises about twenty gestural units, most of them keyed up to suggest that their energy has been packed into the smallest space possible. Only two are direct quotations from *King Priam*, but as 'given' material these influence the whole Sonata, notably its tone, since they are both from the 'war' act. The first impression of the work is of a bruising clash of ideas, as intransigent as they are unending, or of a pent-up aggression always ready to erupt and occasionally doing so. Subsequently this impression may be replaced by one simply of fascination – at the constant realignments and retexturings of little motifs that seem to be attracted to or repelled by each other according to principles known only to themselves. No sooner does the work come into some sort of focus than it re-forms into another. It seems to be in a continual state of transformation, and this doubtless is why Tippett originally thought of calling it 'Mosaics'. He rejected the idea, perhaps because it sounded pretentious, but mostly because he realized that the work is, in its own way, as closely related to the sonata idea as was his Piano Sonata No. 1, about whose titling he had had similar misgivings. Nevertheless, its reinterpretation of the one-movement design pioneered by Liszt is as radical as was Liszt's reinterpretation of classical four-movement design, and in this respect the Sonata is the first fruit of that distinction between 'historical' and 'notional' formal archetypes that Tippett had begun to formulate while writing *King Priam* (see p.351).

The Sonata is a 'circular' work, its ending its beginning (though its last bars are not literally the same as its first, in which respect Tippett already reveals something of the tension in his mind between musical concepts and musical instincts). In addition, the work continually, and often somewhat brutally, stops the flow of time by abrupt pauses, or by unexpected switches into different tempi and different material. It has no transitions, and therefore consists wholly of statements, a pattern of short motivic units sounding like 'first subjects'. So it might seem; and the Sonata is in fact one of the most concentrated of Tippett's attempts to discipline his lyrical impulse. Yet his organization of the units is neither left to chance, nor is it controlled by the then fashionable device of rearranging the units until all possible permutations had been exhausted. Behind it lie the same basic principles of musical behaviour that had guided all his structural thinking. These, in essence, were to shape material according to its function. The Sonata does not, therefore, consist wholly of 'first subjects'.

The table on p.379 lists the main structural divisions. Tippett's small sections are sharply characterized and instantly recognizable: they sound impervious to the influence of their neighbours. It will be observed, however, that literal repetitions of material are almost non-existent, and that Tippett continually adjusts and alters in order to make his sections serve some structural or expressive function. (The numerals in the table merely refer to the tempo indications with which Tippett distinguishes his material: if set out in sequence they do not, therefore, provide any arithmetical key to the work's construction.)

The 'first movement' is designed as a gradual accelerando from *lento* to *allegro*, or from rhetoric to lyricism, a process comparable with Tippett's earlier interpretation of a classical exposition as a transformation of the passionate into the lyrical (see p.88). It contains two transition sections, the first sounding as if the music is being wrenched into another perspective, the second a dramatic flourish, or an impatient confirmation of the new perspective and an anxiety to explore it.

The 'slow movement' is a rondo, whose processes become so automatic that they eventually subside into total inertia.

This is swept away by transition 2, which, apart from engaging in a 'development' of itself along with a development of the semiquavers of section 4, ushers in another new section. This functions both as 'scherzo' and as a means of stabilizing and giving point to 'development 1'. It is the most substantial section in the work and it rises to its own climax, which then spills over into a shimmer of glissandi and harmonics, from which emerges, in complete contrast to the 'scherzo', the lyrical melody from the 'first movement', now allowed to expand and complete itself. Another transition leads to the 'finale', a slow finale whose main pillars (the first of them sonorous chords recalling the piano part of Helen's aria in *King Priam*) frame a 'development 2'. It is here that Tippett's post-*King Priam* technique is at its most condensed. All the material not hitherto accounted for is fused into a climactic amalgam of fragmentary recollections. If the Sonata had not been for a single player, Tippett would doubtless have

Ex. 146 Piano Sonata No. 2

(Ex. 146 cont.)

superimposed rather than juxtaposed his material. The limitations of the piano however forced him to redefine his 'collage' technique by reducing the components to their smallest possible size and then sticking them together. This section is illustrated in Ex. 146. (The numerals over the bars refer to the numerals in the table.)

'first movement'	1	rhetorical opening statement
	2	transition 1 (with cadence)
	3	transition 2 (cadenza-like flourish)
	4	lyrical flow (semiquavers)
	5	interruption of 4
	4[a]	lyrical flow turning into melody
	5	second interruption of 4
	4[b]	lyrical melody expanded
'transition'	2[a]	transition 1 with addition; repeated and extended to double cadence
'slow movement'	6	rondo 'theme' (period construction: antecedent of four motifs, 6abcd)
		episode 1 (two motifs, melodic and harmonic, 6ef)
		rondo, with superimposed 6f
		episode 2 (two motifs, harmonic and melodic, 6gh)
		rondo, with superimposed 6f and 6h

'transition' to	3[a]	transition 2 altered and extended
'development 1'	4	lyrical flow shortened
cum 'scherzo'	3[a]	transition 2 transposed
	4	lyrical flow extended
	5[a]	interruption with new extension
	7	new 'scherzo' theme (two motifs, 7ab, plus continuation to climax)
	4[b]	development and completion of lyrical melody
'transition'	2[b]	transition 1, repeated by inversion
	3[b]	transition 2, simplified and shortened
'slow finale'	8	new chordal theme
with inserted		2[b] transition 1, inversion with repeat leading to double cadence
'development 2'		3, transition 1, leading to fragments: 4b 6cf 7b 7a 6bf 7b 6b 4a 7a 6cf 7b 6d 6a 3b 8 7b becoming 3
	1	shortened recapitulation, with 6h and its liquidation

The motifs from *King Priam* upon which the Sonata is based are 2 and 7a above, those associated with the warrior instincts of Hector and Achilles. These motifs are variants of each other (see Ex. 136(i)*b* and *c*). The three-note cell from which they derive is the intervallic source of the whole Sonata, either in its original semitonal form or expanded diatonically. Motivic coherence of this kind naturally acts as a powerful unifying element, as does tonality; but the principal reason why this apparently sectional and fragmentary work is so intensely of a piece remains firmly anchored in the structural and expressive considerations described above.

In his Concerto for Orchestra Tippett carried the experimentation of the Sonata several stages further. This was not simply a question of applying its creative concepts to a large-scale orchestral work. He approached the subject from a different standpoint, using generous expanses of melodic material, as opposed to the concise motifs of the Sonata, and placing particular emphasis on circular forms. The result was the most sophisticated of his 'collage' treatments and the culmination of his interest in 'non-endings', each of the Concerto's three movements abruptly halting in mid-flight. This latter feature sets the seal on the most endearing characteristic of the work, its mixture of exuberance and 'English' understatement.

By way of compensating for the novelty of these features, Tippett makes no attempt to alter the traditional three-movement concerto design he had already used in his Double Concerto and Piano Concerto; and although his treatment of the orchestra develops the principles of *King Priam* (Tippett has written that the Concerto could be called a 'concerto for various instrumental ensembles') it nevertheless harks back to earlier precedents: to the eighteenth-century concerto grosso (no *ripieno*, but a large number of *concertini*) and to the Concertos for Orchestra of, for example, Hindemith and Bartók. And by dividing his orchestra into two main units (all instruments except strings, and strings alone) and then combining them in the finale, he acknowledges a debt to such a work as Bartók's Piano Concerto No. 2. It was typical that his adventurousness should be rooted in tradition – typical also that he should set his first and decisive break with the Beethovenian dramatic sonata-allegro in so disarming a context as the virtuoso concerto.

That the Concerto's first movement should represent a calculated alternative to the sonata-allegro does not occur to the listener at all. What he hears are sound patterns endlessly wheeling in and around themselves, as if they had been set in motion by some unseen hand and were content to continue doing so until they came to rest. He hears expert performers generously treating their audience to nine recitals in a row and then playing them all together. He is quite happy to sit back and listen to this extravaganza as a child might watch the circus. This indeed is Tippett's purpose – to write a movement in which dramatic conflict is replaced by its opposite, a kind of relaxed enchantment where events seem to mark time and yet where everything is still rich and weighty enough to warrant single-minded attention, or to warrant the cardinal status traditionally accorded the first movement of a concerto. Tippett achieves this remarkable effect through the nature of his material, its treatment and through the overall form of the movement.

His material consists of nine fully worked-out themes, complete and self-sufficient, for nine instrumental ensembles. Seven of the themes are complete only by implication, since their last phrases lead into or overlap with the first phrases of their neighbours. Of the remainder, one (for timpani and piano) functions primarily as timbral modulation and is therefore the least noticeable of the nine. The other, however, the first to be heard, sets the tone for the whole movement. It is a beautifully poised melody for flute and harp (reminiscent of Hermes's aria in *King Priam*, which also featured flute and harp) which runs its leisurely course until it reaches a perfect cadence in D major (the tonic chord being Tippett's favourite 'consonance' of D plus seventh and ninth, C sharp and E). This is the only true cadence in the movement and it isolates the melody, as if to impress on the other ensembles that *this* is the subject of what follows. So it works out. As well as establishing the predominant mood, the three principal phrases of the melody control the overall design.

Tippett's ensembles are also grouped in threes, according to their expressive function. The first (flute and harp, tuba and piano, three horns) creates lyricism; the second (timpani and piano, four reed instruments – oboe, cor anglais, bassoon and double bassoon – two trombones) rhetoric; the third (xylophone and piano, clarinet and bass clarinet, two trumpets) speed. The serene and lyrical becomes pungent, rhythmic and harmonic, a point of tension which is then released in a spate of brilliant semiquavers. Thus the 'exposition' of the movement describes an emotional curve quite different from that of Tippett's other sonata-allegros. It reverses the accepted order of the 'passionate and the lyrical'. But more than that, it reaches a complete and satisfying statement of its own, whose continuation is a development of timbres and textures, rather than the concentrated argument demanded by the open-ended propositions of sonata form.

Tippett's 'exposition' is particularly influenced by dynamics. Each of the three instrumental groups rises to a miniature climax featuring its brass instruments. The first two climaxes relax into brief 'collage' sections, which integrate the material and in the process give notice of the principal feature of the 'development' section, before, with another crescendo on the brass, leading to the next group. The climax of the third group is the climax of the whole 'exposition', the final phrase of the trumpet duet combining lyricism, rhetoric and speed in one gesture. The succeeding collage this time is a diminuendo, leading back to the dynamic level of the opening and completing a dynamic arch which reproduces on a larger scale that of the flute/harp duet. Having returned to the beginning, Tippett now proceeds to an elaborate restatement of his 'exposition' – with a broad section which combines the traditional features of repeated exposition and of development and recapitulation but which cannot strictly be compared with any of these since its principal function is simply to rehearse the premises of the 'exposition'. It is as if Tippett were opening out his box of tricks and exhibiting the contents for all to see. The contents are presented in an apparently arbitrary arrangement. But in fact they are very carefully organized around the three phrases of the flute/harp duet. There are three sub-sections, which take the phrases one by one and surround and extend them with collages of material from the remaining ensembles. All nine are never heard at once: the result would be too confusing. The maximum is four, and three is the norm because each group of ensembles is divided into three textural areas, high, middle and low, a procedure which enables Tippett to people the areas with material from any group he wishes while still retaining clarity. In general, textural density corresponds with expressive behaviour. As in the 'exposition', each sub-section rises to a climax. The first two climaxes fall to short 'resting points', single notes on the tuba, while the third, the climax of the whole movement, returns the music to the beginning once more. These climaxes are marked by the two trombones, whose theme is accordingly divided up, after the manner of the flute/harp duet, into three units, the first two appearing at the climactic points, the third beginning earlier and rising to the most sustained piece of loud music in the movement – trombones overlaid with the major part of the theme for two trumpets, to which is added, with a stroke on the tam-tam, the culminating phrase of the theme for three horns. Thus all three climaxes from the 'exposition' are laid out successively in a controlled dynamic arch. As before, the horns lead back to the first collage of the 'exposition', or to what is, structurally, the first of a series of codas. Part of this climax and of the ensuing coda is illustrated in Ex. 147. The function of the four codas, deriving from Tippett's use of a repeated codetta phrase in the flute/harp melody, is to restore the lyrical influence of that melody. This is accomplished after the xylophone and piano have been invited to release their exuberance in a short cadenza. The opening phrase (bracket *x* in Ex. 147) returns for a third time; the trumpets also are stilled, and all that remains now is for the phrase to give the merest hint of its presence (just one bar) for everything to be in balance – or for the whole movement to start its cycle again.

Ex. 147

Concerto for Orchestra

(Ex. 147 cont.)

This movement has been described in some detail in order to show how deliberate is its construction, to show, that is, how consummate is the art lying behind its apparently wayward exterior and behind its 'non-ending'. The endings of the other two movements do not sound so inevitable, because they end not with the beginning but with the transition and middle section respectively. Their designs are less rigorous and only in retrospect does the first movement acquire its classic status as the most weighty of the three.

The slow movement is one long, continuous melodic line, richly harmonized and treated to some of the most elaborate and beautiful embellishments in the whole of Tippett's output. It is very human music, particularly so after the first movement, whose material responds to circumstances only in so far as it occurs in different contexts. Here, the cellos respond passionately to the aching lament of the soloist among them; the violas offer comfort when the cellos have been driven to the depths; they also carry the music upwards where violins can take charge and sing in rapt delight after the manner of *The Midsummer Marriage*. It is a Tippettian scenario of the 'dark' and the 'light' moving from one to the other – and then back, for when the violins have reached the peak of their delight, the lament of the solo cello returns and the process begins again, while the violins slowly climb down to meet the violas offering comfort once more. This is the point at which the movement stops, for it is now clear that the melodic line can continue describing the same curves indefinitely.

Of special interest are the numbers and proportions of Tippett's string body. Violins and violas are a third of the number of those in a normal symphony orchestra, cellos and basses a half. This reduced size and unusual emphasis on low instruments enables Tippett to focus on the rich tone of the low instruments and the bright one of the violins, and thus to differentiate timbres after the manner of the first movement. More pertinently, it encourages the individual virtuosity that was essential if the work were to sustain its concertante quality and not be weighed down by the sound of strings *en masse*.

Several features in its first two movements have revealed its connections with *King Priam* – the flute/harp duet, the trombones' theme (which is an elaboration of a motif for the Young Guard in Priam's third monologue), the xylophone/piano duet, Andromache's cellos (and double-bass harmonics). Direct quotation from the opera in the Concerto's finale might seem logical therefore. But Tippett has confessed that he quoted from *King Priam* only because he was short of time. If he had equipped his finale with newly composed music it is possible that the result would have been better. But it is difficult to believe that the effect would have been substantially different. Tippett made a virtue out of necessity, and by its looser, more sectional construction, its lighter weight (if more raucous sound) and its flavour of quick-witted extemporization, this finale admirably fulfils what was obviously Tippett's original intention of concluding his Concerto with a traditionally invigorating rondo. Asymmetries within a broadly symmetrical design confirm the impression of a composer thinking on his feet and getting away with it. These asymmetries are caused by the episodes. The first shares some material with the third, the second with the fourth *and* fifth. Tippett committed himself to this additional episode once he had conceived his middle section, a lyrical contrast, which could hardly have been followed by the brash rondo theme for trumpet and violins. The design of the movement could be simplified as follows: A B^1 A B^2 C B^3 A B^4 A B^5 C . . .

Tippett's episodes comprise extended passages (with voice parts suitably orchestrated) from the 'war' scenes of *King Priam*,[45] selected for their

energy and arranged so that both 'pairs' culminate in the same blaze of
trumpets. The middle section is a long theme in canon for flutes and
bassoons, accompanied by distant harmonies and other canonic figures in
the rest of the woodwind which eventually spill out in filigree patterns and
lead into the third episode. The canon is in fact a round, constructed so
that the last of its seven five-bar phrases merges into the second – with
which, on the second appearance of the section, the work ends. It has again
reached the point at which no more can be said.

The Vision of Saint Augustine

Long before he had completed *The Vision of Saint Augustine* (April 1965),
Tippett had given evidence of his preoccupation with musical 'magic', the
idea that music can create an awareness of the transcendent. The
commentator can refer confidently to the visionary quality of such a work
as *The Midsummer Marriage* without feeling it necessary to justify the remark
other than by reference to the sounds of the music. The question remains
however: what is this transcendent, visionary quality, what is this supreme
experience of which we talk so freely? The most remarkable thing about *The
Vision of Saint Augustine* is that it does contain what its title suggests. At the
core of it is a real vision – that vision of eternity, of God, which Augustine
described in his *Confessions*:

> And while we were thus talking of eternal life and panting for it, we
> touched it for a moment with a supreme effort of our heart: and we
> sighed and left the first fruits of our spirit bound to it, and returned to the
> sounds of our mouth, where words begin and end.

Tippett follows Augustine's narrative to the colon in the quotation above
and then fills the pause with sound, giving to that stupendous 'it' a reality
that Augustine, tied to words, could not give.

It is not surprising that Tippett should have wanted to formulate new
answers to the question of what visionary meant, nor that he should have
isolated the question, cleared it of distractions and addressed himself to it
alone; nor that he, an agnostic, should have accepted Augustine's Christian
symbolism. But that he should have embarked on a project of such
immensity – one which Schoenberg, in *Die Jakobsleiter*, had been unable to
finish and which Hindemith, in his opera *Die Harmonie der Welt*, felt could
be realised only in the silence following his last chord – and that he should
then have ventured to identify with one of the most celebrated accounts of
mystical experience in Western literature, all this suggests a degree of
hubris exceeding the limit even Beethoven might have set himself. To
apprehend

> The point of intersection of the timeless
> With time, is an occupation of the saint –
>
> (Eliot, *The Dry Salvages*, V)

Tippett was obviously aware of his presumption in writing *The Vision of Saint Augustine*, as his text's final line, which is spoken not sung, makes clear: 'I count not myself to have apprehended.' Yet this apparently artless ending is not only the composer's confession that he does not fully understand what he has done: it is also his identification with Augustine, who frequently refers to the biblical passage from which it is taken (Philippians 3:12–14). The pretensions lying behind the work cannot, therefore, be glossed over. All that can be said is that their justification lies in the essence of the creative artist, and, of course, in the work itself. *The Vision of Saint Augustine* stands apart in Tippett's output. While it would be invidious to judge it his greatest or even his most characteristic, it is certainly his most extraordinary.

This is not simply because he dares to 'poeticize' the story of Augustine's vision. It is also because he uses the story to explore the meaning of time – to show that through a concentrated mental effort to reach a state in which past, present and future are one, to reach, that is, an experience of timelessness, of ecstasy, the transcendent might be experienced in the temporal world. To the average sensual man, the transcendent is experienced only in love, when it seems that the sun and stars are bound to dance in delight at such sublimity. In *The Vision of Saint Augustine* Tippett is saying that the transcendent might also be experienced through music.

Tippett had read Augustine's *Confessions* in his schooldays and had long been attracted to them, in particular the account in Book IX, chapter 10, of the vision of eternity. He knew the original Latin almost by heart. The vision of eternity is one of two visions described in the *Confessions*. In Book VIII, chapter 12, Augustine relates the circumstances leading up to his first vision, when, after intense emotional turmoil as he struggled to renounce his sensuality and submit to God, he heard, in his imagination, a child singing repeatedly: 'Take it and read it.' The first biblical passage his eyes fell on resolved his conflict and led to his conversion to Christianity. The vision of eternity followed about a year later. In describing this, Augustine explains how he and his mother Monica, resting at a house in the Italian port of Ostia before returning to their native North Africa, found themselves standing at a window overlooking an inner garden. They began discussing what the eternal life of the saints might be like. After a period of deep concentration they suddenly experience eternity. Later they ponder that *if* their souls could have remained silent and the vision have been prolonged for ever, would they not then have experienced what was meant by the words of the parable of the talents: 'Enter into the joy of the Lord?'

Why Tippett should have wanted to convert Augustine's vision into a piece of music in the special circumstances of the early 1960s is discussed above (see p.330). Furthermore, it had instant and intrinsic qualities as a story (whose attractions would, to Tippett, have been heightened by the symbolic significance of the window and the inner garden, the garden doubtless contributing to the *mise-en-scène* of his next major work, *The Knot Garden*). In particular, it was the basis from which were developed, in Book

XI of the *Confessions*, Augustine's ideas on the meaning of time and eternity, ideas which were of deep interest to Tippett. He had for many years been fascinated by writings on the metaphysics of time – from Judaeo-Christian beliefs in time as linear, irreversible and evolutionary, to ancient and oriental beliefs in time as cyclic, the myth of the eternal return; from Bergson's distinction between quantitative 'clock time' and *la durée réelle*, which is a product of memory and the emotional flux, to Stravinsky's transference (in *The Poetics of Music*) of *la durée réelle* to music and the idea of 'psychological' versus 'ontological' time. He had been profoundly impressed by Eliot's struggle in the *Four Quartets* to relate the actual and the transcendent, the temporal and the timeless. As far as can be judged from his writings (see, for example, the quotation on p.330), Tippett's reactions to such ideas were ambiguous. While he naturally sympathized with the idea of time as cyclic, music as 'ontological' – perhaps since this offered more direct access to the transcendent or at any rate to the universal – he was nevertheless unable to reject the alternative viewpoint, even though it was associated with a Christian theology he could not accept and with a Darwinian theory of mindless evolution he found distasteful. What Augustine's writings did, it seems, was offer a solution that was not only rational and credible: it was also entirely in accord with Tippett's inclination to reject neither view and accept both. Augustine showed that time and eternity, the linear and the cyclic, the actual and the transcendent, could be reconciled.

Augustine's reconciliation of time and eternity is founded not on logic but on knowledge, his experience of God in the vision of eternity. This starting point would have been entirely plausible to Tippett. He possessed some understanding of Christian mysticism already, through the writings of Evelyn Underhill; more to the point, he himself had direct knowledge of the 'gods', the archetypes, and, if the switch from a Christian to a Jungian metaphor is extended further, an at least intuitive knowledge of the Self, the godhead. Augustine upheld the Christian conception of time as finite, the unfolding of a divine plan of salvation from its beginning in the Garden of Eden to its end at the Last Judgement, by equating time with creation. The Creation did not occur at a certain point in time: the two are one and the same thing. Thus the provocative question, which Augustine was at pains to demolish since it implied a cyclic conception of time – what was God doing before he created the world? – is meaningless. God is in eternity, not time. Tippett's reaction to this argument was openminded, in that, as an agnostic, he could accept it as a metaphor. What particularly interested him was Augustine's postulation of a dramatic dialogue between God and the world – when, for example, eternity irrupted into time at the birth of Christ and at Augustine's own vision – and the next step in the argument, Augustine's thesis that perception of time is mental. Time is in the mind, the soul (Augustine's Latin, *anima*, would of course have had powerful Jungian resonances for Tippett). Time is perceived by Augustine as memories of the past, experiences of the present and expectations of the future. Our minds are continually distended by the pressures of all three forces. Time is a distension of the soul, a dispersal of energy, and before even that understanding can be grasped it is already lost, for it is only when something is finished that it can be defined and apprehended. How therefore can the soul find itself? Not within itself, but only if it strives to reach outwards ('not by dispersal but by concentration of energy') to that region beyond, that eternal *ante* before time was created, where past, present and future are obliterated by an eternal present (where 'all is always now', as Tippett's motto to his score, a quotation from Eliot's *Burnt Norton*, reads). Augustine's vision told him that this prescription for unity of soul was possible, because true. The distinction between time and eternity is an inner relation between man and God.

The correspondence between these ideas and Tippett's own creative and psychological instincts is close. His music to date had clearly shown his belief that nothing worthwhile can be gained unless it is earned by intense struggle and effort. With hindsight, this effort can be seen as an attempt to resolve the mental clamour of memories, desires and expectations in order to reach some form of inner silence, out of which the soul (the archetypes) can speak direct. What is new about *The Vision of Saint Augustine* is Tippett's deliberate compacting of the contents of the mind into a single force, which is then pushed upwards and outwards into a direct experience of the transcendent – his particular 'Augustinian' technique of combining the present (the baritone solo which follows Augustine's narrative of the vision) and the past and future (the chorus, which recalls or forecasts thoughts prompted by the narrative), out of which density of texture the transcendent moments irrupt or explode. The work becomes therefore the most exemplary and concentrated of Tippett's attempts to show that the transcendent is latent in the human mind and that it is within the power of music to reveal it. Whether his, and Augustine's, prescription for so doing guarantees success is of course another matter. After his music has fallen silent, Tippett acknowledges, like Augustine, that any success he has achieved is not due reward for effort, but a gift: 'I count not myself to have apprehended.' Nevertheless, the unique position which *The Vision of Saint Augustine* has retained in Tippett's output indicates that he made a final, comprehensive and, one might almost say, absolute statement in the work.

Tippett took unusual care over the work's composition, as can be seen in his essay 'Music of the Angels'.[46] This is a preparatory study for the sort of music he would write for his re-creation of Augustine's two visions and for much of the rest of the work as well. It sets out the evidence in Judaeo-Christian writing[47] for what the music of angels actually sounded like, taking as its point of departure the traditional belief that angels are messengers between heaven and earth and that what they sing or play would uncover some of the secrets of the 'music' of transcendence. In many ways the most significant feature of Tippett's essay is an omission – significant because by ignoring what he obviously regarded as irrelevant to his conception of transcendence, Tippett confirmed what was. He makes no reference to the long-standing tradition of the Music of the Spheres, a subject which through its association with magic might be supposed to have had at least some relevance to a composer particularly interested in 'musical magic'. The belief that the cosmos is divided into the three realms of the elements, the planets and the angels (with God at the head) goes back to Plato; from this followed the belief that through correspondences of proportion between the acoustical properties of sound and the supposed proportional hierarchies of the extraterrestrial realms, it is possible to imitate and summon up the 'sounds' or presences of such realms. A 'magician' is one who knows the secrets of the proportional correspondences. Even Augustine was unable entirely to escape the influence of these ideas, for his vision describes a passage through the analogous realms of body, soul and spirit. Tippett certainly followed Augustine's Neoplatonic hierarchy in this respect. But by disregarding considerations of proportion and number in his essay, he made the point that transcendence is not a 'trick' to be manipulated by the proportional quantities of cabalistic magic (not least because quantity, patterns, organized rhythm, are products of time, not eternity) but a mystery in the mind, apprehended by intuitive acts of understanding having nothing to do with the discursive intellect. Augustine's Christian tradition upheld much the same belief. What Tippett sought in angelic tradition, therefore, were stimuli to which his imagination could respond.

Of the ideas his reading uncovered, the one that stimulated him most was that angels use glossolalia. Glossolalia is a Greek term, referring to sounds accompanying ecstasy, the experience of the transcendent – the wordless 'vocalizations, shouts, orgiastic repetitions of vowels'[48] which break out when human vocabulary is no longer able to match up to the expressive demands placed upon it. The central vocal technique of *The Vision of Saint Augustine* is that of glossolalia. Naturally, it is found in the vision of eternity – where two of the three vocal strands extend the 'ia' syllable of 'alleluia' to extreme lengths (after the manner of the jubilus in plainsong *alleluias*) and where the third consists entirely of vowel sounds (taken from a prayer of the risen Christ to God in the Gnostic apocryphal gospel known as the *Pistis Sophia*). The 'shouts' and 'orgiastic repetitions' are also present in good measure. But glossolalia pervades much of the rest of the work as well, which abounds in melismas so long that the word they carry is soon forgotten and turned into pure vocalization.

The music of *The Vision of Saint Augustine* does not, of course, derive solely from the idea of vocalization. In his essay Tippett lists various additional features of angelic singing, which enabled him to define glossolalia more precisely: the use of short note-values in large quantities, antiphony, unbroken continuity, vast numbers singing in unison. Of these, the last appears to have had the most powerful influence on his creative imagination. The image of vast numbers singing in unison can be related to a particularly striking aspect of Tippett's use of the chorus – not as the conventional body of sopranos, altos, tenors and basses whose deployment stems from a basic four-part texture, but as a single sound with a range spreading from the lowest of men's voices to the highest of women's and thus forming enormous arcs, like heavenly vaulting. Add to this the more

familiar though equally extraordinary Monteverdian *trillo* and what results
is that exalted form of coloratura, unique to *The Vision of Saint Augustine*,
which requires no less of its chorus than of its baritone soloist a virtuosity
bordering on the limits of the humanly possible (see Ex. 148).

The idea of glossolalia gave Tippett an *entrée*, as it were, into the music of
transcendence. But how and when he applied the idea depended on his
assessment of the quality and degree of emotional intensity in Augustine's
narrative, or on the way he used his composer's licence to 'poeticize', as he
put it in his preface to the score. A three-part hierarchy of 'transcendent'
music can be distinguished in *The Vision of Saint Augustine*. It ranges from

Ex. 148   **The Vision of Saint Augustine**

* The instrumental doublings of Baritone solo and Chorus are not shown in this example.

(Ex. 148 cont.)

that in which the soul is still tied to the body (as in Ex. 148 above, which despite its rapture is a trope to the 'earthly' music of the Ambrosian hymn in the men's voices), to that in which the body is left behind and the soul is in touch with a higher spiritual realm (as in Tippett's evocation of Augustine's first vision), and finally to that which represents true transcendence (the vision of eternity). The first vision is depicted at the climax of Part 1 of the work, as Augustine's mental torment is finally released in a remarkable passage of high, antiphonal glossolalia culminating in a purely instrumental section which suddenly floods the texture with a stream of light. Tippett has described this section as an 'Angel Symphony'. One of the most intriguing things about it is that it is instrumental. Although 'Music of the Angels' had concentrated on what angels might have sung, when for the first and only time in the work Tippett writes avowedly angelic music, his angels play. Certainly, they use the proper 'technique', as is shown by their appropriation of the dancing choral glossolalia and by the antiphonal yodelling of their trumpets. But nevertheless they play. This is doubly surprising, since the vision they evoke is of a *singing* child – as Tippett seems to acknowledge by echoing the poetic metre of *tolle lege* ('take it and read it') in the musical rhythm of the beginning of his 'Angel Symphony', as well as by the unaffected simplicity of his musical gesture as a whole. The answer to this little enigma illustrates the nice equation Tippett struck between faithfulness to his poetic concept and the expressive demands of his music. Angels are not the godhead; by using instruments at this point he is able to draw a crucial distinction in kind between Augustine's first vision and the vision of eternity, for which Tippett uses his full resources. In addition, his 'Symphony' provides the novelty and brilliance of sound necessary to create a sense of climactic release after the straining complexity of the music that precedes it (see Ex. 149).

Ex. 149   **The Vision of Saint Augustine**

(Ex. 149 cont.)

The distinction between the two visions is further emphasized by differences of structure. The 'Symphony' is in a clear strophic form, its two equal strophes also divided into two parts. The vision of eternity has a form only in as far as it sounds and then ceases to sound. The rhythmic organization of the 'Symphony' includes, as does most of Tippett's 'timeless' music, a set of superimposed ostinati, which at the end of each strophe are adjusted so that each line finishes at the same time and thus the structure is satisfyingly completed. The rhythmic patterns involved are illustrated in Ex. 150, the second part of each strophe.

The vision of eternity is conceived according to quite different premises. Its ostinati are not only more numerous and complex but they are arranged in such a way that there could never be a completion of an implied pattern, with each line finishing at the same time, but that the sound could,

Ex. 150   **The Vision of Saint Augustine**

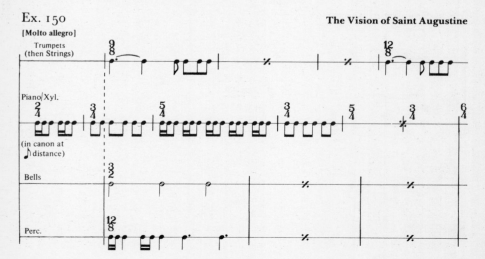

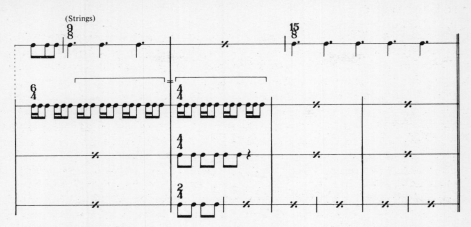

theoretically, go on into infinity. It will be seen from Ex. 151 that the music is held together by an ostinato five semibreves in duration, or twenty crotchets, and that to find a common finishing point for the other, superimposed ostinati (of 16, 21, 26, 32, 34 and 34⅔ crotchets) would defeat the most accomplished of mathematicians.

Ex. 151   **The Vision of Saint Augustine**

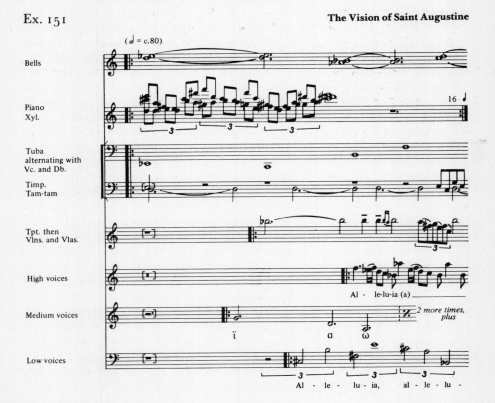

(Ex. 151 cont.)

After its first statement, Tippett's fundamental ostinato becomes alternately softer and louder; the other ostinati follow the same dynamic sequence. This does not serve to impose any 'meaning' on the music: it creates an impression – of the slow breathing of the sea, of vast waves of sound, myriads of songs advancing, receding and engulfing the listener within a swirling mass of sensations so rich and complex that understanding is silenced and the only response acceptance. Tippett has said that he conceived this music as the door of heaven opening and closing – which suggests that its sources are, surprisingly, the angelic choruses in Berlioz's *L'enfance du Christ*. The combined effect of warmth, brilliance and some other unidentifiable quality could be attributed to Tippett's emphasis on the tonalities of E flat, D and something hovering around C. But this is to circumscribe an astonishing conception, which ultimately defies analysis.

Although the vision irrupts unexpectedly and stops just as abruptly (it takes up about one of the work's thirty-five minutes), Tippett's compositional technique had by then created the environment in which the idea of transcendence could be accepted, if not comprehended: the conventional sense of time as succession had, that is, been overtaken by one of simultaneity. Tippett achieves this effect in two principal ways. The first is by going in circles as it were, so that if the beginning is the same as the end there is no real beginning or end. The whole work describes a circle of this kind. The opening and closing harmonies are the same (Ex. 152). Another example is the passage preceding the ascent to the vision – a set of entries following the intervals of a whole-tone scale and thus finishing where it had started.

Ex. 152   **The Vision of Saint Augustine**

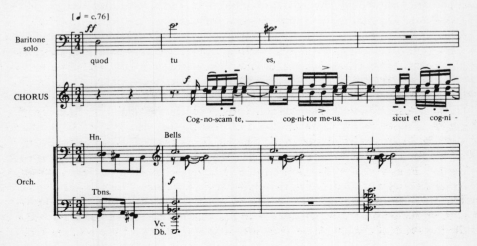

The second and more characteristic way of preparing for timelessness lies at the heart of the work, influencing the structure of its text, its musical resources and its musical technique. It derives from Augustine's thesis that time is a flux of memories, 'sights' and expectations whose tendency to disperse in all directions can be mastered by mental concentration. Augustine exemplifies his thesis in his *Confessions*, by compacting into his narrative thoughts prompted by the immediate details of his discourse – allusions to or quotations from biblical passages or from other events in his life. Tippett adopts this literary technique for his own text by interlacing Augustine's simple account of the vision of eternity with complementary passages chosen from the Bible and from elsewhere in the *Confessions*. The resulting dialogue between Augustine and his *alter ego* naturally dictates the vocal forces of *The Vision of Saint Augustine*, baritone soloist and chorus, and it immediately accounts for the work's pervasive sense of time arrested, the narrative being not so much interrupted as embellished by burgeoning choral parentheses. It is the special province of music to be able to say two things at once. Tippett vastly elaborates Augustine's technique in this respect, frequently combining narrative and added text in a dense collage, which is made even more dense by an orchestral gloss and by the division of the chorus itself into two strands or more. It is in such passages, when past, present and future are superimposed, that perception of time is most radically altered. In Ex. 153, Augustine's '[in the presence of truth] which

Ex. 153   **The Vision of Saint Augustine**

(Ex. 153 cont.)

you are, we were discussing [what the eternal life of the saints might be like]' is combined with the choral 'Let me know you, who know me: let me know you as I am known', a supplication Augustine made *after* the events the baritone is describing (it is from Book X, chapter 1), though it also refers back to Augustine's mental conflict preceding his first vision. As a whole the passage expresses the sense of strain as Augustine grapples with the problem of eternity while at the same time recalling the events preceding that first vision. In Ex. 154, from Part 2, Augustine's 'rising with a more burning affection [towards that ultimate reality]' is combined with two choral strands (from Book X, chapter 34), the complementary 'light' in the low voices, and a particular instance, in the high voices, of that divine light 'which Tobias saw [when with blind eyes he taught his son the way of God]'. This passage also combines past, present and future, and with much greater density since it is closer to the vision of eternity. (In Exx. 153 and 154 the published rhythms are altered in order to illustrate Tippett's dramatically analogous combination of rhythms.)

Ex. 154   **The Vision of Saint Augustine**

Passages of this kind are placed at crucial stages in the work's structure, functioning as marshalling points where energy is condensed so that it can be released in passages of relatively high tessitura which in turn gather density and lead to the focal points, the two visions. One of the most idiosyncratic features of the work is the irruption within this process of passages loud, brutal and apparently senseless (see Figs. 57, 108 and 179 in the score). Tippett has provided some explanation of them by saying that 'you can't have a mystic silence without the god inadvertently bursting out' (an idea he was to rework in the finale of his Symphony No. 3, with its reference to the God of Job thundering from the whirlwind). This is unlikely to have occurred to the commentator without help from the composer. The effect of these irruptions is nevertheless entirely in keeping with the density of the work as a whole.

Such passages as those in Exx. 153 and 154 present Tippett's collage technique at its most radical. Elsewhere he juxtaposes rather than superimposes, a procedure which in the particular terms of *The Vision of Saint Augustine* preserves contact with a conventional, 'teleological' view of musical flow and dramatizes Tippett's *rapprochement* between linear and circular conceptions of time. The work begins with such juxtapositioning, establishing a context in which Tippett's natural instinct to make his music grow and flower can take root. Its division into three parts (the three paragraphs of Augustine's narrative) follows the archetypal patterning he had used in *A Child of Our Time*: the broad details of the situation, the specific subject matter, a meditation on its meaning. So the work continually mixes the traditional and the new. If the new predominates it is still held in place by the traditional.

This is clearly evident in Part 1 of the work, which uses the remarkable features referred to above to articulate a structure that otherwise is unexceptional – introduction, exposition, development and finale. In the introduction Tippett employs an AAB form, each section consisting of solo juxtaposed with chorus, rhythmic coherence between the different tempi of two forces being effected by 'tempo modulation' (the two-quaver beat of the one equalling the three-quaver beat of the other). Between the last two sections is inserted that superpositioning of solo and chorus which first announces the special quality of the work (see Ex. 148) – the setting of the Ambrosian hymn, *Deus creator omnium*, with which Augustine consoled himself after the death of his mother. After a statement of the word *fenestram* (window) the exposition proceeds with main subject, transition and subsidiary subject, which latter, being a recapitulation of the hymn, both absorbs the introduction into the scheme of things and neatly rounds off what now can also be regarded as a ternary form double exposition. The main subject is one of Tippett's most characteristic inventions, a lyrical theme for the tenors in his A-flat pastoral vein followed by an equally beautiful theme for the sopranos. These themes are prompted by the word *hortus* (garden) from the soloist, and, being settings of verses from the *Song of Songs* ('A garden enclosed is my sister, my spouse ... Let my beloved come into his garden ...'), make the point that Augustine's struggles with the power of sensuality were severe indeed. A garden also reminds Augustine (in Tippett's conception) of the garden he had fled to when seeking the privacy in which he could indulge his emotional torment. The 'transition' recounts this experience and signals the imminence of his first vision by highlighting Tippett's 'magical' instruments of xylophone and piano, which themselves had been prepared for by the sound of flutes and celesta and of bells earlier in the work. Augustine's anger with himself for not then submitting to God summons up *Deus creator omnium* once more. The 'development' is conceived as a sequence of six short sections harnessed to a rhythmic momentum which eventually issues in glossolalia (see Ex. 149) – despite the density of texture (see Ex. 153) and the divine irruption referred to above. The 'Angel Symphony' is the exuberant 'finale'.

Part 2 of the work is a ternary design, whose last section, a variation of the first, has been described by Tippett as a 'thrice repeated act of prayer'. Part 3 is a fragmentary recapitulation with coda. Both parts could be described in terms comparable with those used above.

Tippett's collage technique is spiritually related to the medieval concept of troping. It also finds a precedent in Bach's technique of interpreting the meaning of a chorale by adding a simultaneous commentary for a soloist; in fact, *The Vision of Saint Augustine* contains (at Fig. 173) a phrase strikingly similar to that used by Bach in the 'Mein teuer Heiland' movement of his *St John Passion*, which suggests that Tippett may have appropriated Bach's particular as well as general idea. Nonetheless, whatever the work might owe to received ideas, it remains uniquely personal in sound and substance. It may find a contemporary counterpart in such a work as Carter's Concerto for Orchestra. It could be said to belong to the tradition of such works as Elgar's *The Dream of Gerontius* or Delius's *Sea Drift*. But if this is so, *The Vision of Saint Augustine* is one of those very special works that alter existing conceptions of a tradition and demand its reformulation.

Tippett's Expressionism

General Considerations

Tippett's second period concludes with a group of five works, centred on his Symphony No. 3 and bounded on either side by his operas *The Knot Garden* and *The Ice Break*. These works may at first seem to have little to do with one another, since each inhabits so complete and arresting a world of its own. But they share a common parentage in *King Priam* and, like sturdy offspring, proclaim their independence by being collectively more astringent, intense and eruptive than their progenitor. What distinguishes them most from *King Priam* and, particularly, from their immediate predecessor, *The Vision of Saint Augustine*, is their difference in attitude. All Tippett's music is direct in expression, in that it is as lucid and immediate as is compatible with the nature of its subject. But the directness of *The Knot Garden* and its successors is unlike that in his previous music. It is stripped, defenceless, importunate. It lays the emphasis on publicizing rather than 'poeticizing'. It speaks of a composer whose earlier convictions had been placed under serious threat and who now needed to rethink and reassert them with maximum forcefulness in order to make himself heard amid the general clamour of dissenting voices. To harness the power of music to expressive honesty may involve the disturbing and the violent. It may also invite charges of self-indulgence. If this is the case, Tippett seems to be saying, so be it: the matter is too urgent to be compromised by deference to over-refined sensibilities. With these works, he abandoned the fastidiousness of his earlier music and entered what may be described as the expressionist phase in his output.

Tippett's expressionism has much in common with 'classic' expressionism – the angular lines and abrupt gestures, the high level of dissonance, the ruthless yet idealistic paring away of social convention, the intense subjectivity, the probing into the dynamic of the unconscious; it even, in the 'howlings' of the character Dov in *The Knot Garden*, recalls the primal expressionist scream. But naturally it is not a mere repeat of its early twentieth-century counterpart. It is not so self-sufficient, its terms of reference are wider and it neither wages war against a hostile world nor presumes that music can embrace the abstract essence of things by means of an 'absolute' metaphor. On the contrary, it seeks a covenant with real life and is always conditioned by Tippett's preoccupation with the integration of the individual – the individual with himself, with others and with society at large. In addition, it is coloured by an irony which questions its whole basis. In *The Vision of Saint Augustine* Tippett had celebrated the capacity of his music to perform 'magic'. In *The Knot Garden* he casts doubt on the process. Mangus, the controller of the opera, psychoanalyst and would-be Prospero figure, and, like the other characters, a piece of Tippett himself, is eventually shown to be neither the magus of Shakespeare's *The Tempest*, able to dispense beneficent magic, nor even the pompous but effective psychoanalyst of Eliot's *The Cocktail Party*, a play of which the opera is a kind of criticism. He has a modicum of success but at the denouement he confesses to being a fraud. In *The Ice Break*, Astron, the 'messenger figure' and as such the voice of archetypal wisdom, emits some extremely serious remarks while at the same time presenting himself as both ludicrous and unreal. Such inversions of meaning are fundamental to Tippett's expressionist works and give them their most individual slant, that defiant detachment which is precisely what prevents them from degenerating into self-indulgence. Inevitably, Tippett reacted against their vehemence and occasional brashness. Shortly after completing *The Ice Break* he felt that 'all the "knot gardens" and the howlings and the screams and shrieks have altered your ears, they've ruined your style'. This was putting it melodramatically (the quotation is from an unscripted public lecture[49]) but nevertheless clearly enough to explain why, in his more recent works, notably his String Quartet No. 4 and Triple Concerto, he has sought to redress the balance and recover something of that purity and tenderness of expression he finds in late Beethoven and which, after all, is a 'fundamental experience in music'.[50]

The Knot Garden

For all its vehemence *The Knot Garden* is the most intimate of Tippett's operas. It has no chorus, and its seven characters in a 'high-walled house-garden shutting out an industrial city' soon find they cannot conceal their secrets from one another. Small in scale, the opera is correspondingly swift-moving. There are none of the elaborate transitions of *The Midsummer Marriage* or even the interludes of *King Priam*. Its impression of speed is due, paradoxically, to its rapid sequence of stops and starts – abrupt switches from one short, self-contained scene to another, and strident punctuations by means of Tippett's musical equivalent of the television technique of dissolve. This is not the gradual disintegration of a picture and the formulation of another from a void, but a criss-cross of lines which blots out what has just happened and clears the air for something new (see Ex. 155). These 'dissolves' (oddly reminiscent of the 'Joie du sang des étoiles' from Messiaen's *Turangalîla-Symphonie*) are striking evidence of Tippett's continuing and productive dialogue with the innovations of contemporary theatre ('theatre' now extended to include film and television), or, in other words, of his alert recognition of how he could pilfer from modern cutting and lighting techniques and convert apparent discontinuity of dramatic process into its opposite.

Ex. 155 The Knot Garden

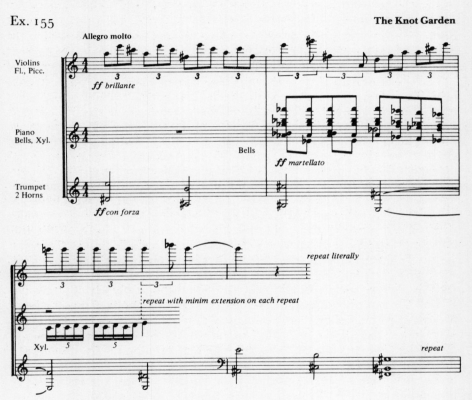

The theatricality of *The Knot Garden*, its visual impact, its dynamic impetus, depends less however on its connections with contemporary theatre than on its treatment of character. Not only are the characters vividly individualized, they interact, and thus spark off dramatic tensions quite new in Tippett's output. In this respect *The Knot Garden* effects a synthesis between *The Midsummer Marriage* and *King Priam*, where characters were, respectively, rather vaguely drawn and concerned only with themselves, and very sharply drawn and still isolated from one another. Here, the characters are thrust into complex interrelationships which necessarily impose real, if modest, changes of outlook on all of them.

The seven characters are obviously designed to form that miniature human universe which, though selective and stylized, would reflect Tippett's anxiety that his music should relate to the actual rather than the conceptual. The characters embody contemporary social problems, including homosexuality, race relations and the torture of political prisoners – already an index of the seriousness with which Tippett views his role as artist in society. These problems are not however at the core of the opera. Rather are they by-products of a much larger, psychological problem which itself needs to be resolved or at least eased before progress can be made elsewhere. The main subject matter therefore is the inner as opposed to the public lives of the characters, and from this emerges the main dramatic idea, which is a question: can people yet learn to live with each other when their personalities and personal relationships have reached a seemingly crippling deadness or bitterness?

The starting point is a crisis in the marriage of Thea and Faber. At the beginning of the opera the characters are 'nothing but a set of obsolete responses' (to quote the diagnosis of the psychoanalyst in *The Cocktail Party*). In order to break open their suppressed emotional turbulence, Mangus engineers a psychological storm and then, having loosened up his charges in a nightmare of painful and unpalatable encounters, he persuades them to project their fantasies on to characters from *The Tempest* and act out, under the protective disguise of stage costumes, a series of 'charades' he has derived from the play. Gradually they are forced to acknowledge what they 'really are' and by the end of the opera they all, with the exception of Dov, the musician, have found a way out of the impasse. The opera is, of course, a re-formulation of Tippett's central artistic belief that illumination of the psyche through music can promote that self-understanding which can leave the individual better equipped to take his place in society. It is couched in the most unequivocal of terms, for as well as casting his presiding genius as a psychoanalyst, Tippett draws his dramatic metaphor from contemporary psychotherapeutic techniques (abreaction techniques and the role-playing of psychodrama).[51] But it differs in several respects from its obvious exemplar, *The Midsummer Marriage*. Even its title, with its allusion to the ambiguous idea of the marriage knot or lovers' knot, shows that Tippett has lost the assurance of the earlier opera. And the distinction between inner and public lives is given an ironic twist, for the ostensibly 'public' lives of the characters – Thea's garden, Faber's factory, Dov's music, etc. – are shown to be projections of their inner fantasies and as such both incomplete and unrelated to the demands of everyday living. Most significantly, when self-understanding does eventually emerge, it is shown to be partial and arbitrary: it is not brought about by personal effort but by external agency – by Denise and by Mangus, who in any case is not fully in control of what he is doing. Some degree of self-understanding is reached all the same, and with it is released that quality of forgiveness which provides the opera with its most obvious 'message', the same as that of *The Marriage of Figaro* or *Così fan tutte* – or Blake: when human nature leads someone to inflict terrible injury on someone else, the only possible resolution is forgiveness.

> Mutual forgiveness of each vice:
> Such are the Gates of Paradise.
> *(For the Sexes)*

Blake's couplet might have served as a motto for the opera. In fact, as he stated in a BBC interview on 3 December 1970, Tippett had these lines at the back of his mind all through the composition of *The Knot Garden*. What he actually used as motto is not, however, so beguiling. When the unspeakable Parolles in *All's Well That Ends Well* is unmasked and brought face to face with his own duplicity, he picks himself up with the comment: 'Simply the thing I am shall make me live'. Through this quotation, Tippett acknowledges his opera's debt to Shakespeare's late 'comedies of forgiveness'.[52] In particular, he identifies himself with the Shakespearian viewpoint that the Christian tradition from which the idea of forgiveness derives needs to be injected with some down-to-earth realism and the idea itself reduced to more practical proportions. Parolles's words here seem to mean that in order to live, man has to learn to forgive not only others but himself. In any event the real message of the opera takes forgiveness one stage further. From forgiveness flows love. In an epilogue Tippett leaves no doubt that what he means by love is the transforming power of physical love. So if *The Knot Garden* is a sadder and wiser version of *The Midsummer Marriage* it still ends on a note of splendour.

The title and setting of the opera derive from the idea that a garden is a projection of someone's inner personality. A knot garden, found in large, formal gardens of Tudor and Elizabethan times, is an intricate 'knotted' pattern of box hedges filled in with sand or gravel, 'looking' like a personality clipped and distorted in order to prevent it from releasing its natural exuberance, or like one so rigid that all it can do is contemplate the arid channels of thought it has imposed on itself. The knot garden may be described as the middle ground of the opera. It falls between two extremes. If it were planted with flowers and grass, it would become more like a rose garden, the lovers' garden where all is warm and fragrant. If its hedges were left to grow very high, it would turn into a maze or labyrinth where the personality gets lost or entangled. When relationships in the opera become tender, the scene moves towards the idea of a rose garden; when harsh, towards that of a labyrinth.

However bleak the proposition that a knot garden is the metaphorical norm for contemporary personal relationships, a garden of whatever colour provides opportunities for attractive staging. It ensures some consistency of verbal imagery. And, since only one of the characters in *The Knot Garden* is cast as a genuine gardener, it helpfully indicates that she, Thea, is the determining factor behind the launching of the action. Tippett's garden setting is an imaginative theatrical conceit. But its real function is simply to create the symbolic environment in which inner personalities may plausibly be explored, a subject that is obviously unsuited to conventional 'plot' and which the setting therefore also helps hold together. This is not to imply that *The Knot Garden* is deliberately obscure. Its novel and even radical approach to dramatic content is the logical outcome of Tippett's thinking about opera in general. What matters in opera is the dramatic and emotional power of the music. Since music is incapable of conveying in its own terms the explanatory trappings of a drama, why have them at all? Why not lay the responsibility for dramatic and emotional argument squarely on the shoulders of the music and leave the listener to provide for himself such explanations as he may need concerning the dramatic context? If the music is worthwhile such explanations will in any case be relatively unimportant. This is the reasoning behind Tippett's apparent unwillingness in either libretto or music to disclose the full details of his scenario. Apart from the fact that it leads to a conception of opera that could prove to be extremely influential, it also explains why, with such emphasis on the expressive, *The Knot Garden* is so concentrated and intense a work and why its scenes are so short. It also of course presents the listener with an intriguing interpretative problem, markedly different from that encountered in other operas. However persuasive the music, he will still, and for that very reason, want to know how these narrative and explanatory gaps are to be filled. His first question will concern the background to the action. What, exactly, has been going on? Here is one answer.

Thea and Faber are a childless couple. It may be assumed that Thea has cast the blame for this on Faber. She has retreated into the privacy of her garden, thus rejecting Faber, who has responded to his supposed freedom by sowing a few wild oats and, in particular, by trying to find some sexual satisfaction from Flora (a flower, virgin), their adolescent ward. In the process he has precipitated the crisis in their marriage. Faber is described as a civil engineer of thirty-five. Other than suggesting that he is reasonably successful with his work at the factory (*faber* = maker) where he can escape from his wife, his name and given profession have no connection with the course of the opera. With Thea however it is different. Her name, as Tippett has pointed out, recalls that of a goddess (though precisely which goddess is not clear[53]) and she often behaves like one, notably in the first act, where she enjoys exercising her impregnable authority. In the final act she is the first person to respond to Mangus's therapy, the first person to melt, which in turn suggests that with the far-sightedness of a goddess she has known all along what is to happen and that she is simply living out the ritual she has set in motion and probably gone through before. It may be deduced therefore that Mangus is present at Thea's invitation. He respects the implied consultant/client relationship, for during the charades Thea is an onlooker. They are presented, as it were, for her critical approval and the parties on whose account she presumably invited Mangus in the first place, Flora and Faber, duly appear in them. (Flora-Miranda is an obvious parallel. By casting Faber as Ferdinand, Mangus seems to have decided to confront the would-be playboy with his own illusions of youthful charm and audacity.) Mangus has seen however that it is not so much the behaviour of Flora and Faber that needs attention as the marriage, and he plans his therapy accordingly, ensuring that Thea be included, even though she, tactfully, will not be cast as a direct participant at the climax of it.

The name Mangus is a conflation of Magnus (perhaps the 'great' King Magnus of Shaw's *The Apple Cart*, the intelligent but autocratic philanthropist who believes he has an historical destiny to fulfil), Mangan (the bluntspeaking tycoon of Shaw's *Heartbreak House*, who is eventually obliged to swallow his pride) and the Renaissance *magus*, the seer who sought to improve the world through his magical 'art'. Frances Yates[54] believed that the figure of Prospero was Shakespeare's attempt to rehabilitate the English magus John Dee, who by the time of *The Tempest* had lost his standing in the English court. Once Mangus is associated with *The Tempest*, the power of art and the predicament of the creative artist, the allusions surrounding the name become extremely complex and stretch far beyond what at first might seem the merely clever Mangus-Prospero pairing. They are examined more closely on later pages.

At their first appearance, Dov,[55] the white musician, and Mel,[56] his black lover, a writer, are already dressed up for the charades, so it may be assumed that Mangus had decided he would need his two 'servants', Ariel and Caliban, before he could fulfil his Prospero role convincingly and had secretly asked Thea to supply the requisite house-guests. With his cast complete, this is the point at which the opera begins.

In Act I, subtitled 'Confrontation', Tippett first lays out the dramatic hypothesis: Mangus with his plan of redemption, Thea in the haven of her garden, and the seemingly lethal relationships between Flora and Faber, and Faber and Thea. To this is added the relationship between Dov and Mel, which by contrast seems to work harmoniously enough, until Thea reappears – at which juncture the development of the action proper begins. She brings a tray of cocktails for her guests, and as the three lift their glasses she entices Mel into her garden – in the libretto, 'like Circe'[57] – and upturns the relationship entirely. Why she should want to assert her sexuality in this way may be construed as her need to convince herself, trapped as she is in a dead marriage, that she is still attractive; or perhaps she has been persuaded to do so by Mangus, who now wishes to initiate the first stage of his therapy. In any event, Dov is thrown over, his world is torn to shreds, and, like Odysseus's companions, he is turned into an animal. He barks and howls like a dog. (The libretto states, obscurely, 'like Ariel's dog'.) In this compromising position he is caught by Faber, who makes an experimental pass at him (certainly, along with its counterpart in Act II, the most provocative moment in the opera). But before anything can happen, Thea and Mel return. The tensions generated by this improbable re-grouping of relationships leave them all voiceless and, with the unexpected entry of Denise, chastened. Denise is Thea's sister. She is described as a 'dedicated freedom-fighter'. The gaudy costumes Mangus has just brought in and what now seem the trivial upsets of the others create an indecent contrast with her, 'twisted or otherwise disfigured from the effects of torture'. Her appearance makes for a dramatic *coup de théâtre*, but it is also the catalyst, the 'fortuitous accident' Mangus was looking for, which will break open the protective shells and provide him with material which can yield to the workings of his psychological storm.

Denise's name suggests that she had been a *maquisarde* (Tippett gives her the feminine version of Denys, the patron saint of France), though she could be generally representative of those women of the present period whose integrity has enabled them not to break under stress nor betray the ideals they hold with such passion. From her position of moral superiority she denounces the whole company. She cannot however live her revolutionary life for ever. She has come home. 'How shall I turn home again to you the beautiful and damned?' At home, the distinction between right and wrong is not so easy to draw. Mel, the black American, who understands her more clearly than anyone else and who perhaps is the least inhibited of the company, is the first to respond – in his inherited language of the blues. But even he cannot be entirely himself, for apart from caricaturing the blues style he still uses the language of Caliban: 'Do not torment me.' Dov sees this in a more personal way and retorts with 'Do not desert me'. A complex ensemble builds up with everyone admitting something of his true feelings – though still in quotation marks. Denise is forgotten. Mangus, realising that his time is ripe and also realising that unless his own self-examination is deep enough his therapy will cause havoc, quotes Prospero: 'And my ending is despair, Unless I be relieved by prayer ...' – to which apparent gobbledeygook Mel provides the obvious comment: 'Sure, baby.' The irony is that Mel probably has fathomed Mangus's posture.

Act II, subtitled 'Labyrinth', is the *Tempest*-like, psychological storm. The labyrinth is understood to be whirling about at a furious speed and Mangus operating a 'huge puppet show', a pattern of duets in which one pair of characters is sucked in to the centre to be confronted with the full extent of their unconscious feelings and then whisked away to leave room for another. Eventually, those most disorientated and least able to absorb the nightmare, Flora and Dov, wake up, as it were, and are left together to make what they can of their situation. The duets progress from the least to the most plausible of pairings. Denise can make no contact with Thea, and little with Faber. Faber tries to rape Flora; Thea attacks Faber with a horse-whip; Faber attempts to kiss Dov. Dov and Mel act out a serious ritual of parting and, finally, Denise and Mel discover what seems a genuine communion of body and spirit. At this point Mangus presumably considers that the characters have learnt enough about themselves for present purposes, and the labyrinth rapidly unwinds, in the process 'ejecting' Flora who is left alone sobbing, until Dov comforts her.

Being a composer he seeks to do so by persuading her to sing. Flora has no songs of her own, so she sings one that expresses the situation for her: alone, rejected by Thea whom she loves, and, like Desdemona, expecting to die – 'Die liebe Farbe' from Schubert's *Die schöne Müllerin*. Dov translates her German. 'I will dress myself in green, In green weeping-willows: My love's so fond of green.' Dov then tries to cheer her up by singing another song of young love, but one less nostalgic and more inspiriting. Being composer as well as singer, he cannot however be so personal as Flora. His compositional experience has taught him that he must transform his own heartbreak into a piece of music quite separate from himself and addressed to a much wider audience than the young girl sitting listening to him. At the climax of his song he is totally engrossed by his own music and its power to summon up the 'fabulous rose-garden'. When Mel, the cause of the heartbreak, taps him on the shoulder and says, 'I taught you that', reality intervenes and the illusion withers away.

Act III is the proposed denouement, when Mangus will stage-manage the charades through which his characters, theoretically at least, will be released from the knots they have got into. The charades cover the history of the island of *The Tempest* from when Prospero first set foot on it until his final departure, thus both pre- and post-dating the action of Shakespeare and showing that Mangus's intention is to present a fully rounded view of the inner world of his charges. He dons his Shakespearean mantle and draws out the circle in which Prospero had charmed his enemies and which the 'audience', Thea and Denise, are now asked to imagine as the magic island. Denise is sceptical about the power of Mangus's 'play': 'Power is in the will.' But Thea instantly sees it as the means to forgiveness and a reawakening of love[58] – a curiously improbable reaction at this point and one of the least convincing moments in the opera. Perhaps it can be explained along the lines mentioned earlier (p.406).

The first charade enacts Prospero's discovery of Caliban and Ariel (*The Tempest*, I.ii. 355–7 and 270–93). He 'civilizes' Caliban by making him stand up (though at this stage Caliban is left still unable to speak) and he releases Ariel from the 'cloven pine'. The charade then nearly gets out of hand, for Ariel's attack on Caliban, ostensibly his retribution for having been imprisoned by Caliban's mother, is of unscripted violence. Miranda becomes very frightened and Mangus-Prospero cuts the proceedings short. It may be presumed that this charade is chiefly for the benefit of Flora, who learns, if only subliminally, that Caliban, the spirit of animal nature, and Ariel, the seemingly anarchic spirit of the imagination, were both present on the island from the beginning and that instead of trying to get rid of them Prospero can tame and control them. The 'audience' respond in their different ways – Thea, as if she is welcoming an insight she possesses already, Denise, irritated by Mangus's equivocation.

The second charade shows how Caliban attempted to 'violate' Miranda (*The Tempest*, I.ii. 349–50). With Prospero watching through a telescope, Caliban steals up on the sleeping girl; when he tries to tear her clothes off, she screams. Ariel has been posted to rescue her, but at this point Denise rushes out of the audience and pulls Mel away. This charade presumably enables Flora, with the connivance of Mangus, to find out at first hand what sensuous nature means and how she can deal with it. With Thea nearly 'cured', it is also directed at Denise. In Act II her dream response to Mel had been founded on an apparent identity of political purpose: her humanitarian commitment linked with his skill with words in the fight for racial equality. But reality now confronts her with an aspect of Mel she was unprepared for and she goes away in tears, struggling with contradictions she will in fact soon assimilate (as the finale of the opera implies). Dov encourages Mel to follow her. If Mel had not been prepared to let Dov go off with Flora at the end of Act II, he, Dov, is prepared to accept the inevitable – that his function has been simply to enable Mel to find out where his sexuality lay.

The third charade derives from the scene in *The Tempest* when Prospero finally mends his quarrels by revealing Ferdinand and Miranda playing chess, the game for royal lovers. Miranda accuses Ferdinand of cheating. As in Shakespeare, he denies it: 'I would not for the world'. But – not in Shakespeare – Flora-Miranda then upturns the chess-board. 'Oh yes you would' she says and cheerfully flies off on Dov-Ariel's wings. Flora has now learnt the value of her imagination, and she is no longer frightened of men, even though, after her experience in the second charade, she knows they may overstep the limits. The outcome of the charade was not however what Faber had been expecting. He has been sharply informed that his illusions of youthful charm are absurd. He must return to his proper wife: she, not least after her rejection by Flora, is ready to return to him. Mangus asks the two of them to set up the chess-board again. Faber finds the king, Thea the queen – and she gives it to him, a symbolic gesture which annoys Mangus because he has yet, in the final charade, to confirm the change in Faber, to confirm, presumably, Faber's willing dependence on a benevolent fate. Left alone, Thea sings of her wonder that she can flower again and be receptive to the mysterious delights of love.

In the final charade Prospero and Miranda are preparing to leave the island, delayed only by the problem of what to do with Prospero's 'servants', Ariel and Caliban. Prospero decides he must put their demands for freedom to the test. This charade is the only one not directly derived from Shakespeare and, as his own invention, it presents therefore Mangus's conception of himself, the omniscient philanthropist who has the power and authority to round up his charges (*The Tempest*, V.i. 9), pass judgement on them and 'set them all to rights'. The role he assigns Faber is his agent, a jailor cum clerk-of-the-court. (Precisely how Faber is to benefit from this role is one of the most cryptic aspects of the opera – unless the interpretation given in the paragraph above is the intended one, in which case Tippett seems to have given Faber short shrift.) Ariel is brought in and duly allowed his liberty. But Prospero wants to keep Caliban: he 'serves in offices that profit us'. Caliban retorts that the island is his and that he is entitled to be his own master, for which challenge to his authority Prospero commits his 'inferior' servant to the penitentiary. Ariel gloats over the humiliation of Caliban like a spoilt schoolboy. Faced with the results of his own pretensions Mangus suddenly realises that his paradise is corrupt. 'The damage the poetic would inflict if it ever succeeded in intruding upon the real'[59] is unthinkable, as are the consequences of projecting his darker instincts on the Calibans of the world. Rather melodramatically, he abandons the whole proceedings: 'Prospero's a fake.'

He is like everyone else; like his charges, he too has reached an impasse. With this startling admission of arrogance and futility, Mangus's universe collapses like a pack of cards. There is nothing left, a void – filled only with the cold fact that, after all, he and the rest of the cast are opera singers in an opera-house. All he can really do, he tells the audience (and here Tippett, in a *Midsummer Marriage*-like *parabasis*, himself comes to the fore) is let music, literally music, effect the therapy. With this extraordinary change of gear, *The Knot Garden* moves into its final ensemble, in which the idea that music, love and forgiveness can bring people together is expressed briefly and tentatively.

The cast then leave, Mel with Denise, Flora out into her 'brave new world' and Dov by himself, until Mel beckons him to follow and thereby underlines both the frailty of the new pairing and the fact that despite everything some changes have occurred during the course of the opera. By way of confirmation, an epilogue depicts Thea and Faber together again, and about to embrace. With a last touch of irony they sing 'The curtain rises'[60] as the curtain falls.

For such a short opera (*The Knot Garden* lasts barely an hour and a half) the above synopsis may seem disproportionately long – especially so, when measured against the inconclusiveness of some of its findings. No synopsis however, whatever its length, can claim to be wholly satisfactory because no synopsis of the opera can claim to be definitive. *The Knot Garden* is one of those intrinsically equivocal, and even contradictory works, which rather than make statements pose questions. Its nature is to provoke rather than assuage. The most straightforward of its questions, those concerning the behaviour of the characters, can be answered tolerably well. But there remain larger questions of meaning which resist neat solutions because they are essentially unanswerable. If, for example, as suggested earlier and as stated in the opera's denouement, music is not only to carry the main burden of meaning but also to be the ultimate and only true therapy, why does the text of the final ensemble refer to love?

> If for a timid moment
> We submit to love ...
>
> We sense the magic net[61]
> That holds us veined
> Each to each to all.

Are music and love to be understood as the same thing, the 'two wings of the soul', as Berlioz put it in his *Memoirs*? And if music (or love) is to be the means whereby man's common identity (which provides the key to 'our salvation'[62]) can be sensed, what value should be ascribed to something that lasts for only a 'timid' moment? Questions of this kind lie at the heart of *The Knot Garden*.

Tippett was obviously aware that they could obstruct understanding of his opera and, accordingly, before its first performance, he circulated two short introductions[63] which sought to pre-empt misleading answers to at least some of them. Though it might appear strange, *The Knot Garden* is in fact derived from two theatrical traditions. The essential characteristic of the first of these is, as Tippett sees it, that action is shaped not so much by plot as by relationships. A pattern of changing character-pairings develops which imposes an abstract structural logic so strong that *it* controls the course of the action, not the plot or the personalities of the characters, who thus lose something of their individuality and become more like counters in a game. The action is complete only when all permutations of the characters, all the 'games', have been played out. Tippett's favourite example of this genre, and the one he specifically refers to, is Shaw's *Heartbreak House*, whose second act contains a sequence of 'duets' prefiguring those in the second act of *The Knot Garden*. (Since its subject matter and technique is closer to that of his opera, Tippett might also have referred to *Dear Brutus* of J.M. Barrie.) In an earlier article[64] he revealed that a crucial stimulus behind the opera had been Fry's *A Sleep of Prisoners*, another example of the genre. Here, he was particularly attracted to Fry's dramatic technique whereby the dream of one character is shared by other, sleeping, characters, because this 'relativity of identity is a universal psychological problem of our time' – from which it may be deduced that Tippett's central artistic objective in *The Knot Garden* was indeed to use music to inculcate a sense of human interdependence. Mozart's *Così fan tutte*, Goethe's novel *Elective Affinities* and, in the present period, the plays of Albee, Pinter, the writings of R.D. Laing and the novels of Iris Murdoch (notably *A Severed Head* of 1961, which includes both a psychoanalyst who knows all the answers and a 'knotted' pattern of relationships, and *A Fairly Honourable Defeat* of 1973, whose 'plot' is even closer to that of *The Knot Garden*) all confirm that the opera belongs to a living genre with a long tradition behind it. In this context, the important question therefore is not whether *The Knot Garden* is an artistic maverick but why Tippett should have used the genre in the first place. An answer may be found in *The Midsummer Marriage*, whose stylized dramatic techniques give body and meaning to material which, left to itself, would break into anarchy. The material of *The Knot Garden* is similarly in need of a distancing, formalizing framework. If the incompatible and potentially explosive emotions of Tippett's basic dramatic idea were wholly 'real' and representative (after all, real life can be far worse than that presented in the opera and would in any case be likely to be complicated by authentic children, not adolescent wards), the opera would become unmanageable. Tippett's intention is not therefore to simulate reality. The opera is hardly less ritualized than *The Midsummer Marriage*.

The second theatrical tradition Tippett refers to is that of Shakespeare's late 'comedies of forgiveness'.[65] In these plays antagonisms caused by perplexingly amoral conduct are resolved not by gradual reform but by sudden repentance, and consequent forgiveness – which might appear a glib evasion of the problem did it not both ring true and lift the dramatic temperature to a level curiously like that of music. Shakespeare's 'modern' refusal to judge his characters, especially the less pleasant ones ('Simply the thing I am shall make me live'), and his idea that in forgiveness lies the key to reconciliation offer strong reasons why Tippett should have become attracted to these plays; but the musical reason was no doubt equally strong, for it automatically singled out *The Tempest*, the play he was already fascinated by (through his involvement in the 1962 Old Vic production) and the play in which music is given a decisive role, not least in promoting the final act of forgiveness.

Tippett's introductions show that he borrowed and adapted from characteristically diverse sources in order to give shape to his dramatic idea, the first tradition articulating it, the second resolving it. The two traditions unite in *The Tempest*: the first in the island setting, an enclosed space comparable with a house (Shaw), church (Fry) or garden (Tippett), and in Tippett's reworking of the 'games' technique in his charades; the second in the idea of forgiveness. Once this is recognized, the influence of *The Tempest* on *The Knot Garden* can be readily understood.

This influence cannot however be limited to these considerations alone. Apart from direct quotations and allusions (Dov and Mel's Act I song 'Ca-ca-Caliban', for example, being an echo of the drunken Caliban's ''Ban, 'Ban, Cacaliban'), there are many parallels of structure and dramaturgy. Prospero's 'glistering apparel' to trap the malefactors may be compared with Mangus's stage costumes; the Act III banquet with Thea's cocktail party. Even Tippett's 'dissolve' sections emanate from the play, where 'dissolve' is a recurring image: Prospero dismisses his Act IV masque, for example, with 'These our actors ... shall dissolve ... and leave not a rack behind'. The most striking parallels are between the masque and the charades: like a masque, the charades spill into both the stage and the real audience; and as Prospero dismisses the masque when he realises he has been bewitched by his own 'art' and in the process forgotten Caliban, so Mangus dismisses the charades for comparable reasons. Parallels of this kind may naturally be extended to include parallels of theme, and it is here that the commentator encounters the links which provide the key to the whole opera.

The Tempest may be interpreted as an allegory about the creative artist, even of Shakespeare himself, in which case it is also a self-criticism. *The Knot Garden* may be interpreted in a similar way, modified only by the fact that the process of self-criticism is effected through a criticism of *The Tempest*. Tippett accepts the basic Shakespearean premise: Prospero-Shakespeare, the artist, who through the transforming imaginative power of his art can fulfil the superhuman task of bringing harmony into the world, though only with the aid of his 'light' and 'shadow', Ariel and Caliban, without whom he can accomplish nothing. Likewise, Mangus-Tippett cannot effect his charade therapy without Dov and Mel, archetypal projections of imagination and sensuality. Obviously it is natural that Dov should be associated with music, though it is less clear why Mel is cast as a writer (though Caliban is given the best poetry in *The Tempest*). Tippett adds various small glosses on Shakespeare, such as the one above, but the largest and most significant occur towards and at the denouement. Prospero abandons his masque and turns to self-questioning, when he suddenly realises that he cannot accommodate Caliban in his arcadian paradise. Mangus abandons his charades when he realises the same thing. The outcome however is different. Both Prospero and Mangus treat Caliban ('on whose nature nurture can never stick') as the nineteenth century treated lunatics; but while Prospero's plan for reconciliation then continues serenely on its way towards the final forgiveness, Mangus's founders at precisely this point. Dov belabours Mel: the hubris of the imagination would stamp out even the sensual if it got the chance. If this is the result of imaginative power Tippett cannot accept it. Dov cannot be allowed his 'freedom', and neither can Mangus his illusions of philanthropy. To admit the favoured role of the creative artist is to admit the us/them dichotomy against which Tippett had been campaigning all his life. Mangus 'breaks his staff' and 'drowns' his book, and puts himself in the same position as his audience – who can find reconciliation only in music. Prospero reaches roughly the same conclusion, but by design, for having relinquished his art he deliberately hands over the responsibility for summoning up forgiveness to 'some heavenly music'. At this point occurs the sharpest divergence between play and opera. Prospero dismisses Ariel, the summoner of music. What is left? – to which the answer is love and forgiveness. But what happens to the creative artist who has forsworn his imaginative power? In Shakespeare's case the answer was, literally, nothing, because *The Tempest* was his last play. In Tippett's case, he certainly had not forsworn his imaginative power: he had to carry on. But having diagnosed his position as creative artist as extremely suspect, if not fraudulent, it is not surprising that his moment of love and forgiveness in *The Knot Garden* should be so short, so insecure, so 'timid'. To have denied it entirely would, on the other hand, have been tantamount to saying that his life's work had been worthless. With this question-mark still hanging over the Dov-Ariel projection, it is not surprising either that Tippett should have continued exploring the projection in the *Songs for Dov* he wrote immediately after completing *The Knot Garden*.

As a stage in Tippett's compositional career, *The Knot Garden* can be seen therefore as a kind of purgation, from which he could once again assess his broad artistic aims and draw strength to renew himself creatively. In other respects, it stands or falls on its quality as opera pure and simple – that is, on the quality of Tippett's answer to its very particular question: can music heal personal (and, by implication, collective) antagonisms? If Tippett's intellectual answer to this question is indecisive, his musical answer is nothing of the kind. *The Knot Garden* is the most tightly constructed of all his operas. It is cast in a language which cuts into the imagination with the precision of laser beams and the dazzle of a kaleidoscope; and it has its moments of release, carefully placed set-pieces which balance the short scenes and stabilize the structure as a whole. Admittedly, the crucial modulation into the final moment of forgiveness threatens to topple the structure and it is not easy to bring off in performance: an extraordinary collage of off-stage howls and wolf-whistles, on-stage declarations spoken by Mangus to the audience and a quotation from Tippett's own setting of 'Full fathom five', to which are added fragments from the earlier music of Faber, Dov and Mel (all this latter signifying that Mangus has consigned his role of omniscient, irreplaceable father-figure to the depths and has identified himself with the common anguish of his fellow men). But a sea-change occurs nonetheless. The texture clears to reveal the pearl at the centre, an exquisitely frosty tenderness of harmony which does indeed lift the music into realms where all is still, alert and receptive. This final moment of forgiveness may be very short, shorter even than the comparable moments in *The Marriage of Figaro* or *Così fan tutte*, and it is enclosed within an exceedingly ambivalent setting of 'Come unto these yellow sands' (another self-quotation, which is both an invitation to love and, through its ribald instrumental comments, a caricature of such an idea). But its musical expression is exact and deliberate (see Ex. 156). Nobody believes that the forgiveness will last long: all they have to be reminded of is that it is possible. This is Tippett's 'message' – applauded by the peal of bells, or what sounds like a peal of bells, which closes the opera.

Ex. 156   **The Knot Garden**

The most striking aspect of the structural layout of *The Knot Garden* (illustrated in the table on p.416) is Tippett's skill in marshalling dramatic material so that each act can lead to its main set-pieces. In Act I there are two, the aria for Denise and the septet, extended forms which together comprise about half the act as a whole. The aria makes its initial impact through its harmony, a reassuringly calm sonority which imposes its authority on the frantic pace of the opera thus far as if to say that *it* represents true humanity and that everything that has preceded it simply scratches the surface. The effect recalls Berg's technique in the last

ACT 1
1 *Prologue*: Mangus
   DISSOLVE
2 *First Exposition*
   a) Scena:
      Thea, Mangus, Flora, Faber
   b) Aria: Thea
   c) Aria: Faber
   d) Monologue: Mangus
   DISSOLVE
3 *Second Exposition*
   a) Scena and Song:
      Thea, Flora
   b) Scena and Song:
      Flora, Dov, Mel
4 *Ensembles*
   a) Tableau 1:
      Thea, Mangus, Flora, Dov,
      Mel
   b) Tableau 2: Mel, Thea, Dov
   c) Monologue: Dov
   d) Scena: Dov, Faber
   e) Tableau 3:
      Thea, Mel, Dov, Faber
5 *Finale*
   a) Scena: add Flora, Mangus
   b) Aria: Denise
   c) Septet

ACT 2
6 *Duets*
   a) Thea, Denise
   b) Denise, Faber
   c) Faber, Flora
   d) Faber, Thea
   e) Faber, Dov
   f) Dov, Mel
   g) Mel, Denise
7 *Trios*
   a) Denise, Mel, Dov
   b) Mel, Denise, Thea
   c) Thea, Flora, Faber
   DISSOLVE
8 *Songs*
   a) Scena and Lied: Flora
   b) Song: Dov

ACT 3
9 *Scena*
   Mangus, Thea, Denise
   DISSOLVE
10 *Charade 1*
   Duet: Thea, Denise
   DISSOLVE
11 *Charade 2*
   a) Duet:
      Denise, Mangus
   b) Scena:
      Mel, Dov
   c) Scena:
      Mangus, Thea
   DISSOLVE
12 *Charade 3*
   a) Scena:
      Mangus, Thea, Faber
   b) Aria: Thea
   DISSOLVE
13 *Charade 4*
   a) Collage
   b) Septet
   DISSOLVE
14 *Epilogue*
   Duet: Thea, Faber

interlude of *Wozzeck*. Denise's opening phrase cadences on the same chord (asterisk in Ex. 157) which resolves the confusion of the Act III collage. Here however it leads not to forgiveness but to perplexity. Denise may be

Ex. 157   The Knot Garden

capable of inspiring confidence, but she also insists on reliving her agonies of torture and thereby on revealing that the moral convictions they give her can find no cause to fasten on to other than rhetoric and, furthermore, that they can sometimes veer distressingly close to cliché: Denise's two brief flights into wordless coloratura show how prepared Tippett was to drain his music of substance in order to achieve dramatic verisimilitude (see Ex. 158) – and how deftly he avoided overstating his case, for they are both very short.

Ex. 158   The Knot Garden

The main impression left by the aria is of contemptuous, concentrated but aimless libido. Its formal metaphor is bipartite, each part containing a fourfold acceleration of tempo and increase in volume, thus creating that open-ended momentum that could drive on indefinitely were it not held in check by the short codetta with which Tippett wrenches the tempo into gear for the septet.

The blues septet is one of his most daring inventions. It fulfils its obvious purpose of providing a stabilizing response to Denise's aria expertly enough, not least through its regular, if not always audible pulse and its closed ABA form. But its effect – the cathartic release of collective emotion – is less easy to account for. You sing the blues to get out of the blues, and in the inter-war years there was a complementary practice by which you went down as low as possible, namely into the shameless desperation of boogie-woogie, in order to do so properly (thus creating the blues-boogie-blues scheme Tippett uses). Whether the blues really have an archetypal power and an immediate therapeutic value depends of course on what they sound like, and not simply on the traditional twelve-bar harmonic framework: it depends, that is, on the tension between the framework and the inventiveness and authenticity of the performer's attempts to escape from it. Tippett keeps strictly to the given structure and its chord sequence (I, four bars – IV and I, two bars each – V and I, two bars each) and he colours and elaborates it with all manner of harmonic enrichments, riffs, instrumental tropes, and piled up vocal melismas and overlaps. His outer sections retain their identity as blues particularly through a set of repeated chords on the piano at the end of each chorus (asterisk in Ex. 159), a feature which lights up the tonic, the pulse, the structure and the style. The central section needs no such point of reference, for it is unmistakably boogie-woogie. The closer music approaches its model the greater the danger that it will sound vulgar. Certainly, the music of Tippett's blues septet is in one sense deliberately unreal, for it cloaks the characters in a borrowed persona behind which they can pretend they are not wholly themselves. But even this would have sounded artificial had not Tippett's language already been profoundly influenced by jazz idioms (for example, the anticipatory rhythms and 'blue' notes in Ex. 159) and had he not already possessed that uncanny sympathy with the spirit of jazz which enabled him to absorb the blues into his own language quite unaffectedly. This is the secret of the septet's success. By the time it has reached its climax, all seven characters contributing to an extraordinary screaming claustrophobia, it has entirely transcended its adopted style and become simply a piece of music, highly charged music, but one whose stylistic label is of no account.

Ex. 159   **The Knot Garden**

It will be seen from Ex. 159 (which illustrates the last four bars of the third chorus and the beginning of the boogie-woogie) that Tippett has no need to quote blues tunes. His text however is almost entirely of quotations. He borrows freely from Bobby Blue Bland,[66] but he ensures that what he borrows is dramatically as well as stylistically pertinent. When, for example, Faber sings ''Cause I'm gonna play the high-class joints ...', he defies Thea to stop him so doing, while at the same time quoting direct from the lyrics of 'Tonk Honky Tonk'; and when Thea gets the message and decides that what is good for Faber is good for her too, she sings 'Well, I walk, talk – but all by myself', direct from 'Loan a Helping Hand'. In general, Tippett's technique draws from his experience with the spirituals of *A Child of Our Time*, when he discovered texts appropriate to any situation he wished to articulate. In blues texts he found equally universal sentiments. (It may be mentioned here that the somewhat alarming tendency of *The Knot Garden*'s libretto to revert to slang simply indicates Tippett's readiness to play tricks with words and risk bathos in order to make a complex point in contemporary terms. When Faber first encounters Dov he says, 'Who in hell are you?'. If the sentence is changed to read 'Who are you in hell?' the meaning is clear but the effect lost.)

The earlier part of the act prepares for these two set-pieces largely by contrasting with them: they are sustained and static, whereas it is volatile and hyperactive. It contains a profusion of short motifs and gestures that initially give the impression of being invented piecemeal in order to capture the rapidly changing thoughts and situations of the text, but which are subsequently revealed as essential material to be deployed to make musical and dramatic points across the opera as a whole. Two of the most important of them are presented in Mangus's prologue. Here he inspects the tools of his trade, as it were, and having satisfied himself that they are in working order puts them aside for future use. The 'tempest' music, at one extreme of his therapy, shows that he can engineer the necessary psychological upheaval; the 'magic island' music, at the other, that he can command a paradise, the hum of 'a thousand twangling instruments' (see Ex. 129). The 'tempest' music is of particular interest since it is based on a twelve-note motif (see Ex. 136(iv)), or, in other words, on the compositional principle Tippett had previously shown every sign of holding in contempt. The motif is however only one of many in the opera, and as such is simply an instance of how he will plunder from any- and everywhere in the search for sounds and techniques that will meet his immediate compositional needs. Its initial conception owed nothing to twelve-note methods and it was only afterwards that he saw what it consisted of and how it might be used. If the motif sounds like something being torn apart and mangled into bits, that no doubt is what Tippett meant it to sound like. And if in the process he implies a correlation between the twelve-note principle and pain, that no doubt is also what he intended.

The two motifs mentioned above may be considered part of the machinery of the opera; but Mangus is a person as well as a manipulator and the prologue is accordingly a character sketch as well as a dramatic hypothesis. Initially, Mangus's estimate of himself is confidently self-deprecating. He 'o-ho-hos' on his assumed name like one of the pirates in *Treasure Island* – to a phrase which, at the opera's denouement, will return to taunt him mercilessly (Ex. 160). Thea is introduced with a motif on horns and lower strings suggestive of the nourishment she draws from the

self-absorption of her garden (Ex 161(i)). This motif can however turn
vicious and self-righteous (ii); it can generate a sense of purpose (iii); it can
even be associated with the well-springs of musical creation (iv).

Ex. 160   The Knot Garden

Ex. 161   The Knot Garden

All the characters are given motifs of this type, material malleable and
eloquent enough to be metamorphosed or added to as the situations
demand, yet not so dominant as to pre-empt the structural function of the
main set-pieces. Sometimes Tippett fashions material of this kind into mini
set-pieces. The 'arias' of Thea and Faber (2b and c in the table) are cases in
point. They are so concentrated that their status as points of structural
articulation is hardly evident. Yet as the first fully-developed musical
statements in the opera, their function closely corresponds with that of
traditional arias. Thea and Faber are shown as fiercely antagonistic
towards one another, able to draw on reserves of resentment far deeper
than their characteristic motifs would suggest. Their music is of a

suppressed violence new in Tippett (see Ex. 137(ii)). The arias are both in closed ternary forms and each concludes with its own codetta. Mangus's monologue (2d in the table) begins with a recapitulation of Thea's codetta, so the 'first exposition', that of the marital drama, is neatly rounded off before the remaining characters are introduced in the 'second exposition'.

Flora, Dov and Mel, for separate reasons, all shrink from reality and their expository statements are songs, as opposed to arias (songs commonly function in opera as intrusions or escapes from the 'real' world and 'real' music of the opera proper). Flora's song employs the baby talk of the nursery. At first she idly hums to herself as she wonders which flower to pick from Thea's garden; then she decides on a familar tactic: 'Eeeny, meeny, miney mo, Catch a nigger by his toe ...' – which seems merely a touch of local colour, until it is realised that had her reverie not been cut short at that point by the real black man and his white lover, her final line would have been, 'let him go'. Before Dov and Mel sing a word therefore, Tippett has already hinted at the precariousness of their relationship – and not by this verbal conceit alone, for the 'fish-like' Mel-Caliban is trying to elude the attentions of Dov, costumed in Ariel's first transformation as a sea-nymph. Musically, Tippett's *coup de théâtre* is accompanied by a rowdy blues fragment, with irregular tempo (5/2) and harmony (I,V,I,IV), and overlaid with figures on electric guitar and clarinet representing the pursuit of Mel by Dov. Like much of the Act I music, it finds its proper place in Act II, where it becomes the chorus of a fast blues number. Here, it serves principally as a stunning mechanism, or as a means by which the emotional temperature of the opera can be abruptly dropped to the level of plain speech. After an astonished silence, Dov and Mel recite the dialogue of Tweedledum and Tweedledee: 'If you think we're waxworks, you ought to pay, you know.' Flora automatically contributes to the make-believe and then gets annoyed with herself for doing so, whereupon Dov and Mel tactfully explain themselves – and sing their song, for which the preceding events can now be seen as a nicely judged rationale (Ex. 162).

Ex. 162   **The Knot Garden**

The arrival on the scene of Thea with her tray of cocktails puts a halt to the merrriment. The music of 'tableau 1' sounds partly like clinking glasses but what it really summons up is a kind of frozen terror, that chilling of the blood and singing in the ears which seizes the body when some emotional calamity is imminent (see Ex. 163(i)). It is the beginning of a sequence of events by which music *is* the drama: Tippett uses the resources of instrumental music to express what cannot be expressed vocally. By these means he creates a kind of vacuum, which will be filled by the vocal music of the aria and septet. The tableaux seem to represent Thea's bewitching of Mel and his attraction to her but they are best understood as the reaction of Dov to the loss of Mel. In the first tableau he senses it. In the second it happens, and Dov is overtaken by a wild desperation which eventually breaks out into howls of anguish – real howls, although he tries to disguise them by prefacing his 'ows' with the 'bow-wows' of the watch-dogs in Ariel's 'Come unto these yellow sands'. The instrumental music that accompanies his howls would sound like a caricature of the crudest examples of 1950s serialism did it not paint so realistic a picture of the disintegration of his emotional universe. The third tableau depicts the pounding of his heart and his 'strange sobbing cry' (the description in a draft libretto) as he watches Mel and Thea return (Ex. 163(ii)). The section is then overtaken by the hysterical cries of Flora as she announces the arrival of Denise; but the tableaux nevertheless remain at the core of the act and the most precise evidence of Tippett's willingness, in *The Knot Garden*, to strip away decorum and rely on the immediacy of naked musical metaphor.

Ex. 163   **The Knot Garden**

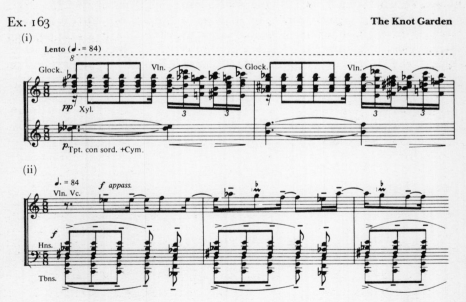

The majority of the Act II duets are distended echoes of music in Act I, a kind of black recapitulation which instead of offering resolution announces that the initial exposition of conflict was understated and the situation far worse than had been proposed. They sound hard, frantic and somewhat chaotic. In fact they are carefully ordered to increase and then decrease in savagery and thus culminate in the duet for Denise and Mel, which is one of the most tender and consoling pieces of music Tippett has written. The duet which makes this possible is that between Dov and Mel. It retains the breathless pace, but since it is a stylized song and dance number in fast blues tempo with a symmetrical scheme of choruses and verses it lays a steadying hand on the music thus far and enables the poignancy of the human situation (Mel's jilting of Dov) to break through despite the tortured exterior: the compensating warmth of the Denise/Mel duet thus emerges as an emotional necessity. The chorus sections of the blues duet use the music of Dov and Mel's entrance in Act I, now with vocal parts added: 'One day we meet together, brother, One day we move apart.'[67] (It is the music which provides two ritornello sections in *Songs for Dov*.) The verse sections retain traditional blues harmony, but so caricatured and distorted by Tippett's frenetic instrumentation that it is barely recognizable as such. The harmony of the Denise/Mel duet, on the other hand, makes an immediate effect (see Ex. 132(ii)). It offers a security so welcome at this point that all the vituperation of the previous scenes seems to drop into it out of sheer exhaustion. Once nerves have been calmed, its protective grip relaxes and the music gradually opens out to reveal a very finely voiced consonance, four points of light picked out like a constellation in the night sky. This is when Mel begins to feel the sound of the protest song 'We shall overcome' stirring inside him (cellos in bar 3 of Ex. 164). Tippett structures this scene like an Ivesian chorale prelude on a hymn tune. The opening section is based on an inverted variant of the protest song, which eventually takes shape so unobtrusively that it is recognized only at the last moment or, in *The Knot Garden*, when Mel actually sings the line, 'Deep in my heart'.

Ex. 164   **The Knot Garden**

Despite its beauty this duet is nevertheless not long enough to ease the oppressive atmosphere nor, therefore, to disturb the design of the act as a whole, which is strong and simple: the 'duets' (followed, when the labyrinth goes into reverse, by miniature 'trios') and the 'songs' (which in effect may be reduced to the song of Dov, the main set-piece of the act). Together they form a unit of tension and release.

The most obviously affecting moment in *The Knot Garden* is when Tippett quotes Schubert's 'Die liebe Farbe'. It arouses complex emotions – relief at encountering something familiar, pleasure at the utmost delicacy with which he does so, and satisfaction with the dramatic appropriateness of the quotation. In Ex. 165, Dov, while pondering the German Flora has just sung, reacts as a composer would, by instinctively appropriating Schubert's original and giving it a sharper relevance – here, by means of an exquisitely acid gloss on the piano. In the process he also effects a transition to the music of his own song.

Ex. 165   The Knot Garden

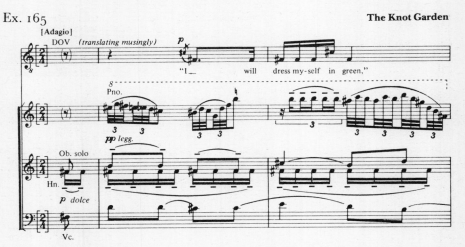

Since Dov's song is a genuine song, formalized as such with melody, accompaniment and strophic shape, it rapidly detaches itself from the stage situation and for a while converts the opera into a concert. This is the stratagem by which Tippett intensifies the impact of the opera. When Mel dismisses Dov's performance as artifice, the shock is extreme and the return to 'reality' only too convincing, precisely because the romantic fantasy conjured up by the song had become so desirable and the rapture of young love so nearly true. The equation set up is finely balanced. The musical reflection of it is a characteristically peppery sweetness – the edgy sounds of an electric guitar with double-basses, and the glowing sounds of clarinets and vibraphone, accompanying a voice part compounded of stuttering *trilli* and *appoggiature*, and fluid melismas (see Ex. 166). By the climax of the song the orchestra has been joined by Tippett's magical apparatus of harp, piano and bells and the music reaches a lyric intensity recalling that of *The Midsummer Marriage*.

The table on p.416 suggests that Act III has a relatively straightforward four-part structure, each charade initiating its consequence (or set-piece) and the consequences themselves forming a sequence which culminates in

Ex. 166   **The Knot Garden**

the final septet. The dramatic content of this act is however too complex to
be condensed so that it makes automatic sense in musical terms, as was the
case in the two previous acts. Here, the dramatic content influences the
structure much more strongly, with the result that the structure does not
fall into place so readily. The consequences do not exhibit that progressive
increase in length and stability which the table might imply and neither do
the charades make room for such a possibility. They, in fact, are patterned
symmetrically, the first and fourth framing the two inner and much shorter
charades; and only one of the consequences, the aria for Thea, is
comparable in emphasis with the set-pieces in the previous acts, the
remaining three making, at least in proportional terms, much less emphatic
statements. All this may be said to place a high premium on the listener's
(and the performers') ability to discriminate qualitatively between two
types of music: the vivid but essentially illustrative music of the charades,
which carry the main interpretative challenge of the opera, and the richer,
more 'musical' music of the set-pieces, which, because they are relatively

short or unsettled in character, are in danger of being overshadowed by the charades.

That Tippett should have been prepared to advance the claims of the illustrative as against the 'musical' is not perhaps surprising in an opera whose denouement will cast doubt on no less a subject than the art of music itself. What is at issue however is whether Tippett's set-pieces serve their structural and expressive functions on the strength of their musical quality alone, however fleeting that might be. This is not easy to answer, for the convoluted expression of the first two of them militates against any quality they might have as points of clarification or release. Yet if the final septet (Ex. 156) sounds as moving as has been suggested, then the other set-pieces, and especially Thea's aria, the one immediately preceding it, must have established the context in which its quality could be responded to. This aria may accordingly be seen as the cornerstone of the act. The remarkable thing about it is its atmosphere – one of rapt serenity, conjuring up a picture of Thea floating in an experience so indescribably beautiful that it would be sacrilege even to acknowledge it. It is hardly the atmosphere upon which a composer would normally load the crucial structural weight of an opera; but it is entirely in accord with Tippett's creative temperament, and the premises of *The Knot Garden,* that he should attempt to bring off this hazardous technical feat. The sounds linger in the imagination long after their short life is over (see Ex. 167).

Ex. 167   **The Knot Garden**

(Ex. 167 cont.)

Tippett's charades' music is unashamedly pictorial. The short motifs from which it is constructed make an unusually direct connection between sound and action. It is designed, perhaps, to compensate for complexity of meaning by clarity of exegesis. Example 168, from the second charade, illustrates Tippett's self-discipline in this respect. He curbs his natural instinct to develop material (though not his instinct to find analogies, for all the material has been heard before) and fashions his language into a kind of glossary of expressive effects. The first two bars represent Caliban stealing up on the sleeping Miranda while the magical sounds of the island hover overhead, the next two bars him pouncing on her, and the final two bars his thrusts, her terrified cries and the impotent alarm signals of Ariel.

Ex. 168   **The Knot Garden**

As has been suggested, the most surprising single feature of *The Knot Garden* is the twelve-note motif at the very beginning. It would be tempting to dismiss Tippett's recourse to serial methods as opportunistic or at best as a temporary expedient, for the motif's subsequent transformations are, in serial terms, primitive and Tippett has not returned to the serial idea since. All this is true. But if his methods are judged by their aural results, then such observations become irrelevant. The most important function of the motif is to create the nightmarish atmosphere of Act II and with it the impression of an ineluctable, malevolent force against which resistance is useless. Examination of the music at the beginning of the act (Ex. 169)

Ex. 169   **The Knot Garden**

suggests that Tippett can escape from the strait-jacket of his series only by parting company with it altogether – an expressive effect that is exactly what his 'tempest' music conveys. It evokes the feeling of being trapped in the workings of some latter-day circle of hell (bracket *a*), where you are kicked repeatedly and with cold savagery (*b*), until, screaming (*c*), you are tossed into another circle (*d*) hardly less grim for being peopled with human beings. The meaning of Tippett's metaphor is so unequivocal that when it returns to break up one duet and initiate the next, the listener's reaction can only be to submit and wait for its brute strength to project him where it will.

The remaining transformations of the motif could be described in similar terms: when the labyrinth goes into reverse there is a grinding clatter, effected by the superposition of the retrograde (on xylophone) on the basic series (piano). All transformations occur at 'tempestuous' moments and all sound equally graphic: Dov's howlings, Denise's descriptions of torture, the withering of the Act II rose-garden, the imaginary tempest conjured up by Mangus for his charades' audience, and Caliban's attempted rape of Miranda.

While it would be correct to say that these transformations are transformations of merely one motif in *The Knot Garden*, which is not therefore a basic series in the Schoenbergian sense, the fact remains that the motif exerts a stronger influence on the opera than any other. This can be seen on a surface level (the four-note cluster at the centre of the motif and the three-note head motif appearing in melodic and harmonic forms at various points), on a more subtle level (the occasional use of heterophony – notably in the way Tippett provides instrumental support for his vocal lines – which reflects his attempt to derive appropriate 'harmony' from an essentially linear and non-harmonic source by accompanying a line with its simultaneous embellishment) and on a decisive structural level, that of tonality. The first note of the motif is B. The other notes seem to grow out of it – and then to reassert it, for the last note in the series is its dominant. In all its transformations the motif remains untransposed (except for its later appearances between the Act II duets), which is another way of underlining the correlation between 'tempestuous' emotions and B. Clearly the note and its associated tonality is of central importance and it is significant that the main points of structural articulation, the set-pieces, are in either B or in very closely related tonalities: Denise's aria begins in a kind of B major, the blues septet is in E, the Schubert quotation in its original key of B minor, Dov's song in F sharp, the first two set-pieces of Act III also in a kind of F sharp, and Thea's aria homes in on B. The tonality of the final septet is difficult to isolate but the epilogue emphatically reaches a vibrant B major. Of course these tonalities do not have the stability of triadic tonality. They offer various ways of approaching a tonality, ranging from one so twisted and distorted that it is hardly audible to one of brilliant clarity. *The Knot Garden*, like *The Midsummer Marriage*, can be seen therefore as a search within a tonality or, in other words, as a familiar Tippettian metaphor of the psyche: the light is contained within the shadow and the seeds of hope present within even the darkest moments of despair. Why Tippett should have used the tonality of B to define the particular metaphor of *The Knot Garden* may be found in the B minor of Schubert's 'Die liebe Farbe'. This song is one of very many works using B minor as an archetypal expression of resignation and despair – the Kyrie of the B minor Mass, Mozart's B minor Adagio for piano, the Unfinished Symphony, Tchaikovsky's 'Pathétique'. Tippett has described B minor as a black tonality, 'the lowest of the low', and given his characteristic use of tonality as expressive colour it was perhaps inevitable that he should have 'heard' *The Knot Garden* in these tonal terms. Given his previous use of B major to represent the 'magic kiss' of *The Midsummer Marriage*, it was perhaps also inevitable that *The Knot Garden* should end with the glowing excitement of B major.

Songs for Dov

This song cycle is a parable about how the creative artist, and by inference Tippett himself, contrives to live with the contradictions of his vocation. There can be no answer to the paradox expressed in *The Knot Garden*. If the imaginative power which makes a creative artist what he is is also capable of corrupting his most humanitarian instincts, then he can only take note of the fact and try to preserve some balance between the two. The realistic question is to what ends, exactly, should his talents be directed? The answer, according to *Songs for Dov*, depends on his age. In youth (Song 1, which is straight from *The Knot Garden*), he should follow his proper inclinations towards romantic idealism; later (Song 2), he should set out on a journey of exploration so that his art may have a basis in experience; in full maturity (Song 3), the artist should attempt to sustain the 'pastoral' – a word evoking a host of ideas from the romantic 'fallacy' to the eternity of the human soul – while acknowledging that unless he also draws from the rough vitality of contemporary urban culture he will lapse into fantasy. *Songs for Dov* thus ends with a considered statement of artistic aims, the 'urban' (the boogie-woogie from *The Knot Garden*) set against the 'pastoral'.

The context in which these aims are placed is narrative. The situations and text of the final song are borrowed or derived from Pasternak's *Doctor Zhivago*, which serves to introduce Russia into Dov's itinerary and show that his imagined journey round the world (or, in other words, his account of rounded experience) has now reached the point from which it can return to the rather nebulous Europe/America it started from. Tippett's borrowings have another and more important purpose, however, which is the characteristic one of articulating a philosophy in terms of a gloss on the philosophy of someone else. What particularly moved him in *Doctor Zhivago* were, it seems, the love-affair between Zhivago and Lara, which epitomized the beauty, the necessity and the transience of love, and Zhivago's poetic ideals, which might have been the ideals Tippett would have had to adopt himself had he been in Pasternak's position, and which were made especially poignant by Zhivago's failure to live up to them. In his posthumous papers were found some notes, including the following:

'... cities are the only source of inspiration for a truly modern, contemporary art ... The living language of our time is urban.'[68] But with the possible exception, as Pasternak pointedly remarked, of 'Hamlet', a poem in which the poet asks to be released from the role he is expected to play and which concludes with the Russian proverb, 'To live your life is not as easy as to cross a field', Zhivago's posthumous poetry contained no evidence of this 'living language'. His poems are all love lyrics or 'pastorals': when it came to the point, and he wrote real poetry rather than theorized about it, Zhivago found that his ideals had changed. In 'The Earth'[69] he explained why. Tippett sets part of this poem in the climactic section of *Songs for Dov*:

> Then why does the horizon weep in mist
> And the dung smell bitter?
> Surely it is my calling
> To see that the distances do not lose heart
> And that beyond the limits of the town
> The earth should not feel lonely?

As if to assure Pasternak that he was right in both precept and practice, Tippett acknowledges the claims of the 'urban' as well as the 'pastoral'. He twice quotes the line 'The living language of our time is urban' and he twice introduces the boogie-woogie. But he is aware of the ambivalence of his position. Boogie-woogie, after all, is outdated, and in *Songs for Dov*, it is prefaced by the Russian proverb – a conjunction which in this context reads like an apologia for its somewhat forced abandon or even for Tippett's presumption in making any comment at all on the work of the novelist whose fate was so appalling. Perhaps, in the end, his calling really is, like Pasternak's, to ensure that the 'distances do not lose heart'.

The uncertainty within Tippett's 'conclusions' is the uncertainty an artist must live with. It is significant that Tippett no longer tries to integrate the 'urban' and the 'pastoral', as he had done (in the Double Concerto, for example), nor does he bend one to the condition of the other. He emphasizes their independence, both of style and of behaviour. The form of the climactic section of *Songs for Dov* is ABAC. The boogie-woogie defies alteration and is repeated literally – perhaps an index of the timeless claims of its animal abandon (it seems to say, What the hell, let's go out and have some *fun*), as well as of the emotional need to be assured that its invitation was not a tease. The 'pastoral' begins (B) with delicate lyricism and then breaks into a cry of yearning (C, see Ex. 170) so heart-rending[70] that it would have cancelled out the boogie-woogie altogether had Tippett not punctuated it with the same ironic note of self-deprecation (the line, 'Sure, baby', from *The Knot Garden*) that had punctuated the boogie. The final bars are therefore a shrug of the shoulders. But the stark juxtapositionings cannot be forgotten. The listener is left to decide for himself whether they can or should be fused into one image, or whether they should remain suspended in a precarious balance. Since most of the cycle is constructed by similar juxtapositionings of material, much of which is, like

Ex. 170   **Songs for Dov**

the boogie, 'given' or quoted, Tippett himself leaves little doubt that he intended the latter effect – an image, maybe, of that hoped-for society whose emblem would be the water-carrier balancing both pitchers and spilling nothing from either.

The uncertainties of *Songs for Dov* are integral to the work, running through all the songs to a greater or lesser extent: the entrancing lyricism of the first is rejected, as in *The Knot Garden*, and in the second Dov continually hesitates to respond to allurements which find so resonant an echo in his affections. But far from representing a failure of nerve, these uncertainties are cause for celebration. The tone of the work suggests that Tippett wrote it eagerly, quickly and confidently (though in fact it required prolonged effort), and that he rejoiced in uncertainty because it could be equated with lack of dogmatism or with a view of the world in which nothing would be excluded and everything could find its place.

It is in this light that the numerous quotations in *Songs for Dov* can best be approached, though in keeping with the undogmatic spirit of the work and with Tippett's conception of the artist as one who steals ideas from wherever he can find them, they are not used in a particularly consistent way. Some flow naturally out of Dov's experiences in *The Knot Garden* (Song 1, the boogie-woogie) and from his Ariel-like capacity to feel without experiencing (passages from Thea's aria, which evoke the depth of Zhivago's love for Lara). Others are more playful, little *trouvailles* which help colour the narrative (Wagner's Dutchman motif which contributes to the 'travelling' railroad refrain of Song 2, and the few bars of Pimen's music from Mussorgsky's *Boris Godunov* which accompany the imagined scene in Song 3 when Zhivago writes about his poetic ideals). The most interesting quotations are those in Song 2; for they have a strongly autobiographical flavour. This song may be described as an interlude between the fantasy of Song 1 and the inescapable uncertainties of Song 3, an exploratory romance in which Dov heeds the calls of the 'warm south' and the 'golden Californian west' of Song 1 and journeys through three stages of his emotional and creative life in pursuit of them. The first stanza opens with quotations from the setting of Mignon's song 'Kennst du das Land' ('Do you know the land where the lemon bushes flower?') by Beethoven – not Schubert, Schumann or Wolf, but Beethoven, Tippett's first and only true master. Tippett starts by transferring Beethoven's refrain ('There, there is where I want to go with you, my love') from voice to solo trumpet, a marvellously exhilarating sound which, if this is how Tippett 'heard' Beethoven, makes it easy to understand why he was so excited by him. In the second stanza the young composer has outgrown acts of reverence and found his own style; but he is still not entirely free from the influence of the master for the quotation here, from 'Come unto these yellow sands' from *Songs for Ariel*, is on its return at the end of the stanza slightly distorted by an echo of the notes and the sound (solo trumpet) of the Beethoven setting. The quotation in the third stanza is pure Tippett (Paris's aria from *King Priam*, 'Carried on the wind of love, if I carry you away [Helen, who will escape the avenging war?]') and is obviously meant to indicate that Dov has now become his own master – though the Beethovenian trumpet which takes the vocal line suggests that this can never be entirely so. He is, however, as mature as he is likely to be and this acounts for the fact that the link between Songs 2 and 3 is the 'dissolve' from *The Knot Garden* and not the chorus section (with 'howls' added) from the blues duet which had preceded the first two songs. Dov has become a grown man and can put away his youthful exhibitions of self-pity.

The quotations in this song thus chart the course of a creative life. This is not the only point of the song, however. It also reveals something of an artist's emotional experiences and of the harsh conclusion he must draw from them. His whole being (see Ex. 171) responds to the marvellous mixture of the sensual and the imaginative he encounters on his journey – to the invitations of a Mignon (the 'boy-girl'), an Ariel (the 'girl-boy'), the Sirens, to Goethe, Shakespeare, Homer. But each time he hesitates and is driven elsewhere by a force stronger than himself. When he reaches the Sirens he realises that if he succumbs to their bewitching song and allows himself (like Paris) to be swept away by the delights of love, he will forfeit his creative power and be reduced to a heap of bones on an inaccessible island. So he must forswear the sensual. But he can feel it, and if he steals the Sirens' song, he can re-create it.

Ex. 171   **Songs for Dov**

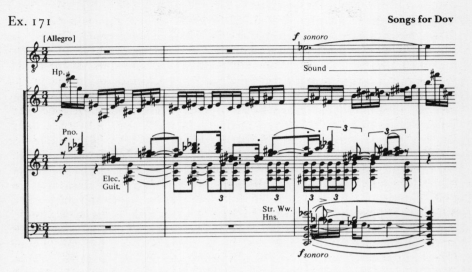

Whereas a significant number of major works appeared in the wake of each of Tippett's first two operas, *Songs for Dov* is the single important product of *The Knot Garden* – an index of how conclusive his musical statements have been since *The Vision of Saint Augustine* and of how he has refused in the later part of his life to allow commissions to divert the main course of his creative development. As for unimportant products, there are two. The *Severn Bridge Variations*, a composite work consisting of six variations on the Welsh melody 'Braint' by three Welsh and three English composers (see p.504), was commissioned to celebrate the first anniversary of the BBC Training Orchestra in Bristol (to Tippett, a sympathetic idea) and the opening of the road link between south Wales and England (less so). Tippett sets the lines of the melody one by one in the heterophonic style he was to use in *The Knot Garden* and introduces them with two somewhat perfunctory gestures, the second of which takes over as a coda. This is, as it were, a draft version of the 'magic island' music from the opera, and it serves to end the work on a questioning note – as if to say that what the bridge will offer is of no particular account. 'Braint' is hardly recognizable as the work of its composer.

This cannot be said of the other work contemporary with *The Knot Garden*, *The Shires Suite* for orchestra and chorus. In the first of its two orchestral interludes there are distinct echoes of Symphony No. 2, and in the second direct quotations from the blues duet and the 'dissolve' sections of the opera. What makes the work so unexpected a contemporary of *The Knot Garden* are its breezy high spirits and the exceedingly roisterous behaviour at the centre of it – hunting and drinking canons in which the chorus tally-ho through loud-hailers, pop their cheeks, drop trays of cutlery and laugh. The more serious moments, the interludes and the mysteriously beautiful epilogue, do not in truth play an especially necessary role in this scheme of things and the work lacks focus. But it is enjoyable and entertaining, a genuine successor to the *Suite for the Birthday of Prince Charles*. Like that work, its material is borrowed. Each of its five movements is based on canons, a nice symbol of the unanimity aspired to in amateur music-making: in the first, headed Prologue, 'Soomer is i-coomen in'; in Interlude I, 'The Silver Swan';[71] in the third movement (a 'Cantata' of three canons, each introduced by one of Tippett's own, 'Come let us sing a song in canon'), the hunting canon attributed to Byrd, 'Hey ho, to the greenwood', Purcell's drinking catch, 'Fie, nay prithee John' and a canon by Alexander Goehr, 'The sword sung on the barren heath' given to Tippett on his sixtieth birthday;[72] in Interlude 2, the round 'Great Tom is cast'; and in the Epilogue, 'Non nobis Domine', attributed to Byrd. It will be seen from the above that Tippett planned the work as a symmetric arch, a procedure that enabled him to compose it piecemeal, returning to it from time to time over a period of five years without fear of disturbing its basic structure. What the above does not make clear is that knowing of the remarkable accomplishments of the members of the Leicestershire Schools Senior Orchestra (for whom the work was written) Tippett gave special prominence to the orchestral part, which is hardly less taxing than his music for professional orchestras. The chorus part does not ask of young voices what they cannot give and is correspondingly easier – though it is still challenging (see Ex. 172).

Ex. 172   **The Shires Suite**

Symphony No. 3

If the theme of *The Knot Garden* is the paradox in the artistic temperament, that of *Songs for Dov* the paradox in artistic intention, the theme of Tippett's Symphony No. 3 is the paradox in artistic value. By the time he came to write this work Tippett had ceased to believe that 'humanist art could achieve that moral power over and within humanity which religious art, and, indeed, traditional religion itself had failed to engender'.[73] The crimes committed in the twentieth century are of such magnitude that whatever

credence was placed by previous centuries on the capacity of art to improve
man's nature or situation, now it is no longer possible to credit it with
anything of the sort, nor gloss over the fact that brutality is an inescapable
component of the human condition. What value can one assign to art when
someone capable of responding to, for example, Goethe is also capable of
mass murder?[74] Yet, and here is the paradox, Tippett must believe that art
has some value and some moral power, or at least that if art is illusion it is a
necessary illusion. To believe otherwise would be to deny his own
humanity, and with it that absolute compulsion to renew the imaginative
and the sensual without which man would cease to be man, and the artist
cease to be an artist. His mandate therefore is still to nourish 'imagination
and desire' (the Blakeian expression Tippett is fond of using,[75] and which
may be regarded as synonymous with the 'pastoral'). But unless his art is
to be gratuitous or irrelevant, he must also acknowledge the brutal context
in which imagination and desire have to be upheld – a context,
furthermore, which cannot lead to integration, since the polarities are
obviously irreconcilable. It can only be of acceptance. And what is
accepted is that while art cannot make man good it might perhaps prevent
him from getting worse. The Symphony concludes with a metaphor of such
acceptance, brutal brass chords answered by tender and, pointedly, more
sustained string chords (Ex. 173).

Ex. 173   **Symphony No. 3**

By attempting to pit 'reality' against 'art' in this way, Tippett draws the
sting from his paradox. He cannot however remove it altogether. The
brutality of his brass chords is an imagined brutality and a work of art is
not to be charmed away by the persuasiveness of its metaphors. The
paradox remains to stare its beholder in the face and remind him that
however laudable his social awareness, what is left is simply the eternal
question of whether art is rhetoric or whether it is autonomous, whether it
can inspire a communion of like-minded souls or whether, as Stravinsky
wrote, it is an 'ontological reality'.[76] 'How is one to explain the "meaning"

of a monument that was produced to satisfy the concerns of one age, survives to meet the different needs of a later age, and yet through it all remains in some sense the same work?[77] How, for example, is one to explain the lasting appeal of Beethoven's Ninth Symphony when its utopian aspirations have been discredited by subsequent history? How, that is, can Tippett reconcile his profound belief in the Stravinskian aesthetic with his equally profound belief that art must speak to its time? It is typical of him that he should ask such questions, and typical also that he should stare back at them and propose an answer. Art is both: it is autonomous and rhetorical. Furthermore, the two depend on each other. In his Symphony No.3, the largest, most ambitious and most heroic of all his symphonies, Tippett uses Beethoven to dramatize this idea. He expresses his love for his master by creating a new child of the Beethovenian symphonic tradition, and he criticizes him, by turning the precepts of the most rhetorical product of that tradition, the Ninth Symphony, upside down. Beethoven's ecstatic vision of a world in which all men will be brothers is confronted with the sober facts of what men actually are and of how their supposed brotherhood has manifested itself. Yet Tippett cannot leave matters there. He must affirm his own belief, deeply ironical though it may be, that, despite everything, Beethoven's ideals remain vital and absolute. What has changed is the context and manner in which they are voiced. Tippett's Symphony No.3 is the paragon and paradigm of his second period.

In design, then, the Symphony is one massive antithesis: a structure in two parts, the first abstract and instrumental, the second dramatic and vocal (a solo soprano), reflecting oppositions between music as unremitting intellectual argument and music as human expression, between disinterested logic and passionate response, cause and effect, fact and message. The simple, almost primitive clarity of this design operates on various subsidiary levels. Thus, Part 1 is itself in two parts, a cumulative, driving allegro followed by a geometric, passive lento, the one impelled by abrupt contrasts between compressed and released energy, the other set in position by spacious contrasts between still, high music and fluid, low music. In describing Part 1 of the Symphony, Tippett has used images of sights and sounds rather than of human feelings (for the allegro, 'the pull and thrust of a jet engine', for the lento, 'the music of a wind-less night sky' and 'the song of the ocean currents'[78]). It does indeed have the quality of a natural phenomenon, impervious to everything save the inexorable cycle of the elements which carve it down to bare essentials, leaving only the framework behind. The bipartite structure of Part 2 is less rigorous, more diverse, human feelings now the direct source of its warmer contours. It consists of a brief scherzo acting as an anacrusis to the extended vocal finale, a sequence of three blues leading to what Tippett has described as a dramatic scena.[79]

The simplicity of Tippett's basic design suggests that he conceived it in an instant. But in fact it evolved slowly over a period of years and did not take its final shape until composition had already begun. Tippett has revealed how the germinal idea behind the Symphony occurred to him during a performance of Boulez's Piano Sonata No. 2 at the 1965 Edinburgh Festival. He was listening in his characteristically piratical way, reflecting that on this occasion he could not appropriate any compositional stimulus from such apparently aimless or 'motionless' music, unless, and this was the point, it could be used in a dialectic of strong contrasts. 'This suddenly clicked and I knew that a symphonic work had begun.'[80] What had happened was not that he had been influenced by Boulez, but that Boulez had sparked off a train of thought which led to the sudden solution of a problem he had been pondering ever since he had completed his Symphony No. 2 of eight years earlier: namely, how to write a modern symphony with the dynamic spirit but not the outdated letter of Beethoven. Tippett had discovered a way of rethinking the archetypal dualities of the Beethovenian prototype in accordance with the dictates of his own recent music. He had replaced the 'passionate and lyrical' (see p.88) with what he called 'arrest and movement',[81] 'arrest' signifying not 'motionless' but compression, with consequent 'movement' or release, the two terms postulating a form consisting of increasingly more extended sections of such 'arrest and movement'. Ironically, this new approach to the sonata-allegro was similar to the Sibelian approach Tippett had experimented with in his unpublished Symphony in B flat and then discarded in favour of the traditional Beethovenian sonata-allegro. In that earlier symphony neither the compositional discipline involved nor the structural idea itself were particularly suited to Tippett's style at the time. The key element in the structural idea, that of a form which could develop organically from the kinetic energy in its material, is however perfectly suited to his second period style and it influenced the design of the new symphony as a whole, as well as that of its opening allegro. Parts 1 and 2 follow the sequence of arrest and movement, as do their component sections. The blues and breaks of the finale are also a kind of arrest and movement.

From the start Tippett had imagined his finale as a set of blues. There were several reasons for this, not the least being that he loved the blues anyway (in particular, Bessie Smith's 1925 recording of the *St Louis Blues*, which he played over and over again in the early 1930s, significantly, the period of composition of the Symphony in B flat). He had also, in *The Knot Garden*, proved that he could write blues himself. Tippett has provided two further reasons: the negative one that he wanted to avoid a finale in which 'you just pile things on' and create 'Shostakovich bombast'[82] (a judgement on Shostakovich he was later to repudiate), and the more positive one that he had always regarded blues as an archetypal form to be compared with Purcellian ground basses[83] – in which case his finale would have been a kind of passacaglia. But there were other and perhaps more important reasons. At a stage in his career when he was more concerned than ever before that his music should communicate on an overtly human level, blues offered a transparently and almost defiantly human music, vitally necessary after the 'pure' music of Part 1 of the Symphony. And what had sanctioned the use of 'impure' music was the crucial distinction he had formulated between 'historical' and 'notional' archetypes (see p.351). Armed with this latter conception he could see how Mahler, for example, had redefined the term symphony not only by dividing it into large-scale parts but also by grafting apparently foreign elements onto it – and how, therefore, the blues could legitimately find their place in his own Symphony.

At first Tippett thought his blues would be instrumental. He then realised that blues are essentially vocal and that he was therefore fully committed to the 'notional' archetype of the symphony, with its allied problems of what words should be sung and how the individual blues should be organized. Beethoven's Ninth Symphony, the progenitor of the 'notional' archetype, did not help him at this point since Beethoven, as Tippett then saw it, had a ready-made text which automatically provided a solution to the formal problem. What did help him was a chance hearing of a radio discussion about Mahler's *Das Lied von der Erde*. Tippett not only adapted Mahler's technique of organizing songs to correspond with the movements of a symphony; he also drew from Mahler's conceptual idea. In a 'Personal Synopsis' of the Symphony of August 1970, Tippett wrote that the 'Song of the Earth' was to become a 'Song of the Body', 'where "Body" has just as much spiritual and philosophical meaning as Mahler's "Earth"'. By this, Tippett presumably meant that while Mahler's work shows that the rift between anguish of soul and escape into the innocent, heavenly delights of nature could eventually be healed by an acceptance of both, or an acceptance of life and mortality on earth, his own work, in a characteristic gloss, would show no such rift: it would show how through his body, from anguished birth to the sensuality of youth, man could develop a physical and a spiritual maturity that would lead to ecstasy. In the 'Personal Synopsis' Tippett outlined the correspondences between his and Mahler's formal and conceptual schemes. (The text in the right-hand column below quotes directly, apart from the italicized headings, from Tippett's synopsis; the left-hand column is added for comparison.)

MAHLER	TIPPETT
[*Sonata-Allegro*]	[*Slow Movement*]
1. Earthly sorrow	1. Slow Blues: the archetypal cry, probably beginning with a quote from the *St Louis Blues*
[*Slow Movement*]	
2. Loneliness	
[*Triple Scherzo*]	[*Scherzo*]
3. Youth and illusion	2. Fast Blues: the flamboyant peacock male (although sung by a woman) going out into the world [*Second Slow Movement*]
4. Beauty, passion and maturity	3. A moderate movement blues: the homecoming maturity, or whatever [*Finale*]

5. Wine as escape

4. A blues that gets progressively faster and wilder: Ecstasy

[*Slow Finale*]
6. Acceptance of sorrow, death and ever-renewing nature

Any analogue to Mahler's No. 6 [opposite] just drops out

In the Symphony as it was finally composed, the first two blues remain broadly as described above. But Tippett changed the others radically. Why he should have done so may perhaps be attributed to the fact that his scheme as it stood was something of a cliché, a self-caricature. The crucial reason though was that he was prompted by some remarks of Colin Davis, after his performance of Beethoven's Ninth Symphony at the Bath Festival in June 1970, to return to the question of what Beethoven had actually done in the 'notional' archetype, to ask himself whether the ecstatic affirmations of universal brotherhood in Beethoven's finale really had relevance any more and whether the proposed 'ecstasy' of his own finale was not therefore gratuitous. He asked himself, that is, the questions posed at the beginning of the present discussion. Tippett's earlier scheme changed course. The third blues would not be about a perfect, mature body, but about bodies deformed and deranged. The fourth blues would be struck out altogether and replaced by a scene in which Beethoven's finale and Schiller's 'Ode to Joy' were confronted head-on and the contradictions in them faced directly. Tippett's finale became therefore what could be described as a 'Song of Man' rather than a 'Song of the Body' and it concluded with that concept of acceptance which, interestingly, is also present in the Mahler finale he had previously disregarded.

The extraordinary thing about all this is not that the genesis of so direct and accessible a work should have been so laboured, nor that the most idiosyncratic feature of the symphony, the blues, should turn out to be a twentieth-century equivalent of the most idiosyncratic feature of Beethoven's symphony, the revolutionary hymn. It is that Tippett should have dared to meet Beethoven on his own ground. His pretensions are made clear from the very first bar, which sounds like a reference to the beginning of the 'Eroica' Symphony. Tippett seems to be saying that the opening chord of *his* third symphony will be both arresting and, unlike Beethoven's two chords, integrated with the tempo and substance of what follows. Technical criticism is really a criticism of expressive intent. So Tippett may be further interpreted as saying that Beethoven's spirit of Promethean endeavour can no longer be cast as a majestic and benevolent humanity roaming freely and bestowing favours where it will: the twentieth century has discovered that Promethean attempts to remake man have ended in horror. The spirit must be identified for what it is. It cannot however be gainsaid. If frightening, it is exhilarating; if harsh, relentless and potentially destructive, it is also a source of vigour and vitality. Tippett proceeds to make a ruthlessly objective musical metaphor of its power, resisting the temptation to humanize it and showing that even if in the end it is doomed to self-annihilation it still has the capacity to release seemingly inexhaustable torrents of energy – now breathtaking, now ugly, now of stark beauty.

Example 174 is 'arrest', music which despite its rasping harmony is still chained to a firm tonality. (In the example an editorial key signature is added to illustrate the point.) A brief codetta (bracket *b* in example) releases the first unit of 'movement' (see Ex. 175). In contrast to the primarily harmonic 'arrest', this is linear, heterophonic and apparently much faster, although the two units are connected rhythmically by the identity of one bar of 3/4 'movement' with one of 2/4 'arrest'. The connection is underlined by the similarity of Tippett's two units to the interior contrasts of an antecedent in traditional period structure. And the traditional basis of the music is underlined still further by the details of 'movement', which comprise an 'introduction', 'first phrase' and 'transition' – not at all the undisciplined rush of activity they seem at first.

Ex. 174   Symphony No. 3

With the return of 'arrest' and 'movement', somewhat extended, the traditional basis of Tippett's thinking is underlined, for the period is now completed with its consequent and Tippett has therefore laid out a 'first subject'. It may be concluded that he conducts an argument on two levels: the more radical one of subjecting the units to progressive extension, and the more traditional one of pursuing the course of a sonata-allegro. The radical level is the more prominent, since it sounds so, 'arrest' being allotted to brass and untuned percussion, 'movement' to the remaining and less obtrusive sections of the orchestra. Proportional relationships between the units are also very striking. The units begin from a position of equality. 'Arrest' expands slowly, but remorselessly, and largely by means of interpolated variants of *a* in Ex. 174, until it finally reaches an apotheosis in which the bottom three notes of its opening chord generate a massive theme in two strophes (the beginning of the theme is shown in Ex. 125(ii)). 'Movement', on the other hand, expands rapidly, and by means of organic development, until in the middle sections it is about twice as long as 'arrest'. Having fulfilled itself, it contracts.

The two processes are not independent of each other. Tippett continually makes one the other's justification – through the inherent qualities of music which embodies his central dialectic of compression and release, and also, significantly, through that compositional will-power that forces

Ex. 175   **Symphony No. 3**

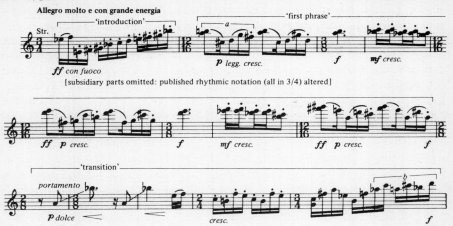

material to function as the dialectic requires. Thus, the codettas (*b* in Ex. 174, *b* and a variant of *a* in Ex. 175) which wrench or thrust the units into their counterparts: thus, in particular, the codetta which breaks the vicious circle of the massive theme mentioned above (whose AABA structure is designed to be self-perpetuating, the final A of strophe 1 overlapping with the first A of strophe 2). Thus, most of all, the background level of sonata form. This is illustrated in the table below.

Arrest		*Movement*	
1. (6 bars) Statement	part of	1. (9 bars) Statement	remain-
2. (9) Complement	first	2. (17) Complement	ing part
	subject		of first
			subject
3. (23) Transition		3. (58) First transition, leading to second subject, the 'exposition' concluded with a reference to 2	
4. (46) Second subject, first group, motivic		4. (90) Development, leading to a varied recapitulation of first subject with stretta coda	
5. (96) Second subject, second group, thematic		5. (30) Second transition	
6. (67) Fragmentary recapitulation, of sections from 4, 4+3, 3+2+1, and 5	*with*	6. (67) Exact recapitulation of second subject in 3 and recapitulation in 4	

In this double sonata form, the logic of Tippett's eventual superposition of units is as inescapable as are its consequences: the hubris of 'arrest' leads to disintegration, the intransigence of 'movement' collides with it, and an accumulation gathers of such density that it 'explodes'. (Ironically, this is a compositional procedure very characteristic of Boulez, the composer with whom Tippett has less in common than with almost any other – Boulez's contribution to the genesis of the Symphony notwithstanding.) The explosion reverberates, settles and eventually reveals the icy vistas at the core of the lento (see Ex. 176). The whole process sounds so natural, even artless, that it comes as quite a surprise to discover how skilfully Tippett has manipulated a *Klangfarben* technique in order to effect the necessary diminuendo, and how he has shown that passivity is not only the obverse of violence but intimately connected with it: here, by a second tempo modulation in which one crotchet beat of the lento equals precisely one bar of the previous allegro.

Ex. 176   **Symphony No. 3**

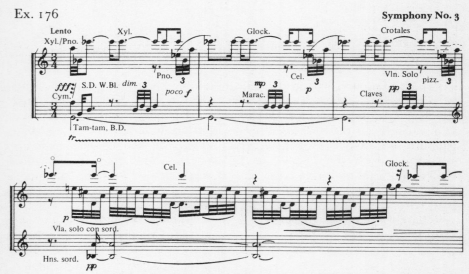

This slow movement is the nearest Tippett has got to impressionism. It is a very particular kind of impressionism. Despite their meticulously analytical approaches to nature, Debussy and Bartók (in his 'night music') still wanted to convey delight in its workings. For Tippett, nature is the subject of dispassionate, almost scientific documentation. It is a universe that appears and then disappears, signifying no more than that it exists. What is documented is extremely beautiful, but so remote, huge and mysterious that it seems out of reach of human contact. This is perhaps overstating the matter. But nowhere else in Tippett's music is one forced to concede that so characteristic a passage as that in Ex. 177, for example, is less a metaphor of human tenderness than an image of something from which such a metaphor might derive, a preternatural organism. Four such organisms form the basis of the movement, and they propagate many others. Again, the warm layer of string tone that emerges out of the centre of the movement is less a metaphor of rising passion than an image of natural growth. Tippett's sound-images 'impress' themselves on the listener's imagination as pictures from the roots of creation.

Ex. 177   **Symphony No. 3**

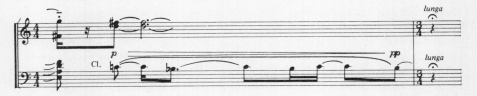

The movement is a palindrome, one of the very few instances of the
technique which can be heard as such – doubtless because Tippett's
original conception was of a phenomenon approaching and receding. The
basis of the palindrome is a thrice-repeated strophe consisting of the four
'organisms' mentioned above: the first two are shown in Ex. 176, the third,
the still centre, in Ex. 177; the fourth is a chilling, stuttering crescendo
which gives birth to further organisms and to the next strophe. The falling
and rising dynamics of the strophe naturally initiate smooth joins between
repeats. Tippett's procedure is not however so automatic nor so symmetric
as this might suggest. In the first place, the sixteen bars of the strophe are
divided asymmetrically, 3+5+6+2, the quasi-repeat within the second
organism preparing for the complete stasis of the third, whose three bars
are isolated by pauses and then, Debussy-like, repeated literally. Secondly,
the accumulation of new organisms at each repeat obscures the original
dynamic shape and converts the three-strophe palindromic unit into one
extended crescendo, whose consequent diminuendo, when the unit goes
backwards, not only contributes to the palindrome's audibility but also
imparts an inevitability to the process entirely in keeping with the
movement's conceptual character. Tippett's most striking departure from
strict palindromic technique occurs at the central turning point, when he
inserts that extended paragraph of rich string harmony already referred to.
This inaugurates a dual formal process, analogous to that in the allegro, in
which cold, sectional music is answered by warm, continuous music and in
which a second dynamic arch, crescendo and diminuendo, pursues an
independent course of its own. When it reaches the peak of its crescendo, it
is met by the second half of the palindrome, whose return journey is
interrupted by fragmentary evidence of the string music as it in turn winds
its way back to the depths. As a whole, the process forms a very
characteristic Tippettian metaphor, the immovable rigour of the palindrome combined with the continuous expansion of the string music.

Of course, none of this would have mattered much had the components of Tippett's formal complex not been so memorable and so suited to their various functions. To conceive music that retains its indentity whether going forwards or backwards is a major imaginative feat, involving further small adjustments to a strict technique, notably in the final strophe where Tippett introduces a trope on the cor anglais, to bind the texture together, and a tiny codetta. And to conceive a neo-tonal harmony that is neither derivative nor nostalgic is, in the latter half of the twentieth century, an even more precious achievement. It may be that Ives was the progenitor of such harmony. But the following excerpt (Ex. 178(i)), quite apart from its typical bitonality, shows that Tippett is not so much alluding to some half-remembered Ivesian battle-hymn as marshalling an argument in his own terms, marking out an area within which the hitherto contemplative melodic line on the violas can gather the determination, weight and support it needs to carry the full string body to the self-realisation of rhythmic and harmonic identity (Ex. 178(ii)), in other words, to the main climax of the movement.

Ex. 178   **Symphony No. 3**

Part 2 of the Symphony starts in a pleasantly crazy way, an acknowl-edgement of the fact that after the concentrated music of Part 1 the listener needs to relax and be assured that the answer to his anxious question of whether such intensity is to be sustained across the complete Symphony is no: Tippett will lower the temperature and introduce an element of playfulness, more precisely, the 'trickster' element, made familiar from the 'false' Sosostris in *The Midsummer Marriage*. So his scherzo has something of the flavour of a practical joke. The joke however turns sour. The music grows frantic rather than entertaining and eventually reaches an almost manic state, comparable with that at the climax of the opening allegro. There it resulted in an explosion. Here, Tippett cuts it short, leaving a dramatic pause – an act of will which announces that henceforth the Symphony is to be conditioned not by the awesome laws of the cosmos but by human decisions and human responses. The compositional technique Tippett uses in his scherzo could be interpreted as a means of dramatizing this turning point – an undisguisedly Ivesian collage technique ranged against a finale in which the Transcendentalist ideals Ives so fervently believed in are held to account and found to be wanting. In context, Tippett's scherzo, too short to qualify as a genuine movement (it lasts five out of a total of fifty-five minutes), serves the specifically musical function of a transition. It is an anacrusis, throwing the main weight of the work onto the finale.

Its most obvious exemplar is less a genuine piece of Ives, such as *The Fourth of July* or the second movement of his Symphony No. 4, than Tippett's own reworking of Ivesian methods in the 'dissolve' music of *The Knot Garden* (see Ex. 155). What distinguishes it from that is the nature and behaviour of its material. The 'dissolve' consists of repetitions of three summary motifs of varying lengths, two of them fixed, the other expanding by arithmetical proportion, all three somewhat machine-like in tone and thus inviting the mechanical permutations of order and relationship Tippett in fact subjects them to. The resulting sequence of textures continually thwarts expectation and the 'dissolve' consequently sounds like a contradiction, both of itself and of what has preceded it. In the Symphony, collage technique generates an analogous but less belligerent effect. Tippett achieves this firstly through the scale and the quantity of his components, five very diverse 'musics', each of them a complete theme or thematic paragraph. The extended time-scale creates a much more leisurely environment than in the 'dissolve', where playfulness can prosper and contradictoriness not take hold of things until the scherzo is well under way. With collage technique 'enlarged' to reveal the way its components breathe, Tippett's manipulation of the components is now far less automatic, far more musical. The main principle is retained: components are added to a given continuum until a saturation of independently repeating 'musics' is reached, here 'like a juggler with five different objects in the air at once'.[84] But the point at which a 'music' is thrown into the fray depends not on a preconceived plan but on its need to adjust itself to the nature and inner structure of the others and on such considerations as harmony, dynamics and texture. Thus, while central stability is provided by a poised and classically developed theme on four horns repeated five times at (more or less) regular intervals, the other, more aggressively single-minded components enter at irregular intervals and none of them is repeated exactly. Tippett's procedure can be illustrated by describing how the five 'musics', whose beginnings are shown in Ex. 179, are introduced.

The horns' theme sounds out unchallenged. Its final cadence is dovetailed with the cellos' and basses' gruff assertion of their presence, which prompts the violins to stabilize the texture by adding a layer of

Ex. 179   **Symphony No. 3**

4 Horns
(basically 7/4)

Cello and Basses
(basically triplet 3/2)

Violins
(basically 5/4)

Woodwinds
(basically 3/4)

Piano
(basically triplet 3/2)

* quadrupled at the octave above and two octaves below.

glittering high semiquavers to the existing middle and low registers; the
cellos and basses ruminate while they do so. Thus neither 'music'
obliterates the other. When the cellos and basses resume their gruff
activities and in the process complete a ternary design, the violins dance
attendance, or, in structural terms, reveal the middle section of a ternary
design of their own, returning to their semiquavers and thus to a
completion of their design when the cellos and basses drop out and the
horns enter for a second time (now *p* as opposed to *f*, in order to
accommodate the small-voiced violins). When the violins in turn have
dropped out and the horns reached their lyrical and less forceful central
phrases, the winds enter, with a theme whose character is a nice mixture of
the cadential and the expository: its sharply punctuated contours, all-
embracing texture (stretching across the whole gamut from high to low
register) and dimensions (it finishes precisely when the repeat of the horns'
theme finishes) put a concluding stamp to the proceedings thus far, while
its traditional sentence structure makes a statement and promises elaboration to come. This Tippett provides in a codetta, a technique of
continuation which enables him to round off the whole of the first stage of
the collage process by bringing back the cellos and basses and the violins in
reverse order and placing an abbreviated repeat of the winds' theme across
them. At the height of this complexity the horns' theme returns for a third
time, and four strands of music are now in play at once. Tippett then both
arrests the confusion and sustains the momentum by abruptly stopping two
of the strands, the violins and the winds, and immediately introducing his
final 'music', a prancing, somewhat frenzied theme on a solo piano.

Tippett's approach is thus dramatic rather than schematic. If his eventual combination of all five strands sounds like anarchy rampant, the deliberation with which he prepares for this state of affairs shows that he meant it to – in order to cut the music short, to say in effect that this is not the way to proceed, and to direct attention, via his dramatic pause, to what *is*, a quotation of the first seven bars from the finale of Beethoven's Ninth Symphony, the so-called 'Schreckensfanfare'.

This is the most celebrated single feature of the Symphony. It at once fulfils two objectives: it wrenches the tone from the abstract to the concrete in almost as startling a way as that achieved in the original, where Beethoven's outburst of impotent rage signalled the dispatch of instrumental music and the introduction of singing into a symphony for the first time; and it also indicates that Tippett's finale is to be a commentary on Beethoven's. This latter is of prime importance. It provides the quotation's true justification, which is not so much that Tippett could not invent for himself a musical gesture with equivalent dramatic force (though he has admitted he could not), nor even that Beethoven's gesture is so archetypal as to be inescapable: it is rather that to do otherwise would have been pointlessly to conceal the subject matter of a finale which if not direct in meaning would be nothing. Tippett put the matter thus: 'I can't reinvent the archetype in such a way that it would work without getting confused.'[85] His use of quotation may therefore be accounted economical. Quoting Beethoven is nevertheless a daring thing to do, and Tippett's tactic has excited much adverse comment. To some, it is a tasteless exhibition of hubris, to others, simply an excrescence: he would seem to have been better advised to have written his own 'Schreckensfanfare' – which is another way of saying that he has overstretched himself and that the Symphony is fatally compromised. Even if based on a misunderstanding, opinions of this kind are unlikely to be influenced by counter-argument. They strike at the roots of Tippett's artistic beliefs and re-open the question of whether the 'notional' archetype is a valid concept at all. Criticism can be levelled against the quotation – in that by choosing the first, the barer and less dissonant of the two outbursts in the Ninth Symphony, Tippett spiked his own guns somewhat. But this is to quibble. His intentions are clear and the quotation's three appearances serve notice of the three stages by which he subjects Beethoven's finale to critical scrutiny in order to recast it and thereby make a pertinent statement through it. Tippett's methods can be illustrated by a comparison between the movements as shown on p.450.

Beethoven's finale is in two main sections, the discursive first section comprising rejection of 'old' themes and discovery of the new one, the core second section a confirmation and celebration of the new, the Ode to Joy. This is not only a new theme but the basis of a new faith as well, an ecstatic vision of universal brotherhood. Tippett's core section is his first. Beethoven's structure is thus stood on its head from the start. The quotation does not sweep away the past, it prompts reflection; and the 'new' is shown to be an illusion: the condition of man, as expressed in the blues, is unchanging and unchangeable and is rooted in sorrow not joy. It

BEETHOVEN

1. *a* Outburst
   b Instrumental recitative (purposeful)
   c Old themes surveyed and rejected
      i. first movement
      ii. second movement
      iii. third movement
   d Instrumental recitative continued (discovery of theme)
   e ODE TO JOY (instrumental)
      i. variation 1
      ii. variation 2
      iii. variation 3 plus codetta

2. *a* Outburst
   b Vocal recitative, conflation of 1*b* and *d* (confident)
   c ODE TO JOY (vocal)
      i. variation 4
      ii. variation 5
      iii. variation 6 plus codetta (plus remainder of Beethoven's finale)

TIPPETT

1. *a* Quotation of Beethoven 1*a*, plus extension
   b Instrumental response (hesitant)
   c 'New' themes: BLUES [blues = variations]
      i. slow blues
      ii. fast blues
      iii. slow blues

2. *a* Quotation, as in 1*a*
   b Quotations from Beethoven 1*b* and 2*b*, eventually with added vocal commentary, leading into quotation of two thirds of 2*c*(i), with continuing commentary
   c Old themes recollected and absorbed
      i. lento of Part 1
      ii. allegro of Part 1
      iii. scherzo of Part 2
      iv. allegro of Part 1
   d Quotation of remaining third of Ode to Joy plus codetta, as in Beethoven 2*c*(iii), with continuing vocal commentary, leading to
   e New development

3. *a* Quotation, as in 1*a*, but with added instrumental and vocal commentary
   b Instrumental response, as in 1*b*, but with added vocal commentary, leading to reprise of introduction to 1*c*(i), as entry to
   c 'Dream of the Peaceable Kingdom', tempered by reminders of allegro and lento from Part 1 and of 1*c*(i)
   d Coda

is in this light that Tippett, in his discursive second section, a parody of Beethoven's first, examines Beethoven's and Schiller's whole premise. His third section begins like a recapitulation of his first. But it swiftly alters course to embody the conclusion he has reached. He does not reject Beethoven's vision outright. But he severely qualifies it, replacing it with a vision so fettered and so tainted by reality that it can hardly claim to be a vision at all. In its own context, however, and its own extremely circumspect terms of reference, Tippett's 'dream' of abounding love and compassion is indeed a visionary, and a moving statement – moving, precisely because its wings are clipped and because it is completed with an acknowledgement of both its practical impossibility and its emotional necessity (see Ex. 173).

Tippett's point therefore is not that Beethoven's vision of humanity was unrealistic. How could it have been, when his music still exerts such irresistible power? And neither is Tippett interested in the alternative view that Beethoven – who of all composers was most denied contact with fellow humanity and who, for this very reason, might have wanted to conjure up a humanity to which he himself could belong – was nevertheless realistic enough to have compromised his vision with a blatantly awkward formal structure, to have greeted Schiller's line 'And the cherub stands before God' with the equivalent of a Blakeian divine fart (see p.455) and to have omitted more than half of Schiller's text, concentrating only on the idea that joy leads to transcendence. What Tippett does not do is assess the Ninth Symphony. He uses it. He fits the work into the eighteenth-century tradition of political utopianism in order to contrast that with what has actually happened since (the labour camps, gas chambers) and thereby define his own position more vividly. A celebration, vision, 'dream' (Tippett has described his third section as a 'dream of the Peaceable Kingdom'[86]) is a no less necessary proof of man's infinite humanity than it was in Beethoven's time but it can no longer serve to disguise the facts of man's incurable inhumanity. If the twentieth century is to see a new faith, this precarious equation is the best that they can be offered. This, of course, is a variation of the Blakean/Jungian philosophy Tippett had been expounding all his creative life and put in a verbal paraphrase such as the above it may suggest that he had ceased to have anything new to say and was content to recite formulae academic or blindingly obvious. Translated into music, however, his philosphy sounds fresh and supremely relevant, as perhaps might be expected from a composer whose ideas were beginning to be shared widely and who was anxious to press home his advantage, even to the extent of risking comparison with Beethoven and losing everything in the process.

Tippett's crucial statement is made in the blues, expecially the first one. Had it not summoned up so authentic an image of the human condition it would have invalidated his whole finale. As it is, Tippett produced here some of his most memorable music. The remainder of the finale is coloured to a considerable extent by the question of whether he will bring this music back, confirm that it does indeed embody a fundamental human experience whose denial would have been a denial of precisely those things with which the Symphony is most deeply concerned. He does bring it back. A mere hint (its introductory two bars) is enough to establish its presence when it unlocks the door to Tippett's 'dream' (in 3*b*), and in the 'dream' itself it appears, in more extended recapitulation, to mend the cracks and show such stuff as dreams are made on.

Naturally, the effect of the first blues is due in part to the associations surrounding its model – a classic recording by Bessie Smith and Louis Armstrong of the *St Louis Blues* (made on 24 January 1925). The harmonium accompaniment of the original is transferred to trombones and tuba (plus supporting bassoons) and the cornet solo to flugelhorn, the latter a brilliant stroke on Tippett's part for the deep tone quality of the flugelhorn serves not only to match the sonority of the accompaniment but also to introduce a new sound to the work precisely when it needs it. (Admittedly, a flugelhorn had been heard in a symphony before, in Mahler's Third and Vaughan Williams's Ninth, for example; but the style Tippett gives it is unprecedented in 'classical' music and was in any case derived from the playing of Miles Davis.) The humanity of the music may also be ascribed to Tippett's adoption of another characteristic feature of the original, the idea of a dialogue between voice and solo instrument, which could be said to symbolize man's dialogue with his soul or, on a more homely plane, the tenderness and encouragement he may expect to find with someone else. None of this, however, can really account for the effect of the music. Tippett has taken the traditional twelve-bar blues and made it his own – a cry of suffering humanity within which is also contained the bright excitement of a humanity ready to break out of suffering and turn it into something inspiriting (Ex. 180).

If the poignancy of this music forces its relationship with Beethoven into the background, its text is a reminder that Schiller, at least, is in the forefront of Tippett's attention. Its first two choruses relate how, from the milk of its mother and the kisses of its father, the baby inherits sorrow – not the joy which, according to the 'Ode to Joy', is to be drunk from the 'breasts of nature' nor the joy which lavishes 'kisses and vines' on all things. 'Blood of their blood/Bone of their bone/What then is me that was not them?' sings the soprano in the final chorus: humanity is born to

Ex. 180   **Symphony No. 3**

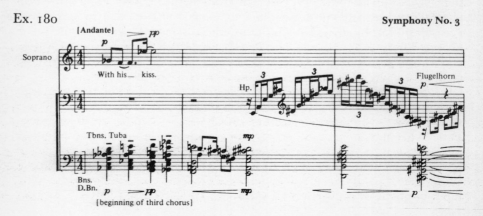

[beginning of third chorus]

sorrow. The text here, with its allusion to the Genesis account of the
creation of woman, is also an indication that if Schiller can use the Bible to
support his eschatology Tippett can use it to support his own – as he does,
more pointedly, later in the finale.

The text of the second blues is influenced not by Schiller but by the
Elizabethan blazon, the poetic tradition of honouring a mistress by
praising the separate parts of her person, from top to toe. Tippett's praise
of physical topography is designed to show that despite its sorrowful
inheritance youth will always be possessed of boundless delight in
sensuality. From the fateful D minor (not Beethoven's D major) of the first
blues, the music now leaps to F sharp, the brilliant fourth 'fifth' (see p.90).
As the stanzas, in three stages, move their attention from the face
downwards, so the tonality follows suit, though with a subtle twist: the next
two tonalities in a descending cycle, B and E, are reversed, presumably so
that B, the most sensual tonality in Tippett's vocabulary, can be reserved
for celebration of dark declivities (see Ex. 141).

This blues does not have the happiest of Tippett's texts, and its music
needs to be taken at a slightly faster metronome mark than that indicated
in the score if it is to generate the appropriate abandon and its interior
repeats are not to sound laboured. Its most attractive feature is a set of

clarinet breaks, solo (see Ex. 181), duet and trio, which cock a snook at proceedings from time to time and in the process effect modulations between stanzas. Since they are not contained within the twelve-bar form, these breaks are not breaks in the classic sense of the term. But their improper behaviour has a structural function nonetheless, for it signals the looser form of the third blues and hence progress towards the dramatic form of the final section of the work.

Ex. 181   **Symphony No. 3**

In the third blues the soprano encounters those who cannot experience youthful delight, the malformed, the dumb and the deaf, the mentally ill. Confronted with the injustice of the world she offers the only comforts she knows, milk and kisses. She then realises that these fruits of her sorrow, even if they are all she can give, are still better than the nothing an indifferent God provides, and her determination to offer them is redoubled. But at this point her thoughts are overtaken by the Beethoven quotation, sounding now like screaming rage at the futility of things.

The disturbing responsibilities of maturity account for the heavy tread of this blues and its less secure design. Only in its final, fourth stanza does it submit to the fundamental twelve-bar structure and just before that Tippett introduces a short section which forsakes blues altogether – as if the soprano momentarily disclaims the moral pressure that has been laid on her. Its wayward tonality is another pointer to the outburst to come. It begins in A, a continuation of the descending cycle of the second blues, and in its second four-bar unit it drops to the fifth below that, the fateful tonality of the first blues. The closing unit of the first chorus abandons the four-bar model and, at the words 'milk and kisses', alights on Tippett's visionary tonality of A flat. The subtlety with which Tippett traces a logical tonal design and at the same time reflects his music's anxiety to avoid its inevitable resting point, D, is illustrated in the diagram below (Ex. 182).

With the irruption of the Beethoven quotation and of D minor, Tippett admits that his portrait of the human condition leads to desperation. Beethoven's ought therefore to be re-examined. In his examination of the

Ex. 182   **Symphony No. 3**

route by which Beethoven reaches the Ode to Joy and of the Ode itself, Tippett treats Beethoven's material as a kind of tenor or cantus firmus. His ironic instrumental and vocal gloss already imparts an air of uncertainty to the proceedings, for it is not clear whether attention is focused on Beethoven or Tippett. When the cellos and basses have reached the notes associated with the words 'All men will be brothers', the music stops short. 'And did my brother die of frost-bite in the camp? And was my sister charred to cinders in the oven?' The music accompanying these words is a reprise of Ex. 177 from the lento – a primal tenderness, therefore, almost too sacred to touch. Yet the compassionate instinct is also too powerful to suppress. With this proof of the interdependence of movements in his Symphony, Tippett has inaugurated a parody of Beethoven's 1c (see p.450), a set of recapitulations and quasi-recapitulations which here are an integral part of the work and not material to be discarded. They culminate in brass and percussion music recalling the opening allegro and underlining the words 'My sibling was the torturer' – a phrase that can be said to epitomize the shift in Tippett's thinking that had taken place since his statement in *A Child of Our Time*.

If, however, even Schiller conceded that 'the worm was given love-lust' (Tippett's translation of 'Wollust'), Tippett cannot dismiss him, or Beethoven, yet. The examination resumes and is taken to the point where Schiller's text runs 'And the cherub stands before God', a major turning-point in the Ninth Symphony and certainly one here. The word 'God' is like a red rag to Tippett. Neither the 'loving father', hallowed by Schiller, nor the jealous God of the Old Testament are worthy of consideration if they are so indifferent to the fate of the men they profess to have an interest in as to permit the suffering and savagery witnessed in recent generations. Tippett counsels the cherub to 'demote himself to man',

> Then spit his curses across the celestial face
> Though he be answered (Answered!?)
> With annihilation from the whirlwind.

Tippett has called this passage a 'burst of Nobodaddy-rhetoric',[87] a reference to Blake's Nobodaddy and to the rhetorical questions with which God assailed Job from the whirlwind. It is a curiously self-deprecating label in view of the vehemence of the music. Blake, in his irreverent moments, used Nobodaddy as a synonym for Jehovah, a 'nobody's daddy' who

> Farted and belched and coughed,
> And said, 'I love hanging and drawing and quartering
> Every bit as well as war and slaughtering!'[88]

Elsewhere, however, notably in his figure of Urizen, Blake took the savage Jehovah extremely seriously and so does Tippett, otherwise there would have been no need to curse him with such passion. But vehemence and passion are not quite the right words to describe music which also has a touch of bravado in it; and in this may be found the true reason for Tippett's reaction. God, or at least the divinity, the God-image, the Jungian self, is a real and frightening presence, an unconscious phenomenon containing both integrative and disruptive forces, both dispassionate good and dispassionate evil. It cannot be humanized by religious dogma. Conscious man can escape from neither its inner presence nor its outward manifestations. He can however assess it, for, as Jung wrote in *Answer to Job*, man has shown himself to be 'superior to his divine partner both intellectually and morally'. If, therefore, Tippett is taking an enormous risk in challenging 'God' and inviting retaliation from within his own psyche, he does so because God's evil is in the ascendant and there is an overriding need to assert the values of man.

This is the final 'message' of the Symphony, and it is presented with some diffidence, for the values of man that Tippett has been at pains to dissect leave only a slender hope that they will be an improvement on the lack of values in God. But hope there is. When the whirlwind – the final appearance of the Beethoven quotation overlaid with rushing triplets – is silenced, what is left is the small voice of suffering humanity. This recapitulation now points in a new direction. It leads not to the desperation following the blues but to Tippett's 'dream' and his coda – a humanistic assertion with none of the confidence of his earlier music but, for this reason, with perhaps greater powers of persuasion.

Piano Sonata No. 3

After completing his Symphony, in April 1972, and before embarking on a fourth opera, Tippett intended to draw back a little and relax – a reasonable precaution and especially so in the case of *The Ice Break*, which, as a dramatized elaboration of the premises set out at the end of the Symphony, would allow him no respite from its cognitive processes and would deny him the creative stimulus he might have gained from an entirely new subject. In the event, Tippett's 'relaxation', his Piano Sonata No. 3, proved more taxing than he had expected. He took almost a year to write it. Something of the strain involved can be deduced from his treatment of its first four themes. Taking his cue from the quirky opening one he could cheerfully have turned them into a set of latter-day Beethoven bagatelles; but instead he fashioned them into a concentrated and somewhat irascible sonata-allegro. It is as if he had been served with an unexpected summons to return to the 'historical' archetype, and had responded only with reluctance because what he really wanted to do was get on with the opera and not be sidetracked by the demands of a full-blown sonata. The intensity of the work, particularly its finale which is almost angry in mood, suggests the same thing, as does its apparently perfunctory design, three simply shaped movements assembled under the mantle of a one-movement sonata.

Another interpretation of the work can be advanced, however, which sets these observations in a different light. The extreme rigour with which

Tippett completes his design suggests that far from indulging in a show of petulance he composed the Sonata with studied deliberation, which in turn suggests that the 'historical' archetype had revealed an approach to large-scale structure he sensed would be of profound importance to him – as indeed has proved the case. All Tippett's subsequent instrumental works are indebted to the Sonata's structural hypothesis, a continuous span of music, strong and simple in outline and allowing room for a great variety of expression to flourish within it. Signs of inner conflict and even of pedagogy may mark out the Sonata as a transitional work; but it is a seminal one nonetheless, its potential vital enough to survive three years in cold storage (while Tippett was writing *The Ice Break*) and emerge fully-realized in his Symphony No. 4.

The change in direction signalled by Sonata No. 3 thus coincides with a shift in attitude towards the 'historical' archetype. Tippett no longer associated this with Beethoven's middle-period symphonies, for example, but with the continuous structures of his late piano sonatas, and, of course, with the spiritual world they embody. The sequence of movements, or sections, in Sonata No. 3 – sonata-allegro, variations, toccata in the form of a palindrome – has no exact parallel in late Beethoven (in fact its closest counterpart is the middle-period 'Appassionata' sonata); but Tippett follows Beethoven's general example in making each movement the immediate and necessary resolution of the previous one, so that the work as a whole is an unbroken unity. The obvious explanation of why Tippett should want to use a formal metaphor emphasizing completeness is the best one: in the latter part of his life he would naturally want to consolidate, distil, summarize. He has described the Sonata as 'more of a summation than a novelty' (programme notes for the first performance). He said this, however, before embarking on the late works which most fully warrant the description. If the Sonata is a summation, what it summarizes is less the experience of a lifetime than the fury of an explorer knowing that his exploring years are slipping out of reach.

Warning signs of the turmoil to come are hoisted at the very beginning of the Sonata – rebarbative two-part counterpoint by free melodic inversion but in strict rhythmic canon, each line vainly seeking to escape from the other despite the fact that the distance which separates them means that there is no hope of aural cohesion anyway (see Ex. 183(i)). Tippett has explained the extraordinary texture here in terms of pianistic virtuosity. He senses virtuosity 'through arms and hands rather than fingers, whose skilled movements are beyond me. I am stimulated by the duality of the hands and their possible perceptible independence in one compositional direction and aural unity in another'.[89] The Sonata thus begins with the hands as far apart as possible, and its subsequent behaviour is conditioned to a considerable extent by a dialectic between open and closed textures, or between furious activity when the hands are far apart and calm when they are close together – or, it could be said, between resistance to and acceptance of the imminent final stage in Tippett's compositional career.

The influence of Symphony No. 3 on the Sonata is apparent in the way

Ex. 183

Tippett expands his first subject, of *King Priam* in the way he isolates and presents his material: first subject, followed by pause; second-subject group, consisting of first theme (harmonic) and second theme (lyrical), followed by another pause; codetta theme (see Ex. 183(i–iv)). The important consideration however is that the material presented in this way is that of a classic sonata-allegro. Tippett has turned full circle and is once again inspecting the components of an allegro under a microscope, as if to remind himself of their true functions and re-acquire that knowledge of first principles which he can put to freer use in subsequent works. Much of the tension in the movement derives from the intellectual effort Tippett expends on fulfilling the strict conditions he imposes on himself. There is tight motivic control, an exemplary formal design and even a classical, or near-classical, tonal scheme. The first subject is in B (shown by the editorial key signature in Ex. 183(i)), the second group in a modally related A. The codetta theme assembles the other tonal regions touched upon thus far, before leading them into a return of the first subject now transposed up a fifth into the 'dominant' of F sharp. The exposition ends with a swing back to the 'tonic', a procedure which confirms the structural importance of tonality in an idiom whose allusive use of tonality would otherwise tend to conceal its presence altogether. In the recapitulation the second group appears, traditionally, in the 'tonic', a procedure that serves the same purpose. Since the recapitulation is almost exact, what this also does is conclude the movement (there is no coda) in a foreign tonality, an unresolved tension which Tippett turns to account by making it the justification for the slow movement.

The most immediately audible justification for the slow movement is that its calmness provides relief from the severity of the allegro. But there is a deeper and more dramatic reason as well. It sounds as if it had emerged unbidden, as if it had almost been stumbled upon. If Tippett needed to convince himself of the richness that was waiting beyond the unresolved tensions of the allegro, he surely did so here for what he stumbles upon is a landscape of exquisite beauty, one, moreover, whose beauty derives from the apparent aridity of its structure. His 'theme', a set of sixteen (or seventeen) chords never heard in their basic form (see Ex. 184(i)), is varied five times, each variation a minor third higher than the previous one, the final variation arriving on the same pitches as the first. The closed circuit of a minor third axis permits therefore no 'escape'. It is a structural metaphor of inevitability. In this context, all the variations can do is move into different aspects of one another. Tippett makes expressive capital out of these limitations by exploring the vertical aspect, as it were, rather than the horizontal, and uncovering vistas of the imagination so intensely sensuous that they lift the movement into an entirely new dimension where time and tension seem not to exist – even though the movement actually lasts as long as the other two put together. The lento is in fact one of those visionary movements so characteristic of Tippett. Its obvious forerunner is the Lento from his Symphony No. 3, at least in so far as it pursues that Lento's contemplation of pure sonority with comparable single-mindedness. But its true ancestry is to be found in the Pre-Scene to Act II of *The Midsummer Marriage*, where Tippett summoned up a dreamy landscape both completely still and profusely alive and where he first discovered his personal technique of decoration. Even that music, however, cannot rival the Sonata for sustained intensity of mood. The remarkable thing is that Tippett achieves his results with so simple a method – subjecting his inert chords to ever more luxuriant decoration (see Ex. 184(ii), chords 10 and 11 in the second variation), activating them, breathing life into them and then allowing them to flower before disappearing in a haze of trills. It is a method recalling that of Beethoven in the variations movement of his

Ex. 184

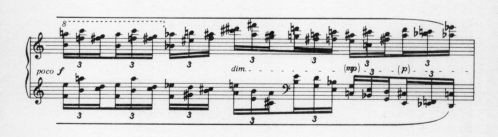

op. 111. To suggest that Beethoven's method is simple is to use the word in a very specialized sense however and not to gloss over the imaginative power which endows technique with meaning. So with Tippett. His Lento combines simplicity and complexity to a degree unparalleled in his output.

The finale springs to life as if anxious to defer to the conventional wisdom that a finale should restore a sense of purpose to things. It quickly becomes apparent however that this finale's impulsive seizure of every inch of the keyboard is no temporary expedient. The music drives on obsessively and relentlessly in a torrent of semiquavers, trills, hammered single notes and hammered chords, until it is finally dispatched with a defiant 'the devil take it'. Admittedly, it could be described in terms of *élan* or exhilaration, but this would be to exercise special pleading. The dominant impression remains of tumult, of someone trapped in a cage frantically rushing from one side to the other and then banging on the sides in a vain attempt to get out. Inevitably it stamps the whole Sonata with its astonishing fury. Why Tippett should have conceived the work in these terms has been considered above. It remains to examine some of the technical means by which he realized his conception.

The finale is a logical consequence of the first movement, as can be heard in its adoption of gaunt, two-part invertible counterpoint as the textural constant. It is also related thematically – at least to the extent that its first bars are a variation of the Sonata's opening theme. The complex derivations here suggest that other passages are related as well but such relationships can only be sensed, for Tippett's variation techniques are too idiosyncratic to yield to analysis. The most obvious technical feature of the movement is its palindrome. In his Symphony No. 3 Tippett had shown that he could put the device to powerful expressive effect, and so he does now. It serves to tighten the screws after the (seemingly) rhapsodic slow movement, to yield a rondo form (albeit somewhat unconventional and only implied – A, B (retrograde of A), A . . .) and to symbolize imprisoned emotions: in whichever direction the music proceeds, the outcome is the same. As with the Symphony, the success of Tippett's tactic depended on his ability to write music that can be instantly recognized, and on his modification of the textbook model. If he had concluded the finale when the palindrome had reached the end of its retrograde, schematic balance would have conflicted with expressive imbalance. The return of the first section enables Tippett to underline the impotence of his rage – and then, significantly, to do the opposite. Perhaps the most important aspect of the whole Sonata is that finally in a brief coda, it does, after all, wrench free of its obsessions (see Ex. 185).

Ex. 185   Piano Sonata No. 3

The Ice Break

Its libretto does not say so, but *The Ice Break* is set unambiguously in the USA of the 1960s, racial tension and hippy culture to the forefront of the action. It is thus the most 'topical' of Tippett's operas. Tippett has never been afraid to give artistic shape to contemporary problems dismissed by most composers as unworkable, and if the opera marks the limit to which he would go in this respect, his concern here with problems of such magnitude as racial conflict, the survival of human values in Soviet Russia, the generation gap and the pursuit of panaceas is not after all so surprising. What is surprising is that he should have treated these problems so realistically. Even *A Child of Our Time*, the one work whose pretensions are of the same order, stops short of stating its subject matter so baldly. As for his other operas, their symbolic atmospheres seem to have been designed precisely so that their meanings should not be circumscribed by the associations of realistic detail. The revolver shots and police sirens of *The Ice Break*, on the other hand, show to what extent Tippett was prepared to divest his music of metaphor, in order that its meaning *should* be circumscribed and made as clear and uncomplicated as possible. That meaning can be summarized as follows. Man should be reminded that entrenched attitudes lead to self-destruction; he should abandon his quest for panaceas and cultivate his humanity whenever the opportunity arises to do so. This of course is neither an original nor a particularly inspiring 'solution' to the problems posed. But its overriding importance to Tippett at this time can be gauged from his anxiety to state it so unequivocally and in such a wide-ranging context, when it was perfectly obvious that by so doing he might be brushed aside by some as naïve or shallow.

The problems posed by *The Ice Break* are indeed enormous. But they are also related to Tippett's intense personal interests (in American life, especially) and the resulting tension between the general and the personal is what gives the opera its most individual quality. It is both large in scope and small in scale, both a disquisition on the ills of contemporary society and a human story, a succession of sudden invasions from the outside world and an intimate narrative pursuing its course as best it can. In order to hold these disparate elements in manageable equilibrium Tippett naturally compressed and simplified his dramatic material. The plot of *The Ice Break* is certainly the most straightforward in his output. It is also, however, the most epigrammatic and the most vulnerable to criticism: its text contains its full share of Tippettisms ('Cool and jivey once; Now touchy and tight') and, in this case, of English-Americanisms ('He'll flick that Whitey out'); some of its characters are underdeveloped (Yuri, Gayle and Olympion tend to caricature the types they represent); and some of its situations are contrived: the eternals of experience may be clichés but they sometimes need less summary treatment if they are to be raised above the level of TV soap opera.[90] It is difficult though to see how Tippett could have wholly avoided these difficulties if he were to present clearly his idea of the stereotype, his principal diagnosis of the problems and his dominant dramatic idea – that of unthinking identity with attitudes so self-righteous that the humanity in opposing ones cannot be conceded. In outline the plot runs as follows.

Lev, a fifty-year-old teacher who has spent the last twenty years of his life in Soviet labour camps and in exile, has been released and is joining his wife Nadia and their son Yuri in the USA, where they had emigrated after his arrest. (Tippett's names are borrowed from the novels of Solzhenitsyn, who, it should be noted, was not exiled to the West until after Tippett had started his opera.) Lev soon discovers that the new world is not what he had expected. Nadia has lost her will to live and is retreating into fantasy (her character has some points in common with the visionary Marfa of Mussorgsky's *Khovanshchina*); Yuri greets his father with hatred, for being a coward and not fighing the Soviet system. In addition, Lev finds himself caught up in an atmosphere of racial tension which eventually flares into a riot. The link with the outside world of crowds, slogan-shouting mobs and racial violence is provided by Yuri's girlfriend, Gayle.

The first scene of the opera is set in an airport lounge. While Nadia is waiting for the arrival of Lev, Gayle, with Hannah, a black nurse, and a large crowd of fans, celebrates the triumphant home-coming of Hannah's lover, Olympion, described as a 'black champion'. Provoked by the sullen behaviour of Yuri, Olympion delivers his creed of black power. Gayle uses the occasion to 'make amends', by bending down on her knees and seeming to wash Olympion's feet with her hair, like Mary Magdalen before Christ.[91] Yuri is incensed, lunges at Olympion, who contemptuously knocks him down. The fans divide into hostile factions of black and white and thus are sown the seeds of the race riot in Act II, which ends with the deaths of Gayle and Olympion and terrible injuries to Yuri, who has been nearly kicked to death.

In the final act, Nadia, unable to withstand the shock of Yuri's injuries, slowly fades away, asking Lev to look after Yuri when she is dead. At this point there is an interlude in the 'Paradise Garden' where 'seekers of all kinds' are visited by a 'psychedelic messenger', Astron. The scene changes to the hospital where Yuri's broken bones have been set and his whole body encased in plaster. The plaster is cut away and Yuri's newborn body is revealed. He is wheeled in by Hannah to a hall where Lev is waiting. He takes some tentative steps. Father and son embrace.

We're not in a magic world, but in a world in which things are pretty grim. My next opera will be about whether or not we can be reborn from the stereotypes we live in ... This is almost the central problem of our time, and the actual rebirth will demand, I know, probably the warmest music I've ever written.[92]

Tippett made these remarks some two years before he started work on *The Ice Break* in March 1973. The interesting thing about them is not simply their evidence of how a single idea (the stereotype) could spark off a whole opera, nor of how at that time, nearly thirty years after completing *A Child of Our Time*, he still held fast to the idea of rebirth. It is rather that when he did come to write his music of rebirth it should be not warm, as he had prophesied, but routine, or at best, ironic: it sounds like a parody of the already parodistic Ex. 158 from *The Knot Garden*. Of course, this music can be judged second-rate Tippett and left at that; but it can also be seen as the consequence of a shift in Tippett's thinking, which made him far less confident that rebirth was a universal remedy or even that it was possible at all. The major cause of such a shift must have been his experience in writing his Symphony No. 3.

That work ends with the proposition that God's values (or a 'god's' values) have been discredited and that man can draw only from his own. He continually perverts or obstructs these values, for which reason their realization is called a 'dream'; but the individual, at least, can still remake them, be reborn to them. *The Ice Break* can be interpreted as a testing of this proposition. Tippett makes little attempt to evade its implications. His gratuitous ridiculing of the idea of a saviour God (in the Paradise Garden interlude) may fit uncomfortably into the general scheme of the opera, but for the rest he presents man at his worst, and in his least flattering aspect – locked in mortal combat because he will not let go of his stereotyped attitudes towards his fellow men. What Tippett concentrates on is the apparently unbridgeable gulf between this mass-man, who is blind to human values, and individual-man, who is not.[93] In these circumstances, is rebirth possible for those who have been submerged in the mass and lost their human identity? Of the three members of his cast who cannot resist the attractions of the mass, two perish and one survives. The survivor is reborn to his humanity. But his rebirth is occasioned by assault and has cost two lives. It cannot therefore be credited to those human values which nevertheless are released by it. Having put his proposition to the test, Tippett discovered that it had weaknesses. Hence his caution towards the idea of rebirth. But he still makes it happen, and with this compromised but proud expression of faith in humanity's ability to renew itself he ends his opera with what can justifiably be called some of his 'warmest' music – a glowing, transfiguring sonority which lights up like a beacon and guides its listeners into areas where the opera's sufferings and brutalities seem not to matter any more (see Ex. 186).

Ex. 186   **The Ice Break**

The most novel structural feature of *The Ice Break* stems directly from Tippett's idea of the stereotype and the blind and arbitrary collective behaviour to which stereotyped attitudes give birth. This idea is projected onto the chorus, which is not only an imaginative solution of what to do with the chorus in a modern opera but also the source of a new kind of dramatic counterpoint. The opera proceeds in two dimensions at once: one the continuous and, as it were, horizontal family story, the other a succession of sudden, vertical impingements by the chorus who blot out the human story altogether before vanishing as abruptly as they arrived. The story is then left to continue from where it left off. It is an approach to dramatic structure that has much in common with Tippett's methods in *The Vision of Saint Augustine*, though the formal metaphor here is of the struggle not for transcendence but for very existence – humanity precariously holding to its course while being buffeted by forces beyond its control.

In order to emphasize that his chorus is an anonymous mass in which individuals lose their identity, Tippett directs that it should be masked. To some extent this edges the opera's realism towards ritual. Tippett has called his chorus scenes surrealistic, partly no doubt because the disrelation between chorus and individuals reflects the aesthetic of early twentieth-century surrealism, but principally because in his original conception he had planned to present his chorus with a heightened, super-realism so that its impact would be not realistic but subliminal. What the masked chorus actually does is create a sense of unease or terror. Their impact is eminently realistic. Tippett got the idea of masks from a production he saw in his twenties of Toller's play *Masse-Mensch*, in which the chorus, a row of figures with their backs to the audience, suddenly turned round and revealed that they were masked – to frightening dramatic effect. In 1969 he saw the Covent Garden production of Berlioz's *Benvenuto Cellini*, whose carnival scene with masked revellers convinced him that the memory he had stored away for so many years could be turned to good account.

An important consequence of unpredictable chorus behaviour is that the steady development of the family scenes is thereby set in relief. Like *The Knot Garden*, *The Ice Break* consists of a large number of short scenes. Unlike the earlier opera, however, these scenes are not self-contained units; rather are they fragments of one large scene which would have been almost continuous had it not been constantly interrupted. The opera has no place therefore for the equivalent of 'dissolve' sections, let alone the interludes of *King Priam*, and if this introduces acute production problems concerned with getting the chorus on and off stage in a matter of seconds (problems Tippett confidently leaves to the producer), it also relieves the opera of the restlessness of *The Knot Garden*. The diagram below illustrates the details of Tippett's dramatic counterpoint in Act I. (In Acts II and III, a second intimate thread is woven into the fabric, that of Hannah and Olympion, then of Hannah alone and finally of Hannah and Lev.)

Scene

1. Nadia waiting, with Yuri, for Lev

2. Gayle and Hannah are swept away
3. by the throng on their way to
4. greet Olympion

5. Nadia and Yuri still waiting

6. The throng returns with Olympion, who feeds their adulation by playing the part expected of him (Yuri joins the throng)

7. Lev arrives and is reunited with Nadia
8. In Nadia's apartment, the two talk together

9. Scene 6 develops into an atmosphere of extreme racial tension

10. Yuri arrives, and reviles his father

This dramatic 'continuity' provides Tippett with a built-in musical continuity, with the result that he has more room for clear set-pieces than in *The Knot Garden* (the scenes in *The Ice Break* are in fact constructed more conventionally, being cast usually in simple strophic or refrain forms) and does not need to use so many recurring motifs as in the earlier opera to hold the work together or to identify its characters. What motifs he does use, however, are correspondingly more conspicuous. Notable among them are a coarse scalic passage hammered out in the orchestra whenever the catch-phrase 'Ain't that so?' is exchanged among members of the younger generation, and brooding harmonies associated with Lev (see Ex. 187).

Ex. 187   **The Ice Break**

In a 'Note' to his score and libretto Tippett refers to two other motifs, describing them as the 'archetypal sounds' of the opera. One is indeed a sound rather than a motif, 'the exciting or terrifying sound of slogan-shouting crowds, which can lift you on their shoulders in triumph or stamp you to death' (see Ex. 188). The opera contains many passages comparable with Ex. 188, whose impact depends not so much on their purely musical substance as on their evocative qualities.

Ex. 188   **The Ice Break**

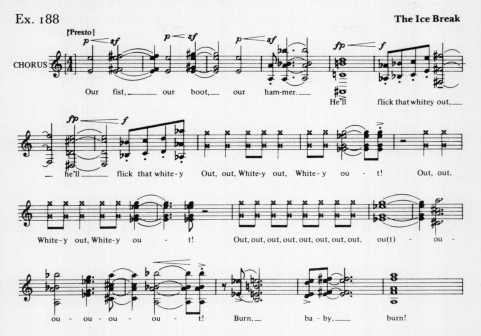

The other motif is the 'title' motif, 'the frightening but exhilarating sound of the ice breaking on the great northern rivers in the spring'.[94] The opera begins with this motif, and though descriptive enough and as such an immediate statement of the philosophy behind the work, it does not, by itself, contain that instantly recognizable, electrifying quality which fully justifies the word archetypal. It is in fact rather prosaic. Only when it is associated with intensely human moments, the reunion of Lev and Nadia and the reconciliation of Lev and Yuri, only, that is, when Tippett adds to it a characteristic trope on violins, flutes and trumpets, does it become truly archetypal (see Ex. 189).

Ex. 189   **The Ice Break**

What Tippett does not draw attention to is the one motif that entirely justifies the term, that illustrated in Ex. 186. It appears only three times in the opera (four, if its smothered appearance in the extremely dense quartet at the beginning of Act II is counted) but from the very first it leaves no doubt of its supreme importance as an image of 'magic', the 'pastoral', 'imagination and desire', the 'dream'. All Tippett's attempts to verbalize what he means by the value and nature of music are encapsulated in this one sound, whose effect reverberates well beyond its short duration. The verbal metaphor he uses here is 'poetry'. The motif is always accompanied by a quotation from Lev of the poetry that has sustained him in the Soviet Union and which now also sustains him in the West. At the beginning of Act III he is heard reading to himself from the final paragraph of Goethe's *Wilhelm Meisters Wanderjahre* (the second version of 1829). Wilhelm Meister sees his son plunge into a river from a cliff top; the son is rescued and lies on the bank, naked and asleep. Then follow the final lines of the novel, and, after Yuri's recovery, of the opera. 'Yet you will always be brought forth again, glorious image of God, and likewise be maimed, wounded afresh, from within and without.' *The Ice Break* ends therefore not only with the reconciliation of Lev with *his* son but also with the sounds of Ex. 186, or in other words with a statement – diffident and pensive perhaps, but little less affirmative than that in *The Midsummer Marriage*.

No doubt it was because of this ending, because, that is, Tippett knew that the essence of his opera would not be compromised by the angular and abrasive music which nevertheless was demanded by most of its scenario, that he felt justified in making his message crystal clear, depicting violence with a realism unparalleled in his output. Inevitably, the scene which casts its shadow over the whole work and comes closest to challenging the validity of the ending is that of the race riot. To lift the taboos on such subjects is one thing, to present them responsibly and to a purpose another. There can be no doubt about Tippett's standpoint in this matter. He wastes no time in explaining why blacks and whites in the crowd scenes are equally at fault in allowing their common humanity to be perverted. If he is pressing a point, it is not that no race has special claims to compassion or brutality but the much larger one that intolerance breeds in mass behaviour and leads to catastrophe. This is the idea *The Ice Break* presents so starkly. In dramatizing it, Tippett naturally courted the danger that his opera would promote the opposite of what he had intended, and to that extent his tactics may be judged irresponsible. This, however, would be to discount his music and his ability to weigh its qualitative effect. One of the most striking features of *The Ice Break* is what may be termed its hierarchy of values, at one extreme the 'poetry' motif, at the other, the music of the crowd scenes. When Tippett reaches the scene of the killings, he ceases to write music, in his sense of the word, altogether. What 'music' there is, is callously descriptive noise, as if by way of underlining that what is happening on stage is real and that to equate that with art would be blasphemy. In the previous scenes, in which blacks and whites assemble, then confront each other in a 'tribal ritual', Tippett keeps art at a distance by putting his music in quotation marks. Summoned by, respectively, tuned drums and muted trumpets (this latter a peculiarly blood-curdling wail[95]), the two groups are identified by the 'Burn, baby, burn' chant which greeted the firing of buildings during the 1965 riots in the Watts district of Los Angeles (see Ex. 188) and by a cold distortion of a Methodist hymn[96] appropriated by the Ku Klux Klan, now given new words (the first four lines in Tippett's text are authentic, the remainder his own – see Ex. 190). The groups then taunt and provoke each other, the blacks led by

Ex. 190   The Ice Break

a clarinettist and dancing what Tippett has described as the 'violent dancing of Voodoo' (his tune is authentic), the whites led by a violinist[97] and dancing a hoe-down – all this, cardboard music, crude, vulgar and two-dimensional. It is platitudinous. When, however, animal-like itera-tions on the voices force their way into the texture and turn the sound into a nightmarish racket, questions of artistic quality become irrelevant: the stage is simply a source of menace and terror (see Ex. 191).

Tippett thus makes no attempt to 'poeticize' these events and elevate them through musical argument. All he does is label his groups and then combine them in the most primitive of collages. It is a moot point whether

Ex. 191   The Ice Break

the crowd music of *The Ice Break* represents a failing of his creative imagination or the necessary consequence of his scenario. Certainly this music is short-winded; but it is bold and eventful as well. It is unmemorable but recognizably individual. In any event, the brevity of Tippett's crowd scenes ensures that they do not squander their theatricality.

The most idiosyncratic of them is that in Act III, where drug-sodden hippies, awaiting the answer to the riddle of the universe, are rewarded by the appearance of Astron, a double-voiced androgynous spirit (sung by mezzo-soprano and high tenor). Astron emits some cryptic quotations, rebukes those who would place him in the seat hitherto occupied by God ('Saviour?! Hero?! Me!! You must be joking.') and vanishes in a puff of smoke. At best he is a pipe-dream, at worst nothing at all. The scene is attractive to look at and if its nod in the direction of rock music summons up a lusty operatic chorus instead, it is none the less entertaining for that. Tippett went to considerable trouble to justify the scene dramatically. He reveals that the 'paradise' Nadia's soul has supposedly just entered is a fiction; he uses the scene to emphasize the futility of Gayle's deification of Olympion by showing that there is nothing to deify in a fantasy world either; and he subsequently contrasts the unreality of Astron's emergence with the reality of Yuri's rebirth. Special pleading of this kind is however inconsistent with Tippett's basic idea that the chorus erupt irrationally and it only serves to underline a fundamental defect in the scene – which is that it is out of character and out of place. It introduces entirely new personnel (hippies, as opposed to the previous racial groups) and an entirely new dimension (that of a vision), neither of them possible to integrate because neither is developed. Why, then, did Tippett introduce the scene? As has been suggested, one reason must be that he wanted to restate the agnosticism of his Symphony No. 3. The more important reason however is frankly autobiographical. Astron is the last in line of Tippett's 'messenger' figures. Tippett's opinions on the status of messenger figures may seem to have changed radically since he first articulated them through the person of Sosostris. Astron is not awesome, he is absurd. All the same, Tippett cannot resist introducing him. Even if he is appalled at the pretentiousness of imagining the creative artist could be of any significance at all, at the same time he is driven by his belief that what the artist actually says is supremely significant and must not be suppressed. This is the irony of the artist's position. Astron is a send-up and in any case his messages are not original but quotations from Jung and Shakespeare; they are however deadly serious and the essence of what Tippett would wish his music to say. 'Take care for the Earth. God will take care for himself' – adapted from a Jung letter;[98] 'Spring come to you at the farthest in the very end of the harvest' – from the masque in *The Tempest*: miracles can occur and the renewal of spring take place in the cold of winter.

Solo music within crowd scenes represents an intermediate stage in the opera's hierarchy of values, more individual than the crowd music itself but still affected by artificiality. Astron's messages are delivered in the halting and rather stilted manner of someone who can only just remember what he has been told to say. Gayle offers herself to Olympion with such fervour that it is not surprising that Yuri thinks she protests too much. Olympion greets his fans with an aria whose self-posturing is as transparent as it is engaging (see Ex. 192).

Ex. 192 The Ice Break

The most clear illustration of Tippett's treatment of the remaining stages in his hierarchy is provided by the family scenes of Act II, which range from ensembles and duets, where individuality is to a greater or lesser extent held in check, to an aria, in which Tippett writes some of the most haunting and moving music in the opera. The act is designed symmetrically (quartet, duet, aria, duet, quartet, with interspersed crowd scenes and a coda), rather like the middle act of *The Midsummer Marriage*, and perhaps for the same reason, in that the most deeply archetypal material, here the eruption of violence, must be contained within the most abstract of structures. The difference is that, presumably to achieve maximum clarity of meaning, Tippett now imposes symmetry less rigidly. The second quartet, for example, is far less obviously a quartet than the first.

The first quartet is the only true ensemble in the opera, a family quarrel in which Gayle, Nadia, Yuri and Lev are able to break out of the isolation of their private thoughts only by means of impulsive outbursts of moral rectitude. Constructive dialogue is therefore impossible. Tippett's super-position of four vocal strands, in the declamatory style made familiar from *The Knot Garden*, and two additional orchestral strands (the 'poetry' motif and, at the other extreme, the cocky motif of the easy-going Gayle) creates the most dense texture he has written since the slow movement of his Piano Concerto, impenetrable to the point of perversity but an exact metaphor of the situation on stage. Although the second quartet (the arrival of a police lieutenant, a hospital doctor, Hannah and Lev on the scene of the murders) is as straightforward as the first is not, its characters are hardly less boxed in by their fixed attitudes and the music hardly less communicative of Tippett's idea that the individual is compromised by the group.

The duets are on a higher level of quality, particularly the first, a love scene between Hannah and Olympion in which Tippett writes music of great beauty, betraying, however, a reluctance on the part of the lovers to yield fully to their own or each other's humanity. It is an intellectualized expression of the memory of love rather than an expression of love itself (see Ex. 193).

Ex. 193   **The Ice Break**

The most completely human music occurs only when a character is alone – the aria for Hannah, in which she explores the 'blue night' of her soul after her lover has been swept away by his masked followers to what she senses will be his death. Hannah's aria may seem disproportionately long; but apart from the fact that it thereby makes a key contribution to the act's structure, its length is really a way of underlining Tippett's idea that true humanity is to be sought in the individual. In the process he discloses the kind of music in which he himself is at his most personal and by which *The Ice Break* is most sharply distinguished from his previous output. The real novelty of the opera lies in its daring simplicity of line and harmony, notably in Hannah's aria (Ex. 194(i)), also in the Act III aria of Nadia as, on her deathbed, she regresses into childhood (Ex. 194(ii)), and most of all in those moments when thoughts are expressed not vocally but instrumentally. The 'poetry' motif represents the apex of Tippett's hierarchy of values, but the Act II coda comes close to it: a silent eloquence as the bereaved Hannah and the distraught Lev seek comfort in one another (Ex. 194(iii)).

Of all Tippett's operas *The Ice Break* is the least easy to assess. Its scope is enormous; inevitably therefore, its contents are too large for its form. In attempting to remedy this, Tippett deprived his specifically human contents of the chance of establishing themselves convincingly (Lev, for example, remains a disturbingly inert figure and Yuri, around whose rebirth the whole opera revolves, does not even have an aria to his name)

Ex. 194   **The Ice Break**

(i) Act II

(Ex. 194 cont.)

(iii) Act II

and thus left his work with something of the flavour of a tract, whose manner is more persuasive than its matter. In the process he also weakened the impact of his most fascinating structural idea – continuous narrative splintered by choral eruptions – because the narrative scenes are too short and the eruptions too frequent to allow the idea to register dramatically. Add to this Tippett's dangerous use of 'inferior' music and *The Ice Break* might seem fatally flawed. It might perhaps be judged an heroic failure. If so, this would not be to dismiss it. Rather would it be to recognize that Tippett has dared to embrace subjects of such magnitude and say something important and moving about them.

1976-

Ex. 195   Symphony No. 4

The example above is of the opening of Tippett's Symphony No. 4: a click
in the lock and the listener is ushered into a realm of feeling where
everything is resonant, lucid and alert and where is unfolded a seemingly
endless succession of distances. Tippett's gesture is both profoundly
familiar and marvellously surprising. It would perhaps be stretching a
point to suggest that it continues from where his Piano Sonata No. 3 left off
(compare with Ex. 185) but there is no doubt that it marks the assuage-
ment of the fury of the Sonata, that it relegates its composer's anxious
involvement with contemporary sociology in *The Ice Break* to another
planet, in short, that Tippett has signposted as clearly as a composer can
his entry into a new world of expression where the distinctive features will
be expansiveness, inclusiveness, the intrinsic. The Symphony then proceeds to generate a single-movement design, whose component sub-

sections are broad and purposeful rather than erratic (as in *The Ice Break*, for example). And while its language contains nothing that is strictly new, its scope is wide (stretching back as far as the beginning of his String Quartet No. 1: compare Ex. 195 with Ex. 25); and it is productive as well, for the work abounds with the creative excitement of a composer who has accepted that his pioneering days are over and who now finds that such acceptance leads not to sterility but to richness. The dominant idea embodied in the Symphony is thus of acceptance.

It would be misleading to suggest by this that the Symphony is serene or resigned, though it does contain moments of deep serenity and even, at the end, of true resignation. In fact the immediate impressions it gives are of mass, of boldness, of toughness and exertion, dramatic contrasts, prodigal invention, orchestral virtuosity extended to its limits. These characteristics could be interpreted as Tippett's salute to the Chicago Symphony Orchestra who commissioned the work – and he is unlikely to have included six horns, two tubas and a large percussion section in his scoring had there been no such commission. But he is not really the kind of composer who trades in social courtesies and the Symphony's character, like that of all his major works, must be taken as the product of creative necessity. It remains therefore to consider why so strenuous a work should embody the idea of acceptance. The key to this question lies in Tippett's treatment of his main climax. On the analogy of his other symphonies this might have been expected to uncover the revelation to which all else had been leading. What actually happens is a literal repeat of Ex. 195 – an anticlimax, in the normal course of events. The quality of the opening music is however so deep-rooted that its recall instantly fires that shiver of recognition which is the seal of the numinous: the climax *is* a revelation. In other words it is an acceptance, that what opened the Symphony is an untranscendable and unsurpassable mystery. It is in this context that Tippett's idiosyncratic use of a wind machine can best be understood,[1] for it represents not wind but the 'wind of the spirit', or, less poetically, breathing, the ultimate metaphor of life. The opening bars are the ineffable, primary impulse which breathes life into things. When these bars return, within a recapitulation in which the diverse events of the Symphony pass, as it were, under review, they confer a kind of ritual benediction. Tippett seems to be saying, quite simply, that he accords supreme meaning and value to nothing less than life itself and that the efforts, trials, consolations, delights, agonies that have been enacted during the course of his work will now be sanctified. Once this has been done he gives a final assurance that new life will always be born and there remains only a gradual, resigned, though peaceful extinction of life. The breathing stops: there is a death. No threnody, no despair. Tippett accepts the condition of mortality, the human condition *per se*. Most of his music may be said to have been concerned with the idea of acceptance. Now he expresses it not as something to be campaigned for but as an experience to be embraced in its totality and rejoiced in.

Tippett was seventy-two when he completed the Symphony and it is perhaps too easy to read into it the natural instinct of an old man to encapsulate the knowledge of a lifetime. But by referring to his Symphony as a 'birth to death piece', by adopting the formal metaphor of a single movement (which inevitably signifies unity and comprehensiveness), by combining within this structure the classical procedures of his first period with the fantasia-like ones of his second, by combining the abstract with the programmatic – by all these things and, in particular, by the tone of the Symphony, Tippett leaves little doubt that the work was indeed conceived in the terms outlined above. To reduce its expressive effect to the single word acceptance is of course to court misunderstanding. If, however, acceptance implies passive submission, the strenuousness of the music quickly asserts an active involvement in accommodating the diverse components of life. If acceptance seems a somewhat limp conclusion to draw from the knowledge of a lifetime, it is actually a profoundly considered philosophy which rejects religious and political dogma, the attitudes of either/or, and puts in their place the overriding need to include everything and recognize that if the humanist position is to be strengthened through music, this can be done only with great effort and in very small stages. The faith which makes this possible is kindled by the transcendent – which is why the opening of the Symphony is so crucial a moment and why a work of such strenuousness and diversity should nevertheless sound less like an expression of these things than a celebration of them. Despite its craggy surface, at its heart there is calm and assurance.

This is the predominant tone of the Symphony and in the two instrumental works Tippett has completed since, his String Quartet No. 4 and Triple Concerto for violin, viola, cello and orchestra, it has grown steadily more pronounced. In fact, the three works have so many points in common that Ex. 195 can already be interpreted as an open sesame to not only a symphony but to a 'late' period as well. To examine such a period along the lines adopted in earlier chapters of this book would be premature. Tippett's creative energies show no signs of abating (his *The Mask of Time*, completed in 1982, promises to be the most extended and ambitious of his non-operatic works) and it is obviously impossible to predict where a late period would ultimately lead. But the three instrumental works offer some indication of its broad direction and they at least can be surveyed briefly by way of postscript.

Each covers a complete cycle of experience and each is an unbroken span of music; each is lit up by its moments of transcendence. Collectively, therefore, they speak of a single artistic purpose – in which respect Tippett's late music may seem to have reached a kind of stasis, a constant reformulation of the same thing. A verbal summary of this 'thing' tends to make it sound pretentious: continually to testify to a comprehensive experience of value and meaning in life, or to fulfil an imperative moral obligation to uphold the humanist position. Nevertheless his purpose certainly is of high pretension, and given the example of the rest of his output, it could hardly be otherwise. What this means is simply that his late music in no way represents a weakening of creative ambition. Whether it represents a withdrawal into a more personalized view of the composer's mandate than had earlier been the case is an open question. Tippett's late works appear more concerned with voicing a personal philosophy than with responding to the 'feel of the time'; yet they could also be understood as characteristic attempts to 'project into our mean world [an increasingly mean and polarized world] music which is rich and generous'.[2] Perhaps personal and public responsibilities in his make-up have become so integrated that they are one and the same. In any event, if the common purpose of his late works suggests that his creative imagination is running dry, the individuality and imaginative richness of the works themselves tell of creativity refreshed.

The source of this refreshment may be said to lie in his discovery of a structural archetype, new to his music and no less vital and insistent than were the sonata (the 'historical') and the fantasia (the 'notional') archetypes of his first and second periods. It may be called the cyclic archetype. Tippett's late works are conditioned by the demand not only for variety and unity, for comprehensiveness and synthesis, but also for aural and thus structural clarity. They are not particularly radical manifestations of the cyclic archetype, as in, for example, Sibelius's Symphony No. 7 or the one work of Tippett himself which anticipates his later practice, his Piano Sonata No. 2. Rather are they an interlocking, an acceptance, of both the sonata and the fantasia, of Tippett's earlier instinct to preserve and distinguish between classical genres and his subsequent one to discard them. In these respects, and in their use of thematic and sectional interrelationships and recurrences, his late works of course reflect a nineteenth-century inheritance and as such mark his eventual coming to terms with the Romantic tradition he had dismissed in his youth as irrelevant. But the true significance of the cyclic archetype lies solely in the fact that it can generate metaphors of comprehensiveness. Each of the three works is a different metaphor, the Symphony of life itself, the String Quartet of an individual life, ending, after passion has receded, in a vision of transcendence, and the Concerto of a natural cycle from one day to the next. Each has a different structure, Tippett's inventiveness deriving particularly from his varied treatment of the sonata-allegro, itself a product of his re-examination of the form in his Piano Sonata No. 3.

The Symphony combines the 'historical' four-movement design with the freer sectional construction of a symphonic poem, comprising slow introduction and sonata exposition (first movement), development 1, slow movement, development 2, scherzo and trio, development 3, recapitulation (finale). The sonata exposition here serves to establish the proportions of the whole work and accordingly it drives forward in one extended paragraph, even though it divides neatly into the traditional components of first subject, transition, second subject and codetta. Before and after development 1 Tippett introduces a structural brake, a three-part landmark consisting of climactic tutti semiquavers, punctuating chords on the six horns and a passage of release, which is an index both of his desire to have his design followed easily and of the confidence with which he conceives simple, bold gestures in his late works. This landmark does not return until it ushers in the recapitulation, so the central four sections form a unit on their own. They are an exemplary series of causes and effects. The profoundly beautiful slow movement eventually drifts into a state of lethargy. The music is then forcibly shaken into life again and to such an extent that it gains an inflated sense of its own power and importance. Very characteristically, Tippett now pricks the bubble and provides a somewhat inane, self-deprecating waltz as scherzo. With the trio (for three pairs of horns) the music recovers its self-respect and that authentic vitality which is recapitulated as a symbol of life reborn near the end of the Symphony. The return of the landmark music now defines the central sections as an extended 'development' and the Symphony itself as one vast sonata-allegro: exposition, two developments and recapitulation.

The four movements of the String Quartet are more closely related to the 'historical' archetype than are the principal sections of the Symphony, in that they include a genuine finale, and lead directly into one another, following the spirit, if not the letter, of Beethoven's op. 131. But the sequence of movements is unusual and recalls Tippett's own String Quartet No. 1 rather than any obvious classical precedent: extended slow introduction, sonata-allegro, main slow movement, palindromic finale. The format of the sonata-allegro is nicely geared to its status as a movement carrying major but not crucial structural weight. It is cast in three strophes – three expositions, each with first- and second-subject and codetta groups. These expositions are adapted to function as quasi-exposition, -development and -recapitulation but they are not argued through in such a way as to pre-empt the effect of the last two movements. The finale is another example of how Tippett adapts the palindrome to his own expressive purposes. Here the material is full of Promethean struggle, a point underlined by a reference to Beethoven's *Grosse Fuge*. But Tippett does not continue the struggle, in a Beethovenian way, to a point of resolution. At the centre of the palindrome he introduces a new element, a strange, disembodied slow theme on high harmonics. The main allegro material is organized in three pairs and the pairs now retreat in reverse order, while, in between, the 'other' music grows into the vision of transcendence with which the Quartet ends. If the work seems to finish on a note of irresolution, the struggle abandoned and the transcendence not properly won, this is not a sign of weakening compositional resolve but another way of expressing the philosophy of acceptance.

The Concerto does perhaps show some signs of weakening resolve. It opens with a sub-Wagnerian gesture that is disturbingly ordinary compared with the 'birth-motifs' introducing the Quartet and, especially, the Symphony, and the second part of its finale is perfunctory. Yet the work contains some of the most enchanting music Tippett has written and these defects ultimately are submerged within that calm and measured progress which comes only to the composer who has unquestioning confidence in his own creativity. The most striking feature of the Concerto is a rapt lyricism, notably in the slow movement, which is focused on an exquisitely beautiful tune in F major. The lyricism derives from the soloists, representatives of each member of the string family (bar the double-bass) accepted for what they are and allowed to explore their individual identities without being pressurized into an artificial unity. The choice of three string players presumably derives from Tippett's conceptual basis. He has revealed that he conceived the work as a progress from one day to the next, or, in other words, as a natural cycle flowing from beginning to end and admitting none of the sharp contrasts associated with more individual experience. The cyclic design of the Concerto is accordingly a continuous flow: sonata-allegro linked by an interlude to the slow movement, which itself is linked to the finale by a second interlude. In this scheme of things the first interlude evokes twilight, the slow movement night (a nocturne) and the second interlude dawn – hence Tippett's quotation in the latter from the dawn chorus in *The Midsummer Marriage*. Dawn imagery also explains the otherwise gratuitous clatter on percussion and trumpets, which precedes the quotation, for this is a musical equivalent of the sudden streaks of red that shimmer across the dark colours of a night sky. What gave him the idea of painting dawn in this way was the phrase 'night splits' from Yeats's poem *High Talk*.

All metaphor, Malachi, stilts and all. A barnacle goose
Far up in the stretches of night; night splits and the dawn breaks loose;
I, through the terrible novelty of light, stalk on, stalk on;
Those great sea-horses bare their teeth and laugh at the dawn.[3]

Tippett's fascination with the phrase 'gong-tormented sea' from another late poem of Yeats, *Byzantium*, could provide a strong reason for the presence of tuned gongs in the Concerto – even though his visit to Indonesia shortly before composing the work was the real stimulus behind its many, if unobtrusive orientalisms (its scoring, occasional pentatonicism and its re-creation of Javanese gamelan performing practice, notably at the end, where the players simply put their instruments down, as it were, and stop). In keeping with its conceptual basis, all movements are open-ended. The sonata-allegro consists of an exposition and a recapitulation which is also a development; the slow movement is a rondo which could repeat indefinitely; the finale is in two discrete sections. What turns this into a cyclic organism is the reappearance at the end of the work of the opening paragraph (the 'birth-motif'; the material introducing each instrument in turn; and the material marking their hushed communion – this latter borrowed from the Quartet's coda) and of the sonata-allegro's codetta. Tippett's procedure may suggest the truism that things will always begin and end in the same way but that their middles will be different; it gains significance here because it is in the middle, the slow movement, that the transcendent moments occur. In the process Tippett shows that transcendence is a gift that can occur anywhere – at the beginning (the Symphony), the middle (the Concerto) and the end (the Quartet).

Structural novelties are of course not the only novelties yielded by

Tippett's adoption of the cyclic archetype. Perhaps the most immediately audible are those of sound and harmony – the continual enlargement of his timbral vocabulary (as in the *tremulo sul ponticello*, the pizzicato glissandos and the very rich eight-part sonorities of the Quartet, or the sweet and sharp brilliance of celesta and glockenspiel accompanying alto flute, and the magical octave doubling of the soloists in the slow movement of the Concerto) and his enriched harmonic palette, deriving ultimately from the colouring of a blues chord. But these novelties do not alter the fact that Tippett's late music remains unmistakably of its composer, that it celebrates the *status quo*, that it is all acceptance.

The eventual contents of Tippett's late period can only be guessed at. As for his existing work, that is *there* – solid, imposing, multifarious, demanding of its commentator that he stand back a little, take a look at it and attempt some final assessment of its stature and status. An invidious task: the work of a composer of genius should properly be the subject of understanding rather than the object of value-judgements. To suggest that Tippett is a genius is however to make a value-judgement from the start, thus to evoke the truism that commentaries on music are intrinsically and irredeemably subjective. Luckily one does not need to be a solipsist to live with that, for if music teaches anything at all it is that behind every division humanity has contrived to impose on itself there lie deep areas of universal feeling which bind it together. So, while my 'assessment' is a report of personal opinions, it is also an attempt to persuade.

Certain characteristics of a composer of genius can be taken for granted – the vision which enables him to pursue his own priorities whether or not they correspond with received opinion, the individuality which gives precision to what he has to say and the highly developed technique which enables him to say it. Thus far, Tippett fits the prescription very well. At this point we might add complexity of musical language. The single theme of music is human experience and if a composer is to say anything worthwhile about that, he will struggle to find some meaning in its tensions, diversities, paradoxes – its complexity. (Certainly there are composers who have turned their backs on these things and retreated into fantasy or an equivalent of that scientific method which finds meaning in information: but their art is deficient.) Here Tippett continues to fit the prescription, especially in his rhythmic polyphony, a musical analogue of tension. It is only when we consider the particular quality of a composer's approach to meaning that assessment of his stature becomes more subjective. The meaning of life is in the living of it, more particularly in the experience of those transcendent moments of timeless illumination, resolution of tension, which fully define the words meaning and value. The search for transcendence is the terrifying, supreme task of the genius. If he succeeds, the listener too experiences something of that terror, when his hair stiffens or his spine tingles. It is part of Tippett's genius that he can make your spine tingle. It is a special part of his genius that he can do so

within contexts which might seem inimical to the idea of transcendence.
He belongs to that generation of composers, born in the 1900s, which
witnessed in two world wars a rape of civilized values more horrible and
protracted than had ever been known before. What sort of art could be
created in a world that had barbarized everything it apparently stood for?
The challenge of this question could be ignored and the nineteenth-century
tradition of the 'egotistical sublime' perpetuated in a kind of apathetic
nostalgia. Or it could be accepted. And what would be accepted would be
that the artist has a moral responsibility to try to preserve or remake those
values which have been perverted, while at the same time never losing sight
of the contemporary reality that they might yet again be perverted. The
point, therefore, was not what to do but how to do it. Tippett's own
answers to this question – his discovery of a tradition he could belong to
and rejuvenate, his relating of the eternal with the actual – have been
examined in the previous pages of this book. The point to be made now is
the delicate one that the value of great art is to be measured in terms of its
moral standpoint. Art is not a plaything. A vitally important message
imperfectly transmitted is greater than an unimportant one perfectly
transmitted. Faults can be found in some of Tippett's works; but they are
swallowed up in his emotional and intellectual eloquence. What he has had
to say has not of course won easy acceptance, because that is the way with
music which demands active involvement from its listeners. But he has
achieved enough, I think, to stand as the composer who has contributed
more to the English tradition than any other since Purcell and, alongside
three others of his generation, Carter, Messiaen and Shostakovich, as one
of the giants of the century.

Herschel Grynspan

Herschel Fiebel Grynspan (born on 28 March 1921) was the youngest of three surviving children of a family of eight. His father[1] was a tailor, born in Russian-dominated Poland, who had settled in Hanover before the 1914–18 war, first retaining his Russian nationality and then changing to Polish when the Versailles Treaty restored Polish independence. After leaving school Herschel Grynspan planned to emigrate to Palestine. He was granted a passport valid until June 1937, and he obtained from the Hanover police a re-entry permit – the official document he needed before he could obtain a visa for Belgium, where an uncle lived and where he hoped to obtain a visa for Palestine. At this point a chance meeting with an old man at a synagogue persuaded him that he should change his plans, leave Germany as soon as possible and settle in France. His father then wrote to another uncle, in Paris, who said he would take the boy and even adopt him. In July 1936 Grynspan all the same went to Brussels, where the Belgian uncle was unwelcoming but where a charitable neighbour took him in. In September the neighbour's sister, who lived in Paris, paid a short visit to Brussels and allowed Grynspan to travel with her back to Paris, even though he did not have the necessary papers. He crossed the border by taking a tram reserved for railway employees, and arrived at his uncle Abraham's house later in the month. His uncle arranged a residence permit and his Polish passport was renewed by the Polish Consulate until February 1938. But from that date no attempt was made to preserve his status. He was consequently living in France illegally, as well as having forfeited the possibility of legal residence in three other countries: Poland, Belgium and Germany.

On 11 August 1938 he was served with an expulsion order from the French Ministry of the Interior and his uncle was now obliged to shelter him in a servant's room at the top of the house. Grynspan's relatively free and easy existence came to an abrupt end when, on 3 November, he received a postcard dated 31 October from his sister at Zbonszyn, telling him of his family's arrest and deportation and how they were now penniless. His anguish was intensified by reports in the Jewish paper *Journée Parisiènne* (*Pariser Haint*) of the persecutions on the Polish frontier. He talked of suicide but abandoned the idea because he thought that the death of one Jew would not attract attention. His uncle tried to pacify him by giving him money but he was not to be pacified and began to reproach his uncle and aunt for being indifferent to his family. On the evening of 6

November he left the house in a fury and booked himself in a hotel. Later that evening he wrote a message to his parents asking their forgiveness for the protest he was about to make. On the following morning, 7 November, he bought a revolver and went to the German Embassy in Paris saying that he wanted to hand over some important documents to the ambassador's first secretary. No credentials were asked for and he was admitted. Since the secretary was out, he was taken to the third secretary, Ernst vom Rath. Grynspan protested about the treatment of the Jews at the frontier, and then fired five shots, two of which hit vom Rath. Grynspan made no attempt to escape. Vom Rath died on 9 November, two days after the shooting.

Later that month Grynspan's uncle and aunt were sentenced to four months' imprisonment plus a fine each, on appeal altered to six months for the uncle and three months for the aunt. The Nazis wanted the French to try Grynspan secretly. But world opinion (co-ordinated in the USA by Dorothy Thompson, wife of the novelist Sinclair Lewis, who set up a Herschel Grynspan Defense Fund and engaged a prominent lawyer, Vincent de Moro-Giafferi) urged a public trial. The trial was delayed by the French authorities, firstly on the grounds that feeling against Germany would prejudice impartiality and then, with the outbreak of war, on the grounds that the plaintiffs, vom Rath's family, could not be admitted to France until the war was over. A month after war was declared Grynspan wrote from Fresnes prison in Paris to the French Minister of Justice appealing for release so that he could go out to fight Nazism. But by the time he was actually released he had evidently become a changed person. During the confusion preceding the armistice, prisoners from Paris, including Grynspan, were evacuated first to Orléans in southern central France and then, because of the German advance, were earmarked for a prison at Bourges. But the police escort abandoned the convoy on the way and left the prisoners to fend for themselves. Most of them disappeared into the countryside but Grynspan asked to be taken to Bourges prison. Perhaps he did this to avoid capture by the Germans or perhaps he was so full of remorse that he craved for punishment. In any event at Bourges he was quickly told to slip away and after being refused admission at the prison in Châteauroux was finally taken in at Toulouse. The Vichy government traced him and handed him over to the Nazis. In October 1940 he was sentenced, ostensibly by a Vichy court, to twenty years in a penitentiary. Later that month he was sent to Berlin. In January 1941 he was in Sachsenhausen concentration camp, where however he was treated mildly because the Nazis wanted him in good shape for a spectacular public trial they were planning. He returned to a Gestapo prison in Berlin in the summer of that year to be at hand for the trial. The trial was eventually fixed for May 1942 but in fact it never took place. Grynspan suddenly claimed to have had homosexual relations with vom Rath, a ruse which was too clever even for Goebbels who feared that testimony of this kind would sabotage the whole point of the trial. It has been suggested[2] that Grynspan survived the war and then lived in Paris under an assumed name, but no material evidence of his fate has yet come to light.

Tippett's Choice of Poetry

For the BBC programme 'With Great Pleasure', Tippett chose the following: 'Is my team ploughing?' from Housman's *A Shropshire Lad*, 'Drum Taps' from Whitman's *Leaves of Grass*, Goethe's 'Marienbad Elegie' and 'Wanderers Nachtlied', Shakespeare's sonnet 'Shall I compare thee to a summer's day', Blake's 'The Tyger', the first movement from Eliot's 'Burnt Norton', Yeats's 'Lapis Lazuli', the 'Tempest' chapter from Dickens's *David Copperfield* and the 'First Day of Creation' chapter from Solzhenitsyn's *Cancer Ward*.

For 'Personal Anthology', he chose the following: the section beginning 'Oh, what is life and what is man?' from the first chapter of Blake's *Jerusalem*, 'Anthem for Doomed Youth' and 'The End' by Owen, 'The Windhover' and 'Felix Randal' by Hopkins, 'Lay your sleeping head' by Auden, the beginning of *The Waste Land*, the third section of *Ash Wednesday* and *The Journey of the Magi* by Eliot, 'Leda and the Swan', 'Among School Children', 'The Second Coming' and 'Lullaby' by Yeats and Ulysses's speech on degree from Shakespeare's *Troilus and Cressida*.

NOTES TO THE TEXT

INTRODUCTION

1. Michael Tippett, *Moving into Aquarius* (London ^{2}1974), p. 118; subsequent references are to this edition
2. George Clement Boase, *Collectanea Cornubiensia* (Truro 1890), p. 994
3. *The Times*, 17 January and 10 February 1899
4. See Fred Hitchen-Kemp, *The Kemp(e) Family of Thanet, Chislet, Whitstable and other parts of Kent* (London 1903)
5. In August 1943, when Tippett was thirty-eight and shortly before his release from prison, he wrote to Evelyn Maude: 'She [his mother] had better face up to the fact that she will just spoil my (& her) homecoming – for the old usual mother-ish moral reasons wh. spoilt so much of childhood'. *Michael Tippett: A Man of Our Time* (London 1977), p. 52
6. Lieut.-Commander Peter Kemp is now a distinguished naval historian
7. Later in life she became an adherent of the anthroposophy of Rudolf Steiner, she attended churches of every denomination and eventually she became a believer in spiritualism and faith-healing. Her belief in spiritualism derived from an experience during a severe illness in her early forties, in which, in her delirium, she thought she had entered 'the other side' of life. Her bible was the *Aquarian Gospel of Jesus the Christ*, the 'philosophical and practical basis of the religion of the aquarian age of the world and the church universal', transcribed from 'God's remembrances known as the Akashic records' by Levi [Levi H. Dowling] (London 1908). See I.C. Kemp, *God Within* (Bala, North Wales 1965)
8. R.O. Morris, *Contrapuntal Technique in the Sixteenth Century* (London 1922)
9. See Phyllis Kemp, *Healing Ritual: Studies in the Technique and Tradition of the Southern Slavs* (London 1935)
10. See also Michael Tippett, *Music of the Angels*, ed. Meirion Bowen (London 1980), pp. 117ff
11. After the Second World War she, and her Indian husband, eventually settled in East Berlin. Her major work, *Englische Arbeiterliteratur vom 18. Jahrhundert bis zum ersten Weltkrieg* (Berlin and Weimar 1980), is published under her married name of Phyllis Mary Aschraf.
12. See Francesca Allinson, *A Childhood* (London 1937)
13. See Rolf Gardiner, *Water Springing out of the Ground* (Shaftesbury 1972). Gardiner was a remarkable man of lofty idealism. He came to maturity in the aftermath of the First World War and was extremely sensitive to Anglo-German bitterness. He believed that the only way to heal the wounds of the war was to encourage England and Germany to accept a common destiny as part of a commonwealth of nations linked by a Celtic-Germanic culture, a commonwealth that would create some independent unit of strength between the USA and the USSR. In an attempt to achieve this he bypassed conventional political methods and appealed direct to the aspirations of young people. He found a model method in the work-camps which took place in Silesia in 1928–30. Here there had also been severe unemployment and a successful attempt had been made to replace industrialization with a return to a land economy and a campaign of

self-help and self-government which cut across class barriers. Peasants, workers and students joined in releasing the latent talent and energy of the indigenous people. A land economy implied a rural culture, and music and dancing found a natural place in the scheme of things. The Cleveland camps imitated the Silesian pattern: physical work in the mornings (clearing the land of rocks and gorse and then double-digging it for allotments) and cultural activities during the rest of the day (meetings and discussions of local matters, choral singing, sword dancing, country dancing, concerts, plays). The students who came to the camps were mostly English and German but included Danes and Norwegians.

14. Reg Groves, *The Balham Group* (London 1974)
15. See, for example, Alan Bush and Randall Swingler (eds.), *The Left Song Book* (London 1938)
16. *Music of the Angels*, pp. 34–6
17. Jeffrey Mark, *The Modern Idolatry* (London 1934) and *Analysis of Usury* (London 1935)
18. Evelyn Underhill, 'Men and Books', *Time and Tide*, xix, 2, 8 January 1938, pp. 46–7 (review of William Blake, *Illustrations of the Book of Job*, with a note by Philip Hofer, London 1938)
19. In the first, which took place in a new and unfamiliar estate of his, a huge lorry and tractor were backing down a slope threatening to crush roses and fruit trees he had planted near a river. He then saw that the machines were digging a trench for a water pipe and that they had carefully avoided disturbing his roses and fruit trees. Walking back to his house he noticed that builders had left logs for his winter fires. In the final dream he was in bed in a strange room of a strange house unable to sleep. A young man came in bringing an early breakfast and saying that he had woken him because the men downstairs knew that Tippett had the money to 'pay them out'. He noticed that the young man was holding a medical syringe, actually a revolver. He then understood that he would not have to pay out and could keep the money, which had belonged to his comrades who had been killed during the previous week. Then two of these 'dead' men came in. He realised that a fourth was missing, the last to 'die', at which point the fourth man came through the door. Tippett said to himself 'Let what must be happen'. The fourth man gave him both his hands and signalled to the other three, who began to strangle him. A bell rang (his alarm clock) and, still dreaming, he said to himself 'This is where we wake up'.
20. *Moving into Aquarius*, p. 23
21. Ibid., p. 121
22. Tippett's routine in his Oxted cottage is vividly described by John Amis and Priaulx Rainier in Ian Kemp (ed.), *Michael Tippett: A Symposium on his 60th Birthday* (London 1965), pp. 74–5 and 77
23. Ibid., p. 20
24. Reprinted in *Moving into Aquarius*, p. 22
25. An episode recounted in 'Britten by Tippett', *The Observer*, 17 November 1963, p. 29
26. Four of Tippett's letters from prison (to Evelyn Maude) are reproduced in *Michael Tippett: A Man of Our Time*, pp. 40–53
27. See Michael and Mollie Hardwick, *Alfred Deller: A Singularity of Voice* (London 1968), especially pp. 71–7
28. Earlier in 1948 he had visited Budapest, as a member of the jury for the Bartók competition and as a conductor of his own music, and had soon discovered that Stalinism was still flourishing, contrary to the hopes of Western idealists for the 'popular front' government. What struck him most forcibly was a remark of an orchestral player: 'The reason we like you is because when *you* say B flat and not B natural we know that that is not a political question.'
29. See Nicolas Nabokov, *Bagázh* (London 1975), pp. 232–8 and Dmitri Shostakovich, *Testimony*, ed. Solomon Volkov (London 1979), pp. 111–12 and 152, in which Shostakovich describes his part in the affair. 'I felt like a dead man. I answered all the idiotic questions in a daze, and thought, when I get back it's over for me.'
30. *Moving into Aquarius*, p. 83

31. Ibid., p. 129
32. *Monthly Musical Record*, lxix, March–April 1939, pp. 73–6
33. Michael Tippett, 'A Personal View of Music in England', in Carl Dahlhaus (ed.), *Festschrift für einen Verleger: Ludwig Strecker zum 90. Geburtstag* (Mainz 1973), p. 63
34. Ibid.
35. Michael Tippett, 'Music for Our Time', *The Sunday Telegraph*, 3 January 1965
36. *The Times*, 4 September 1953
37. Ibid., 29 November 1951
38. 'The BBC's duty to society', *The Listener*, 26 August 1965, pp. 302–3
39. The script is printed in *Moving into Aquarius*, pp. 148–59
40. 'The BBC's duty to society', op. cit.
41. Adrian Ball (ed.), *Food of Love* (London 1971)
42. Ian Kemp, op. cit., pp. 64–8
43. See Appendix 2
44. See, however, Antony Hopkins in Ian Kemp, op. cit., pp. 78–9
45. *Moving into Aquarius*, p. 148
46. Ibid., p. 148
47. Ibid., p. 118

CHAPTER ONE

1. See Colin Mason, 'Michael Tippett', *The Musical Times*, May 1945, pp. 137–41
2. Allinson wrote a book on the whole subject, *The Irish Contribution to English Traditional Tunes*, which so offended the Sharp school that it was never accepted for publication. The MS is now, ironically, in the Vaughan Williams Memorial Library, London, having been presented by Tippett.
3. A.L. Lloyd, *Folk Song in England* (London 1975), p. 44
4. See Michael Tippett, 'Holst: Figure of Our Time', *The Listener*, lx, 13 November 1958, p. 800

CHAPTER TWO

1. Rimington, Van Wyck advertisement for the recording of Tippett's Piano Sonata No. 1, *The Gramophone*, August 1941
2. Pierre Boulez, *Conversations with Célestin Deliège* (London 1976), p. 56
3. Sleeve note to recording on Nonesuch H-71249
4. Vincent d'Indy, *Cours de Composition Musicale*, deuxième livre (Paris 1912). pp. 241–61
5. Michael Tippett, 'Music and Life – 1938', *Monthly Musical Record*, lxviii, July–August 1938, pp. 176–7
6. 'Tippett's Piano Concerto', *The Score*, 16 (June 1956), pp. 63–8
7. Tippett's published rhythms are usually a compromise in the interests of ensemble. Notational problems are similar to those discussed by Olivier Messiaen in *Technique of My Musical Language* (Eng. trans. 1957), Chapter VII.
8. Revised edition, *Jazz: A History* (New York 1964)
9. *Rhythm and Tempo* (London 1953), pp. 21–32
10. Edward T. Cone, *Musical Form and Musical Performance* (New York 1968), pp. 26–31
11. Howard E. Smither, 'The Rhythmic Analysis of 20th-Century Music', *Journal of Music Theory*, viii, 1964, pp. 54–88
12. Tippett himself has suggested that certain elements in his style derive from Northumbrian bagpipe music ('The Composer Speaks', *Audio and Record Review*,

February 1963, pp. 27–8). Northumbrian bagpipes, known as small pipes, are pitched higher than Scottish bagpipes and can produce a clear staccato. Tippett's discovery of this subject was the fruit not of academic study but of the enthusiasm of Jeffrey Mark, who thought he had found a model for a new diatonicism in it. At first glance there seems little in common between a Northumbrian dance-tune, such as 'The Broken-Legged Chicken' illustrated below and, for example, Ex. 10.

From J. Collingwood Bruce and John Stokoe, *Northumbrian Minstrelsy* (Newcastle upon Tyne, 1882), p.149

But on closer inspection the Scotch snap at the opening of the tune could be interpreted as a distant relative of the opening of the fugue subject, the trills as the origin of the semitonal clashes in the String Quartet's heterophony; rapid articulation of quavers is common to both. Without a lead from the composer it is unlikely that a commentator could have ferreted out such correspondences.

13. No. 8 from *Nine Fantasias in Three Parts* [c.1620]
14. Reprinted in 'Purcell and the English Language' in Watkins Shaw (ed.), *Eight Concerts of Henry Purcell's Music* (London 1951), pp. 45–9
15. Tippett's op. 1 was his Symphony in B flat. He gave his next four major works opus numbers but he had abandoned the practice before any of his music was in print.
16. After Phyllis Sellick's 1941 recording of the Sonata Tippett shortened the penultimate variation in the first movement and incorporated this alteration in the 1942 first publication of the work. The 1954 edition, although published as a 'revised edition', is in fact the same as the 1942 edition, apart from some changes in notation and a more elegant appearance.
17. Sleeve note by the composer for the recording on Philips 6500 534
18. See *The Listener*, 18 January 1945, p. 66 for a shortened version of a radio talk Tippett gave on 14 January about *A Child of Our Time*
19. At the suggestion of his friend Paul Dienes, a Marxist refugee from Horthy's Hungary, who was both mathematician and poet
20. *Ein Kind unserer Zeit*, reprinted Frankfurt am Main 1973
21. Drawn from contemporary reports in *The Times* and the *New York Times*, and from Rita Thalman and Emmanuel Feinermann, *Crystal Night*, trans. Gilles Cremonesi (London 1974) and F.K. Kaul, *Der Fall des Herschel Grynszpan* (Berlin, DDR 1965)
22. A fuller account is given in Appendix 1
23. Much of the information here and elsewhere is taken from Tippett's article on *A Child of Our Time* in R.S. Hines (ed.), *The Composer's Point of View* (Oklahoma 1963), pp. 111–22, which is reprinted in an extended version in *Music of the Angels*, pp. 117–26
24. Printed in *Music of the Angels*, pp. 127–87
25. Quoted by Tippett in 'The Composer as Librettist', *The Times Literary Supplement*, 8 July 1977
26. See however William McGuire and R.F.C. Hull, *C.G. Jung Speaking* (London 1978), pp. 273–5
27. *Moving into Aquarius*, p. 50
28. C.G. Jung, *Symbols of Transformation* (London 1967), p. 23
29. C.G. Jung, *Aion* (London 1968), p. 226
30. C.G. Jung, *Psychology and Religion* (London 1969), p. 79
31. *Moving into Aquarius*, p. 23
32. Ibid., p. 23
33. C.G. Jung, *Psychology and Alchemy* (London 1968), p. 186
34. 'Music for Our Time', *The Sunday Telegraph*, 3 January 1965
35. Sleeve note (1975) for Philips recording 6500 985
36. James Weldon Johnson (ed.), *The Book of American Negro Spirituals* with music arranged by Rosamund Johnson (New York 1926)

37. R.S. Hines, op. cit., p. 118
38. Ibid.
39. Sleeve note (1975). In the 'Sketch' Tippett indicated that he was also thinking of these lines from Owen's *The Seed*: 'But now the exigent winter, and the need/Of sowings for new spring, and flesh for seed.' Tippett's comments may also be compared with the following sentences of Jung, written in 1946. 'Never before has mankind as a whole experienced the numen of the psychological factor on so vast a scale. In one sense this is a catastrophe and a retrogression without parallel, but it is not beyond the bounds of possibility that such an experience also has its positive aspects and might become the seed of a nobler culture in a regenerated age.' *The Practice of Psychotherapy* (London 1954), p. 231
40. R.S. Hines, op. cit., p. 118
41. Ibid.
42. C.G. Jung, *Psychological Types* (London 1971), p. 467
43. The preceding paragraphs contain a hazardously incomplete summary of Jung's (and Tippett's) understanding of the psyche and the reader is referred to the literature on the subject: *The Collected Works of C.G. Jung*, trans. R.F.C. Hull (London 1953–71) and C.G. Jung, *Memories, Dreams and Reflections* (London 1963); Frieda Fordham, *An Introduction to Jung's Psychology* (London 1953); Jolande Jacobi, *The Psychology of C.G. Jung* (London 1968); Anthony Storr, *Jung* (London 1973)
44. *Music of the Angels*, p. 182
45. Michael Tippett, programme note for York Festival, April 1963
46. R.S. Hines, op. cit., p. 118
47. This spiritual was, ironically, the only one not taken from the James Weldon Johnson book (see note 36 above). There the tune begins with a falling sixth. Jeffrey Mark dictated the present tune to Tippett.
48. A view held by Tippett himself. See Murray Schafer (ed.), *British Composers in Interview* (London 1963), p. 101
49. Poole had been so moved by a BBC broadcast of Tippett's String Quartet No. 2 that he wrote asking for a work for Canterbury
50. In 1953 Tippett wrote a second Fanfare, for four trumpets, for the St Ives Festival of the Arts (of which he, along with Barbara Hepworth and Priaulx Rainier, was an artistic director) because the original Fanfare proved too difficult for the local players. This new Fanfare also proved too difficult, so he wrote a third – of extreme simplicity.
51. Despite his knowledge of the Chrysander edition of Handel, Tippett accepted the corrupt text of *Erewhon*. This is taken from a nineteenth-century edition of Handel's harpsichord music omitting sixteen bars of bravura passage-work after the first cadence. (In its original context the theme is the Prélude in a 'Suite' in B flat first published in London in 1733 in *Suites de Pièces pour le Clavecin*.) All the same the Fantasia abounds with keyboard bravura.
52. Ian Kemp, op. cit., pp. 200–1
53. Michael Tippett, 'Conclusion' in Denis Stevens (ed.), *A History of Song* (London 1960), p. 464
54. BBC Third Programme, April 1973
55. R.S. Hines (ed.), *The Orchestral Composer's Point of View* (Oklahoma 1970), p. 210. See also p. 21 above.
56. To the Liverpool Philharmonic Arts Club. Reported by Scott Goddard in 'Michael Tippett and the Symphony', *The Listener*, 12 January 1950
57. H.E. Wooldridge, 'The Polyphonic Period of Music', *The Oxford History of Music*, i, Part 1, rev. Percy C. Buck (London [2]1929), pp. 148–59
58. R.S. Hines, *The Orchestral Composer's Point of View*, p. 209
59. The note-values of Wooldridge's transcription have been halved. It should be mentioned that it was not known at the time that the texted part of a conductus would have been given to all voices – which explains Tippett's reference to plainsong. His use of the word hoquet is the result of a misunderstanding. The 'flying hoquets' are characteristic melismatic *caudae*. Hockets are vocal ornaments in which one rhythmic

value in a medieval rhythmic mode is missed out. Wooldridge's transcription does not in fact contain any (although a more recent transcription does: see Ethel Thurston, *The Works of Pérotin*, New York 1970). Tippett's 'bumpy quavers' refer to the short-long rhythm of the rhythmic modes 2, 3 and 4, which appears in Ex. 68(i) (mode 4, bars 5–6) and in later parts of Wooldridge's transcription not given here.

60. Significantly, this motif recurs at the climax of the fourth ritual dance in *The Midsummer Marriage* (see Ex. 100*a*)

61. In an unpublished letter of December 1940 to Francesca Allinson. The Man of the title is an irresponsible widower who leaves money-making to his daughters – except the youngest who still goes to school. Most of his time is spent in the pub. The unexpected arrival of a handsome cousin from the north provides the necessary catalyst. The cousin enrages everyone by taking the youngest daughter to the cinema, whereupon the other six turn on their father with such ferocity that they inadvertently kill him. It then becomes clear that despite his behaviour the father was the real centre of the household, for the daughters promptly proceed to break away. Before they depart however the news attracts the pub regulars and the scenario ends with a sozzled barman sentimentalizing over his dead friend.

62. T.S. Eliot, 'Shakespeare and the Stoicism of Seneca', *Selected Essays* (London 1932)

63. *Moving into Aquarius*, pp. 50–66. Jung would have called it a product of the 'active imagination'.

64. An apparently slovenly expression (Kantian in origin) but one that had the sanction of Eliot. In his essay 'The Three Voices of Poetry' (*On Poetry and Poets*, London 1957) Eliot refers with approval to a lecture by the German poet Gottfried Benn, paraphrasing Benn's account of the creative process as follows: 'When you have the words for it, the "thing" for which the words had to be found has disappeared, replaced by a poem.'

65. *Moving into Aquarius*, p. 107

66. 'The Composer as Librettist', *The Times Literary Supplement*, 8 July 1977

67. Susanne Langer, *Feeling and Form* (London 1953), p. 157

68. Denis Stevens, op. cit., pp. 462–3. See also 'Music and Poetry' in *Recorded Sound*, xvii, January 1965, pp. 287–93.

69. 'Music and Poetry', op. cit.

70. Douglas Newton. See Newton's article 'The Composer and the Music of Poetry' in *The Score*, 1, August 1949, pp. 13–20.

71. Erich Neumann, 'Art and Time', Bollingen Series XXX, *Man and Time* (New York 1957), pp. 29–30. See also *Moving into Aquarius*, p. 123.

72. See Jane Harrison, *Prolegomena to the Study of Greek Religion* (Cambridge ³1922), pp. 572ff and W.K.C. Guthrie, *Orpheus and Greek Religion* (London 1935), pp. 171ff

73. Susanne Langer, op. cit., p. 193

74. Described briefly in *Psychology and Alchemy*, pp. 376–96. The book was first published in 1944 in Zürich as *Psychologie und Alchemie*.

75. C.G. Jung, *The Archetypes and the Collective Unconscious* (London 1968), p. 22

76. C.G. Jung, *Two Essays on Analytical Psychology* (New York 1953), pp. 225–39

77. C.G. Jung, *Aion*, pp. 233–4

78. C.G. Jung, *The Archetypes and the Collective Unconscious*, p. 20

79. Ibid., pp. 255–72

80. He was particularly fascinated by the concept as formulated in an ancient Chinese book of religion: *The Secret of the Golden Flower* [the lotus], trans. Richard Wilhelm with commentary by C.G. Jung (London 1962). See also *Psychology and Alchemy*, pp. 95–222 and *The Archetypes and the Collective Unconscious*, pp. 355–84.

81. *Moving into Aquarius*, p. 143. Tippett's ideas derived from Heinrich Zimmer, *Myths and Symbols in Indian Art and Civilization* (New York 1946), especially pp. 11–19. This book also showed him how he could represent his 'sacred marriage' or symbol of the self. One of its illustrations (plate 34) is of a tenth-century Bengalese relief, now in the British Museum, of Shiva-Shakti – the god Shiva and his consort Shakti seated on a throne of lotus. In *The Midsummer Marriage* the transfigured Mark and Jenifer are

directed to be 'seated facing the audience, but with their heads turned to each other. The outside of her right thigh is resting on the inside of his left thigh.' This is an exact description of the pose in the relief. Zimmer's commentary includes the following: 'Gazing with a deep and everlasting rapture, they are imbued with the secret knowledge that, though seemingly two, they are fundamentally one. For sake of the universe and its creatures, the Absolute [represented by the lotus] has apparently unfolded into this duality, and out of them derive all the life polarities...'

82. See also Robert Donington, 'Words and Music' in Ian Kemp, op. cit., pp. 87–113
83. Jane Harrison, *Themis* (London [2]1912)
84. Ibid. p. xxi
85. Ibid., 'Excursus on the ritual forms preserved in Greek Tragedy', pp. 341–63
86. F.M. Cornford, *The Origins of Attic Comedy* (London 1914). Current scholarship attempts to discredit Cornford, but this would not have worried Tippett. See also G.R. Levy, *The Gate of Horn* (London 1948), pp. 313–30.
87. *Moving into Aquarius*, p. 53
88. As described in Jessie L. Weston, *From Ritual to Romance* (London 1920)
89. 'The Composer as Librettist', op. cit. The poem was 'put into my hands by a Hungarian mathematician [Paul Dienes, see note 19 above], who said: "There is the answer to what you are looking for" – and it was.' ('Music and Poetry', op. cit.)
90. They are from an essay by Schiller, 'Die Sendung Moses'. See A.W. Thayer, *The Life of Ludwig van Beethoven*, ii (New York 1921), pp. 167–8.
91. Robert Graves, *The White Goddess*, rev. ed. (London 1961), p. 448
92. Maud Karpeles (ed.), *Cecil Sharp's Collection of English Folk Songs*, i (London 1974), No. 109 Hares on the Mountains.
93. *Moving into Aquarius*, p. 21
94. J.G. Frazer, *Balder the Beautiful*, i (London 1913), p. 168. This is Part VII of *The Golden Bough*.
95. According to Frazer's understanding of primitive belief, fire was associated with resurrection by means of the following argument. The great god manifested himself most spectacularly through lightning and lightning seemed to favour oak trees. The great god therefore resided in the oak. It was on an oak that mistletoe was most frequently found. Mistletoe is evergreen, it grows not out of the earth but out of the oak and its berries glow with the golden light of the sun (it is the golden bough Aeneas plucked as talisman for his journey into the underworld). The mistletoe is therefore the heart and soul of the great god. If a pretender managed to slaughter the guardian of the sacred oak he would inherit the power of the mistletoe and be next in line for the sacred marriage with the earth goddess. In this way Frazer solved the riddle of the King of the wood and the priesthood of Diana at Nemi.
96. J.G. Frazer, *Adonis, Attis, Osiris* (London 1913), pp. 146–8. This is Part V of *The Golden Bough*.
97. C.G. Jung, *Symbols of Transformation*, p. 166
98. *I Ching*, trans. R. Wilhelm (London [3]1968), p. 269. Trigrams are blocks of three lines, some continuous, some broken, that function as images of the continually changing forces which shape life; pairs of trigrams form the characteristic hexagrams with which the book is chiefly concerned.
99. The manner of King Fisher's death owes much to the final scene in Part IV of *Back to Methuselah*. There the Oracle knows that the Elderly Gentleman's desire for a life of transcendence would be too much for him: 'He stiffens; a little convulsion shakes him: his gaze relaxes; and he falls dead.'
100. This *parabasis* is a personal reproof as well. Paul Dienes (see note 19) and his wife had been living with Tippett at Tidebrook Manor ('the broken house') and it was there that Dienes developed a fatal illness. While writing Act III of the opera Tippett had neglected his friend. 'Players and painted stage took all my love,/And not those things that they were emblems of.' (W.B Yeats, 'The Circus Animals' Desertion')

101. In the Introduction to his *Oxford Book of Modern Verse* (Oxford 1936) Yeats wrote that 'passive suffering is not a theme for poetry', thereby explaining the omission from his anthology of Owen, for whom the key word was 'pity'. For Yeats the key word was 'gay', referring to that intellectual passion through which a creative artist can transform suffering into joy. Tippett's identity here with Yeats marks his own shift from the 'pity' of *A Child of Our Time* (see above, p. 163) to the 'gaiety' of the opera.

CHAPTER THREE

1. 'An Englishman Looks at Opera', *Opera News*, 2 January 1965, pp. 7–9
2. And always for the same purpose: a kind of 'open sesame' to the world of the imagination. The pedigree of the motif for the god Hermes in *King Priam*, for example, can be traced by reference to Exx. 101(i), 103(iii), 116, 119 (harp and piano) and 130.
3. Better known as the hymn 'Let saints on earth in concert sing'
4. Tippett's programme note for the first performance
5. See E.W. White, 'Crown of the Year' in Ian Kemp, op. cit., pp. 50–2, for the work's compositional background
6. 'O mistress mine' from *Twelfth Night*, in the version of Byrd and Morley; 'Malbrough s'en va–t–en guerre', which of course sounds like 'For he's a jolly good fellow'; the Austrian carol 'O wie wohl ist mir am Abend', known in English as 'Oh how lovely is the evening'; 'Frankie and Johnny' in the less familiar version introduced by the Leighton Bros.
7. Variations on an Elizabethan Theme (Sellinger's Round) for string orchestra, first performed on 20 June 1953. After a transcription, by Imogen Holst, of the theme – Byrd's version from the *Fitzwilliam Virginal Book* – there follow variations by Arthur Oldham (*Allegro non troppo*), Tippett (*Andante espressivo*), Berkeley (*Andante*), Britten (*Quick and gay*), Searle (*Adagio*) and Walton (*Presto giocoso*).
8. Tippett's editions of Purcell's songs are not so informative, since they are largely the work of his collaborator, Walter Bergmann. See Ian Kemp, op. cit., p. 82.
9. See note 13 to Chapter Two
10. The aria 'Preach me not your musty rules' from Arne's music for the masque in *Comus*; Field's Nocturne No. 13 in D minor; 'I have a song to sing, O' from Gilbert and Sullivan's *The Yeomen of the Guard* (this last set in an expert pastiche of the Stravinsky of *Danses Concertantes*)
11. Tippett's sleeve note to the recording on L'Oiseau Lyre DSLO 14
12. See p. 25
13. The passage may also be interpreted as a tribute to Britten, for Tippett borrowed the idea of intoning on a single note, and the note in question (E), from the aria 'Now the Great Bear and Pleiades' from *Peter Grimes*
14. 'Music and Poetry', op. cit., pp. 287–93
15. Ibid.
16. See Peter Evans, 'The Vocal Works' in Ian Kemp, op. cit., pp. 154–60, for an examination of Tippett's treatment of the strophic principle
17. Taken from the second movement of Corelli's Trio Sonata in B minor, op. 3, No. 4. Further background information can be found in the preface to the Eulenburg miniature score of the *Fantasia Concertante* (London 1985).
18. Ernö Lendvai, *Béla Bartók* (London 1971), pp. 1–16
19. Extreme technical and ensemble difficulties have gained the work some notoriety, and unless performed well and in a good acoustic it can indeed sound confused, like incoherent but vaguely animated burblings from a musty clubroom
20. This despite the fact that Tippett has described the first two movements as a 'Domenico Scarlatti sonata' and 'tiny sonata-allegro', respectively (programme note)
21. Tippett has explained (sleeve note to the recording on Argo ZRG 535) that the 'exact moment of conception' of the Symphony was stimulated by some music of Vivaldi. He was in a studio of Radio Lugano (see p. 56), listening to tapes, when some 'pounding

cello and bass C's, as I remember them, suddenly threw me from Vivaldi's world into my own'. This is remarkable evidence of the archetypal nature of musical gesture, for the beginning of Tippett's Symphony derives from no particular Vivaldi original.

22. The expression coined by Leonard B. Meyer in *Music, the Arts, and Ideas* (Chicago 1967), p. 72

CHAPTER FOUR

1. See the 'Notes' Brecht appended to his libretto for Weill's *Aufstieg und Fall der Stadt Mahagonny*. Tippett had in fact been influenced by Brecht, as is discussed on p. 357.
2. *Moving into Aquarius*, pp. 101 and 130
3. Ibid., p. 132
4. Ibid., p. 141
5. 'The Composer as Librettist', op. cit. and *Music of the Angels*, p. 223
6. Paris 1955; English translation by Philip Thody, *The Hidden God* (London 1964)
7. Tippett's programme note for the first performance of *King Priam*
8. *Moving into Aquarius*, p. 100
9. Ibid., p. 134
10. Leonard B. Meyer, *Music, the Arts, and Ideas*, p. 183
11. *Moving into Aquarius*, p. 144
12. Ibid., p. 153
13. Ibid., p. 118
14. Ibid., p. 143
15. From the text of Tippett's Symphony No. 3
16. See Jacob Bronowski, *The Ascent of Man* (London 1973)
17. R.S. Hines, *The Orchestral Composer's Point of View*, pp. 210–11
18. Ibid.
19. Susanne Langer, *Philosophy in a New Key* (Cambridge, Mass. [3]1957) p. 238
20. In R.S. Hines, *The Orchestral Composer's Point of View*, pp. 203–19, especially pp. 204–5
21. *Music of the Angels*, p. 223
22. Subsequently published as 'Drum, Flute and Zither', *Moving into Aquarius*, pp. 67–84
23. Ibid., p. 70
24. *Music of the Angels*, p. 223
25. Ibid., p. 226
26. In this connection, see Tippett's remarks quoted on p. 330
27. *Music of the Angels*, p. 232
28. Ibid., p. 224. Eight, because Tippett originally thought that the eight trigrams of the *I Ching* could help articulate the separate stages of an 'eight ages of man', the turning point being marked by the conjunction of the all-male and all-female trigrams.
29. In this connection it is worth pointing out that Berlioz's *Les Troyens* was performed at Covent Garden in 1957
30. *Music of the Angels*, p. 231. Having completed *King Priam*, Tippett found a book which neatly expressed his thoughts on the matter. Here is a relevant passage from Eric Bentley, *The Life of the Drama* (London 1965), p. 36: 'The distinction we live with each day remains (since babyhood) simply that between oneself and other people. And the primordial group of other people – our family – makes up the original cast of characters in the drama of life, a drama that we keep on reviving later with more and more people cast for the same few parts.' Tippett provides a fuller quotation in *Music of the Angels*, pp. 211–12.
31. 'At work on *King Priam*', *The Score*, 28 (January 1961), pp. 58–68
32. *Moving into Aquarius*, p. 65
33. *Music of the Angels*, pp. 224–5
34. Ibid., p. 205
35. See Tippett's descriptions of his characters in *Music of the Angels*, pp. 227–30

36. As in *The Merchant of Venice* (three caskets = three women), *King Lear*, Psyche, the Judgement of Paris. See Siegmund Freud, 'The Theme of the Three Caskets', in *The Complete Psychological Works*, xii (London 1958), pp. 291–301.

37. 'The composer as Librettist', op. cit.

38. W.B. Yeats, 'The Statues' from *Last Poems*

39. For example: 'Ah, but life is a bitter charade'; 'Prince Hector will want his bath the moment he comes in from fighting'; and these two exchanges between Paris and Priam: 'Achilles has killed him, and shamefully misused him' – 'Say that again' and 'I will leave the doomed city to found another Troy' – 'You are not the founding sort'.

40. See also William Mann, in Ian Kemp. op. cit., pp. 127–34 and Francis Routh, *Contemporary British Music* (London 1972), pp. 282–91

41. A standpoint which suggests that Tippett's sung interludes derive as much from Yeats's dance plays as from Brecht. In *The Tragic Drama of William Butler Yeats* (New York and London 1965, p. 176) Leonard E. Nathan writes that Yeats's chorus of Three Musicians (playing drum, flute and zither, see note 22 above) 'creates the scene, prepares for the action, explains or generalizes on both, and naturalizes the incredible, all without entering the action. In all its functions it operates as a human imagination given special insight into the depths of the mind, yet reacting to the tragic struggle with a horror springing from a normal sense of life ...'

42. 'The Composer as Librettist', op. cit.

43. Some are taken from another Yeats collection, *A Woman Young and Old*. The full sequence comprises 'After Long Silence', 'Crazy Jane talks with the Bishop', 'Crazy Jane Grown Old looks at the Dancers', 'A First Confession', 'His Bargain', 'Girl's Song', 'Young Man's Song', 'Her Anxiety', 'Consolation', 'Her Dream', 'Parting', 'Three Things' and 'A Last Confession'.

44. Two female and one male. They took the parts of, respectively, 'Crazy Jane', 'Young Girl', and of 'The Poet' and 'Young Man' together.

45. Act II, scenes 1 and 2, and Act III, scene 3

46. *Music of the Angels*, pp. 60–6

47. Culled largely from Reinhold Hammerstein, *Die Musik der Engel* (Berne 1962)

48. *Music of the Angels*, p. 63

49. *E. William Doty Lectures in Fine Arts*, 2nd series 1976 (Austin, Texas 1979), p. 45

50. Ibid., p. 44

51. At least this would seem to be the case. But Tippett has told the present writer that *The Knot Garden* is also influenced by *Lila*, a remarkable and little-known Singspiel of Goethe, in which the heroine's psychological problems are cured by the technique of what is now known as psychodrama. Masterminded by a doctor disguised as 'Der Magus', Lila meets the figures of her fantasy world – who are her own family and friends disguised as fairies, demons, etc – and is restored to health and to her husband.

52. See Robert Grams Hunter, *Shakespeare and the Comedy of Forgiveness* (New York 1965). The quotation itself is included in Eliot's essay 'The Three Voices of Poetry'.

53. It could be Theia, the sun-goddess wife of Hyperion; or Thea (sometimes also known as Thetis), the prophetess daughter of Cheiron, the centaur king; or even Thetis herself, the sea-goddess. The latter two both had difficulties with their offspring. Thea's daughter was turned into a foal by Poseidon before it was born, because Poseidon wanted to help conceal the pregnancy and the mortal seducer, Aeolus, from Cheiron. It was then turned back into a girl and adopted. Thetis could not find a husband because the gods had been told that any son born to her would be greater than its father. She was married off to Peleus, by whom she had seven sons. Six she burned to make them immortal but the seventh, Achilles, was rescued by Peleus, whereupon Thetis retreated in fury to her private sea-house. In both cases the goddesses lost their children because they had slept with a mortal. Could this imply that Tippett's Thea was harbouring her own daughter disguised as a ward, or that she felt she had married beneath her? The allusiveness of much of Tippett's work often prompts speculations of this kind. He himself would not say whether they were relevant or not, characteristically refusing to

limit himself to any one interpretation. If, therefore, the individual listener finds them helpful, well and good; if not, it does not really matter.

54. *Shakespeare's Last Plays* (London 1975)

55. Tippett encountered the name in a newspaper report of the wedding of General Dayan's son-in-law. Dov is a diminutive of David. The biblical David was psalmist and musician, an allusion which pleased Tippett, as did the idea that the dove symbolizes peace, the soul, or, in Christian symbolism, the Holy Spirit.

56. The name derives from *miel*, the French for honey. Mel suggests the USA, where 'honey' is a common form of endearment. The name also recalls the situation in Shelagh Delaney's *A Taste of Honey*.

57. Later, having completed the opera, Tippett commented that she is 'for a moment the goddess Calypso' (thought by some authorities to be the daughter of Thetis, see note 53 above). At the same time he explained that he had taken the idea of cocktail glasses lifted as libations from Eliot's *The Cocktail Party*. Calypso can 'take you into the garden with the sexual power, and the glass is the eternal image of the female'. (See *Sir Michael Tippett*, a brochure issued by Phonogram International n.d.)

58. Her obscure comment here, 'Blood from my breast', is a reference to the pre-Shakespearean 'comedy of forgiveness', *The Rare Triumphs of Love and Fortune*, in which Fidelia pierces her breast so that her despicable brother may be cured of dumbness and thereby forgiven for his part in banishing her lover. See Robert Grams Hunter, op. cit., p. 70.

59. W.H. Auden, 'The Sea and the Mirror', in *Collected Longer Poems* (London 1968), p. 234

60. From the final lines of Virginia Woolf's *Between the Acts*

61. An image borrowed from Goethe's poem *Das magische Netz*

62. Tom Sutcliffe, 'Tippett and The Knot Garden', *Music and Musicians*, xix, December 1970, p. 53

63. One is reprinted in David Matthews, *Michael Tippett* (London 1980), pp. 81–2; the other appears almost verbatim in Francis Routh, op. cit., pp. 292–3

64. 'An Englishman Looks at Opera', *Opera News*, 2 January 1965, p. 9

65. See note 52 above

66. See Charles Keil, *Urban Blues* (Chicago 1966), pp. 125–8 and 141, from which all the blues texts are taken

67. A characteristic excerpt from the libretto which, if it reads on paper like an advertisement for glue, has in performance the necessary clarity and immediacy to prevent it holding up perception of the music

68. Boris Pasternak, *Doctor Zhivago*, trans. Max Hayward and Manya Harari (London 1958), p. 436

69. Ibid., p. 499

70. Tippett has dismissed his pastoralism here as rhetoric, but it is difficult to believe that he meant to. *Music of the Angels*, p. 237

71. By John Smith. See *The Catch Club* (London 1762, reprinted Ridgewood, New Jersey 1965)

72. See Ian Kemp, op. cit., p. 70. The final line of Goehr's canon yielded, to Tippett, such peculiar harmonies that he changed it.

73. *Moving into Aquarius*, p. 163

74. Ibid.

75. Ibid., p. 164. 'Man is All Imagination', the aphorism from Blake's annotations to Berkeley's *Siris*, is echoed by Faber in the epilogue to *The Knot Garden*

76. Igor Stravinsky, *Poetics of Music* (London 1947), p. 117

77. F.E. Sparshott, 'Aesthetics of Music', *New Grove Dictionary of Music and Musicians*, i (London 1980), p. 128

78. From an unpublished 'Fore-note' of February 1971

79. *Moving into Aquarius*, p. 158

80. 'Tippett's Third Symphony', *Music and Musicians*, June 1972, pp. 30–2

81. The terms are borrowed from a book on Egyptian and Cretan art by H.A.

Groenewegen-Frankfort, *Arrest and Movement* (London 1951), whose title is itself borrowed from Eliot's 'Burnt Norton', II

82. 'Tippett's Third Symphony', op. cit.
83. 'Michael Tippett', *Hi-Fi News and Record Review*, January 1975, pp. 115–17
84. 'Fore-note', op. cit.
85. 'Michael Tippett', op. cit.
86. *Moving into Aquarius*, p. 158
87. Ibid.
88. LII from 'Poems from the Notebook'. Nobodaddy also figures in XX of the collection and in 'When Klopstock'.
89. Programme note for the first performance, 7 June 1973
90. An amusing hatchet job may be found in Eric Sams's *New Statesman* review of 22 July 1977
91. Tippett has explained the significance of the scene. 'An English girl called Gayle (and I've called her that here) decided that Malcolm X, the Black Power leader, was God. He had a black wife and they all went off to Trinidad with him when he fled back home. Then he murdered Gayle. In that case the catastrophe was sown by trying to turn a human being into God.' *The Observer*, 3 July 1977
92. Tom Sutcliffe, 'Tippett and The Knot Garden', pp. 53–4
93. See C.G. Jung, *The Practice of Psychotherapy*, p. 321. 'The mass-man is good for nothing – he is a mere particle that has forgotten what it is to be human and has lost its soul.'
94. Tippett's description obviously recalls Stravinsky's recollections of the 'violent Russian spring that seemed to begin in an hour and was like the whole earth cracking'. *Memories and Commentaries* (London 1960)
95. Meetings of the Ku Klux Klan were summoned by a man on horseback who rode around blowing (wailing) a trumpet
96. Lowell Mason's 'Missionary Hymn', known in England as 'From Greenland's Icy Mountains', and used by Ives in his String Quartet No. 1 and Symphony No. 4. Tippett's setting, the tune in the tenor, was suggested to him by a film of a barber shop contest in Portland, Oregon.
97. Suggested by an old print of the famous fiddler Fiddlin' Jim Carson playing at the gallows of men murdered by the Ku Klux Klan
98. C.G. Jung, *Letters*, I, 1906–50 (London 1973), pp. 64–6. The relevant passage reads: 'One must be able to suffer God. That is the supreme task for the carrier of ideas. He must be the advocate of the earth. God will take care of himself' (to Walter Robert Corti, 30 April 1929).

POSTSCRIPT

1. Tippett miscalculated here. Despite his indications of 'gently breathing', 'like a prolonged sharp intake of breath', etc., an orchestral wind machine cannot avoid sounding like real wind. Its substitution by actual or synthesized human breathing serves his intentions more faithfully.
2. *Moving into Aquarius*, p. 99
3. In his foreword to *Michael Tippett: A Man of Our Time*, Colin Davis urged Tippett: 'Long may you "through the terrible novelty of light, stalk on, stalk on".' This was how Tippett was led to the poem. The text of *The Mask of Time* begins with the Yeats lines quoted above.

APPENDIX I

1. He survived the war and emigrated to Israel. In 1962 he was taken from his kibbutz to Haifa to hear the first Israeli performance of the work inspired by his son.
2. *Der Spiegel*, xxxvi, 31 August 1960

LIST OF WORKS AND WRITINGS

Dates in square brackets after the title of a work are autograph MS completion dates.

Unpublished Works

This list comprises (a) works or fragments whose MSS have survived and (b) works whose MSS cannot be traced but which were publicly performed.

Arrangements for piano trio (Bolsters – a ballet: The House that Jack Built: Cheerly Men: Yang-Tsi-Kiang: Three Jovial Huntsmen), *c.* 1926–7; *The Undying Fire* (H.G. Wells) for baritone, chorus and orchestra, *c.* 1927; *The Village Opera*: Ballad Opera in Three Acts (Charles Johnson 1729) – performing arrangement, 1927–8; Sonata in C minor for piano, *c.* 1928; String Quartet in F, 1928 rev. 1930; Concerto in D for flutes, oboe, horns and strings, 1928–30 [MS lost]; String Quartet in F minor, 1929; Variations for Dudley [Parvin] for piano, 1929; Ten Variations on a Swiss Folksong as harmonized by Beethoven [WoO64], 1929; Three songs (Charlotte Mew) for voice and piano (Sea Love, Afternoon Tea, Arracombe Fair), 1929 [MS lost]; Jockey to the Fair: Variations for piano, 1930; Overture and Incidental Music to *Don Juan* (James Elroy Flecker), 1930 [MS lost]; Psalm in C: *The Gateway* (Christopher Fry) for chorus and orchestra, 1930; Sonata in E minor for violin and piano, *c.* 1930 [fragments]; Symphonic Movement for full orchestra, *c.* 1930–1; String Trio in B flat, 1932; Orchestration of preceding, 1932 [fragments]; Symphony in B flat, 1933 rev. 1934 [16 November 1933; spring 1934]; *Robin Hood*: A Folk-Song Opera in Two Acts (David Michael Penniless – pseudonym for David Ayerst, Michael Tippett and Ruth Pennyman), 1934; *Miners* (Judy Wogan) for chorus and piano, *c.* 1935; *A Song of Liberty* (William Blake, 'The Marriage of Heaven and Hell') for chorus and orchestra, 1937 [May Day 1937]; *Robert of Sicily*: A Play for Children (Christopher Fry), 1938; *Seven at One Stroke*: A Play for Children (Christopher Fry), 1939.

Published Works

Details of first performances are given in the last entry under each work.

1934–5   String Quartet No. 1 [23 September 1935] rev. autumn 1943 'To Wilfred Franks'

        9 December 1935, Brosa Quartet, Lemare Concert, Mercury

Theatre, Notting Hill Gate, London; revised version, 26 February 1944, Zorian Quartet, Wigmore Hall, London

1936–8 Sonata No. 1 for piano [July 1938]
'To Francesca Allinson'
11 November 1938, Phyllis Sellick, Queen Mary Hall, London

1938–9 Concerto for Double String Orchestra [6 June 1939]
'To Jeffrey Mark'
21 April 1940, South London Orchestra conducted by the composer, Morley College, London

1939–41 Fantasia on a Theme of Handel for piano and orchestra [11 November 1941]
'To Phyllis Sellick'
7 March 1942, Phyllis Sellick and the London Symphony Orchestra conducted by Walter Goehr, Wigmore Hall

1939–41 A Child of Our Time: Oratorio for SATB soloists, chorus and orchestra with text by the composer
19 March 1944, Joan Cross, Margaret McArthur, Peter Pears, Roderick Lloyd, London Region Civil Defence Choir, Morley College Choir and the London Philharmonic Orchestra conducted by Walter Goehr, Adelphi Theatre, London
[In 1958 Tippett arranged the five spirituals for unaccompanied chorus]

1941–2 String Quartet No. 2 in F sharp [5 December 1942]
'To Walter Bergmann'
27 March 1943, Zorian Quartet, Wigmore Hall

1942 Two Madrigals for unaccompanied chorus SATB:
The Source (Edward Thomas)
The Windhover (Gerard Manley Hopkins)
'To Morley College Choir'
17 July 1943, Morley College Choir conducted by Walter Bergmann, Morley College

1943 Boyhood's End (W.H. Hudson): Cantata for tenor and piano
'To Peter Pears and Benjamin Britten'
5 June 1943, Peter Pears and Benjamin Britten, Morley College

1943 Fanfare No. 1 for four horns, three trumpets and three trombones
Commissioned for the 50th anniversary of the consecration of St Matthew's Church, Northampton
21 September 1943, Band of the Northamptonshire Regiment conducted by Bandmaster C. Marriott, St Matthew's Church

1943–4 Plebs Angelica: Motet for double choir
'For the choir of Canterbury Cathedral, January 1944'
Commissioned by Canterbury Cathedral

16 September 1944, Fleet Street Choir conducted by T.B. Lawrence, Canterbury Cathedral

1944–5   Symphony No. 1 [25 August 1945]
10 November 1945, Liverpool Philharmonic Orchestra conducted by Malcolm Sargent, Philharmonic Hall, Liverpool

1944   The Weeping Babe (Edith Sitwell): Motet for soprano solo and mixed choir SATB [Christmas 1944]
'In memory of Bronwen Wilson, August 8th 1944'
Commissioned by the BBC for 'Poet's Christmas'
24 December 1944, BBC Singers conducted by Leslie Woodgate, BBC Home Service

1945–6   String Quartet No. 3
'To Mrs Mary Behrend'
Commissioned by Mary Behrend
19 October 1946, Zorian Quartet, Wigmore Hall

1946   Preludio al Vespro di Monteverdi for organ [5 July 1946]
'For Geraint Jones'
5 July 1946, Geraint Jones, Central Hall, Westminster.

1946   Little Music for string orchestra
'For the 10th anniversary of the Jacques String Orchestra'
9 November 1946, Jacques Orchestra conducted by Reginald Jacques, Wigmore Hall

1946–52   The Midsummer Marriage: Opera in Three Acts with text by the composer
27 January 1955, Covent Garden Opera conducted by John Pritchard, produced by Christopher West, scenery and costumes by Barbara Hepworth, choreography by John Cranko, Royal Opera House, Covent Garden

Ritual Dances from The Midsummer Marriage for orchestra with optional chorus
'To Walter Goehr'
13 February 1953, Basel Kammerorchester conducted by Paul Sacher, Musiksaal, Basel

1948   Suite for the Birthday of Prince Charles (Suite in D)
Commissioned by the BBC in celebration of the birth of Prince Charles
15 November 1948, BBC Symphony Orchestra conducted by Sir Adrian Boult, BBC Third Programme

1950–1   The Heart's Assurance (Sidney Keyes and Alun Lewis): Song-cycle for high voice and piano
'In memory of Francesca Allinson (1902–1945)'
Commissioned by Peter Pears
7 May 1951, Peter Pears and Benjamin Britten, Wigmore Hall

1952 Dance, Clarion Air (Christopher Fry): Madrigal for five voices SSATB
From 'A Garland for the Queen' [a collection of madrigals by Bliss, Bax, Tippett, Vaughan Williams, Ireland, Howells, Finzi, Rawsthorne and Rubbra], *commissioned by the Arts Council of Great Britain to mark the occasion of the coronation of Her Majesty Queen Elizabeth II*
1 June 1953, Golden Age Singers and the Cambridge University Madrigal Society conducted by Boris Ord, Royal Festival Hall, London

1953 Fantasia Concertante on a theme of Corelli for string orchestra
Commissioned by the Edinburgh International Festival 1953, in celebration of the tercentenary of the birth of Arcangelo Corelli
29 August 1953, BBC Symphony Orchestra conducted by the composer, Usher Hall, Edinburgh

1953 Fanfare No. 2 for four trumpets
Fanfare No. 3 for three trumpets
Written for the St Ives Festival, Cornwall
6 June 1953 [Fanfare No. 3], trumpeters from RAF St Mawgan, St Ives Church Tower

1953–4 Divertimento on 'Sellinger's Round' for chamber orchestra
'Dedicated to Paul Sacher'
Commissioned by Paul Sacher
5 November 1954, Collegium Musicum Zürich conducted by Paul Sacher, Tonhalle, Zürich

1953–5 Concerto for piano and orchestra
'To Evelyn Maude'
Commissioned by the City of Birmingham Symphony Orchestra in conjunction with the John Feeney Charitable Trust
30 October 1956, Louis Kentner and the City of Birmingham Symphony Orchestra conducted by Rudolf Schwarz, Town Hall, Birmingham

1954 Four Inventions for descant and treble recorders
Written for the Society of Recorder Players
1 August 1954, Freda Dinn and Walter Bergmann, Froebel Institute, London (Recorder in Education Summer School)

1955 Sonata for Four Horns
20 December 1955, Dennis Brain Wind Ensemble, Wigmore Hall

1956 Bonny at Morn: Northumbrian Folksong set for unison voices and recorders (two descants and treble) [April 1956]
Written for the 10th Birthday of the International Pestalozzi Children's Village at Trogen, Switzerland

1956　　　Four Songs from the British Isles for unaccompanied chorus
　　　　　SATB:
　　　　　　　England: Early One Morning
　　　　　　　Ireland: Lilliburlero
　　　　　　　Scotland: Poortith cauld
　　　　　　　Wales: Gwenllian
　　　　　Commissioned by the Nordwestdeutschland Sängerbund, Bremen
　　　　　6 July 1958, London Bach Group conducted by John Minchin-
　　　　　ton, Abbaye de Royaumont, Seine-et-Oise, France (Royaumont
　　　　　Festival)

1956–7　　Symphony No. 2 [13 November 1957]
　　　　　'To John Minchinton'
　　　　　Commissioned by the BBC
　　　　　5 February 1958, BBC Symphony Orchestra conducted by Sir
　　　　　Adrian Boult, Royal Festival Hall

1958　　　Crown of the Year (Christopher Fry): Cantata for chorus SSA,
　　　　　recorders or flutes, oboe, clarinet, cornet or trumpet, string
　　　　　quartet, percussion, handbells and piano
　　　　　*Commisioned by Eric Walter White for the centenary celebrations at
　　　　　Badminton School, Bristol*
　　　　　25 July 1958, Badminton School choir and ensemble conducted
　　　　　by the composer

1958　　　'Unto the Hills' (John Campbell): Wadhurst (Hymn Tune)
　　　　　Written for The Salvation Army

1958–61　King Priam: Opera in Three Acts with text by the composer
　　　　　'To Karl Hawker'
　　　　　*Written for the Koussevitsky Foundation in memory of Mrs Natalie
　　　　　Koussevitsky*
　　　　　29 May 1962, Covent Garden Opera conducted by John
　　　　　Pritchard, produced by Sam Wanamaker, scenery and costumes
　　　　　by Sean Kenny, Coventry Theatre (Coventry Cathedral Fes-
　　　　　tival)

1959　　　Lullaby for Six Voices (Yeats) or alto solo and small choir
　　　　　SSTTB
　　　　　'For the 10th birthday of the Deller Consort'
　　　　　31 January 1960, Deller Consort, Victoria and Albert Museum,
　　　　　London

1960　　　Music (Shelley): Unison Song for voices, strings and piano or
　　　　　voices and strings
　　　　　*Written for the jubilee of the East Sussex and West Kent Choral Festival
　　　　　1960*
　　　　　26 April 1960, Combined Choirs of the East Sussex and West
　　　　　Kent Choral Festival conducted by Trevor Harvey, Assembly
　　　　　Hall, Tunbridge Wells

1960   Words for Music Perhaps (Yeats): A sequence of love poems for speaking voice or voices and chamber ensemble
Commissioned by the BBC
8 June 1960, Bee Duffell, Sheila Manahan, Allan McCelland, ensemble conducted by the composer, produced by Anthony Thwaite, BBC Third Programme

1961   Songs for Achilles for tenor and guitar
7 July 1961, Peter Pears and Julian Bream, Great Glenham House (Aldeburgh Festival)

1961   Magnificat and Nunc Dimittis for chorus SATB and organ, (Collegium Sancti Johannis Cantabrigiense)
Composed for the 450th anniversary of the foundation of St John's College, Cambridge
13 March 1962, St John's College Chapel Choir conducted by George Guest

1962   Sonata No. 2 for piano [March 1962]
'To Margaret Kitchin with affection and esteem'
3 September 1962, Margaret Kitchin, Freemason's Hall, Edinburgh (Edinburgh Festival)

1962   Incidental Music for Shakespeare's *The Tempest*
29 May 1962, produced by Oliver Neville, music directed by John Lambert, Old Vic, London

1962   Songs for Ariel for voice and piano or harpsichord
21 September 1962, Grayston Burgess and Virginia Pleasants, Fenton House, Hampstead, London
[1964: arr. for voice, fl./picc., cl., hn., perc., hpd.]

1962   Praeludium for brass, bells and percussion
Commissioned for the 40th anniversary of the BBC
14 November 1962, BBC Symphony Orchestra conducted by Antal Dorati, Royal Festival Hall

1962–3   Concerto for Orchestra [June 1963]
'To Benjamin Britten with affection and admiration in the year of his 50th birthday'
Commissioned by the Edinburgh International Festival 1963
28 August 1963, London Symphony Orchestra conducted by Colin Davis, Usher Hall, Edinburgh

1963–5   The Vision of Saint Augustine for baritone solo, chorus and orchestra [10 April 1965]
'Matri, patrisque in memoriam'
Commissioned by the BBC
19 January 1966, Dietrich Fischer-Dieskau, BBC Chorus and Symphony Orchestra conducted by the composer, Royal Festival Hall

1965–70   The Shires Suite for orchestra and chorus
           Written for the Leicestershire Schools Symphony Orchestra
           8 July 1970, Schola Cantorum of Oxford and the Leicestershire
           Schools Symphony Orchestra conducted by the composer,
           Cheltenham Town Hall (first complete performance)

1966   Braint: the final variation in 'Severn Bridge Variations', a com-
           posite work on the traditional Welsh melody by Arnold,
           Hoddinott, Maw, Jones, Williams and Tippett
           Commissioned by the BBC West Region
           11 January 1967, BBC Training Orchestra conducted by Sir
           Adrian Boult, Brangwyn Hall, Swansea

1966–9   The Knot Garden: Opera in Three Acts with text by the
           composer [20 February 1969]
           'To Sir David Webster of the Royal Opera House, Covent
           Garden'
           Commissioned by the Royal Opera House, Covent Garden
           2 December 1970, Royal Opera conducted by Colin Davis, pro-
           duced by Peter Hall, scenery by Timothy O'Brian, costumes by
           Tazeena Firth, Royal Opera House, Covent Garden

1969–70   Songs for Dov for tenor and small orchestra [9 February 1970]
           'To Eric Walter White'
           Commissioned by the Music Department, University College, Cardiff,
           with assistance from the Welsh Arts Council
           12 October 1970, Gerald English and the London Sinfonietta
           conducted by the composer, University College, Cardiff

1970–2   Symphony No. 3 for soprano and orchestra [30 March 1972]
           'To Howard Hartog'
           Commissioned by the London Symphony Orchestra
           22 June 1972, Heather Harper, London Symphony Orchestra
           conducted by Colin Davis, Royal Festival Hall

1971   In Memoriam Magistri for flute, clarinet and string quartet
           Commissioned by Tempo magazine in memory of Igor Stravinsky
           17 June 1972, London Sinfonietta conducted by Elgar Howarth,
           St John's, Smith Square, London

1972–3   Sonata No. 3 for piano [1 March 1973]
           'To Anna Kallin'
           Commissioned by Paul Crossley
           26 May 1973, Paul Crossley, Assembly Rooms, Bath (Bath
           Festival)

1973–6   The Ice Break: Opera in Three Acts with text by the composer
           [27 January 1976]
           'To Colin Davis'
              'Chastened, together,
              We try once more.'

Commissioned by the Royal Opera House, Covent Garden
7 July 1977, Royal Opera conducted by Colin Davis, produced
by Sam Wanamaker, scenery and costumes by Ralph Koltai,
choreography by Walter Raines, Royal Opera House, Covent
Garden

1976–7   Symphony No. 4 [18 April 1977]
          'To Ian Kemp'
          Commissioned by the Chicago Symphony Orchestra
          6 October 1977, Chicago Symphony Orchestra conducted by Sir
          Georg Solti, Orchestra Hall, Chicago

1977–8   String Quartet No. 4 [26 September 1978]
          'To Michael Tillett, colleague and friend'
          20 May 1979, Lindsay String Quartet, Assembly Rooms, Bath
          (Bath Festival)

1978–9   Triple Concerto for violin, viola, cello and orchestra [30 November
          1979]
          'To Herbert and Betty Barrett'
          Commissioned by the London Symphony Orchestra with funds provided by
          the Ralph Vaughan Williams Trust
          22 August 1980, György Pauk, Nobuko Imai, Ralph Kirshbaum,
          London Symphony Orchestra conducted by Sir Colin Davis,
          Royal Albert Hall, London

1980   Wolf Trap Fanfare for three trumpets, two trombones and tuba
          Commissioned for the 1980 Wolf Trap Festival
          29 June 1980, members of National Symphony Orchestra of
          Washington conducted by Hugh Wolff, Wolf Trap Festival,
          Virginia

1980–2   The Mask of Time for voices and instruments (SATB soloists,
          chorus and orchestra) with text written and compiled by the
          composer [16 December 1982]
          'To Meirion Bowen'
             'Parce que c'était lui; parce que c'était moi'
          Commissioned for the 100th anniversary of the Boston Symphony Orchestra
          5 April 1984, Faye Robinson, Yvonne Minton, Robert Tear,
          John Cheek, Tanglewood Festival Chorus, Boston Symphony
          Orchestra conducted by Sir Colin Davis, Symphony Hall,
          Boston

1982–3   The Blue Guitar for solo guitar
          'To the memory of Calvin Simmons (1950–1982)'
          Commissioned by the Ambassador International Cultural Foundation in
          Celebration of the Tenth Anniversary of the Ambassador Auditorium,
          Pasadena, California
          9 November 1983, Julian Bream, Ambassador Auditorium,
          Pasadena

1983   Festal Brass with Blues for brass band [16 September 1983]
            Commissioned by the Hong Kong Arts Festival Society
            6 February 1984, Fairey Engineering Band conducted by
            Howard Williams, Hong Kong Arts Festival
1983–4   Sonata No. 4 for piano [December 1984]
            'To Michael Vyner'
            Commissioned by the Los Angeles Philharmonic Association
            14 January, 1985, Paul Crossley, Japan America Theatre, Los
            Angeles

Addendum

1985   'A Vision of the Island': an adaptation for radio by Andrew
            Parrott and Ian Cotterell of the Incidental Music for *The
            Tempest*, for speakers, four men's voices and chamber ensemble
            25 October 1985, Robert Eddison, Stephen Boxer and others,
            members of the Taverner Consort and Nash Ensemble conducted
            by Andrew Parrott, produced by Anthony Burton and Ian
            Cotterell, BBC Radio 3

Writings

Moving into Aquarius (London 1958: [2]1974)
Music of the Angels, ed. Meirion Bowen (London 1980)

Important articles, conversations and lectures not included in the books
listed above are:

'A Child of Our Time', *The Listener*, xxxviii (1945), p.66
'Purcell and the English Language', *Eight Concerts of Henry Purcell's Music*,
    ed. Watkins Shaw (London 1951), pp.46–9
'Holst: Figure of Our Time', *The Listener*, lx (1958), p.800
'Our Sense of Continuity in English Drama and Music', *Henry Purcell:
    Essays on his Music*, ed. Imogen Holst (London 1959), p.42
'Conclusion', *A History of Song*, ed. Denis Stevens (London 1960)
'At Work on King Priam', *The Score*, 28 (1961), pp.58–68
'The Gulf in our Music', *The Observer* (14 May 1961), p.21
'King Priam: Some Questions Answered', *Opera*, xiii (1962), p.297
'The Composer Speaks', *Audio and Record Review* (February 1963), pp.27–8
'Michael Tippett', *British Composers in Interview*, ed. Murray Schafer,
    (London 1963), pp.92–102
'Music on Television', *The Listener*, lxxi (1964), p.629
'Music and Poetry', *Recorded Sound*, xvii (January 1965), pp.287–93
'An Englishman Looks at Opera' *Opera News*, xxix (2 January 1965),
    pp.7–9
'Music for Our Time', *The Sunday Telegraph* (3 January 1965)
'The BBC's Duty to Society', *The Listener*, lxxiv (1965), p.302
'Waiting for the Public Ear', *The Guardian*, (6 April 1968)
'The Festival and Society', *Musical Times*, cx (1969), p.589
'A Personal View of Music in England', *Festschrift für einen Verleger: Ludwig*

Strecker zum 90. Geburtstag, ed. Carl Dahlhaus (Mainz 1973) pp.61–4

['Concerto for Orchestra'], *The Orchestral Composer's Point of View*, ed. R.S. Hines (Oklahoma 1970), pp.203–19

in Tom Sutcliffe, 'Tippett and Knot Garden', *Music and Musicians*, xix (December 1970), pp.52–4

in Bayan Northcott, 'Tippett's Third Symphony', *Music and Musicians*, xx (June 1972), pp.30–2

'My Kind of Music', *The Observer* (17 October 1973)

'Michael Tippett talking about the PPU', *The Pacifist*, xiii/3 (October 1974) pp.11–14

'Michael Tippett', *Hi-Fi News and Record Review* (January 1975), pp.115–17

'Michael Tippett on Ice', *The Observer* (3 July 1977)

'The Composer as Librettist', *Times Literary Supplement* (8 July 1977)

'Back to Methuselah and The Ice Break', *Shaw Review*, xxi/2, May 1978, pp. 100–3

E. William Doty Lectures in Fine Arts, 2nd series 1976 (Austin, Texas 1979)

['Shostakovich's Testimony'], *Quarto*, No.3 (February 1980), p.7

'*The Mask of Time*: Work in progress', *Comparative Criticism: A Yearbook*, iv, ed. E.S. Shaffer (Cambridge 1982), pp.19–30

SELECT BIBLIOGRAPHY

Books and Monographs

Ian Kemp (ed.), *Michael Tippett: A Symposium on his 60th Birthday* (London 1965)

Michael Hurd, *Tippett* (London 1978)

Eric Walter White, *Tippett and his Operas* (London 1979)

David Matthews, *Michael Tippett* (London 1980)

Meirion Bowen, *Michael Tippett* (London 1982)

Arnold Whittall, *The Music of Britten and Tippett* (Cambridge 1982)

Nicholas John (ed.), *Operas of Michael Tippett* (London 1985)

Geraint Lewis (ed.), *Michael Tippett O.M.: A Celebration* (Tunbridge Wells 1985)

Articles

John Amis, 'New Choral Work by Michael Tippett', *Musical Times*, lxxxv (1944), p.41

Colin Mason, 'Michael Tippett', *Musical Times*, lxxxvii (1946), p.137

Scott Goddard, 'Michael Tippett and the Symphony', *The Listener*, xliii (1950), p.84

John Amis, 'A Child of our Time', *The Listener*, xliv (1951), p.436

A.E.F. Dickinson, 'Round about The Midsummer Marriage', *Music and Letters*, xxxvii (1956), p.50

Colin Mason, 'Michael Tippett's Piano Concerto', *The Score*, 16 (1956) p.63

Wilfrid Mellers, 'Michael Tippett and the String Quartet', *The Listener*, lxvi (1961), p.405

Edmund Rubbra, 'The Vision of Saint Augustine', *The Listener*, lxxvi (1966) p.74

Tim Souster, 'Michael Tippett's Vision', *Musical Times*, cvii (1966), p.20

John Warrack, 'The Knot Garden', *Musical Times*, cxi (1970), p.1092

Bayan Northcott, 'Tippett Today', *Music and Musicians*, xix (November 1970), pp.34–40

A.E.F. Dickinson, 'The Garden Labyrinth', *Music Review*, xxv (1971), pp.176–80

Francis Routh, 'Michael Tippett' in *Contemporary British Music* (London 1972), pp.282–91

David Cairns, 'The Midsummer Marriage', in *Responses* (London 1973), pp. 33–45

John Clapham, 'Tippett's Concerto for Double String Orchestra', *Welsh Music*, v/6 (1977), p.47

David Fingleton, 'The Ice Break', *Music and Musicians*, xxv (July 1977), pp.28–30

John Warrack, 'The Ice Break', *Musical Times*, cxviii (1977), p.553

'Tippett at 75' – essays by Peter Gellhorn, Paul Crossley, Symon Clarke, Peter Garvie, Stephen Aechternacht and Francis Routh, *Composer*, 70 (Summer 1980), pp. 1–37

Lyudmila Kovnatskaya, 'Makyl Tippet,' *Sovetskaye Muzyka*, xi (1980), p. 123

Frederick Sternfield and David Harvey, 'A Musical Magpie: Words and Music in Michael Tippett's Operas', *Parnassus: Poetry in Review* (New York), x/2 (Fall/Winter 1982), pp. 188–98

Arnold Whittall, 'The Transcendental Guest', *Times Literary Supplement*, (28 December 1984), p. 1493

Paul Driver, 'The Mask of Time', *Tempo*, 149 (June 1984), pp. 39–44

Meirion Bowen, 'Travels with my art', *The Guardian* (2 January 1985)

Andrew Clements, 'Tippett at 80', *Opera*, xxxvi/1 (1985), pp. 16–24

Peter Dennison, 'Reminiscence and Recomposition in Tippett', *Musical Times*, cxxvi (1985), pp. 13–18

Geraint Lewis, 'Tippett: the Breath of the Life – an Approach to Formal Structure', *Musical Times*, cxxvi (1985), pp. 18–20

Malcolm Wren, 'A Piece for our Time: Theological Reflections on Sir Michael Tippett's 'The Mask of Time'', *Theology*, lxxxviii (1985), pp. 209–215

Heleen Mendl-Schrama, 'Michael Tippett als operacomponist', *Mens & Melodie*, xl/11 (November 1985), pp. 494–505

Unpublished postgraduate dissertations

Margaret Andrew Sheppach, 'The Operas of Michael Tippett in the light of twentieth-century opera aesthetics', Ph.D., Rochester 1975

J. Agar, 'An Approach to the Operas of Michael Tippett', M.Mus., East Anglia 1976

Richard Elfyn Jones, 'The Operas of Michael Tippett', Ph.D., Cardiff 1977

George N. Odam, 'Michael Tippett's Knot Garden: an exploration of its musical, literary and psychological construction', M.Phil., Southampton 1977

R.E. Rodda, 'The symphonies of Sir Michael Tippett', Ph.D., Case Western Reserve 1979

B.V. Vaughn, 'The hope of reconciliation: a stylistic characteristic of Sir Michael Tippett culminating in The Ice Break', D.M.A., Ohio State 1982

H. Gerald Anderson, 'The Derivation of Michael Tippett's Piano Works from His Operas', D.M.A., Chicago 1985

Miscellaneous

Michael Tippett: A Man of Our Time (London 1977) [exhibition catalogue]

Paul Andrews, 'Sir Michael Tippett – A Bibliography', *Brio* (Autumn 1978), pp.33–46 [reprinted with addenda by Bedfordshire County Library (1980)]

Alan Woolgar, 'A Tippett Discography', *Records and Recording*, xxiii/5 (1979–80), p.26

Eric Hughes and Timothy Day, 'Discographies of British Composers: 4 Sir Michael Tippett', *Recorded Sound*, 78 (July 1980), pp. 73–89 [supplement available from the British Institute of Recorded Sound]

INDEX

Italic figures indicate main references; superior figures indicate endnote numbers.